Entrepreneurship IN ACTION

SECOND EDITION

MARY COULTER
SOUTHWEST MISSOURI STATE UNIVERSITY

Upper Saddle River, New Jersey 07458

Library of Congress Cataloging-in-Publication Data
Coulter, Mary K.
Entrepreneurship in action / Mary Coulter.--2nd ed.
p. cm.
Includes bibliographical references and index.
ISBN 0-13-101101-4
1. New business enterprises. 2. Entrepreneurship. I. Title.

HD62.5 .C65 2003
658.1'1--dc21

2002029080

Vice-President/Editor-in-Chief: Jeff Shelstad
Managing Editor (Editorial): Jessica Sabloff
Editorial Assistant: Jill Wasiowich
Media Project Manager: Michele Faranda
Marketing Manager: Shannon Moore
Marketing Assistant: Christine Genneken
Managing Editor (Production): Judy Leale
Production Editor: Theresa Festa
Permissions Coordinator: Suzanne Grappi
Associate Director, Manufacturing: Vincent Scelta
Production Manager: Arnold Vila
Manufacturing Buyer: Diane Peirano
Design Manager: Maria Lange
Designer: Michael J. Fruhbeis
Interior Design: Setting Pace
Cover Design: Michael J. Fruhbeis
Cover Illustration/Photo: Santokh Kochar, Getty Images Inc.
Illustrator (Interior): Accurate Art
Manager, Print Production: Christy Mahon
Composition: Preparé
Full-Service Project Management: Preparé

Credits and acknowledgments borrowed from other sources and reproduced, with permission, in this textbook appear on appropriate page within text.

Pearson Education LTD.
Pearson Education Australia PTY, Limited
Pearson Education Singapore, Pte. Ltd
Pearson Education North Asia Ltd
Pearson Education, Canada, Ltd
Pearson Educación de Mexico, S.A. de C.V.
Pearson Education–Japan
Pearson Education Malaysia, Pte. Ltd

ISBN 0-13-101101-4

To Jan Strube and the late Curt Strube—
the two best entrepreneurs I know!

Brief Contents

Contents

CHAPTER 9: MANAGING GROWTH AND OTHER ENTREPRENEURIAL CHALLENGES 326

Preface

Welcome to the second edition of *Entrepreneurship in Action*! Entrepreneurship continues to be a significant part of our economic health and vitality in the United States. And in this book, I've tried to bring to you the excitement and challenges of what it's like to be an entrepreneur in today's world. I believe my book is unlike any other entrepreneurship textbook available. Why? Because it emphasizes, explains, and celebrates the realities of being an entrepreneur—it shows entrepreneurship in action. I first wrote this book because I felt there was a definite need for a book that conveyed the exciting realities of entrepreneurship; now after finishing the second edition, I still believe that! Entrepreneurship is such a fascinating topic—why not have a book that brings that excitement to students studying entrepreneurship? How does the second edition of *Entrepreneurship in Action* do this? Through many of the unique features introduced in the first edition which have been retained and enhanced. These features include the following:

Chapter-Opening Entrepreneurship in Action Case

Every chapter opens with a description of a real entrepreneur in action, facing the challenges that entrepreneurs must deal with, and making good and even some not-so-good decisions. The entrepreneurs profiled are Daymond John of FUBU (Chapter 1), Gary Hirshberg of O'Naturals (Chapter 2), Sara Blakely of Spanx (Chapter 3), Lisa Joronen of SOL Cleaning Service (Chapter 4), Karen Drakenberg of StrawberryFrog (Chapter 5), Nicholas Graham of Joe Boxer Company (Chapter 6), Joe Montgomery of Cannondale Corporation (Chapter 7), Glen Kelman of Plumtree Software (Chapter 8), and Corinna Lathan of AnthroTronix (Chapter 9). Each case ties in to the chapter material and is referenced at various points throughout the chapter. These fun stories relate the excitement of the entrepreneurial adventure. It certainly is an adventure that you're embarking on!

Entrepreneurship in Action

This chapter box provides examples of entrepreneurs from different types and sizes of entrepreneurial ventures. You'll discover what's involved with being an entrepreneur, and you'll read about different entrepreneurial approaches and philosophies. Again, it's another way to see entrepreneurship in action.

Rapid Review

In multiple places throughout each chapter, you'll find a box that lists review questions addressing the material that you've just read. These questions will help you review and assess whether you understand the material. I've also used this innovation in my other textbooks (*Management* [with Stephen P. Robbins] and *Strategic Management in Action*), and I believe that you'll find it to be a convenient and useful way to review and reinforce key chapter information.

FYI (For Your Information)

This chapter box provides information about a particularly interesting entrepreneurial topic or idea. Each chapter has a number of FYI Boxes. Some of the topics covered in the FYIs include male versus female entrepreneurs, gazelles, combating sexual harassment, building customer loyalty, budgeting basics, values-based management, developing your creativity, and the ABCs of trademarks and patents. I think you'll find the information included in these FYI Boxes to be timely and useful in your entrepreneurial journey.

The Grey Zone

As I sit writing this preface in the summer of 2002, the collapse of Enron and WorldCom and other well-publicized business scandals are reinforcing the importance of ethical decision making in business. Entrepreneurs do (and will) face ethical and social responsibility challenges as they pursue their entrepreneurial dreams. This chapter box describes some of these issues. You won't just read about these issues, you're asked to think critically about what you would do in this situation. As you'll find out, there are no easy answers when it comes to these grey zone dilemmas.

BizPlan Pro Exercises

Business Plan Pro software provides students with a step-by-step approach to creating a comprehensive business plan. The software is designed to stimulate students thinking about the many tasks and decisions that go into planning and running a business. Preformatted templates, charts, and tables do the mechanics so students can focus on the thinking.

The end-of-chapter Business Plan Pro exercises included in *Entrepreneurship in Action*, 2e, focus on chapter-related material. By working through the exercises, students will gain a practical business-planning skill as they begin to craft a winning business plan.

Sweat Equity

You may have heard the term sweat equity before. It refers to the hard work and effort—the sweat—an entrepreneur puts into an entrepreneurial venture in order to build equity value. This end-of-chapter feature presents six to ten assignments that you must "sweat" to complete. These sweat equity assignments cover a broad spectrum of entrepreneurial topics. Many involve writing brief research papers or researching a topic on the Web. I tried to design these assignments to show you the reality of entrepreneurship—again, entrepreneurship in action.

Entrepreneurship in Action Cases

These Entrepreneurship in Action cases provide descriptions of entrepreneurs and the challenges and issues they're facing. Discussion questions at the end of each case get you "into" the case and ask for your input on the challenges, issues, and dilemmas that are presented. Five of these cases are in every chapter—one is the chapter-opening Entrepreneurship in Action case—and they cover a broad spectrum of entrepreneurial businesses. Some examples of the entrepreneurial ventures described include an online jewelry retailer, a CPA firm, an artisan bread bakery, and a bike bag manufacturer. These cases are fun to read and provide another dose of entrepreneurship in action.

Video Cases

In addition to the written cases, one video case is included in every chapter. These video cases, which are video segments from Business Now (**www.businessnow.com**), are an excellent way to really see entrepreneurship in action. You'll hear the voices and see these real-life entrepreneurs as they deal with current issues and challenges. The written cases include discussion questions for you to answer.

Appendix

The Appendix provides some additional information to help you in your journey to being a successful entrepreneur. There are two major parts included in the Appendix. The first section is an annotated list of entrepreneurship Web sites. The Web sites included in the listing provide all kinds of information about starting and managing an entrepreneurial venture. The second section includes five additional Entrepreneurship in Action cases that you can read for your own enjoyment or that your professor may assign you to read and analyze.

As you can see by the descriptions of all the unique features in *Entrepreneurship in Action,* I've tried to provide you as close an experience to what it's like to be an entrepreneur in action, other than actually being one. I truly hope that the excitement and exhilaration of being an entrepreneur comes through and motivates you to pursue the fun, but demanding, journey of becoming one.

Supplements

- **Instructor's Manual with Test Item File and Video Guide**
  The Instructor's Manual contains Learning Objectives, Expanded Chapter Outlines with teaching tips and highlighted text features, and teaching notes to end-of-chapter material for each chapter in the text. Each Test Item File chapter contains true/false, multiple choice, chapter essay, and case essay questions. Also included is a Video Guide that includes summaries and teaching notes for the chapter-ending Business Now video cases.
- **Companion Web Site**
  The Prentice Hall Companion Web site features an interactive online student study guide with multiple choice, true/false, and Internet-based essay questions that accompany each chapter in the text. Professors will also find downloadable versions of the Instructor's Manual, Test Item File, Video Guide, and PowerPoints.
- **Business Now Videos**
  Brand new to this edition, Prentice Hall is pleased to offer exciting new BusinessNOW video cases. BusinessNOW is a fast-paced television news magazine that takes viewers on location and behind closed doors to look at America's most interesting companies and the corporate executives who run them. These videos offer interesting, up-to-date content pertaining to the topics raised in *Entrepreneurship in Action*, 2e, and were chosen specifically for their tie-ins to topics related to entrepreneurship.
- **Instructor's Resource CD-ROM**
  Included on one CD-ROM, professors will find the Instructor's Manual, Test Item File, Video Guide, and PowerPoint presentation.

Acknowledgments

I need to thank a number of people for their contributions to this book. Without them, *Entrepreneurship in Action* wouldn't be here. First and foremost, I'd like to thank my students, past and present, who always challenge me to think about how I convey information to them. They have made me a better communicator because I then try to write in such a way that topics and concepts are explained clearly—and, in an interesting and fun way! I'd also like to thank my department head, Barry Wisdom, and my college dean, Ron Bottin. Your support and encouragement of my writing efforts mean a lot to me. Of course, I must thank my departmental secretaries, Carole Hale and Anita Looney. You ladies are super to work with!

I'd also like to recognize the individuals who provided me with intelligent and thorough reviews. These individuals are as follows: Brent Strong, Brigham Young University; Timothy Stearns, California State University; Richard Huttner, Northeastern University; Charles Boyd, Southwest Missouri State University; Tim Berry, University of Oregon; and Maryellen Kelly, Waynesburg College. I sincerely appreciate your thoughtful insights into the first edition of the book and how I could make the second edition better. I know the final product is much improved because of your suggestions. Thank you! Then, I'd like to thank Tim Berry of Business Plan Pro for writing the end-of-chapter Business Plan Pro assignments. Thank you, Tim, for your hard work!

I'd also like to thank the wonderful people at Prentice Hall, my publisher. As usual, all of you have been just super to work with. First off, I'd like to thank Shawna Kelly, who used to be my local sales representative and is now a representative in the St. Louis area. Shawna, thanks for believing in me and being such a good friend! Then, a big thank you to Jessica Sabloff who took on this project! Jess, you have been great to work with and I hope this is not the last time we get to work together! I'd also like to thank Theresa Festa for her great work as my production editor! Theresa, thanks for all your patience with me and keeping me on track! Then, there's Kevin Glynn, Judy Leale, and the other team members at Upper Saddle River who deserve a big thank you, as well! And, of course, I must thank my marketing manager, Shannon Moore, who is absolutely wonderful! Thanks for all your great ideas!

Finally, I'd like to say THANKS to my family—my wonderful and supportive husband, Ron, and my bright, beautiful, and remarkably well-adjusted daughters Sarah and Katie. Ron, Sarah, and Katie, thank you for being patient with me and my hectic schedule. Thanks for everything you do to help and for not complaining about all the take-out meals we've eaten! All three of you provide that much-needed balance to my life. What I've been able to do, I couldn't have done without the three of you! I love you all very much!

Mary Coulter
Southwest Missouri State University

Entrepreneurship IN ACTION

SECTION 1 INTRODUCTION TO ENTREPRENEURSHIP

1 ENTREPRENEURS AND ENTREPRENEURSHIP

LEARNING OBJECTIVES

After reading and studying this chapter, you should be able to:

1. Define entrepreneurship.
2. Describe the historical perspectives of entrepreneurship.
3. Distinguish between entrepreneurship and intrapreneurship.
4. Explain what entrepreneurial ventures are and how they're different from small businesses.
5. Explain why entrepreneurship is important.
6. Discuss entrepreneurial activity around the globe.
7. Outline the steps in the entrepreneurial process.
8. Describe who entrepreneurs are and what they do.
9. Discuss the different types of entrepreneurs.
10. Discuss the rewards and challenges of being an entrepreneur.

ENTREPRENEURSHIP IN ACTION

FUBU—For Us By Us. As one of the New York area's top-rated privately held companies, FUBU makes trendy sportswear that appeals to a particular cross section of America's youth.[1] Daymond John, FUBU's current President and CEO, started the company in 1992 in the basement of his home in Hollis, Queens, New York. Hip-hop street fashion was just becoming popular, and while shopping for a particular style of hat, Daymond realized that no neighborhood retail shops had exactly what he was looking for. So he did what many entrepreneurs do when they can't find a product or service they want—he decided to make and sell his own. Daymond mortgaged his home for $100,000 and turned to a group of neighborhood friends

Maybe you've had an experience like Daymond Johns did—wanting a product or service that simply did not exist. Did you do something about it? Maybe that's your dream: to create and market a product yourself. Or maybe *your* personal dream is to be your own boss and not have to answer to someone else at work; to have control over what you do, how you do it, and how much you earn. Whatever your personal reason is for taking this class and reading this book, there's no doubt that entrepreneurs and entrepreneurship are playing important roles in today's global business environment. What *is* entrepreneurship and who *are* entrepreneurs? These are the main topics we're going to explore in this chapter. So whether you want to be the next Michael Dell, Bill Gates, Leslie Blodgett, or Daymond Johns, or whether you just want to pursue your own personal dreams, understanding entrepreneurship in action is an important first step!

WHAT IS ENTREPRENEURSHIP?

Practically everywhere you turn these days, you'll read or hear about entrepreneurs. Pick up a current newspaper or newsmagazine. Tune into a radio or TV news broadcast. Or log onto one of the Web's news sites. Chances are you'll find at least one story (and probably many more) about an entrepreneur or an entrepreneurial business. Entrepreneurship is a popular topic these days! But exactly what is it? Let's see if we can answer this by looking at how entrepreneurship is defined.

Definition of Entrepreneurship

If someone asked you right now to define entrepreneurship, what would you say? How would you go about describing it? Defining entrepreneurship might seem simple, but it isn't! There are about as many definitions of entrepreneurship as there are people who have written about the subject. Everyone seems to have his or her own ideas about what it is and how best to define it. Let's look at some of the various ways that entrepreneurship has been defined.

Entrepreneurship has long been described by researchers and writers with terms such as *new, innovative, flexible, dynamic, creative,* and *risk-taking*. Many authors have said that identifying and pursuing opportunities is an important part of entrepreneurship.[2] Other authors have said that entrepreneurship involves the creation of value, the process

who shared his vision. Calling themselves Team FUBU, the group of friends turned half of John's house into a factory to make fashionable street-wise tie-top hats.

From that modest beginning, FUBU is now a fashion empire with annual sales of its oversized shirts, leather jackets, baggy jeans, and other cool clothes estimated at $380 million. As a major innovator and leader in the youth market, FUBU has a savvy clientele *and* a savvy entrepreneurial team. In fact, FUBU is continuing its entrepreneurial tradition as it makes a major push into online retailing and FB Entertainment, a full-fledged entertainment company including a record label (FUBU Records).

of starting or growing a new profit-making business, the process of providing a new product or service, and the intentional creation of value through organization by an individual contributor or a small group of partners.[3] Another definition of entrepreneurship that's been used is "the process of creating something different with value by devoting the necessary time and effort, assuming the accompanying financial, psychological, and social risks, and receiving the resulting rewards of monetary and personal satisfaction."[4] Even the professional association for management academics (the Academy of Management) has its own broad definition of entrepreneurship: "the creation and management of new businesses, small businesses, and family businesses."[5] And there are many other definitions that we could cite. However, even given this wide variety of definitions of entrepreneurship, we can detect some common themes.[6] (See Exhibit 1-1.) Let's look closer at these common themes so we can begin to better understand what entrepreneurship is.

One of the common themes found in the definitions of entrepreneurship recognizes the important role that the entrepreneur plays. There's no doubt that without a person who's willing to do what an entrepreneur does, there would be no entrepreneurship! Because the person—the entrepreneur—is a critical element in entrepreneurship in action, we'll be discussing who entrepreneurs are and what they do later in this chapter. But keep in mind that entrepreneurship wouldn't be possible without an entrepreneur.

Another common theme in the definition of entrepreneurship is innovation. Entrepreneurship involves changing, revolutionizing, transforming, and introducing new approaches. Think back to what Daymond Johns did initially with his tie-top hats. These products weren't available in the marketplace—this particular customer need wasn't being met. So he innovated, created a new product, and in the process, revolutionized the urban hip-hop fashion industry. Entrepreneurship involves innovation.

The third common theme that we see in definitions of entrepreneurship is organization creation. What is this, and what does it have to do with entrepre-

EXHIBIT 1-1 Common Themes in Definitions of Entrepreneurship

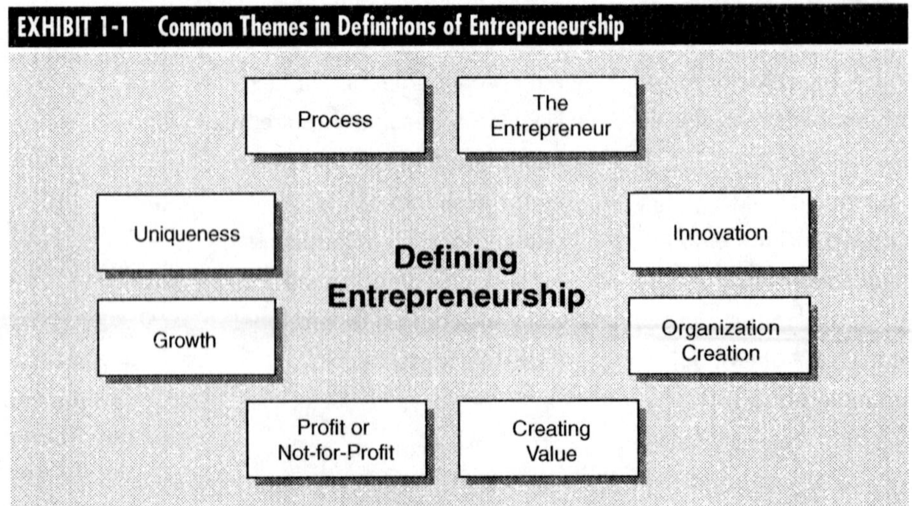

Source: Based on W. B. Gartner, "What Are We Talking About When We Talk About Entrepreneurship?" *Journal of Business Venturing,* Vol. 5, 1990, pp. 15–28.

neurship? In order to pursue the perceived opportunities for innovation and to create value, there must be organized efforts and actions. Someone must take the initiative to do something—take action to get the entrepreneurial venture up and running. Without some type of organized effort—whether as an individual or as a team of individuals (think of Team FUBU)—the ability to obtain resources to pursue the entrepreneurial opportunity will be limited, if not completely closed off.

Next, we find that the process of creating value is a common theme in describing entrepreneurship. What does it mean to "create value"? One interpretation is that through entrepreneurship, new products, services, transactions, approaches, resources, technologies, and markets are created that contribute some value to a community or marketplace.[7] We can also see value created when, through entrepreneurship, resources are transformed into outputs such as products or services. During this transformation process, value is created because the entrepreneur is fashioning something worthwhile and useful. Another way to view this is that value also is created through the financial exchange as customers purchase the entrepreneurial organization's products or services.

Another theme often found in definitions of entrepreneurship is a recognition that entrepreneurship can take place in both profit and not-for-profit environments. Although we tend to assume that entrepreneurial activity is geared at making a profit (and we agree that much of it is), entrepreneurship also occurs in social service agencies, in community arts organizations, or in other types of not-for-profit settings. For example, Susana Valadez, an anthropologist by training but now an avid entrepreneur, established an enterprise to help revitalize the Huichol Indian tribe's jewelry-making tradition. The intricately beaded jewelry pieces created by artisans at the Huichol Center for Cultural Survival and Traditional Arts

Entrepreneurs in Action

Would you eat pasta shaped like a football, a cat, a sailboat, or a ghost? Well, that's what John and Carey Aron of Nashville, Tennessee, decided to do with plain old ordinary pasta. These pasta shapes are just a few of the many gourmet products that the Arons' company, The Pasta Shoppe, produces and markets. (Check out their Web site at **www.pastashoppe.com**.) Determined to fulfill their dream of starting their own company, the Arons' left corporate life and New York City in 1993. Pasta was their passion and they felt they could make pasta products that were unique and of higher quality than was being marketed by the mass producers. So, they took an essentially commodity-type product, gave it an unusual twist, and created a valuable product variation. In the process, this entrepreneurial couple turned a unique idea into a viable business.

Sources: The Pasta Shoppe Web site (**www.pastashoppe.com**), April 8, 2002; and S. Sansoni, "Spaghetti Deluxe," *Forbes*, October 20, 1997, p. 240.

are big fashion hits in the United States, Europe, and Japan, especially among movie stars. (Check out their products at **www.huicholcenter.com**). Revenues from jewelry sales are used to help Huichol Indian families and to preserve the ancient culture and arts of this tribe.[8]

The next common theme in entrepreneurship definitions is growth.[9] One major difference between entrepreneurial ventures and other small businesses is the emphasis on growth. Entrepreneurship is about growing a business and pursuing opportunities as they arise. It's not about standing still or being content to stay in one market or with one product. Entrepreneurship implies growth.

Another theme commonly found in definitions of entrepreneurship is that of uniqueness. Entrepreneurship involves new combinations and new approaches with which entrepreneurs are willing to experiment. Therefore, the very nature of entrepreneurship infers differences, not the norm.[10] Through entrepreneurship, unique products are created and unique approaches are tried. Entrepreneurship isn't merely imitating what others have done. It's doing something new, something untested and untried—something unique.

The final theme commonly found in definitions of entrepreneurship is the recognition that it is a process. A process, very simply, is a set of ongoing decisions and actions. Entrepreneurship is not a one-time phenomenon; it occurs over time. It involves a series of decisions and actions from initial start-up to managing the entrepreneurial venture to even, at some point, exiting it. Later in this chapter, we'll look at the specific steps involved in the entrepreneurial process.

Now that we've explored many of the common themes found in definitions of entrepreneurship, how are we going to define it? Our definition of **entrepreneurship** is the process whereby an individual or group of individuals use organized efforts to pursue opportunities to create value and grow by fulfilling wants and needs through innovation and uniqueness, no matter what resources the entrepreneur currently has. This definition captures the unique nature of entrepreneurship and encompasses many of the important elements we just looked at.

Now that we have a good grasp of how entrepreneurship is defined, let's look at how it has evolved. Why look at the past? Examining the past can give us a deeper appreciation and understanding of how we view entrepreneurship today. When and how did entrepreneurship theory evolve? Exhibit 1-2 provides a summary time line of the development of entrepreneurship theory.

Historical Perspectives on Entrepreneurship

Entrepreneurship is not a twentieth- or twenty-first-century phenomenon, although the current popularity of entrepreneurial exploits would tend to make you think that it was. Early in the eighteenth century, the French term *entrepreneur* was first used to describe a "go-between" or a "between-taker."

Richard Cantillon, a noted economist and author in the 1700s, is regarded by many as the originator of the term *entrepreneur*.[11] Cantillon used the term to refer to a person who took an active risk-bearing role in pursuing opportunities. This individual—the entrepreneur—served as the bridge between someone who had the capital, or money, who chose not to personally pursue those opportunities. Instead an individual (or group of individuals) financed the pursuit of oppor-

EXHIBIT 1-2 Time Line of the Development of Entrepreneurship Theory

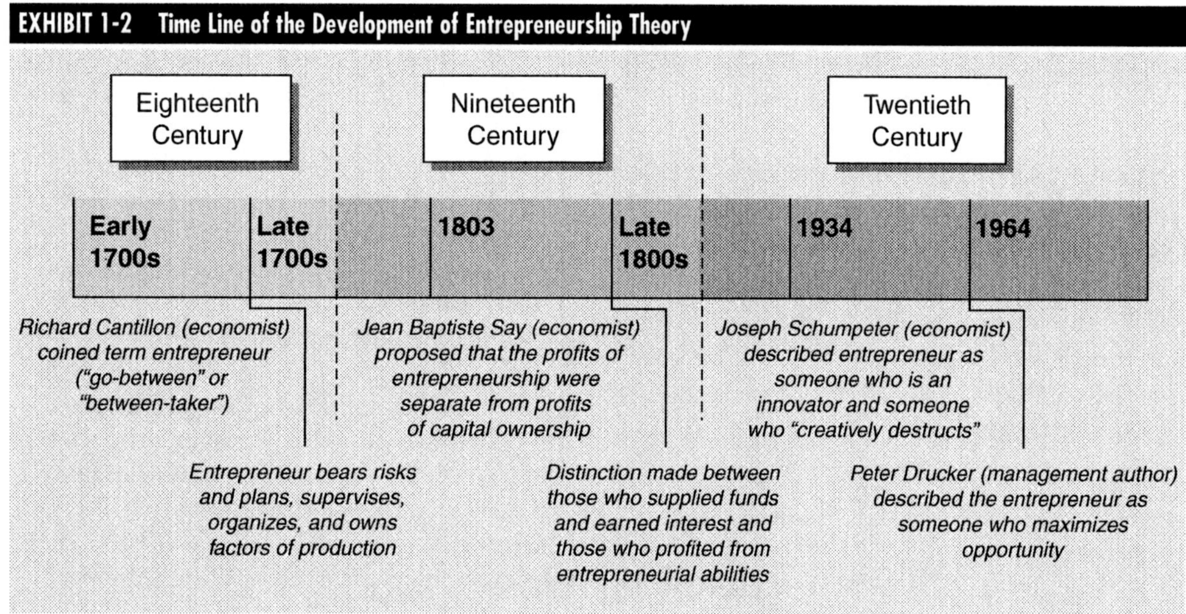

tunities and the entrepreneur served as the go-between—the actively involved risk-taker. Late in the eighteenth century, the concept of entrepreneurship was expanded to include not only the bearing of risks but also the planning, supervising, organizing, and even owning the factors of production.

The nineteenth century was a fertile time for entrepreneurial activity because technological advances during the industrial revolution provided the impetus for continued inventions and innovations. Early in this century, the view that the entrepreneurial process was a unique set of actions became even more prevalent when economist Jean Baptiste Say proposed that the profits of entrepreneurship were distinct and separate from the profits arising from the ownership of capital. (This distinction is still relevant today if you consider the role that venture capitalists play—that is, owning and providing capital—in supporting entrepreneurial activities.) Then, toward the end of the nineteenth century, the concept of entrepreneurship changed slightly again to distinguish between those who supplied funds and earned interest and those who profited from entrepreneurial abilities.

During the early part of the twentieth century, entrepreneurship was still believed to be distinct and different from the management of organizations. However, in the mid-1930s the concept of entrepreneurship expanded. That's when economist Joseph Schumpeter proposed that entrepreneurship involved innovations and untried technologies or what he called **creative destruction**, which is defined as the process whereby existing products, processes, ideas, and businesses are replaced with better ones. Schumpeter believed that through the process of creative destruction, old and outdated approaches and products were replaced with better ones. Through the destruction of the old came the creation of the new. He also believed that entrepreneurs were the driving forces behind this process of creative destruction.[12] They were the ones who took the breakthrough ideas and innovations into the marketplace. Schumpeter's description of the

The Grey Zone Continual changes in technology have cut the "shelf life" of many employees' work skills. As wave after wave of technological innovations appear (Schumpeter's creative destruction process at work), what ethical obligations do entrepreneurs have toward workers whose skills have become obsolete? Should an entrepreneur be concerned with the possibility that his or her innovations might eliminate the need for certain work skills? What do you think?

process of creative destruction served to highlight further the important role that innovation plays in entrepreneurship. As our earlier definition of entrepreneurship showed, the concepts of innovation and uniqueness are (and always have been) integral parts of entrepreneurial activity.

The final development from the twentieth century we'll look at is Peter Drucker's contention that entrepreneurship involves maximizing opportunities. Drucker is a well-known and prolific writer on a wide variety of management issues. What his perspective added to the concept of entrepreneurship is that entrepreneurs recognize and act on opportunities. Drucker proposed that entrepreneurship doesn't just happen out of the blue but arises in response to what the entrepreneur sees as untapped and undeveloped opportunities.

Although we've looked at only a small portion of entrepreneurship's long and colorful past, keep in mind that the history of entrepreneurship continues to unfold. Its history is still being written today. In the early years of the twenty-first century, researchers continue to study entrepreneurs and entrepreneurship.[13] Although no generally accepted theory of entrepreneurship has emerged from these studies, what we *do* know about successful and not-so-successful entrepreneurship continues to evolve.[14] We'll highlight many of these important research findings as we cover material throughout the rest of this textbook.

As we continue our exploration of what entrepreneurship is, it may help to clarify the concept by explaining what it *isn't*. Although entrepreneurs and entrepreneurial activities have been studied for well over three centuries, there are some misconceptions about it.[15]

Misconceptions About Entrepreneurship

1. *Successful entrepreneurship needs only a great idea.* Having a great idea is only part of the equation for successful entrepreneurship. Understanding the demands of the different phases of the entrepreneurial process, taking an organized approach to developing the entrepreneurial venture, and coping with the challenges of managing the entrepreneurial venture are also key ingredients to successful entrepreneurship.
2. *Entrepreneurship is easy.* You may think that because you're pursuing your passion and have an intense desire to succeed that it's going to be easy. However, be forewarned that entrepreneurship is *not* easy! It takes commitment, determination, and hard work. And even if you have these qualities, it still isn't effortless! Entrepreneurs often encounter difficulties and setbacks, but the successful entrepreneurs are those who push on in spite of the difficulties.
3. *Entrepreneurship is a risky gamble.* Because entrepreneurship involves pursuing new and untested approaches and ideas, it must be a gamble. Right? Not really. Although entrepreneurs aren't afraid to take risks, entrepreneurship

Entrepreneurs in Action

Terry Black, president of Super Smokers BBQ (**www.supersmokers.com**), a $7 million food, catering, and restaurant company in O'Fallon, Missouri, knows firsthand the effort that goes into building a successful business. Black and his college roommate, Skip Steele, used to barbecue for themselves and crowds at their fraternity's annual spring bash. In 1987, Steele contacted Black and proposed that they enter a barbecue competition in Little Rock. Using an old propane tank they found abandoned in a field, Black and Steele came in 13th of 14 teams. However, the duo decided to do it better, and they experimented with seasonings, temperatures, and wood chips. They kept entering competitions, and in 1994 Black and Steele took sixth place in the World Championship Barbecue Cooking Contest in Memphis. Their success led to weekend catering gigs and the addition of a third partner, Ron Skinner. In May 2000, Super Smokers took home the ultimate prize—first place out of 247 teams participating in the Memphis competition. Today, Super Smokers BBQ has three free-standing stores, four grocery store BBQ outlets, three concession stands at the Dome (St. Louis's football stadium), a 500-seat outlet at Busch Stadium, a thriving catering business, and an e-commerce Web site. These three guys know that entrepreneurship isn't easy, but sure is a whole lot of fun!

Sources: Super Smokers Web site (**www.supersmokers.com**), April 8, 2002; and L. Buchanan, "Pork Chaps," *Inc.*, January 2002, p. 24.

involves calculated risks, not unnecessary ones. In fact, there are times when successful entrepreneurship means avoiding or minimizing risks.

4. *Entrepreneurship is found only in small businesses.* Many people have the mistaken idea that entrepreneurship is associated only with small organizations. The truth is that entrepreneurship can be found in any size organization. On the other hand, just because an organization is small doesn't automatically make it entrepreneurial.
5. *Entrepreneurial ventures and small businesses are the same thing.* This misconception is so widespread that we're going to address it more completely in the next section.

Entrepreneurial Ventures and Small Businesses—The Differences

Many people think that entrepreneurial ventures and small business are one and the same. However, there are some important differences between the two. Let's look first at what a small business is.

What constitutes a "small" business? Although there is no universally accepted definition of a small business, most use some quantitative measure of the number of employees or annual sales. The Small Business Administration (SBA),

FYI: Entrepreneurship Versus Intrapreneurship

How can a large organization be entrepreneurial in nature? Well, given an environment characterized by turbulent and chaotic markets, technological complexity, and global opportunities and threats, being entrepreneurial just may be the key to long-term success and survival! In large organizations, the process of using organized efforts and means to pursue opportunities to create value and grow by fulfilling wants and needs through innovation and uniqueness is called **intrapreneurship**. It's the pursuit of entrepreneurship within the confines of a large organization. Intrapreneurship provides large organizations the opportunities to adapt quickly to changes in the marketplace, to go in new directions without having to acquire or merge with an existing business, and to try out new products and processes. For example, at Texas Instruments Inc., its IDEA program, in which individual employees are encouraged to pursue new ideas in areas that might not be related to their assigned job responsibilities has contributed an estimated $500 million in profits and cost savings to the company's bottom line during its more-than-25-year existence. Other large organizations that are well known for their emphasis on intrapreneurship include Charles Schwab, GE Capital, AT&T, DuPont, 3M, and Hewlett-Packard.

Sources: M. Robinson, "The Ten Commandments of Intrapreneurs," *Management*, December 2001, pp. 95–97; G. Hamel, "Reinvent Your Company," *Fortune*, June 12, 2000, found online at **www.fortune.com**; N. Enbar, "Where Big Shots Learn to Think Like Hotshots," *Business Week*, October 18, 1999, found online at **www.businessweek.com**; R. D. Russell, "Developing a Process Model of Intrapreneurial Systems: A Cognitive Mapping Approach," *Entrepreneurship Theory & Practice*, Spring 1999, pp. 65–84; T. Stevens, "Idea Dollars," *Industry Week*, February 15, 1998, pp. 47–49; G. Carrier, "Intrapreneurship in Small Business: An Exploratory Study," *Entrepreneurship Theory and Practice*, Fall 1996, pp. 5–20; and T. D. Schellhardt, "David in Goliath," *Wall Street Journal*, May 23, 1996, p. R14.

a federal agency of the U.S. government that provides, loans, advice, and assistance to small businesses, has different definitions for a small business depending on what industry it's in. For instance, the cutoff point for a small business in the office machinery manufacturing industry is 1,000 employees, whereas in the confectionery wholesalers industry, it's 100 employees.[16] In this book, we're going to define a **small business** as one that is independently owned, operated, and financed; has fewer than 100 employees; doesn't engage in any new or innovative practices; and has relatively little impact on its industry.[17]

Rapid Review

- ✔ List the common themes found in the definitions of entrepreneurship.
- ✔ Define entrepreneurship.
- ✔ What are some of the key developments in the history of entrepreneurship?
- ✔ What role does creative destruction play in entrepreneurship?
- ✔ List the misconceptions about entrepreneurship and explain why these are misconceptions.
- ✔ How is entrepreneurship different from intrapreneurship? How are they the same?
- ✔ Differentiate between an entrepreneurial venture and a small business.

Now, what is an entrepreneurial venture? As we discussed previously, entrepreneurship involves using organized efforts to pursue opportunities to create value and grow by fulfilling wants and needs through innovation and uniqueness, no matter what resources the entrepreneur currently has. Therefore, we're going to define an **entrepreneurial venture** as an organization that is pursuing opportunities, is characterized by innovative practices, and has profitability and growth as its main goals.

Although there are some definitional and actual overlaps between small businesses and entre-

EXHIBIT 1-3 Differences Between Small Businesses and Entrepreneurial Ventures

Small Business	Entrepreneurial Venture
• Independently owned, operated, and financed	• Innovative practices
• Fewer than 100 employees	• Goals are profitability and growth
• Doesn't emphasize new or innovative practices	• Seeks out new opportunities
• Little impact on industry	• Willingness to take risks

preneurial ventures, we are going to view them as different. (See Exhibit 1-3.) A small business isn't necessarily entrepreneurial in nature just because it's small. To be entrepreneurial means being innovative and seeking out new opportunities. Even though entrepreneurial ventures may start small, they do pursue growth. Some new small firms may grow, but many will remain small businesses, by choice or by default.

The Current Importance of Entrepreneurship

Using any number of sources, you can find statistics about how many small businesses there are, how many workers they employ, and how much of the gross national economic output they're responsible for. The headlines scream the information: Small businesses "represent over 99% of all employer firms and employ 52% of all private workers. They account for 51% of the private-sector output and are responsible for virtually all new jobs through creation of new firms as well as expansion of existing small businesses."[18] These statistics, as collected by various research firms and government agencies, reflect the economic activity of *all* small businesses, not just that of entrepreneurial ventures. Because we've made a point of distinguishing between small businesses and entrepreneurial ventures, these statistics don't tell the entire story. Instead, let's try to look at what entrepreneurship contributes. Then the questions become: How can we measure the importance of entrepreneurship? Does entrepreneurship contribute to economic vitality? How does it do so?

Entrepreneurship is, and continues to be, important to every industry sector in the United States and in other global economies. Its importance can be shown in three areas: innovation, number of new start-ups, and job creation and employment.

Innovation. Innovating is a process of creating, changing, experimenting, transforming, and revolutionizing. As we know from our earlier definition, innovation is one of the key distinguishing characteristics of entrepreneurial activity. The "creative destruction" process of innovating leads to technological changes and employment growth.[19] Entrepreneurial firms act as these "agents of change" by providing an essential source of new and unique ideas that might otherwise go untapped.[20] Statistics back up this assertion. New small organizations generate 24 times more innovations per research and development dollar spent than do *Fortune* 500 organizations, and they account for over 95 percent of new and "radical" product developments.[21]

The passionate drive and intense hunger of entrepreneurs to forge new directions in products and processes and to take risks set in motion a series of decisions that lead to the innovations that are important for economic vitality. Without these new ideas, economic, technological, and social progress would be slow indeed.

Number of New Start-ups. All businesses—whether they fit the definition of entrepreneurial or not—at one point in time were start-ups, the most convenient measure we have of the role that entrepreneurship plays in this economic statistic is to look at the number of new firms over a period of time. The assumption that we have to make, then, is that some of these new firms engage in activities that are entrepreneurial in nature.

Getting data on the number of new start-ups isn't as easy as it may appear because there are different opinions on what constitutes the birth of a new company. Is a new company "born" when it opens an office, when it makes its first sale, or when it files its first tax return? Government estimates and private organization estimates tend to vary greatly.[22] The latest data available from the U.S. Small Business Administration are shown in Exhibit 1-4. Looking at the data in the exhibit, we see that the number of new firms has stayed relatively steady. During the late 1990s, there were some slight decreases; however, the estimates for 2000 (the latest information available) show an increase of around 4 percent over 1999. Again, if we assume that some of these new businesses engage in innovative practices and pursue profitability and growth as main goals—that is, they're entrepreneurial ventures—we propose that the pursuit of entrepreneurship contributed to the overall creation of new firms. Why is the creation of new firms so important? It's important because these new firms contribute to economic development through benefits such as product-process innovations, increased tax revenues, societal betterment, and job creation.

Job Creation. We know that job creation is vital to the overall long-term economic health of communities, regions, and nations. Just how important are entrepreneurial ventures to job creation? Once again, getting accurate measures of job creation isn't easy. The only data we have to answer that question cover all small businesses. (But presumably some of these small businesses would be considered entrepreneurial ventures.) According to the U.S. Small Business Administration, small companies created 76.5 percent of net new jobs from 1990 to 1995 and 75.8 percent of net new jobs from 1996 to 1997 (the latest data available).[23] The creation of jobs by small businesses is expected to continue into the future as new firms start small and grow.[24]

EXHIBIT 1-4 Number of New Businesses, 1995–2000

1995	1996	1997	1998	1999	2000
594,369	597,792	590,644	589,982	587,700*	612,400*

*Estimates

Source: "Small Business Economic Indicators, 2000," Office of Advocacy, U.S. Small Business Administration, p. A–8, accessed at **www.sba.gov/advo/stats**, March 15, 2002.

Entrepreneurs in Action

Jose Reategui, CEO of Rego Realty Corporation (**www.regorealty.com**), has built a successful growing business by taking old dilapidated inner-city buildings in Hartford, Connecticut, renovating them, and turning them into income-producing rental apartments. In just six years, Rego's inner-city holdings have grown from one five-family unit generating $30,000 to 32 residential buildings generating $1.5 million in rentals annually. The company, which is continuing to grow, has had to move to larger offices and has even added a construction subsidiary—and employees—to renovate the buildings the company buys.

Sources: Rego Realty Web site (**www.regorealty.com**), April 8, 2002; and "These Old Houses," *Inc.*, May 2001, p. 60.

Although small companies do have a significant impact on the creation of *net* new jobs, data collected by the U.S. Small Business Administration indicates that for the first time, big businesses appear to employ more U.S. workers than do small businesses.[25] The data, collected in 1999 (the latest year available), says that big companies employed 49.7 percent of the 111 million U.S. workers. And, the SBA predicted that the share of the workforce employed by big companies probably surpassed 50 percent in 2000. Yet, the SBA also predicted that with all the jobs downsized and restructured by large companies in 2001 small firms may temporarily regain an edge on total job employment when data for 2001 are released. Even though small companies' total share of employment may be shifting, there's no doubt that they will continue to have economic clout.

The Impact of Entrepreneurship Globally

What about entrepreneurial activity outside the United States? What kind of impact has it had? An annual assessment of global entrepreneurship called the Global Entrepreneurship Monitor (GEM) studied the impact of entrepreneurial activity on economic growth in various countries. What did the researchers find? The GEM 2000 report covered 21 countries that were divided into three levels of entrepreneurship. (See Exhibit 1-5.) As you can see from this data, the highest levels of entrepreneurial activity were found in five countries (Australia, Canada, Korea, Norway, and the United States). Average levels of entrepreneurial activity were found in 14 countries and the lowest levels of entrepreneurial activity were found in two countries—France and Japan.

In addition, the researchers found among the major industrialized G-7 countries (group of seven countries including Canada, France, Germany, Italy, Japan, the United Kingdom, and the United States), in particular, a very strong relationship between the level of entrepreneurial activity and annual economic growth. "The GEM report provides conclusive evidence that promoting entrepreneurship and enhancing the entrepreneurial dynamics of a country should be an integral element of any government's commitment to boosting economic well-being."[26]

EXHIBIT 1-5 Level of Entrepreneurial Activity Around the Globe

Top Level	Middle Level	Lowest Level
Australia	Argentina	France
Canada	Belgium	Japan
Korea	Brazil	
Norway	Denmark	
United States	Finland	
	Germany	
	India	
	Israel	
	Ireland	
	Italy	
	Singapore	
	Spain	
	Sweden	
	United Kingdom	

Source: Based on "Economic Growth Linked to Levels of Business Start-Ups," *GEM2000 Report*, accessed at **www.babson.edu/press/gemGrowth2000.html**, December 22, 2000.

From a global perspective, we also can conclude that entrepreneurship plays an important role in a country's economic growth.

Now that we've established how important entrepreneurship is to the rate of product and process innovations, to the number of new start-ups, and to new job creation, we need to look at how entrepreneurship takes place. Does it consist of simple, unconnected, and random actions, or are there specific and identifiable steps that entrepreneurs follow as they start and proceed through the entrepreneurial experience? Although each entrepreneurial experience is going to be different because of differing situations and circumstances, there do appear to be common decisions that entrepreneurs face as they get their entrepreneurial ventures up and running.

The Entrepreneurial Process

What's involved in the entrepreneurial process? Exhibit 1-6 illustrates the main decisions that entrepreneurs confront as they pursue their entrepreneurial ventures. From exploring the various aspects of the entrepreneurial context to identifying opportunities and possible competitive advantage(s) to starting and managing the entrepreneurial venture, entrepreneurs make decisions and engage in activities that *are* entrepreneurship in action. Let's take a closer look at each of these decisions and activities.

Exploring the Entrepreneurial Context. Why is it important to look at the entrepreneurial context? Because the context determines the "rules" of the game and what decisions are likely to be successful. The coach of a baseball team, for instance, analyzes its specific context (factors such as the condition of the playing

EXHIBIT 1-6 Entrepreneurship in Action—The Entrepreneurial Process

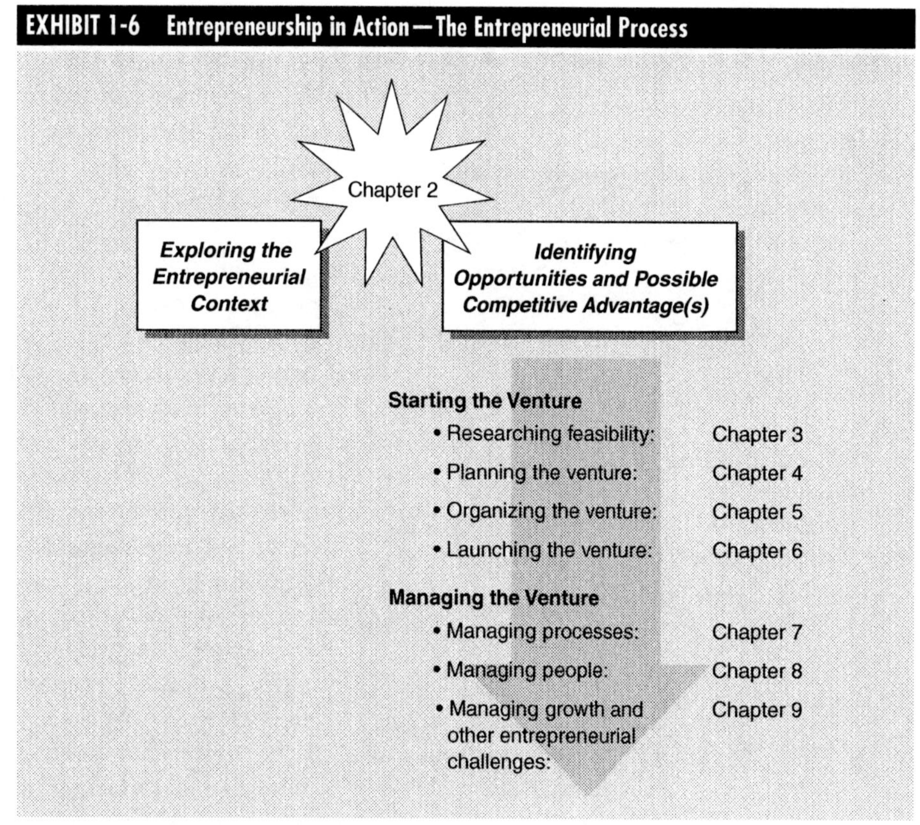

field, the cohesiveness of the team's players, injuries to players on the other team, or maybe even the team's current rankings in its division) in deciding what players to play, the best batting order, pitchers to start, etc. So, too, must entrepreneurs be aware of the context within which entrepreneurial decisions are made. Only through exploring the context can entrepreneurs discover the untapped opportunities and competitive advantage(s) that may lead to the development of a potentially successful entrepreneurial venture.

Identifying Opportunities and Possible Competitive Advantage. A crucial aspect of entrepreneurship is the pursuit of perceived opportunities. What are **opportunities**? They're positive external trends or changes that provide unique and distinct possibilities for innovating and creating value. Think back to our chapter-opening case. Daymond John recognized the hip-hop fashion trend as an opportunity to create clothing that would appeal to fashion-conscious teens and young adults. However, just identifying an opportunity isn't enough. The entrepreneurial process also involves pinpointing a possible competitive advantage. A **competitive advantage** is what sets an organization apart; it's an organization's competitive edge. Having a competitive advantage is crucial for an organization's long-term success and survival. Even not-for-profit organizations (such as governmental agencies, community arts organizations, or social service groups) need something that sets them apart—something unique that they offer in order to continue in business. We'll cover the related aspects of exploring the entrepreneurial context and identifying opportunities and competitive advantage in Chapter 2.

Rapid Review

- ✔ What role does entrepreneurship play in innovation?
- ✔ Why is entrepreneurship important in the number of new start-ups?
- ✔ How does entrepreneurship contribute to job creation?
- ✔ What does the GEM2000 report say about the importance of entrepreneurship around the globe?
- ✔ Draw the entrepreneurial process model and explain it.
- ✔ What are opportunities and competitive advantage? Why are they important to entrepreneurship?
- ✔ What is a world-class organization? Why might this concept be important to entrepreneurship?

Starting the Venture. Once entrepreneurs have explored the external context and identified possible opportunities and competitive advantage(s), they must look at the issues involved with actually starting up their entrepreneurial venture. Included in this phase of the entrepreneurial process are the following activities: researching the feasibility of the venture (Chapter 3), planning the venture (Chapter 4), organizing the venture (Chapter 5), and launching the venture (Chapter 6). Each of these activities is important to being an entrepreneur, and we'll cover each more thoroughly in the chapter indicated.

Managing the Venture. Once the entrepreneur has the entrepreneurial venture up and running, then what? We have to recognize and understand that there's more to entrepreneurship in action than just starting the venture. An entrepreneur also must effectively manage the venture by managing processes (Chapter 7), managing people (Chapter 8), and managing growth (Chapter 9). We'll cover the aspects of managing the entrepreneurial venture in the chapters indicated.

In addition, we'll look at some special issues facing entrepreneurs. Given the dynamic nature of the external environment and the volatility of market opportunities, entrepreneurs constantly need to keep on top of the changing landscape. One way to do this is by being a **world-class organization**, which very simply is an organization that is the best in its world at what it does. We'll cover what it means to be a world-class organization in Chapter 7. Finally, in Chapter 9, we'll look at some unique entrepreneurial situations such as minority- and women-owned entrepreneurial ventures, family businesses, and challenges in the entrepreneur's personal life.

Although you may think it odd that we look at the person—the entrepreneur—in a textbook on entrepreneurship in action, actually it's that person who makes it all happen. Without that individual who makes the effort and who is willing to take the risk to pursue an opportunity, entrepreneurship wouldn't occur! In the next section, we want to focus more closely on the person by looking at who entrepreneurs are and what they do.

WHO ARE ENTREPRENEURS AND WHAT DO THEY DO?

Describing *who* entrepreneurs are has been (and continues to be) a favorite pursuit of researchers and business journalists. One thing we need to get straight first as we look at the entrepreneur as an individual is our definition of **entrepreneur**. We're going to define an entrepreneur as someone who initiates and actively operates an entrepreneurial venture.[27] Inherent in this definition is the idea that the entrepreneur is not just the person who identifies the opportunity(ies) that are the basis for pursuing and initiating the entrepreneurial venture, but is also that person who operates the entrepreneurial venture. The entrepreneur "does" the venture as well as "dreams" it up.

Types of Entrepreneurs

When FUBU's Daymond John decided to start his own business making hip-hop urban fashions, he became an entrepreneur. A continent away in Madrid, Spain, Martin Varsavsky, also an entrepreneur, has founded not one, but six successful companies and his personal net worth is estimated somewhere between $300 million to $600 million.[28] Both can be considered entrepreneurs, but are they the same *types* of entrepreneurs? Probably not. Researchers who have studied entrepreneurial behavior suggest that there are different types of entrepreneurs. These types include nascent, novice, habitual, serial, and portfolio.[29] A **nascent entrepreneur** is an individual who is in the process of starting a new business. A **novice entrepreneur** is an individual who has no prior business ownership experience as a business founder, inheritor of a business, or a purchaser of a business. A **habitual entrepreneur** is an individual who has prior business ownership experience. The nascent entrepreneur can either be a novice or a habitual entrepreneur. A **serial entrepreneur** is an individual who has sold or closed an original business, established another new business, sold or closed that business, established another new business, sold or closed that business, and continues this cycle of entrepreneurial behavior. A **portfolio entrepreneur** is an individual who retains an original business and builds a portfolio of additional businesses through inheriting, establishing, or purchasing them.

Of these types of entrepreneurs, the concept of a nascent entrepreneur appears to most closely reflect the chaotic and complex entrepreneurial process. Exhibit 1-7 summarizes some interesting research results found in studies of nascent entrepreneurs. As we attempt to further understand entrepreneurship, the concept of nascent entrepreneurs will continue to be a popular subject of entrepreneurship researchers.[30]

EXHIBIT 1-7 What Do We Know About Nascent Entrepreneurs?

- They have significantly higher expectations about: the desirability of starting a business, the extent to which doing so would help achieve other goals, and the extent to which their skills and abilities would contribute to the success of the business.
- They use entirely different styles of problem solving, decision making, and creative discovery than do non-nascent entrepreneurs.
- Most nascent entrepreneurs start as small reproducers (ventures that offer products and services not all that different from what is already available) and not as innovators (ventures that offer products and services that vary significantly from those of existing organizations).
- Most nascent entrepreneurs draw upon their own savings and personal assets in putting together their organizations.
- Having strong relationships (high levels of trust and emotional closeness) with contacts (business associates, close friends, and family members) can help nascent entrepreneurs in their efforts.

Sources: H. E. Aldrich and M. A. Martinez, "Many Are Called, But Few Are Chosen: An Evolutionary Perspective For the Study of Entrepreneurship," *Entrepreneurship Theory & Practice*, Summer 2001, pp. 41–56; K. Johnson, W. Danis, and M. Dollinger, "The Impact of Cognitive Styles of Decision Making in New Venture Creation on the Expectations and Perceptions of the Nascent Entrepreneur," *Academy of Management Proceedings*, 2001, Entrepreneurship Division Abstracts, p. 4; and K. Shaver, E. Gatewood, and W. Gartner, "Differing Expectations: Comparing Nascent Entrepreneurs to Non-Entrepreneurs," *Academy of Management Proceedings*, 2001, Entrepreneurship Division Abstracts, p. 16.

Now that you know how we define an entrepreneur and have a better understanding of the types of entrepreneurs, you might be asking yourself, Am I (or could I be) an entrepreneur? Maybe we can better answer that question by looking at the characteristics of entrepreneurs.

Characteristics of Entrepreneurs

How would you describe well-known entrepreneurs such as Bill Gates (of Microsoft fame), Michael Dell (founder of Dell Computer), or Dineh Mohajer (founder of Hard Candy)? Would you be apt to describe their background (demographic profile) or their personality characteristics? Or might you focus more on their intention to be entrepreneurs—that is, what made them want to be entrepreneurs? Each of these approaches can be (and has been) used to describe entrepreneurs.[31]

Demographic Profile of Entrepreneurs. If we wanted to use the demographic approach to describe who entrepreneurs are, we'd look at the characteristics of the individual's personal background. Some of the more popular demographic factors that have been studied include:

1. *Family birth order.* Studies have shown that firstborn children tend to seek out more responsibility and be high achievers, which researchers say is likely to correlate with being an entrepreneur.[32]
2. *Gender.* Overall, studies have shown that men are much more likely (in fact, twice as likely) to start a business than are women.[33]
3. *Work experience.* There's some evidence that having worked in a small business or having had prior entrepreneurial experience is positively related to being an entrepreneur.[34]
4. *Education.* Studies have shown that having a high school diploma sharply raises a person's odds of trying to start a business.[35]
5. *Entrepreneurial family.* Various studies have found that entrepreneurs tend to have parents who were entrepreneurial.[36]

Other demographic traits that have been studied by entrepreneurship researchers include marital status, age, education level of parents, and socioeconomic status.[37]

Although it's interesting to look at these demographic characteristics (and perhaps to see how your own personal background measures up), the problem with trying to create a demographic profile of a typical entrepreneur is that these models aren't widely applicable and don't account for every situation. Just because people may have these demographic characteristics doesn't automatically mean that they will be entrepreneurs. Likewise, just because others don't have these characteristics doesn't mean that they won't be entrepreneurs. Because there are drawbacks to using demographic characteristics to describe entrepreneurs, perhaps we can learn something about who entrepreneurs are by looking instead at their personality characteristics.

Personality Profile of Entrepreneurs. What types of personality traits do entrepreneurs have that might distinguish them from nonentrepreneurs, and what traits do they have that might predict who will be a successful entrepreneur? Is there a classic "entrepreneurial personality?" Those are the questions that the personality approach has attempted to answer. Researchers and writers long have

FYI

Male Versus Female Entrepreneurs

Although the 1990s were a decade in which women launched companies in record numbers, studies show that females are significantly less likely than males (62 percent to 72 percent) to want to start a business of their own. But, just how different are male and female entrepreneurs in the way they run their businesses? One study looked at the differences between male and female entrepreneurs in the areas of planning, controlling, internal communication, human resources management, work-related tasks, customer service, networking, and on-the-job personal time. The results showed that women tended to engage in the following behaviors more often than their male counterparts:

- Controlling behavior
- Internal communication
- Human resources management
- General work-related tasks

The most surprising result? That of controlling behavior, which has long been thought to be predominantly a male trait. In this study, women actually reported more instances of assertive and controlling behavior than did the men. Another interesting result was that male entrepreneurs tended to use more on-the-job time for personal matters such as reading the newspaper, talking with drop-in visitors, and so forth.

Sources: P. Thomas, "Today's Women-Owned Ventures Are Cutting-Edge Enterprises," *Wall Street Journal Online*, August 17, 1999, accessed at **www.startupjournal.com**; C. Mulhern, "A Different World," *Entrepreneur*, July 1998, p. 36; and M. L. Kourilsky and W. B. Walstad, "Entrepreneurship and Female Youth: Knowledge, Attitudes, Gender Differences, and Educational Practices, *Journal of Business Venturing*, vol. 13, 1998, pp. 77–88.

tried to pinpoint entrepreneurial personality characteristics.[38] Although the personality approach has the same types of descriptive concerns as the demographic approach—that is, being able to pinpoint specific personality characteristics that all entrepreneurs share—this hasn't stopped researchers from trying to identify common traits.[39] For instance, one list of personality characteristics included the following: high level of motivation, abundance of self-confidence, ability to be involved for the long term, high energy level, persistent problem solver, high degree of initiative, ability to set goals, and moderate risk-taker.[40] Another list of characteristics of "successful" entrepreneurs included high energy level, great persistence, resourcefulness, the desire and ability to be self-directed, and relatively high need for autonomy.

Another development was the proposed use of a proactive personality scale to predict an individual's likelihood of pursuing entrepreneurial ventures. What is a **proactive personality**? Very simply, it describes an individual who is more prone to take actions to influence his or her environment—that is a person who is more proactive. Obviously an entrepreneur is likely to exhibit proactive actions as he or she searches for opportunities and acts to take advantage of those opportunities.[41] Items on the proactive personality scale found to be good indicators of a person's likelihood of becoming an entrepreneur included gender, education, having an entrepreneurial parent, and possessing a proactive personality.

The personality approach to describing entrepreneurs, like the demographic approach, isn't flawless, but it has helped us better understand who entrepreneurs

Type E's

Is there a Type E (entrepreneurial) personality? One study suggests that entrepreneurs tend to share certain characteristics that set them apart from their corporate counterparts. According to this study, these common traits included the following:

1. Aggressively pursues goals; pushes both self and others
2. Seeks autonomy, independence, and freedom from boundaries; very individualistic
3. Sends consistent messages; very focused and doesn't deviate from purpose
4. Acts quickly, often without deliberating
5. Keeps distance and maintains objectivity; expects others to be self-sufficient and tough-minded
6. Pursues simple, practical solutions; able to cut through complexity and find the essential and important issues
7. Is willing to take risks, comfortable with uncertainty
8. Exhibits clear opinions and values; makes quick judgments, often finding fault and having high expectations
9. Impatient regarding results and with others; "just do it" mentality
10. Positive, upbeat, optimistic; communicates confidence

What do you think of this list? Does *your* personality fit this profile?

Source: J. Chun, "Type E Personality," *Entrepreneur*, January 1997, p. 10.

are. Perhaps we can get an even clearer picture by looking at entrepreneurs from the perspective of their behavioral tendencies (intentions) toward creating and starting an entrepreneurial venture.

Intentions Profiles of Entrepreneurs. Given the limitations of both the demographic and personality profiles for describing entrepreneurs, the current focus of entrepreneurship researchers has been on attempting to understand the decision (intention) to become an entrepreneur. How do studies of entrepreneurial intention relate to understanding who entrepreneurs are? They can help us better understand the situational context, the person, *and* the process the individual goes through as he or she contemplates becoming an entrepreneur.

An underlying anchor behind the entrepreneurial intention approach is that becoming an entrepreneur clearly represents planned, intentional behavior.[42] Proponents of this approach believe that the decision to be an entrepreneur isn't accidental, but instead is the result of a combination of personal and contextual factors. Exhibit 1-8 shows these relationships in an early model of entrepreneurial intentionality. As you can see, the entrepreneurial action (decision) by an individual is preceded by the intention to do so, which in turn is influenced by both contextual factors (social, political, economic opportunities) and personal factors (history, personality, abilities).

Another approach to determining entrepreneurial intentions proposed using the ACE (Appropriateness–Consistency–Effectiveness) model from communication theory. (See Exhibit 1-9.) The ACE model suggests that mass media and interpersonal messages can influence an individual's perception of the appropri-

EXHIBIT 1-8 Bird's Model of Entrepreneurial Intentionality

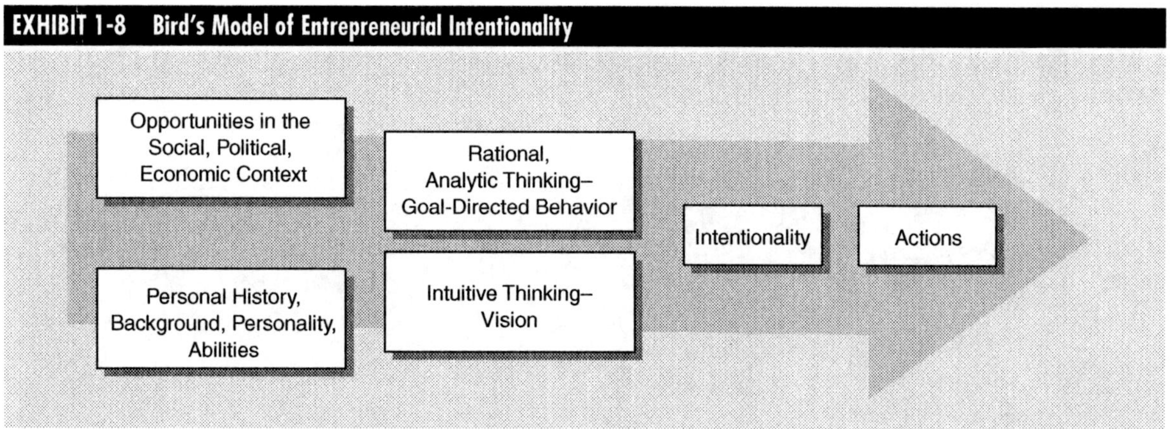

Source: Republished with permission of *Academy of Management Review*, from "Implementing Entrepreneurial Ideas: The Case for Intention," Vol. 13, No. 3, 1988, p. 444.

ateness, consistency, and effectiveness of starting a business. These perceptions then influence an individual's intention to become an entrepreneur. How effective is the ACE model at predicting a person's intention to start a business? In one study of U.S. and Irish citizens, the ACE model effectively predicted intention to start a business for both groups.[43]

Do these intentionality approaches make sense for understanding who entrepreneurs are? One important thing they do is helps us recognize the interplay of personal *and* contextual factors in being an entrepreneur. Researchers continue to look at entrepreneurial intentions and are helping us refine our knowledge of entrepreneurs and the factors that influence the entrepreneurial decision.[44]

By now, you should have a fairly good grasp of who entrepreneurs are and the various ways to describe them. But knowing *who* entrepreneurs are doesn't tell us anything about *what* they do. That's the next topic we're going to explore.

EXHIBIT 1-9 ACE Model of Intention to Start a Business

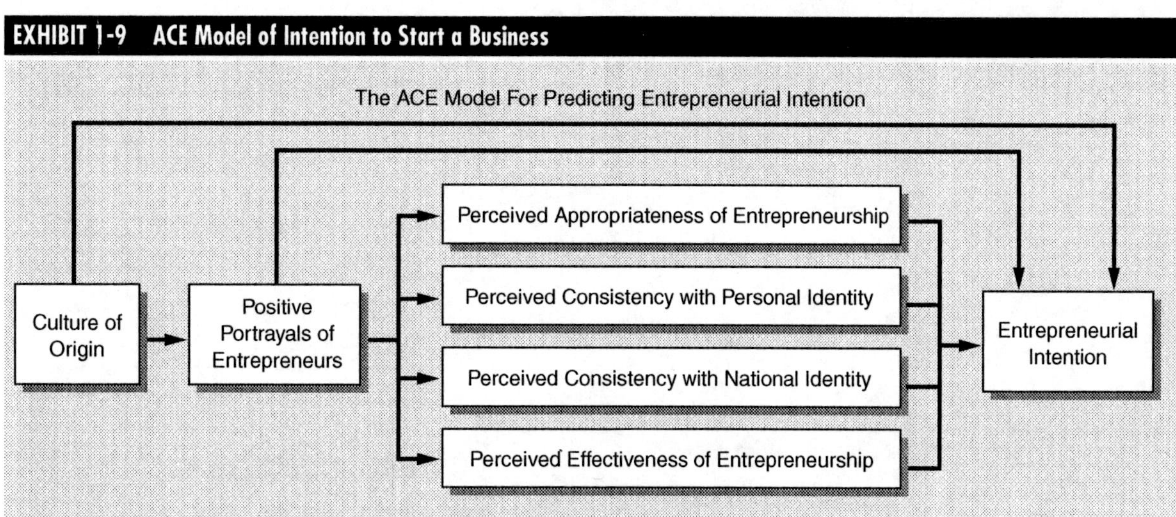

Source: Reprinted with permission from E. G. DePillis and K. K. Reardon, "Culture, Personality, Role Models, Persuasion: What Makes One Want to Become an Entrepreneur?" *Academy of Management National Meeting Paper*, August 2001, p. 10.

FYI

Have You Got What It Takes?

Do you think you've got what it takes to be an entrepreneur? Take the following quiz!

Answer these questions to see if you're cut out to run your own show.

1. Can you look at an inkblot that clearly represents a ship and see a horse or a lamppost as well?

- **Yes**
- **No**

A Rorschach test may be the best way to spot an entrepreneur. Management gurus cite a tolerance for ambiguity as one of the crucial intellectual assets needed to run a company.

2. You're in the front row at a comedy club. The headliner beckons you onstage to be part of the act. What do you do?

- **Plead laryngitis.**
- **Step up to the mike.**

Being able to think on your feet is a must for a business owner (and having a sense of humor doesn't hurt). Entrepreneurs have to constantly sell themselves and their company—to employees, customers, investors, the media, and the general public.

3. You are considering taking a cycling vacation. Which would you prefer?

- **Mountain biking on rugged terrain.**
- **A gentle cruise on a smooth road.**

When you own a business, there's no such thing as coasting. The path to success is filled with massive potholes, bumps, hills, hazards—and competitors who are pedaling just as furiously.

4. Can you take no for an answer?

- **Yes**
- **No**

If you can, forget it. Venture capitalists may turn down your proposals 25 times before you strike pay dirt. Skepticism should not leave you feeling rejected—it should motivate you to learn from the experience, change your pitch, and try again.

5. You're ready to buy a new home. Which do you do?

- **Find an existing house you're happy with.**
- **Find a vacant lot and supervise the construction of your dream house.**

Entrepreneurs are, at root, builders. In fact, creating a business from scratch is a lot like building a house. You've got to carve out your territory, plan a structure that will withstand the elements, and hire specialists to do the labor, all the while staying within your budget.

6. Your neighbor's daughter shows up at your door in full Girl Scout regalia, selling cookies. You already have a cabinet full of Thin Mints. Can you resist?

- **Yes**
- **No**

If you can, that's a big plus. Running a company means saying no just as often as saying yes—to friends, neighbors, and even kids asking for money.

7. Can you simultaneously watch—and absorb—the nightly news, edit a presentation, and conduct a three-way conference call with your brother and sister?

- **Yes**
- **No**

Start-up companies are not distinguished by a division of executive labor. One minute you're the CFO, the next you're handling a marketing issue, then you're dealing with a personnel problem. And, more often than not, you're doing them all at once.

8. You've planned a long-weekend getaway for months. The night before departure, your plumbing explodes. Now you've got to stay home and bail out the basement. What do you do?

- **Go into a deep funk.**
- **Roll up your sleeves and take it in stride.**

If nothing else, entrepreneurs must be flexible. When you're the boss, owner, and chief investor, no problem is too small for your attention. "If you're rigid about what you want to do, it's not going to work," says Ralph Subbiondo, a partner in Ernst & Young's entrepreneurial services group. "That doesn't mean you can't be rigid in your ideals and goals, but you have to be flexible on a day-to-day basis."

Entrepreneurial Aptitude

If you answered all eight correctly, what are you waiting for?

Say goodbye to your boss, fire up your business, and don't look back.

Half right? Start up in your spare time but keep a paycheck coming in. Or find a co-conspirator to help you kick-start your company.

Fewer than four? Keep your day job. Some of us just aren't cut out to be our own boss.

Sources: *Working Woman*, July–August 1998, p. 46. Reprinted with permission of MacDonald Communication Corporation. Copyright © 1999 by MacDonald Communication Corporation.

What Entrepreneurs Do

Describing what entrepreneurs do isn't an easy task! No two entrepreneurs' specific work activities are exactly alike. In a general sense, entrepreneurs are creating something new, something different. They're searching for change, responding to it, and exploiting it.[45] Yet, maybe we can get a clearer picture if we look at what entrepreneurs do in terms of broad categories of entrepreneurial activities. We can also find some similarities by re-examining what happens in the entrepreneurial process. (Refer back to Exhibit 1-6.) Those activities are good descriptions of what entrepreneurs do.

Initially, an entrepreneur is engaged in assessing the potential for the entrepreneurial venture and then dealing with start-up issues. In exploring the entrepreneurial context, entrepreneurs are gathering information, identifying potential opportunities, and assessing possible competitive advantage(s). Then, armed with this information, the entrepreneur begins researching the venture's feasibility—uncovering business ideas, looking at competitors, and exploring financing options. After looking at the potential of the proposed venture and assessing the likelihood of a successful pursuit, the entrepreneur proceeds to planning the venture. What's involved with planning? It includes activities such as developing a viable organizational vision and mission, exploring organizational culture issues, and very importantly, creating strong and effective business plans. Once the entrepreneur has resolved these planning issues, then he or she must look at organizing the venture, which involves choosing a legal form of business organization, addressing other legal issues such as patent or copyright searches, and coming up with an appropriate organizational design for structuring how work is going to be done. After these start-up activities have been completed, the entrepreneur is ready to actually launch the venture. What happens during this phase? It includes setting goals and strategies. It also includes identifying the technology-operations methods, marketing plans, information systems, financial-accounting systems, and cash flow management systems to be used in performing the work of the entrepreneurial venture.

Entrepreneurs in Action

Have you ever been on one of those tour boats where you could view the fish and other fascinating aquatic life underneath you? Many of these semisubmersible boats are made by Sub Sea Systems, Inc. (**www.subseasystems.com**) of Sacramento, California. Co-owners Jim Mayfield and Patrick and Michael Stafford decided that building these boats for the tourism industry was a pretty good bet. However, launching the idea was anything but smooth sailing. They built their first semisubmersible boat on speculation and mortgaged their homes to pay the design expenses. In addition, they had the formidable task of getting approval from the U.S. Coast Guard for the boat's design specifications. That process alone took 18 months. However, before the first boat was completed, the company had signed contracts to design and build two more. Now, Sub Sea Systems is the largest supplier of these specialty vessels in the United States. The company is known worldwide for its quality craftsmanship, attention to detail, and engineering. Finding a niche in this industry has required the owners to adjust to the changing demands of the tourism industry. But through it all, the owners have maintained their sense of humor. Mayfield says laughingly, "We like to say we're going under every day and loving it."

Sources: Sub Sea Systems Web site (**www.subseasystems.com**), April 8, 2002; and C. Goodman, "The View From Below," *Nation's Business*, September 1998, p. 79.

Once the entrepreneurial venture is up and running, the entrepreneur's attention switches to managing it. (Remember what we said earlier: Entrepreneurs "do" as well as "create.") What's involved with managing the entrepreneurial venture? There are three main responsibilities: managing processes, managing people, and managing growth. When managing processes, entrepreneurs are concerned with things such as making decisions, establishing action plans, analyzing the venture's internal and external environments, measuring and evaluating performance, and stimulating and making needed changes. When managing people, entrepreneurs are concerned with things such as selecting and hiring, appraising and training, motivating, managing conflict, delegating tasks, and being an effective leader. Finally, when managing growth, entrepreneurs do things such as developing appropriate growth strategies, dealing with crises, exploring ways to finance growth, determining the venture's value, and perhaps even eventually preparing to harvest or exit the venture.

As you can tell from the above descriptions, being an entrepreneur is an exciting proposition! Entrepreneurs do a variety of things and deal with a multitude of challenges. In fact, one writer concluded that "there are no easy answers" in being an entrepreneur. "Like parenting, like teaching, like singing a song, the act of starting a business can be done well or disastrously—but it's done best

EXHIBIT 1-10 The Rewards and Challenges of Being an Entrepreneur

Rewards	Challenges
▲ High degree of independence—freedom from constraints	▼ Must be comfortable with change and uncertainty
▲ Get to use a variety of skills and talents	▼ Must make a bewildering number of decisions
▲ Freedom to make decisions	▼ May face tough economic choices
▲ Accountable to only yourself	▼ Must be comfortable with taking risks
▲ Opportunity to tackle challenges	▼ Need many different skills and talents
▲ Feeling of achievement and pride	▼ Must be comfortable with the potential of failure
▲ Potential for greater financial rewards	

when it's on your own terms, for your own reasons, using your own skills."[46] Another writer proposed that entrepreneurial behavior was complex, intentional, and passionate.[47] Yet, it's primarily because of these qualities that it's prudent for you to know, from the start, the rewards and challenges of being an entrepreneur.

The Rewards and Challenges of Being an Entrepreneur

Would you enjoy being an entrepreneur? Are you prepared to deal with the rewards and challenges? Although many entrepreneurs "fell into" their roles, the fact that you're reading this book indicates that you're interested in studying entrepreneurship and trying to learn all you can about it. Part of that education is understanding the upside and downside of entrepreneurship. Exhibit 1-10 summarizes the major rewards and challenges of being an entrepreneur.

There are many rewards associated with being an entrepreneur! Many individuals pursue entrepreneurship primarily because of the high degree of independence that it allows them. In fact, researchers have found that the freedom from others' constraints—that is, being independent—is the dominant attraction for entrepreneurs.[48] Other positive aspects of being an entrepreneur include getting to use a variety of skills and talents, having the freedom to make decisions, being accountable only to yourself, having the opportunity to tackle challenges, experiencing feelings of achievement and pride in accomplishing goals, and, of course, having the potential for greater financial rewards. Yes, the potential to make loads of money can be quite tempting. However, the financial rewards, which for most entrepreneurs are a nice secondary benefit, are not the primary reason for being an entrepreneur.

What about the challenges associated with being an entrepreneur? Successful entrepreneurs will tell you that it's an all-consuming passion, that it's hard work, that it involves sacrifices (both personal

Rapid Review 

- ✔ How do we define an entrepreneur?
- ✔ What focus does each of the three approaches to describing entrepreneurs have?
- ✔ How do male and female entrepreneurs differ?
- ✔ Describe the different types of entrepreneurs.
- ✔ What are the drawbacks of the demographic and personality approaches to describing entrepreneurs?
- ✔ How does the entrepreneurial intentions approach contribute to describing entrepreneurs?
- ✔ Discuss the two entrepreneurial intentions models introduced in the chapter.
- ✔ Describe what entrepreneurs do.
- ✔ List the major rewards and challenges of being an entrepreneur.

and professional), and that it's never the same from day to day. To be an entrepreneur means that you must be comfortable with change and uncertainty. In fact, the very essence of entrepreneurship (remember our definition) implies that change is the normal state of affairs for entrepreneurs. With change comes uncertainty and risk. Entrepreneurs must be comfortable with change and with taking risks. In addition, many of the challenges associated with being an entrepreneur involve making choices. Entrepreneurs face a bewildering array of decisions, which may, at times, mean making tough economic choices and dealing with the reality of failure.

As we said at the beginning of the chapter, entrepreneurship is attracting a lot of attention these days. After reading this chapter, you should now have a better understanding of this strong interest in entrepreneurs and entrepreneurship. And you, hopefully, have begun to decide whether entrepreneurship is the correct career choice for you.

CHAPTER SUMMARY

This summary is organized around the chapter-opening objectives.

1. Entrepreneurship is the process whereby an individual or group of individuals use organized efforts to pursue opportunities to create value and grow by fulfilling wants and needs through innovation and uniqueness, no matter what resources the entrepreneur currently has.
2. Richard Cantillon, an economist in the early 1700s, originated the term *entrepreneur* to describe someone who took an active risk-bearing role in pursuing opportunities. During the 1800s, economist Jean Baptiste Say proposed that the profits of entrepreneurship were separate from the profits of capital ownership. In the mid-1930s, economist Joseph Schumpeter proposed that entrepreneurship involved creative destruction—a process whereby existing products, processes, ideas, and businesses are replaced with better ones. Another development in the historical perspective of entrepreneurship from the twentieth century involved the view of Peter Drucker, a management author, who said that entrepreneurs recognize and act on opportunities.
3. We defined *entrepreneurship* as the process whereby an individual or group of individuals uses organized efforts and means to pursue opportunities to create value and grow by fulfilling wants and needs through innovation and uniqueness, no matter what resources are currently controlled. Intrapreneurship is the pursuit of entrepreneurship within the confines of a large organization.
4. An entrepreneurial venture is an organization that is pursuing opportunities, is characterized by innovative practices, and has profitability and growth as its main goals. They're different from small businesses in that small businesses do not emphasize new or innovative practices and do not seek growth.
5. The importance of entrepreneurship can be seen in three areas: innovation, number of new start-ups, and job creation. Research has shown that entrepreneurial firms play an important role in innovation because they are an essential source of new and unique ideas. In addition, the pursuit of entrepreneurship contributes to the overall creation of new firms. This is impor-

tant because new firms contribute to economic development. Finally, new small firms create an overwhelming majority of net new jobs.

6. The Global Entrepreneurship Monitor (GEM) report studies the impact of entrepreneurial activity on economic growth in various countries. The GEM 2000 report showed that among the major industrialized G-7 countries, there was a very strong relationship between the level of entrepreneurial activity and annual economic growth.
7. The steps in the entrepreneurial process include exploring the entrepreneurial context in order to identify opportunities and possible competitive advantage(s); starting the venture through researching its feasibility and planning, organizing, and launching it; and managing the venture (which includes managing processes, managing people, and managing growth) and other entrepreneurial challenges.
8. An entrepreneur is someone who initiates and actively operates an entrepreneurial venture. Entrepreneurs can be described by their characteristics using things such as demographic profiles, personality profiles, or entrepreneurial intentions profiles. Entrepreneurs engage in a variety of activities, including exploring the entrepreneurial context, researching the venture's feasibility, planning the venture, organizing the venture, launching the venture, and managing the venture.
9. There are different types of entrepreneurs. A nascent entrepreneur is an individual who is in the process of starting a new business. A novice entrepreneur is an individual who has no prior business ownership experience. A habitual entrepreneur is an individual who has prior business ownership experience. A serial entrepreneur is an individual who has sold or closed an original business, established another business, sold or closed that business, established another business, sold or closed that business, and continues this cycle of entrepreneurial behavior. A portfolio entrepreneur is an individual who retains an original business and builds a portfolio of additional businesses.
10. The rewards of being an entrepreneur include having a high degree of independence, getting to use a variety of skills and talents, having the freedom to make decisions, being accountable to only yourself, having the opportunity to tackle challenges, experiencing feelings of achievement and pride, and having the potential for greater financial rewards. The challenges of being an entrepreneur include being comfortable with change and uncertainty, making a bewildering number of decisions, facing tough economic choices, being comfortable with taking risks, needing many different skills and talents, and being comfortable with the potential of failure.

KEY TERMS

- *Entrepreneurship:* The process whereby an individual or group of individuals uses organized efforts to pursue opportunities to create value and grow by fulfilling wants and needs through innovation and uniqueness, no matter what resources the entrepreneur currently has.
- *Creative destruction:* The process whereby existing products, processes, ideas, and businesses are replaced with better ones.

- *Intrapreneurship:* The pursuit of entrepreneurship within the confines of a large organization.
- *Small business:* A business that is independently owned, operated, and financed; has fewer than 100 employees; doesn't engage in any new or innovative practices; and has relatively little impact on its industry.
- *Entrepreneurial venture:* An organization that is pursuing opportunities, is characterized by innovative practices, and has profitability and growth as its main goals.
- *Opportunities:* Positive external trends or changes that provide unique and distinct possibilities for innovating and creating value.
- *Competitive advantage:* What sets an organization apart; its competitive edge.
- *World-class organization:* An organization that is the best in its world at what it does.
- *Entrepreneur:* Someone who initiates and actively operates an entrepreneurial venture.
- *Nascent entrepreneur:* An individual who is in the process of starting a new business.
- *Novice entrepreneur:* An individual who has no prior business ownership experience as a business founder, inheritor of a business, or a purchaser of a business.
- *Habitual entrepreneur:* An individual who has prior ownership experience.
- *Serial entrepreneur:* An individual who has sold or closed an original business, established another new business, sold or closed that business, established another new business, sold or closed that business, and continues this cycle of entrepreneurial behavior.
- *Portfolio entrepreneur:* An individual who retains an original business and builds a portfolio of additional businesses through inheriting, establishing, or purchasing them.
- *Proactive personality:* An individual who is more prone to take actions to influence his or her environment.

SWEAT EQUITY

1. You've been asked to make a presentation before the local chapter of the Young Entrepreneur's Organization (**www.yeo.org**) about the advantages and drawbacks of the Internet and the World Wide Web for entrepreneurial ventures. After doing some research on this topic, draw up a detailed outline of the key points you want to make. Be sure to cite your sources.
2. Studies are showing that many formerly self-employed Americans are returning to work in established companies. Locate a self-employed person and interview them regarding the advantages and drawbacks of being self-employed. Ask about the person's experiences and if he or she has ever considered returning to work in an established company and what factors might enter into that decision.

3. The participation of women in the overall workforce during the latter part of the twentieth century has had a profound impact on the general economy. The latest numbers from the National Foundation for Women Business Owners (**www.nfwbo.org**) state that as of 2002, there were an estimated 6.2 million majority-owned, privately held women-owned firms in the U.S., accounting for 28 percent of all privately held firms in the country. Between 1997 and 2002, the number of women-owned firms increased by 14 percent nationwide, sales grew by 40 percent, and employment increased by 30 percent. Using your library or the Internet, find three examples of women-owned entrepreneurial ventures. Describe their businesses, and, if enough information is given, describe the challenges they have faced. Be sure to cite your sources.
4. A large-scale study of nascent entrepreneurs (the National Panel Study of U.S. Business Start-Ups) proposes that a key difference between entrepreneurs and nonentrepreneurs isn't personality traits; it's the fact that entrepreneurs have learned to take the steps required to set up a business. And it appears that the actual sequence of events doesn't seem to matter much. Success comes from momentum, from taking action—meeting with potential customers, potential investors, potential suppliers, potential employees, and so on. What are the implications of these findings? Interview two or three entrepreneurs about their experiences in starting their businesses.
5. If entrepreneurship and stories about entrepreneurship are such hot topics, just how popular is entrepreneurship education? Research how and where entrepreneurship is being taught today. (Your focus might be on the elementary, secondary, or college level.) Write a report (at least two pages in length) on your findings. Be sure to include at least two visual representations of data in the form of tables, graphs, charts, or maps.
6. How has the role of an entrepreneur changed? According to Tom Richman (see "The Evolution of the Professional Entrepreneur," in *Inc.'s State of Small Business Special Issue*, 1997, pp. 50–53), today's entrepreneur is more of a *professional* entrepreneur who relies on intellect, not gut instincts. Here are some other comparisons Richman provided of the "then" entrepreneur versus the "now" entrepreneur:

Then:	*Now:*
Boss	Leader
Secretive	Open
Self-reliant	Inquisitive
Lone ranger	Networker
Quick decisions	Takes time to build consensus

   Based on what we discussed in this chapter, do you agree with these characterizations? Why or why not? How do you think these "new" characteristics might change our description of what entrepreneurs do?
7. Experts say that the number of teenage entrepreneurs is growing. Research the topic of teen entrepreneurs. What special challenges do teens face in launching and managing entrepreneurial ventures?

ENTREPRENEURSHIP IN ACTION CASES

FUBU (www.fubu.com)

This case can be found at the beginning of Chapter 1.

Discussion Questions

1. Is entrepreneurship evident in Daymond John's story? Explain.
2. Is FUBU an example of Schumpeter's creative destruction? Why or why not?
3. Put yourself in John's shoes, and describe what you initially had to do as an entrepreneur and what you do now in your role as an entrepreneur.

Hussey Seating Company (www.husseyseating.com)

1835. That's the year that Hussey Seating was founded by the great-great-great grandfather of the current CEO, Tim Hussey. The company initially began as a manufacturer of agricultural plow blades. But one thing that distinguishes this long-running business is its inventiveness. As markets and customers have changed, the company has reinvented itself by either redefining a market position or by creating new uses for its original core competency—shaping steel. When the agricultural plow blade business began declining, Hussey capitalized on its steel-forming expertise and moved into the steel-ladder and steel-fire-escape businesses. And today, Hussey is the leading manufacturer of seating for arenas and stadiums and bleacher and seating platforms used in gyms and auditoriums.

Yet, even as the market leader, Tim Hussey knows there are no long-term guarantees. He says, "We are constantly looking at ways that we can change the rules. It is an aggressive approach that has helped the company thrive." For example, Tim launched a full-scale redesign of the biggest portion of the company's business, indoor folding bleachers, even though they were the leaders in that business. He explained to his employees that the next-generation product was needed while the company was in the strong position of industry leader. In the summer of 2000 Hussey's MAXAM bleacher line was introduced. The bleachers contain 50 percent fewer parts, can be installed much more quickly (one-third less time), have no sharp edges, and are more accommodating to people with disabilities. Then, in November of 2001 Hussey introduced an innovative seating solution for arenas that allows super-fast and super-simple conversions between basketball and ice hockey seating configurations. Developing solutions to difficult seating challenges isn't anything new to Hussey. John Poyner, Vice President of Marketing at Hussey says, "Our goal is to be the total seating solution provider of choice among stadiums and arenas around the world. Responding to the needs of our customers and introducing new products . . . is part of our strategy to accomplish that goal." In many ways, these product redesigns exemplify the company's entrepreneurial spirit. It's that boldness that will help the company continue to be successful.

However, Hussey Seating isn't just about sustaining product leadership, it's also concerned with treating employees with respect, keeping a persistent focus on customers, and maintaining a commitment to its community, North Berwick, Maine, where it has been located from the beginning. The company's culture has its roots in the family's Quaker ancestors who felt strongly about "a sense of equity, business ethics, and a . . . connection to employees and the community." The company has had an employee profit-sharing plan since 1956. It also has supported the community with school funding, revamping sewage systems, and being the "cheerleader" for economic development.

Under Tim's leadership, the company's annual revenues have nearly doubled, to an estimated $110 million. He expects 10 percent growth in the two key North American markets for at least the next five years. But Tim has other goals as well. "I want to be recognized as the industry leader. I want to have a workplace that is productive and to be the employer of choice in our community. I want to be able to grow to be a strategic player in the overseas market. . . . We need to keep our eyes open for the next opportunity." Yes, Hussey Seating Company has ambitious plans. But as its history should show, it's not content to "sit" on its successes.

Discussion Questions

1. Would you classify Hussey Seating as an entrepreneurial venture? Explain.
2. What role do you think innovation plays at Hussey Seating Company?
3. What do you think the keys to Hussey's long-standing success are? Why do you think these elements are necessary?
4. What types of challenges do you think Hussey might face as it moves more and more into the global market? How would an entrepreneurial approach help them address these challenges?
5. What could other entrepreneurs learn from Hussey's experiences?

Sources: Hussey Seating Company Web site (**www.husseyseating.com**), April 5, 2002; and M. A. Verespej, "Sitting Pretty," *Industry Week*, March 5, 2001, pp. 48–54.

E*Trade Access (formerly Card Capture Services, Inc.) (www.ccsexpress.com)

If "an entrepreneur is someone who knows how to turn a setback into an opportunity," then Jeffrey Jetton and Steven Wright would definitely be entrepreneurs! As partners in Card Capture Services, they faced significant challenges in getting their venture up and running.

In 1993, CCS sold credit-card-processing machines to restaurants, grocery stores, and department stores around Portland, Oregon. Many of these merchants would accommodate customers by advancing cash against credit cards. However, credit card issuers didn't like this practice because they were being deprived of that revenue. If the card issuer caught a merchant doing this, it would drop them. Needless to say, this practice was highly risky for both the retail merchants and for CCS! Wright and Jetton figured there had to be a better solution. What these merchants needed was an inexpensive machine that would dispense cash just like an ATM. Out of a potential crisis came an opportunity!

Wright and Jetton helped found a new industry of independent ATMs. Now there are thousands of these machines dispensing cash at locations such as convenience stores, casinos, bars, and bowling alleys. Wright and Jetton's company became the nation's largest supplier of these machines. Sensing another opportunity, the company's ATMs now do other things than just spit out cash. The ATMs' video screens promote in-store specials, and customers also can get stamps and phone cards.

All in all, the initial crisis faced by Wright and Jetton, although risky, seemed pretty mild. But it wasn't quite as easy to get this entrepreneurial venture up and running as it sounds. To make their idea work, they had to find an inexpensive machine. Every manufacturer they went to said there was no market for low-end ATMs. But finally, they located a small company in Mississippi that made a strange-looking terminal (tall, narrow, tacky beige color), but the price was right! Another crisis resolved! The popularity of the machines with merchants triggered the next crises—managing rapid growth and the surge of new competitors coming into the market. Wright and Jetton knew that this was a pivotal point for their venture. Their solution? Bringing in professional help. They hired an old college pal, David Grano, who was in management at Nextel Communications. Grano brought his marketing background and fresh ideas to the table. The company was well-positioned to capture its place in the market, which it did throughout the late 1990s. Then, its successes attracted the attention of E*Trade Group, which acquired CCS Inc. in May 2000. E*Trade renamed the subsidiary E*Trade Access. Today, E*Trade Access is the operator of more than 10,000 ATMs across the United States.

Discussion Questions

1. Do you agree with the description of an entrepreneur as someone who knows how to turn a setback into an opportunity? How does this fit in with our chapter definitions of entrepreneur and entrepreneurship?
2. Using the model of the entrepreneurial process (Exhibit 1-6), describe the evolution of CCS/E*Trade Access.
3. What do you think contributed to the success of CCS?
4. What can other entrepreneurs learn from Jetton and Wright and their experiences with CCS?

Sources: Information on company from Hoover's Online (**www.hoovers.com**), April 8, 2002, and E*Trade Access's Web site (**www.ccsexpress.com**), April 8, 2002; J. Helyar, "At E*Trade, Growing Up Is Hard to Do," *Fortune,* March 18, 2002, accessed at **www.fortune.com**, and C. Hawn, "The Soul of a New Machine," *Forbes,* April 20, 1998, pp. 74–76.

C.F. Martin Guitar Company (www.cfmartin.com)

For well over a century and a half, the C. F. Martin Guitar Company (established in 1833) of Nazareth, Pennsylvania, has been producing acoustic instruments considered to be among the finest in the world. Like a Steinway grand piano, a Rolls Royce automobile, a Buffet clarinet, or a Baccarat crystal vase, a Martin Guitar—which can cost more than $10,000—is among the best that money can buy. This family business has managed to defy the odds and survive through six generations. Current CEO Christian Frederick Martin IV—better known as Chris—continues to be committed to the guitar maker's craft. He even travels to Martin dealerships around the world to hold instructional clinics. Few companies have had the staying power of Martin Guitar. Why? What are the keys to the company's success? A primary one has to be the entrepreneurial leadership and skills of a talented leader who has kept employees focused on important issues such as quality.

From the very beginning, quality has played an important role in everything that C. F. Martin Guitar Company does. Even through dramatic changes in product design, distribution systems, and manufacturing methods, the company has remained committed to making quality products. The company's steadfast adherence to high standards of musical excellence and providing a product to meet the needs of a demanding customer base permeates everything that happens in the organization, top to bottom and in all work areas. Part of that quality approach includes a long-standing ecological policy. Because the company depends on natural-wood products to make its guitars, it has embraced the judicious and responsible use of traditional natural materials and encouraged the introduction of sustainable-yield alternative wood species. Based on thorough customer research, Martin introduced guitars that used structurally sound woods with natural cosmetic defects that were once considered unacceptable. In addition, Martin follows the directives of CITES, the Convention on International Trade in Endangered Species of Wild Fauna and Flora (**www.cites.org**).

C. F. Martin Guitar Company is an interesting blend of old and new. Although the equipment and tools may have changed over the years, employees remain true to the principle of high standards of musical excellence. Building a guitar to meet these standards requires considerable attention and patience. Family member Frank Henry Martin explained to potential customers in the preface to a 1904 catalog, "How to build a guitar to give this tone is not a secret. It takes care and patience. Care in selecting the materials, laying out the proportions, and attending to the details which add to the player's comfort. Patience in giving the necessary time to finish every part. A good guitar cannot be built for the price of a poor one, but who regrets the extra cost for a good guitar?" Now, a century later, this statement is still an accurate reflection of the company's philosophy.

Although the company is rooted in its past, Chris isn't afraid to take the company in new directions. For instance, in the late 1990s, he made the decision to start selling guitars in the under-$800 market segment. This segment accounts for 65 percent of the acoustic guitar industry's sales. Although the company's DXM model doesn't look, smell, or feel like the company's pricier models, customers claim it has a better sound than most other instruments in that price range. Chris justified his decision by saying that "If Martin just worships its past without trying anything new, there won't be a Martin left to worship." And this commitment to trying new things continues. In early 2002 more than 25 new stock models, special guitars, and limited editions were introduced.

Discussion Questions

1. What do you think has contributed to the success of this business?
2. Would you call C. F. Martin Guitar Company an entrepreneurial venture? Explain your choice.
3. What do you think of CEO Chris Martin's direction for the company? What are the advantages? The drawbacks?
4. Chris made the statement that, "If Martin just worships its past without trying anything new, there won't be a Martin left to worship." What are the implications for other entrepreneurs looking to learn something from Martin's successes?

Sources: C. F. Martin Web site (**www.cfmartin.com**), April 8, 2002; and S. Fitch, "Stringing Them Along," *Forbes*, July 26, 1999, pp. 90–91.

Whirlpool Corporation/Inspired Chef (www.inspiredchef.com)

Whirlpool Corporation is a $10 billion company that's encouraging its employees to innovate like entrepreneurs. CEO David R. Whitwam believes that any one of Whirlpool's 55,000 employees can, with guidance, come up with innovative products or services that will make money. Inspired Chef is one of these employee-founded startups. Josh Gitlin, president of Inspired Chef, was chief of acquisitions and product development at Whirlpool's KitchenAid unit when he dreamed up the business that he now heads: in-home cooking classes taught by a branded network of chefs. He wrote up a business proposal, took it to an investor (none other than Whirlpool itself), and got money to launch the venture in September 2000. Inspired Chef is in 33 states and plans to continue growing to other states and adding more instructors and students. And Gitlin believes the company is on target to break even later in 2002.

Whitwam's notions about innovation are somewhat radical. He acknowledges that most employees won't have the time or the insight to create a new business or product line. And analysts worry that the company will neglect its manufacturing strengths by shifting its focus to untried ventures. Yet, Whitwam insists that his employees must think like entrepreneurs. If not, he believes Whirlpool will be resigned to a future of ever-slowing sales growth, diminishing profit margins, and sluggish share prices. Whitwam fostered this push toward innovation after rival Maytag Corporation blindsided the industry with a revolutionary new product, the front-loading Neptune washing machine. He countered Maytag's startling innovation by dispatching Whirlpool's research and development engineers to customers' homes so they could see firsthand how customers behaved. And this new focus on innovation appears to be paying off. Whirlpool is rolling out a wide array of innovative products. But Whitwam wants employees to get even more innovative in their thinking. To encourage creativity, he set aside 20 percent of the company's $400 million capital budget in 2001 for innovations. By 2003 that amount will increase to at least 35 percent. To claim a piece of that money requires inventive ideas. And he's even linking executives' pay to revenue derived from new products or services.

To facilitate this push to intrapreneurship, Whirlpool now has 35 "innovation consultants" around the world whose full-time job is to help employees turn ideas into action. These consultants are assisted by 177 part-time innovation mentors who also act as sounding boards and facilitators. The company also has an innovation intranet (in-house Web site) on which any employee can post an idea, volunteer to help on someone else's project, or correspond with the innovation consultants or mentors. The innovation Web site has recorded as many as 300,000 hits a month (about five per employee). And last, but not least, the innovation push has one other crucial characteristic. It's structured to sift through suggestions quickly and at minimal cost. Once senior managers judge an employee proposal worth pursuing, the employee(s) and innovation consultants have just 100 days and $100,000 to get it up and going by producing product prototypes or conducting customer research. This emphasis on speed and cost is premised on the fact that most concepts are doomed to fail. Yet, you have to do it again and again and again to hit the eventual winners.

Besides the Inspired Chef venture, others are coming soon. One idea being tested is a spin-off from Inspired Chef—teaching corporate team building by preparing meals in the kitchen. A new line of outdoor-grilling equipment is being pushed by a unit of KitchenAid. And the company is testing an Internet-enabled mini-refrigerator that can be turned into an oven.

Discussion Questions

1. Is Whitwam's push toward employee innovation intrapreneurship? Why or why not?
2. What do you think of Whirlpool's actions?
3. What types of steps is Whitwam taking to make sure his intrapreneurship efforts have a chance of success?
4. What advantages do you see to Whirlpool's approach? Drawbacks?
5. Do some research and find two other examples of corporate intrapreneurship. Describe what these companies are doing. Compare and contrast them with Whirlpool's approach.

Sources: Inspired Chef Web site (**www.inspiredchef.com**), April 8, 2002; and M. Arndt, "Whirlpool Taps Its Inner Entrepreneur," *Business Week Online*, February 7, 2002.

BUSINESS PLAN PRO

EXERCISE 1-1: Entrepreneurs and Their Business Plans

Install Business Plan Pro™, and start a new plan. Find the "Sample Plans" icon on the main toolbar, and click it once to open the built-in Sample Plan Browser. Instructions for this are in Chapter 4 of the Business Plan Pro manual. After you install the software, you can open the digitized manual from the Help menu in Business Plan Pro.

Experiment with the Sample Plan Browser's search facilities to find the following sample plans:

1. Southeast Health Plans. The plan name is "Plan Administration—Health." Its SIC code is 6411.
2. The Athlete's Foot. Athletic shoe store chain. The plan name is "Shoe Store—Athletic—Franchise" and its SIC code is 5661.
3. The Daily Pere. The plan name is "Café—Coffee Kiosks" and its SIC code is 5812.

These are actual business plans with real names, as they were developed by entrepreneurs as part of their start-up process. All three plans were funded, and the companies they envisioned were actually established. As you read through these plans, consider these questions:

- Among all the entrepreneurs described in the management summaries of these different plans, who would you most want as a partner in a new business? Who would you be most willing to invest in? Who of them is the most likely to succeed?
- Which of these plans was most entrepreneurial? Why? How does this plan illustrate entrepreneurship?
- Would you invest money in one or more of these plans? Which ones? What would you ask of the entrepreneurs in return?
- Which of these plans was most likely to succeed? Why?

BUSINESS NOW Myteam.com

Elliot Katzman is a serial entrepreneur. He has played key roles in several successful start-ups. His latest entrepreneurial venture—Myteam.com (**www.myteam.com**)—is a labor of love. With two sons playing on six different sports teams, Katzman saw the market need for a place where coaches, parents, and kids could come for information on schedules, rosters, directions, and other stuff associated with coordinating kids sports. Myteam.com was Katzman's solution. According to the company's Web site, Myteam is a direct marketing company that utilizes the Internet to enable communication, administration, and commerce among those involved in the amateur sports marketplace. Katzman felt that this was a perfect opportunity to combine his professional background in other tech-oriented entrepreneurial ventures and his personal passion for kids sports.

Myteam has had the support of a strong group of investors including Charles River Ventures. Ted Dintersmith, a partner at Charles River says that Myteam is the clear category leader in amateur sports communication and administration. His investment group found Myteam appealing on multiple dimensions: clear sense of mission, its values, and the potential to be a big commercial success. In addition, they recognized that Katzman had a great track record and a clear vision of what he wanted Myteam to be.

Myteam is building relationships with several key partners. It has exclusive multiyear agreements with over 30 premier amateur sports organizations such as Little League Baseball, Amateur Softball Association, and Amateur Athletic Union. These relationships cover more than 30 sports and give Myteam's sponsors access to more than 13 million sports participants. In addition, it has a team of professional advisers including noted athletes such as Bobby Orr and Gary Carter.

Discussion Questions

1. What do you think has contributed to the success of Myteam.com? Why do you think these elements are necessary?
2. Does Myteam.com fit the definition of an entrepreneurial venture? Explain.
3. Do some research on organized kids sports. Is the popularity continuing? Which kids sports seem to be growing in popularity? Which seem to be declining? What would the implications be for Myteam.com?
4. What types of challenges might Myteam.com face as it continues to grow?

Sources: Company information from company Web site (**www.myteam.com**), July 10, 2002; and *Business Now* video segment.

ENDNOTES

1. Information on FUBU from company's Web site (**www.fubu.com**), March 1, 2002; Hoover's Online (**www.hoovers.com**), March 1, 2002; and "Start Me Up," *Smart Money*, January 2001, p. 113.
2. E. G. Flamholtz and Y. Randle, *Growing Pains* (San Francisco: Jossey-Bass, 2000), p. xvii; S. Venkataraman, "The Distinctive Domain of Entrepreneurship Research: An Editor's Perspective," in *Advances in Entrepreneurship, Firm Emergence and Growth*, vol. 3, ed. J. A. Katz (Greenwich, CT: JAI Press, 1997), pp. 119–138; L. W. Busenitz, "Research on Entrepreneurial Alertness," *Journal of Small Business Management*, vol. 34, no. 4, October 1996, pp. 35–44; D. Krackhardt, "Entrepreneurial Opportunities in an Entrepreneurial Firm: A Structural Approach," *Entrepreneurship Theory and Practice*, vol. 19, no. 3, spring 1995, pp. 53–69; M. Warshaw, "The Entrepreneurial Mind: An Interview with Jeffrey A. Timmons," *Success*, April 1994, pp. 48–51; N. F. Krueger Jr. and D. V. Brazeal, "Entrepreneurial Potential and Potential Entrepreneurs," *Entrepreneurship Theory and Practice*, vol. 18, no. 3, spring 1994, pp. 91–104; J. C. Huefner and H. K. Hunt, "Broadening the Concept of Entrepreneurship: Comparing Business and Consumer Entrepreneurs," *Entrepreneurship Theory and Practice*, vol. 18, no. 3, spring 1994, pp. 61–75; W. D. Bygrave, "Theory Building in the Entrepreneurship Paradigm," *Journal of Business Venturing*, vol. 8, no. 3, 1993, pp. 255–80; J. R. Van Slyke, H. H. Stevenson, and M. J. Roberts, "The Start-Up Process," in *The Entrepreneurial Venture*, ed. W. A. Sahlman and H. H. Stevenson (Boston, MA: Harvard Business School Publications, 1992), pp. 1 and 81.
3. S. Shane and S. Venkataraman, "The Promise of Entrepreneurship as a Field of Research," *Academy of Management Review*, January 2000, pp. 217–26; and B. J. Bird, *Entrepreneurial Behavior* (Glenview, IL: Scott, Foresman and Company, 1989).
4. R. D. Hisrich, "Entrepreneurship and Intrapreneurship: Methods for Creating New Companies That Have an Impact on the Economic Renaissance of an Area," in *Entrepreneurship, Intrapreneurship, and Venture Capital*, ed. R. D. Hisrich (Lexington, MA: Lexington Books, 1986), p. 89.
5. S. A. Shane, "Who is Publishing the Entrepreneurship Research?" *Journal of Management*, vol. 23, 197, pp. 83–95.
6. W. B. Gartner, "What Are We Talking About When We Talk About Entrepreneurship?" *Journal of Business Venturing*, vol. 5, 1990, pp. 15–28.
7. Bird, *Entrepreneurial Behavior*, p. 3.
8. Web site for Huichol Center for Cultural Survival and Traditional Arts (**www.huicholcenter.com**), March 13, 2002; and L. Taylor, "Accidental Entrepreneur," *Working Woman*, April 1999, p. 17.
9. P. Davidsson and J. Wiklund, "Entrepreneurship as Growth; Growth as Entrepreneurship," *Academy of Management Proceedings*, 2001, Entrepreneurship Division Abstracts, p. 17.
10. W. B. Gartner, "Words Lead to Deeds: Towards an Organizational Emergence Vocabulary," *Journal of Business Venturing*, vol. 8, 1993, pp. 231–40.
11. R. D. Hisrich and M. P. Peters, *Entrepreneurship* (Boston, MA: Irwin McGraw-Hill, 1998), p. 7.
12. F. Rose, "The Father of Creative Destruction," *Wired*, March 2002, p. 94; and R. Mitchell, "Creative Destruction," *Business 2.0*, May 1, 2001, p. 9.
13. P. Davidsson, M. B. Low, and M. Wright, "Editor's Introduction: Low and MacMillan Ten Years On: Achievements and Future Directions for Entrepreneurship Research," *Entrepreneurship Theory and Practice*, summer 2001, pp. 5–15; M. B. Low, "The Adolescence of Entrepreneurship Research: Specification of Purpose," *Entrepreneurship Theory and Practice*, summer 2001, pp. 17–25; and W. B. Gartner, "Is There an Elephant in Entrepreneurship? Blind Assumptions in Theory Development," *Entrepreneurship Theory and Practice*, summer 2001, pp. 27–39.
14. Gartner, 2001, p. 28.
15. J. Chun, "To Tell the Truth," *Entrepreneur*, April 1998, pp. 106–13; and D. Kansas, "Don't Believe It," *Wall Street Journal*, October 15, 1993, p. R8.
16. Title 13 (Business Credit and Assistance) , Chapter 1 (Small Business Administration), Part 121 (Small Business Size Regulations) of the Code of Federal Regulations, Revised as of January 1, 2001, found on Small Business Administration's Web site (**www.sba.gov**), March 15, 2002.
17. T. L. Hatten, *Small Business: Entrepreneurship and Beyond* (Upper Saddle River, NJ: Prentice Hall, 1997), p. 5; and J. W. Carland, F. Hoy, W. R. Boulton, and J. C. Carland, "Differentiating Entrepreneurs from Small Business Owners: A Conceptualization," *Academy of Management Review*, vol. 9, no. 2, 1984, pp. 354–59.

18. "United States Business Facts," *U. S. Chamber of Commerce Statistics and Research Center,* accessed on U.S. Chamber of Commerce Web site (**www.uschamber.org**), February 15, 2002.
19. "The Third Millennium: Small Business and Entrepreneurship in the 21st Century," Office of Advocacy, U.S. Small Business Administration, accessed on U.S. Small Business Administration Web site (**www.sba.gov**), February 15, 2002.
20. P. Almeida and B. Kogut, "The Exploration of Technological Diversity and Geographic Localization in Innovation: Start-up Firms in the Semiconductor Industry," *Small Business Economics*, vol. 9, no. 1, 1997, pp. 21–31.
21. R. J. Arend, "Emergence of Entrepreneurs Following Exogenous Technological Change," *Strategic Management Journal*, vol. 20, no. 1, 1999, pp. 31–47.
22. "Counting Start-Ups," *Inc. State of Small Business*, May 29, 2001, pp. 62–63.
23. "The Job Factory," *Inc. State of Small Business*, May 29, 2001, pp. 40–43.
24. "The Third Millennium: Small Business and Entrepreneurship in the 21st Century," Office of Advocacy, U.S. Small Business Administration, accessed on U.S. Small Business Administration Web site (**www.sba.gov**), February 15, 2002, p. 32.
25. J. Hopkins, "Workforce Shifts to Big Companies," *USA Today*, March 18, 2002, accessed at **www.usatoday.com**.
26. "Economic Growth Linked to Levels of Business Start-Ups," *GEM 2000 Report*, accessed at **www.babson.edu/press/gemGrowth2000.html**, December 22, 2000. GEM 2000. Report also available at **www.entreworld.org/GEM2000**.
27. J. Cunningham and J. Lischeron, "Defining Entrepreneurship," *Journal of Small Business Management*, January 1991, pp. 45–61.
28. M. M. Moore, "Start Me Up," *Darwin Magazine Online* accessed at **www.darwinmag.com**, March 20, 2002.
29. D. Ucbasaran, P. Westhead, and M. Wright, "The Focus of Entrepreneurial Research: Contextual and Process Issues," *Entrepreneurship Theory and Practice*, summer 2001, pp. 57–80.
30. H. E. Aldrich and M. A. Martinez, "Many Are Called, But Few Are Chosen: An Evolutionary Perspective for the Study of Entrepreneurship," *Entrepreneurship Theory and Practice*, summer 2001, pp. 41–56.
31. P. B. Robinson, D. V. Simpson, J. C. Huefner, and H. K. Hunt, "An Attitude Approach to the Prediction of Entrepreneurship," *Entrepreneurship Theory and Practice*, summer 1991, pp. 13–31.
32. Ibid.
33. "The Founder Next Door," *Inc. State of Small Business*, May 29, 2001, pp. 72–73; L. Kolvereid, "Prediction of Employment Status Choice Intentions," *Entrepreneurship Theory and Practice*, fall 1996, pp. 47–56; and M. Selz, "Study Scrutinizes People Who Would Be Entrepreneurs," *Wall Street Journal*, December 14, 1995, p. B2.
34. Kolvereid, "Predictions of Employment Status Choice Intentions," and Selz, "Study Scrutinizes People Who Would Be Entrepreneurs."
35. Selz, "Study Scrutinizes People Who Would Be Entrepreneurs," p. B2.
36. Kolvereid, "Prediction of Employment Status Choice Intentions," p. 47.
37. Robinson et al., "An Attitude Approach to the Prediction of Entrepreneurship," p. 15.
38. G. d'Amboise and M. Muldowney, "Management Theory for Small Business: Attempts and Requirements," *Academy of Management Review*, vol. 13, no. 2, 1988, p. 230.
39. Robinson et al., "An Attitude Approach to the Prediction of Entrepreneurship," p. 15.
40. B. M. Davis, "Role of Venture Capital in the Economic Renaissance of an Area," in *Entrepreneurship, Intrapreneurship, and Venture Capital*, ed. R. D. Hisrich, pp. 107–118.
41. J. M. Crant, "The Proactive Personality Scale as a Predictor of Entrepreneurial Intentions," *Journal of Small Business Management*, July 1996, pp. 42–49.
42. N. F. Krueger Jr. and D. V. Brazeal, "Entrepreneurial Potential and Potential Entrepreneurs," *Entrepreneurship Theory and Practice*, spring 1994, pp. 91–104.

43. E. DePillis and K. Reardon, "Culture, Personality, Role Models, Persuasion: What Makes One Want to Become an Entrepreneur?" *Academy of Management Proceedings*, 2001, Entrepreneurship Division Abstracts, p. 38.

44. Krueger and Brazeal, 1994.

45. P. F. Drucker, *Innovation and Entrepreneurship: Practice and Principles* (New York: Harper & Row), 1985.

46. "Your Way," *Inc.*, January 2001, p. 37.

47. Bird, *Entrepreneurial Behavior*, pp. 7–8.

48. M. Jamal, "Job Stress, Satisfaction, and Mental Health: An Empirical Examination of Self-Employed and Non-Self-Employed Canadians," *Journal of Small Business Management*, October 1997, pp. 48–57.

2 The Context of Entrepreneurship

LEARNING OBJECTIVES

After reading and studying this chapter, you should be able to:

1. Discuss the various aspects of today's economy including the driving forces, the implications, and the critical success factors.
2. Explain the legal factors that are part of the context of entrepreneurship.
3. Describe the changing world of work and its impact on entrepreneurship.
4. Discuss the role that social responsibility and ethics play in the context of entrepreneurship.
5. Explain opportunities and their role in entrepreneurship.
6. Describe competitive advantage and explain why it's important.

ENTREPRENEURSHIP IN ACTION

When you think of fast food, what do you think of? A double cheeseburger, super-sized fries, and a soda large enough to float a battleship? The calories and fat content in that lunch are enough to make any nutritional expert cringe. But fast food is popular—Americans spent an estimated \$118 billion on it in 2001. Gary Hirshberg, Mac McCabe, and Pam Solo hope to capture a portion of that by using a different approach.[1]

Hirshberg is president and CEO of Stonyfield Farm, a national organic yogurt company based in Londonderry, New Hampshire. With a strong belief that food should be of high quality and healthy, and dismayed by the fast-food choices available to his family, Gary wanted to develop a natural food quick-serve restaurant. Partnering with Mac and Pam, O'Naturals (**www.onaturals.com**) was born. Believing there are

Staking a claim in the competitive world of fast food isn't going to be easy for the O'Naturals team. Yet, they feel there are enough opportunities in the market to take the plunge. With the organic market growing at 20 percent and the natural market growing 10 percent annually, O'Naturals' team of entrepreneurs can, if done properly, position themselves in a fast-growing category that has good demographics supporting it. Their story offers an appropriate illustration of the importance of considering, interpreting, and understanding the context in which entrepreneurship takes place. It's a story of recognizing how the "rules of the game" are changing and then jumping in to take advantage of those changes. In this chapter, that's what we want to look at: how the rules are changing and the various factors that influence when, where, how, and why entrepreneurs pursue their vision. We'll be discussing some important contextual topics (including the characteristics of today's economic climate, legal issues, the changing world of work, and social responsibility and ethics) that are affecting entrepreneurial organizations. In addition, we're going to discuss the important concepts of opportunity and competitive advantage. Just as Gary, Mac, and Pam did, you need to understand the context that entrepreneurs face as they pursue their entrepreneurial dreams.

ISSUES AFFECTING ENTREPRENEURSHIP IN ACTION

No one could argue with the fact that it's an exciting world out there! To be a successful entrepreneur, you're going to have to understand what "that exciting world" consists of. What's happening that could have an impact (positive or negative) on your entrepreneurial venture? What changes and trends are evident or not so evident? Contextual factors are so important to understand that entrepreneurship researchers have studied them in relation to the overall development of entrepreneurial activity and found that, in general, environmental conditions do have an impact on the emergence and growth of entrepreneurial enterprises in a country.[2]

What are these contextual issues that have the potential to affect entrepreneurship in action? The main ones we're going to look at include characteristics of today's economy, legal factors, the changing world of work, and social responsibility and ethics.

untapped opportunities in the marketplace for such an approach, their dream is to turn the company into a profitable nationwide chain over the next few years.

What makes O'Naturals unique, other than its obviously healthy alternatives to fast food, is its commitment to being socially responsible. The company's mission statement says: "[We want] To be the leading nationwide alternative to mainstream fast-food restaurants, providing delicious meals from natural and organic ingredients; As a community member, we will provide a comfortable place for people to meet; We will educate customers about the world in a way that is fun and informative for the entire family; and We will provide our staff with a caring and learning environment." A company with a mission *and* on a mission!

Characteristics of Today's Economy

The economic context facing today's entrepreneurial organizations is a lot different from what it used to be. Current and potential entrepreneurs face new challenges and opportunities in a time when the conventional wisdom regarding ways of doing things and what it takes to be successful no longer holds. Here in the first decade of a new century, we need to examine some important characteristics of this economy: What forces are "driving" it? What are the implications? What will it take to be successful in this context? Exhibit 2-1 provides an overview.

Driving Forces of Today's Economy. What are the driving forces of today's economy? Four seem to be the most critical: (1) the role of information, (2) technological trends, (3) globalization, and (4) changing demographics.

1. If there's one driving force that has set the tone for today's economy, it's the role of information. Information is now readily available to practically anyone from anywhere on the globe at any hour of the day and in almost any format. An investor in Los Angeles at 3 A.M. can check currency exchange rates for the yen, click on another software program, and e-mail instructions to a broker in London. A shopper in Shanghai with a fondness for maple syrup can indulge that passion by purchasing products from a small retail store in Vermont without ever physically stepping foot in the United States. How? By linking to its virtual storefront on the Internet. The almost instant availability of almost any type of information has radically changed the nature of the economy. This in turn affects the context of entrepreneurship.

   Although information has always been a factor in producing goods and services, previously it had been applied only to the design and use of work tools, organizational processes, management systems, and products. History shows us that from the early days of the industrial revolution (in the 1700s) up through what has often been called the "productivity" revolution (the

EXHIBIT 2-1 Today's Economy

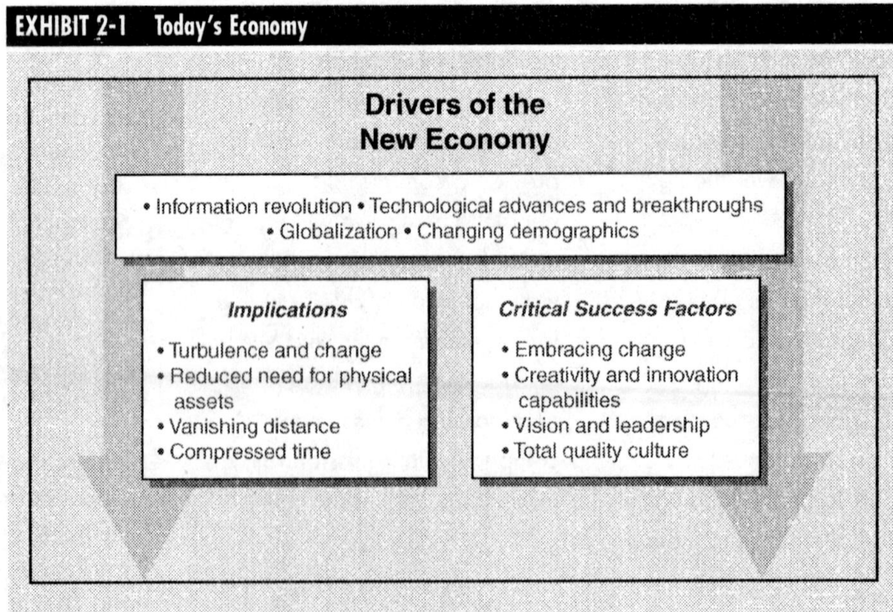

early 1900s), information was primarily used as a tool to achieve organizational efficiency and effectiveness. However, what we're seeing today is information as *the* essential resource of production, not simply as a means to an end. In fact, today's economy is often described as the *Information Age.*

Since the development of the first transistors in the 1940s, information accessibility has flourished primarily because of technological developments. We now have **telecommuters** (individuals who work from home and are linked to the workplace by computers and modems); **virtual organizations** (organizations with little or no physical work space, no formal hierarchical structure, and individuals who contract to perform specific work as needed); and the Internet, where individuals communicate, research information, and conduct business transactions. It's a world made possible by the availability of information through technology. But information isn't the only area in which we're seeing important technological trends, which brings us to the second driving force of today's economy.

2. All organizations—regardless of size, type, or location—use some form of technology to do their work. For instance, in a college classroom, a professor can access different forms of technology for presenting information. He can use an overhead projector, a DVD player, a smart board, or even that low-tech approach, a chalkboard and chalk. Although some industries are by necessity more technology-intensive than others, all organizations use some type of technology. And there's no doubt that trends in technology are changing the way we work and the type of work we do.[3] Four key technological trends (see Exhibit 2-2) that are affecting the context of entrepreneurship are the increasing rate of technological change and diffusion, the increasing commercialization of innovations, increasing knowledge intensity, and increasing recognition that advanced information technologies are the cornerstone of successful businesses.

   The increasing rate of technological change and diffusion is a recognition that not only are technological advances happening more frequently, but they're also being more rapidly adopted by organizations. This trend is important because it means that there are significant opportunities for creating and capturing value as new technologies are created and diffused throughout the economy. However, it also means that entrepreneurs need to keep up with technological change or be left behind.

   The rapid rate of technological change also has had an impact on the competitive protection offered by patents, which brings us to our second

EXHIBIT 2-2 Major Technological Trends

- Increasing rate of technological change and diffusion
- Increasing commercialization of innovations
- Increasing knowledge intensity
- Increasing recognition that advanced information technologies are critical

FYI

Dot-Com to Dot-Bomb

From boom to bust. From billions of dollars to pennies. What happened to the Internet revolution? And does this mean that the dreams for profitable e-commerce strategies were just that—fanciful dreams?

The rush to sell products over the Internet during the late 1990s has been compared to the gold rush boom of the mid-1800s in California—people willing to risk it all to get there first and hit it big. What did the boom in dot-coms look like? Thousands of Web sites selling everything from pet food to barbecue sauce to toys were created by young, tech-savvy entrepreneurs intent on getting funding for their start-up and making millions by going public through an IPO (initial public offering of a company's stock) or by selling out to someone else. During the period from 1994 to the first quarter of 2000, more than 500,000 dot-com business plans were marketed to venture capitalists (venture capitalists are investors who provide capital to entrepreneurial ventures and who hope for some type of financial return on their investment). Only a scant one-half to one percent of those proposed entrepreneurial ventures actually received any venture capital funding. But, the amount of dollars those venture capitalists invested in Internet companies was pretty impressive: $19.9 billion in 1999 and $35.2 billion in 2000. Even established businesses felt pressured to have an Internet presence. The www.com addresses that we're all so familiar with soon became an ever-present feature on all of a company's communications and "e-" became a ubiquitous descriptor of a company's strategies. All seemed golden in the Internet world. Golden that is, until things began to fall apart—slowly at first, but snowballing until the bottom eventually fell out. The bust (which many pundits called the dot-bomb) took down companies and decimated stock market values. From boo.com's (**boo.com** was a Web site started by two young Swedes whose vision was to create the ultimate Internet global fashion site) meteoric rise and spectacular fall to pets.com's stock burnout (from $14 per share to 6 cents), the e-commerce landscape was changed. During 2000 alone, 75 percent of dot-com companies in the B2C (business-to-customer) segment shut down. And the average percentage of stock value lost by dot-coms in 2000 was 88 percent. Yes, things got pretty bad. But, does this mean that the whole Internet revolution was a fantasy? Were the statements that the Internet would change everything about the way business is conducted just empty promises? Probably not. There are still numerous obvious applications for the Internet and all its attendant possibilities for linking companies, customers, suppliers, and other stakeholders. Despite the dot-bombs, e-commerce is not dead. What the dot-com to dot-bomb experience taught us is that entrepreneurs will need to stick to the basics—continual innovation, a good business plan, and a strong management team. (We'll cover e-business essentials more thoroughly in Chapter 7.)

Sources: R. Spiegel, "Where Have All the Dot-Coms Gone?" *Electronic News,* March 25, 2002, p. 30; Editors, "About This Issue," *Black Enterprise,* March 2002, p. 18; S. Luckett, " Despite Dot-Bombs, E-Commerce Is Not Dead," *Aftermarket Business,* September 2001, p. 42; J. Useem, "And Then, Just When You Thought the 'New Economy' Was Dead," *Business 2.0,* August/September 2001, pp. 69–75; L. Cavanagh, "From Dot Coms to Dot Bombs: Have We Learned Anything?" *Seybold Report Analyzing Publishing Technologies,* June 4, 2001, pp. 28–29; "The Dot-Com Riches-to-Rags Index," *Inc. State of Small Business,* May 29, 2001, pp. 30–31; K. B. Begun, K. Stroup, and A. Moller, "Looking Beyond the Dot Bomb," *Newsweek,* April 30, 2001, pp. 62–64; and J. Fischer and M. Tharp, "The Dot-Bomb Survivors Club," *Newsweek,* March 19, 2001, pp. 34–36.

EXHIBIT 2-3 Number of Patents Granted, 1990–2000

Year	Number Granted
2000	176,087
1999	169,146
1998	163,207
1997	125,516
1996	122,561
1995	114,425
1994	114,126
1993	110,053
1992	107,663
1991	106,839
1990	98,937

Sources: U.S. Patent and Trademark Office (**www.uspto.gov**), "Issues and Patent Numbers." April 2002.

major technological trend: the increasing commercialization of innovations. **Innovation** is the process of taking a creative idea and turning it into a product or process that can be used or sold. Some experts have suggested that the U.S. economy is in the early stages of a powerful new wave of innovation.[4] One possible measure of the increasing commercialization of innovations is the number of patents granted by the U.S. Patent and Trademark Office. Exhibit 2-3 shows these numbers. A **patent** is a legal property that allows its holder to prevent others from employing this property for their own use for a specified period of time. (We'll cover the different types of patents in Chapter 5.) Although the use of patents traditionally provided inventors and organizations with protection for technological discoveries that were the basis for proprietary products or services, this advantage is declining in significance because new technological discoveries can rapidly replace the technology that's currently protected by the patent.

Another significant trend in technology is the increasing dependence on knowledge. Because technology—both the creation and the use of it—involves knowledge, its importance for entrepreneurial ventures has increased significantly. The implication is that as the use of technology increases, so does the need for knowledge. The reverse is true as well. As knowledge increases, so does the use of technology. For instance, even employees in traditionally labor-intensive jobs now must have more than manual dexterity skills and physical stamina. They need knowledge to operate the sophisticated equipment often found in today's manufacturing and service jobs. Successful entrepreneurial ventures in today's economy will capture and capitalize on knowledge.

Rapid Review

- ✔ What are the four driving forces of today's economy?
- ✔ Describe the impact of information on the context facing entrepreneurs.
- ✔ Who are telecommuters? What are virtual organizations?
- ✔ Define technology. What technological trends are evident in today's economy?
- ✔ What is innovation, and how is it affecting the entrepreneurial context?
- ✔ What are patents? Why are they important in technology?

The last important technological trend we want to look at is the reality that advanced information technologies are the cornerstone of successful businesses.[5] What kinds of information do organizations need? Information about customers, inventories, distribution, and other specific business functions is vital to compete successfully in today's economy. Think back to our chapter-opening case. As the entrepreneurs behind O'Naturals plan their strategy for the nationwide rollout of their chain of restaurants, they'll need to make sure they have reliable and appropriate information technologies in place to monitor operations, to make sure everything goes as planned, and to detect any potential or actual problems. Entrepreneurs who recognize how important it is to use advanced information technologies in their organizations will be better positioned for success.

3. The third driving force of today's economy is **globalization**, the linkage of economies and cultures that fosters a business and competitive situation in which organizations have no national boundaries. You've probably heard about the concept of globalization for so long now (undoubtedly in every business class you take), that it almost seems cliché. However, it is important and continues to be a dominant characteristic of today's economic and business environment. More than ever, entrepreneurs are witnessing the globalization of the business landscape and are taking part in it as they find increasing opportunities in international trade.[6] Here's one person's view of what this continuing global economic environment is all about: "Free trade agreements and alliances like the EU [European Union] and NAFTA [North American Free Trade Agreement] are really creating an environment in which some small businesses should look at international issues. Otherwise they'll face stiff competition from businesses in countries that are U.S. trading partners."[7]

   However, globalization is more than just producing, marketing, and distributing goods and services throughout the world. "It is a new way of thinking."[8] It's solving customers' needs no matter where the customer is. It's segmenting markets on a global basis and sourcing people, capital, technologies, and ideas from anywhere in the world. Globalization has transformed and continues to transform today's economy.

4. The fourth and final major driving force of today's economy is changing demographics. **Demographics**, very simply, are the vital statistics of a population. They include the kinds of information that the U.S. Census Bureau typically collects in its census survey, such as gender, age, income levels, ethnic makeup, level of education completed, family composition, geographic locations, birthrates, employment status, and so forth. Gathering and analyzing demographic information isn't something that's done just in the United States. All industrialized, and most semi-industrialized, countries collect census information. In addition, the United Nations collects a considerable amount of demographic information from around the world.

FYI

What Are These FTAs Anyway?

International competition used to be best described in terms of country against country—the United States versus Japan, France versus Germany, Mexico versus Canada. Now, global competition has been reshaped by the creation of regional trading and cooperation agreements—free trade agreements. There are four main ones: the European Union (EU), the North American Free Trade Agreement (NAFTA), Mercosur, and the Association of Southeast Asian Nations (ASEAN), although other regions of the world are getting into the act, as well.

The European Union, formed in 1992, consists of 15 countries—Belgium, Denmark, France, Greece, Ireland, Italy, Luxembourg, the Netherlands, Portugal, Spain, the United Kingdom, Germany, Austria, Finland, and Sweden. Six countries (Poland, Hungary, the Czech Republic, Cypress, Slovenia, and Estonia) are in membership negotiations to join the EU but won't be admitted before 2003. And seven other countries (Turkey, Romania, Slovakia, Bulgaria, Latvia, Lithuania, and Malta) are considering starting membership negotiations. As a single market, the European Union alliance has no national barriers to travel, employment, investment, or trade. And the EU took a big step toward full unification in 1999 when 11 of the 15 countries began sharing the same currency, the euro. The primary motivation for the joining of these European nations was to reassert their economic position against the strength of the United States and Japan. As a unified economic and trade entity, the EU covers a population base of over 374 million people (and that number would increase to 437 million with the addition of the seven countries in membership negotiations). That's a significant source of economic power.

The North American Free Trade Agreement (NAFTA) is an agreement among the Mexican, Canadian, and U.S. governments in which barriers to free trade have been eliminated. Eliminating the barriers to free trade (tariffs, import licensing requirements, and customs users fees, among other things), has resulted in a strengthening of the economic power of all three countries.

Because of NAFTA, other Latin American nations are moving to become part of free-trade blocs, also. Colombia, Mexico, and Venezuela signed an economic pact in 1994 that eliminated import duties and tariffs. Another free-trade bloc known as the Southern Cone Common Market, or Mercosur, consists of Argentina, Brazil, Bolivia, Chile, Paraguay, and Uruguay. In addition, 36 countries in the Caribbean region, South America, and Central America are negotiating a Free Trade of the Americas (FTAA) trade agreement.

The ASEAN is a trading alliance of 10 Southeast Asian nations including Indonesia, Singapore, Malaysia, Brunei, the Philippines, Vietnam, Cambodia, Thailand, Laos, and Myanmar. Because of the population growth, this region promises to be one of the fastest-growing economic regions of the world.

And these aren't the only regions looking at free trade alliances. Nine African nations (Djibouti, Egypt, Kenya, Madagascar, Malawi, Mauritius, Sudan, Zambia, and Zimbabwe) have combined into a free trade area. These nine countries also are members of the 21-nation Common Market for Eastern and Southern Africa (COMESA).

Sources: E. L. Andrews, "European Union's Tough but Relentless Drive to Expand," *New York Times*, December 20, 1999, p. C22; H. Cooper, "The Euro: What You Need to Know," *Wall Street Journal*, January 4, 1999, pp. A5+; C. Sims, "Chile Will Enter a Big South American Free-Trade Bloc," *New York Times*, June 26, 1999, p. C2; and T. Purdum, "Africa Zone Created," *Industry Week*, November 20, 2000, p. 12.

EXHIBIT 2-4 The World's Largest Markets by the Year 2015

Country	Population (in millions)
China	1,513
India	1,442
United States	300
Russia	300
Indonesia	286
Nigeria	281
Pakistan	267
Brazil	246
Bangladesh	235
Mexico	150
Japan	127
Ethiopia	127
Vietnam	117
Philippines	112
Zaire	99

Sources: Reprinted from *The Shape of Things to Come* by R. W. Oliver. Copyright © 1999 McGraw-Hill. Reprinted by permission of the McGraw-Hill Companies.

What kind of picture is this demographic information painting?[9] We can see five interesting trends emerging. The first significant trend is that *the world's population is growing geometrically and at a very fast rate.* It took until about 1880 for the world's population to reach 1 billion people. It took only another 85 years to reach 3 billion. But it took less than 30 years to reach 5 billion people in 1994. By the year 2020 (a mere 26 years later), the world's population is expected to increase by another 3 billion people. Exhibit 2-4 shows a forecast of the world's largest markets by the year 2015. Are you surprised by some of the countries? They may not be what you initially expected.

The second significant demographic trend is that *the world's population is getting older and younger at the same time.* In countries north of the equator, the average age of the population is increasing. However, in countries south of the equator, the average age of the population is going down as birthrates skyrocket. These southern locations are where you'll find the greatest concentration of young consumers, the fastest-growing incomes, and most of the world's unmet needs.

The third interesting demographic trend is that *the world's population continues on the move.* Migration within and between countries has always been a part of human history. However, even today, major migrations still occur, with approximately 60 million people worldwide moving annually. Ethnicity is no longer a clue to a person's residence. For instance, the growing proportion of Hispanics in the U.S. population reflects one of the most dramatic demographic shifts in American history. The number of Hispanics is increasing almost four times as fast as the rest of the population and is expected to surpass African Americans as the largest minority group by the year 2005. But the label *Hispanic* doesn't begin to

Entrepreneurs in Action

They present a striking futuristic profile on the horizon. Described as "origami architecture," the small shelter pods developed by entrepreneur Sanford Ponder were inspired by geodesic principles. (Check out the photos at **www.icosavillage.net**.) The pods were developed as a line of refugee shelters for relief organizations, but potentially could be used where any types of temporary shelters are needed. Because they can be constructed from any ready supply of foldable materials (cardboard, corrugated plastic, or whatever), they can be assembled whenever, wherever, and however needed. This type of flexibility is often critical in relief efforts. The shelters are well insulated, waterproof, and resistant to high winds. Why shelter pods? Ponder said that if people had to live in boxes, he wanted to invent a better box. And so it seems, he did.

Sources: Icosavillage Web site (**www.icosavillage.net**), April 24, 2002; and A. Rose, "Mobile Home," *Wired*, March 2002, p. 34.

capture the unique subcultures of this ethnic group. One estimate is that there are 17 different Hispanic subcultures, including these examples: In Los Angeles, you'll find immigrant Mexicans, middle-class Mexicans, and barrio dwellers; in Texas, you'll find south Texans and Texas Guatemalans; in Miami, you have Miami Cubans and Miami Nicaraguans; and in Chicago, there are Chicago Puerto Ricans. These are just a few of the different subcultures in this one ethnic group.[10]

The fourth significant demographic trend is that *most of the world's economically active people live in cities and urban areas.* The vast majority of the world's population is urban. The world's five largest cities (Tokyo, Japan—26.4 million; Mexico City, Mexico—18.1 million; Mumbai [Bombay], India—18 million; São Paulo, Brazil—17.7 million; and New York City, United States—16.6 million) are more populous than many countries.[11] This urban population is economically active, meaning most inhabitants are engaged in economic functions, including producing, selling, and purchasing goods and services.

The final significant demographic trend we want to look at is *the division of the world's population into three broad groups.* Increasingly, the world's population can be defined by annual per capita income and lifestyle. Using these measures, we can identify three broad groups:

- The poor, which includes individuals with household incomes of less than $700 per year (about 1.1 billion people); these individuals account for 2 percent of the world's income.
- The middle class, which includes individuals with family incomes of between $700 and $7,500 per year (about 3.5 billion people); these individuals earn about 33 percent of the world's income.
- The consumer class, which includes individuals with household incomes above $7,500 per year (about 1.1 billion people); these individuals claim about 64 percent of the world's income.

Each of these demographic trends is coloring the nature of today's economy. Like the other driving forces of the twenty-first century economy, they affect the context within which entrepreneurs pursue their entrepreneurial ventures. What are the implications of these forces for entrepreneurs?

Implications of These Driving Forces. As you look back at Exhibit 2-1, you'll see that there are four major implications arising out of the driving forces of today's economy. These include continual turbulence and change, the reduced need for physical assets, vanishing distance, and compressed time.

1. *Continual turbulence and change.* Change, and for many organizations, turbulent change, is a fact of life in today's business context. [12] All organizations must deal with change, if not on a daily basis, then on an increasingly frequent basis. **Change** can be defined as any alteration in external context or internal organizational factors. Often changes in external factors stimulate the need to make organizational changes. For instance, changes in information technology (such as electronic mail and the Internet) have opened up new avenues for entrepreneurs. For example, executives at Maytag Corporation knew that salespeople at appliance stores sometimes directed customers to other brands even though those customers had intended to buy a Maytag.[13] Through Web-services software developed by a small entrepreneurial venture called Comergent, Maytag found a way to get those sales without alienating their dealers (the appliance stores). Comergent connected the inventory and pricing systems of 3,200 stores with Maytag's internal software. Now, at maytag.com, a customer can select a machine, find local retailers who carry it, get up-to-the-minute information on availability and prices, and place an order. One year after the system was installed, Maytag was thrilled with the results. Why? Customers who bought via the Web site spent an average of 50 percent more than did walk-in customers, Maytag got valuable information about its customers, and the Web site without alienating the retailers. And there are numerous other examples of entrepreneurs who've recognized and acted on opportunities presented by changing technology. Or, take for instance, changing demographic trends. The baby boomlet (resulting from the large group of baby boomers who have had and are now having children), the increasing Hispanic population, and other demographic changes have forced entrepreneurs and other large consumer goods companies to alter the types of products they offer, the packaging of these products, and the promotional techniques used to sell these products. Organizations—entrepreneurial or not—are looking for ways to prosper in today's economy in which change is the norm, not the exception. Turbulence and change are the realities of the external context that entrepreneurs face.
2. *Reduced need for physical assets.* It used to be that having a large number of physical assets (buildings, factories, equipment, inventory, and so forth) was essential for financial success. The more physical assets you had, the more economically powerful you were. However, that's not the case in today's economy. Success in today's economy isn't reliant simply on physical assets. Instead, value is found in intangible factors such as information, people, ideas, and knowledge. For instance, eBay, the Internet auction site, is the

Entrepreneurs in Action

Searchspace Corporation doesn't have, or need, a big investment in physical assets yet it helps financial institutions track trillions of dollars every day. Using its proprietary pattern-recognition software, Searchspace looks for suspicious patterns in financial transactions such as credit-card use, bank deposits and withdrawals, and funds transfers. Looking for suspected illegal activity amid the millions of legitimate financial transactions every day has been compared to finding a needle in a haystack. Yet, Konrad Feldman, Searchspace's CEO, says that the company's software can pick out unusual patterns in transactions, down to single-digit dollars. Searchspace was founded in 1993 by four doctoral students at London's University College Intelligent Systems Laboratory. Using their knowledge about neural networks, genetic algorithms, and fuzzy logic, the partners initially consulted for British utilities and supermarkets predicting product and electricity demand. However, their focus these days is on data security, as they help financial institutions look for check fraud, credit-card fraud, money laundering, and even terrorist financing.

Sources: Information on company from Hoover's Online (**www.hoovers.com**), April 26, 2002; and T. Kellner, "Cybersleuth," *Forbes*, November 16, 2001, pp. 202–204.

prototype of success in the twenty-first century. It has used customer information exchange, proprietary online bidding systems, and other intangible factors to create a successful entrepreneurial venture. With minimal investment in physical assets and just 2,500 employees, the company did $749 million in revenues for 2001.

3. *Vanishing distance.* The influence of physical distance on organizational decisions has disappeared. Although geography traditionally played an important role in determining customers and competitors, that's no longer the case. An entrepreneur's potential market can be found anywhere. The limitations once imposed because of physical distance have vanished. The world is your customer. But this also means that the world is your competitor. The opportunities—and challenges—for entrepreneurs have never been greater.

4. *Compressed time.* As the limitations of physical space have disappeared, so have the limitations of time. It used to take Pony Express riders weeks to deliver information via the mail, but the U.S. Postal Service now delivers mail in two to three days, and even overnight. But, as you already know, the time frame is even more compressed than that now. With electronic mail and interactive Web sites, we have almost instantaneous delivery of information. The instant interactivity (between customer and business, between employees, between companies and suppliers, or even between friends and family) has created a context in which if an organization doesn't stay alert to

Rapid Review

- ✔ What is globalization, and how is it affecting the entrepreneurial context?
- ✔ Why is it important for entrepreneurs to understand demographics?
- ✔ Describe five significant demographic trends that are having an impact on today's economy.
- ✔ What are the four major implications arising out of the driving forces of today's economy?
- ✔ What is change, and how is it having an impact on the entrepreneurial context?
- ✔ Why is there a reduced need for physical assets in today's economy?
- ✔ Describe how the concepts of vanishing distance and compressed time impact the entrepreneurial context.

changes, its marketplace advantage will be temporary, at best. Although it isn't easy to do, it's important. Take, for example, Dell Computer. It's been able to hold on to its marketplace advantage by understanding the benefits and challenges of compressed time. Michael Dell, founder and CEO of Dell Computer, built a successful entrepreneurial venture on the basis of staying alert to changes through instantaneous interactivity. The company builds computers directly from customers' requests. Then, using its lightning-fast inventory and purchasing cycles, Dell builds and ships out computers not long after the customer's order is received. Also, Dell uses information from customers' orders to adapt to emerging trends way ahead of the curve. They listen to what customers are asking for and move quickly to address those needs. Dell is a good example of an organization that understands the external context and what it takes to be successful in today's economy. What *does* it take to be successful given the realities of today's economy?

Critical Success Factors. Four critical success factors for succeeding in today's economy include the ability to embrace change, the ability to be creative and innovative, vision and leadership, and total quality culture. (Refer to Exhibit 2-1.) Let's look at why each of these success factors is critical.

If there's one word that captures the essence of today's economy, it's *change.* Do you like change? Few people enjoy, or even seek out, change. Most of us think change is scary. We like order, not chaos. We like the old and comfortable, not the new or the unknown. But change is a given in today's economy. Being successful in this kind of turbulent context means not only being tolerant of change but also seeking it out and embracing it. As we know from Chapter 1, entrepreneurs are comfortable with change. They know that change brings not only opportunities but also challenges in dealing successfully with the changes. These uncertainties don't faze successful entrepreneurs, however, as they seek out change and enjoy the thrill of trying something new and different.

The second critical success factor for today's economy is the ability to be creative and innovative. Here's a short statement of just how critical this is: "Create and innovate or lose!" It's that simple. In today's dynamic, chaotic world of technological change, information revolution, globalization, and changing demographics, entrepreneurs must be prepared to create new products and services and adopt state-of-the-art technology if their ventures are to compete successfully and survive. **Creativity**, the ability to combine ideas in a unique way or to make unusual associations between ideas, is an important capability.[14] A creative person or organization develops novel approaches to doing work or unique solutions to problems. But, it doesn't stop there. We know from our earlier chapter discussion that innovation is the process of taking a creative idea and turning it into a useful

Developing Your Creativity

If asked, many of us would say that we're not very creative. However, in a dynamic and turbulent environment, where changes are fast and furious, creativity is crucial! How can you become more creative? It's easier than you think!

Researchers who have looked at creativity say that being creative is a matter of deciding what you want to do, how you can do it, and how you can do it better. It involves the *process,* not just the outcome. So now that we've taken some of the pressure off—you don't *have* to be a Michelangelo or a Beethoven to be creative—what steps can you take to develop your creativity? Here are some specific suggestions you might use to help develop your own creative abilities.

1. *Relax.* Some relaxation techniques include clearing your mind mentally, listening to classical music, meditating, telling a joke to someone, going off by yourself to someplace quiet, or stopping thinking about the problem and returning to it later.
2. *Exercise your mind.* This includes activities such as playing freely with ideas without any specific problem to solve, practicing concentrating on a single issue, trying to think of unique solutions to personal or work-related problems, and practicing becoming comfortable with not having complete control over problems or outcomes.
3. *Determine what you want to do.* This includes such things as taking time to understand an issue before even beginning to try resolving it, getting all the facts in mind, and trying to identify the most important facts.
4. *Look for ways to tackle issues.* This can be done by setting aside a block of time to focus on the issues; working out a plan for attacking them; establishing subgoals; imagining or actually acting out the issues; thinking of similar issues and how you solved them before; using analogies whenever possible (for example, could you approach your problem like a fish out of water and how it copes, or can you use what you do to find your way when it's foggy) to help you resolve them; using different problem-solving approaches such as verbal, visual, mathematical, theatrical (for example, you might draw a diagram of the issue to help you visualize it better, or you might talk to yourself out loud describing the problem, or you might tell it as a story to someone else); trusting your intuition; and playing with different possible ideas and approaches (for instance, ask yourself what your grandmother might do if faced with this issue).
5. *Look for ways to do things better.* This may involve trying consciously to be more original, not worrying about looking foolish, eliminating or ignoring cultural taboos (like gender stereotypes) that might influence your possible solutions, keeping an open mind, being alert to odd or puzzling facts, thinking of unconventional ways to use objects and the environment (for example, could newspaper or magazine headlines help you be more creative), discarding usual or habitual ways of doing things, and striving for objectivity by being as critical of your own ideas as you are of others'.

Source: S. P. Robbins and M. Coulter, "Developing Your Creativity," *Management* 5th ed. (Upper Saddle River, NJ: Prentice Hall, 1996), p. 209.

product. An innovative person or organization is able to channel creativity into useful outcomes. Both abilities, being creative and being innovative, are critical to entrepreneurial success in this new economy.

The third critical success factor involves vision and leadership. Think back to our chapter-opening case and Gary Hirshberg's strong belief that food should (and could) be high in quality and healthy. His interest in organic and natural foods led him initially to found a company (Stonyfield Farm) that made organic yogurt and eventually to co-found O'Naturals as a way to provide tasty natural fast food—an alternative to greasy burgers and fries. Success in today's economy means visualizing what can be and pursuing that dream. A **vision** is a broad comprehensive statement of what an entrepreneur wants his or her organization to become. It's a statement of what the organization stands for, what it believes in, and why it exists. The vision provides a vibrant and compelling picture of the future. It presents a view beyond what the entrepreneurial venture "is" to what it "can be."[15] The vision is the embodiment of the entrepreneur's dream. You may think the concept of a "vision" is rather strange—something that sounds good on paper, but isn't at all realistic or useful in improving an organization's performance. However, when an organizational leader—the entrepreneur—is able to articulate a distinct vision, all current and future decisions and actions are guided by that vision. By articulating a vision, the entrepreneur maps out an overall picture of where he or she would like the entrepreneurial venture to be positioned in the future. Being successful in today's tumultuous economy requires this type of vision and the leadership to create, embrace, and convey it.

The final critical success factor for today's economy is having a **total quality culture**, an organizational culture in which all resources and capabilities are directed at the pursuit of greater quality in all parts of the organization.[16] Why is having a total quality culture so important? Because customers demand—and expect—it. There are too many other options available to them. You ignore quality at your own peril! Those who do, risk losing out. But, then, the question becomes, what is quality? How would *you* define it? Granted, the concept isn't an easy one to describe. Each of us probably has his or her own perspective on what a "quality" product or service is—each correct in its own way. To help clarify this definition dilemma, five different views of quality are described in Exhibit 2-5. No matter which view you agree with, it's important that an entrepreneurial venture focuses all its resources and capabilities on the pursuit of quality in everything it does—in every decision and action. A total quality culture facilitates this pursuit. (We'll discuss how to have a total quality culture in Chapter 6.)

There are many entrepreneurial opportunities and challenges associated with the realities of today's economy. However, not only do entrepreneurs need to be aware of these issues, they also need to know how legal factors affect the entrepreneurial context.

Rapid Review

- ✔ What are the four critical factors for succeeding in today's economy?
- ✔ Why is it important for entrepreneurs to be comfortable with change?
- ✔ What is creativity, and why is it important?
- ✔ How can you develop your creativity?
- ✔ What is vision? What role does it play in helping an entrepreneur succeed?
- ✔ Describe what a total quality culture is. Why is having one important?

Legal Factors

As we explore the context facing entrepreneurs, we can't ignore the impact of the legal environment. A

EXHIBIT 2-5 Different Views of Quality

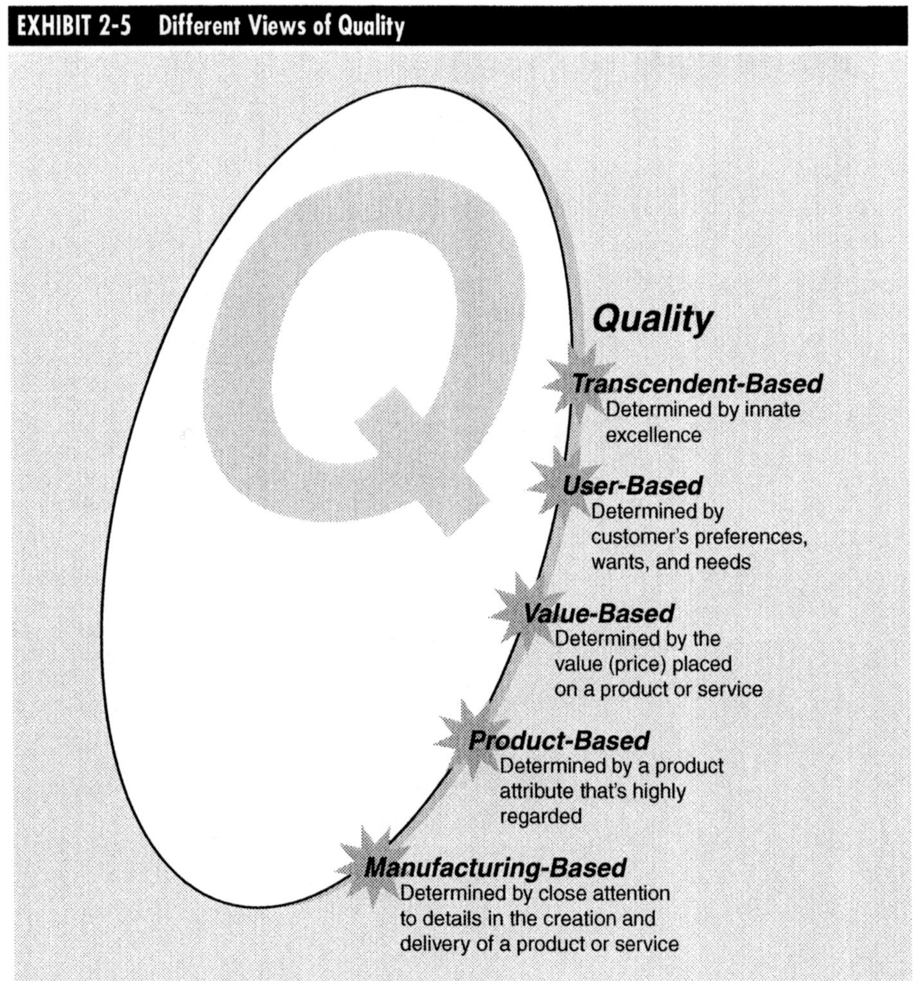

Source: Based on D. Garvin, ***Managing Quality*** (New York: Free Press, 1988).

society's laws and regulations provide the framework within which its citizens can do or not do certain things. The legal environment both allows and prohibits certain decisions and actions. Obviously, entrepreneurs are affected by these legal issues and need to be aware of these factors before embarking on an entrepreneurial journey.

What comes to mind when you think of the legal environment? Is it laws and regulations and all the "red tape" that are a hassle to deal with whenever, for example, you have to renew your driver's license or car tags? Maybe it's forms and documents that must be completed, signed, and submitted by certain deadlines, such as the Internal Revenue Service's Form 1040. Perhaps it's Judge Judy and her strict courtroom rules, comments, and judgments. Believe it or not, the reality of the legal environment entrepreneurs must deal with isn't quite this cynical or negative! Yes, there are going to be certain things that you must do, by law, and certain things you absolutely cannot do, by law. Pursuing your entrepreneurial dream means you'd better know and understand the legal constraints. Exhibit 2-6 illustrates several important legal issues affecting an entrepreneurial venture.

EXHIBIT 2-6 Legal Issues at Different Stages

Entrepreneurial Venture

Legal Issues in Start-up	Legal Issues in Managing the Ongoing Business
• Determine form of business organization	• Human resource management laws and regulations
• Set up record keeping for tax purposes	• Safety laws and regulations (product, workplace, environmental)
• Conduct lease and financing negotiations	• Financial and accounting laws and regulations
• Draw up contracts	• Marketplace laws and regulations
• File for patents, trademarks, and copyright protection	

During the start-up stage, an entrepreneur faces certain legal issues. These can include determining the form of business organization, setting up appropriate records for tax purposes, negotiating leases and financing, drawing up contracts, and filing for patents, trademarks, or copyright protection. In each of these start-up activities, certain laws and regulations affect what an entrepreneur can and cannot do. An entrepreneur must be familiar with the relevant laws and regulations affecting the proposed venture. But the impact of the legal context on the entrepreneurial context doesn't end there. When the entrepreneurial venture is up and running, there are legal issues associated with managing the business. For instance, human resource laws and regulations may affect hiring, compensation, and performance appraisal decisions. Or, for example, safety laws and regulations may have an impact on product design and packaging, workplace and equipment design and use, and environmental pollution control and species protection. Exhibit 2-7 provides a brief description of some of the more recent laws (those enacted since 1970) that can have an impact on businesses. Although many laws may apply only when an organization reaches a certain size, the fact that entrepreneurial ventures pursue growth means that entrepreneurs can face these legal issues fairly quickly. Entrepreneurs also must recognize that federal laws aren't the only ones with which they may have to deal. State and local laws are likely to influence the entrepreneurial venture as well.

EXHIBIT 2-7 Selected Significant Legislation Regulating Business Since 1970

Legislation	Purpose
Occupational Safety and Health Act of 1970	Requires employer to provide a working environment free from hazards to health
Consumer Product Safety Act of 1972	Sets standards on selected products; requires warning labels, and orders product recalls
Equal Employment Opportunity Act of 1972	Forbids discrimination in all areas of employer–employee relations
Americans with Disabilities Act of 1990	Prohibits employers from discriminating against individuals with physical or mental disabilities or the chronically ill; also requires organizations to reasonably accommodate these individuals
Civil Rights Act of 1991	Reaffirms and lightens prohibition of discrimination; permits individuals to sue for punitive damages in cases of intentional discrimination
Women's Business Development Act of 1991	Assists the development of small business concerns owned and controlled by women through a training program and a loan program that eases access to credit through the Small Business Administration (SBA) loan program
Family and Medical Leave Act of 1993	Grants 12 weeks of unpaid leave each year to employees for the birth or adoption of a child or the care of a spouse, child, or parent with a serious health condition; covers organizations with 50 or more employees
North American Free Trade Agreement of 1993	Created a free trade zone between the United States, Canada, and Mexico
U.S. Economic Espionage Act of 1996	Makes theft or misappropriation of trade secrets a federal crime
Electronics Signatures in Global and National Commerce Act of 2000	Gives online contracts (those signed by computer) the same legal force as equivalent paper contracts

It should be clear to you by now that legal factors do play an important part in the entrepreneurial context. Before an entrepreneur proceeds, it's important to know the pertinent laws and regulations. We'll discuss these legal issues more thoroughly in Chapter 5. The next thing we need to study in relation to the entrepreneurial context is how the world of work has changed and the implications for entrepreneurs.

Changing World of Work

Most people define *work* in terms of a job. You've probably worked at a job sometime during your life. Stop for a minute and think about what a "job" is. For most people, having a job implies regular work hours, written or orally communicated job descriptions that specify certain work responsibilities, regular and routine tasks that must be completed, and bosses who tell workers what needs to be done. Jobs could be described as the essence of predictability and security. There's only one problem with this view. It's no longer realistic in today's dynamic and turbulent environment! This image we have of organizations with specific, rigid "jobs" that people work at just isn't appropriate anymore. This view might have been realistic in a context that was relatively stable and predictable. However, today's world of work is changing, and these changes are affecting the entrepreneurial context. We're going to look at two major areas of changes that have had an impact on the way people work. The first is the nature of the work they do; the second concerns the organizational setting within which work takes place.

The major change in the nature of work that people do in organizations is that work is much more knowledge-intensive. Knowledge has become an important component of task accomplishment, even in jobs that you think traditionally might not require it—for instance, waiting tables or driving a truck. Today, employees are expected to use their mental abilities in addition to their physical ones. The application of knowledge to everything an organization's employees do is essential for prospering and even surviving in today's dynamic environment. In fact, an organization that has developed the continuous capacity to adapt by acquiring information and knowledge and incorporating this knowledge and learning into decisions and actions is called a **learning organization**. A learning organization is one in which people think in new ways, are open to each other, understand how the organization really works, have a vision with which everyone agrees, and work together to achieve that vision.[17] It's the type of organizational atmosphere that an entrepreneur needs to cultivate if he or she wants to be successful in today's context.

A good example of how an emphasis on learning can lead to success can be found on the shores of the Mississippi River in the Memphis, Tennessee, headquarters of Buckman Laboratories (**www.buckman.com**). Buckman Labs manufactures over 500 specialty chemicals and employs over 1,300 individuals in 70 countries. The company's innovative entrepreneurial founder, Bob Buckman, first began to appreciate the power of knowledge and learning long before others did. Buckman and his associates began treating knowledge as the company's most important asset back in 1984. Since that time, they've organized all associates (employees) and their work around the company's knowledge network, known as K'Netix®. This global electronics network provides company associates with a constant stream of the latest information about products, markets, and customers. It's a key to Buckman's success in a highly competitive global market. (You can learn more

Entrepreneurs in Action

Most franchise operations are run as clones of the original business. After all, that's the idea—find the best ways of doing things and copy those ways again and again so that customers everywhere have a predictable experience. However, Great Harvest Bread Company (**www.greatharvest.com**), a franchisor of retail bread bakeries headquartered in Dillon, Montana, doesn't do things that way. In fact, after a one-year apprenticeship, Great Harvest allows its franchisees to run their business as they see fit. The company encourages them to be unique, to experiment, and to be themselves. But there is one main aspect that makes all the difference. Every owner in the chain is encouraged to be a part of Great Harvest's "learning community." Franchisees who join (and most have) must share information, financial results, observations, and ideas. If asked questions, they must give answers. They must share openly with each other. The result—a true learning organization.

Sources: Great Harvest Bread Company Web site (**www.greatharvest.com**), April 26, 2002; and "True Learning Organization," *Inc.*, November 15, 2000, accessed at **www.inc.com**, April 26, 2002.

about Buckman Labs and its emphasis on learning in one of the Entrepreneurship in Action cases at the end of this chapter.) Although the knowledge-oriented nature of work today is a good example of how work has changed, it's also characteristic of the changed organizational setting within which work takes place.

As we know from our earlier discussion of the driving forces behind today's economy, it's a fast-moving world out there! Traditional approaches to getting work done through rigid and inflexible job assignments just won't cut it anymore. Instead, an organization that hopes to succeed in today's business context is one characterized by flexibility, temporariness, and independence. Instead of a "job," entrepreneurs need to think in terms of packets of skills and abilities applied to specific tasks. In fact, many of today's successful entrepreneurial organizations contend with the rapidly changing environment by getting work done through projects. A **project** is a temporary set of work tasks that has a definite beginning and ending point in time. As a work need arises, people with the necessary skills are assigned to complete the project. As each project is completed, employees move to another one. It's an approach to work that recognizes the need to be flexible, temporary, and independent.

About now you may be asking yourself, so what? I just want to start my own business. How could these changes in how we view work possibly affect me? And that's a good question. Again, keep in mind that in this chapter we're looking at the context that's affecting entrepreneurial organizations. The demands imposed by the context will influence choices that you make about how work is going to get done in your entrepreneurial venture. The facts that the nature of work and the organizational setting within which work gets done have changed will affect the way you do your work and if you have additional employees, the way they do their work. So, yes, the characteristics of the changing world of work are important to recognize and understand.

The final aspect of the entrepreneurial context that we need to look at involves the concepts of social responsibility and ethics. These are never easy topics to discuss, but they do play a significant role in influencing entrepreneurial decisions and actions.

Rapid Review

- ✔ Why is the legal environment an important part of the entrepreneurial context?
- ✔ What legal issues affect an entrepreneurial venture?
- ✔ Describe some of the important federal laws that have an impact on businesses.
- ✔ How is the world of work changing?
- ✔ What impact is being made on entrepreneurial ventures by the changes in the way work is done?
- ✔ What is a learning organization, and why is this concept of importance to entrepreneurs?
- ✔ How might entrepreneurs use projects?

Social Responsibility and Ethics

How much and what type of social responsibility an organization should pursue has been a topic of heated debate for a number of years. **Social responsibility** is the obligation of organizational decision makers to act in ways that recognize the interrelatedness of business and society.[18] Social responsibility assumes the existence of **stakeholders**, individuals or groups of individuals who have a stake in or are significantly influenced by an organization's actions and who, in turn, can influence the organization. However, it's in the definition of to "whom" organizations are responsible that we find a diversity of opinions.

The traditional view of social responsibility was that organizations existed solely to serve the

EXHIBIT 2-8 Possible Organizational Stakeholders

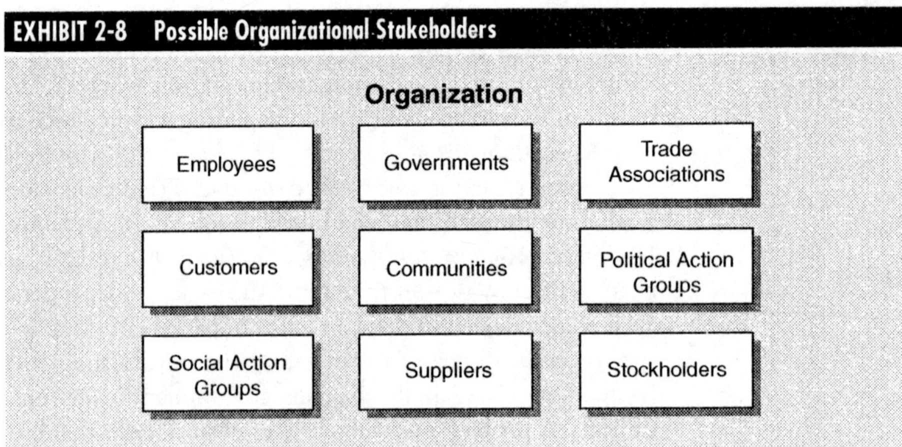

interests of one stakeholder group—stockholders.[19] Milton Friedman has been the biggest advocate of this view. He argued that organizational social programs and actions must be paid for in some way, which adds to the costs of doing business. These costs either have to be passed on to customers in the form of higher prices or absorbed internally, thus increasing organizational expenses. In either case, profits might suffer because customers might buy less at higher prices or costs would increase. Stockholders, the true "owners" of the organization, are interested in increasing profits and the return they're earning on their investments. You do need to understand, however, that Friedman didn't say that organizations shouldn't be socially responsible. In fact, he said they *should* be. Yet his argument was that the extent of the organization's responsibility was to maximize stockholder returns.

However, the traditional—and purely economic—view of social responsibility has given way to a belief that organizations have a larger societal role to play and a broader constituency to serve than stockholders alone. Possible organizational stakeholders are illustrated in Exhibit 2-8. Balancing the demands of these various stakeholders is, as you can well imagine, a difficult process because they often have a wide range of needs and conflicting expectations. Take a minute and think about how an entrepreneurial organization could be socially responsible in each of these stakeholder relationships.

There are numerous examples of organizations that believe in strong and socially responsible stakeholder relationships. For example, Ben & Jerry's Homemade Inc., a successful entrepreneurial venture best known for its premium ice cream, has been a role model for social responsibility with its efforts to promote world peace, preserve the

The Grey Zone Littleton, Colorado. Springfield, Oregon. Pearl, Mississippi. Paducah, Kentucky. Places we remember because of the tragic school violence that happened there. The national debate that ensued from these events focused on the violence to which children and teens are exposed through film, music, video games, and the Internet. The video game industry, an industry made up mainly of entrepreneurs and entrepreneurial ventures, is trying to strengthen voluntary measures to shield children from inappropriate games. What social and ethical responsibilities do entrepreneurs have when there are tough societal questions being raised about the products being marketed? What would you do if you were an entrepreneur? How would you respond to the societal concerns being raised?

environment, and support local businesses.[20] Ben Cohen and Jerry Greenfield (co-founders of Ben & Jerry's) along with fellow entrepreneurs Anita and Gordon Roddick (Body Shop International), Paul Hawken (Smith & Hawken), and Yvon Chouinard (Patagonia) were early pioneers in socially responsible business practices. Today, entrepreneurs such as Jeff Mendelsohn of New Leaf Paper LLC (www.newleafpaper.com), Daniel Grossman of Wild Planet Toys, Inc. (www.wildplanet.com), and Seth Goldman of Honest Tea Inc. (www.honesttea.com) are following the lead of those early entrepreneurs who took their responsibilities to society seriously. How are these entrepreneurs showing their commitment to social responsibility? New Leaf Paper manufactures and distributes recycled paper. Wild Planet Toys designs and manufactures nonsexist, nonviolent, and imagination-inspiring toys. And Honest Tea makes fully biodegradable tea bags filled with whole tea leaves. Although social responsibility emphasizes the broad picture of an organization's societal interactions, it's also important that these interactions take place in a context of "doing the right thing" or doing things ethically.

By this time in your life, you've undoubtedly faced a number of ethical dilemmas, both in school and, if you're employed, at your job. For instance, is it ethical to make a copy of expensive computer software for a friend who's short of money or to "donate" copies of completed homework assignments to your sorority or fraternity? Or, say you're a part-time telemarketing representative. Is it ethical for you to pressure customers to purchase a product they don't really need or can't really afford just so you can win a prize? **Ethics** involves the rules and principles that define right and wrong decisions and behaviors. In other words, as we live our lives—attend school, go to work, engage in hobbies, go out with friends, and so forth—certain decisions are ethically "right" and others are ethically "wrong." Considering the varied interpretations of right and wrong, you can see how ethics is a complex topic to address. However, ethical considerations do play a role in the decisions you make and the actions you take with your entrepreneurial venture. You need to be aware of the ethical consequences of these. The example you set, especially if you have other employees, can be significant in influencing behavior. For example, Charlie Wilson, founder of Houston-based SeaRail International Inc., made ethics a consideration in putting together guidelines for his sales representatives. He says, "Ethics is what's spearheading our growth. It creates an element of trust, familiarity and predictability in the business. You don't get a good reputation doing things that way [unethically]. And, if you do [act unethically], eventually customers won't want to do business with you."[21] The importance that entrepreneurs place on ethics can be seen in the results of a study of approximately 300 business owners and corporate managers. It showed that entrepreneurs generally have stricter ethical standards than do managers and are also better able to live by their beliefs, probably because entrepreneurs typically have more control over their decisions and actions. Only half of the entrepreneur respondents said they would sacrifice personal ethics to achieve business goals, as compared with 71 percent of the corporate managers.[22]

We've now looked at all the various contextual issues that might affect entrepreneurs and their entrepreneurial ventures. Within this context, entrepreneurs need to be alert to certain trends and changes because of the potential opportunities they present.

FYI

Being Ethical

As an entrepreneur, you'll undoubtedly face ethical dilemmas. How will you deal with them? Knowing what to do isn't always easy. However, the following guidelines might help you evaluate the ethical situation more clearly.

1. Is the ethical dilemma what it appears to be? If you're not sure, you need to find out all you can about it.
2. Is the action you're considering legal? Is it ethical? If you're not sure, find out.
3. Do you understand the position of those who might be opposed to the action you're considering? Does their opposition sound reasonable?
4. Whom will your action(s) benefit? Harm? How much will it benefit or harm others? For how long?
5. Have you sought out the opinions of others who might have knowledge, training, or information about the situation and who could be objective?
6. Would you be embarrassed to have your action(s) made known to family, friends, neighbors, or others around you? How would you feel about having your action(s) reported in the local newspaper or on the evening news?

There are no correct answers to these questions. But by using these guidelines, you should be better able to clarify whether your action(s) are ethically and socially responsible.

Sources: A. M. Pagano and J. A. Verdin, *The External Environment of Business*, (New York: Wiley, 1988), Chapter 5; and J. L. Badaracco Jr. and A. P. Webb, "Business Ethics: A View From the Trenches," *California Management Review*, winter 1995, pp. 8–28.

IDENTIFYING ENVIRONMENTAL OPPORTUNITIES

2,300 percent. That was the impressive number that caught Jeff Bezos's attention in 1994.[23] It reflected the explosive growth in the use of the Internet—a rate of about 2,300 percent a month. Bezos recognized that something dramatic was happening, and he wanted to be a part of it. He decided to quit his job as a successful stock market researcher and hedge fund manager and pursue his vision for online retailing. Narrowing a long list of products he believed could be sold over the Internet down to two—books and music—he finally settled on books for two simple reasons: More products to sell and the publishing companies were not as ferociously competitive as the record companies. And Amazon.com, the world's largest on-line retailer, was born.

Rapid Review 

- ✔ What is social responsibility?
- ✔ What are stakeholders, and what role do they play in entrepreneurial ventures?
- ✔ List the different types of stakeholders.
- ✔ Describe the traditional and more contemporary views of social responsibility.
- ✔ What are ethics, and why are ethical considerations important to entrepreneurs?
- ✔ Describe the guidelines an entrepreneur can follow in order to be ethical.

The skyrocketing Internet use that Bezos observed is a prime example of identifying environmental opportunities. What exactly are **opportunities**? They're positive external trends or changes that provide unique and distinct possibilities for innovating and creating value. Entrepreneurs need to be able to pinpoint these pockets of opportunity that a changing context provides. How might they do this? Peter Drucker, a well-known management author, has identified seven potential sources of opportunity in the external context.[24]

1. *The unexpected.* When situations and events are unanticipated, opportunities can be found. The event might be an unexpected success (positive news) or an unexpected failure (bad news). Either way, there can be opportunities for entrepreneurs to pursue. For instance, when Sonny Bono (famous singer) and Michael Kennedy (member of a famous political family) were killed in skiing accidents, ski helmet manufacturers scored an unexpected bonanza as skiers rushed to purchase protective headgear. And, after the terrorist attacks of September 11, many entrepreneurs in security-related fields found their businesses booming. These are examples of unexpected events in which opportunities to innovate and create value arose.
2. *The incongruous.* When something is incongruous, there are inconsistencies in the way it appears. Things "ought to be" a certain way, but aren't. When conventional wisdom about the way things should be no longer holds true, for whatever reason, there are opportunities to capture. Entrepreneurs who are willing to "think outside the box"—that is, to think beyond the traditional and conventional approaches—may find pockets of potential profitability. For instance, Fred Smith, founder of FedEx, recognized the incongruities in the delivery of documents. His approach was: Why not? Who says that overnight delivery is impossible? Smith's answer to those incongruous questions was the creation of FedEx, now the world's leading express package delivery organization.
3. *The process need.* What happens when technology doesn't come up with the "big discovery" that's going to fundamentally change the very nature of some product or service? What happens is that there can be pockets of entrepreneurial opportunity in the various stages of the process as researchers and technicians continue to work for the monumental breakthrough. Because they've not been able to make the full leap, opportunities abound in the tiny steps. A good example of this can be seen in the medical products industry. Although researchers haven't yet discovered, for example, a cure for cancer, there have been many successful entrepreneurial ventures created as our knowledge about genetics' role in fighting cancer continues to expand. The "big breakthrough" hasn't happened, but there have been numerous entrepreneurial opportunities throughout the process of discovery.
4. *Industry and market structures.* When changes in technology change the structure of an industry and market, existing firms can become obsolete if they're not attuned to the changes or are unwilling to change. Changes in social values and consumer tastes also can shift the structures of industries and markets. These markets and industries become open targets for nimble and smart entrepreneurs. Take, for example, the Internet's impact on the recorded music industry. When Shawn Fanning, founder of Napster, created the technology to share music files over the Internet, the recorded music industry changed forever. As Napster struggled to create its future after being forced to curtail its business after a lawsuit was filed by the music industry, other entrepreneurs jumped on perceived opportunities to do what Napster had done. Even the big five music companies that comprise the industry

Entrepreneurs in Action

Stressed-out and overworked moms are paying people to do things they can't do or don't have time to fit into their frantic schedules. And entrepreneurs are finding ways to respond to the opportunities in this family time crunch by creating unique businesses. For instance, families can hire people to pay bills, plan birthday parties, provide transportation for the children, cook, offer back-up babysitting services, baby-proof the house, sort and organize papers and photos, and so forth. There are even family chaos consultants and nanny surveillance businesses. In today's families, in which both parents are pursuing demanding full-time careers, having someone else take care of the household chores and errands is a real time- and sanity-saver. And, for creative entrepreneurs, the opportunities for meeting the needs of these families can be quite attractive.

Source: R. Sharp, "Nannies on Speed Dial," *Business Week*, September 18, 2000, pp. 108–110.

were being entrepreneurial by innovating their own versions of online music subscription services.

5. *Demographics.* We know from our earlier chapter discussion that the vital statistics of the world's population—that is, demographics—are changing. These changes influence industries and markets by altering the types and quantities of products and services desired and customers' buying power. Although many of these changes are fairly predictable if you stay alert to demographic trends, others are not as obvious. Either way, there can be significant entrepreneurial opportunities in anticipating and meeting needs of the population. For instance, one population group (another term for this is *cohort*) that you've probably heard a lot about is the baby boomers. This group typically includes individuals born between 1946 and 1964. You hear so much about the boomers because there are so many of them. Through every life stage they've entered (going to elementary school, teenage years, climbing the career ladder, and now the middle-age years), they've had an enormous impact because of their sheer numbers. Other age cohorts besides boomers that have been identified include the Depression group (born 1912–1921); the World War II group (born 1922–1927); the Postwar group (born 1928–1945); the Generation X group (born 1965–1977); and Generation Y (born between 1978 and 1994; also called echo boomers or millennials). Analysts predict that there are enormous opportunities for providing goods and services to the boomers and to Gen Y. For instance, Gold Violin (www.goldviolin.com) and Scriptsave (www.scriptsave.com) have positioned themselves to profit as the baby boomers age. Two other entrepreneurial ventures have targeted Gen Y consumers. Alien Workshop (www.alienworkshop.com) designs and distributes skateboards and other skate apparel. Paul Frank Industries (www.paulfrank.com) designs and dis-

tributes trendy fashion clothing and accessories.[25] And age is just one demographic! Astute entrepreneurs can find opportunities by tracking trends in any of the demographics.

6. *Changes in perception.* Perception is one's view of reality. When changes in perception take place, then facts do not vary, but their meaning does. Changes in perception get at the heart of people's psychographic profiles—what they value, what they believe in, and what they care about. Changes in these attitudes and values create potential market opportunities for alert entrepreneurs. Our chapter-opening case is a good example of this. As customers begin to demand tastier and healthier alternatives to fast food (think of Burger King's introduction of the Veggie Burger), market opportunities will abound. O'Naturals is preparing to exploit these opportunities presented by changes in perception.
7. *New knowledge.* New knowledge can be a significant source of entrepreneurial opportunity. As what we know about how the world works continues to increase, pockets of entrepreneurial opportunity can be exploited. For instance, as knowledge about energy-conservation technology continues to expand, entrepreneurial ventures are exploiting opportunities. Solar Attic (www.solarattic.com) has discovered a way to recover heat from home attics to heat swimming pools, for use in heating hot water, and for space heating. And Real Goods Trading Corporation (www.realgoods.com) uses knowledge about wind turbines and photovoltaic systems to market these products to customers.[26] It does take more than just *having* new knowledge, though. It often takes the convergence of several pieces of new knowledge. And you have to be able to do something with that knowledge—create products, improve processes, and so forth—and to protect your proprietary information from competitors.

FYI

The Entrepreneurial Mindset

To prosper in today's changing context, entrepreneurs have to be fast and smart. They have to be able to recognize opportunities and be willing to jump on them. A book by Rita Gunther McGrath and Ian MacMillan called *The Entrepreneurial Mindset: Strategies for Continuously Creating Opportunity in an Age of Uncertainty* provides an extremely practical approach for doing this. One of the unique strategies these authors discuss is creating an "opportunity register—an inventory of opportunities, a list of your ideas for improving, or even completely reinventing, your current business model or for going into entirely new opportunity spaces." And they point out that these opportunities are found in five categories: (1) redesigning products or services, (2) redifferentiating products or services, (3) resegmenting the market, (4) completely reconfiguring the market, and (5) developing breakthrough competitive strengths. The suggestions given in this book will provide any potential or current entrepreneur with plenty to think about. It might be something you want to invest in!

Source: R. G. McGrath and I. MacMillan, *The Entrepreneurial Mindset* (Boston: Harvard Business School Press), 2000, pp. 4–5.

The importance of understanding the entrepreneurial context and being alert to potential opportunities can't be overemphasized! In assessing the context, it's also important for entrepreneurs to understand the concept of competitive advantage.

UNDERSTANDING COMPETITIVE ADVANTAGE

Competitive advantage is important to successful entrepreneurial ventures. What is it? **Competitive advantage** is what sets an organization apart—in other words, its competitive edge. When an organization has a competitive advantage, it has something that other competitors do not, does something better than other organizations do, or does something that others can't.

Competitive advantage is a necessary ingredient for long-term success and survival. However, getting and keeping a competitive advantage isn't easy. The ability to create a competitive advantage leads to organizational success or failure. Although success is the preferable choice, entrepreneurs don't consciously choose failure. Instead, poor performance of an entrepreneurial venture typically can be traced to poor or nonexistent competitive advantage. What does it take to get, and keep, a competitive advantage? There are three different views on this.[27]

The first perspective is called the industrial organization, or I/O, approach. It says that competitive advantage arises out of the organization's ability to look at important external factors, analyze those factors for potential opportunities, and then base organizational decisions on what was discovered. The focus of analysis in the I/O view is external. According to this view, getting and keeping a competitive advantage is dependent on the ability to see external trends and changes and to interpret and act on them.

The second view of competitive advantage is called the resource-based view (RBV) and emphasizes exploiting organizational resources and capabilities. The focus of this view is internal. According to the RBV, getting and keeping a competitive advantage is dependent on developing or acquiring unique organizational resources and capabilities.

Resources are simply the assets an organization has for doing whatever work it's in business to do. These resources can be financial, physical, human, intangible, and structural/cultural. Financial resources include cash reserves, credit lines, ability to borrow money, available equity (stock), and other monetary assets. Physical assets are tangible assets such as buildings, equipment and fixtures, raw materials, office supplies, manufacturing facilities, and so forth. Human resources include the experiences, knowledge, skills, accumulated wisdom, and characteristics of the organization's employees. Intangible resources are things such as brand names, patents, trademarks, databases, copyrights, or registered designs. Finally, structural/cultural resources include things such as organizational history, culture, work systems, policies, relationships with stakeholders, and the structure (informal or formal) being used. The resources are the "whats"—what the organization has or owns.

Capabilities, on the other hand, are the "hows"—the organizational routines and processes that determine how efficiently and effectively the organization transforms its inputs (resources) into outputs (products and services). A good example to illustrate how resources and capabilities differ is someone who's con-

Entrepreneurs in Action

John Wall, president of a woodworking shop in rural Vermont, Wall/Goldfinger (**www.wallgoldfinger.com**), started in 1971 making rolltop desks and four-poster beds. Today, his company creates furniture for the most prestigious businesses in the United States. *Fortune* 500 corporations, leading financial and insurance businesses, nationally known law firms, and numerous leading universities are Wall/Goldfinger customers. With capabilities perfected over the years, the company has carved out a niche making lecterns, credenzas, reception desks, and its specialty—exquisite high-tech furniture for corporate conference and meeting rooms. In 2001 Wall/Goldfinger received the Governor's Award for Environmental Excellence in Pollution Prevention. Why? A redesign of the company's finishing facility by company employees reduced the generation of hazardous waste by 20 percent. And, new air units and furnaces that reduced air pollution and fuel usage were installed, thus creating a cleaner environment for employees *and* a better product for customers.

Sources: Wall/Goldfinger Web site (**www.wallgoldfinger.com**), April 26, 2002; and J. Lardner, "Chairman of the Boards," *Business 2.0*, February 2002, p. 29.

sidered an excellent cook. This cook will own pots and pans, spices, equipment, and other cooking materials (that is, resources) to be used in preparing delicious meals. However, to get a reputation as an excellent cook, it takes more than just owning a bunch of resources. That person has to be able to do something with those resources. A good cook has to be able to transform the raw materials (food, spices, and so forth) using equipment (pans, utensils, and other cooking paraphernalia) into a fabulous meal. Likewise, an organization possesses resources that can be used (transformed) to put together a competitive advantage. Although an organization's resources can be considered its "pantry of goodies," these assets are much more valuable as they're used by the entrepreneur or other organizational members in doing their work. By themselves, the resources aren't productive. Remember our gourmet cook—he has to combine the spices and food using the appropriate equipment to put together the delicious meals. Likewise, the organization's resources have to be combined and used through capabilities in order to do whatever it's in business to do. As organizational members work, combining resources within the structure of the organization's work routines, they accumulate knowledge and experience about how best to get the most out of the resources.

The third perspective on competitive advantage—the guerrilla view—is relatively new. What do you think of when you hear the term *guerrilla?* Do you envision rapid and continual sneak attacks on an enemy position by a well-trained, competent, and skilled force? That's very much the analogy behind the guerrilla

Rapid Review

- ✔ What are opportunities? Why do entrepreneurs need to care about opportunities?
- ✔ Describe the seven potential sources of opportunities in the external environment.
- ✔ What is competitive advantage, and why do entrepreneurs need to care about it?
- ✔ Discuss the three perspectives on getting and keeping competitive advantage.
- ✔ What are resources? What are capabilities?
- ✔ Describe the five types of resources an organization has.
- ✔ Describe the connection between resources and capabilities.

view of competitive advantage. The main premise of the guerrilla view is that an organization's competitive advantage is temporary. Why? Because the external context is characterized by continual, radical, and often revolutionary changes. For instance, disruptions in technological know-how, market instabilities, and other types of significant and unpredictable changes can challenge entrepreneurs' attempts to create a long-term sustainable competitive advantage. Under these types of chaotic conditions, it's difficult to develop a permanent competitive advantage. Instead, according to this view of competitive advantage, successful entrepreneurial ventures must be more adept at rapidly and repeatedly disrupting the current situation and radically surprising competitors with actions that keep them off balance—in other words, acting like a guerrilla unit. And, the successful entrepreneurial organization will repeatedly form new competitive advantages based on different approaches and different asset combinations from the current ones being used.

The thing for entrepreneurs to remember is that all three views of competitive advantage are important to getting a sustainable competitive advantage. Because the external context is continually changing (for instance, new competitors come and go, customers' tastes change, technology changes, and so forth), the source of sustainable competitive advantage—the "edge" an organization has over its competitors—is probably found at different points over time. The organizational resources and capabilities needed to exploit those changes will vary also. Pursuing a sustainable competitive advantage by taking advantage of any positive changes (or protecting against negative trends) with the entrepreneurial venture's resources and being ready to change as conditions warrant is what it all boils down to. That's the ever-changing, and constant, challenge for the entrepreneur.

CHAPTER SUMMARY

This summary is organized around the chapter-opening objectives.

1. The economic arena facing entrepreneurs is a lot different from what it used to be. Four driving forces characterize today's economy. These include the role of information, technological trends, globalization, and changing demographics. Information is now readily available anytime, anywhere, to anyone. It has become the essential resource of production, not simply a means to an end. Next, all organizations use some form of technology to do their work. Within this area, four technological trends affecting the context of entrepreneurship include the increasing rate of technological change and diffusion, the increasing commercialization of innovations, increasing knowledge intensity, and increasing recognition that advanced information technologies are the cornerstone of successful businesses. The third driving force, globalization, is the linkage of economies and cultures that fosters a business and competitive situation in which organizations have no national boundaries.

Entrepreneurs will continue to find increasing opportunities in global markets and increasing challenges in global competitors. The final driving force of today's economy is changing demographics. As the world's demographics change, they affect the context within which entrepreneurs pursue their entrepreneurial ventures.

There are four major implications arising out of the driving forces. These include continual turbulence and change, reduced need for physical assets, vanishing distance, and compressed time. Change is a fact of life in today's business context. In addition, success in today's economy doesn't rely simply on physical assets. Value can be found in intangible factors such as information, people, ideas, and knowledge. Also, the influence of physical distance on organizational decisions has disappeared. An entrepreneur's potential market can be found anywhere, but so can competitors. As the limitations of physical space have disappeared, so have the limitations of time. The instant interactivity between customers and businesses, between employees, and between companies and suppliers has created a context in which marketplace advantage can be temporary if an organization doesn't stay on top of the changes.

What does it take to be successful given the realities of today's economy? Four critical success factors include the ability to embrace change, the ability to be creative and innovative, vision and leadership, and a total quality culture.

2. The context facing entrepreneurs includes legal factors. A society's laws and regulations provide the framework within which citizens can do or not do certain things. The legal environment both allows and prohibits certain decisions and actions. Several important legal issues affect an entrepreneurial venture at different stages. During the start-up stage, legal issues might include determining the form of business organization, setting up appropriate records for tax purposes, negotiating leases and financing, drawing up contracts, and filing for patents, trademarks, or copyright protection. When the entrepreneurial venture is operating, legal issues might include human resource laws and regulations, safety laws and regulations, financial and accounting laws and regulations, and marketplace laws and regulations.

3. Today's work world is different from what it used to be. Two major areas of change that have had an impact on the way people work include the nature of the work that people do and the organizational setting within which work takes place. Work today is much more knowledge-intensive. Employees are expected to use their mental abilities in addition to their physical ones, and this is true in all kinds of jobs, not just in those that you think might require knowledge work. And, traditional approaches to getting work done through rigid and inflexible job assignments aren't appropriate anymore. An organization that hopes to succeed in today's context is one characterized by flexibility, temporariness, and independence. Instead of a "job," entrepreneurs need to think in terms of packets of skills and abilities applied to specific tasks. In fact, many entrepreneurial organizations are using projects—a temporary set of work tasks that has a definite beginning and ending point in time—to perform work.

4. Social responsibility is the obligation of organizational decision makers to act in ways that recognize the interrelatedness of business and society. The traditional and purely economic view of social responsibility has given way to a belief that organizations have a larger societal role to play and many stakeholders to serve. Ethics involves the rules and principles that define right and wrong decisions and behaviors. Ethical considerations do play a role in decisions and actions in an entrepreneurial venture. Entrepreneurs need to be aware of the ethical consequences of their decisions and actions.
5. Opportunities are positive external trends or changes that provide unique and distinct possibilities for innovating and creating value. Entrepreneurs need to be able to pinpoint pockets of opportunity provided by a changing context. Seven potential sources of opportunity include the unexpected, the incongruous, the process need, changing market and industry structures, demographic trends, changes in perception, and new knowledge.
6. Competitive advantage is what sets an organization apart; its competitive edge. When an organization has a competitive advantage, it has something that other competitors do not, does something better than other organizations do, or does something that others can't. Competitive advantage is important for long-term success and survival.

KEY TERMS

- *Telecommuters:* Individuals who work from home and are linked to the workplace by computers and modems.
- *Virtual organizations:* Organizations with little or no physical work space, no formal hierarchical structure, and individuals who contract to perform specific work as needed.
- *Innovation:* The process of taking a creative idea and turning it into a product or process that can be used or sold.
- *Patent:* A legal property that allows its holder to prevent others from employing this property for their own use for a specified period of time.
- *Globalization:* The linkage of economies and cultures that fosters a business and competitive situation in which organizations have no national boundaries.
- *Demographics:* The vital statistics of a population.
- *Change:* Any alteration in external context or internal organizational factors.
- *Creativity:* The ability to combine ideas in a unique way or to make unusual associations between ideas.
- *Vision:* A broad comprehensive statement of what an entrepreneur wants his or her organization to become.
- *Total quality culture:* An organizational culture in which all resources and capabilities are directed at the pursuit of greater quality in all parts of the organization.

- *Learning organization:* An organization that has developed the continuous capacity to adapt by acquiring information and knowledge and incorporating this knowledge and learning into decisions and actions.
- *Project:* A temporary set of work tasks that has a definite beginning and ending point in time.
- *Social responsibility:* The obligation of organizational decision makers to act in ways that recognize the interrelatedness of business and society.
- *Stakeholders:* Individuals or groups of individuals who have a stake in or are significantly influenced by an organization's actions and who, in turn, can influence the organization.
- *Ethics:* The rules and principles that define right and wrong decisions and behaviors.
- *Opportunities:* Positive external trends or changes that provide unique and distinct possibilities for innovating and creating value.
- *Competitive advantage:* What sets an organization apart; its competitive edge.
- *Resources:* The assets an organization has for doing whatever work it's in business to do.
- *Capabilities:* The organizational routines and processes that determine how efficiently and effectively the organization transforms its inputs (resources) into outputs (products and services).

SWEAT EQUITY

1. In today's intensely competitive and "post-Enron" world, ethical business behavior isn't just something that's good to do—it's a valuable necessity. One thing an entrepreneur can do to behave ethically, and to encourage employees to behave ethically, is to have a written code of ethics. Research what should be in a code of ethics. Get at least three real examples of codes of ethics. Then, create your own proposed code of ethics for an entrepreneurial venture. Be prepared to present your work to the class. And be sure to include your list of reference sources.
2. As an entrepreneur you need to recognize opportunities. Refamiliarize yourself with the seven potential sources of opportunity. Then, read through the five latest issues of any business or general news periodical (*Business Week, Inc., Fast Company, Time, Fortune, Wall Street Journal,* and so forth). Use the same one or any combination of these magazines. Based on your reading, make a bulleted list of potential opportunities. Note the source of opportunity under which each of your items falls. This assignment is going to require you to be really creative and open-minded. Look for the unusual connections and the unseen, yet potential, linkages. Have fun!
3. "We're from the government and we're here to help you." Does this phrase make you chuckle? Well, an entrepreneur's best friend just may be the government. As we have discussed, legal factors both allow and prohibit certain behaviors and actions and, as such, affect the entrepreneurial context.

But, the government can also be a source of immense help. Your assignment is to do some research into the help for entrepreneurs offered by your local and state governments. Find out what types of entrepreneurial programs, assistance, and help are available in your community. Once you have collected this information, sort it according to start-up assistance and assistance for ongoing businesses. Write up a report describing what you have found.

4. Although violence and terrorist attacks aren't anything new, the events of September 11, 2001, made many people more aware of their vulnerability. Although most entrepreneurial businesses are unlikely targets, what can entrepreneurs do to protect their businesses against any forms of violence? Research this topic. You might even want to interview some local entrepreneurs about what steps they have taken. Come up with a list of suggestions. (*Hint:* Keep in mind that violence doesn't have to hit you directly for you to be affected by it. Don't forget to think about the ripple effects of violence aimed at someone else—your customers, suppliers, or even the general economy.) Be prepared to share your suggestions with your class.
5. How can entrepreneurs become aware of potentially important external changes that might be sources of opportunities or even threats to their entrepreneurial ventures? Experts say that some of the more popular techniques aren't crystal balls or tea leaves, but do include Delphi interviews, environmental scanning, and scenario development. Research these techniques and write at least one page describing each. Be sure to look at what the technique involves, the advantages and drawbacks of the technique, and how entrepreneurs might use it.
6. The state of the economy obviously plays an important role in an individual's decision to start a business. Your professor will divide your class into two groups. One group will come up with arguments why a slowing economy is a good time to start a business. The other group will come up with arguments why a slowing economy is not a good time to start a business. Each side should prepare a list of arguments and be prepared to debate this topic in class.
7. An article in *Business 2.0* ("Minds over Matter," January 1999) proposed that today's economy is based on brains, not brawn. In this economy, intellectual (knowledge) capital is critical. According to author Don Tapscott, the only assets that count are people assets—those with brains, knowledge, and the ability to think and innovate. People serve as the key to a sustainable competitive advantage. Your assignment is to research the topic of people as a competitive advantage. Using your research results, type up a bulleted list of important points you found (at least one page). Then, write up what you think the implications of this perspective might be for entrepreneurs (good *and* bad). Be sure to cite your research sources.

ENTREPRENEURSHIP IN ACTION CASES

O'Naturals (www.onaturals.com)

This case can be found at the beginning of Chapter 2.

Discussion Questions

1. What source of opportunity seems to describe Gary Hirshberg's idea for starting O'Naturals? Explain your choice.
2. What types of legal and work design issues might O'Naturals have to deal with as they prepare to expand nationally? What might the entrepreneurial team do to prepare for these issues?
3. Go to the O'Naturals Web site (**www.onaturals.com**) and read their mission statement. Does the mission statement reflect social responsibility? Explain. Now, take each of the statements and describe how the company might actually practice what it states. For instance, how could it "provide staff with a caring and learning environment?" In addition, as the company grows, how can it ensure that each restaurant outlet continues these commitments?

Crosslink Polymer Research (www.crosslinkresearch.com)

You probably don't know a whole lot—if anything—about polymers. Yet, scientific researchers say that polymers have the potential to improve daily life in numerous ways. According to the enlightening tutorial, Polymers 101, on Crosslink Polymer's Web site, polymers are "large molecules built up by the repetition of small, simple chemical units and are naturally occurring or can be created." At Crosslink Polymer Research, the expanding technology of polymer applications is contributing to new and exciting directions for this Fenton, Missouri-based entrepreneurial venture.

Crosslink's chairman and chief executive officer Brent St. John is hoping to revolutionize the use of polymers in all kinds of illumination (lighting) applications. In 2000, St. John's company created a patented printing process called Lumimove™ that made it possible to print electrically charged inks on polymers. Although these "excitable inks" (inks that conduct electricity) had been around for years, the application of these inks on plastic panels (polymers) has opened up some interesting new markets especially given the fact that these inks have a complete color palette and use one-hundredth the power of neon signs. Crosslink's revolutionary Lumimove system overcame the constraints of traditional forms of lighting including incandescent, fluorescent, and neon illumination. Product and store advertising signs made using Crosslink's process are sophisticated enough to flash letters, words, or images in a desired sequence. So far, Crosslink's two production lines have turned out Lumimove products for bars and restaurants including tables and hanging signs advertising food and beer. However, the company is looking at new markets and new applications for its products. For instance, the vending-machine market is one area Crosslink is thinking about pursuing. Since the light sources currently used in vending machines are power hungry and prone to break, Crosslink's Lumimove technology could reduce those problems. And think of the incredible number of vending machines in the United States alone!

However, the most interesting application for Crosslink's technology may be in visual alarms that could emit a flashing light if people or products came in contact with a dangerous chemical or bacteria. The idea for this product came to St. John after the terrorist attacks on September 11, 2001. Since that time, his company's researchers have been trying to figure out how to integrate the illumination technology into a type of delivery system similar to nicotine patches. How would this product work? Say, for example, if a bioterrorist attack occurred, the patch would flash alerting the wearer and also potentially could trigger the release of an antidote. Another application of the illumination concept is thought to be on packages of meat to signal contamination. If, for instance, beef or chicken were tainted with *E. coli* or *Salmonella* bacteria, the package would flash a light warning against use.

Crosslink Polymer Research is poised to exploit the wonders of polymer technology. Its bright future has caught the eye of investors who have put $4 million in the company since 1998.

Discussion Questions

1. Would knowing something about the entrepreneurial context be important to Crosslink's executives? Why or why not?
2. What competitive advantage(s) would you say Crosslink has? Describe the company's competitive advantage from the three different perspectives.
3. How could Brent St. John use Drucker's approach to identify additional opportunities?

Sources: Information on company from company Web site (www.crosslinkresearch.com), September 20, 2002, and Hoover's Online, September 20, 2002; and M. Hofman, "Bright Writes," *Inc.*, March 2002, p. 28.

JobDirect (www.jobdirect.com)

Whereas most college graduates are concerned (and justifiably so) about getting that first job, two women stressing out over their own job searches decided to pursue a vision for helping students make their own job searches as stressless as possible. In 1996 Rachel Bell and Sara Sutton started JobDirect (now called True Careers), a Stamford, Connecticut-based Internet job service for entry-level positions.

After researching their idea and raising money from family and friends, they purchased a recreational vehicle, had it spray-painted to look like their Web site, and took off on a promotional tour of college campuses. The RV was equipped with 15 laptops for students to type in their résumés. That first year, after cruising around 43 campuses, their database contained the résumés of 5,000 young job seekers. Today, résumés from college students pour into JobDirect's database at a rate of more than 1,000 per day.

How does their business work? Students seeking entry-level jobs put their résumés into the database. Soon after, JobDirect e-mails back jobs that they're qualified for. Students never have to do the searching—that's the service that JobDirect provides. In addition, students can access a multitude of career resources on JobDirect's Web site. And students can do this without ever having to pay a fee.

What about employers? What does JobDirect do for them? Primarily, help them find the best person for a job. Employers from a wide array of industries and from *Fortune* 500 companies to start-ups pay a fee to access JobDirect's database and other services. On the Web site, recruiters can look at prequalified résumés, comment on them or forward them to colleagues, respond to them, set up phone or in-person interviews, and publicize campus visits. JobDirect also has hundreds of campus representatives who solicit student résumés and who market JobDirect's service. In addition, JobDirect has an eight-person Campus Relations team that's responsible for forging alliances with campus career centers and other national collegiate organizations. JobDirect also provides employers with account managers who train recruiters on how to use JobDirect's services and how to make the most out of the software. Because many companies often have a hard time finding qualified diverse applicants, JobDirect has established a diversity initiative by developing career partnerships with the Historically Black Colleges and Universities (**www.hbcu-central.com**), the Hispanic Association of Colleges and Universities (**www.hacu.net**), the National Association for Equal Opportunity in Higher Education (**www.nafeo.org**), and *Black Enterprise* magazine (**www.blackenterprise.com**).

Although JobDirect has evolved from its early days of simply sending out brightly colored RVs across the country on road trips, its culture and organizational style still reflect the original by-students, for-students focus. In fact, JobDirect says on its Web site that "we do one thing—we match great students to great jobs. We do it every day, we do it all day, we've done it since 1996—and because we're so completely focused, we learn how to do it a little bit better every single day. Every dime of our research money, every minute of our focus groups, and every last one of our employees is dedicated to matching great students to great jobs." And that single-minded devotion may be the key to its success.

Discussion Questions

1. How did the realities of today's economy contribute to the idea for this entrepreneurial venture? Given these realities, is JobDirect doing what it should be to continue its success? (*Hint*: You might want to check out Exhibit 2-1.)
2. There are a number of online recruiting sources, so competitive advantage is obviously something about which JobDirect is concerned. What would you tell the company about getting and keeping a competitive advantage? What do you think JobDirect's competitive advantage might be?
3. How might the changing world of work affect the services that JobDirect provides? Are these potential impacts positive or negative? Explain.

Sources: JobDirect Web site (**www.jobdirect.com**), April 29, 2002; and C. Adler, "Have Resumes, Will Travel," ***Business Week Enterprise***, May 25, 1998, p. ENT18.

Green Mountain Coffee Roasters (www.greenmountaincoffee.com)

Long before Starbucks started its ubiquitous march from Seattle east across the United States, there was Green Mountain Coffee Roasters. Started in 1981 in a small café in Waitsfield, Vermont, Bob Stiller roasted his own coffee beans on the premises. It didn't take long for his high-quality, freshly roasted coffee to become a favorite of locals. And Green Mountain Coffee Roasters was on its way to becoming one of the nation's leading specialty coffee companies. Today, Green Mountain is headquartered in Waterbury, Vermont, and produces more than 70 varieties of arabica coffee. It sells this coffee to more than 6,700 wholesale accounts, such as grocery stores, convenience stores, resorts, and office delivery services. ExxonMobil (through its convenience stores) is Green Mountain's largest customer. The company also markets its coffees and related accessories through direct-mail catalogs and its Web site. Unlike Starbucks, Green Mountain closed its retail outlets in order to concentrate on wholesale customers. In 2001, *Forbes* named founder Bob Stiller Entrepreneur of the Year and called his company "one of the smartest small companies in America."

Revenues for 2001 reached $95.6 million and net profits reached $5.9 million (an increase of 37.2 percent over 2000). But it isn't just the company's success at growing sales an average of 24 percent per year over the past five years, nor the fact that its stock more than doubled during 2001 (outperforming both Starbucks and rival Peet's Coffee & Tea) that make it a great company. It's Green Mountain's commitment to being a socially responsible and ethical company that distinguishes it.

The company's commitment to social responsibility and ethics is seen up front and boldly in its statement of Core Values and Beliefs. It states: "We share a commitment to improve the environment and to make our local and global communities better," and "We act with honesty and integrity in all our actions and relationships." And these aren't just statements. The company actually does what it professes as it acts in ways consistent with an environmental conscience in all aspects of its business operations.

Discussion Questions

To answer these questions, you'll need to log on to Green Mountain's Web site at (**www.greenmountaincoffee.com**).

1. What other core values and beliefs, aside from social responsibility and ethics, does Green Mountain hold?
2. What core values does Green Mountain have specifically in relation to its environmental commitment?
3. Describe several examples (at least five) of how Green Mountain shows its commitment to social responsibility and ethics. Be specific.
4. Green Mountain is an active supporter and participant in the Businesses for Social Responsibility (BSR) organization. Log on to BSR's Web site (**www.bsr.org**) and do some reading about it. What does BSR do? How can organizations join BSR?
5. What can other entrepreneurs learn from Green Mountain's experiences?

Sources: Green Mountain Coffee Roaster's Web site (**www.greenmountaincoffee.com**), February 25, 2002; Hoover's Online Web site (**www.hoovers.com**), May 1, 2002; and L. Krull, "Java Man," *Forbes*, October 29, 2001, pp. 142–145.

Buckman Laboratories (www.buckman.com)

Buckman Laboratories, headquartered in Memphis, Tennessee, manufactures over 500 specialty chemicals and employs over 1,300 individuals in 70 countries. Its annual revenues exceed $300 million. Although this small, privately held company depends on its research laboratories for the innovative products that bring in its revenues, the whole company itself is a learning laboratory.

What is it about Buckman Labs that attracts executives from AT&T, 3M, Champion International, US West, and other *Fortune* 500 companies, who trek to Memphis to see and learn? They're coming to see how the company stays so fast, global, and interactive. Bob Buckman, founder and CEO from 1978 to April 2000, recognized the power of knowledge and information long before others did. Buckman and his associates began treating knowledge as the company's most important corporate asset back in 1984. They believed that being (and remaining) competitive in a knowledge-intensive global environment required three things: (1) closing the gap between the organization and the customer; (2) staying in touch with each other; and (3) bringing *all* of the company's brainpower together to solve problems for each customer. Beginning in the early 1980s, Buckman was concerned with staying connected, sharing knowledge, and functioning anytime, anywhere, no matter what.

Buckman has organized its associates and their work around its knowledge network, K'Netix®. This global electronic communications network resulted from Buckman's desire to close the gap between his associates and his customers—instantly. He started thinking about how important information and knowledge were—not just to him but to *all* of Buckman Labs' associates. What he needed and what his associates needed was a steady stream of the latest information about products, markets, and customers. And this information needed to be easily accessible and easily shared. As an ardent reader of business and management literature, Buckman remembered a comment of Jan Carlzon (former CEO of Scandinavian Airlines) that stuck in his mind, "An individual without information cannot take responsibility; an individual who is given information cannot help but take responsibility."

Buckman realized that the way to maximize each individual associate's power was to connect each associate to the world. He wrote down the characteristics of his ideal knowledge transfer system. Here's what he wrote: (1) It would be possible for people to talk to each other directly one on one, to minimize distortion. (2) It would give everyone access to the company's knowledge bases. (3) It would allow each individual in the company to enter knowledge into the system. (4) It would be available 24 hours a day, seven days a week. (5) It would be easy to use. (6) It would communicate in whatever language was best for the user. (7) It would be updated automatically, capturing questions and answers for a future knowledge base. But the technology of the system wasn't the most important barrier to knowledge sharing. Such a system would require a total cultural transformation—literally turning the organization upside down by getting associates to be deeply involved with knowledge sharing and collaboration. And that's what Bob Buckman set out to do. It wasn't easy, however, to transform the company from an old top-down, bureaucratic, command-and-control organization into an organization in which every associate had complete access to all information and one in which no one would be controlling associates by telling them what to do all the time.

Getting the physical hardware and software in place to support such a system was the easy part. Getting associates to use the knowledge base *and* to contribute to it were the challenges. After all, a knowledge-based company is successful only if knowledge is shared among all its organizational members, because knowledge has value only when it moves across and throughout the organization. What was particularly difficult about this type of change was that employees had always been rewarded on their ability to hoard knowledge, and thus gain power and recognition. This is how the situation at Buckman Labs was described: "There were people whose file cabinets were locked and filled with everything they knew, and that was the source of their power." But that philosophy had to change if the knowledge system was going to work. Not long after K'Netix® went online, Buckman made his expectations clear: "Those of you who have something intelligent to say now have a forum in which to say it. Those of you who will not or cannot contribute also become obvious. If you are not willing to contribute or participate, then you should understand that the many opportunities offered to you in the past will no longer be available." What ultimately emerged at Buckman Labs has been a mixture of visible incentives and invisible pressure to use K'Netix®.

Because Buckman Labs competes in a variety of markets, often against competitors much larger than it is, its commitment to knowledge takes on a new urgency. Salespeople need the right answer for each customer and they need it fast. K'Netix® has made getting answers simple and fast. But the company's commitment to associate interactivity and knowledge sharing, and its embrace of globalization wouldn't be possible without a recognition of the learning that is taking place.

Discussion Questions

1. Is Buckman Labs a learning organization? Explain.
2. Is Buckman Labs' commitment to sharing knowledge and learning important in light of the driving forces of today's economy, the implications of these driving forces, and the critical success factors? Explain.
3. Go to Buckman's Web site. Answer the following:
   - Find the statement of mission. What is it?
   - Locate the company's code of ethics. Summarize some of the company's basic principles.
   - Find the Knowledge Nurture page. What is the Buckman Room? What is the Library?
   - Find the page that describes the Buckman Knowledge Network. What does it say?
4. What could other entrepreneurs learn from Buckman Labs' experiences?

Sources: Buckman Laboratories Web site (**www.buckman.com**), April 15, 2002; S. Thurm, "What Do You Know?" *Wall Street Journal*, June 21, 1999, pp. R10+; B. P. Sunoo, "How HR Supports Knowledge Sharing," *Workforce*, March 1999, pp. 30–32; G. Rifkin, "Buckman Labs Is Nothing but Net," *Fast Company* Web page (**www.fastcompany.com**), April 17, 1997; and A. Bruzzee, "Sharing Knowledge Breaks Hierarchy," *Springfield News-Leader*, October 17, 1997, p. 7A.

BUSINESS PLAN PRO

EXERCISE 2-1: The Guided Tour

Chapter 3 of the Business Plan Pro manual contains a guided tour, introducing the main steps in creating a business plan. Find this chapter in the manual and follow the steps laid out in the chapter to create the bare bones of a business plan for a small graphic design company.

- Read the chapter and start the software, create the plan, and type in the suggested texts and numbers.
- When you're done you'll have a start on a plan text and projections. Save it on your computer as "Graphico.bpd."

EXERCISE 2-2: Graphico Example

Complete Exercise 2-1. As you look at the software view, you are probably still looking at the Wizard Tasks view. If not, click the "Wizard Tasks" icon in the toolbar to return to the Wizard Tasks view.

While there are not a lot of details in the manual text, think of the Graphico example in the Business Plan Pro guided tour as a graphic design business to be started by a single person.

- Imagine what kind of person starts a business like this, and why. Try to guess what this person's background and experience might be. What might the founder's résumé include? Has this person worked for a graphic design company as an employee? Does this person have business knowledge, familiarity with bookkeeping? Could this business be bigger than the projections in the guided tour?
- Find the "Management Summary" topic (in the "Your Management Team") section and write the management summary that should go with this plan, describing either a person you know, or a person you can imagine, who might be starting the small graphic design company.

EXERCISE 2-3: Graphico Competitive Advantage

Complete Exercises 2-1 and 2-2. Ask yourself what kinds of clients a business like Graphico might expect to develop. Should Graphico be trying to sell to local businesses, or national, or international? Should it be trying to sell to individuals? Schools? Government agencies?

- Consider the driving forces of today's economy. How do they affect Graphico?
- Find the "Market Analysis" topic in "Your Market" and describe the kinds of target customers you think might be appropriate for Graphico. How would you differentiate the most important potential customers from the rest of the world? Why would that be important? What might be the driving forces, as explained in this chapter, affecting Graphico's chances of success?
- Find the "Keys to Success" topic in the "Concept Kick Start" section and write about the critical success factors as

suggested in this chapter. Keep it short, use bullet points, and include no more than 3–4 keys to success.
- Find the "Competitive Edge" topic in the "Your Marketing Plan" section and write about a competitive edge you can imagine a hypothetical small graphics design company might be able to develop. As you do, consider the discussion of competitive advantage in this chapter.

EXERCISE 2-4: An Environmental Opportunity

Chapter 3 of the Business Plan Pro manual contains a guided tour, introducing the main steps in creating a business plan. Find this chapter in the manual and follow the steps laid out in the chapter to create the bare bones of a business plan for some company you'd like to start, or a company you know, or a company you'd like to work with. Use your imagination to invent a company that doesn't exist, or to imagine what the starting business plan might have been like, for a company that does exist.

- Start the software, create the plan, and type into your new plan the same elements the tour shows for its small graphic design company. That would include text for the text topic "Objectives," a sales forecast, a personnel forecast, and expenses in profit and loss. Then look at the cash flow, and, if necessary, use the start-up table to add investment to support cash needs. Use the Business Plan Pro Chapter 3 Guided Tour as a guide, but invent your own numbers and your own situation instead. When you're done you'll have a start on a plan text and projections. Save it on your computer as a business plan file.
- As you look at the software view, you are probably still looking at the Wizard Tasks view. If not, click the "Wizard Tasks" icon in the toolbar to return to the Wizard Tasks view.
- Find the "Keys to Success" topic in the "Concept Kick Start" section and write about the keys to success as suggested in the instructions. Keep it short, use bullet points, and include no more than 3–4 keys to success. These are the same as critical success factors in this chapter.
- Find the "Management Summary" topic (in the "Your Management Team") section and write the management summary that should go with this plan, describing either a person you know, or a person you can imagine, who might be starting the company you are inventing.
- Find the competitive edge section. Imagine the competitive advantages your hypothetical company might seek to develop.

BUSINESS NOW Crunch Fitness International

Cardio Strip Tease. Urban Rebounding. Circus Sports. Hip Hop Aerobics. These are just a few of the unique classes that fitness enthusiasts can take at Crunch Gyms (**www.crunch.com**). In 12 years, Crunch has grown from one gym in a dusty basement studio in Manhattan's East Village to 22 clubs in 7 U.S. cities (New York, Los Angeles, San

Francisco, Miami, Chicago, Atlanta, and Mission Viejo). And, unlike the fitness industry average that says 66 percent of new gym members quit within the first 90 days of joining, Crunch keeps the customers coming back. How? By constantly reinventing the fitness classes offered. Their goal is to make people forget they're working out.

Jim Solomon, President and CEO, says that Crunch's philosophy revolves around an irreverent attitude and cutting-edge fitness workouts. For instance, one of their newest classes isn't offered on solid ground. It's called "Airplane Yoga" and is offered to passengers aboard all JetBlue Airways flights. In the seatback pocket is a Crunch Fitness Airplane Yoga card illustrating four yoga poses that can be done while seated.

Solomon recognizes that Crunch's classes are not for everyone. However, they have identified a profitable niche—one that probably works only in heavily urban areas where the crowd it appeals to live and work. The average Crunch club generates around $5 million in revenues annually, whereas the industry average for a fitness club is approximately $1 million to $1.5 million. Solomon says that his Crunch clubs have significantly more productivity and creativity than the average club. And these urban gyms with classes taught by drag queens and firefighters prove that an approach that isn't just about taking off weight, but about putting on an exotic show, can be an entrepreneurial success.

Discussion Questions

1. What types of change might Crunch Fitness International have to deal with? How might these changes have an impact on what Crunch does?
2. Would you describe Crunch as creative and innovative? Would creativity and innovation be important in this industry? Explain.
3. Using material from this video case and from the company's Web site (**www.crunch.com**), write a vision statement for Crunch Fitness International.
4. To continue its successful growth, what sources of potential opportunity might Solomon need to look at?
5. Does Crunch have a competitive advantage? If so, what is it? If not, what might they need to do to develop one?

Sources: Company information from company Web site (**www.crunch.com**), July 10, 2002; and *Business Now* video segment.

ENDNOTES

1. Information on O'Naturals from company's Web site (**www.onaturals.com**), April 5, 2002; and D. Fenn, "Veggie-Burger Kings," *Inc.*, November 2001, pp. 42–44.
2. D. R. Gnyawali and D. S. Fogel, "Environments for Entrepreneurship Development: Key Dimensions and Research Implications," *Entrepreneurship Theory and Practice,* summer 1994, pp. 43–62.
3. J. Ellis, "Many Things Matter and Here's What Matters Most," *Fast Company,* June 2001, pp. 70–74; S. Kerr and D. Ulrich, "Creating the Boundaryless Organization: The Radical Reconstruction of Organizational Capabilities," *Planning Review*, September–October 1995, pp. 41–45.
4. M. J. Mandel, "You Ain't Seen Nothing Yet," *Business Week*, August 31, 1998, pp. 60–63.
5. "The Third Millennium: Small Business and Entrepreneurship in the 21st Century," Office of Advocacy, Small Business Administration, found on U.S. Small Business Administration Web site (**www.sba.gov/advo**), February 15, 2002; and J. Ellis, "Many Things Matter and Here's What Matters Most."

6. "One World: How Will Globalization Affect Small Businesses?" *Inc. State of Small Business*, May 29, 2001, p. 92.
7. Ibid.
8. R. W. Oliver, *The Shape of Things to Come: 7 Imperatives for Winning in the New World of Business*, (New York: McGraw-Hill, 1999), p. 23.
9. Ibid., pp. 42–45.
10. L. Robinson, "Hispanics Don't Exist," *U.S. News & World Report*, May 11, 1998, pp. 26–32.
11. W. McGeveran (editorial director) and K. Park (publisher), *World Almanac* (New York: World Almanac Education Group, Inc.), 2002, p. 869.
12. "The Third Millennium: Small Business and Entrepreneurship in the 21st Century," p. 3.
13. D. Kirkpatrick, "Beyond Buzzwords," *Fortune*, March 18, 2002, p. 164.
14. This definition is based on T. Amabile, "A Model of Creativity and Innovation in Organizations," in *Research in Organizational Behavior*, vol. 10, ed. B. M. Staw and L. L. Cummings (Greenwich, CT: JAI Press, 1988), p. 126.
15. D. I. Silvers, "Vision—Not Just for CEOs," *Management Quarterly*, winter 1994–1995, pp. 10–14.
16. J. Batten, "A Total Quality Culture," *Management Review*, May 1994, p. 61.
17. B. Dumaine, "Mr. Learning Organization," *Fortune*, October 17, 1994, p. 148.
18. D. J. Wood, "Corporate Social Performance Revisited," *Academy of Management Review*, October 1991, pp. 691–718.
19. M. Friedman, *Capitalism and Freedom* (Chicago: University of Chicago Press, 1962).
20. T. Singer, "Can Business Still Save the World?" *Inc.*, April 2001, pp. 58–71.
21. G. S. Stodder, "Goodwill Hunting," *Entrepreneur*, July 1998, p. 119.
22. E. Updike, "The Straightest Arrows," *Business Week Enterprise*, October 12, 1998, p. ENT2.
23. G. B. Knight, "How Wall Street Whiz Found a Niche Selling Books on the Internet," *Wall Street Journal*, May 15, 1996, p. A1.
24. P. Drucker, *Innovation and Entrepreneurship* (New York: Harper, 1985).
25. "Graying Boomers, Booming Teens," *Inc. State of Small Business*, May 29, 2001, pp. 86–87.
26. "Opportunity Knocks," *Inc. State of Small Business*, May 29, 2001, pp. 94–95.
27. Discussion of industrial/organization perspective based on K. R. Conner, "A Historical Comparison of Resource-Based Theory and Five Schools of Thought within Industrial Organization Economics: Do We Have a New Theory of the Firm?" *Journal of Management*, vol. 17, no. 1, 1991, pp. 121–154; M. Porter, *Competitive Advantage: Creating and Sustaining Superior Performance* (New York: Free Press, 1985); and M. Porter, *Competitive Strategy: Techniques for Analyzing Industries and Competitors* (New York: Free Press, 1980). Discussion of resource-based view based on D. Miller and J. Shamsie, "The Resource-Based View of the Firm in Two Environments: The Hollywood Film Studios From 1936–1965," *Academy of Management Journal*, June 1996, pp. 519–543; J. M. Liedtka, "Collaborating Across Lines of Business for Competitive Advantage," *Academy of Management Executive*, May 1996, pp. 20–34; C. C. Markides and P. J. Williamson, "Corporate Diversification and Organizational Structure: A Resource-Based View," *Academy of Management Journal*, April 1995, pp. 340–367; L. W. Lam, "Does Competence Really Matter? An Empirical Investigation of the Resource-Based Explanation of Firm Performance," *SWFAD Proceedings*, March 1996, pp. 19–23; J. B. Barney, "Looking Inside for Competitive Advantage," *Academy of Management Executive*, November 1995, pp. 49–61; J. B. Barney and E. J. Zajac, "Competitive Organizational Behavior: Toward an Organizationally-Based Theory of Competitive Advantage," *Strategic Management Journal*, winter 1995, pp. 5–9; R. Ashkenas, "Capability: Strategic Tool for a Competitive Edge," *Journal of Business Strategy*, November/December 1995, pp. 13–15; P. C. Godfrey and C. W. L. Hill, "The Problem of Unobservables in Strategic Management Research," *Strategic Management Journal*, October 1995, pp. 519–533; S. L. Hart, "A Natural Resource-Based View of the Firm," *Academy of Management Review*, October 1995, pp. 986–1014; J. B. Black and K. B. Boal, "Strategic Resources: Traits, Configurations, and Paths to Sustainable Competitive Advantage," *Strategic Management Journal*, summer 1995, pp. 131–138; P. Shrivastava, "Environmental Technologies and Competitive Advantage," *Strategic Management Journal*, summer 1995, pp. 183–200; D. J. Collis and C. A. Montgomery, "Competing on Resources: Strategy in the 1990s," *Harvard Business Review*, July–August 1995, pp. 118–128; W. B. Werther and J. L. Kerr, "The Shifting Sands of Competitive Advantage," *Business Horizons*, May–June 1995, pp. 11–17; B. Wernerfelt, "The Resource-Based View of the Firm: Ten Years After," *Strategic Management Journal*, March 1995, pp. 171–174; J. Pfeffer, "Producing Sustainable Competitive Advantage Through the Effective Management of People," *Academy of Management Executive*, February 1995, pp. 55–69; D. Schendel, "Introduction to Competitive Organizational Behavior: Toward an

Organizationally Based Theory of Competitive Advantage," *Strategic Management Journal,* winter 1994, pp. 1–4; C. K. Prahalad and G. Hamel, "Strategy as a Field of Study: Why Search for a New Paradigm?," *Strategic Management Journal,* summer 1994, pp. 5–16; O. Harari, "The Secrety Competitive Advantage," *Management Review,* January 1994, pp. 45–47; I. Bogaert, R. Martens, and A. Van Canwenbergh, "Strategy as a Situational Puzzle," in *Competence-Based Competition,* ed. G. Hamel and A. Heene (New York: Wiley, 1994), p. 58; R. Hall, "A Framework for Identifying the Intangible Sources of Sustainable Competitive Advantage," in Hamel and Heene, pp. 151–154; P. J. Verdin and P. J. Williamson, "Core Competences: Competitive Advantage and Market Analysis: Forging the Links," in Hamel and Heene, p. 81; D. J. Collis, "Research Notes: How Valuable are Organizational Capabilities," *Strategic Management Journal,* winter 1994, pp. 143–152; R. Hall, "A Framework Linking Intangible Resources and Capabilities to Sustainable Competitive Advantage," *Academy of Management Journal,* November 1993, pp. 607–618; M. A. Peteraf, "The Cornerstones of Competitive Advantage: A Resource-Based View," *Strategic Management Journal,* March 1993, pp. 179–191; R. Amit and P. J. H. Schoemaker, "Strategic Assets and Organizational Rent," *Strategic Management Journal,* January 1993, pp. 33–46; R. M. Grant, "The Resource-Based Theory of Competitive Advantage: Implications for Strategy Formulation," *California Management Review,* spring 1991, pp. 114–135; J. B. Barney, "Firm Resources and Sustained Competitive Advantage," *Journal of Management,* vol. 17, no. 1, 1991, pp. 99–120; K. R. Conner, "A Historical-Based Comparison of Resource-Based Theory and Five Schools of Thought within Industrial Organization Economics: Do We Have a New Theory of the Firm?," 1991; J. B. Barney, "Asset Stocks and Sustained Competitive Advantage: A Comment," *Management Science,* December 1989, pp. 1511–1513; I. Dierickx and K. Cool, "Asset Stock Accumulation and Sustainability of Competitive Advantage," *Management Science,* December 1989, pp. 1504–1511; R. P. Rumelt, "Towards a Strategic Theory of the Firm," in *Competitive Strategic Management* ed. R. B. Lamb (Upper Saddle River, NJ: Prentice Hall, 1984), pp. 556–570; and B. Wernerfelt, "A Resource-Based View of the Firm," *Strategic Management Journal,* vol. 14, 1984, pp. 4–12. Discussion of guerrilla view is based on C. A. Lengnick-Hall and J. A. Wolff, "Similarities and Contradictions in the Core Logic of Three Strategy Research Streams," *Strategic Management Journal,* December 1999, pp. 1109–1132; V. Rindova and C. J. Fombrun, "Constructing Competitive Advantage: The Role of Firm-Constituent Interactions," *Strategic Management Journal,* August 1999, pp. 691–710; K. M. Eisenhardt and S. L. Brown, "Patching: Restitching Business Portfolios in Dynamic Markets," *Harvard Business Review,* May–June 1999, pp. 72–81; B. Chakravarthy, "A New Strategy Framework for Coping with Turbulence," *Sloan Management Review,* winter 1997, pp. 69–82; R. A. D'Aveni, *Hypercompetition: Managing the Dynamics of Strategic Maneuvering* (New York: Free Press, 1994); D. J. Collis, "Research Note: How Valuable Are Organizational Capabilities?" *Strategic Management Journal,* Winter Special Issue, 1994, pp. 143–152; and K.M. Eisenhardt, "Making Fast Strategic Decisions in High-Velocity Environments," *Academy of Management Journal,* December 1989, pp. 543–576.

SECTION 2 ENTREPRENEURIAL VENTURES—START-UP ISSUES

3 Researching the Venture's Feasibility

LEARNING OBJECTIVES

After reading and studying this chapter, you should be able to:

1. Identify misconceptions about and realities of great ideas.
2. Describe the four main sources of ideas.
3. Describe different ways to generate ideas for entrepreneurial ventures.
4. Explain how to evaluate ideas.
5. Explain what the break-even point is and how to calculate it.
6. Define competition and describe the different ways to view competitors.
7. Discuss how to do a competitive analysis.
8. List and explain the various financing options from which entrepreneurs may choose.
9. Explain how to evaluate the various financing options.
10. Discuss the guidelines for seeking financing.

ENTREPRENEURSHIP IN ACTION

Sara Blakely knew that she loved to wear pantyhose under her fitted Capri pants and slim skirts because it gave her such a smooth profile. But she hated the look of footed hosiery with the strappy sandals she'd wear with these tight-fitting outfits.[1] So she did what many women would do—she cut the feet off her pantyhose. The result was constricting, hot pantyhose that tended to creep up her legs. And, needless to say, the frayed edges quickly unraveled. Sara said, "I looked all over the place for footless pantyhose, and they didn't exist. Clerks would always say what a great idea it is, but that was as far as it went."

Blakely's frustration led her to do what many "accidental" entrepreneurs do—solve the problem herself. Unfortunately, she had no experience in the pantyhose industry. However, working around her two jobs as a sales/motivational speaker and

The story of Sara Blakely and Spanx is a fun illustration of the importance of researching an entrepreneurial venture's feasibility. It tells how an entrepreneur spotted an idea, evaluated its potential, and started a company. Even given the challenges, Blakely persisted in her belief that her idea was a good one. Yes, it is important for entrepreneurs to research the venture's feasibility. That's what we're going to cover in this chapter. We'll be looking at different ways to generate ideas for entrepreneurial ventures, how to evaluate those ideas, how to research and evaluate the competition, and finally, we'll look at the various financing options that entrepreneurs have.

GENERATING AND EVALUATING BUSINESS IDEAS

Even though research tells us that newer and smaller firms are less likely to engage in formal or structured environmental research, the fact is that generating and evaluating business ideas is an important step in the entrepreneurial process.[2] Some of you may already have fairly specific ideas about potential entrepreneurial ventures; others may know only in a broad sense in what entrepreneurial direction they'd like to go; and the rest may have no clue whatsoever! But, no matter what your stage of entrepreneurial idea readiness, it's important for you to be able to generate and evaluate potential business ideas. Before we discuss how to do this, however, we need to address some misconceptions that you may have about ideas and what makes them great.

Misconceptions About and Realities of Great Ideas

Entrepreneurship books and magazines are filled with stories of entrepreneurs striking it rich because they had a good idea. These stories, however, tend to give the wrong impressions about great ideas—what they are and where they come from. These misconceptions about great ideas are summarized in Exhibit 3-1.[3]

1. *Great ideas just appear out of nowhere.* Do you buy into the notion that a "light bulb" goes off as someone all of a sudden sees a unique, creative approach? That the whole process is almost an epiphany? The reality is that the best idea generators tend to do so in a structured, systematic way. They don't wait for the bolt of lightning to hit, but instead approach idea generation as a top-priority activity by devoting set periods of time to it.

stand-up comedienne, Blakely started sketching designs and researching patents. She saved up enough money to hire a patent attorney, but most laughed when she presented them with her idea. The attorney who ultimately agreed to work with her actually thought his friends were playing a joke on him or that Blakely was working for *Candid Camera*. But that was only one of many challenges. Finding a manufacturer, picking a name, designing packaging, and getting the product into stores were all part of the process. Blakely persisted and Spanx (**www.spanx.com**) was launched. The product was an instant hit! Even Oprah Winfrey picked Spanx as one of her favorite new products in 2001. Today, Spanx can be found at high-end department stores, in specialty boutiques, and of course, on the company's Web site.

EXHIBIT 3-1 Common Misconceptions About and the Realities of Great Ideas

Misconception #1	**Reality #1**
• Ideas just appear out of nowhere.	• The most successful idea generators do so in a structured, systematic way.
Misconception #2	**Reality #2**
• There are no stupid ideas.	• The most powerful ideas often are resoundingly bad, at first glance.
Misconception #3	**Reality #3**
• Customers will tell you what to do if you'll only listen.	• Although customers can help identify unmet needs, there's much more involved with making an idea workable.
Misconception #4	**Reality #4**
• We can generate all the ideas we'll ever need if we just sit down at a meeting.	• Great ideas are best shaped through an ongoing dialogue.
Misconception #5	**Reality #5**
• Getting ideas isn't the problem; implementing them is.	• The problem is not carefully screening the ideas that are generated.

Source: Based on S. Greco, "Where Great Ideas Come From," *Inc.*, April 1998, pp. 76–86.

2. *There are no stupid ideas.* In order to avoid hurt feelings or to prevent others from feeling that their contributions aren't valued, the belief is that all ideas should be approached as worthy. The reality is that many ideas are bad. However, there's nothing wrong with that! Sometimes, the most powerful ideas come from what, at first glance, seemed stupid or illogical.
3. *Customers will tell you what to do if you'll only listen.* Who better to have as a source of ideas than the people who will purchase your products? The only problem with this belief is that although customers can help identify unmet needs, there's much more involved with making a great idea workable than simply listening to your customers.
4. *We can generate all the ideas we'll ever need if we just sit down at a meeting.* Getting people together for a meeting to discuss ideas and to feed off of each other's enthusiasm and creativity seems like a great thing to do. However, generating great ideas shouldn't be restricted to a meeting. Great ideas are best shaped through an ongoing dialogue, not simply relegated to a specific place and time.
5. *Getting ideas isn't the problem; implementing them is.* There's a misconception that generating ideas is the easy part of the process and that putting those ideas into action is the difficult part. However, the reality is that problems with implementation arise from not screening carefully enough the ideas that are generated. If this were done, a lot of frustration could be minimized as ill-thought-out ideas could be screened out before even being implemented.

Now that we've cleared up some of the initial misconceptions you may have about ideas, it's time to look at the process involved with generating ideas.

Generating Ideas

Entrepreneurs need ideas to start and to grow their entrepreneurial ventures. Generating ideas is an innovative, creative process. It's also one that will take some time, not only in the beginning stages of the entrepreneurial venture but also throughout the life of the business. As we look at the process of generating ideas, we're going to discuss where ideas come from, ways to generate ideas, and the roles of structured analysis and intuition.

Where Ideas Come From. Various entrepreneurship researchers have looked at the source of an entrepreneur's ideas. These studies have shown that the sources of their ideas are unique and varied. In one survey, 60 percent of respondents said working in the same industry was the major source of ideas for a business.[4] For example, Vance Patterson, CEO of Patterson Fan Co. (www.pattersonfan.com), a manufacturer of industrial fans, discovered two of his employees cooking hamburgers on an odd-looking grill one day at lunch.[5] They had created the device out of spare parts, and it seemed that the odd shape of the flared fan parts kept the unit cooler than other grills and allowed air to circulate more evenly. Recognizing the uniqueness of the idea, Patterson patented the grill in his name and the names of the two inventors, James Ballentine and Robert Carter. In 1998 Down South Inc. was formed to manufacture and sell the unique Town and Country grill. Another survey of 100 entrepreneurs who created some of the fastest-growing private companies in the United States showed similar results.[6] The overwhelming majority (71 percent) of the respondents replicated or modified an idea gained through previous employment. The next largest percentage of survey respondents in this particular study (20 percent) said they got their ideas for an entrepreneurial venture from a serendipitous (coincidental) discovery. Included in this set of responses were comments such as "built temporary or casual job into a business," "happened to read about the industry," "thought up idea during honeymoon in Italy," and "wanted product or service as an individual consumer." Think back to our chapter-opening case about Spanx footless pantyhose. That's exactly where Sara Blakely's idea came from—a product she wanted but wasn't available. And, although a honeymoon in Italy may seem like a fun, but unusual, place to get an idea, actually it just confirms the fact that an entrepreneur needs to be open to ideas anyplace and at any time. But, as important as being alert and open to ideas is, it really doesn't tell you anything about where to look for ideas.

Entrepreneurs might use numerous idea sources. Exhibit 3-2 illustrates some of the more common sources and what to look for as you explore them. Let's look more closely at the four main sources of ideas.

First on the list is personal interests or hobbies. Many entrepreneurial ventures were formed because of an entrepreneur's love of doing something—restoring antique automobiles, scuba diving, baking grandma's scrumptious praline chocolate brownies, or whatever. A successful entrepreneurial business might be built around your personal interests in a particular product or activity.

Another potential source of ideas, and a popular one as shown by the results of the entrepreneurial surveys described earlier, is an entrepreneur's work experiences, knowledge, and skills. By tapping into the knowledge of a particular industry or market gained by working in it, an entrepreneur can pinpoint areas of potential opportunity. For example, if you've ever traveled, you've undoubtedly

EXHIBIT 3-2 Potential Sources of Entrepreneurial Ideas

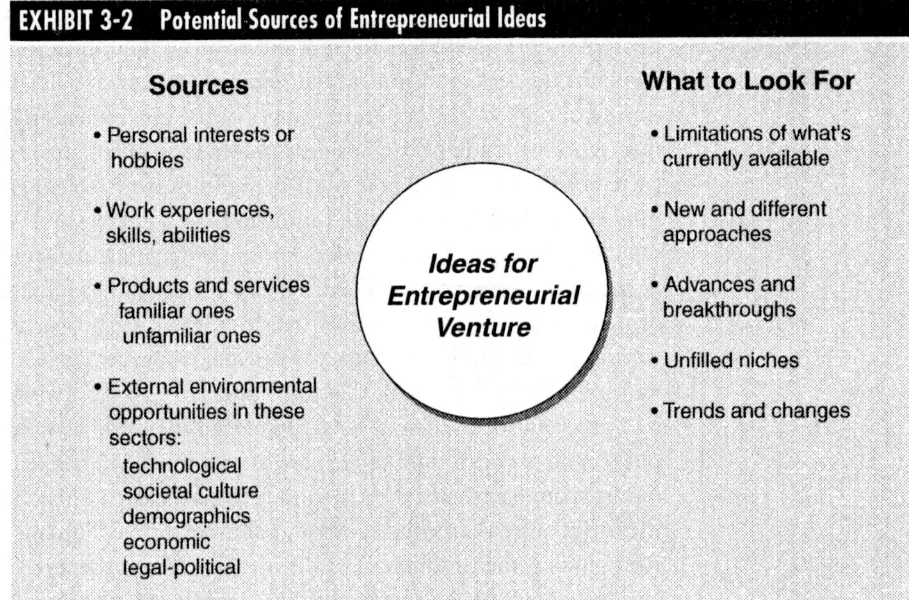

seen those suitcases with wheels. Now wasn't that a great idea! Well, Robert Plath created the first wheeled suitcase, the Travelpro Rollerboard, because in his job as an airline pilot he was constantly carrying his bags from one place to another, and he was looking for a more convenient, comfortable way to do so. In the process of using his work-related experiences and knowledge, he created not only a new product but also a new industry!

The third source of possible ideas is to look at products and services currently available, both familiar and unfamiliar ones. What products do you use every day? Do they do everything that you wished they would? What about products you're not familiar with? Can you take what you're familiar with and apply it to those unfamiliar ones?

The final source of potential entrepreneurial ideas is the external environment. As we discussed in Chapter 2, there are certain to be opportunities—positive trends or changes that provide unique and distinct possibilities for innovating and creating value—in the entrepreneurial context. You just have to look for them. These opportunities can be found in the technological, societal culture, demographics, economic, and legal-political sectors.

Now that you know the potential sources of entrepreneurial ideas, what specific things should you look for? (Refer to Exhibit 3-2.) Basically, you should look for the limitations of what is currently available, for new and different approaches, at scientific and technological advances and breakthroughs, for unfilled niches, and at trends and changes. Any of these could be a potential idea for an entrepreneurial venture. But, perhaps even this isn't enough. Even with the wide variety of idea sources, maybe you're finding it difficult to come up with an idea for your entrepreneurial venture. At this point, you may want to use some different, more structured approaches to help generate ideas.

Ways to Generate Ideas. In this section, we're going to describe four different structured approaches you might use to help generate ideas: (1) environmental scanning, (2) creativity and creative problem solving, (3) brainstorming, and

Entrepreneurs in Action

As is the case with many entrepreneurs, Sacramento physician Steven Marcum got the idea for SportEYZ (**www.sporteyz.com**) from his own experiences—in this instance, while recuperating from corrective eye surgery. After the surgery, his doctor gave him two pairs of sunglasses—one was the clunky, wraparound type usually worn by elderly patients after cataract surgery and the other pair was too flimsy to be useful. Marcum thought both were unappealing and unattractive, but when he wore his own sunglasses, the daylight hurt his eyes. So he decided to make his own sunglasses. Attaching a piece of UV-blocking window film bought at a hardware store to a piece of transparency film and using a pair of Dr. Scholl's footpads for padding, Marcum's invention provided complete protection while looking stylish. And—the fun part—when he took off the "glasses," he rolled them up for easy storage in a small film canister he stashed in his pocket.

Marcum patented his design and founded Marcum Industries to distribute his SportEYZ glasses. Each pair costs about $1.50 to make and are sold for a price between $5 and $10, which includes the carrying canister. Athletes have been the primary customers for the product because they find it to be lightweight and effective.

Sources: Company Web site (**www.sporteyz.com**), May 15, 2002; and M. Hofman, "Sight for Sore Eyes," *Inc.*, October 16, 2001, p. 22.

(4) focus groups. Keep in mind that although we're discussing these techniques in relation to generating entrepreneurial ideas, they're also useful for resolving any type of entrepreneurial problem for which an imaginative solution or new idea is needed.

Do you know the latest scoop on what's happening in the business world? Are you aware of the latest news headlines? Do you know what books or movies are popular right now? One technique that entrepreneurs can use to generate ideas is **environmental scanning**, the screening of large amounts of information to detect emerging trends. Here are some "ideas" to stimulate your own idea creation by scanning the world around you: Read your local and other major metropolitan newspapers (the *New York Times,* the *Washington Post, USA Today,* and others); read business publications (the *Wall Street Journal, Business Week, Fast Company, Fortune, Financial Times,* and others); read popular consumer and news magazines; review

Rapid Review

- ✔ What common misconceptions do people have about great ideas? What are the realities of great ideas?
- ✔ What have various entrepreneurship researchers found with regard to the source of an entrepreneur's ideas?
- ✔ Describe the four main sources of entrepreneurial ideas.
- ✔ What types of things should entrepreneurs look for as they explore ideas?

the fiction and nonfiction best-seller lists; review government and consumer publications; subscribe to relevant trade publications; pay attention to commercials; watch and review top prime-time television shows; browse through the magazine section of a bookstore; walk through a local shopping mall to see what's there; and so forth. The challenge of this method is not having too little information to scan; it's having too much. But, how are you going to know what's happening in the world, what people are thinking, what people are doing, if you're not staying alert to these things? Yes, it may seem like a lot of effort and work, but if you're serious about being a successful entrepreneur in action, it's energy well spent.

We introduced the concept of creativity in Chapter 2. We defined it as the ability to combine ideas in a unique way or to make unusual associations between ideas. Whereas traditional logical thinking is like parallel railroad tracks—going on forever, but never crossing—creative thinking means linking new concepts in unusual ways. It means cross-thinking by seeing new angles, connections, and approaches.[7] The whole area of creativity has been extensively researched and studied, resulting in a lot of information—too much for us to cover here. Instead,

FYI

Trend Spotting

The skill of observing. Do you have it? Can you pick up on what people think is "hot" or popular? Faith Popcorn, an author and probably today's best known trend spotter, actually says that you don't have to be a pro to be good at it: In fact, professionals may be constrained by rigid organizational structures and their past successes. So, how can you get in tune with what's happening and hone your skills at trend spotting? Here are some suggestions:

1. Remember that valuable information is everywhere around you. Look for it everywhere and anywhere. Read magazines you don't normally read. Watch television shows or movies in which you might not personally be interested. Go to places. Do things. Talk to people. Information is the bread-and-butter of a good trend spotter.
2. File that information away. If your memory isn't as good as it should be, use note cards. What you write down doesn't have to be long and complex. It could be something so simple as "avocado seems to be a hot color" or "teens seem to be flocking to fitness programs" or whatever.
3. Determine whether the fads seem to be part of deeper, wider trends that can be good sources of entrepreneurial opportunity. You can do this by assessing whether the fad seems to have staying power, whether the fad is a reflection of a change in people's attitudes or behaviors, and whether you see the fad in more than a few places.
4. Test your ideas about trends on intelligent friends of various ages and incomes. Bounce your ideas off of them. What do they say? But, make sure that these people will be honest with you.
5. Don't expect trends to jump out at you. After all, if they were easy to spot, everyone would be doing it. You have to be alert, be open to new and unusual possibilities, and be willing to work at it. And, don't worry if you miss a trend. After all, there will be more.

Source: R. Furchgott, "Trend-Spotting: Anyone Can Play," *Business Week Enterprise*, 3/2/98, pp. ENT12–ENT16.

what you need to understand about the role of creativity and creative problem-solving as a structured technique for generating ideas is that a number of specific creativity approaches can be used. For instance, here are a few specific techniques: the checklist method, in which an entrepreneur uses a list of questions or statements to develop new ideas; free association, whereby an entrepreneur develops a new idea through a chain of word associations; attribute listing, in which an entrepreneur develops a new idea by looking at the positive and negative attributes of a product or service; and so on. Using any of these structured creative problem-solving approaches can help you unlock your creativity and generate potential entrepreneurial ideas. If you need more information on how to be creative, research the topic at your library or on the Internet.

One of the most familiar and widely used approaches to generating ideas is **brainstorming**, an idea-generating process for developing creative solutions that encourages as many alternatives as possible while withholding criticism. Brainstorming is a relatively simple technique that is typically done with a group of people. (You could do this with friends or colleagues.) In a brainstorming session, a group of people gets together in a room, preferably one with a relaxed environment, where everyone would be free to stretch their minds and think beyond the ordinary. A group leader states the issue or problem to be addressed and ensures that all participants understand it. Then members contribute as many ideas as they can in a given time by describing them verbally (often shouting them out). Participants are encouraged to come up with as many ideas as possible and to build on each others' ideas. In brainstorming sessions, talking is often non-stop as participants suggest ideas. No criticism of ideas is allowed during the brainstorming session. Instead, all ideas, no matter how illogical or crazy, are recorded for later discussion and analysis. The purpose of brainstorming is to be an idea-generating process that opens up as many alternatives as possible as other people's remarks act to stimulate others in a sort of chain reaction of ideas. It can be a frenzied, yet productive way to generate numerous ideas.

The final structured approach to generating ideas we want to look at is the use of **focus groups**. These groups of individuals provide information about proposed products or services in a structured setting. In a typical focus group, a moderator focuses the group discussion on whatever issues are being examined. For instance, a focus group might look at a proposed product and answer specific questions asked by the moderator. In other instances, the focus group might be given a more general issue to discuss and the moderator simply leads the discussion based on comments made by the group. Either way, a focus group can provide an excellent way to generate new ideas and to screen proposed ideas and concepts.

The Role of Intuition. We can't leave our discussion of generating ideas without looking at the role of intuition. **Intuition** is a cognitive process whereby we subconsciously make decisions based on our accumulated knowledge and experiences. It's been called that "'Aha' feeling you get when your internal search engine hits its mark."[8] You may have heard it called "gut feeling." Researchers have shown that a person's intuition can be measured. Measure yours using the FYI box entitled "As Good As a Guess?" Although structured, methodical approaches to generating ideas are important, intuition also can play an important role. Intuition can be a powerful source of new ideas if you learn to use it.

FYI

As Good As a Guess?

Rate your intuitive powers by taking the following quiz.

Complete the following quiz as honestly—and quickly—as you can. It will give you a gauge of how strong your gut instinct is.

1. When working on a project, do you prefer to:
a) Be told what the problem is but left free to decide how to solve it?
b) Get very clear instructions about how to go about solving the problem before you start?

2. When working on a project, do you prefer to work with colleagues who are:
a) Realistic?
b) Imaginative?

3. Do you most admire people who are:
a) Creative?
b) Careful?

4. Do the friends you choose tend to be:
a) Serious and hardworking?
b) Exciting and often emotional?

5. When you ask a colleague for advice on a problem, do you:
a) Seldom or never get upset if he questions your basic assumptions?
b) Often get upset if he questions your basic assumptions?

6. When you start the day, do you:
a) Seldom make or follow a specific plan?
b) Usually make a plan to follow first?

7. When working with numbers, do you find that you:
a) Seldom or never make factual errors?
b) Often make factual errors?

8. Do you find that you:
a) Seldom daydream during the day and really don't enjoy it when you do?
b) Frequently daydream during the day and enjoy doing so?

9. When working on a problem, do you:
a) Prefer to follow the instructions or rules when they are given to you?
b) Often enjoy circumventing the instructions or rules when they are given to you?

10. When you are trying to put something together, do you prefer to have:
a) Step-by-step written instructions for assembly?
b) A picture of how the item is supposed to look once it's assembled?

11. Do you find the person who irritates you the most is the one who appears to be:
a) Disorganized?
b) Organized?

12. When a crisis that you have to deal with comes up unexpectedly, do you:
a) Feel anxious about the situation?
b) Feel excited by the challenge?

HOW TO SCORE

First, total the number of "a" responses you circled for questions 1, 3, 5, 6, and 11. Second total the number of "b" responses you circled for questions 2, 4, 7, 8, 9, 10, and 12. Add the totals.

If you scored above an 8, your intuition is humming. If you scored above 10, you are an intuition superstar, in the top 10 percent of all Americans.

Source: By permission of Weston Agor, Ph.D. ENFP Enterprises, 5525 North Stanton Street, #18-D, El Paso, TX 79912.

Rapid Review

- ✔ What is environmental scanning? How can it be used to generate ideas?
- ✔ Define creativity. Describe some specific techniques for enhancing creativity.
- ✔ What is brainstorming? How can it be used to generate ideas?
- ✔ How could focus groups be used to generate ideas?
- ✔ What is intuition, and what role does it play in generating ideas?

Maybe the best approach of all would be to combine the structured with the intuitive. After all, the two complement each other. Listen to that "inner voice" and then use more structured approaches to fine-tune your ideas.

Although generating ideas is an important process for entrepreneurs, it's only half the battle! You must look at your ideas carefully before taking action and proceeding any further with your entrepreneurial venture.

Evaluating Ideas

When you're in the market for a new computer or maybe a new car, do you take the first one that you see? Most of us wouldn't. We shop around. We look at each possibility in order to determine which is going to best meet our needs and fit within our available budget. This process is just as important in evaluating entrepreneurial ideas. After all, we want to pursue the option that's going to allow us to best meet our goal(s) given the resources we have available. In this section we discuss why evaluation is important and then look at some different ways to evaluate ideas.

Why Is Evaluation Important? When the environment is changing rapidly (as we discussed in Chapter 2), it may seem that evaluating ideas is a big waste of time. You may think that if you take the time to evaluate your entrepreneurial idea you'll miss the quickly closing window of opportunity. However, there are four reasons why idea evaluation is an important step in researching the venture's feasibility. (See Exhibit 3-3.)

The first reason that idea evaluation is important is that it forces the entrepreneur to decide what's important in the entrepreneurial venture. What are the goals of the entrepreneur in pursuing this venture? Think back to our chapter-opening case. Sara Blakely's goal was to make footless pantyhose a reality for herself and other consumers. Any entrepreneurial decisions she had to make along the way would be evaluated against this goal. Other entrepreneurs will have their own unique reasons behind wanting to pursue an entrepreneurial venture. Potential ideas should be evaluated against what's important to the entrepreneur.

EXHIBIT 3-3 Why Idea Evaluation Is Important

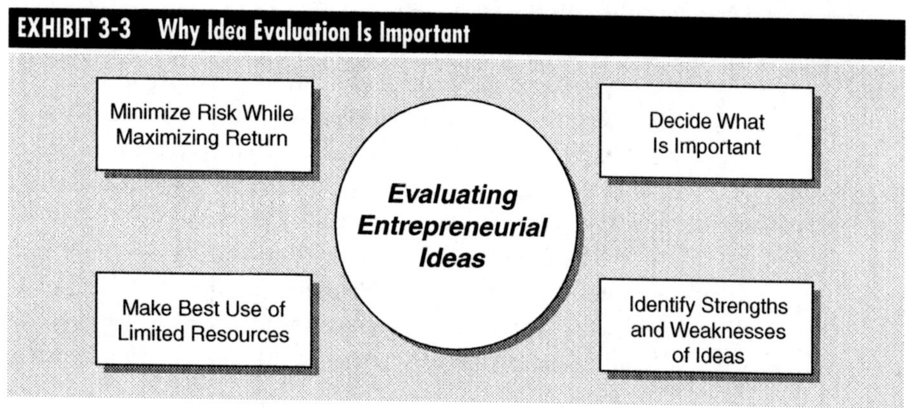

Entrepreneurs in Action

Jennifer Maxwell, cofounder and owner of PowerBar Inc., knows firsthand the importance of evaluating ideas. PowerBar got its start because of a bad case of stomach cramps. Brian Maxwell, a college athlete and top-ranked runner, was competing in the London Marathon. About halfway through the race—which, by the way, he was leading by about a minute—Maxwell began to experience stomach cramps. He ended up in seventh place. Back in the United States, he met Jennifer Biddulph, also an accomplished runner and nutrition-food science student at the University of California at Berkeley. Trying to find a way to combat the cramp problem faced by athletes in all sports, Jennifer and Brian mixed hundreds of combinations of raw ingredients, trying to find a snack bar that would digest easily and provide quick energy. They tried out the test bars on friends. After several "tests," they finally hit on the right combination of fructose, oat bran, and milk protein. Today, the firm sells its energy bars and other products in supermarkets and health foods and sports stores in the United States, Canada, and 30 other countries. After struggling to expand distribution, the Maxwells opted to sell the company to Nestlé, the Swiss food company, in 2000.

Sources: Information on company from Hoover's Online (**www.hoovers.com**), May 15, 2002, and company's Web site (**www.powerbar.com**), May 15, 2002; and "Entrepreneurial Excellence," *Working Woman*, May 1999, p. 48.

The second reason that idea evaluation is important is that all ideas are not created equal. Some ideas that an entrepreneur comes up with will have better chances of success than others. By evaluating the strengths and weaknesses of each idea, the entrepreneur is forced to identify and assess the strong and weak points. Think again of a time when you made a major purchase. Did you look at the features of each alternative and assess the advantages and disadvantages? Why did you do this? Because in looking at the strengths and weaknesses of each alternative, you were getting information to help you make a better decision. When evaluating the strengths and weaknesses of entrepreneurial ideas, you're also getting and using information to help you make a better decision.

The next reason idea evaluation is important has to do with the reality of limited resources. Most entrepreneurs have limited amounts of money, time, people, or other resources that will be needed to pursue their entrepreneurial ideas. By evaluating your entrepreneurial ideas, you can make sure your choice(s) make the best use of those limited resources.

The final reason why idea evaluation is important has to do with the desire to minimize risk while maximizing return. What is **risk**? It's the uncertainty surrounding decisions and actions about what will happen. **Return**, on the other hand, is the payback (financial or otherwise) that an entrepreneur hopes to gain from the entrepreneurial venture. Naturally, we'd like to have the least amount of uncertainty (risk) while getting the largest payback (return) from our entrepreneurial decisions and actions. When an entrepreneur puts in the effort to evaluate potential entrepreneurial ideas, there's an opportunity to minimize the level of risk exposure while maximizing the possible amount of payoff.

Here's some advice from a successful entrepreneur that summarizes the importance of idea evaluation. "In addition to having an idea for a better mousetrap, you have to understand it in a business context. You have to understand the industry, the market, the competition, and the necessary technology."[9] Now that we know why idea evaluation is important, let's look at how it's done.

How to Evaluate Ideas. Evaluating entrepreneurial ideas revolves around personal and marketplace considerations. Each of these assessments will provide the entrepreneur with key information about the idea's potential.

In an entrepreneurial venture, the entrepreneur is the pivotal point around which all other decisions and actions happen. Therefore, in evaluating potential ideas, it's important to measure them against the personal considerations of the entrepreneur. Here are some questions to consider[10]:

- Do you have the capabilities for what you've selected?
- Are you ready to be an entrepreneur?
- Do you have a passion for what you're considering?
- Are you prepared emotionally to deal with the stresses and challenges of being an entrepreneur?
- Are you prepared to deal with rejection and failure?
- Are you ready to work hard?
- Do you have a realistic picture of the proposed venture's potential?
- Have you educated yourself about financing issues?
- Are you willing and prepared to do continual analyses (financial and other types) of your venture?

Although it's extremely important for an entrepreneur to evaluate ideas against personal considerations, it's equally important to assess them against marketplace considerations. Your decision about which entrepreneurial direction to go should not take place without considering market factors. Your idea will have to be viable in a competitive and dynamic marketplace. Consequently, the choice you make needs to be made with an eye to the market. The more market-driven your venture, the greater the chances of success.[11] Here are some general questions to ask in relation to evaluating the marketplace potential:

- Who are the potential customers for your idea (not just who, but where and how many)?
- What similar or unique product features does your proposed idea have in relation to what's currently on the market?
- How and where will potential customers purchase your product?
- Have you considered how you will price your proposed idea? Have you calculated your break-even point?
- Have you considered how you will need to promote and advertise your proposed entrepreneurial venture?

FYI

Pointing Out Break-even

An entrepreneurial venture's break-even point could be an important piece of information in determining the feasibility of the venture. When a business is breaking even, it is earning enough revenue to cover its costs. Any level of revenue below the break-even point and the business will experience a loss; any level of revenue above the break-even point and the business will earn a profit.

Break-even point is calculated by looking at the unit price of the product being sold (P), the variable cost per unit (VC), and total fixed costs (TFC). Variable costs are those that change in proportion to level of output and typically include raw materials, labor costs, and utility costs. Fixed costs are expenses that do not change regardless of volume. Typical examples are rent, insurance premiums, and property taxes. This information is plugged into this formula:

$$BE = \frac{TFC}{P - VC}$$

Let's work through an example. Suppose that Michelle's Photocopying Service charges $0.10 per photocopy. If fixed costs (rent + insurance premiums + property taxes) are $27,000 per year and variable costs (raw materials, labor, and utilities) are $.04 per copy, Michelle can compute her break-even point as follows: $27,000 divided by ($0.10 – $0.04) = 450,000 copies, or when annual revenues are $45,000 (450,000 copies × $.10). Any revenue amount below this and Michelle will not be covering her expenses. Any revenue amount above this and Michelle will be earning a profit.

These broad-based questions force an entrepreneur to at least think about the viability of the proposed entrepreneurial idea. Although the idea may appear great on paper, if there's no market for it, the chances of success are zero.

The final things we want to look at in this section on evaluating entrepreneurial ideas are two specific evaluation techniques an entrepreneur might use. One is the four-questions approach and the other is a feasibility study.

The four-questions approach very simply suggests that evaluating entrepreneurial ideas revolves around four basic questions: (1) Do you love the business? (2) Are you skilled at the business? (3) Do you have experience at the business? (4) Is the business simply a fad or trend?[12] Each of these questions forces the potential entrepreneur to get beyond dreaming and to focus on specific issues. By answering these simple yet thought-provoking questions, the entrepreneur must examine whether or not he or she really has the personal characteristics (desires, skills, abilities) and marketplace considerations (fad, trend, or relatively long-term demand) in his or her favor. Another more thorough evaluation technique is the feasibility study.

A **feasibility study** is a structured and systematic analysis of the various aspects of a proposed entrepreneurial venture designed to determine its workability. A well-prepared feasibility study can be an effective evaluation tool to determine whether an entrepreneurial idea is a potentially successful one. In addition, the feasibility study can serve as a basis for the all-important business plan.(We'll cover business plans in Chapter 4.)

What does a feasibility study include? It should give descriptions of the most important elements of the entrepreneurial venture and the entrepreneur's analysis

EXHIBIT 3-4 Example of a Feasibility Study

Feasibility Study

A. Introduction, historical background, description of product or service:
   1. Brief description of proposed entrepreneurial venture
   2. Brief history of the industry
   3. Information about the economy and important trends
   4. Current status of the product or service
   5. How you intend to produce the product or service
   6. Complete list of goods or services to be provided
   7. Strengths and weaknesses of the business
   8. Ease of entry into the industry, including competitor analysis

B. Accounting considerations:
   1. Pro forma balance sheet
   2. Pro forma profit and loss statement
   3. Projected cash flow analysis

C. Management considerations:
   1. Personal expertise—strengths and weaknesses
   2. Proposed organizational design
   3. Potential staffing requirements
   4. Inventory management methods
   5. Production and operations management issues
   6. Equipment needs

D. Marketing considerations:
   1. Detailed product description
   2. Identify the target market (who, where, how many)
   3. Describe place product will be distributed (location, traffic, size, channels, etc.)
   4. Price determination (competition, price lists, etc.)
   5. Promotion plans (role of personal selling, advertising, sales promotions, etc.)

E. Financial considerations:
   1. Start-up costs
   2. Working capital requirements
   3. Equity requirements
   4. Loans—amounts, type, conditions
   5. Break-even analysis
   6. Collateral
   7. Credit references
   8. Equipment and building financing—costs and methods

F. Legal considerations:
   1. Proposed business structure
      a. Type
      b. Conditions, terms, liability, responsibility
      c. Insurance needs: property, liability, personal, etc.
      d. Buyout, succession issues
   2. Contracts, licenses, and other legal documents

G. Tax considerations:
   1. Sales, property, employee
   2. Federal, state, and local

H. Appendix—charts, graphs, diagrams, layouts, résumés, etc.

of the viability of these elements. Exhibit 3-4 provides an outline of one possible approach to a feasibility study that covers eight different sections. These eight sections include an introductory section covering historical background and brief summary of product, potential strengths and weaknesses, and other key information; accounting considerations; management considerations; marketing considerations; financial considerations; legal considerations; tax considerations; and an appendix with supporting charts, graphs, diagrams, layouts, resumes, and so forth.

Yes, the feasibility study covers a lot of territory. It takes a significant amount of time, effort, and energy to prepare it. However, isn't your potential future success worth an investment of time, effort, and energy? As stated previously, if done effectively, the feasibility study can make preparing and writing the business plan a whole lot easier.

Rapid Review

- ✔ Why is evaluating ideas important?
- ✔ What role do risk and return play in evaluating entrepreneurial ideas?
- ✔ What role do personal considerations play as an entrepreneur evaluates potential ideas?
- ✔ What role do marketplace considerations play?
- ✔ What is break-even point? How is it calculated? Why is it important in evaluating entrepreneurial ideas?
- ✔ Describe the four-questions approach to evaluating entrepreneurial ideas.
- ✔ What is a feasibility study? Why is it a valuable tool in evaluating entrepreneurial ideas?

Now that you've thoroughly investigated your entrepreneurial idea(s) and have a fairly good assessment of the idea's strengths and weaknesses, it's time to look at others who might be doing the same or similar things that you're pursuing. That's the second part of researching the venture's feasibility—researching competitors and competitive advantage.

RESEARCHING COMPETITORS

Competition is everywhere. Very few industries or markets haven't experienced some form and degree of competitiveness. Researching your competition through competitor intelligence can be a powerful tool for entrepreneurs.[13] **Competitor intelligence** is a process of gathering information on who competitors are, what they are doing, and how their actions will affect your organization. In this section, we're going to discuss these competitor intelligence issues: what competition is, how to determine who your competitors are, and competitive information—what information to get about your competitors and how to get it.

What Is Competition?

Competition is defined as organizations battling with each other for some desired outcome—customers, market share, survey ranking, or needed resources. Although individuals also compete for desired objects or outcomes—getting the highest grade in class, winning a race, or getting a desired job—our focus is on competition as it relates to organizations. What types of competition might an entrepreneurial venture face? This can be answered by looking at who competitors are.

Who Are the Competitors?

There are three ways to define possible competitors. The first approach, the industry perspective, identifies competitors as organizations making the same product or providing the same service. For instance, there's the oil industry, the supermarket industry, the pantyhose industry, and the dental care industry. The competitors in each of these industries are producing the same or similar types of products or services. (To make sure you understand this approach, take a minute to try to name competitors in the personal computer industry, the cosmetics industry, and the automobile industry.) Using this approach, an entrepreneur could assess the intensity of competition by looking at how many organizations are in the industry and how they differ from each other. Competition would be highest when there are numerous, similar competitors. In other words, these competitors are all using the same approaches in fighting for the same desired outcome—for example, getting a customer to purchase their product or service, and not another organization's.

Another approach to defining who competitors are is the marketing perspective, which says that competitors are organizations that satisfy the same customer need. For example, if the customer need is entertainment, potential competitors might range all the way from video game producers to theme parks to movie theaters to the local community symphony orchestra. These are different industries but ones that are attempting to satisfy the same customer need. (Think about the different industries that might satisfy a customer's need for food, need for transportation, or need for financial security.) Under this perspective, the intensity of competition depends on how well the customer's needs are understood or defined and how well different organizations are able to meet that need.

The final approach to defining who competitors are is the strategic groups perspective. **Strategic groups** are groups of competitors following essentially the same strategy in a particular market or industry.[14] Within a single industry, you might find a few or several strategic groups, depending on what strategic factors are important to different groups of customers—that is, what factors customers use in making purchase decisions. For instance, two strategic factors often used in grouping competitors are price (low to high) and quality (low to high). Competitors would then be "grouped" according to their price-quality strategies, with those following the same or similar approaches in the same strategic group. To illustrate, let's use the automobile industry as an example. Saturn is not in the same strategic group as Mercedes-Benz, but Lexus, BMW, and Jaguar are. The Kia Sportage sport utility vehicle wouldn't be in the same strategic group as the Mercedes-Benz, BMW, or Lexus SUVs, but others such as the Honda CRV or the Subaru Forester would be. Keep in mind that the important strategic factors used to determine an organization's competitors are different for every industry and can be different even for various industry groups. Exhibit 3-5 lists some common factors that might be used to distinguish strategic groups.

EXHIBIT 3-5 Possible Dimensions for Identifying Strategic Groups

- Price
- Quality
- Geographic scope
- Product line breadth—depth
- Market share
- Product characteristics
- Profits
- Any other relevant factor

This approach suggests that strategic groups are important to understanding who your competitors are because your most relevant competitors are those in your particular strategic group. Although competition might come from organizations in other strategic groups, your main competitive concerns are the organizations in your own strategic group. The intensity of competition according to this perspective depends on how effectively each competitor has been able to develop a competitive advantage and on the specific competitive actions being used by each competitor to capture the desired outcome—be it customers, resources, or whatever.

No matter how we define our potential competitors, the fact remains that there will be other organizations working hard to secure the same customers, resources, and other desired outcomes that you also want. Now that we know how to define "who" our competitors are, we need to look at what type of competitive information to get and where to get that information about what our competitors are doing.

Getting Competitor Information

Keep in mind that at this point you're still researching the feasibility of your entrepreneurial venture. By looking at what other competitors are doing, you can better understand how your proposed product or service would fit into the competitive mix and whether it's feasible. The first thing you need to decide is what type of competitive information you'd like. What would you like to know about your potential competitors?

What Type of Competitive Information Should You Look For? What you want to do is get a good feel for what your potential competitors are doing. Here are some possible questions you might use to guide your research:

- What types of products or services are competitors offering?
- What are the major characteristics of these products or services? What are their products' strengths and weaknesses?
- How do they handle marketing, pricing, and distributing?
- What do they attempt to do differently from other competitors? Do they appear to be successful at it? Why? Why not?
- What are they good at? That is, what competitive advantage(s) do they appear to have?
- What are they not so good at? What competitive disadvantage(s) do they appear to have?
- How large and profitable are these competitors?
- How do these competitors react when something (or someone) new comes into the marketplace?

These are just a few of the questions you might ask about your potential competitors. Your goal is to get a good understanding of each one's competitive strengths and weaknesses. Then, you want to assess how your proposed entrepreneurial venture is going to "fit" into this competitive mix. Will you be able to compete successfully or is the level of competition too intense? Once you've decided what type of competitive information you'd like to have, you're ready to find it. Now, where can you find this type of information?

Where to Get Competitive Information. It's not as difficult as you might think it would be to find information on competitors. You can use published financial sources; former employees; dealers, representatives, and distributors; suppliers; professional meetings; market surveys; trade fairs and exhibits; competitors' brochures; competitors' Web pages; technical analysis of competitors' products (called **reverse engineering**); comparison shopping; news stories found in newspapers or other printed publications and on broadcast media news programs; competitive intelligence firms; interviews with consultants; and so forth. One thing you should be concerned with as you gather competitive information, however, is whether or not your information gathering is ethical.

Questions and concerns that often arise about competitor intelligence pertain to the ways in which competitor information is gathered. Competitor intelligence becomes illegal business spying when it involves the theft of any proprietary materials or trade secrets by any means. That's an easy one to understand. However, there's often a fine line between what's considered *legal and ethical* and what's considered *legal but unethical*. For instance, questioning competitors' employees at technical meetings by disguising who you are and who you work for,

The Grey Zone Here are some other techniques that have been suggested for gathering competitor information: (1) Pretend to be a journalist writing a story. Call up competitors' offices and interview knowledgeable personnel. (2) Dig through a competitor's trash. (3) Sit outside a competitor's place of business and count how many customers go in. (4) Get copies of your competitors' in-house newsletters and read them. (5) Call the Better Business Bureau and ask if competitors have had complaints filed against them and if so, what kind of complaints. (6) Have a friend call your competitors for a price list, brochure, or other marketing information. Do you think these methods are ethical or unethical? Why? What ethical guidelines would you propose for entrepreneurs when gathering competitor intelligence?

going on false job interviews with a competitor in order to get information, or conducting false job interviews with competitors' employees might be legal actions, but they are also ethically questionable. In gathering competitor information, consider whether or not the way you're getting the information is both legal *and* ethical.

Once you've gathered information on your competitors, you might want to organize it in some type of competitor analysis matrix. (See Exhibit 3-6 for an example.) List the competitors along the horizontal axis and the type of competitive information along the vertical axis. Fill in the actual information for each competitor in the appropriate cell. In this way, you would be able to compare your potential competitors easily. Also, this type of competitor analysis becomes an important part of your feasibility study and your business plan.

The final part of researching the venture's feasibility is to look at the various financing options. This is not the final determination of how much funding you will need, where you will obtain these funds, or other specific financing

EXHIBIT 3-6 Example of a Competitor Analysis Matrix

Competitive Information	***Business 1***	***Business 2***	***Business 3***	***Business 4***
Products or Services Offered				
Product Strengths				
Product Weaknesses				
Competitive Advantage(s)				
Competitive Disadvantage(s)				
Other Competitive Information				

Rapid Review

- ✔ What is competitor intelligence?
- ✔ What is competition?
- ✔ Describe the three different ways to define possible competitors.
- ✔ What are strategic groups, and what types of strategic factors might be used to define a strategic group?
- ✔ What type of competitive information should an entrepreneur get, and what are some sources of competitive information?
- ✔ What is reverse engineering?
- ✔ What role should ethics play in competitor intelligence gathering?
- ✔ How might a competitor analysis matrix be helpful?

information. However, it is important when researching the venture's feasibility to be aware of the various financing alternatives.

RESEARCHING FINANCING OPTIONS

Getting financing for your entrepreneurial venture is a lot like painting a room. A lot of the hard work is in the preparation. But if prepped right, the job goes fairly easily. What we're going to do in this section is "prep" the venture by looking at possible financing options. We're first going to describe the various options, then look at how to evaluate the options to determine what's best for your particular situation, and finally provide some general guidelines for preparing to seek funding.

Possible Financing Options

Chances are you're going to need funds to start your entrepreneurial venture. Where will those funds come from? A number of financing options are available to entrepreneurs—ranging all the way from personal resources to funds provided by others. Exhibit 3-7 lists the various options. Let's take a closer look at each.

Entrepreneur's Personal Resources. The entrepreneur's personal resources can be a good source of financing. What types of personal resources might an entrepreneur have access to? The most common are personal savings, home equity, cash proceeds from the sale of personal assets, life insurance policy loan, personal loans, credit cards, and loans from family or friends.

Of these possibilities, the credit card option has become a popular choice for entrepreneurs. Today, almost half (48 percent) of all entrepreneurs use credit cards as a financing option.[15] Credit cards are easy to obtain, quick to use, and widely

EXHIBIT 3-7 Possible Financing Options

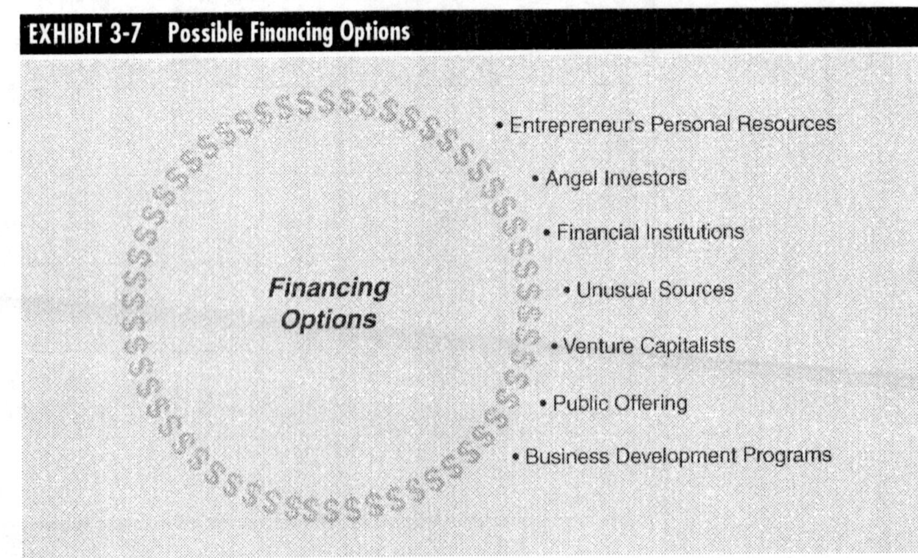

available. They also offer a way to track expenses efficiently. And, many entrepreneurs "rate surf"—looking for the cards with the lowest introductory rate and, before that rate expires, transferring the balance to another card with a low introductory rate, and so on. However, you need to be cautious in using credit cards to finance your entrepreneurial venture. It's easy to get overextended, and trying to find the lowest interest rates can consume a large amount of time and energy.

Each of these personal sources of funds allows the entrepreneur to maintain more control over the entrepreneurial venture but also exposes the entrepreneur to more personal risk. You need to decide if you can live with this risk. You're risking your personal financial assets, your credit record, and your personal relationships with family and friends. Is this acceptable? Keep in mind, however, that some entrepreneurs have no other options. They can't get a loan, provide sufficient equity ownership, or qualify for other types of assistance. Under those circumstances, the entrepreneur's personal resources are the only choice.

Financial Institutions. Another possible alternative for financing the entrepreneurial venture is to look to financial institutions. Financial institutions provide **loans**, financial resources made available by a financial institution that are paid back, including the principal amount plus interest, by the borrower over a certain period of time. The borrower is charged a certain interest rate as the cost for borrowing the funds. Financial institutions that provide loans include banks, savings and loan institutions, credit unions, life insurance firms, other commercial lenders, and finance companies.

Entrepreneurs in Action

Fred Calloway and his brother Richard know firsthand how difficult it can be to get financing for a new entrepreneurial venture. Their business concept, Male Care (based in Augusta, Georgia), was designed around the fact that professional men have very little time for taking care of mundane necessities such as haircuts, dry cleaning, and getting the car washed. So why not provide a place where all of those things could be done in one place at one time? In 1998, using approximately $30,000 in personal savings, the brothers created Male Care. The start-up money was quickly spent on leasing a building, renovating the interior, and purchasing supplies. The pair sought bank financing to finish the job, but were turned down for business loans and lines of credit. But, the brothers were determined to succeed. So, they used sweat equity—rolling up their sleeves and doing the work themselves. Richard said, "We weren't going to give up, so we made it happen through sweat equity and personal funds until the cash flow started." Today, the company serves approximately 1,800 customers each month, 80 percent of whom are repeat customers.

Source: B. McCrea, "Taking Care of Business," *Black Enterprise*, July 2001, p. 46.

Getting a loan can be tricky, particularly for new start-ups. A new entrepreneurial venture represents uncertainty, and financial institutions like certainty. They want to know that any financial resources loaned are going to be paid back in full and on time. Usually, the loan will have to be secured (backed) by either business or personal assets. If the loan is not repaid, these assets become the property of the financial institution and can be sold to pay off the loan. Loan decisions are made only after a careful review of the borrower and the financial track record of the entrepreneurial venture. Often, these decisions are based on both quantifiable information and subjective information. The entrepreneur has to make a good impression and provide adequate supporting documentation that justifies why the loan is a good idea. This is where the feasibility study and the business plan will be useful. These written reports document that you have thought through your proposed venture and are aware of the opportunities and challenges awaiting you. What if you just do not have the necessary track record, assets, or other factors necessary to get a loan from a bank or financial institution? This is where a U.S. Small Business Administration (SBA) guaranteed loan might be an appropriate alternative. The **Small Business Administration (SBA)** is a government agency devoted to the enhancement, support, and education of entrepreneurs and small business owners-managers. (Check out its Web page at www.sba.gov. It's full of great information!) The SBA enables its lending partners (usually banks) to provide financing to small businesses when funding is otherwise unavailable by guaranteeing major portions of loans made to small businesses.

The SBA has a number of loan guarantee programs. It can guarantee as much as 85 percent on loans up to $150,000 and 75 percent on loans of more than $150,000. This guarantee permits the bank to make a more risky loan than it might otherwise make. The procedure to obtain an SBA loan is similar to that of a regular bank loan in that the entrepreneur has to complete loan application forms. But, in addition, government forms and documentation are required. Often, there are banks in a community that specialize in these types of loans and are equipped to assist the entrepreneur in filling out the needed loan forms correctly, minimizing the amount of time for governmental processing and approving (or denying) the loan. An entrepreneur would need to find a financial institution in his or her community that specializes in SBA loans.

Although banks are the most common source for obtaining loans, entrepreneurs shouldn't overlook other types of financial institutions—savings and loans, credit unions, life insurance firms, other commercial lenders, and finance companies. Although the decision criteria may be stricter at these financial institutions, the process for getting a loan would be similar to getting one from a bank.

Venture Capitalists. The next source for potential financing is **venture capital**, which is external equity funding provided by professionally managed pools of investor money. Banks and other financial institutions provide debt (loan) financing that is paid back, but venture capitalists provide equity (ownership) financing. In other words, the entrepreneur gives up some amount of ownership in the entrepreneurial venture in return for financing from the venture capitalist. Venture capitalists get their funds and additional financial returns back if and when their equity stake in the entrepreneurial venture rises in value.[16] Many venture capitalists also provide more than access to funding; they provide consulting

FYI

New Sources for Funding

While most of the traditional funding sources for entrepreneurial ventures are the most likely ones to pursue, there are some sources that provide new solutions to the perennial financing challenge faced by entrepreneurs. Here are just a few:

1. **SBA Express.** This is another initiative of the U.S. Small Business Administration. It's a streamlined process for bank-qualified business owners. They can borrow up to $150,000 through an SBA-backed loan without going through the typical application process. And, an answer is guaranteed within 36 hours. One difference, though, is that these loans are guaranteed at only 50% of their value, so many lending institutions have yet to offer this service.
2. **Community banks.** As competitors in the banking industry continue to merge with each other, entrepreneurial ventures looking for financing often get shortchanged. Many times, the best chance for these businesses is to look to local, community banks, where a long-term banking relationship can be established.
3. **Micro-loans.** These are loans that typically range from hundreds of dollars to the low six figures. Because many financial institutions consider micro-loans too small to be worth the effort, these may be difficult to find. But, if you need only a small amount of financing, ask about one.
4. **Third-party loan guarantees.** Sometimes a loan approval can be gained if a third party (family or close friend) cosigns for the loan. If this is something you're reluctant to ask someone close to you to do, there are financial sources that will consider cosigning your loan for a fixed fee or a percentage of the face value of the loan.
5. **Strategic partnership.** Perhaps a financing alternative might be to look to a corporate partner. The corporate partner benefits by having access to new technology or a niche market that's too small for them to pursue profitably on their own. And, of course, the entrepreneur benefits by getting the needed financing.

Source: J. A. Fraser, "How to Finance Anything," *Inc.*, March 1999, pp. 32–48.

services to entrepreneurs. Although each venture capital fund has its own investment criteria, most will provide capital only to entrepreneurial ventures that are "well beyond a scribble on a napkin."[17] As with any attempts to obtain any type of external financing, debt or equity, the entrepreneur needs to be well prepared with a thorough feasibility study and business plan.

Is venture capital financing a good source of funding for an entrepreneurial venture? Here's something to think about. A study by the Stanford Business School of venture financing practices concluded that venture-capital-financed companies did better over the long term than those funded by other investors.[18] However, the study also showed that founders who funded their companies with venture capital were more than twice as likely to be removed from the CEO (chief executive officer) position than those who chose other forms of financing.

Angel Investors. An **angel investor** is a private investor, a wealthy individual, who offers financial backing usually in high-risk/high-reward opportunities in return for an equity stake in the business. The angel is looking to invest in

Rapid Review

- ✔ What types of personal resources might an entrepreneur have access to for financing?
- ✔ What types of financial institutions provide funds to entrepreneurs? How do they provide these funds?
- ✔ Describe an SBA-guaranteed loan.
- ✔ What is venture capital? Why would venture capitalists be interested in financing entrepreneurial ventures?
- ✔ What is an angel investor? What cautions are appropriate when dealing with an angel investor?

entrepreneurial ventures that have the potential to provide high rates of return but also have the risk of failing dramatically without any chance of earning back the investment. But the angel is willing to take that risk because of the potentially high reward.

As with venture capital financing, an angel investor is an equity investor. The angel provides funds in return for some ownership stake in the entrepreneurial venture. If the venture is profitable and its market value rises, the angel's investment increases in value. Because they're dealing personally with the entrepreneur, many angels do have a personal interest in the venture as well. They want to see the entrepreneurial venture succeed and are willing to provide advice and assistance as needed. Although angels may indeed seem like the answer to an entrepreneur seeking funds, there are some cautions about angel investors.[19] Some angels may be looking for a quick turnaround of their money and will, in effect, destroy the business to get it back out. Some supposed angels are less-than-desirable individuals with suspicious backgrounds and intentions. In other instances, angel investors may feel that their equity investment permits them to tell the entrepreneur how to run the business. So, just be cautious. Although an angel investor can, indeed, seem to be the answer to funding, be aware up front what the angel's motivation, stipulations, and intentions are.

Public Offering. Rather than offering equity stakes to private venture capitalists or angel investors, an entrepreneur may choose to do a public offering of ownership stakes in the entrepreneurial venture. This is done through an **initial public offering (IPO)**, an investment vehicle that is the first public registration and sale of a company's stock. The IPO allows an entrepreneur to raise a much larger pool of funds than is possible through the other approaches. In fact, during the dot-com boom, stories of Internet companies going public and raising hundreds of millions of dollars in funds had many entrepreneurs with big dollar signs in their eyes salivating at the prospect! (Exhibit 3-8 lists the number of IPOs between 1994 and 2001.) However, keep in mind that what is being offered for sale is ownership—ownership of the entrepreneurial venture. With the acquired funds come certain requirements and expectations. A brand-new start-up would face overwhelming hurdles in going the IPO route. Without a proven track record, the new entrepreneurial venture has nothing with which to entice potential investors. Underwriters (an investment banking firm that actually manages the whole stock-offering process) and attorneys want to see a strong management team, a competent board of directors, standardized procedures, outstanding employees, and a host of other characteristics. Often, an IPO—the process and event of "going public"—is the culmination of years of hard work and long-delayed financial rewards for an entrepreneur. However, this doesn't mean that a young entrepreneurial venture can't pull it off, but the probability of obtaining financing through an IPO is highly unlikely.

EXHIBIT 3-8 Number of IPOs between 1994 and 2001

Year	Number
2001:	101
2000:	451
1999:	545
1998:	362
1997:	603
1996:	786
1995:	557
1994:	539
Total:	3,944

Source: www.venturecoach.com/resources/ipo-stats.htm, May 15, 2002.

Business Development Programs. The next type of financing can be found in various business development programs. These programs are designed to help entrepreneurs get their feet on the ground—to provide funding and other types of assistance in those crucial early stages of the entrepreneurial venture. We're going to look at four different programs and what they offer: Small Business Investment Companies (SBICs), Small Company Offering Registration (SCOR), business incubators, and Angel Capital Electronic Network (ACE-Net).

1. *Small Business Investment Companies (SBICs).* The U.S. Congress authorized the creation of SBICs in 1958.[20] Since then, SBICs have invested over $30 billion in entrepreneurial businesses.[21] Some of those businesses—such as FedEx, America Online, Apple Computer—have gone on to become huge market successes. The Small Business Administration licenses private investment firms as SBICs. These SBICs get their money from their owners and from individual investors. To become an SBIC, a firm must have $5 million of its own capital ($10 million if they intend to use participating securities) and obtain a special license from the government.[22] The SBIC can then sell certain government-guaranteed bonds and borrow money at attractive rates from the SBA to put into entrepreneurial ventures. An SBIC generally will take more risk than a bank will. The funds are repaid through a regular stream of payments, but the SBIC also may reserve the right to purchase stock in the new venture if it succeeds. However, SBICs are barred by federal law from buying a controlling interest in the entrepreneurial venture. A specialized type of SBIC called an SSBIC (Specialized Small Business Investment Company) offers financing to businesses owned by socially or economically disadvantaged individuals. These programs offer help to entrepreneurial ventures that might have no other financial options to pursue.
2. *Small Company Offering Registration (SCOR).* A SCOR is a do-it-yourself public offering.[23] The concept was created by the North American Securities Administrators Association and the American Bar Association to encourage entrepreneurs and other small business owners to take advantage of the U.S. Securities and Exchange Commission's Rule 504. Rule 504 permits the sale of securities worth up to $1 million in a 12-month period without being subject to SEC reporting requirements. The registration form is called a U-7 and was designed to be completed by business owners rather than by securities lawyers and investment banking firms. (For more information, check out the North American Securities Administrators Association Inc. Web site at www.nasaa.org. At the Main Menu button, click on Corporate Finance and look for SCOR information.) Sounds like an entrepreneur's financing dream, right? Not so fast! Despite its many professed advantages, nothing about a SCOR is simple. Although the form is the same in all the states that allow SCOR financing, the SCORs are administered by state securities commissions, and laws vary from state to state. In addition, there are expenses associated with the document's preparation. Most states require that financial statements be reviewed or audited by a certified public accountant. Then, there's the time spent on becoming familiar with the program and completing the preparation, filing, and marketing processes. Because of the lack of publicity about it and the lack of standardization among states, the SCOR

program hasn't been as popular as first envisioned. However, it does provide another financing option for an entrepreneur.

3. *Business incubators.* Are you familiar with an incubator? It protects newborn animals (and humans) in a controlled environment and ensures that they're off to a healthy start. **Business incubators** serve much the same purpose—they nurture new entrepreneurial ventures in a controlled environment and ensure that they get off to a strong start. Many incubators are found in conjunction with universities, although not always. Most incubators provide their start-up companies with common office space, equipment, professional services (such as attorneys and accountants), managerial advice, and encouragement. We're including this as a financing option because it is a way for an entrepreneur to minimize his or her initial financial investment.
4. *Angel Capital Electronic Network (ACE-Net).* The ACE-Net is sponsored by the Small Business Administration's Office of Advocacy. It's simply a listing service that provides information to private investors on promising entrepreneurial ventures seeking to raise $250,000 to $5 million.[24] For anyone seeking less than $250,000, the SBA warns that the costs involved may offset a significant amount of the funding received. Investors must have a net worth of at least $1 million or an annual income of more than $200,000. Entrepreneurs pay $450 annually to be listed and must meet certain qualifications. You can access the site at www.ace-net.org. Entrepreneurs and investors wishing to have access to this service must first enroll in the system. An application may be downloaded from the ACE-Net Web site. Once the form is completed, it must be mailed, along with the enrollment fee, to the nearest network operator. The local network operator will then issue a password providing access to the secure ACE-Net Web site. A majority of states have adopted new initiatives that allow companies raising less than $1 million on ACE-Net to use a short-form listing that significantly reduces the amount of effort required to get listed. This allows a company to file a simplified single listing along with its business plan. ACE-Net is fast becoming the primary information source linking entrepreneurs to angel investors.[25]

Other Sources of Financing. Although we've covered traditional and even some Internet-based financing sources, there are other, more unusual sources. For instance, on the television show *MoneyHunt* (www.moneyhunt.com) entrepreneurs get 10 minutes to tell their story and persuade a panel of experts why they deserve financing. There are also judged business plan competitions, which provide opportunities for student entrepreneurs to get exposure to potential investors. Finally, entrepreneurs might look to federal grant programs for possible financing. Through programs such as Small Business Innovation Research (SBIR) and Small Business Technology Transfer (STTR), entrepreneurs can receive funding.[26] The SBIR and STTR are designed especially for small businesses that develop products or services that can be used by the 10 federal agencies that participate in the grant program: Agriculture, Commerce, Defense, Energy, Education, Health & Human Services, Transportation, the Environmental Protection Agency (EPA), the National Aeronautics and Space Administration (NASA), and the National Science Foundation.

Entrepreneurs in Action

Marshall Rafal, president of OLI Systems Inc., looked to the federal government for funding after a yearlong effort to raise $5 million in equity financing didn't work. OLI Systems (**www.olisystems.com**), a New Jersey–based software and technology business, helps industrial companies forecast the environmental consequences of the way they do business. For instance, one of the company's software programs helps chemical companies predict the effects of corrosion, which causes $250 billion of damage annually to equipment. Despite the attractive potential market, investors weren't interested. So Rafal turned to the National Institute of Standards and Technology (NIST), an agency that awards millions of dollars every year through its Advanced Technology Program (ATP). He was able to obtain nearly $2 million in grants from the ATP investment fund. However, to win this grant, Rafal had to show that his project had both scientific and technological significance and could have a broad-based impact on the national economy. Grant applicants prepare thoroughly researched proposals and then, if they make it to the final round, must pass a rigorous oral examination, in which they explain the impact that their new technology will have on the economy. Despite the challenges, Rafal went for it and succeeded. Today, OLI Systems continues to provide technical assistance and support to companies around the world.

Sources: Company Web site (**www.olisystems.com**), May 22, 2002; and A. M. Bornego, "Seed Capital from Uncle Sam," *Inc.*, May 2001, p. 102.

Evaluating Financing Options

Remember, at this point in time, the entrepreneur is still looking at and assessing the venture's feasibility. It isn't enough just to know what financing options there are. Which option(s) are the best? Evaluating financing options boils down to three words: control, risk, and reward.

One issue in evaluating the financing options is the amount of control the entrepreneur wants. To keep the highest level of personal control means financing the entrepreneurial venture through personal resources. When the entrepreneur has to look elsewhere for financing, some level of control is sacrificed because he or she either is in debt or someone has been offered ownership (equity) percentages in the business. However, the flip side to the control issue is that of risk. Using personal resources to finance the entrepreneurial venture exposes the entrepreneur to personal risk. But, this doesn't mean that there are no risks involved with the other sources of financing either. Debt (loan) financing and equity (ownership) financing also carry degrees of risk. What the entrepreneur has to do is

EXHIBIT 3-9 Evaluating the Financing Options

	Personal Control	Personal Risk	Potential Reward
Personal resources	High	High	High
Financial institutions (debt financing)	Low to medium	Low	Low to medium
Venture capitalists (equity–debt financing)	Low to medium	Low	Low to medium
Angel investors (equity financing)	Low to medium	Low	Low to medium
Public offerings (equity financing)	Low	Low	Low to high
Business development programs	Low to medium	Low	Low to medium
Unusual sources	Low to high	Low	Low to high

weigh the risk he or she is willing to live with. Another important consideration in weighing the risk is the potential reward. If the entrepreneur hopes to maximize personal reward(s) from the entrepreneurial venture, personal resources would be the best choice. Under this option, the rewards (profits or business value) are not "shared" with anyone else. The other financing options require sharing some percentage of the rewards in return for putting up the money for the business.

The various combinations of control, risk, and reward are different for each of the financing sources we've covered. Exhibit 3-9 summarizes these combinations.

Guidelines for Seeking Financing

You can take certain steps to ease the difficulties of researching potential financing. As we said earlier in this section, *preparation* is the key.

1. *Write a feasibility study and then a business plan.* These two documents show potential financing sources that you have thought through your idea, you've researched the competition and marketplace, and you've identified the key elements of getting this proposed entrepreneurial venture up and running.
2. *Get professional advice and help.* Although the last thing you may want to do is spend resources, this is important. Getting the advice of an accountant, attorney, or other professional consultant can pay for itself by saving you time and making sure you've covered every possible detail and have what you will need. Usually a financing source (bank, venture capitalist, or other source) will want to see financial projections or statements and other documents with verified information.
3. *Get references.* Even entrepreneurs need references—someone who is willing to attest to their character, skills, experiences, or whatever. Be ready to provide these names and contact information.

Rapid Review 

- ✔ Why is it important for entrepreneurs to evaluate the various financing options?
- ✔ What role do control, risk, and reward play in an entrepreneur's evaluation of the financing options?
- ✔ Describe the various combinations of control, risk, and reward for each of the financing sources.
- ✔ What role does preparation play in seeking financing? Explain.
- ✔ List and explain the guidelines for seeking financing.

4. *Go do it.* You've researched the venture's feasibility. You've prepared whatever supporting documents and information you can. If your research shows that your proposed entrepreneurial venture is feasible, it's time, as the popular advertising slogan says, to "Just Do It!"

CHAPTER SUMMARY

This summary is organized around the chapter-opening objectives.

1. The misconceptions and realities of great ideas include the following: (a) Great ideas appear out of nowhere. The reality is that the best idea generators tend to do so in a structured, systematic way. (b) There are no stupid ideas. The reality is that many ideas are bad. However, keep in mind that sometimes the most powerful ideas come from what, at first glance, seemed stupid or illogical. (c) Customers will tell you what to do if you'll only listen. The problem with this belief is that although customers can help identify unmet needs, there's much more involved with making a great idea workable. (d) We can generate all the ideas we'll ever need if we just sit down at a meeting. The reality is that generating great ideas shouldn't be restricted to a meeting. (e) Getting ideas isn't the problem; implementing them is. The reality is that problems arise from not screening carefully enough the ideas that were generated.
2. There are four main sources of ideas. First is personal interests or hobbies. Many entrepreneurial ventures got their start because of an entrepreneur's love of doing something. Another popular source is an entrepreneur's work experiences, skills, and abilities. The third source is to look at products and services currently available, both familiar and unfamiliar, and see if there are needs that aren't being met. Finally, opportunities—positive trends or changes that provide unique and distinct possibilities for innovating and creating value—in the external environment can be a source of potential entrepreneurial ideas.
3. Entrepreneurs can generate ideas by environmental scanning, creativity and creative problem-solving, brainstorming, and focus groups. In addition, intuition can play an important role in generating ideas. Environmental scanning is screening large amounts of information to detect emerging trends. Entrepreneurs can also use specific techniques of creativity and creative problem-solving to help generate ideas. Brainstorming is an idea-generating process for developing creative solutions that encourages as many alternatives as possible while withholding criticism. Focus groups are groups of individuals who provide information about proposed products or services in a structured setting. Finally, intuition is a cognitive process whereby we subconsciously make decisions based on our accumulated knowledge and experiences.
4. Evaluating entrepreneurial ideas revolves around personal and marketplace considerations. In evaluating potential ideas, it's important to measure them against the personal considerations of the entrepreneur by looking at issues such as: Do you have the capabilities for what you've selected? Are you ready to be an entrepreneur? Do you have a passion for what you're considering?

Are you prepared emotionally to deal with the stresses and challenges of being an entrepreneur? Are you prepared to deal with rejection and failure? Are you prepared to work hard? Do you have a realistic picture of the proposed venture's potential? It's also important to look at marketplace considerations by evaluating things such as: Who are the potential customers? What similar or unique product features does your proposed idea have in relation to what's currently on the market? How and where will potential customers purchase your product? Have you considered pricing and break-even point? Have you considered how you will promote and advertise your proposed idea? Two specific approaches for evaluating entrepreneurial ideas are the four-questions approach and a feasibility study. The four-questions approach asks: (a) Do you love the business? (b) Are you skilled at the business? (c) Do you have experience at the business? and (d) Is the business simply a fad or trend? A feasibility study is a structured and systematic analysis of the various aspects of a proposed entrepreneurial venture designed to determine its feasibility.

5. Break-even point is the point at which total revenues are just sufficient to cover total costs. To calculate break-even point (BE), an entrepreneur needs to know the unit price of the product (P), the variable cost per unit (VC), and total fixed costs (TFC). The formula for computing break-even point is:

$$BE = \frac{TFC}{P - VC}$$

6. Competition is organizations battling with each other for some desired outcome—customers, market share, survey ranking, or needed resources. There are three ways to define possible competitors. The industry perspective identifies competitors as organizations making the same product or providing the same service. The marketing perspective defines competitors as organizations that satisfy the same customer need. The strategic groups perspective says that competitors are the organizations in your strategic group. Strategic groups are groups of competitors following essentially the same strategy in a particular market or industry.

7. A competitive analysis can be done by deciding what types of competitive information you'd like. For instance, what types of products or services are competitors offering? What are the major characteristics of these products or services and what are their products' strengths and weaknesses? How are competitors handling marketing, pricing, and distributing? What are they good at? What are they not so good at? You can find this competitive information in many different places, such as published financial sources, former employees, market surveys, trade fairs and exhibits, reverse engineering, news stories, and so forth. Once you've gathered information on your competitors, you might want to organize it in some type of competitor analysis matrix.

8. There are a number of financing options available to entrepreneurs. The first type is an entrepreneur's personal resources, including personal savings, home equity, cash proceeds from the sale of personal assets, life insurance policy loan, personal loans, credit cards, and loans from family or friends. Another option is financial institutions that provide loans—financial resources made available by a financial institution that are paid back, including the principal amount plus interest, by the borrower over a certain period of time. Venture capital, another financing option, is external equity provided by professionally managed pools of investor money. An angel investor is a private investor, a wealthy individual, who offers financial backing, usually in high-risk/high-reward opportunities in return for an equity stake in the business. An initial public offering (IPO) is a source of funds that comes from the first public registration and sale of a company's stock. Business development programs—including Small Business Investment Companies (SBICs), Small Company Offering Registration (SCOR), business incubators, and the Angel Capital Electronic Network (ACE-Net)—are designed to help entrepreneurs get their feet on the ground by providing funding and other types of assistance in the crucial early stages of the entrepreneurial venture. Finally, some other unusual sources of financing might include the television show *MoneyHunt*, judged business plan competitions, and federal grant programs.

9. Evaluating financing options involves looking at control, risk, and reward. How much control does the entrepreneur want? How much risk is the entrepreneur prepared to assume? Does the entrepreneur hope to maximize personal reward(s) from the entrepreneurial venture? Each of the financing options has different combinations of control, risk, and reward.
10. Preparation is the key in seeking financing. Being prepared means following these steps: write a feasibility study and then a business plan; get professional advice and help; get references; and go do it.

KEY TERMS

- *Environmental scanning:* The screening of large amounts of information to detect emerging trends.
- *Brainstorming:* An idea-generating process for developing creative solutions that encourages as many alternatives as possible while withholding criticism.
- *Focus groups:* An approach to generating ideas that uses groups of individuals who provide information about proposed products or services in a structured setting.
- *Intuition:* A cognitive process whereby we subconsciously make decisions based on our accumulated knowledge and experiences.
- *Risk:* The uncertainty surrounding decisions and actions about what will happen.
- *Return:* The payback (financial or otherwise) that an entrepreneur hopes to gain from the entrepreneurial venture.
- *Feasibility study:* A structured and systematic analysis of the various aspects of a proposed entrepreneurial venture designed to determine its workability.
- *Competitor intelligence:* A process of gathering information on who competitors are, what they are doing, and how their actions will affect your organization.

- *Competition:* Organizations battling with each other for some desired outcome.
- *Strategic groups:* Groups of competitors following essentially the same strategy in a particular market or industry.
- *Reverse engineering:* Technical analyses of competitors' products.
- *Loans:* Financial resources made available by a financial institution that are paid back, including the borrowed amount and interest charges, by the borrower over a certain period of time.
- *Small Business Administration (SBA):* A government agency devoted to the enhancement, support, and education of entrepreneurs and small business owners/managers.
- *Venture capital:* External equity financing provided by professionally managed pools of investor money.
- *Angel investor:* A private investor who offers financial backing usually in high-risk/high-reward opportunities in return for an equity position in the business.
- *Initial public offering (IPO):* An investment vehicle that is the first public registration and sale of a company's stock.
- *Business incubators:* A business development program that nurtures new entrepreneurial ventures in a controlled environment to ensure that they get off to a strong start.

SWEAT EQUITY

1. "It is important to choose a business or profession that fulfills your unique purpose or passion in life. It is much easier to succeed at something you enjoy." Do you agree with this statement? Why or why not? Write a paper explaining your position. Be sure to examine your personal philosophy about this and how this might affect your pursuit of an entrepreneurial venture.
2. Trends can be a powerful source for entrepreneurial ideas. However, how do you know when something is really a trend and not simply a fad? Do some research on trends and fads. Write a report on suggestions for entrepreneurs in understanding trends and fads.
3. One important place to start looking for ideas is by looking at population groups (known as cohorts). One particular population group that you've probably heard a lot about is the baby boomers. This group includes individuals who were born between the years 1946 and 1964. You hear so much about the baby boomers because there are so many of them. However, another population group that is attracting attention is Generation Y or the baby-boomlet generation (born between 1978 and 1994). This group is predicted to be as large as, if not larger than, its boomer parents. Do some research on Generation Y. What are its characteristics? Look for things such as values, attitudes, beliefs, demographics, purchasing tendencies, and so forth. Using a bulleted-list format, write a report summarizing your findings.

Also, discuss how an entrepreneur might use such information in generating ideas. Be sure to cite your sources.

4. Robert Pagliarini popularized the term *elevator pitch* to describe the need for an entrepreneur to be able to describe his or her entrepreneurial idea in the approximate amount of time for an average elevator ride. He suggests that an elevator pitch must answer six questions: What is your competitive advantage? Who is behind the company? How do you expect to make money (your revenue model)? What is your product or service? Who is your market? and Who is your competition? Compare and contrast these questions to what was discussed in the chapter. What do you think is the purpose behind each of these questions? Are there any others you would add to the list? Explain. What are the advantages and disadvantages of being able to describe your business idea succinctly?
5. Research the topic of competitor intelligence. Try to focus on specific information and suggestions that potential entrepreneurs could use. Write a paper describing what you found. (Be sure to cite your sources.) Be prepared to share your findings with your class.
6. When the economy is in poor shape, entrepreneurs often have to look at some unusual financing options. Two such options are having your venture bankrolled by a giant corporation (funding provided by a large company in return for stock or exclusive rights to future products) or selling off a part of your business (such as a product line). Think about the advantages and disadvantages of such approaches. Write them down and be prepared to debate why you think these options would be positive or negative.
7. "Barriers to entry" is a concept taken from strategic management that describes the obstacles to entering an industry. Do some research on barriers to entry. What are barriers to entry? What do entrepreneurs need to know about barriers to entry as they research the feasibility of their ventures? Write a report describing your findings. Be sure to cite your sources.
8. "Coming up with a killer idea isn't enough. You have to put it in the right place—the right market—to extract value from it." What do you think this statement means? How does it relate to what we discussed in this chapter?
9. We know that economic, demographic, and social trends provide significant opportunities for entrepreneurship. However, trends in business do, too. Here's a list of business trends. Think of how each of these trends has an impact on entrepreneurship and some potential entrepreneurial ideas that could arise from it. (Unless you're familiar with them, you will probably have to research these topics.)

   Business Trends:
   - The wireless revolution
   - The Internet–World Wide Web
   - Downsizing
   - Outsourcing
   - Globalization
   - Quality improvement programs
   - Value-chain management

ENTREPRENEURSHIP IN ACTION CASES

Spanx (www.spanx.com)

This case can be found at the beginning of Chapter 3.

Discussion Questions

1. Where did the idea for Spanx come from? Is this a good source of entrepreneurial ideas? Why or why not?
2. What examples of researching a venture's feasibility do you see in this story?
3. Because no other organization was doing what Sara Blakely wanted to do, would she still need to research competitors? Explain.
4. What other information might Sara have looked at as she researched the feasibility of her idea? What would this information have provided her?

Sonicare (www.sonicare.com)

The battlefield is your mouth. Or more precisely, your teeth and gums. Helping people keep their teeth and gums clean and healthy is a huge market! David Giuliani, an engineer by training, was about to stake his career and personal savings on the home-dental-care appliance of the future. Giuliani had spent 12 years at Hewlett-Packard, working his way up to section manager. But he wanted more. He wanted to "try his hand at the tiller." He left HP for an executive position with a medical-imaging company and when an opportunity came to head up one of its subsidiaries, a digital radiography business, he jumped at it. However, because he still wanted something more entrepreneurial, he quit. Now on his own, Giuliani invented a handheld ultrasound device that could measure bladder volume. He eventually built that product into a 70-employee division of a company that was eventually acquired by Abbott Laboratories. Although he stayed on as an executive, Giuliani was searching for his next entrepreneurial challenge.

Meanwhile, two University of Washington professors, David Engel and Roy Martin, were looking for someone with entrepreneurial experience to help them market a prototype sonic toothbrush they'd developed. A sonic toothbrush is based on the premise that a sound-wave-based device could effectively clean the plaque and tartar that are the major causes of dental disease. Engel and Martin had hoped that a large personal health care company would pick up their technology and bring it to market. However, industry giants such as Procter & Gamble, Johnson & Johnson, Sunbeam, Squibb, and 25 other companies declined, pointing to the fact that the U.S. Patent Office was filled with the sad stories of other home sonic toothbrushes that had been tried and failed. What Engel and Martin felt they had, though, was a technology that did work—that did blast teeth and gums with sound waves to keep them clean and healthy. But they needed someone to help them get their prototype up and running. When they spread the news around that they were looking for a sharp businessperson with a knowledge of high-tech medical equipment who could help them build a company, Giuliani's name kept coming up. The three met, and Giuliani's introduction to the prototype in the lab sold him on the deal. The University of Washington, to which Engle and Martin had assigned the patent rights under a standard employee agreement, granted the new company lifetime rights to the patent in exchange for partial ownership.

At the beginning, Giuliani kept his day job with Abbott, but his free time was spent tinkering with the prototype. The results were discouraging. The strip of metal and ceramic that held the toothbrush bristles kept breaking, and it required too much power to produce the needed vibrations. Giuliani was about to give up. But one day, while walking along the beach, he watched as the waves washed over the sand, slowly eroding the beach. That process of nature was the key product design breakthrough Giuliani had been looking for! Maybe what the product needed was sound waves traveling through fluid, which would then erode away plaque. Giuliani went back to his cofounders and told them the idea of a sonic toothbrush was a great one, but they had to abandon the prototype and try a new approach.

After consulting with various engineers, Giuliani came up with a new design: sort of like a tuning fork driven by a vibrating electromagnetic field that would provide power to the brush head. Engel and Martin spent hours in the lab observing how the vibrating brush head churned up a mixture of toothpaste and saliva on artificial teeth. When the vibrations were tuned to 520 strokes per second (middle C on the musical scale), the churned-up fluid would start to erode plaque, even when the brush itself wasn't making contact with the teeth. In theory, this meant that the plaque-cleaning action could take place between teeth and under the gum line, the places where other toothbrushes failed to go. The trio began to believe that their product could really work!

The next step was finding financing, always a big challenge. But Giuliani was able to get nearly half a million dollars from about 25 different investors. He didn't want to bring in venture capital or angels because he didn't want to risk losing control of the company down the road.

It was more than a year after getting financing that the toothbrush design was perfected into one that was manufacturable. The product became Sonicare, and the company, now called Optiva Corporation, set up its first assembly line in August 1992. For a high-tech product, production was pretty low-tech. A high-school student on summer vacation was hired to cut the brush-head bristles with a pair of tiny scissors and to assemble the rest of the product. Eventually, they began producing about 20 units a day. Since that time, Optiva's Sonicare toothbrush has become a best-seller. In August 2000, Optiva Corporation was acquired by Philips Domestic Appliances and Personal Care, a division of Netherlands-based Royal Philips Electronics. The company, now called Philips Oral Healthcare Inc., employs more than 600 people and has annual sales exceeding $200 million.

Discussion Questions

1. Describe the process of idea development behind Sonicare, the company's sonic toothbrush.
2. Would research-oriented universities be a good source of potential entrepreneurial ideas? Do some research on this topic and write up a short report outlining the advantages and drawbacks of this idea source.

3. One of the misconceptions about great ideas is that they come out of nowhere. How do you explain the fact, then, that Giuliani "saw" the connection between a process of nature (waves hitting the beach and eroding the sand) and his redesign of the company's prototype?

4. What is your opinion of Giuliani's approach to the company's financing needs? What suggestions might you have given him?

Sources: Company Web site (**www.sonicare.com**), May 22, 2002; C. Caggiano, "A Simple Plan in a Complex World," *Inc.*, February 1999, p. 45; and D. H. Freedman, "Sonic Boom," *Inc. 500 1997*, 1997, pp. 36–41.

Accuship (www.accuship.com)

"If you want to create a business, go to a party and listen. You'll hear people complain. Every complaint equals a need, a problem, a vacuum. Meet it, solve it, fill it—and there's your business." Mason C. Kauffman heard this bit of advice in an M.B.A. class at the University of Memphis from legendary entrepreneur, Fred Smith, founder of FedEx. After graduating with his M.B.A., he went to work for FedEx and spent 16 years in various jobs, including sales, operations, engineering, and information management systems. He also learned a lot about Smith's approach to the logistics and shipping business. In 1994 Kauffman decided that he was ready to try something on his own. Thinking back to Smith's advice, Kauffman began listening to what customers said. What they were saying is that they were extremely frustrated with every aspect of shipping—the large number of carriers; the broad range of services, rules, and costs; and the constantly changing and complex process of shipping. Complaints = business need. Was this the beginning of a business that Kauffman could pursue?

Believing that most businesses could use expert guidance in finding faster, cheaper, and easier ways to ship and account for their products, Kauffman left his $100,000-a-year FedEx job in 1994 and founded Express Logistics Inc., a consulting business that helped customers with their shipping operations. He started the company with his own savings and didn't receive any outside funding until the business was six years old. For the first year, Kauffman worked alone out of the attic in his home and took no salary. He built his staff slowly, making sure he had new accounts lined up before hiring new people. Expansion was funded through cash flow.

Today, the company (now called Accuship) with 100 employees provides an online logistics information management system that integrates all shipping, tracking, accounting, and reporting capabilities. In a way, Accuship is a virtual company—it owns no planes, trucks, or warehouses. All of its transactions—about 850,000 a day, worth a daily average of $5 million—are electronic. The company provides its customers (Coca-Cola, Hoffmann-LaRoche, and Home Shopping Network are just a few) with a convenient and efficient way to ship and track packages. In 2000 the company turned to outside investors for the first time, receiving $7.6 million in a single round of financing. The capital infusion was part of the company's goal to become the largest player in its field. Although Kauffman's goal is to continue growing his company, he intends to do it slowly and deliberately. He says, "Growth can kill companies. So I'm reminding everyone that we can't be in every country tomorrow and we can't be in every company tomorrow. Timing is everything."

Discussion Questions

1. What do you think of Fred Smith's advice about creating a business? How does this fit in with what we discussed in this chapter?
2. In evaluating the potential of his idea, what would Kauffman want to look at? Explain.
3. What do you think of Kauffman's approach to financing? What are the advantages and drawbacks of financing growth only through available cash?
4. Kauffman stated in relation to company growth that "timing is everything." How might this approach affect the way that an entrepreneur researches a venture's feasibility? Explain.

Sources: Company Web site (**www.accuship.com**), May 22, 2002; and A. Stuart, "Express Delivery," *Inc. Tech 2001*, No. 1, pp. 55–56.

Nobody in Particular Presents (www.nipp.com)

It's a fight that NIPP really didn't want. Yet, as a tiny fish in a big pond, NIPP knew it had to defend its turf. NIPP is an independent concert promoter, a 25-person company based in Denver that promotes lesser-known acts. Some of the touring musical acts listed on its Website include Big Head Todd and the Monsters, The High Rollers, The Garage Doors, and Kottonmouth Kings. Not exactly well-known bands with wide appeal, but ones with loyal regional fans. And NIPP's owners Jesse Morreale, Doug Kauffman, and Chris Swank had carved out a nice niche promoting these types of acts around Colorado and surrounding states. Since 1997 NIPP had promoted the Van's Warped Tour, a punk rock concert. However, in Denver during summer 2001, NIPP found itself facing off against a huge competitor—Clear Channel Communications. Clear Channel was a national radio powerhouse that had made a big move into live concert promotion in 2000. In Denver, NIPP had watched its share of live-entertainment business steadily erode. Then on a bright summer evening in 2001 at the Denver stop on the Warped Tour, Morreale saw a van from a Denver rock station owned by Clear Channel parked at the venue. For Morreale, that was the last straw. He'd purchased advertising time for the Warped Tour on this radio station but says that the station ran the spots at the wrong time or not at all. He also had tried to promote the show with an on-air ticket giveaway, but says the radio station gave the tickets to its own employees instead. And now here, right in his face, the radio station had the nerve to hang its banners at his concert. Morreale went over and kicked the employees off the grounds.

However, that decision would come back to haunt him. Within days, some bands on the Warped Tour found that they were being dropped from the radio station's playlists. Being on a playlist is crucial for a band—without it, you don't get heard. Record executives scrambled and eventually got their bands back on the air. But NIPP found out how far Clear Channel was willing to go to dominate.

For independent concert promoters like NIPP, having a national company with enormous power is changing everything. The number of independents has shrunk from several dozen to around ten. Most merged or sold out to SFX Entertainment, an entertainment consolidator that itself was acquired by Clear Channel in 2000. Figuring that it had nothing to lose, NIPP filed a lawsuit against Clear Channel charging that it violated antitrust laws by leveraging its radio playlists and promotional airtime to freeze out competing promoters. "Specifically, the lawsuit alleges that Clear Channel has built a 'monopolistic multimedia empire' that has decreased competition, reduced consumer choice, and driven up ticket prices." Clear Channel, of course, denies the charges. But NIPP knows that it faces steep odds in its battle. Antitrust charges are notoriously difficult to prove in court. And, so far, it's only NIPP against the corporate giant. Other independent promoters, record executives, and agents may complain privately about Clear Channel's tactics, but aren't willing to join a public fight. No matter how the lawsuit turns out, NIPP and its cofounders are discovering just how competition can change an industry—for better or worse.

Discussion Questions

1. Define who the competitors are using the industry perspective, the marketing perspective, and the strategic groups perspective.
2. What type of competitive information should NIPP have gathered? Be specific.
3. Do some research on Clear Channel Communication. Find out its sales revenues, number of employees, and top managers. In addition, try to find specific information about its live concert business. Would this information have been valuable to NIPP? Why or why not? (Be sure to cite your sources.)

Sources: Company's Web site (**www.nipp.com**), May 22, 2002; and C. Adler, "Backstage Brawl," *Fortune*, March 4, 2002, pp. 170C–170H.

Papa Murphy's Pizza (www.papamurphys.com)

The take-out pizza industry is probably one of the most competitive you'll find. Yet, that didn't stop Robert Graham from pursuing his idea for take-and-bake pizza. From his convenience store in Petaluma, California, Graham knew a vendor who peddled uncooked pizza for customers to take home and bake. He asked him how he made a crust that cooked in a 425-degree home oven instead of a 600-degree professional oven, and the vendor said he'd tell him for $10,000. Rather than part with that kind of money, Graham decided to try his hand at creating a crust. After a year of experimentation and hundreds of under-cooked crusts, Graham finally created a pizza crust that worked—one that baked into a crust that tasted like the delivery pizzas. Although Graham knew nothing about the restaurant business, he spent $100,000 opening up seven outlets, calling them Murphy's Pizza. For three years, Murphy's Pizza struggled. That's when Graham decided to team up with a fast-food-industry veteran, Terry Collins. Seeing potential in the take-and-bake chain concept, Collins bought a 51 percent share of

Graham's company for about $500,000. Then, Collins bought another larger take-and-bake pizza chain called Papa Aldo's out of Portland, Oregon, for almost $1 million. The two companies operated separately until 1995, when they combined as Papa Murphy's.

Today, Papa Murphy's is the seventh-largest pizza chain, with 628 stores in 21 states, most of which are franchise operations. At Papa Murphy's, there is no cooking, no table service, and no delivery. However, no-frills and low prices have contributed to the company's unique niche. CEO Collins says "We've got a real niche here." And, for now, Papa Murphy's owns it. Bigger chains, including Pizza Hut and Little Caesars, have tried the take-and-bake business without success. But competition in the pizza industry is intense. Industry sales have been almost flat for a couple of years. Papa Murphy's doesn't cater to an affluent market and when consumers have more disposable income, they're willing to pay extra for the convenience and variety offered by other full-service pizza chains.

Discussion Questions

1. Do a competitive analysis of the pizza industry. Put your information in a competitor analysis matrix. This will require you to do significant outside research.
2. What approach did you use in identifying your competitors? How did you choose the competitors that you did?
3. What could other entrepreneurs learn from Graham's and Collins's experiences?

Sources: Company Web site (**www.papamurphys.com**), May 22, 2002; and D. Pomerantz, "Raw Deal," *Forbes*, December 25, 2000, pp. 238–239.

BUSINESS PLAN PRO

EXERCISE 3-1: Concept Kick Start and Evaluating Ideas

This chapter talks about generating and evaluating new business ideas. For this exercise, come up with a business idea. This might be a business you've already thought of, one you'd like to start, an idea that came up as you read the chapter, or something from discussions with friends or class discussions.

- Open your Business Plan Pro and start a new plan. Follow the Task Wizard steps to set up the plan by answering the wizard questions about the type of business and some business details. When the setup phase is finished, save the plan with a file name as suggested by the final step.
- Continue on to the "Concept Kick Start" section.
- Complete the five steps included in the Concept Kick Start:

1. objectives,
2. mission,
3. keys to success,
4. break-even analysis table, and
5. break-even analysis text.

For each step, follow the Wizard instructions and click on the examples link (within the instructions) to help you complete the step. The break-even table will require guessing some hard numbers for a business, but let the wizard help you, and make educated guesses.

- You can print the Concept Kick Start alone, without the rest of the plan. Use the Print command in the file menu, or the option included in the Section Conclusion for Concept Kick Start. Print your concept kick start for the new business.

EXERCISE 3-2: Graphico and Competition

Complete the Graphico example in Exercises 2-2 and 2-3. This is a small graphics design business. What competition does a business like this have? How would it research the competition?

- Open Business Plan Pro. Use a new or existing plan, it doesn't matter in this case. Open the Sample Plan browser. Use the keyword search for the term "graphics" to find the sample plan for Graphics Design, SIC 7336. The company is named the Metolius Agency.
- Use the **File>Open in the Business Plan Pro** command to open the Metolius Agency plan in Business Plan Pro.
- Switch to the Outline View. Click the "Plan Outline" icon on the toolbar.
- Read through this sample plan's examination of the market and competition. Compare its discussion of competition, including sections 4.3, Service Business Analysis; 4.3.1, Competition and Buying Factors; and 5.1, Competitive Edge. How does this analysis compare to your imaginary analysis of Graphico in Exercises 2-2 and 2-3? How would you research your competition and factors of competition for a plan for Graphico?

EXERCISE 3-3: Understand the Competition

Choose one of the plans you've started from a previous Business Plan Pro exercise. It might be the Graphico plan used in several exercises, the plan you did for Exercise 2-3, or the one in Exercise 3-1.

- Consider the competitive landscape for graphic design in your area. How does it compare to the plan for the Metolius Agency? How would you go about finding out, for your market area, the nature of competition in graphics design?
- Consider the competitive landscape for whichever plan you choose for this exercise. Open the plan in Business Plan Pro and find "The Business You're In" section in the Easy

Plan Wizard. Fill in the topics in that section. The titles of those topics will depend on the plan setup. For example, "Service Business Analysis" will show for some businesses, and "Industry Analysis" for others. "Factors in Competition" is included regardless. *Hint: the* Plan Setup *includes a choice between more or less detail. If you chose* More Detail *in the* Plan Setup, *you will have more topics in this section.*

Wherenet

"I can't find it." A dreaded phrase for any business. However, a Santa Clara, California-based company called Wherenet (**www.wherenet.com**) is hoping to erase that phrase. How? Through a tracking technology it has developed that locates parts, products, and people with surprising accuracy. In today's Internet-based economy, knowing where your assets are is crucial. Wherenet is helping businesses do just that.

Dave Wisherd—founder, chairman, and chief technology officer—calls the company's technology radical, change-the-world stuff. Wherenet has capitalized on advances in wireless technology to make the first affordable and accurate tracking systems—systems that can get the right parts to the assembly line or locate containers of crucial parts in a warehouse or vehicles in a parking lot. For instance, one of its products, Wherecall, is a wireless device that instantly orders replenishments when assembly-line components run low, thereby keeping excess inventory to a minimum and controlling costs. The company also makes a tagging device that sends out a unique, very-low-power radio frequency that is picked up by antennas, relayed to a database server, and displayed in a map form, allowing any physical object to be located with an accuracy of within 10 feet. Dan Doles, President and CEO, says that Wherenet can solve customers' business problems and provide them with a cost-effective solution. He believes that Wherenet is the definitive market leader and that the sky is the limit as far as applications. One of the company's newest devices, Park Watch, is a wristband tracking device that helps families or groups at a theme park locate each other. And the company's Walk Mate can be used by college students who sense they're in danger to instantly alert security personnel about who and where they are. Although every start-up faces challenges and eventual competition, Wherenet feels its technology will transform the business world, thus helping it successfully track down people, products, and profitability.

Discussion Questions

1. Where do you think the idea for Wherenet came from?
2. What types of competitive information would Wherenet want to have? Be specific.
3. Dave Wisherd described the company's product as radical and change-the-world. How important do you think these characteristics are in researching the feasibility of an entrepreneurial venture?

4. Wherenet's Web site lists several venture capitalists as investors. Look up two of these investors and describe what it says about them. Then, discuss how this information might help an entrepreneur in researching a venture's feasibility.

Sources: **Company information from company Web site (www.wherenet.com), July 10, 2002, and Hoover's Online (www.hoovers.com), July 10, 2002; and *Business Now* video segment.**

ENDNOTES

1. Information on Sara Blakely and Spanx from company's Web site (**www.spanx.com**), May 6, 2002; and L. Gallagher, "Footless and Fancy-Free," *Forbes*, April 2, 2001, pp. 120–121.
2. S. I. Mohan-Neill, "The Influence of Firm's Age and Size on Its Environmental Scanning Activities," *Journal of Small Business Management*, October 1995, pp. 10–21.
3. S. Greco, "Where Great Ideas Come From," *Inc.*, April 1998, pp. 76–86.
4. S. Greco, "The Start-Up Years," *Inc.500*, October 21, 1997, p. 57.
5. R. Rosenwein, "Hiding in Plain Sight," *Inc.*, January 2001, pp. 54–55.
6. A. Bhide, "How Entrepreneurs Craft Strategies That Work," *Harvard Business Review*, March–April 1994, pp. 150–61.
7. A. H. Anderson and P. Woodcock, *Effective Entrepreneurship* (Cambridge, MA: Blackwell Publishers, 1996).
8. R. Wild, "Naked Hunch," *Success*, June 1998, p. 54.
9. D. Phillips and C. E. Griffin, "Good Advice," *Entrepreneur*, December 1997, p. 58.
10. M. Marchetti, "Start Me Up: Stage 1—The Idea," *Smart Money*, January 2001, pp. 108–109; and A. W. Hiam and K. W. Olander, *The Entrepreneur's Complete Sourcebook* (Paramus, NJ: Prentice Hall, 1996), pp. 23–37.
11. T. Burns, *Break the Curve: The Entrepreneur's Blueprint for Small Business Success* (London: International Thomson Business Press, 1999), p. 21.
12. T. Severance, *Business Start-Up Guide* (Oceanside, CA: Tycoon Publishing, 1998), p. 31.
13. R. M. Beal, "Competing Effectively: Environmental Scanning, Competitive Strategy, and Organizational Performance in Small Manufacturing Firms," *Journal of Small Business Management*, January 2000, pp. 27–47.
14. See M. E. Porter, *Competitive Strategy* (New York: Free Press, 1980), Chapter 7.
15. N. A. Mangi, "Credit-Card Mania," *Business Week*, September 10, 2001, accessed at **www.businessweek.com**, May 15, 2002.
16. B. Zider, "How Venture Capital Works," *Harvard Business Review*, November–December 1998, pp. 131–39.
17. B. Solomon, "Something Ventured, Something Gained," *Working Woman*, May 1999, p. 64.
18. D. M. Osborn, "Dear John," *Inc.*, May 2001, pp. 44–48.
19. S. Gruner, "The Trouble with Angels," *Inc.*, February 1998, pp. 47–53.
20. J. Pryde, "A Lending Niche Helps Small Firms," *Nation's Business*, February 1998, pp. 52–53.
21. "Regular and Specialized SBICs Financing to Small Businesses Reported for Years Ending March 31, 1960, to March 31, 2001," accessed at **www.sba.gov/INV/**, May 15, 2002.

22. D. R. Evanson, "Lending Over Backwards," *Success*, July 1998, pp. 54–58.

23. R. Reynes, "Financing for Do-It-Yourselfers," *Nation's Business*, May 1998, pp. 38–40.

24. S. Nelton, "Using the Internet to Find Funds," *Nation's Business*, August 1998, pp. 35–36.

25. "SBA's ACE-Net Pairs Small Companies with Investors," *Springfield Business Journal*, March 1–7, 1999, p. 13.

26. K. E. Klein, "How to Win at the Grant Game," *Business Week Online*, March 8, 2002, accessed at **www.businessweek.com**, March 12, 2002.

4 Planning the Venture

LEARNING OBJECTIVES

After reading and studying this chapter, you should be able to:

1. Describe what organizational vision and mission are.
2. Explain the importance of having an organizational vision and mission.
3. Discuss how to develop an organizational vision and mission.
4. List the four components of a vision statement and the nine components of a mission statement.
5. Define organizational culture.
6. Describe the seven dimensions of organizational culture.
7. Discuss where an organization's culture comes from.
8. Describe how employees learn an organization's culture.
9. Explain why it's important for an entrepreneur to understand organizational culture.
10. Describe the five purposes of a business plan.
11. Explain the various components of a business plan.
12. Prepare a business plan.

ENTREPRENEURSHIP IN ACTION

SOL Cleaning Service, located in Helsinki, Finland, isn't what you might expect.[1] The company's headquarters, located in a renovated film studio, positively "explodes" with color, creativity, and chaos. Walls are painted bright red, white, and yellow, and employees wander the halls talking on bright yellow high-tech portable phones. These bright and energetic surroundings might seem tailor-made for creative, artistic businesses, but SOL competes in a grungy and unglamorous business—industrial cleaning. It's a high-energy, fast-paced, knowledge-driven organization whose business is scrubbing hospital floors, making hotel beds, and sweeping grocery store aisles.

The philosophy of Lisa Joronen, SOL's owner, is "In a service business, if you're not happy with yourself, how can you make the customer happy?" And Joronen has shaped SOL's culture around that philosophy.

SOL's culture is characterized by five values. The first is that *hard work has to be fun.* Joronen believes that because few people dream of becoming

Although it may seem far-fetched to view a company whose revenues are derived from industrial cleaning as entrepreneurial, SOL Cleaning Service is about as entrepreneurial as they come. The company is pursuing opportunities, is characterized by innovative practices, and has profitability and growth as its main goals—all hallmarks, we know, of entrepreneurial ventures. As an entrepreneurially oriented company, SOL recognizes the importance of cultural values in guiding what it does and how it operates. In this chapter we're going to look at organizational culture issues as well as at the importance of developing a vision and mission and developing and writing the business plan. These activities are important steps in planning the entrepreneurial venture that need to be addressed before the venture is formally organized and launched.

DEVELOPING ORGANIZATIONAL VISION AND MISSION

The importance of an organization's vision and mission is perhaps best stated by Peter Drucker, a noted management author, who said, "A business is not defined by its name, statutes, or articles of incorporation. It is defined by the business mission. Only a clear definition of the mission and purpose of the organization makes possible clear and realistic business objectives."[2] Before a new entrepreneurial venture is organized and launched, the entrepreneur should give serious thought to the organizational vision and mission. In this section, we're going to look at what the organizational vision and mission are, why they're important, and how you develop them.

What Are the Organizational Vision and Mission?

Although many people view organizational vision and mission as one and the same, we don't. There are some distinct differences between the two concepts, and we're going to address them separately.

We introduced the concept of organizational vision in Chapter 2 as one of the critical factors for succeeding in today's economy. Just to review, a **vision** is a broad comprehensive picture of what an entrepreneur wants his or her organization to become. The vision provides a vibrant and compelling picture of the future, and presents a view of what the entrepreneurial venture can be. The vision is the statement of the entrepreneur's dream. When an organizational leader—in this case, the entrepreneur—articulates

a cleaner, the keys to keeping her employees satisfied are fun and individual freedom. The second value is that *there are no low-skill jobs.* The company invests significant amounts of time and money in training employees. Another unique value is that *people who set their own targets shoot for the stars.* SOL employees have significant responsibilities because Joronen's philosophy is that people will set targets higher for themselves than what anyone would set for them. The fourth value that SOL stresses is that *loose organizations need tight measures.* Although Joronen believes in employee autonomy, she is a fanatic about performance measurement and accountability. Finally, SOL believes that *great customer service demands cutting-edge technology.* SOL may be in a "low-end" business but that doesn't mean that it's low-tech.

a distinct vision, all current and future decisions and actions will be guided by this vision. By articulating the vision, the entrepreneur maps out an overall picture of where he or she would like the entrepreneurial venture to be in the future. For instance, at Microsoft, Inc., a highly successful entrepreneurial organization, the vision of "a computer on every desk" has guided organizational decisions throughout the company's history of rapid and turbulent growth.

While an organization's *vision* provides an overall picture of where the entire organization would like to be in the future, a **mission** is a statement of what the various organizational units do and what they hope to accomplish in alignment with the organizational vision. Organizational units include work groups, projects, departments, and so forth—for instance, a customer service team, a product development project, or an employee training work group. An organization will have only one vision, but potentially several missions that contribute to the pursuit of the vision. A work unit's mission statement provides a focus for that particular area. Although the mission is not as comprehensive and broad as the statement of vision, it still provides an overview of the unit's purpose, what it does, and its goals. Each of the specific mission statements also should align with the organizational vision. Exhibit 4-1 provides some examples of companies' vision and mission statements.

Why Are the Organizational Vision and Mission Important?

The organizational vision and mission are vitally important to the venture's success. Why? They provide clear direction, they guide the management team, and they create a sense of shared endeavor and purpose. In short, the vision and mission statements establish a general tone or climate for the organization.

Ideally, by creating an organizational vision and mission, an entrepreneur will have a broad framework that allows him or her and any additional organizational members to know what they're doing and why they're doing it. What results is a comprehensive and unified view of these important elements—that is, what the entrepreneurial venture is doing and what it hopes to become. The vision and affiliated missions provide direction and guidance for making decisions and taking actions. By expressing and clarifying the desired values, these statements also serve to establish a general tone or climate for the venture. These desired values also become an important basis for the organizational culture as we'll discuss in an upcoming section. In addition, these statements serve as a focal point for the entrepreneur and other organizational members to identify and clarify the organization's purpose and direction. There are no misunderstandings about what this venture is going to do (or is doing) and what it hopes to become. A final point about the importance of organizational vision and mission statements is that researchers who have studied organizational vision and mission statements have found that high-performing organizations have more comprehensive and thorough statements than do low-performing organizations.[3] How much better is performance? Rarick and Vitton found that organizations with formalized mission statements had twice the average return on shareholders' equity than did organizations without formalized mission statements; Bart and Baetz found a positive relationship between mission statements and organizational performance; and *Business Week* reported that firms using mission statements had a 30 percent higher return on certain financial measures than those without such statements.[4]

EXHIBIT 4-1 Sample Vision and Mission Statements

PRIME INC.

OUR MISSION

Is to prosper while providing excellent service to our customers

PRIME VALUES

CUSTOMERS: Finding, serving, and keeping customers guarantees our existence.

SERVICE: We will provide quality service that meets or exceeds our customers' requirements.

VALUE: We will price our service at rates that are a true value to our customers.

PROFIT: To remain free and provide security for our company and associates, we must earn a profit.

Courtesy of Prime Inc.

THE BAMA COMPANIES, INC.

OUR MISSION

People helping people be successful.

OUR VISION

Create and deliver loyalty, prosperity and fun for all, while becoming a billion dollar company.

Courtesy of The Bama Companies, Inc.

AIRE-MASTER

MISSION

To provide invaluable services that enhance the customer's image of quality.

VALUES

Positive mental attitude • Teamwork and communication • Concern for others • Going the extra mile • Innovative thinking • Training and education • Honesty • Reliability • Excellence • Constant improvement

Courtesy of Aire-Master

BASS PRO SHOPS

MISSION STATEMENT

To be the leading merchant of outdoor recreational products, inspiring people to love, enjoy, and conserve the great outdoors.

Courtesy of Bass Pro Shops

Knowing this, there should be no doubt in your mind about how important it is for you to develop viable and appropriate organizational vision and mission statements. But how? That's what we're going to discuss next.

How Do You Develop Vision and Mission Statements?

In order to answer this question, we first need to look at the process an entrepreneur can follow in developing the organizational vision and mission statements. Then, we address what should be included in these statements. The assumption

Entrepreneurs in Action

Bruce Brown's vision involved bugs. Not the creepy, crawly types with feelers and feet, but the types that invade computers. Computer bugs are Brown's passion. As these bugs have proliferated and as good technical help has become scarce, his *BugNet* newsletter fills an important need for corporate and personal computer users. (You can check out the company's newsletter at **www.bugnet.com**.) *BugNet* makes its money from subscriptions, syndication, and licensing deals, and has been profitable almost from the very beginning. Each week, *BugNet*'s editors wade through numerous user complaints. The approximately 10 percent of problems that are judged to be the most serious or widespread are researched and reported to subscribers. From a vision to a viable venture—now there's nothing "buggy" about that at all!

Sources: Company Web site (**www.bugnet.com**), May 27, 2002; and E. Updike, "Killer Applications," *Business Week Frontier*, April 26, 1999, pp. F28–F29.

we're making is that these statements do need to be *written*. If the proposed dreams, desires, values, and ideas remain only in the entrepreneur's head and are never written down in some formal document, having a unified direction and framework will be hard.

The Process of Developing Organizational Vision and Mission. It can be difficult to express in writing the things that are important parts of the organizational vision and mission. The entrepreneur may have a good idea of what the entrepreneurial venture is going to do but describing that "vision" in words can prove frustrating. The best way to start is first of all to believe in and commit to the importance of having these formal written documents. Unless an entrepreneur is personally "sold" on this, he or she won't be willing to commit the time or energy to develop them. There's no doubt that it will take some effort to create statements that capture the essence of the entrepreneurial venture and that do so in a way that's clear, concise, and motivational. But the effort is worth it! Once an entrepreneur has accepted that vision and mission statements are important, what next?

The next step is finding examples of statements already used by other organizations large and small. These statements usually can be found in brochures, posted on walls at an organization's place of business, printed in annual reports, outlined on a Web site, and in a variety of other places. If there are organizations that you particularly admire, ask the owners for a copy of their vision and mission statements. Look at what these organizations have included in their statements. Use these as guides to the key points or important values you want to include in your own statements.

Rapid Review

- ✔ What is an organizational vision?
- ✔ What is an organizational mission?
- ✔ How are the organizational vision and mission similar? Different?
- ✔ Why is it important for entrepreneurs to develop organizational vision and mission statements?

Finally, once you've had an opportunity to study sample statements, it's time to write your own, on paper. Don't just keep them in your head. Actually put them in writing. Then, look carefully at what you've written. Have other people close to you and whose judgment you trust—family, friends, professional advisers—look at what you've written. Do your statements capture the spirit of what you want your entrepreneurial venture to be and to become? Do the statements describe what is unique about your organization? One other suggestion: If there are other key decision makers in the entrepreneurial venture, involve them in developing and writing the vision and mission statements as well. Their input is essential.

Important Components of Organizational Vision and Mission Statements. As you examine other organizational vision and mission statements, one thing may strike you immediately—the fact that they vary in length, content, format, and specificity. However, as you develop your venture's vision and mission statements, there are some common components that they should include.

Four components have been identified as important to organizational vision.[5] (See Exhibit 4-2.) First is that the vision should be built on a foundation of the organization's core values and beliefs. These values and beliefs address what's fundamentally important to the organizational founder(s), such as conducting business ethically and responsibly, satisfying the customer, emphasizing quality in all aspects, or being a leader in technology. The vision should emphasize whatever those core values are. Although a statement of values won't guarantee success for an entrepreneurial venture, it establishes expectations for the entrepreneur and any other future or current employees. For example, if employees know that outstanding customer service is valued by the organization, they can make decisions and act in ways that champion customer service. Look back at our chapter-opening case and reexamine SOL's core values and the ways in which work decisions and actions are affected.

Second, the vision should elaborate a purpose for the organization. Any organization—large or small, profit or not-for-profit—should have a unique purpose or reason for existing. Specifying the purpose entails asking questions such as: Why is this organization in business? What is its intent? What is its *reason for being* in existence as an organization? This may seem an easy thing to do, but it's not! An entrepreneur must think long and hard about the purpose of the entrepreneurial venture.

The third component of organizational vision is a brief summary of what the organization does. Although the vision shouldn't provide explicit details about

EXHIBIT 4-2 Important Components of Organizational Vision

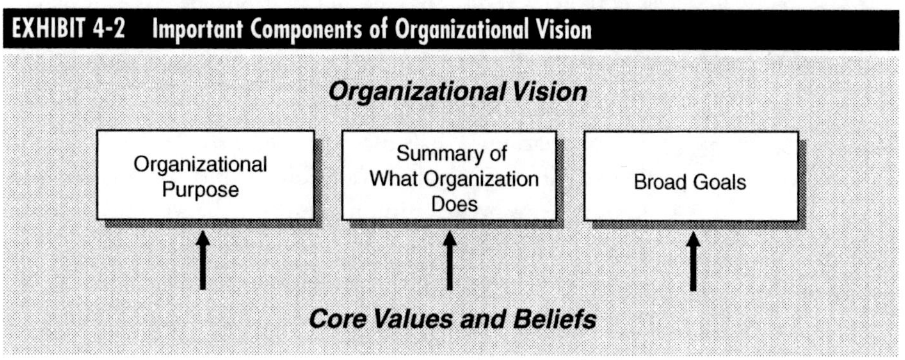

FYI

Values-Based Management

Having a core set of values can influence the way an organization does its business. **Values-based management** is an approach to managing an entrepreneurial venture that entails establishing, promoting, and practicing shared values. An organization's values reflect what it stands for and what it believes in. For example, at Tom's of Maine, an entrepreneurial manufacturer of natural personal care products, the company's shared values have become part of the overall way the business is operated. Every decision at Tom's is evaluated in light of the values found in its Statement of Beliefs and Mission Statement.

Shared organizational values serve at least four main purposes: (1) these shared values guide decisions and actions; (2) the shared values shape employee behavior; (3) shared organizational values influence marketing efforts; and (4) these values help build team spirit in organizations. As you can see, shared organizational values can prove highly beneficial to an organization. Now, how can these shared values be developed?

As any venture that uses values-based management will tell you, it's not easy to establish the shared organizational values. At Tom's of Maine, the process involved everyone in the company. All the employees, working in groups of four to six, took a long, hard look at defining "who we are" and "what we are about." But the commitment by Tom's employees to developing shared values didn't stop there. They realized that they were to actually *use* the values they had helped define. They realized that those shared values really mattered. Entrepreneurs who believe in the importance of shared values might follow these suggestions in developing them: (1) Involve everyone in the company. (2) Allow individual departments or units to customize the values. (3) Expect and accept employee resistance or uncertainty. (4) Keep the statement of values short. (5) Avoid trivial statements of values. (6) Leave out religious references. (7) Challenge the stated values. (8) Live the stated values.

Sources: G. P. Alexander, "Establishing Shared Values Through Management Training Programs," *Training and Development Journal,* February 1987, pp. 45–47; A. Farnham, "State Your Values, Hold the Hot Air," *Fortune,* April 19, 1993, pp. 117–124; and R. Kamen, "Values: for Show or for Real," *Working Woman,* August 1993, p. 10.

what the organization does (this is best done through the mission statements, which we'll discuss shortly), it should explain what it's doing to fulfill its purpose. This is a good time to say that although the concepts are related, there *is* a difference between an organization's purpose and what it does. For example, there may be several organizations that have the purpose of ecological preservation, but the way they go about carrying out that purpose (that is, what they do) may be entirely different.

The last component of organizational vision is that it should specify broad goals. **Goals** are outcomes or end results that are desired by individuals, groups, or organizations. Goals provide targets that all organizational members work toward meeting. Goals serve to direct the entrepreneur and other organizational members toward a common and unified end. The organization's vision can and should be a guiding force in every decision as goals are developed and pursued.

We've covered all the important elements of an organizational vision statement. Now, what about the mission statement(s)? What should be included in them?

EXHIBIT 4-3 Components of Organizational Vision and Mission Statements

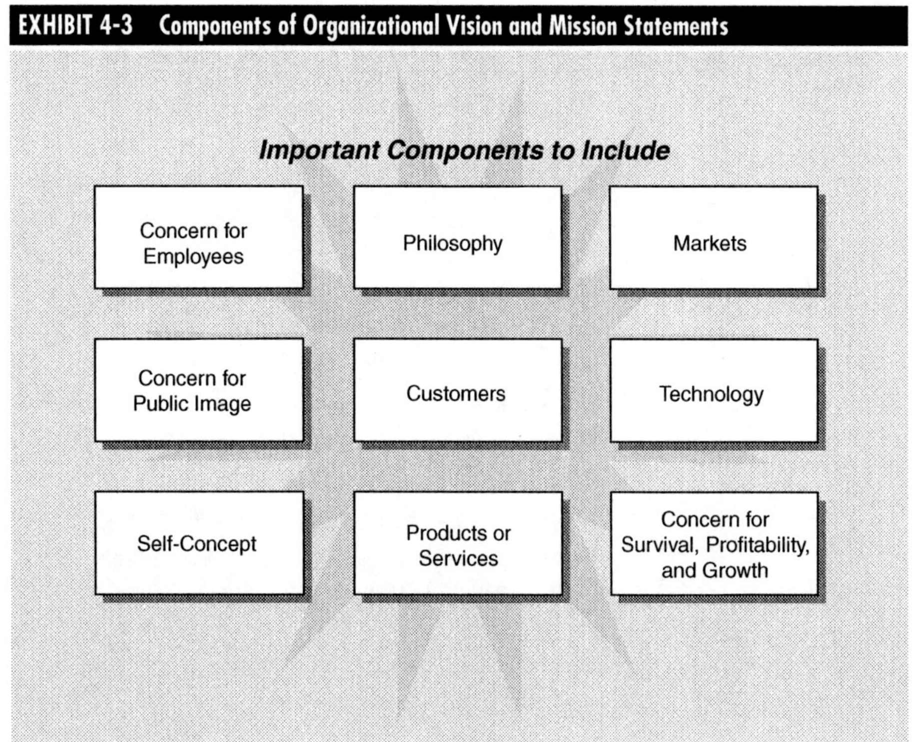

Nine specific components might be included in a mission statement.[6] (See Exhibit 4-3.) What are these nine components?

1. *Customers.* Describe the specific customers of the organizational unit.
2. *Products or services.* Define the major products or services of the organizational unit.
3. *Markets.* Explain where the organizational unit competes geographically.
4. *Technology.* Describe how the organizational unit uses technology.
5. *Concern for survival, profitability, and growth.* Explain how the organizational unit is committed to growth and financial viability.
6. *Philosophy.* This may be one of the harder ones to write because it describes the basic beliefs, values, aspirations, and ethical priorities of the organizational unit. However, this philosophy should, and does, reflect the vision statement. The values that are expressed in the mission statement(s) should align with those in the vision statement.
7. *Self-concept.* Describe the organizational unit's competitive advantage. Explain what it has that competitors do not or what it does better than competitors.
8. *Concern for public image.* Tell how the organizational unit is responsive to societal, community, and environmental issues.
9. *Concern for employees.* If the organizational unit has employees, explain the role of employees in the organizational unit. Describe how and why employees are valuable assets.

These nine components are simply recommendations for what should be included in the mission statement(s). Some may apply; others may not. It is

Entrepreneurs in Action

Reginald Ball saw a lot of action up close as a Secret Service agent for the U.S. Treasury Department—from living through the failed assassination attempt on President Ronald Reagan to coordinating 80 agents for President Bill Clinton's visit to Sydney, Australia. After retiring from the Secret Service, Ball decided he didn't want to just collect retirement checks. He began to look at businesses he could go into. Security would have been an obvious choice, but Ball wanted more of challenge. So, in 1997 he started RB Industries, a general-line industrial products distributor company in Sterling Heights, Michigan. Today, Ball's company supplies industrial products ranging from hand tools to high-tech testing equipment, mainly to the automotive industry. In the company's early days, Ball found that client trust—something that was automatic when he served as a Secret Service agent—wasn't easy to come by. That experience shaped his business philosophy, which is simple—to be worthy of the customer's trust and confidence. That philosophy has served him well as RB Industries now employs around 30 people and has annual revenues approaching $12 million.

Sources: Q. L. Lewis, "A Different Kind of Service," *Black Enterprise*, October 2001, p. 54; and M. Hofman, "In the Line of Pliers," *Inc.*, October 2001, pp. 24–25.

important, however, for an entrepreneur to at least examine each of these areas even though they may not be appropriate for describing what is happening in a specific organizational unit.

Much of what is expressed in the written vision and mission statements are reflected in the organizational culture. It's important for entrepreneurs to understand what organizational culture is and how it influences the entrepreneurial venture. We're going to look at organizational culture issues next in our exploration of planning the entrepreneurial venture.

Rapid Review 

- ✔ Describe the process of developing organizational vision and mission.
- ✔ What four components should an organizational vision include?
- ✔ What is values-based management, and what role might it play in organizational vision?
- ✔ What are goals?
- ✔ List the nine specific components that are recommended to be included in mission statement(s).

ORGANIZATIONAL CULTURE ISSUES

When you walk into a particular business, do you get a certain impression about what is important and about the way work is done there? Do you get the feeling that employees are excited and motivated by what they do, or that employees are there just because it provides a paycheck? Does it seem that customers are important and valued, or that customers are seen as intrusions on getting work done? Do you get the feeling that this organization is warm, relaxed, and open, or that this organization is structured, inflexible, and set in its ways? Do you get the feeling that this organization is more formal or more informal? Just as individuals have personalities, so does an organization. This personality is called *culture.* Just as every person has his or her own unique personality, every organization has a unique personality. In this section, we're going to explain what organizational culture is, describe the different dimensions of organizational culture, look at the source of culture, examine how culture is learned by organizational members, and discuss why it's important for entrepreneurs to understand organizational culture.

What Is Organizational Culture?

Exactly what is **organizational culture**? It's the beliefs, values, and behavioral norms shared by organizational members that influence the way they do their work. Even in an entrepreneurial venture that includes only the entrepreneur, certain beliefs, values, and behavioral norms will influence how decisions are made and how work is completed. These shared values, beliefs, and norms that make up an organization's culture determine, to a large extent, what organizational members think is important and the way they do their work. When confronted with a problem, the culture influences what organizational members do about it because of the "way things are done around here."

This definition of culture implies a couple of things. First, culture *is* a perception. Individuals perceive the culture of the organization based on what they see, hear, or experience within the organization. Also, even though organizational members may have different backgrounds or work in different areas in the organization, they tend to describe the organization's culture in similar terms. That's what we mean by the *shared* aspect of culture. Organizational members share these values, beliefs, and behavioral norms. Finally, organizational culture is a *descriptive* term. This means that culture is concerned with how organizational members perceive an organization, not with whether they like it. Culture describes rather than evaluates. What exactly, though, is the culture describing?

Dimensions of Organizational Culture

Research into organizational culture suggests that seven dimensions capture the essence of an organization's culture.[7] These dimensions, as illustrated in Exhibit 4-4, have been described as follows:

1. *Innovation and risk-taking.* The degree to which employees are encouraged to be innovative and take risks.
2. *Attention to detail.* The degree to which employees are expected to do their jobs with precision, thorough analysis, and attention to detail.
3. *Outcome orientation.* The degree to which results or outcomes are considered more important than the techniques and processes used to achieve those outcomes.
4. *People orientation.* The degree to which organizational decisions take into consideration the effect on the organization's people.
5. *Team orientation.* The degree to which organizational work is done in teams rather than by individuals.
6. *Aggressiveness.* The degree to which organizational members are aggressive and competitive instead of easygoing and cooperative.

EXHIBIT 4-4 Dimensions of Organizational Culture

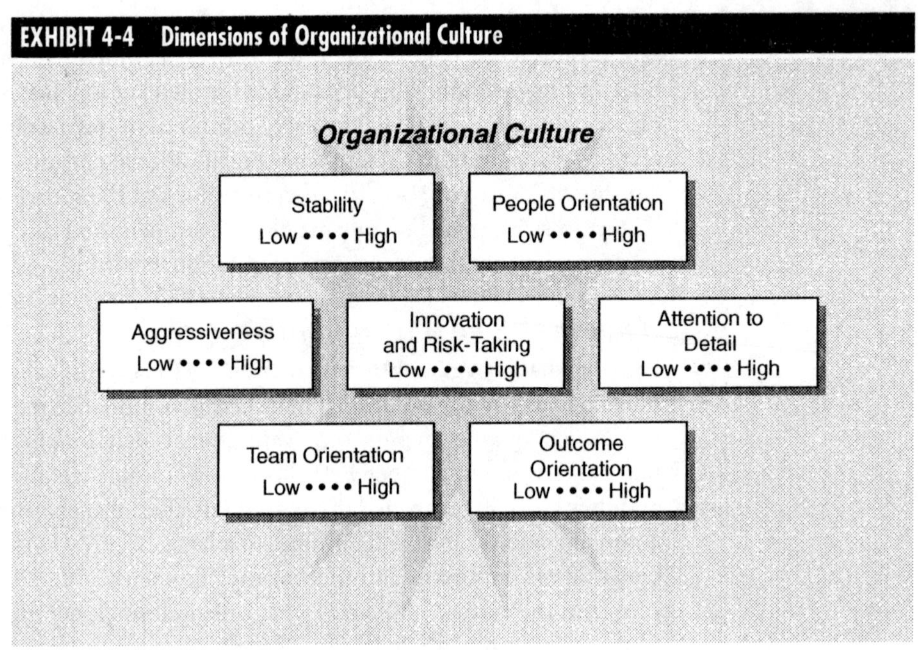

7. *Stability.* The degree to which organizational decisions and actions emphasize maintaining the status quo as opposed to changing.

As shown in Exhibit 4-4, the degree of each of these cultural dimensions will range from low to high. For instance, an organization might be high on team orientation, but low on aggressiveness. Describing whether an organization is high or low on these seven dimensions provides a composite picture of its culture. In many organizations, one cultural dimension may overshadow all the others and essentially shape the organization and the way organizational members do their work. The personalities of these organizations reflect the cultural dimension that is valued and prized. For instance, an organization may have a strong innovation and risk-taking personality, as shown by employees who are continually on the lookout for new approaches and new ideas. Or, an organization might have a strong people-orientation personality, as shown by the way employees are valued and encouraged for their contributions and inputs. Look back at our chapter-opening case on SOL. What type of personality would you say SOL has? Which cultural dimensions do you think are valued and highly regarded?

The Source of Culture

Where do these shared beliefs, values, and behavioral norms come from? An organization's values, customs, traditions, and ways of doing things are largely due to what's been done before and the degree of success it has had with these. The original source of an organization's culture reflects the beliefs, values, and vision of the founder(s). Because the founder (the entrepreneur) has the original idea, he or she also may have certain beliefs and biases about how best to pursue the idea. The founder isn't constrained by previous customs or approaches. Thus, this person establishes the early culture of the organization by projecting an image of what the organization should be. The small size of the new organization also helps the

Entrepreneurs in Action

Hewlett-Packard, founded by Bill Hewlett and David Packard, is one of the great names in American corporations. Early in 1957 the company was at a crossroads. It was growing rapidly and was about to go public. However, as HP grew, its founders feared it would lose its "small-company atmosphere." To keep its all-important innovative spirit alive, Hewlett and Packard realized it was important to nurture an esprit de corps among employees. But how? Hewlett and Packard, along with 20 managers, went off-site to the Sonoma Mission Inn & Spa, where the employees debated what kind of culture HP should cultivate. By the end of their meeting, the group had drafted "values" and "objectives" they thought the company should embrace. That list became the basis for the renowned "HP Way"—the organizational culture for which Hewlett-Packard is still highly regarded today.

Source: "Hewlett-Packard Soaks in Small-Company Culture," *Inc.*, April 2002, p. 132.

founder(s) instill the values and vision in organizational members as they come on board. These people either "buy into" the culture or they don't join the organization.

Let's look at an example of an individual who had an immense influence on shaping his organization's culture. Yvon Chouinard is the founder of the outdoor gear company Patagonia, Inc. (Check out how the company describes its culture at **www.patagonia.com**. Click on "About the Company" and follow the links from there.) Chouinard is an avid extreme adventurer and approached the business in a laid-back, casual manner. For instance, he hired employees not on the basis of any specific business skills they might have had, but because he had climbed, fished, or surfed with them. Employees were friends, and work was treated as something fun to do. In a speech Chouinard gave a few years ago, he uttered his now legendary line, "Let my people go surfing!" Although Patagonia is now a $220-million-a-year company with more than 1,000 employees, its culture still reflects Chouinard's values and philosophy. How did Patagonia's employees "learn" the organizational culture? As an entrepreneurial organization grows and employees are hired, they soon learn the "way things are done around here." How? That's what we're going to discuss next.

Rapid Review

- ✔ What is organizational culture?
- ✔ Describe the implications of the definition of culture.
- ✔ List and explain the seven dimensions of organizational culture.
- ✔ How do these dimensions describe an organization's personality?
- ✔ Where does an organization's culture come from?

How Organizational Culture Is Learned

The culture of an organization is transmitted to members in a number of ways—most importantly, through stories, rituals, material symbols, and language. These stories, rituals, material symbols, and language give the culture life. They are the ways in which employees see, experience, and learn about an organization's culture. In this section, we'll also look at the role that physical surroundings play in reinforcing and supporting the organizational culture.

Stories. Organizational "stories" are narratives that describe significant events or people, such as the founders and how they started the business, organizational members breaking the rules and succeeding through taking risks, rags-to-riches successes, reactions to past mistakes and what happened to employees who made mistakes, and other key organizational events. These stories help tie together the present with the past, provide explanations and legitimacy for current practices, and exemplify what's important to an organization. Organizational stories can play an important role in passing on key values and expectations to organizational members.

Rituals. Rituals are repetitive sequences of activities that express and reinforce the key shared values of the organization and what goals are most important. (Commencement ceremonies would be an example of a ritual with which you're familiar.) In the business world, one of the best-known organizational culture rituals takes place at the annual meeting of another well-known entrepreneurially oriented company, Mary Kay Cosmetics. Looking like a cross between a circus and a Miss America pageant, the meeting takes place over a couple of days in a large auditorium, on a stage in front of a large, cheering audience, with all the participants dressed in glamorous formal evening wear. Salespeople are rewarded for their successes in achieving sales goals with an array of flashy gifts, including gold and diamond pins, furs, and pink cars. This ritual serves as a motivator to employees by publicly acknowledging outstanding sales performance. It also reinforces the determination and optimism of the late founder, Mary Kay Ash, who overcame personal hardships, founded her own company, and achieved material success. It conveys to all salespeople that they too can achieve success through hard work and reaching their sales goals. But a ritual doesn't have to be elaborate to instill and reinforce the key corporate values. It may be something as simple as a Friday afternoon celebration at the end of a successful week. The important thing is that the rituals express and reinforce the desired values.

Entrepreneurs in Action

Auditioning for a job. Sounds like something that actors, singers, or comedians might have to do. But auditioning for a software engineer's job? Yet, at Athene Software Inc. in Boulder, Colorado, potential employees have to audition for jobs. CEO Eric Johnson, a serial entrepreneur on his fifth start-up, says that it's a good way to find out what a person is really like and whether they'll fit in. All employees are invited to the auditions and their opinions matter in the final decision on hiring. Everyone gets to question the auditioner and to comment afterward by e-mail.

Sources: Company information from Hoover's Online (**www.hoovers.com**), May 31, 2002; and R. D. Schatz, "Showtime at Athene," *Business Week Frontier*, March 5, 2001, p. F26.

Material Symbols. Material symbols can include, for example, office location, office furnishings, office size, employee lounges and workout facilities, technological equipment, or reserved parking spaces. Who gets these material symbols conveys to employees who's important and the kinds of behavior (for example, risk-taking, conservative, individualistic, team player) that are expected. If the organization takes the approach that all organizational members share in the material symbols, it's conveying that egalitarianism is important. For example, a story on the national evening news told about the owner of a long-distance phone company in New Jersey who provided all his employees who had been there a certain number of years with a year's lease on a brand-new BMW.[8] The founder explained his actions by saying that he wanted to reward employees who stayed with him because he was spending around $1 million a year to train new employees. It was actually cheaper for him to lease, insure, and license these cars to keep his current employees than it would have been for him to retrain new ones continually. What expectations, values, and behavioral norms would these BMWs convey to new employees and to employees who hadn't yet been there the specified number of years?

Language. Many organizations and even work units within organizations use a special language as a way to identify members. By learning this "language," members attest to their acceptance of the culture, and in so doing, help preserve it. Over time, organizations often develop unique terminology to describe equipment, key personnel, suppliers, customers, or products that are related to the business. This unique terminology can act as a common denominator that unites members of the organization. In turn, this special language makes people feel like they're part of something unique and that they need to preserve that uniqueness by "using" the language.

Role of Physical Surroundings. As we're looking at planning the entrepreneurial venture, we can't forget that the organization's physical work space plays a role in its culture. The way an organization arranges and decorates its physical surroundings should reinforce its culture. For instance, if collaboration among employees is an important and valued behavior, then the work space should be arranged to support and facilitate open discussion. Or, if innovativeness is an important company value, the work space should support people in experimenting and being innovative. Think back to our chapter-opening case and how SOL's physical surroundings—bright, colorful, open, high-tech—reinforced its core values. There's no doubt that the physical work space can play an important role in reinforcing and supporting the shared values, beliefs, and behavioral norms.

The Importance of Understanding Culture

Many people don't like to think about organizational culture because it's not an easy thing to see, describe, or explain. Yet, when you walk into a business, you *do* get a feeling for its culture. You can tell *something* about what the people there think is important. That's one reason why an entrepreneur needs to understand organizational culture—because culture defines what's important and what's not important. Every organization has some kind of culture because every organization is made up of people and people have values, beliefs, and expectations. These values, beliefs, and expectations become the organizational culture, which, in

FYI

Building a Healthy Culture

A healthy organizational culture—one that nurtures, supports, encourages, and motivates organizational members—can be an important advantage for companies. If organizational members don't feel as strongly about the organization as the founders or the key decision makers do, then it's time to take action to get them to feel that way. In other words, it's time to give your organizational culture a check-up and to prescribe some healing medicine! How can you build a healthy culture? Even though every organizational situation is different, there are some general guidelines that you can follow to achieve a healthy culture. These guidelines include: (1) *Change has to start at the top.* If the present organizational culture is sick—that is, it's not working—and cultural change is needed, the person at the top is the one who will have to champion this change. (2) *Think about your culture when hiring.* Job applicants need to be aware of the organization's values, beliefs, and expectations so they know what they're getting into. Cultural "fit" between employee and organization is critical. (3) *Two-way communication is important.* Sharing information is a way to discover problems and to resolve them. It's a way of acknowledging that "we're all in this together." (4) *If you don't believe in it, don't fake it.* If certain values and beliefs are important, make sure that your actions support your words. For instance, don't profess to believe in individual participation in decision making and then not ever give employees the opportunity to make decisions. Nothing can sicken an organizational culture faster than not backing up your words with actions. Although nurturing your organizational culture may seem a waste of time and effort, keep in mind that a healthy culture can support a long and productive organizational life—just as a healthy body supports a long and productive personal life!

Sources: J. Case, "Corporate Culture," *Inc.*, November 1996, pp. 42–53; and M. Barrier, "Building a Healthy Company Culture," *Nation's Business*, September 1997, pp. 57–59.

turn, influences what people do and say, and how they do it because they know it's important or unimportant.

Another reason understanding culture is important is that culture can be a source of competitive advantage. Maybe an entrepreneurial venture can't compete on the basis of having the most complete product line with every style, color, and variation under the sun or by having numerous locations, but maybe it can have a culture that rewards employees for innovativeness or teamwork or whatever else the organization thinks is important. For example, Amy's Ice Creams (**www.amysicecream.com**), a chain of premium ice cream shops in central Texas, has a unique culture that sets the stores apart and contributes significantly to their success.[9] Employees are encouraged to entertain customers. They juggle with their serving spades, toss scoops of ice cream to one another behind the counter, and dance on the countertops. They often offer free ice cream to anyone who will sing, dance, recite a poem, or mimic a barnyard animal (cows are especially encouraged!). They might be wearing pajamas (because it's sleepover night) or there might be colorful pulsating strobe lights throughout the store (because it's disco night). They wear costumes. They express their individuality. They create fun. It's a culture that employees embrace as enthusiastically as do the customers. Amy Miller, the entrepreneur behind Amy's Ice Creams, had to find a way to keep

Rapid Review

- ✔ List and describe each of the ways that culture is learned by organizational members.
- ✔ What role do physical surroundings play in organizational culture?
- ✔ Why is it important for entrepreneurs to understand organizational culture?
- ✔ What does it take to build a healthy organizational culture?

her ice cream shops from becoming just another commodity product amid a vast array of competitors. She believed that the way to do that was to sell an experience that the customer wouldn't forget. In order to do that, she had to create and nurture a culture that made employees *want* to provide those unforgettable customer experiences. As Amy Miller discovered, having the right culture can help an organization resolve critical competitive advantage issues.

The final reason it's important for entrepreneurs to understand organizational culture is that the culture serves as a powerful guide for decisions and actions. As we said earlier, the shared values and beliefs that are the organizational culture should be stated in the organizational vision and mission statements. Organizational members know from these statements what the organization believes and what it values. They know what's expected of them and what guidelines they should use as they make decisions and do their work. In this sense, the culture shapes behavior and serves as a guide to what's acceptable and what's not.

Although planning for the vision and mission statements and the organizational culture may entail looking at factors (including values, beliefs, and so forth) that are hard to describe and explain, the final aspect of planning the entrepreneurial venture isn't quite as abstract, although it, too, may involve some uncertainties! And that's the process of developing and writing the business plan.

DEVELOPING AND WRITING THE BUSINESS PLAN

For many would-be entrepreneurs, developing and writing a business plan is a daunting task. However, a good business plan is essential. It pulls together all the elements of the entrepreneur's vision into a single document. The business plan requires careful planning and creative thinking, but, if it is done well, it can serve many functions. In this section, we're going to look at what's involved with developing and writing an effective business plan.

Why Is a Business Plan Important?

Satchel Paige, the famous baseball player, once said, "If you don't know where you're going, any road will take you there." As an entrepreneur, you *want* to know where you're going. You want to *choose* that road, not just take any one. The process of developing and writing a business plan will help you identify and clarify many of the issues that need to be addressed as an entrepreneurial venture is organized, launched, and managed. Preparing the business plan is an important outcome of the planning process.

The process of planning involves deciding where you want to go, how to get there, and what to do to reduce (as much as possible) any uncertainties. It's a way of thinking about the future in which planning serves as the bridge between the present and the future—that is, where we currently are and where we would like to be. For instance, think of the college degree you'd like to get someday. You've had to plan your classes semester by semester so that you complete the required ones in the correct sequence for getting that desired degree. Perhaps you've followed a degree program—a type of planning document—that outlines where you are currently and where you would like to be. That "plan" serves as the bridge between the present and the future until one day that goal of graduating with a college degree is attained. For an entrepreneurial venture, one document that results from the planning process is a **business plan**, which is a written document that summarizes a business opportunity and defines how the identified opportunity is to be seized and exploited. The process of developing and writing a business plan involves critically analyzing where your venture currently is and where it's headed. That business plan, then, becomes a blueprint and road map for operating the ongoing business, and not just simply done for the start-up phase. Instead, the business plan serves as a "living" document that guides the entrepreneur as he or she makes decisions throughout the life of the entrepreneurial venture.

As you might be able to conclude so far, the business plan *is* an important document for entrepreneurs. It serves five main purposes, as shown in Exhibit 4-5.

The first purpose of a business plan is that it's a development tool for the organizational founders. As the founders identify and assess opportunities, the structured outline of a business plan forces them to address important issues. Rather than just blindly and wildly pursuing ideas, the business plan provides a check and balance for the founders. This type of structured start-up planning by entrepreneurs has been widely studied by researchers who, for the most part, agree that this type of planning can be beneficial.[10]

The business plan's second purpose is that it is useful for helping to clarify the venture's vision and mission. As we discussed earlier in this chapter, organizational vision and mission statements are important elements in planning the entrepreneurial venture. When included in the business plan, these statements describe and explain to others what this entrepreneurial venture is about. Again, the founders are "forced" to carefully consider their organizational purpose, values, and expectations.

The third purpose that the business plan serves is that it defines planning and evaluation guidelines for managing the ongoing entrepreneurial venture. As we stated earlier, the business plan is a working document that should be used beyond the start-up phase. It should guide decision makers on planning and evaluating issues throughout the life of the business. It also should help clarify what the goals and plans are, and it should help to define how goal attainment is going to be measured. However, we need to be aware of the fact that although a business plan attempts to define a desirable future path for the venture, unexpected factors can—and often do—significantly alter that path. But even given the fact

EXHIBIT 4-5 Purposes of a Business Plan

- Development tool for organizational founders
- Vision and mission clarification
- Planning and evaluation guidelines
- Tool for securing financial resources
- Tool for guiding growth

Criticisms of Planning

Formalized planning became popular in businesses in the 1960s and, for the most part, remains so today. It makes sense for an organization to establish some direction. But critics have challenged some of the basic assumptions of planning. These criticisms include:

1. *Planning may create rigidity.* Formal planning efforts can lock an organization into specific goals to be achieved within specific timetables. If the environment changes during that period, an entrepreneur who continues to follow a rigid plan may be in trouble.
2. *Plans can't be developed for a dynamic environment.* Most organizations today—large and small—face dynamic, often chaotic, environments. How can you make plans in that type of environment?
3. *Formal plans can't replace innovation and creativity.* Successful organizations are typically the result of someone's innovative vision. Yet, those visions have a tendency to become formalized as they evolve. Formal planning efforts involve a thorough investigation of the venture's opportunities and capabilities and a mechanical analysis that reduces the vision to some type of programmed routine. That type of analysis can kill creativity and innovation.
4. *Planning focuses entrepreneurs' attention on today's competition but not on tomorrow's survival.* Formal planning tends to focus on how best to capture existing business opportunities within existing industries. It may not allow entrepreneurs to consider reinventing or creating an industry.
5. *Formal planning reinforces success, which may lead to failure.* Success breeds success. If it's not broken, don't fix it, right? Maybe not! Success may, in fact, breed failure in an uncertain environment. It's hard to change or discard previously successful plans—to leave the comfort of what works for the anxiety of the unknown.

How valid are these criticisms? Should entrepreneurs just forget about doing business plans? No, entrepreneurs shouldn't forget about planning! Although the criticisms may be true for rigid, inflexible planning, today's entrepreneurs can be effective planners if they recognize that the business plan is just a road map, not a definitive statement that is followed to the letter.

Sources: J. Moore, "The Death of Competition," *Fortune,* April 15, 1996, pp. 142–43; G. Hamel and C. K. Prahalad, *Competing for the Future* (Boston: Harvard Business School Press), 1994; and H. Mintzberg, *The Rise and Fall of Strategic Planning* (New York: Free Press), 1994.

that uncertainties exist, *not* having some type of plan would make managing the uncertainties even more challenging for an entrepreneur.

Helping an entrepreneur secure needed financial resources is the next purpose served by business plans. Potential lenders and investors will require some type of financial analysis and projections before making a decision on whether to provide a loan or to invest capital in the business. These people aren't going to provide money without some type of analysis of current and future financial data. Again, the structured nature of the business plan forces an entrepreneur to do these important calculations and projections. This is often the hardest part for an entrepreneur in preparing a business plan, but it is critical to include because it will be absolutely necessary to obtain any potential outside financing.

Entrepreneurs in Action

The best way to describe CARS (Comprehensive Automotive Reclamation Services) is that they're an auto manufacturer in reverse. CARS is the largest salvage yard in the country and can dismantle up to 30,000 vehicles a year and reclaim about 99 percent of the car. When founder William Hyman needed financing, he knew he'd have to be prepared. "I went in with a really detailed business plan." That plan included a design of the disassembly line, signed agreements from insurance companies and other organizations that would provide the cars, as well as letters from metal processors and rebuilders that agreed to buy the scrap. Today, General Motors is CARS's largest customer, buying all the scrap metal, 60 percent of the reclaimed batteries, and all the catalytic converters from the dismantled automobiles.

Source: C. Ghosh, "Junkyard Dog," *Forbes*, April 16, 2001, pp. 314–315.

The final purpose of the business plan is that it's an effective tool for guiding growth. We know that what characterizes an entrepreneurial venture is its focus on growth. Although some entrepreneurs may get lucky and growth just sort of "happens," you don't want to bank your future on luck. A well-written business plan can lay the foundation for growth to happen. As we've said before, the business plan provides the road map for pursuing the opportunities that await. A successful entrepreneur doesn't want to "take just any road," but needs to plan for the future and the future growth of the venture through developing a strong business plan.

What Should the Business Plan Include?

A thorough, complete, and *effective* business plan can be lengthy—often 10–15 pages or even longer. Yes, it takes time and effort to prepare, but as we've just seen, the business plan is important. It's a critical tool for successfully launching and managing the business. Practically all authors who have written about entrepreneurs and entrepreneurial issues have their own ideas about what should be included in a business plan.[11] We think a good business plan should include six major areas. These are the executive summary, analysis of the opportunity, analysis of the context, description of the business, financial data and projections, and supporting documentation. Let's look at each.

Executive Summary. Some experts recommend that the executive summary go at the beginning of the business plan so that readers will know the key points being made in the document; others recommend that it go at the end in order to summarize what's been presented. Both of these arguments make sense, so you need to decide which you feel more comfortable doing. The key thing is that the report includes an executive summary. What information should be included in the executive summary? It should summarize the key points the entrepreneur wants to make about the entrepreneurial venture. These might include brief state-

The Grey Zone When putting together your business plan, how truthful should you be? When putting together the analyses of the opportunities and the context, is it okay to "creatively enhance" the research you've done—to make the situation look better than it might be? Are there any circumstances when it *might be* acceptable to use creative enhancements? Is distorting information always wrong, or might it be acceptable under certain circumstances?

ments of vision and mission; primary goals and objectives; history of the venture, including, perhaps, a time line; key people involved in the venture; nature of the business; concise product or service descriptions; explanation of market niche, competitors, and competitive advantage; proposed strategies; and a summary of financial information. Some have suggested that obvious concerns and challenges be presented in the executive summary as well. The important thing to remember about the executive summary is that it should be concise yet comprehensive. The reader should be able to obtain all the significant information highlights about the venture from this section. The rest of the business plan, then, fleshes out this information.

Analysis of Opportunity. Remember our discussion in Chapter 3 about how important the identification and analysis of opportunities are? In this section of the business plan, you want to present the detail of your analysis of the perceived opportunity. Essentially, this means (1) sizing up the market by describing the demographics of the target market—who the customers are, how many of them there are, what values and expectations they may have, how the product or service will meet their needs, and so forth; (2) describing and evaluating industry trends—what the current status of the industry is, what the trends in the industry are, evaluation of the industry growth rate (is it a growing, stable, or declining industry), what it takes to be successful in this industry, and so forth; and (3) identifying and evaluating competitors—who they are, what competitive strengths and weaknesses they have, what they are doing currently, and so forth. If, in the process of researching the venture's feasibility, a feasibility study was completed—as we recommended—the information included in it can be the basis for the material in this section of the business plan. You must show that you have thoroughly researched this market and that you know as much as possible about the advantages and drawbacks of this proposed opportunity.

Analysis of the Context. Whereas the opportunity analysis focuses on the opportunity(ies) in a specific industry and market, the context analysis takes a much broader perspective. Entrepreneurial opportunities exist in a context, and in this section of the business plan, you want to address this context. What should be included here? You should describe broad external changes and trends. These external factors might include an analysis of the macroeconomic environment such as the state of the economy, current and forecasted interest rates or inflation, trends in consumer spending, or any other important economic trends that might have a significant impact on the entrepreneurial venture; an evaluation of any current or proposed governmental rules and regulations that might potentially have an impact on the entrepreneurial venture; an analysis of broad technological trends not related to the specific market or industry that might affect the entrepreneurial venture; and, if appropriate, a description of global changes and trends that might have an impact on the entrepreneurial venture.

Entrepreneurs in Action

When Patricia Adams, CEO of College Capital (**www.collegecapital.com**), first started looking for outside funding, it was two months before the dot-com meltdown. She had prepared a business plan that was just 15 pages long, as investors were looking for "a short, quick, fast read explaining what the business is and explaining how much money you want." But when the Internet bubble popped, that short business plan wasn't working. Adams knew that when the market changed, she had to change her business plan. And she did. Her business plan now fills two three-inch binders. It's thorough, comprehensive, and covers the gamut from descriptions of the market to descriptions of her business.

Sources: Company information from **www.collegecapital.com**, May 31, 2002; and E. Barker, "The Bullet-Proof Business Plan," *Inc.*, October 16, 2001, pp. 102–104.

Description of the Business. In the previous sections of the business plan, you've described the "whats"—what you see as the potential opportunity you hope to capture and exploit. You've described and evaluated the significant trends and changes that might affect your entrepreneurial venture. Now, you're ready to explain the "hows"—the specifics of how you will capture and exploit the opportunity(ies). Specifically, what this section describes is how you're going to organize, launch, and manage the venture. This section provides a thorough explanation of the following: vision and mission statements and a description of the desired organizational culture; marketing plans, including overall marketing strategy, pricing, sales tactics, service-warranty policies, and advertising and promotion tactics; product development plans, such as an explanation of development status (prototype availability) and tasks, difficulties and risks, and anticipated costs; manufacturing and operations plans, such as description of proposed geographic location, facilities and improvement, equipment, and work flow; human resource plans, including a description of key employees, composition of the board of advisers, including their background experience and skills, current and predicted future staffing needs, compensation and benefits, and training needs; and an overall schedule and timetable of events.

Financial Data and Projections. Every effective business plan contains financial data and projections. You must have these! Although these calculations and interpretations may be difficult, they are absolutely critical. No business plan is complete without financial information. What, then, should be included in this section? Financial plans should cover at least three years and contain projected income (profit-and-loss) statements, pro forma cash-flow analysis (monthly for the first year and quarterly for the next two), pro forma balance sheets, break-even analysis, and cost controls. If you anticipate equipment purchases or other major capital expenditures, list the items, costs, and what collateral you have available. In your financial projections and analyses, provide explanatory notes whenever the data seem contradictory or unclear. Try to make your financial projections as realistic as possible. Do your research. Research costs, prices being charged by competitors, and any other quantitative information that will add to the validity and reliability of your data. Although much of your financial analysis is based on assumptions, if you back up your assumptions with logical reasoning and appropriate analysis, you can minimize the inherent problems of making assumptions.

Supporting Documentation. You may have had professors say to you, "Support what you say—support, support, support." I know I've said this to my students many times! Supporting documentation *is* an important component of an effective business plan. Back up your descriptions with charts, graphs, tables, photographs, or other visual tools. In addition, you'll want to provide information (personal and work-related) about the key participants in the venture. Through these supporting documents, you can provide additional details about the information being presented in the actual business plan.

Writing the Business Plan

Explaining your business idea on paper can be an intimidating challenge! Moving from the unabashed exuberance and excitement over the potential of "this great idea" to the harsh reality of describing it in concrete, specific, and explicit terms can prove to be exhausting physically, mentally, and emotionally. However, there is help! Software templates (such as BizPlan Pro), books, and Web sites (check out the following: **www.inc.com**, **www.moneyhunt.com**, **www.bplans.com**, and **www.lowe.org**, to name a few) can help entrepreneurs write business plans. Keep in mind, however, that when you're using these tools, you're using a standardized format that might not adequately describe your unique situation. Be sure to tailor and amend any business plan templates to fit what you're doing.

Just as the idea for an entrepreneurial venture takes time to germinate, so does the writing of a good business plan. It's important to put serious thought

FYI

Writing a Successful Business Plan

We now know that a business plan is a critically important document. How can you create a business plan that's going to win a Pulitzer Prize? Okay, so they don't give Pulitzers for business plans. How *can* you write a business plan that's going to "wow" whoever reads it and that's going to serve as an effective road map for the long-term success of your entrepreneurial venture? What makes for a successful business plan? Here are 10 characteristics:

1. Clear, realistic financial projections
2. Detailed market research
3. Detailed competitor research
4. Descriptions of key decision makers
5. Thorough summary
6. Proof of vision
7. Good formatting and clear writing
8. Brief and concise
9. Writing that demonstrates an understanding of the importance of the bottom line
10. A plan that captures "you"

Sources: P. Gallagher, "Getting Down to Business," *Success,* April 2001, pp. 50–53; and L. Elkins, "Tips for Preparing a Business Plan," *Nation's Business,* June 1996, pp. 60R–61R.

Rapid Review

- ✔ What is a business plan?
- ✔ Why is a business plan important?
- ✔ What five purposes does the business plan serve?
- ✔ List and describe the six major areas that should be included in a business plan.
- ✔ What are some things to remember about the actual writing of the business plan?

and consideration into the plan and to develop one that has all the necessary elements. Because this process can take several days, if not weeks, be prepared to spend whatever time and effort is needed. You don't need to be a professional writer to come up with a solid business plan, but you do need to be able to write clearly and concisely. The resulting document should be something that will serve as a road map for current decisions, and if revised and updated as needed, for future decisions as well.

CHAPTER SUMMARY

This summary is organized around the chapter-opening objectives.

1. The organizational vision is a broad comprehensive picture of what an entrepreneur wants his or her organization to become. The vision is the statement of the entrepreneur's dream. The organizational mission is a statement of what the various organizational units (work groups, projects, departments, and so forth) do and what they hope to accomplish in alignment with the organizational vision. A venture will have only one vision, but potentially several missions that contribute to the pursuit of the vision.
2. The organizational vision and mission are important because they provide direction and guidance for making decisions and taking actions. In addition, they provide the means for expressing and clarifying the organization's values. The vision and mission also help the entrepreneur and other organizational members identify and clarify the venture's purpose and direction. Finally, research has shown that high-performing organizations have more comprehensive and thorough vision and mission statements than do low-performing organizations.
3. Although it can be difficult to express the organization's vision and mission in writing, entrepreneurs should, first of all, be committed to the importance of having these formal written documents. The next step in developing the vision and mission is finding examples of statements used by other organizations. Use these as guides to key points or important values. After studying the sample vision and mission statements, write your own. Finally, have trusted associates (friends and family) critically evaluate your statements. Continue to revise and rewrite until you have vision and mission statements that you feel best capture the essence of your entrepreneurial venture.
4. The four components of organizational vision are a description of the venture's core values and beliefs, which stem from what the founder(s) believes is important, a statement of the purpose of the organization, a brief summary of what the organization does, and a general description of the organization's goals. The nine components of a mission statement include descriptions of customers; products or services; markets; technology; concern for survival, profitability, and growth; philosophy; self-concept or competitive advantage; concern for public image; and concern for employees.

5. Organizational culture is the values, beliefs, and behavioral norms shared by organizational members that influence the way they do their work.
6. Research into organizational culture suggests that seven dimensions capture the essence of an organization's culture. These seven dimensions are innovation and risk-taking, attention to detail, outcome orientation, people orientation, team orientation, aggressiveness, and stability. The degree of each of these dimensions will range from low to high, and an organization's personality will reflect which of these dimensions are valued and prized.
7. An organization's culture (shared beliefs, values, and behavioral norms) comes originally from the founder. This person establishes the early culture of the organization through his or her beliefs and biases about how best to pursue the venture.
8. The culture of an organization is learned by employees in a number of ways, mainly through stories, rituals, material symbols, and language. Stories are narratives that describe significant events or people in the organization. Rituals are repetitive sequences of activities that express and reinforce the key shared values of the organization and what goals are most important. Who in the organization receives and does not receive certain material symbols such as office furnishings, reserved parking spaces, or technological equipment conveys to employees what's important or not important. Many organizations and work units use a special language as a way to identify members. By learning this language, members attest to its importance and their acceptance of it.
9. It's important for an entrepreneur to understand organizational culture because culture defines what's important and what's not important. Also, culture can serve as a source of competitive advantage. Finally, it's important to understand culture because the culture serves as a powerful guide for decisions and actions.
10. The business plan serves five main purposes. First, it's a development tool for the organizational founders. Second, it's useful for helping to clarify the venture's vision and mission. Next, it defines planning and evaluation guidelines for managing the ongoing entrepreneurial venture. In addition, the business plan helps an entrepreneur secure needed financial resources. Finally, the business plan is an effective tool for guiding growth.
11. The business plan contains six major components. First, is the executive summary, which summarizes the key points the entrepreneur wants to make about the entrepreneurial venture. Next, is the analysis of opportunity section, which presents a detailed analysis of the perceived opportunity. Third, is the analysis of context, which focuses on broad external changes and trends. Then, the description of business section describes the specifics of how the opportunity will be captured and exploited. The fifth section is the financial data and projections. Finally, the sixth section includes all the supporting documentation such as graphs, tables, photographs, résumés, and so forth.
12. Actually preparing a business plan entails putting it on paper. Help in writing the business plan can be found through software templates, books, and

Web sites. In addition, it's important for an entrepreneur to recognize that writing a good business plan takes serious thought and consideration. Be prepared to spend the time and effort that's needed.

KEY TERMS

- *Vision:* A broad comprehensive picture of what an entrepreneur wants his or her organization to become.
- *Mission:* A statement of what the various organizational units do and what they hope to accomplish in alignment with the organizational vision.
- *Goals:* Outcomes or end results that are desired by individuals, groups, or organizations.
- *Organizational culture:* The beliefs, values, and behavioral norms shared by organizational members that influence the way they do their work.
- *Business plan:* A written document that summarizes a business opportunity and defines how the identified opportunity is to be seized and exploited.

SWEAT EQUITY

1. Do you agree or disagree with the following statements? Discuss.
   - "A good business plan won't make you succeed."
   - "A business plan has the ability to prevent you from wasting your time on something that can't succeed."
   - "You should write a business plan even if you don't need outside financing."
2. Do an Internet search of five different company sites (large or small). Look for the following information and then write a report describing what you found. Be sure to provide the Web site addresses for each of the companies you research.
   - What can you tell about this company's culture from its Web site? What clues did you observe?
   - Were there any descriptions of stories, rituals, material symbols, language, or physical surroundings included on the Web site? If so, describe, If not, create and describe an appropriate ritual and material symbols that this company might use.
   - Was a vision or mission statement included on the Web site? If so, what is it? Do you think it's a good vision or mission statement? Why or why not? If there are no vision or mission statements, write one for the company.
3. Get into teams of three or four people. Select one of the two companies described below. Then complete the required tasks at the end of the descriptions.

   Company A

   Yes, pet owners tend to be a pretty sentimental bunch, and yes, they tend to buy lots of stuff for their beloved pets. (Every year people spend over $9 billion worldwide to feed their pets.) However, there's little competition for gourmet pet snacks—custom-blended snacks made of all-natural ingredients. Three Dog Bakery (**www.threedog.com**) of Kansas City, Missouri, is out to change the face of pet snacks by offering gourmet doggy biscuits made up of a delicious blend of garlic, spinach, and carrots.

Company B

Timeless beauty, practicality, and flexibility. All words used to describe Cleveland Glass Block's (**www.clevelandglassblock.com**) products—glass blocks used by residential homeowners and in commercial applications. The company is an MD—Master Distributor—for Pittsburgh Corning Glass Block products, handling the complete product line and no others. In addition, the company is one of only a few MDs that also manufactures the glass blocks.

To Do:

Write an organizational vision statement and a mission statement(s) for your chosen company. Write an executive summary for the company you chose. Write an abbreviated business plan outline. Your team must be prepared to present its information to the rest of the class. Make sure you cover all the necessary areas because others will be trying to find "holes" in your business plan material.

4. Do an Internet search using any search engine for the phrase *business plan.* Link to 10 entries from your search and write an analysis of what each site has to offer. Be thorough, descriptive, and critical. Be sure to identify the Web site address in your analysis.

   Now, do the same thing for the phrase *organizational culture*. Also, write an analysis using the above guidelines of 10 entries from this search.
5. Organizations have their own unique personalities—that is, their cultures. Visit seven different organizations (you might even want to try one or two not-for-profit ones) and observe the physical surroundings. Make note of work arrangements, what's on the walls, how you're greeted or treated, interactions between employees, and any other cultural clues that you might observe about this organization. Write up a description of what you observed at each business. Now, compare this information to the seven dimensions of organizational culture we discussed in the chapter. What type of organizational culture would you say each organization exhibits? How did you come to that conclusion?
6. The responses to a survey of equity investors as to the most important elements of a business proposal, in order of importance, were as follows:
   - Strong management team—83 percent
   - Strong return on investment—39 percent
   - Good business idea—39 percent
   - Solid financial projections—36 percent
   - Insightful market analysis—17 percent

   How do these responses relate to what was discussed in this chapter? How might these responses affect what an entrepreneur includes in a business plan?
7. "The environment we operate in is changing so rapidly and is so unpredictable that the time spent on preparing a business plan is wasted." What do you think? Come up with arguments for both sides of this issue—yes, planning is a waste of time, and no, planning is not a waste of time. Be prepared to debate your points.

8. Using the Internet, what information can you find that would help you prepare a business plan for: a new line of long-lasting lipsticks and eye shadows; a new manufacturer of golf clubs; and a new kitchen housewares retailing business? Provide a brief summary of each of the sites you find (including the Web site address).
9. Research goal setting. What do the experts say about setting goals? What guidelines can you come up with for setting goals? Are these guidelines applicable to entrepreneurial ventures? If so, why? If not, rewrite them so they are.

ENTREPRENEURSHIP IN ACTION CASES

SOL Cleaning Services

This case can be found at the beginning of Chapter 4.

Discussion Questions

1. Using Exhibit 4-4, describe SOL's organizational culture.
2. Would the five values that characterize SOL's culture be as effective in other types of organizations? Why or why not?
3. Describe how you think new employees at SOL might learn the culture.

Empower Trainers & Consultants, Inc.

At Empower Trainers and Consultants, associates (there are no "employees") take organizational culture very seriously. Michael and Caroline May have built a successful company in which people dress up as "sparkle" fairies, candy is tossed around at meetings, Foosball competitions are held in the hallways, and mistakes are publicized, not ridiculed or criticized. Culture is an important component of Empower's way of doing business.

Empower provides computer training, applications development, and Internet instructions to clients around Shawnee Mission, a suburb of Kansas City, where it is based. When May started his company, he brought with him thoughts and ideas from previous jobs and from reading about and interacting with other successful entrepreneurs. He knew what he wanted his company to be like. The company's 21-word mission statement—To become number one or number three in all markets we serve and to make this company fun, fast, and fulfilling—can be recited by everyone at Empower. Now, you may be asking yourself, why number one or number three? May explains that you should never settle for second best and being number three gives you something to shoot for (ideas he borrowed from Jack Welch, retired CEO of global powerhouse General Electric).

There are numerous other unusual cultural characteristics of Empower. For example, there's Sparkle. Sparkle captures in one word the sort of personality an Empower associate is always expected to project. Sparkle the Fairy (a character dreamed up by Susan Burden, the first employee hired by Michael and Caroline) will appear and shower associates with glitter and recite a poem: "This Sparkle Power I give you today/ Will empower you in a special way/We hope you will always keep this in mind/To make Empower one of a kind." Every other Tuesday at the company's regular companywide team meeting, everyone recites the poem and new associates get sparkled by a team of Sparkle Fairies. Or, take, for instance, what happens if someone uses the word *employee, boss,* or *manager.* The offender must pay $5 a word into a big yellow crayon bank. The money collected (averaging about $75 a year) goes to charity. Issues that affect everyone are put to a majority-rule vote. Written policies are few and far between. One important written policy, however, is the Cookie and Bagel–Doughnut Policy (68 words long—more than three times as long as the mission statement), which prohibits raids on the refreshments served to client students who are at the company's offices taking computer training. Then, there's the shared belief that to be successful, first and foremost, business should be fun. Finally, there's the attitude toward making mistakes. May says, "If you're not making seven mistakes a day, you're just not trying hard enough." Associates at Empower are encouraged to post "Today's List of Mistakes" on a piece of paper that has, of course, seven lines. The feeling is that mistakes that are hidden can become real land mines ready to explode at any time.

Although Empower's culture may sound curiously strange (to be polite), it works for the company. The company's distinctive and effective culture has enabled it to build the kind of workplace that attracts and keeps top-of-the-line technical talent.

Discussion Questions

1. Evaluate Empower's mission statement. How would you interpret it? Does it include what it should? According to our definitions, would this be a mission or a vision statement? Explain.
2. Describe and evaluate the examples of organizational rituals, language, and shared values. Would these work in other types and sizes of organizations? Explain.
3. Some busy entrepreneurs know that culture is important but feel they don't have the time to create a distinctive culture. They outsource (hire outside consultants) to come in and do it. What would be the benefits and drawbacks of this approach?

Sources: Information on company from Hoover's Online (**www.hoovers.com**), May 31, 2002; and N. K. Austin, "The Cultural Evolution," *Inc. 500,* 1997, pp. 72–80.

Digital Mafia Entertainment (www.digitalmafia.com)

You might wonder about a company with a name like "Digital Mafia." Darien Dash started the company in 1994 when he realized that large cable companies weren't committed to bringing digital services to urban communities. In his job as vice president of sales for Digital Music Xpress, which provided CD-quality music through a regular cable box, Dash was repeatedly rejected by upper-level managers when he suggested bringing the service to inner cities. So he left the company and formed DME. His mission was to expand the hardware and software infrastructure of minority communities. Today DME is a total Internet services company based in Englewood Cliffs, New Jersey. Its employees provide network design, e-commerce, Web site maintenance, and advertising for a variety of clients, including HBO Home Video, the New York Knicks, Lugz, and MSBET. As the company has evolved into a well-rounded information technology company, Dash's vision has remained the same: "Expanding the hardware and software infrastructure within minority communities." However, doing that hasn't been easy.

Although wiring inner cities was an admirable social goal, and one to which Dash remains steadfastly committed, it has not been the quickest way to generate revenues. Like many new businesses, DME initially didn't have sufficient cash flow to pay employees and to develop important business relationships. To pay the bills, Dash began consulting with other companies on how best to leverage multimedia and Internet technology. Soon the Web development side of the business was bringing in much-needed cash flow. That side of the business remains an important part of DME. Yet, Dash remains committed to being more than just a business making a buck—he wants to provide a service to inner cities that others have been unwilling to do.

Discussion Questions

1. What is DME's vision? What was the source of this vision statement?
2. Does DME's vision statement adequately capture what DME is? Explain. How might you rewrite the vision statement without losing the essence of Dash's dream?
3. What does an entrepreneur do when his or her business vision collides with reality—when he or she realizes that the vision may not be viable?
4. Darien Dash would like to build a values-based organization. How might he go about developing values that all DME employees could share?

Sources: Company Web site, **www.digitalmafia.com**, May 31, 2002; and T. K. Muhammad, "Talking Tech and the Stock Market," *Black Enterprise*, January 2000, pp. 45–46.

Burt's Bees (www.burtsbees.com)

Beeswax candles, lip balm, and baby oil. These are just a few of the unique personal care products manufactured by Burt's Bees, Inc., of Durham, North Carolina. And sell, they do—to the tune of some $30 million in 2000.

Burt's Bees was founded in 1984, when Roxanne Quimby met reclusive beekeeper Burt Shavitz in rural Maine. They began making candles, furniture polish, and lip balm from the beeswax, which obviously was in great abundance thanks to Burt's bees. Roxanne and Burt began selling their products at crafts fairs throughout New England. Sales exploded, and they soon had to move their factory from Roxanne's kitchen to an abandoned schoolhouse and then to three trailers parked on her front lawn. When sales hit the $3 million mark in 1993, Roxanne and Burt realized that they had outgrown the rural Maine landscape, where future growth would be restricted by high taxes and unskilled labor. However, fast-paced urban life wasn't at all appealing. To maintain that simple down-home atmosphere that was so important to the company, Roxanne looked at different locations, eventually settling in Raleigh, North Carolina, a hub of cosmetics manufacturing.

Roxanne is the current President and CEO, having bought out Burt, who still lives in his turkey coop in rural Maine. Roxanne and Burt's commitment to a simple lifestyle always was reflected in the way they ran their business. Roxanne says that living off the land was actually good training for running a business, especially a start-up—you're always undercapitalized and looking for ways to survive. But after the move to North Carolina, Quimby got more serious about the business of Burt's Bees. She automated manufacturing and recruited an experienced management team. These changes have helped the company triple its sales over the last three years. Although Burt's Bees products may still have Burt's wrinkled old face on them, there's nothing old-fashioned about the way Burt's Bees is doing business.

Discussion Questions

1. Draw up an outline of a business plan that Roxanne and Burt might have used. You don't need to find or have the information to complete the business plan, but put some thought into explaining what information they might have wanted.
2. Would it be possible for a company such as Burt's Bees to keep its down-home, simple, and uncomplicated culture as it continues to grow? Explain.
3. There is no mention of a vision statement on the company's Web site. From what you know about the company, write a vision statement for Burt's Bees.
4. One of the things mentioned on the company's Web site is the company's commitment to conservation acquisitions. Check out what the company's Web site says about their efforts. How might this information affect the development of a vision statement, mission statement(s), organizational culture, and any future business plans?

Sources: Information from company's Web site (**www.burtsbees.com**) and Hoover's Online (**www.hoovers.com**), May 31, 2002; and J. Sloane, "From Maine to Mainstream," *Fortune*, October 16, 2000, pp. 312[J]–312[N].)

Megatoys (www.megatoys.com)

The toy industry, like all others, has its good points and its bad points. One person who's trying to take advantage of the good points—what he sees as the many growth opportunities in the toy industry—is an individual by the name of Charlie Woo, of Los Angeles.

Woo and his family came to the United States from Hong Kong in the late 1970s. To support the family, his mother and father initially opened a restaurant, but they found that venture to be too time consuming. They looked to start another business; they decided that the toy business looked like a good one. By using their contacts in Hong Kong and by bringing their four sons into the business, the Woo family opened ABC Toys. The company's initial goal was to manufacture and distribute toys to small wholesalers who couldn't get products from the large toy makers because they didn't buy enough volume. ABC Toys had identified a specific niche and hadn't intended to compete with Mattel, Hasbro, or other major toy manufacturers. Charlie, who was about to complete his Ph.D. in physics, found himself making a major career switch—from physics to toys.

ABC Toys purchased several dilapidated warehouses on a blighted corner of downtown Los Angeles. Charlie's vision was to encourage other small toy manufacturers and distributors to rent these buildings and by all working together, to create a "Toy Town." At first, ABC Toys was the only tenant. However, Charlie believed that this wholesale district would enable customers to come to one location, shop comparatively, and he hoped, end up buying more products than they would if they had to travel to separate stores. As more and more small toy companies joined ABC Toys in Toy Town, word soon spread and customers started coming in from all over. Today, this specialized commercial district has created a bustling marketplace that employs over 4,000 people, boasts revenues estimated at roughly $500 million a year, and controls the distribution of roughly 60 percent of the $12 billion in toys sold to U.S. retailers.

In 1989 Charlie and one of his brothers spun off a separate business called Megatoys. Employing approximately 30 people, this distribution company has annual sales in excess of $30 million. And Charlie isn't finished yet! Part of his plan for Toy Town and Megatoys involves expanding the number of customers they serve. Why? He believes that there is still good potential for growth in his business because the changing global trade environment is opening up many potentially profitable opportunities.

Discussion Questions

1. What role does a founder play in the vision for an entrepreneurial venture? Assess Charlie Woo's role in ABC Toys, Megatoys, and Toy Town.
2. Charlie wants to continue Megatoys' growth. Would a business plan be necessary? Explain. What would a business plan for his business need to include?
3. We know that growth is a distinguishing characteristic of entrepreneurial ventures. What challenges does an entrepreneur face in maintaining an organization's culture as it grows? How can an entrepreneur meet these challenges?
4. Charlie has asked you to make a presentation to his employees about the importance of organizational vision and mission. Draw up a list of the main ideas you'd want to tell them.
5. Write a vision statement for Toy Town and for Megatoys.

Sources: J. Kotkin, "Movers and Shakers," ***Reason Magazine***, December 2000, accessed at **www.reason.com**, June 3, 2002; and A. Wooldridge, "Toy Story," *Fortune*, June 26, 2000, pp. 258–72.

BUSINESS PLAN PRO

EXERCISE 4-1: Adding an Organization Vision Statement

Business Plan Pro's default outline includes a mission statement, but not an organizational vision statement. This exercise adds the vision statement to the outline.

- Using any one of the business plans you've worked on for previous exercises, or a new plan of your choosing, click the "Plan Outline" icon in the tool bar to view the plan outline. Add a topic for the Organizational Vision, wherever you think appropriate (*Hint: probably either in the first or the second chapter*). You can get more details on how to add a topic to the outline in Chapter 5 of your Business Plan Pro manual, or by searching the Business Plan Pro Help Index for "Add topic."

- Complete an organizational vision statement for this plan, in the new added topic.
- If the plan doesn't already have a mission statement, from a previous exercise, add one. If it does, review the mission statement for the content suggestions included in this chapter. Revise the mission statement as you see fit.

EXERCISE 4-2: Exploring the Metolius Plan

Open Business Plan Pro, start a new plan or open an existing one, and open your Sample Plan Browser. Do a keyword search on "graphics" to find the Metolius River Graphics plan, listed as "Graphic Services" in SIC code 7336.

- Use the Sample Plan Browser's **File>Open in Business Plan Pro** command to open this business plan inside Business Plan Pro.
- Use Business Plan Pro navigation to go to the Balance Sheet (*Hint:* you can find the Balance Sheet in the Task list in the Easy Plan Wizard, in the Plan Outline View, or with the **Views>Tables** command). Execute the **Edit>Formula** Reset command to reset standard formulas in the balance sheet (sample plans come with hard-coded data in these areas).erify.
- Use the **View>Charts>Cash (planned)** command to access the Cash Flow chart.

  According to this plan, Metolius will have sufficient cash for its first year of business. The cash balance will be less than $15,000 in April and May. You can view the Cash Flow table to verify.
- Use the **View>Charts>Profit Monthly (planned)** command or other navigation to view the Monthly Net Profit chart. It should show losses for most of the first six months, and profits for most of the last six months of the year.
- Use the Easy Plan Wizard to find the sales on credit question in Plan Setup and change the answer to "yes." Make sure to click the "Next" button.
- Find the General Assumptions table. You can find it in the Easy Plan Wizard section called "The Bottom Line," or you can use the View>Tables>General Assumptions command, or use the Plan Outline view. Change the Sales on Credit % assumption to 100%. A graphics design company sells to businesses, and businesses expect to pay invoices a few weeks later.
- Use the **View>Charts>Profit Monthly (Planned)** command to view the Profit Monthly Chart. Has it changed?
- Use the **View>Charts>Cash (Planned)** command to view the Cash Flow chart. Has it changed? In what direction? Why?
- Read the Metolius Graphics' plan market analysis describing its target market. Do you think its customers pay for graphics in cash, or do they expect to receive an invoice and pay later? Do you think the change suggested in this exercise is important? What do you think about the value of a plan in this case?

BUSINESS NOW Zoots

Dropping off and picking up your dry cleaning probably isn't one of your favorite tasks, especially if your days are filled with family activities and work responsibilities. Zoots (**www.zoots.com**), based in Newton, Massachusetts, understands time-starved customers and wants to help them win the race against the clock by making one personal essential easier—getting their dry cleaning done. From working moms to entrepreneurs, busy people are just the customers that Zoots wants to serve. With 45 stores in 10 states, Zoots' President and CEO Todd Krasnow says that Zoots aims to surpass the convenience and quality expectations of time-starved consumers. How? By offering customers lots of options. What kinds of dry cleaning options do Zoots' customers have? Here are just a few: home pick-up and delivery, retail stores with extended hours, 24-hour drop-off and pick-up service, courtesy calls, and online reminders. In addition, to the convenience provided by Zoots, Rick Simoneau, director of retail operations, says that added values—such as replacing lost buttons, tacking hems, and providing standout customer service—are key.

Teri McNamara, vice president of human resources, says that the company's mission is to provide the best possible experience for customers. In doing so, Zoots is dedicated to making dry cleaning as convenient as possible while providing high-quality and reliable service. Zoots wants to be the best dry cleaner available.

One of the most interesting and unusual arrangements that Zoots has developed is one with Goodwill Industries. Customers can drop off their Goodwill donations at any Zoots outlet. Once Zoots has cleaned the clothes, they're donated to Goodwill. It's just another example of how Zoots is helping its customers win the race against the clock by making the essentials easier.

Discussion Questions

1. If Zoots wants to continue expanding, would a business plan be necessary? Explain. What would a business plan for this business need to include?
2. What do you think of Zoots' mission? Is it a mission or a vision? Explain. Using information from the company's Web site (**www.zoots.com**), write a vision statement for Zoots.
3. Because Zoots has numerous outlets, how difficult is it going to be for the company to instill its cultural values in employees? What suggestions would you give Krasnow for transmitting the important cultural values to its employees?

Sources: Company information from company Web site (**www.zoots.com**), July 10, 2002, and Hoover's Online (**www.hoovers.com**), July 10, 2002; and *Business Now* video segment.

ENDNOTES

1. G. Imperato, "Dirty Business, Bright Ideas," *Fast Company Online* (**www.fastcompany.com**), April 16, 1997.
2. F. David, *Strategic Management* (Upper Saddle River, NJ: Prentice Hall, 2001), p. 52.
3. J. Pearce II and F. David, "Corporate Mission Statements: The Bottom Line," *Academy of Management Executive,* May 1987, p. 110.
4. "Mission Possible," *Business Week*, August 16, 1999, p. F12; C. Bart and M. Baetz, "The Relationship Between Mission Statements and Firm Performance: An Exploratory Study," *Journal of Management Studies,* vol. 35, 1998, p. 823; and C. Rarick and J. Vitton, "Mission Statements Make Cents," *Journal of Business Strategy*, vol. 16, 1995, p. 11.
5. D. I. Silvers, "Vision—Not Just for CEOs," *Management Quarterly*, winter 1994–1995, pp. 10–14.
6. This section is based on information in David, *Strategic Management*, pp. 64–65.
7. J. A. Chatman and K. A. Jehn, "Assessing the Relationship Between Industry Characteristics and Organizational Culture: How Different Can You Be?" *Academy of Management Journal*, June 1994, pp. 522–53; and C. A. O'Reilly III, J. Chatman, and D. F. Caldwell, "People and Organizational Culture: A Profile Comparison Approach to Assessing Person–Organization Fit," *Academy of Management Journal*, September 1991, pp. 487–516.
8. T. Brokaw, *NBC Nightly News*, June 18, 1999.
9. J. Case, "Corporate Culture," *Inc.,* November 1996, pp. 42–53.
10. P. Phan and G. Markman, "An Institutional Theory of Business Plans," *Academy of Management Proceedings,* 2001, Entrepreneurship Division Abstracts, p. 2; and G. J. Castrogiovanni, "Pre-Startup Planning and the Survival of New Small Businesses: Theoretical Linkages," *Journal of Management*, vol. 22, no. 6, 1996, pp. 801–22.
11. There are numerous sources about writing business plans. Here's a short list: W. A. Sahlman, "How to Write a Great Business Plan," *Harvard Business Review*, July–August 1997, pp. 98–108; S. Hodges, "How to Write a Business Plan," *Nation's Business*, August 1997, p. 36; L. Elkins, "Tips for Preparing a Business Plan," *Nation's Business*, June 1996, pp. 60R–61R; and C. M. Brown, "The Do's and Don'ts of Writing a Winning Business Plan," *Black Enterprise*, April 1996, pp. 114–22.

5 ORGANIZING THE VENTURE

LEARNING OBJECTIVES

After reading and studying this chapter, you should be able to:

1. List the three basic ways to organize a business.
2. Explain the benefits and drawbacks of each of the six forms of business organization.
3. Describe what a trademark does.
4. Contrast the three types of patents.
5. Describe the other legal issues that entrepreneurs face.
6. Explain the importance of choosing an appropriate organizational structure.
7. Describe the six decisions in organizational design.
8. Discuss the characteristics of each of the two broad types of organization structure and when each might be appropriate.
9. Describe virtual and boundaryless organizations.

ENTREPRENEURSHIP IN ACTION

"We're revolutionizing the world of international advertising." A pretty bold goal for a small ad agency with just a small team of core people in its offices in Amsterdam.[1] Yet, for Karen Drakenberg, the Swedish chief executive of StrawberryFrog (**www.strawberryfrog.com**), the goal is not only ambitious but, she feels, also achievable. "StrawberryFrog is dead set on not becoming or being just a local player."

The team at StrawberryFrog depends on a network of people around the globe who can pitch in when they're needed on various projects. With no cumbersome administrative bureaucracy to slow it down, the agency has landed some large global ad campaigns. Other potential clients, though, have gone elsewhere for their global ad campaigns because they felt that bigger global agencies had the advantage in putting together

Karen Drakenberg's StrawberryFrog is a successful experiment in using an unusual organizational design to pursue her entrepreneurial vision. Once the venture's organizational vision and mission statements have been written, the organizational culture issues addressed, and the business plan written, it's time to put the plan into action. And one of the first steps in executing the plan is deciding the best way to organize the venture. Organizing the venture involves determining the legal form of business organization, addressing other legal issues, and then choosing the most appropriate organizational design.

LEGAL FORMS OF BUSINESS ORGANIZATION

The first organizing decision that an entrepreneur must make is a critical one! It's the form of legal ownership for the venture. The two primary factors that affect this decision are taxes and legal liability. As an entrepreneur, you want to minimize the impact of both of these factors on your entrepreneurial venture. So, it's important to know, examine, and evaluate the advantages and drawbacks of each of the legal forms of business organization. You want to make an educated decision—a decision in which you choose a form of legal organization that's going to help you fulfill your goals for the entrepreneurial venture. The right choice can protect you from legal liability as well as save tax dollars, in both the short and the long run.

What alternatives are available? There are three basic ways to organize your entrepreneurial venture: sole proprietorship, partnership, and corporation. However, when you include the variations of these basic organizational alternatives, you end up with six possible choices, each with its own tax consequences, liability issues, and pros and cons. These six choices are sole proprietorship, general partnership, limited liability partnership, C corporation, S corporation, and limited liability company. Let's look carefully at each choice. Exhibit 5-1 summarizes the basic information about each organizational alternative.

Sole Proprietorship

A **sole proprietorship** is a form of organization in which the owner maintains sole and complete control over the business and is personally liable for business debts. There are no legal requirements for establishing a sole proprietorship other than obtaining necessary local business licenses and permits. In a sole proprietorship, income and losses "pass through" to the owner and

sophisticated and integrated ad campaigns. The team at StrawberryFrog, however, feels that good global campaigns are found in big ideas, not in big bureaucracies.

The key to StrawberryFrog's approach is its new model of virtual work. By relying on a web of computer-connected freelancers around the globe, the agency has access to a network of talent without all the unnecessary overhead and complexity of work arrangements. The inspiration for this approach came from the film and construction industries. If you look at the film industry, people are essentially "free agents" who move from project to project applying their skills as needed. And the construction industry has mastered the art of managing multiskilled teams all working together on one shared vision. Those are the hallmarks of what Drakenberg is trying to do.

EXHIBIT 5-1 Legal Forms of Business Organization

Structure	Ownership Requirements	Tax Treatment	Liability	Advantages	Drawbacks
Sole proprietorship	One owner	Income and losses "pass through" to owner and are taxed at personal rate	Unlimited personal liability	• Low start-up costs • Freedom from most regulations • Owner has direct control • All profits go to owner • Easy to go out of business if necessary	• Unlimited personal liability • Personal finances at risk • Miss out on all kinds of business tax deductions • Total responsibility • May be more difficult to raise financing
General partnership	Two or more owners	Income and losses "pass through" to partners and are taxed at personal rate; flexibility in profit–loss allocations to partners	Unlimited personal liability Personal assets of partners are at risk	• Ease of formation • Pooled talent • Pooled resources • Somewhat easier access to financing • Some tax benefits	• Unlimited personal liability • Divided authority and decisions • Potential for conflict • Continuity of transfer of ownership
Limited liability partnership (LLP)	Two or more owners	Income and losses "pass through" to partners and are taxed at personal rate; flexibility in profit–loss allocations to partners	Limited, although one partner must retain unlimited liability	• Good way to acquire capital from limited partners	• Cost and complexity of forming can be high • Limited partners cannot participate in management of business without losing liability protection
C corporation	Unlimited number of shareholders; no limits on types of stock or voting arrangements	Dividend income is taxed at corporate and personal shareholder levels; losses and deductions are corporate	Limited	• Limited liability • Transferable ownership • Continuous existence • Easier access to resources	• Expensive to set up • Closely regulated • Double taxation • Extensive record keeping • Charter restrictions
S corporation	Up to 75 shareholders; no limits on types of stock or voting arrangements	Income and losses "pass through" to partners and are taxed at personal rate; flexibility in profit–loss allocations to partners	Limited	• Easy to set up • Enjoy limited liability protection and tax benefits of partnership • Can have a tax-exempt entity as a shareholder	• Must meet certain requirements • May limit future financing options
Limited liability company (LLC)	Unlimited number of "members"; flexible membership arrangements for voting rights and income	Income and losses "pass through" to partners and are taxed at personal rate; flexibility in profit–loss allocations to partners	Limited	• Greater flexibility • Not constrained by regulations on C and S corporations • Taxed as partnership, not as corporation	• Cost of switching from one form to this can be high • Need legal and financial advice in forming operating agreement

Entrepreneurs in Action

Patti Glick is known as the Foot Nurse of Silicon Valley (**www.footnurse.com**). Her work—presenting seminars called "My Aching Feet: Is It My Feet or My Shoes?" And no, this isn't a joke! It's a serious business covering a topic that employers obviously find valuable. She charges $600 for a two-hour presentation up to $2,000 for a day-long seminar. Glick made the decision to be a sole proprietor and says she wouldn't have it any other way. Why? She delights in the fact that her business succeeds or fails based on her own actions. Although her business's growth potential is limited by what she personally is able to do, Glick wouldn't have it any other way.

Sources: Company Web site (**www.footnurse.com**), June 6, 2002; and S. Greco, "Balancing Act," *Inc.*, January 2001, pp. 56–60.

are taxed at the owner's personal income tax rate. However, the liability issue is the major concern of sole proprietorships. The sole proprietor has unlimited personal liability for any and all debts of the business.

The advantages of the sole proprietorship revolve around the ease of formation and the freedom to run your business as you please. There are low start-up costs associated with a sole proprietorship. As the owner and proprietor, you have direct control over what you do, when you do it, and how you do it (within legal and regulatory guidelines, of course). Another advantage of the sole proprietorship is the fact that all profits and losses go directly to the owner. A final advantage of this form of business organization is that it is easy to shut down if that becomes necessary. There are no buyout agreements with other owners or shareholders to worry about. If you choose to go out of business, you just do it.

The biggest disadvantage of the sole proprietorship is **unlimited liability**—the obligation to personally repay all debts incurred by the business, which means the potential to lose more than just what the owner has invested in a business. Personal assets, such as a house or a car, may have to be sold to cover the business debts. Although this is the primary disadvantage of the sole proprietorship—and it's a major one—there are also other disadvantages. One is the fact that as a sole proprietor, you forfeit different kinds of business deductions on income taxes that are available only to corporations. Because these deductions lower the amount of income taxes paid, the effective tax rate increases. Another disadvantage is that although you have the freedom and control to run your business the way you want to, you also have total responsibility. You are limited by your personal skills and capabilities, which can prove overwhelming at times. Finally, another disadvantage of the sole proprietorship is the fact that it may be more difficult to get financing. Many financial institutions are reluctant to lend money to sole proprietors because the ability to repay the loan is dependent solely on that individual.

General Partnership

A **general partnership** is a form of business organization in which two or more business owners share the management and risk of the business. Legally, you can have a partnership without a written agreement. However, problems are inevitable in any partnership, no matter whether the partners are family members or good friends. A written partnership agreement drafted by legal counsel is highly recommended. Without a written partnership agreement, a partnership operates according to the rules of the Uniform Partnership Act (UPA) in the state in which the partnership is operating. The intent of the UPA is to resolve issues and problems among partners. Rather than relying on some standardized solution, however, it's a good idea to invest the necessary resources and money to draft a solid partnership agreement up front. Each partner has much to gain from making sure that the partnership starts off with a written partnership agreement.

How does a general partnership compare in terms of the two major organizational issues—taxes and liability? In a general partnership, income and losses "pass through" to the partners and are taxed at each partner's individual personal tax rate. As with the sole proprietorship, the partners are exposed to unlimited personal liability. Each partner's personal assets are at risk under this arrangement as well.

One advantage of this form of organization is that, even with a written partnership agreement, it is relatively easy to form. As with the sole proprietorship, the partnership simply needs the appropriate business licenses and permits. Another advantage of the general partnership that the sole proprietorship does not have is the pooling of talent and resources. Working together, the partners may be able to do more than each partner is able to do on his or her own. Along these lines, the pooling of resources may make it easier to access outside financ-

Entrepreneurs in Action

After selling his commercial photo-labs company for a nice sum of money, David Ross, a Chicago-based entrepreneur, found his newest challenge in a place he never imagined—turning around a long-time boat-building business in Manitowoc, Wisconsin. Burger Boat Company (**www.burgerboat.com**) had been constructing boats since 1863. During most of the 1980s, however, Burger Boat had struggled, until one day in November 1990 the owner shut it down. Ross heard of the company's situation. Since he had always admired Burger, he felt maybe there was an opportunity to purchase the company. As he found out more about the company, he knew that this, indeed, was an opportunity. To pursue that opportunity, Ross chose to partner with friend Jim Ruffolo. Together, the two purchased Burger Boat Company in 1993. Today, Burger Boat Company is thriving!

Sources: Company Web site (**www.burgerboat.com**), June 6, 2002; and "Rescuing Tradition," *Inc.*, August 2001, pp. 48–49.

ing. Financial institutions may be more willing to provide funds because there's more than one person involved. Finally, there are some tax benefits to the general partnership. Each partner reports partnership income on an individual income tax return, and the business does not pay any taxes as its own entity.

What about disadvantages of the general partnership? As with the sole proprietorship, the biggest disadvantage is the unlimited personal liability. Each partner is liable for all business debts, which means personal assets are at risk. In a partnership, you can be held liable for the negligence of your partner(s). Because each partner has the ability to enter into contracts to incur debt, sell assets, or take other actions, you should know what you're getting into with a partner. (Another reason why a partnership agreement is a good idea!) In addition, a big drawback of the partnership arrangement is the divided authority and decision making. In a sole proprietorship, *you* are the decision maker. In a partnership, there are other viewpoints and perspectives to consider. The divided authority and decision making can lead to conflicts. This can be particularly serious if the partners disagree on important core business issues such as future business direction or philosophy. Finally, other disadvantages of this form of organization are the facts that the continuity of the partnership and the transfer of ownership are more complicated. What happens when one partner wants to sell out and the other one

FYI

The ABC's of Perfect Partnerships

Setting up a partnership involves some interesting and challenging issues. One of these issues is the use of a written partnership agreement. The formal contract between the partners forming a partnership is called the **articles of partnership.** In the articles of partnership, the obligations and responsibilities of each business owner are outlined. It's also a good idea to cover the following issues in the partnership agreement: name, location, and purpose of the partnership; the personal contribution of each partner in cash, services, or other assets; the decision-making authority of each partner and situations when consensual decision making is required; work responsibilities of each partner; duration of the partnership; distribution of profits or losses; compensation of each partner; dispute-resolution procedure; procedure for adding any new partner(s); procedure for dissolution of partnership; and procedure for dealing with death or disability of a partner.

Another issue that partners need to be aware of, particularly if they do *not* have a written partnership agreement, is the provisions of the Uniform Partnership Act (UPA). The UPA covers most legal issues concerning partnerships and provides a minimal amount of protection and regulation, especially in the following areas: agreement between partners regarding assignment of partnership property; voting rights because each partner is to have one vote, regardless of ownership percentage; keeping accurate records, with each partner having the right to examine them; the responsibility of each partner to be loyal to the partnership and not do anything to harm the partnership intentionally; the right of partners to draw on their share of their profits; and agreement about salaries and dealing with losses. The intent of this law was to settle potential problems that came up between partners who had no written partnership agreement.

Source: T. Hatten, *Small Business* (Upper Saddle River, NJ: Prentice Hall, 1997), pp. 50–53.

doesn't? What happens when one partner wants to shut down the business and the other one doesn't? Or what happens if one partner dies or becomes incapacitated in some way? These dissolution scenarios should be dealt with up front at the creation of the partnership. Although it may seem strange to talk about dissolving a partnership right when it's being formed, that's the best time to address these issues.

Limited Liability Partnership (LLP)

The **limited liability partnership (LLP)** is a form of business organization in which there are general partner(s) and limited liability partner(s). The general partners actually operate and manage the business. They are the ones who have unlimited liability. There must be at least one general partner in an LLP. However, there can be any number of limited partners. These partners are usually passive investors, although they can make management suggestions to the general partners. They also have the right to inspect the business and to make copies of business records. The limited partners are entitled to a share of the business's profits as agreed to in the partnership agreement, and their only risk is the amount of their investment in the LLP.

An LLP faces a similar tax situation as a general partnership. Income and losses "pass through" to the partners and are taxed at personal rates. The partnership agreement outlines the percentage each partner is to receive. The liability issue is a distinguishing feature of the LLP. Although at least one general partner must have unlimited liability, the limited partners are liable only up to the amount of their investment in the LLP.

The main advantage of the LLP is that it is a good way for an entrepreneur to raise capital. Because the limited partners are risking only a "limited" amount of liability, they view the investment in the LLP as a good source of potential financial returns, and the general partners have the opportunity to obtain funds without having to go through a financial institution.

The biggest disadvantage of this form of organization is the cost and complexity of forming the LLP. A written agreement among all partners is required by most states under the Revised Uniform Limited Partnership Act. Drafting this agreement can be almost as complex as the process involved with incorporating a business. Another disadvantage is the stipulation that limited partners cannot participate in the management of the partnership without losing their liability protection.

Rapid Review

- ✔ What are the two primary factors that affect the decision about type of legal ownership, and what are the three basic ways to organize an entrepreneurial venture?
- ✔ What is a sole proprietorship, and what are its advantages and disadvantages?
- ✔ What is a general partnership, and what are its advantages and disadvantages?
- ✔ What are articles of partnership? What does the Uniform Partnership Act do?
- ✔ What is a limited liability partnership, and what are its advantages and disadvantages?

C Corporation

Of the three basic types of ownership (sole proprietorship, partnership, and corporation), the corporation (also known as a C corporation) is the most complex to form and operate. A **corporation** is a legal business entity that is separate from its owners and managers. Many entrepreneurial ventures are organized as a **closely held corporation**, which, very simply, is a corporation owned by a limited group of people who do not trade the stock publicly. Whereas the sole proprietorship and partnership forms of organization do not exist separately from the person(s) who owns and manages them, the corporation does. The corporation functions as a distinct legal entity and, as such, can make contracts, engage in business activities, own property, sue and be sued, and of course, pay taxes. A corporation must operate in accordance with its charter and the laws of the state in which it operates. These laws do vary by state. What does it take to incorporate?

The process of incorporation can be quite complex. Although many states do allow entrepreneurs to incorporate without legal assistance, this may not be the wisest thing to do. Getting an attorney to help with this process can save a lot of frustration. Even though you may not want to spend the money to get legal assistance, making a mistake in incorporating could end up costing you more in the long run than the legal fees charged for the job. The process of incorporation involves some specific activities. You must prepare **articles of incorporation**, a document that describes the business and is filed with the state in which the corporation is formed. Articles of incorporation typically include the following information:

1. *The name of your company.* This name must be registered with the state in which it will operate. By registering your company name, you're preventing others from using your name and ensuring that you're not using another company's name. Your chosen corporate name must reflect the type of business you are in and should not be deceptive.
2. *The purpose of your business.* You must state the intended nature of your business. This should not be a problem to include if you have written organizational vision and mission statements. Some states do allow very general information in this section, which lets the entrepreneur change the nature of the business without going through the process of reincorporating.
3. *The names and addresses of the incorporators.* This is pretty self explanatory. Be aware that some states require at least one of the incorporators to reside in the state.
4. *The names and addresses of the corporation's initial officers and directors.* The individuals elected as corporate officers and directors must be identified.
5. *The address of the corporation's home office.* You must establish corporate headquarters or offices in the state from which you receive your charter or register as an out-of-state corporation in your own state.
6. *The capital required at the time of incorporation.* Some states require that a newly formed corporation deposit in a financial institution the specific percentage of the stock's par value prior to incorporating.
7. *Capital stock to be authorized.* The types of stock and the number of shares the corporation wants to be authorized to issue must be specified. This doesn't mean that this number of shares must be issued, but the corporation is authorized to issue up to this amount. In addition, the rights, preferences, or limits of each class of stock must be specified in this section.
8. *Corporate bylaws.* **Bylaws** are the rules and regulations that govern the management and operation of the corporation. The bylaws must stipulate the rights and powers of shareholders, directors, and officers; the time and place for the annual shareholder meeting; the number needed for a quorum

Entrepreneurs in Action

Dorothy Julian's business, Henry Marine Service Inc., owns two tugboats that work the harbors of New York City 24 hours a day, 7 days a week. Because of the serious liability issues involved, Julian is looking to incorporate each of her tugboats separately. That way, if one boat has an accident, liability would be limited to that boat and would not jeopardize Julian's total source of income.

Source: R. Feemster, "In Praise of the Unbalanced Life," *Inc.*, June 2002, pp. 46–50.

(the number of people who must be present at corporate meetings in order to conduct business); the process for election and compensation of the board of directors; the dates of the corporation's fiscal year; and the individuals within the corporation who have the authorization to sign contracts.

9. *Corporation's time horizon.* Most corporations are set up with the intent of operating indefinitely. However, you may specify a duration for the corporation's existence.

10. *Miscellaneous information.* Some other information that may be included in the articles of incorporation is restrictions on transferring shares (many closely held corporations want to maintain control over their ownership) and provisions for preemptive rights (if shareholders are granted any).

The main tasks involved in writing the articles of incorporation are naming a **board of directors** (individuals elected by the shareholders to represent their interests), adopting bylaws, electing corporate officers, and issuing stock. You must also decide whether to incorporate as a C corporation, an S corporation (described in the next section), or a limited liability company (described in a later section).

The tax treatment of a corporation is one of the considerations an entrepreneur must look at in deciding whether to incorporate. If business profits are distributed as dividend income, this income is taxed at both the corporate and the personal shareholder levels. This is often referred to as the problem of double taxation. However, the trade-off is that the entrepreneur has limited personal liability because as a legal entity, the corporation assumes any liabilities of the business.

The corporation has other advantages in addition to the major one—that is, limited liability. One of these other advantages includes transferable ownership. Because the corporation's shares can be bought and sold, ownership can be transferred. This also means that the corporation enjoys continuous existence. If something happens to one of the owners, the business does not have to cease operations as is the case with sole proprietorships and partnerships. In addition, corporations typically have easier access to financial and other types of resources. Because the corporate entity has its own assets, which could be sold if necessary, financial institutions are often more willing to lend money.

However, there are some significant disadvantages to the corporate form of organization. We've already discussed one of the major ones—the double-taxation problem. Other disadvantages include the fact that corporations are expensive to set up, they're more closely regulated, extensive records must be kept, and the corporate charter restricts what can and cannot be done.

S Corporation

The **S corporation** (also often called a subchapter S corporation) is a specialized type of corporation that has the regular characteristics of a C corporation, but is unique in that the owners are taxed as a partnership as long as certain criteria are met. The S corporation has been the classic mechanism for getting the limited liability of a corporate structure without incurring corporate tax. New legal interpretations by federal agencies have relaxed some of the strict criteria for being an S corporation. What are the current criteria regarding S corporations?[2]

1. S corporations can now have as many as 75 shareholders (150 including spouses) instead of the former 35 (70 including spouses). This means that several families plus employees can now share ownership of a business.
2. An S corporation can now how have a tax-exempt entity (such as an employee stock ownership plan or pension plan) as a shareholder.
3. Any trust that owns shares in an S corporation can now have multiple beneficiaries rather than just one. This new type of trust is called an "electing small business trust" and it can "sprinkle" income—that is, it can allocate its income unevenly to the owners.

Some legal criteria for being an S corporation have remained the same. These include the following:

1. The S corporation must be a domestic corporation.
2. The S corporation cannot have a nonresident alien as a shareholder.
3. The S corporation can issue only one class of common stock, which means that all shares carry the same rights, except in the case of voting rights, which may differ. Very simply, this means that an S corporation can issue both voting and nonvoting common stock.

Violating any of these criteria (new or old) automatically terminates a company's S status. If the criteria are satisfied, the business owner(s) must annually elect S status within 75 days of the beginning of the tax year—which is usually around March 15. This is done by filing Internal Revenue Service Form 2553. All the corporation's shareholders must consent to being an S corporation. Getting legal and accounting advice on this decision is highly advised because there are some legal loopholes that can be used during the annual S status election.

The tax treatment for an S corporation is the same as for a partnership. Income and losses are not incurred at the corporate level, but instead "pass through" to the owners, who are taxed at their personal rate. However, the S corporation does enjoy the limited liability of a regular corporation. In fact, this limited liability is a significant advantage of the S corporation form of organization. Another advantage is the fact that it's relatively easy to set up as an S corporation as long as the legal criteria are met. In addition, the new stipulation that tax exempt entities can be a shareholder in the S corporation is a significant advantage. This means that a business's employees can be owners through an employee stock ownership plan or a pension plan.

The disadvantages of the S corporation are few. One is, of course, the fact that to be an S corporation, your business has to meet certain criteria. If these criteria are not met, the S election is jeopardized. The other disadvantage is that an S corporation may limit future financing options because of its treatment of income and losses. Because income flows through to the owners, financial institutions may be reluctant to lend money.

Limited Liability Company (LLC)

The **limited liability company (LLC)** is a relatively new form of business organization that's another hybrid between a partnership and a corporation. The LLC offers the liability protection of a corporation, the tax benefits of a partnership, and no restrictions such as those on an S corporation. For instance, an LLC is not limited to 75 shareholders, it can have foreigners as shareholders, and it can have more than one class of stock. An LLC should be seriously considered if the owner(s) needs flexibility in the legal structure of the business, desires limited liability, and prefers to be taxed as a partnership rather than as a corporation.

Most states require that an LLC have at least two owners (called "members"). These members are offered limited liability, just as in a corporation. In addition, the LLC does not pay income taxes. Income and losses "flow through" to the owners, who are taxed on their share of the LLC's income.

The biggest advantage of the LLC is the flexibility that it gives owners. In addition, the fact that the LLC is not constrained by the regulations on C and S corporations is an advantage. Finally, the absence of double taxation is an advantage of this organizing approach.

The main drawback of this approach is the fact that it's quite complex and expensive to set up. Legal and financial advice is an absolute necessity in forming the LLC's **operating agreement**, which is the document that outlines the provisions governing the way the LLC will conduct business. The operating agreement is similar to a corporation's bylaws.

Summary of Legal Forms of Organization

The decision on the legal form of organization is a major one, and it should not be approached lightly. This decision can have significant tax and liability consequences down the road. Although the legal form of organization *can* be changed, it's not an easy thing to do. An entrepreneur needs to think carefully about what's important, especially in the areas of flexibility, taxes, and amount of personal liability. As we've mentioned, it's a good idea to get legal and accounting advice on this decision. There are also other legal issues that an entrepreneur must deal with for which professional advice may be necessary or highly recommended.

Rapid Review ◀◀|

- ✔ What is a corporation? A C corporation? A closely held corporation?
- ✔ What are articles of incorporation, and what do they typically include?
- ✔ What are bylaws? What is a board of directors?
- ✔ What is an S corporation, and what criteria must be met in order to be an S corporation?
- ✔ What is a limited liability company? What criteria does an LLC have? What is an operating agreement?
- ✔ List the advantages and disadvantages of the corporate form of organization, the S corporation, and the LLC.

OTHER LEGAL ISSUES

It's often said with a laugh that entrepreneurs have three choices when it comes to legal issues: learn nothing but hire good lawyers; learn nothing and

Entrepreneurs in Action

Douglas Clark is a veteran inventor who chose *not* to use a lawyer when filing for each of his 11 patents. However, he didn't attempt the patent application process without help. He did have an intellectual-property lawyer review his work. Rather than turning over the entire process to the lawyer, Clark used him as more of a coach and guide. But taking this approach wasn't easy. Filing patent applications is tedious and time-consuming and must be done carefully to avoid legal complications down the road. So, yes, it is possible to save the legal fees, but that doesn't mean there isn't a price to pay.

Source: S. B. Goldberg, "Do-It-Yourself Law," *Business Week*, January 31, 2000, pp. F20–F22.

avoid lawyers; or learn enough to know when legal advice is needed. The best approach is the last—know enough about legal issues to know when professional legal advice is needed. You don't want to bury your head in the sand when it comes to legal issues. There are too many risks associated with doing something illegal, even unintentionally. Ignorance of the law is not a valid excuse. We're going to discuss four legal issues that have an impact on organizing the entrepreneurial venture: choosing a business name, patents, contracts, and employment law. In addition, we're going to look briefly at some miscellaneous legal topics.

Choosing a Business Name, Slogan, or Design

You may be asking yourself why choosing a business name, slogan, or design is a legal issue with which entrepreneurs must deal. Although it may seem that your business is entitled to pick any name it wants, that's not the case. In fact, it's an important legal issue. Legal problems can arise if you choose a name that another company has trademarked or has registered as a corporate name with the appropriate state agency. A **trademark** is a form of legal protection for a distinctive word, name, phrase, logo, symbol, design, slogan, or any combination of these elements. It's a good idea to do a trademark search before choosing a name, logo, or slogan. Doing a trademark search has gotten a lot easier thanks to the Internet. Two of the biggest trademark search companies on the Internet are Thomson & Thomson (**www.thomson-thomson.com**) and CCH Trademark Research Corporation (**www.corsearch.com**). Although these Web sites charge a fee, what you'll get for that fee is a check of federal and state registrations, Internet domain names, and common-law listings found in phone books and trade publications.[3] You also can conduct a trademark search yourself using *The Trademark Register of the United States*, which is available in many libraries or by using other similar directories. A search of registered corporate names would have to be done through the state agency with which corporations are registered. By investigating name and trademark information, you'll have a good basis for arguing that you did act with due diligence if you should ever get in trouble for using another business's name. But, hopefully, if you've conducted a thorough search, you won't ever have to worry about that.

Entrepreneurs in Action

Larry Reinstein, CEO of the Souper Salad chain of takeout restaurants based in Newton, Massachusetts, learned the hard way how important it is to do a national trademark search. In 1976 when he opened his first Souper Salad, he wasn't thinking of going national. However, when he began looking to expand nationally, he discovered that another Souper Salad, based in Dallas, owned the national trademark. Expansion plans were put on hold while another name was researched. Having settled on the name, Fresh City, Reinstein retained the services of top-notch trademark lawyers before rolling out his new restaurants.

Source: S. Greco. "Hot Tips," *Inc.*, January 2001, p. 102.

Once you've found a name that you like and that's not used by others, what then? You can choose that name for your business and do nothing, but it's probably worthwhile to register the name with the federal government. The cost (as of mid-2002) is $325 to apply to the U.S. Patent and Trademark Office for a trademark name that will cover you anywhere in the United States as well as on the Internet. All kinds of information and the forms needed for filing are available on the agency's Web site (**www.uspto.gov**) and are so user friendly that you probably won't even need legal advice to fill them out.

Patents

In Chapter 2, we briefly covered patents. We defined a **patent** as a legal property that allows its holder to prevent others from employing this property for their own use for a specified period of time. A patent protects an invention. It's valid for up to 20 years from the date you file for the patent. There are three different types of patents. A **utility patent**, the most common type of patent, covers inventions that work uniquely to perform a function or use. For instance, if you invented a new device to administer medications, you'd apply for a utility patent. However, if you came up with a unique or new form, shape, or design of an existing object, you'd want to get a **design patent**. For instance, if you came up with a stapler that performed the standard function of stapling but looked like a frog, you'd want to apply for a design patent. The final type of patent is a **plant patent**, which covers new strains of living plants such as flowers, trees, or vegetables.

You need to know that you can't patent everything. You can't patent, for example, an abstract idea, a purely mental process, or a process that you can simply perform using pencil and paper. Also, naturally occurring things cannot be patented. To be patentable, an invention must be a process, a machine, a manufacture, a composition, or an improvement in these. In addition to meeting the requirement of being in this "statutory" class (that is, being a process, a machine, a manufacture, a composition, or an improvement in these), an invention must satisfy three additional requirements to be patentable. These include: (1) *novelty*—the invention must be a new idea and physically different in at least some small way from what already exists; (2) *nonobviousness*—the invention must

The ABC's of Trademarks and Patents

Here are some frequently asked questions and answers about trademarks and patents:

- *Is a service mark the same as a trademark?*

  A service mark is the same except that it identifies and distinguishes the source of a service rather than a product.
- *How are trademarks, patents, and copyrights different?*

  A trademark protects a distinctive word, name, phrase, logo, symbol, design, slogan, or any combination of these elements. A patent protects an invention. A copyright protects an original artistic or literary work.
- *When can I use the "TM," "SM," and "®" symbols?*

  Anyone who claims rights in a mark may use the TM (trademark) or SM (service mark) designation with the mark to alert the public to the claim. It isn't necessary to have a registration or even a pending application to use these designations. This claim may or may not be valid. The registration symbol (®) may be used only when the mark is registered in the Patent and Trade Office.
- *How long does a trademark registration last?*

  For a trademark registration to remain valid, an Affidavit of Use ("Section 8 Affidavit") must be filed between the fifth and sixth year after registration. Assuming that this affidavit of use is filed correctly, registrations granted before November 16, 1989, have a 20-year term and registrations granted on or after November 16, 1989, have a 10-year term. These timing periods are also true for the trademark renewals.
- *What do the terms "patent pending" and "patent applied for" mean?*

  These terms are used by a manufacturer or seller of an article to inform the public that an application for a patent on that article is on file in the Patent and Trademark Office. The law imposes a fine on anyone who uses these terms falsely to deceive the public.
- *If two or more persons work together to make an invention, who is granted the patent?*

  If each person had a share in the ideas forming the invention, they are joint inventors and a patent will be issued to them jointly on the basis of a proper patent application. If one person has provided all of the ideas of the invention and the other has only followed instructions in making it, the person who contributed the ideas is the sole inventor and the patent application and patent will be in his or her name alone.

Source: Information found on the Web pages of the U.S. Patent and Trade Office (**www.uspto.gov**).

be a new or unexpected development, which means that it would not be obvious to someone skilled in the technology of a particular field; (3) *usefulness*—the invention must have some obvious use, or in the case of design, must be ornamental. Once you feel that your invention has met these tests, what then?

The first thing to do before filing a patent application is to conduct a patent search. This search will tell you whether other patents have already been issued that reveal or suggest your invention. You can either do the search yourself or hire a patent agent or patent attorney. If you choose to do the search yourself, you can go to a library that has been designated as a Patent and Trademark Depository Library, or if you have Internet access you can search online (see **www.uspto.gov**). If you want to hire someone to do this search, professional patent researchers will do the search for you. Whichever approach you take, this search should be thorough in order to prevent later problems.

If you complete your search and find nothing that indicates that your invention already has been patented, you're ready to submit a patent application. A patent application is a complex legal document and the federal agency (the United States Patent and Trade Office, or USPTO) responsible for reviewing these applications highly recommends they be completed by someone trained to prepare such documents. There are specific requirements set forth by the USPTO for both content and format of the patent applications. (You can read through the requirements at the USPTO Web site at **www.uspto.gov**.) If you've invented a new way to do something or a new design, doesn't it make sense to protect it? Although this professional advice may be expensive, not having it may be even more so. Protecting your invention(s) that you hope to turn into a viable—and potentially profitable—entrepreneurial venture is absolutely critical. One thing you can do is adhere to the rigorous patent application process requirements.

Contracts

A **contract** is an agreement that creates legal obligations and is enforceable in a court of law. Organizing and then managing an ongoing entrepreneurial venture may entail executing different types of contracts. The commonness and potential variety of contracts that an entrepreneur may deal with means knowing something about contract law. Although it's highly recommended again that you enlist professional legal advice regarding the writing and execution of contracts, there's some basic knowledge about contracts with which you should be familiar.[4]

There are four essentials of a contract. One is *mutual assent*, which means that both parties must agree to the contract. Another is *consideration*, which means that both parties must do or pay something as stated in the contract. The third is *legality of object*, which means that the contract cannot force the parties to do something illegal. The final contract essential is *capacity of the parties*, which means that all parties to the contract must be legally able to perform their part of the contract. For instance, minors, people of unsound mind, intoxicated persons, or drugged persons can legally get out of contracts. In addition, contract law has specific understandings about which contracts must be in writing to be legally binding, what a breach of contract is, and interpretation of contracts. There's much more to contract law than what we've discussed here, and that's why it's a good idea to get legal advice on preparing any contracts that your business may need.

Employment Laws

Employment laws cover hiring and firing, employee policies, employee compensation and benefits, discrimination, workers' compensation, workplace health and safety, family and medical leave, and other employer–employee relationships. New rulings and interpretations in any of these areas further complicate what you can and cannot do regarding any aspect of employment. If you're a sole proprietor, you obviously do not have to worry about employment laws. However, as your venture grows and adds employees, you need to become familiar with employment law. Again, it's highly recommended that you seek professional legal advice in employment law matters. It can be an expensive proposition if an

EXHIBIT 5-2 A Survey of Ways Small Business Owners Are Preventing Employee Lawsuits

Action	Approximate percentage of respondents who have done this
• Wrote employee manual or handbook	80% +
• Trained supervisors	60% +
• Wrote grievance policies	58%
• Hired consultants	53%

Source: "Staying on the Right Side of the Law," *Business Week Frontier*, April 26, 1999, p. F7.

employee sues and you're found to be at fault. A survey of executives at small companies indicated that most were attempting to forestall legal complaints by establishing clear guidelines and procedures. (See Exhibit 5-2.)

Other Miscellaneous Legal Issues

You may have to deal with other miscellaneous legal issues when organizing your entrepreneurial venture or while managing the ongoing venture. These may include sales laws, trade secrets laws, securities laws, credit laws, consumer protection laws, pension and fringe benefit laws, and antitrust laws. In any of these areas, professional legal advice can be valuable, particularly if it relates to a major business concern. The key is to be aware of when you need legal advice—that is, learn enough to know when legal advice is needed.

Entrepreneurs in Action

Stanley Day, his brother F. K. Day, and Samuel Patterson thought nothing of it when a representative of Shimano Corporation, a huge Japanese-based global bicycle products company, visited their tiny Chicago bicycle parts shop, SRAM Corporation, in 1989. In fact, they said, "We were so excited and honored that Shimano was coming to talk to us." The Days and Patterson had invented a new kind of gear shifter to replace the traditional thumb-controlled levers. In retrospect, that friendly visit was probably the worst thing they could have done. Shimano didn't like competition and SRAM was a threat. Throughout the 1990s, as SRAM grew and expanded its line of innovative bicycle gadgets, Shimano took SRAM to court several times over product designs. However, SRAM eventually took the offensive and fought back, filing suits that charged Shimano with anticompetitive actions.

Source: D. Armstrong, "A Stick in the Spokes," *Forbes*, March 5, 2001, pp. 148–149.

Rapid Review

- ✔ What legal issues might arise in choosing a business name, slogan, or design?
- ✔ What is a trademark, and how can entrepreneurs do a trademark search?
- ✔ What is a patent? Describe the three different types of patents.
- ✔ What are the requirements for being able to patent an invention, and what steps are involved in getting a patent?
- ✔ What is a contract? Describe the four essentials of a contract.
- ✔ How might employment laws affect an entrepreneurial venture?
- ✔ What other miscellaneous legal issues might an entrepreneur have to deal with?

ORGANIZATIONAL DESIGN ISSUES

The choice of an appropriate organizational structure is an important activity when organizing the entrepreneurial venture. No other topic in creating and designing organizations has undergone as much change in the past few years as that of organizational structure. Think back to our chapter-opening case on StrawberryFrog and its unique structural design. What did that type of structural design do for this organization and why does it seem to work? Those are some of the topics we want to look at in this section. We first need to understand something about the process of organizing.

What Is Organizing?

When Karen Drakenberg of StrawberryFrog chose to use a virtual global network of experts whose skills were used as needed in creating advertising campaigns, she was organizing. In the field of management, **organizing** is one of the four basic functions of managers (planning, leading, and controlling are the other three), and is defined as the process of deciding how best to get the venture's work done by grouping organizational activities and resources within some type of organizational structure. Just what is an organization's structure? An **organizational structure** is the formal framework within which work is divided, grouped, and coordinated. A visual representation of an organization's structure is called an **organizational chart**. The organizational chart simply portrays the division and grouping of various work activities (horizontal levels) throughout the organization and who's in charge of what areas (vertical levels) in the organization. The process of developing or changing the organizational structure is called **organizational design**. Knowing something about organizational design is important for entrepreneurs because the work that the people in the entrepreneurial venture will perform must be divided, grouped, and coordinated in some way. As the entrepreneurial venture is organized, decisions must be made about the most appropriate organizational design.

Organizational Design Decisions

The whole purpose behind organizational design is making sure that the organization's work gets done efficiently and effectively. In a sole proprietorship, there's not much to organizational structure because the sole proprietor is the one who makes sure the work gets done. There's no need to divide, group, or coordinate the work. However, if an entrepreneurial venture has more than one person involved, decisions about who does what need to be made. As the venture grows, design decisions arise as more employees join the organization. Organizational design involves decisions about six key elements: (1) How much work specialization is needed? (2) Do we need specific departments and if so, what type? (3) Who's going to be in charge, and who reports to whom? Or, in other words, what is the chain of command? (4) How many employees will supervisors manage—that is, what is the span of control? (5) Who's going to make organizational decisions—that is, are organizational decisions going to be centralized or decentralized? (6) How much formalization—rules and procedures—is necessary?[5] Let's take a closer look at each of these important organizing elements.

Work specialization. **Work specialization** describes the degree to which work tasks are divided into separate jobs—also known as division of labor. The essence of work specialization is that an entire job is not done by one individual but instead is broken down into various steps, and each step is completed by a different person. Individual employees perform one part of an activity rather than the entire activity. Work specialization has been around for a number of years and has both advantages and drawbacks. (See Exhibit 5-3.) The advantages are mainly economic and include increasing work efficiency and productivity. The drawbacks are mainly human and stem from the fact that individuals don't want to do the same thing over and over. Although work specialization is important to organizing work, it shouldn't be seen as a source of endlessly increasing productivity. There *will* come a point in the entrepreneurial venture when work responsibilities must be divided. However, keep in mind the potential drawbacks of making jobs too narrowly specialized.

Departmentalization. When an organization grows to the point at which more than one person is working on a particular function, it may be time to departmentalize. **Departmentalization** very simply describes the basis by which specialized work tasks (jobs) are grouped. Once jobs have been divided up through work specialization, they may have to be grouped back together so that common tasks can be coordinated. Although every organization will have its own unique way of classifying and grouping common work activities, there are some general approaches to departmentalization. One of these approaches is by *job function*. For instance, a hotel might be departmentalized around housekeeping, front desk, maintenance, restaurant operations, reservations and sales, human resources, and accounting. Departmentalization by function can be used in all types of organizations and will reflect each organization's unique work functions. Another approach to departmentalization is by *product,* in which jobs are grouped by product line. For example, an accounting firm might have departments oriented toward its "products"—tax preparation, management consulting, auditing, and so forth. An organization also might choose to departmentalize on the basis of *geography* or location. For instance, it might have a southwest region, a midwest

EXHIBIT 5-3 Advantages and Drawbacks of Work Specialization

Advantages—Economic	Drawbacks—Human
• Efficient use of employee skills	• Boredom
• Employee skills can improve because of repetition	• Stress
• Easier and less costly to train employees	• Fatigue
• Minimizes resource waste	• Poor work quality
• Encourages development of specialized equipment and machinery	• Lower productivity
	• May lead to absenteeism and turnover

region, and a southeast region. Another approach to departmentalization is on the basis of *process* or grouping jobs on the basis of how products or customers "flow" through the business. For example, a cabinet manufacturer may have departments for the various work processes involved in designing and manufacturing wood cabinets: sawing, planing, milling, assembling, lacquering, sanding, finishing, inspecting, and shipping. Finally, the *customer* approach might be used if there are common groups of customers that the organization seeks to serve. For instance, an office supply firm might be departmentalized on the basis of retail customers, wholesale customers, education customers, and governmental customers.

One popular trend is the use of **cross-functional teams**. These teams are hybrid groupings of individuals who come from various specialties or functions and who work together on tasks. Those tasks might include designing a new product, preparing a long-term marketing plan, or creating a new layout for the office. Entrepreneurial ventures are particularly fertile grounds for cross-functional teams because of the need for flexibility in assigning and coordinating work.

Chain of command. In designing an appropriate organizational structure, it's important to know who has the ultimate decision-making authority, who has the authority to perform what tasks, and who reports to whom. These are all issues in determining the chain of command. Strict adherence to a formal chain of command, in which individuals have to get permission from their supervisor before doing something, may not be the best approach for an entrepreneurial organization that needs to remain flexible. Instead, the solution to the command-and-control issue for many entrepreneurial organizations is to empower employees. **Empowerment** is increasing the decision-making discretion of individuals. In an empowered organization, employees are free to resolve problems as they arise, are encouraged to approach doing their work the way they feel is best because they do have more detailed knowledge about it, and are encouraged to think for themselves rather than being told what to do. Being empowered, however, doesn't mean making decisions and doing work just any way. All decisions and actions should be aligned with the venture's purpose and goals. However, that's where the vision and mission statements and the behavioral expectations inherent in the organizational culture help shape what employees do and how they do it. Although employee empowerment can be an attractive alternative in resolving organizational chain of command issues, keep in mind that effective empowerment doesn't just happen by itself. It's not a coincidence that empowerment efforts are almost always coupled with extensive employee training. Enhancing employees' skills, abilities, and confidence through training increases the likelihood that any empowerment efforts will succeed.

Span of control. As the venture grows and employees are added, a structural decision may have to be made regarding the

The Grey Zone

Organizational behavior theorists (experts who study the behavior of people in organizations) tell us that there are people who don't want to be empowered at work. They want to come in to work, do their jobs, and go home. They don't want to make decisions, participate in employee-involvement programs, or take on additional responsibilities. As an entrepreneur, what will you do if you're faced with this? What responsibility do you have to your business, and what responsibility do you have to your employees? What if your other employees want to be more involved in decision making? What ethical implications might you face in such a situation?

number of employees the venture's supervisors can effectively and efficiently manage. This organizational design concept is called **span of control**. The span of control concept is important in organizational design because, to a large degree, it determines how many supervisors an organization will need. Wider spans (supervising a greater number of people) are more efficient in terms of cost because fewer supervisors are needed. But at some point, wider spans become inefficient because the supervisor loses track of what's going on and employees may make costly mistakes. Organizational design theorists now recognize that many factors influence the appropriate number of employees a supervisor can efficiently and effectively manage. These factors are the skills and abilities of the supervisor, the skills and abilities of the employees, and the work that must be done. The more skilled the supervisor and the employees, the wider the span can be. The trend in organizations, large and small, has been toward wider spans of control. These wider spans of control allow organizations to control costs, speed up decision making, increase flexibility, and empower employees.

Centralization–decentralization. In an organization, decisions are continually being made—decisions that determine what gets done, when, how, and so forth. The organizational design concept of centralization-decentralization addresses who makes these decisions. **Centralization** describes the degree to which decision making is concentrated in the hands of a few people, usually the founder and other top-level executives. **Decentralization** describes the degree to which decision making is delegated to other organizational members. Our earlier discussion of employee empowerment is an example of how decision making is being decentralized in entrepreneurial organizations. The nature of the entrepreneurial environment favors a more decentralized approach because entrepreneurial ventures need the ability to respond quickly to rapidly changing circumstances. The entrepreneurial venture needs to be nimble and flexible, and decentralization supports this. In addition, the small size of an entrepreneurial organization may limit any attempts to centralize decision making. When there are not many members in the organization, it's hard to keep decision making concentrated with just a few people. In addition, in a small organization, the overlapping job duties and high need for coordination would not be conducive to centralization.

Formalization. The last organizational design element we need to look at is **formalization**, the degree to which jobs are standardized and the extent to which employee behavior is dictated by rules and procedures. If an organization is highly formalized, employees will have little discretion over what is to be done, when it's to be done, and how it's to be done. In organizations with high formalization, there would be explicit job descriptions, numerous organizational rules, and clearly defined procedures for work activities. On the other hand, when formalization is low, the way employees do their jobs is fairly nonstructured, and employees have a great deal of discretion in how they do their work. There are few rules and procedures. Even in organizations with low formalization, however, this doesn't mean that the workplace is a free-for-all. Some degree of formalization is necessary for planning and controlling purposes. Employees have to know what they're supposed to be doing and how their work performance is being measured. Within these parameters, though, employees would be free to do their work in the way they felt was best. The nature of entrepreneurial organizations tends to make them less formalized.

Entrepreneurs in Action

Scott Lutz, president and CEO of 8th Continent (**www.8thcontinent.com**), presides over a company with an unusual structure. 8th Continent is a soy-milk company based in Minnetonka, Minnesota. What's so unusual about its structure is that it's a 50–50 joint venture between two corporate giants, DuPont and General Mills. Lutz says that 8th Continent "aims to combine the power of the big with the spirit of the small—to create a fresh new brand and a nimble new company using the technology and financial resources of two major players."

Sources: Company Web site (**www.8thcontinent.com**), June 6, 2002; and L. Tischler, "Deep Pockets, Open Minds," *Fast Company*, May 2002, pp. 32–33.

Summary. As we stated at the beginning of this section, organizational design decisions revolve around the amounts and types of work specialization and departmentalization, the approach to chain of command, the width of the span of control, the amount of centralization or decentralization, and the degree of formalization. We've discussed the various design options. Now, how do these design options translate into actual organizational structures? What types of organizational structures might an entrepreneur use?

Types of Organizational Structures

An entrepreneur might choose from two generic types of organizational structures.[6] (See Exhibit 5-4 for a comparison.) One is the **mechanistic organization**, which is a rigid and tightly controlled structure characterized by high specialization, rigid departmentalization, clear chain of command, narrow spans of control, high formalization, limited information networking throughout the organization, and little participation in decision making by employees. A mechanistic-type structure tends to be focused on efficiency and cost minimization. The impact of differing personalities, human judgments, and ambiguity are minimized because these are seen as inefficient and inconsistent. In direct contrast is the **organic organization**, which is a structure that's highly adaptive and flexible, with little work specialization, minimal formalization, and little direct supervision of employees. Rather than having standardized jobs and regulations, the organic organization is flexible, which allows it to change rapidly as needs require. Although organic organizations do have work specialization, the jobs are not standardized. Organizational employees are highly trained and empowered to handle diverse job-related problems. Employees in this type of organization require minimal formal rules and little direct supervision. Their high levels of skills and training and the support provided by other highly skilled and trained team members make formalization and rigid organizational controls unnecessary. When is a mechanistic design preferable and when is an organic one more appropriate?

EXHIBIT 5-4 Mechanistic and Organic Organization Structures

Mechanistic	**Organic**
Characteristics: • High specialization • Rigid departmentalization • Clear chain of command • Narrow span of control • Centralized • High formalization	**Characteristics:** • Cross-functional teams • Free flow of information • Wide span of control • Decentralized • Low formalization
Appropriate for these situations: • Cost efficiencies are critical • Large organization (2,000 or more employees) • Standardized products produced in a routine fashion • Relatively stable and certain external environment	**Appropriate for these situations:** • Innovation is critical • Smaller organizations • Customized products produced in a flexible setting • Dynamic, complex, and uncertain external environment

A mechanistic structure would be preferable when cost efficiencies are critical to the organization's competitive advantage; for large organizations in which more specialization, departmentalization, centralization, and rules and regulations are needed for control; if the organization produces standardized products in a routine fashion; and where the external environment is relatively stable and certain. An organic structure would be more appropriate when innovation is critical to the organization's competitive advantage; for smaller organizations in which rigid approaches to dividing and coordinating work aren't necessary; if the organization produces customized products in a flexible setting; and where the external environment is dynamic, complex, and uncertain.

Given the realities of today's economy and the changing world of work (as we discussed in Chapter 2), it's not surprising that many entrepreneurial organizations are looking for more flexible and adaptable organizational designs. For instance, Karen Drakenberg's company, StrawberryFrog, described in the chapter-opening case, is a perfect example of a company that's uniquely organized to take advantage of the dynamic realities of global communication. It moves rapidly to capture market opportunities that it sees. Although its virtual arrangement *is* rather unusual, it fosters and supports the effective and efficient accomplishment of the organization's work. StrawberryFrog's structural design is one of the new types of structural designs entrepreneurial organizations are using that doesn't fit the traditional mold. This design is called a **virtual organization**, which is a network of independent people linked by common goals and information technology. In a virtual organization, each person contributes his or her skills as markets are pursued. The benefit of the virtual organization is that it's extremely fluid and

FYI

Structuring the Entrepreneurial Firm

At some point, successful entrepreneurs find that they cannot do everything alone. More people are needed. The entrepreneur must then decide on the most appropriate structural arrangement for effectively carrying out the organization's activities. Without some type of suitable organizational structure, the entrepreneurial venture may soon find itself in a chaotic situation.

In many small firms, the organizational structure tends to evolve with very little conscious and deliberate planning by the entrepreneur. For the most part, the structure may be very simple—one person who does whatever is needed. As the entrepreneurial venture grows and the entrepreneur finds it increasingly difficult to go it alone, employees are brought on board to perform certain functions or duties that the entrepreneur cannot handle. These individuals tend to keep doing those same functions as the company continues to grow. Then, as the entrepreneurial venture continues to grow, each of these functional areas may require managers and employees.

With the evolution to a more deliberate structure comes a whole new set of challenges for the entrepreneur. All of a sudden, he or she must share decision-making and operating responsibility. This is typically one of the most difficult things for an entrepreneur to do—letting go and allowing someone else to make the decisions. After all, he or she reasons, how can anyone know this business as well as I do? Also, what might have been a fairly informal, loose, and flexible atmosphere that worked well when the organization was small may no longer be effective. Many entrepreneurs are greatly concerned about keeping that "small company" atmosphere alive even as the organization grows and evolves into a more structured arrangement. But having a structured organization doesn't necessarily mean giving up flexibility, adaptability, and freedom. In fact, the structural design may be as fluid as the entrepreneur feels comfortable with and yet still have the rigidity it needs to operate efficiently.

flexible. As opportunities arise, the virtual organization ramps up to take advantage of them. The virtual organization is possible only because of the information technology that links the various people. Sharing information both within and across the organization is important to the ultimate success of a virtual organization. Another of these "new" organizational designs is called a **boundaryless organization**. This type of organization is one whose design is not defined by, or limited to, horizontal, vertical, or external boundaries imposed by a predefined structure.[7] Both boundaryless organizations and virtual organizations are similar in terms of being flexible and fluid. The term *boundaryless organization* was coined by an entrepreneurially oriented executive of a large and successful corporation: Jack Welch, former chairman of the global giant, General Electric. Despite GE's enormous size, Welch wanted to eliminate vertical and horizontal boundaries *within* GE and break down barriers *between* the company and its external stakeholders. He passionately believed that by getting rid of these boundaries, his company could be more responsive and flexible and ultimately, more successful. Although the idea may sound odd, many of today's most successful organizations are finding that they can effectively operate best in today's environment by remaining flexible and *un*structured. The ideal structure for them is *not* having a

Rapid Review

- ✔ What are an organizational structure, organizational chart, and organizational design?
- ✔ What are the six key decisions in organizational design? Describe the main issues to be addressed in each of these areas.
- ✔ Compare and contrast mechanistic and organic organizations.
- ✔ What is a virtual organization? A boundaryless organization?

rigid, predefined structure. Instead, the boundaryless organization seeks to eliminate the chain of command, have limitless spans of control, and replace rigid department lines with empowered teams.[8] The boundaryless organization functions efficiently and effectively by breaking down the artificial boundaries created by a fixed structural design.

Throughout this chapter, we've looked at the issues involved with organizing the entrepreneurial venture. From deciding the legal form of business organization to dealing with other important legal issues to choosing an appropriate organizational design, an entrepreneur has important organizing issues to address. Rather than haphazardly or mindlessly jumping into an entrepreneurial venture, it's important to think carefully about the best approach—that is, the approach that will allow work to be performed efficiently and effectively.

CHAPTER SUMMARY

This summary is organized around the chapter-opening objectives.

1. The three basic ways to organize a business are sole proprietorship, partnership, and corporation.
2. The advantages of the *sole proprietorship* are low start-up costs, freedom from most regulations, the owner has direct control, all profits go to the owner, and it's easy to go out of business if necessary. The drawbacks are unlimited personal liability, personal finances at risk, miss out on all kinds of business tax deductions, total responsibility for business, and it may be more difficult to raise financing. The advantages of a *general partnership* are ease of formation, pooled talent, pooled resources, somewhat easier access to financing, and some tax benefits. The drawbacks are unlimited personal liability, divided authority and decisions, potential for conflict, and continuity of transfer of ownership. The advantages of a *limited liability partnership (LLP)* are similar to that of a general partnership and also include the fact that it's a good way to acquire capital from limited partners. The drawbacks are that the cost and complexity of forming can be high and limited partners cannot participate in the management of the business without losing liability protection. The advantages of a *C corporation* are limited personal liability, transferable ownership, continuous existence, and easier access to resources. The drawbacks are expense to set up, closely regulated, double taxation, extensive record keeping, and charter restrictions. The advantages of an *S corporation* are easy to set up, enjoy limited personal liability protection and tax benefits of partnership, and can have a tax-exempt entity as a shareholder. The drawbacks are it must meet certain requirements and it may limit future financing options. The advantages of a *limited liability company (LLC)* are greater flexibility, not constrained by regulations on C and S corporations, and taxed as a partnership, not as corporation. The drawbacks are the cost of switching from another form to this can be high and there is a definite need for legal and financial advice in forming the operating agreement.

3. A trademark is a form of legal protection for a distinctive word, name, phrase, logo, symbol, design, slogan, or any combination of these elements. It's a good idea to do a trademark search before choosing a name, logo, or slogan.
4. A utility patent covers inventions that work uniquely to perform a function or use. A design patent covers a unique or new form, shape, or design of an existing object. A plant patent covers new strains of living plants.
5. One legal issue that entrepreneurs might face includes contracts. A contract is an agreement that creates legal obligations and is enforceable in a court of law. Organizing and managing an entrepreneurial venture may entail executing different types of contracts. Another legal issue entrepreneurs might face includes employment laws, which cover hiring and firing, employee policies, employee compensation and benefits, discrimination, workers' compensation, workplace health and safety, family and medical leave, and other employer–employee relationships. Other legal issues that may arise when organizing an entrepreneurial venture include sales laws, trade-secrets laws, securities laws, credit laws, consumer-protection laws, pension and fringe-benefit laws, and antitrust laws.
6. Knowing something about organizational structures is important because the work that people in the entrepreneurial venture will perform must be divided, grouped, and coordinated in some way. The whole purpose behind organizational design is making sure the venture's work gets done efficiently and effectively.
7. There are six decisions in organizational design. *Work specialization* describes the degree to which work tasks are divided into separate jobs. An entrepreneur needs to determine how much job specialization will be necessary. *Departmentalization* describes the basis by which specialized work tasks (jobs) are grouped. The ways to departmentalize include by job function, by product, by geography, by process, or by customer. One popular trend in departmentalization is the use of cross-functional teams, which group individuals from various functions to work together on tasks. The *chain of command* determines who has ultimate decision-making authority, who has the authority to perform what tasks, and who reports to whom. Many entrepreneurial organizations use empowerment to increase the decision-making discretion of individuals. The *span of control* determines how many people a venture's supervisors can effectively and efficiently manage. In *centralization-decentralization*, a decision is made as to who makes decisions about what gets done, when, and how. In a centralized organization, decision making is concentrated in the hands of a few people. In a decentralized organization, decision making is delegated to other organizational members. The degree of *formalization* determines how standardized jobs are and the extent to which employee behavior is dictated by rules and procedures.
8. A mechanistic organization is a rigid and tightly controlled structure characterized by high specialization, rigid departmentalization, clear chain of command, narrow spans of control, high formalization, limited information networking throughout the organization, and little participation in decision making by employees. A mechanistic structure is focused on efficiency and

cost minimization and would be appropriate when cost efficiencies are critical to the organization's competitive advantage; for large organizations, in which more specialization, departmentalization, centralization, and rules and regulations are needed for control; if the organization produces standardized products in a routine fashion; and when the external environment is relatively stable and certain. An organic organization is a structure that's highly adaptive and flexible with little work specialization, minimal formalization, and little direct supervision of employees. The organic organization is more appropriate when innovation is critical to the organization's competitive advantage; for smaller organizations, in which rigid approaches to dividing and coordinating work aren't necessary; if the organization produces customized products in a flexible setting; and when the external environment is dynamic, complex, and uncertain.

9. A virtual organization is an organizational design that is a network of independent people linked by common goals and information technology. A boundaryless organization is an organizational design that is not defined by, or limited to, horizontal, vertical, or external boundaries imposed by a predefined structure.

KEY TERMS

- *Sole proprietorship:* A form of organization in which the owner maintains sole and complete control over the business and is personally liable for business debts.
- *Unlimited liability:* The obligation to personally repay all debts incurred by the business.
- *General partnership:* A form of business organization in which two or more business owners share the management and risk of the business.
- *Articles of partnership:* The formal contract between partners forming a partnership.
- *Limited liability partnership (LLP):* A form of business organization in which there are general partner(s) and limited liability partner(s).
- *Corporation:* A legal business entity that is separate from its owners and managers.
- *Closely held corporation:* A corporation owned by a limited group of people who do not trade the stock publicly.
- *Articles of incorporation:* A document that describes the business and is filed with the state in which the corporation is formed.
- *Bylaws:* The rules and regulations that govern the management and operation of the corporation.
- *Board of directors:* Individuals elected by the shareholders to represent their interests.
- *S corporation:* A specialized type of corporation that has the regular characteristics of a C corporation, but is unique in that the owners are taxed as a partnership as long as certain criteria are met.

- *Limited liability company (LLC):* A form of business organization that's a hybrid between a partnership and a corporation.
- *Operating agreement:* The document that outlines the provisions governing the way an LLC will conduct business.
- *Trademark:* A form of legal protection for a distinctive word, name, phrase, logo, symbol, design, slogan, or any combination of these elements.
- *Patent:* A legal property that allows its holder to prevent others from employing this property for their own use for a specific period of time.
- *Utility patent:* A patent that covers inventions that work uniquely to perform a function or use.
- *Design patent:* A patent that covers a unique or new form, shape, or design of an existing object.
- *Plant patent:* A patent that covers new strains of living plants.
- *Contract:* An agreement that creates legal obligations and is enforceable in a court of law.
- *Organizing:* The process of deciding how best to get the venture's work done by grouping organizational activities and resources within some type of organizational structure.
- *Organizational structure:* The formal framework within which work is divided, grouped, and coordinated.
- *Organizational chart:* A visual representation of an organization's structure.
- *Organizational design:* The process of developing or changing the organizational structure.
- *Work specialization:* The degree to which work tasks are divided into separate jobs.
- *Departmentalization:* The basis by which specialized work tasks (jobs) are grouped.
- *Cross-functional teams:* Hybrid groupings of individuals from various specialties or functions who work together on tasks.
- *Empowerment:* Increasing the decision-making discretion of individuals.
- *Span of control:* The number of employees a venture's supervisors can effectively and efficiently manage.
- *Centralization:* The degree to which decision making is concentrated in the hands of a few people.
- *Decentralization:* The degree to which decision making is delegated to other organizational members.
- *Formalization:* The degree to which jobs are standardized and the extent to which employee behavior is dictated by rules and procedures.
- *Mechanistic organization:* A rigid and tightly controlled structure that's characterized by high specialization, rigid departmentalization, clear chain of command, narrow spans of control, high formalization, limited information networking, and little participation in decision making by employees.

- *Organic organization:* A structure that's highly adaptive and flexible, with little work specialization, minimal formalization, and little direct supervision of employees.
- *Virtual organization:* An organizational design that's a network of independent people linked by common goals and information technology.
- *Boundaryless organization:* An organizational design that's not defined by, or limited to, horizontal, vertical, or external boundaries imposed by a predefined structure.

SWEAT EQUITY

1. A custom-made candle business owned and operated by high-school students in Ozark, Missouri, broke a national Junior Achievement sales record when it surpassed $16,000 in sales in its first year of operation. The student president of the company said, "Organization was the toughest part. You learn real quick what works and what doesn't."
   - What is your interpretation of this remark? Do you agree or disagree? Why?
   - What are the implications for entrepreneurs who are looking at organizing their entrepreneurial ventures?
   - Contact your local Junior Achievement office to set up interviews with one or two student-run businesses. Discuss with them their experiences in organizing their business. What problems did they run into? How did they resolve these problems?
2. Go to the U.S. Patent and Trademark Office Web site (**www.uspto.gov**). Pick any of the topics there and compile a bulleted list of 10 items of important information. Be prepared to share your information with the class.
3. Visit with a business law professor or an attorney and ask about the importance for entrepreneurs of understanding contracts. What types of contracts might an entrepreneur face? What types of problems might arise? How can these problems be minimized or averted? Write a short report detailing the information you learned. Be prepared to share your information with the class.
4. Interview five different entrepreneurs as to their form of legal business organization. Ask them why they chose that particular form of legal organization. A survey will be conducted in class to see what the most common forms of organization are.
5. Discuss the statement below in a short paper. What's your interpretation? What are the organizational implications for entrepreneurs?

   "Over the course of time, many entrepreneurs can build their business to a particular size. But then they're unable to get it to the next level."
6. The performance of a partnership depends on the performance levels of each of the partners. How should business partners evaluate one another's performance? Research this topic and come up with a recommendation for a peer performance evaluation that would be viable in a business partnership. Be sure to support your ideas.

7. The Occupational Safety and Health Administration (**www.osha.gov**) develops guidelines for workplace health and safety. One of the issues OSHA is currently involved with is ergonomic injuries. Research the current regulations in this area and what impact they have on small businesses. Prepare a bulleted list summarizing your findings.
8. Current entrepreneurship research suggests that businesses owned by entrepreneurial teams generally have more diversified skills and competence bases to draw on, wider social and business networks, which can be used to acquire additional resources, and increased legitimacy especially when trying to secure financial backing. Explain each of these. What are the implications for organizing the entrepreneurial venture?
9. Solo workers face particular challenges in launching and managing their entrepreneurial ventures. Research this topic and write a 2- to 3-page report describing what solo workers can do to be successful.
10. Are patents an outdated idea for entrepreneurial ventures? The U.S. Patent and Trademark Office is struggling with an ever-increasing number of patent applications. Is it time to rethink the patent process? Research this issue. Your professor will divide the class into two. One half of the class will take the perspective that "yes, patents are an outdated idea and are not useful in today's economy" and the other half will take the perspective that "no, patents are not outdated and still play a viable role in today's economy." Be prepared to debate your side of the issue.

ENTREPRENEURSHIP IN ACTION CASES

StrawberyFrog.com (www.strawberryfrog.com)

This case can be found at the beginning of Chapter 5.

Discussion Questions

1. Check out StrawberryFrog's Web site (**www.strawberryfrog.com**). Describe the company's unique approach to what it does.
2. Is StrawberryFrog's organizational design more of a mechanistic or an organic organization? Explain.
3. How might StrawberryFrog deal with the six key elements of organizational design?
4. Why do you think StrawberryFrog's unique structural design works?

Soho, Inc.

Selling ergonomic computer desks in retail superstores such as OfficeMax and Wal-Mart doesn't exactly sound like a chaotic business in which adaptability and flexibility in organizational structure would be critical to success. However, Mahmoud (Max) Ladjevardi and Bibi Kasrai (a husband-and-wife team), co-owners of Soho, have found that being a virtual organization has been a wise decision.

Although Ladjevardi didn't enter the business with the intent of being a virtual company, he thought to himself, "Can I add that much value building all aspects of the company myself?" His answer was a clear and resounding "no!" So, Max and Bibi chose to handle sales and marketing out of their home office in La Jolla, California. Two employees in Milford, Massachusetts, handle orders and back-office operations. Everything else is outsourced. The company has contracts with 14 suppliers around the country: a wood fabricator in North Carolina, a metal manufacturer in Georgia, a bracket supplier in Ohio. These suppliers ship finished parts to a warehouse in Chicago, where the components are boxed and shipped to customers. The company spends no money on advertising but instead offers promotional discounts to retailers to garner premium shelf space or full pages in catalogs. With the approach Max and Bibi have chosen, they can fill orders for 10 desks or 10,000. Says Max, "If I can earn a profit with four people, why would I want to do it with ten?" Their biggest expense is the variable cost of materials. However, they have no money tied up in a factory, machinery, or warehousing space.

Max and Bibi know that their most valuable asset is the patent on their wood-and-metal desk units with adjustable shelves. A Soho desk allows users to set their own keyboard and monitor heights even if they choose to sit on the floor or stand up. In the huge market for computer desks, ergonomic designs appeal to individuals concerned about the repetitive motion injuries arising from sitting in front of a computer for an extended period. Well aware of the fact that the ergonomic desk patent expires in 2013, the duo is dreaming up new devices for Soho.

Discussion Questions

1. Using information from the chapter, describe Soho's organizational design.
2. Why do you think this type of organizational structure has worked for Soho? Would it work for other types of organizations? Why or why not?
3. This case is a good example of the importance of patent protection. What will Max and Bibi have to do to protect that asset now and in the long run?
4. Research outsourcing. What are its advantages? Its drawbacks?

Sources: L. Gallagher, "The Virtual Start-Up," *Forbes,* August 9, 1999, p. 78; and D. Morse, "Where's the Company?" *Wall Street Journal,* May 21, 1998, p. R19.

Who Needs an Attorney?

Thoughts of drowning while surfing in Baja, California, prompted James Evans to purchase a surfboard quick-release device. After finding nothing suitable on the market, Evans decided to invent one himself using fabric and rubber. When his fellow surfer pals enthusiastically endorsed his invention, Evans decided to patent it. Many people have this type of inspiration but when faced with the sum (anywhere from $3,000 to $10,000) they would spend on a patent attorney—more than they would possibly ever earn from the patent invention—they don't pursue their idea.

As a journalist for a California legal public publication and author of *Law on the Net,* a book about legal resources on the Internet, Evans knew how to avoid the expense. He first checked the U.S. Patent Office Web site (**www.uspto.gov**). He searched the site using the keywords *surfboard, leash,* and *quick release* and found only four patents for inventions similar to this. With a few more clicks, he had the names of the patent holders, the dates of issuance and patent numbers, and summaries of how the inventions worked. After his Web search, Evans decided that the four other surfboard leash snaps weren't similar enough to be a threat to his idea. (One used a buckle, another a pin, a third a snap, and the fourth a foot-activated pressure release. Evans's invention used Velcro.)

The next step Evans took was to file a patent application using a book and software sold by Nolo Press (**www.nolo.com**). With this, he wrote a detailed description of his invention. This information, two pages of graphics, four Patent Office forms, and the filing fee were submitted to the Patent Office. Once this required material is submitted, it takes at least a year for the government agency to decide whether to issue a patent.

Discussion Questions

1. Do you think it's a good idea for individuals to do their own patent search and application? Why or why not? (Discuss the advantages and disadvantages of doing so.)
2. Pretend you're an official at the USPTO looking over this application. Using the information in the chapter, does this invention meet the requirements to be patentable? Explain.
3. Go to the Nolo Press Web site. Search for information on patents. What information did you find there? Did you find this information helpful? Why or why not?

Source: S. Adams, "Be Your Own Patent Lawyer," *Forbes*, October 20, 1997, pp. 188–90.

Glory Foods (www.gloryfoods.com)

William Williams, cofounder of Glory Foods, followed his own recipe for success. Glory Foods, Inc., based in Columbus, Ohio, has annual revenues of over $14 million. It sells "down-home tasting" southern cuisine specialties that are quick and easy to prepare, a delicious alternative to the traditional southern cooking that takes hours. The company has successfully cornered a market niche by following a conservative path to growth.

Williams founded the company after he saw all the ethnic foods being sold—Hispanic, Asian, Jewish, everything but African-American food—while walking down a grocery store aisle. As the owner of a soul food restaurant in Columbus, Williams "smelled" opportunity. Traditional southern cuisine—foods such as black-eyed peas, collard greens, grits, peppered vinegar, and hot sauce—are all very labor-intensive to prepare. Because people are busy, they don't have the time or energy to spend hours cooking and baking, even though they love these kinds of food. Williams felt there had to be a market for ready-prepared African-American food. The big food manufacturers such as Swanson and Green Giant weren't targeting any specific niches, and the companies that were had overlooked this particular food market. Williams decided to pursue his entrepreneurial idea.

Williams brought together two partners, all with food industry experience. They pooled their money and launched Glory Foods. From the beginning the founders followed a conservative path. They all kept their day jobs until the business was financially stable. That way no one would be taking a salary out of the business because capital was scarce in the early days. The threesome worked two years to develop their recipes. They took their time because their goal was making food that tasted delicious and authentic, yet would be healthier, and lower in fat, cholesterol, and salt. Throughout that time, Williams tested recipes at his restaurant to see how customers responded. The partners deliberately chose not to go to market with their products until they had all 17 specialties ready.

Once the products were of the desired quality, Glory Foods test-marketed its products in Kroger grocery stores for 90 days. Although Kroger wanted to place the products in all 90 of its stores in central Ohio, Williams decided to take only part of the order—enough for 40 stores. His rationale was that he felt that Glory Foods was underfinanced for such a large order. Although it was a difficult decision to make at the time, it turned out to be a smart one. With the Kroger order, Williams was able to get a bank line of credit. He then went to South Carolina and contracted with farmers to grow fresh vegetables and with a factory to process the produce. At that time there was no money left for advertising, so Williams resorted to down-home marketing. He recruited women's auxiliary groups from local black churches to give out food samples in the Kroger stores. For their services, Glory made donations to the churches and paid the women $10 an hour. For the first six months of their debut, Glory Foods' products sold slowly. However, another large grocery chain, Food Lion, heard of Glory Foods and placed an order for its 1,400 stores. Cash flow constraints kept Glory from taking on the full order, but it did stock 600 Food Lion stores with its products.

Even with its calculated, careful growth, the time was fast approaching when the company would need more capital to continue in business. The three partners each agreed to invest additional money and to sell 17 percent of the company to 40 investors, mainly friends and a few family members.

Williams's decision to move slowly was based mostly on the fact that he didn't want to dilute the founders' equity portions down to minority levels. Several venture capitalists expressed strong interest in the company, but the partners turned them down. Although the slow-growth approach may have taken more time, Glory Foods' partners felt it was worth it.

In December 2001 Glory Foods faced a crisis that any entrepreneurial venture fears—the death of one of its partners, founder William Williams. Would the business be the same without Williams, the energetic and dynamic founder? Today, Glory Foods distributes a full line of canned vegetables, frozen entrees and side dishes, and fresh vegetables to over 140 supermarket chains throughout the United States. Williams had the foresight to build a company that would withstand time. In fact, in May 2002 one of Glory Foods' products was nominated for a prestigious international award. Glory Foods' director of sales said, "This is quite an honor for Glory Foods and validates that we have indeed successfully captured the authentic taste of the South."

Discussion Questions

1. What organizing implications do you see in Glory Foods' story?

2. What are the advantages and drawbacks to the partnership approach to organizing?
3. Succession issues are something that every entrepreneur needs to think about. Research the topic of succession planning. Prepare a bulleted list of your findings.

Sources: Information on company from company's Web site (**www.gloryfoods.com**), June 10, 2002; Hoover's Online (**www.hoovers.com**), June 10, 2002; and C. Shook, "Making Haste Slowly," *Forbes*, September 22, 1997, pp. 220–22.

Eclipse Aviation (www.eclipseaviation.com)

It's been described as the future "Checker Cab of the skies." Eclipse Aviation of Albuquerque, New Mexico, aims to change the face of aviation with its Eclipse 500 aircraft. Founded by a former Microsoft executive, Eclipse's CEO Vern Raburn is an air buff and pilot. His company is applying revolutionary propulsion, manufacturing, and electronics systems to produce aircraft that cost less than a third of today's small jet aircraft, will be significantly safer and easier to operate than those of today, and have the lowest cost of ownership ever achieved in a jet aircraft. Eclipse's goal is to bring the word "personal" into aviation, by making it possible for passengers to move directly between cities on a quick, affordable, and convenient basis. That dream is embodied in the Eclipse 500, the company's twin-engine microjet. The six-seater will be able to go about 400 miles per hour and have a range of 1,500 miles.

What has made Eclipse's dream possible is a handful of technological breakthroughs, the most critical being an engine that has the highest thrust-to-weight ratio of any commercial jet. Also, to save manufacturing costs, the Eclipse 500's aluminum skin is made of panels that are friction-stir welded rather than riveted. Raburn also chose to merge navigation and weather systems into digital displays and to replace the units that control the plane's flaps and gears with computers that do it at a fraction of the weight. Estimated operating costs for the Eclipse are just 56 cents per mile, compared with $1.75 per mile for the Cessna CJ1, the plane's closest competitor. And at a selling price of $837,500, the Eclipse costs a fourth of what the CJ1 does.

Bringing Eclipse to this point has been the result of several partnerships with other organizations. For instance, Avidyne Corporation of Lincoln, Massachusetts, is supplying avionics and integrated electronics for the Eclipse 500, Williams International created the jet engine that powers the aircraft, and Argo-Tech Corporation will be providing the entire integrated fuel system for the jet. These strategic alliances have been crucial to the company's ability to pursue its dream.

Will the company's flight plan get off the ground? With its first test flight scheduled for July 2002, the Eclipse 500 has been an interesting work in progress. If all goes as planned, the future of commercial air travel just may be drastically changed.

Discussion Questions

1. One of the most critical elements in the development of the Eclipse 500 has been the partnerships with various organizations that are supplying components of the aircraft. These organizational partnerships can be viewed as a type of strategic alliance. Research the topic of

strategic alliances and write a bulleted list of information you find.

2. Take a look at the description of the company's team of managers on its Web site. How would you describe the company's approach to departmentalization? Explain why you chose what you did.
3. Eclipse Aviation's board of directors has played an important role in the development of the company. (The board of directors is profiled on the company's Web site.) What would be the advantages and drawbacks of having a heavily involved board?

Sources: Company information from Web site (**www.eclipseaviation.com**), June 10, 2002; H. Kestin, "The Plane Truth," *Inc.*, June 2002, pp. 64–74; M. Stibbe, "The Checker Cab of the Skies?" *Business 2.0,* May 2002, p. 26; and R. Karlgaard, "Business Travel Battleground," *Forbes*, May 13, 2002, p. 45.

BUSINESS PLAN PRO

EXERCISE 5-1: The Company Chapter

Business Plan Pro's list of business plan tasks in the Easy Task Wizard includes a section called "Your Company," which is normally used to describe the formation and organization of a new company, the history of an existing company, ownership, legal background, and related details.

- Using any one of the business plans you've worked on for previous exercises, or a new plan of your choosing, click the "Wizard Tasks" icons to show the task view. Find the "Your Company" section and fill in the details. That will include sections for a general introductory paragraph, a description of the legal entity and ownership, and either a Start-up or a Past Performance table, depending on whether the plan is for a start-up company or an existing company. (*Hint: the Guided Tour in Chapter 3 of the Business Plan Pro manual, which we used in Exercise 2-1, includes a useful sample start-up table for Graphico.*). Use your judgment and the contents of this chapter to create an appropriate plan for establishing the legal identity, whether it be corporation, sole proprietor, or some other form.

BUSINESS NOW — SAVVIS Communications Corporation

Savvy. When a person has savvy, they're confident, proficient, and competent. When SAVVIS (**www.savvis.com**) chose its corporate name, it was making a play on the word "savvy," and banking on people thinking it was confident, proficient, and competent. What does SAVVIS do?

SAVVIS, founded in St. Louis, Missouri, in 1995, is a global network service provider that supplies access, data transport, and related services to over 2,500 medium and large businesses and Internet service providers. Its customers include world leaders in the financial services industry, including companies such as the New York Stock Exchange, the Chicago Board Options Exchange, the Montreal Derivatives Exchange, Reuters, The Royal Bank of Scotland, and MoneyLine Telerate, among others. Billions of dollars in transactions rely on SAVVIS's networks every single day.

According to Rob McCormick, CEO and chairman, SAVVIS was created out of two different pieces: a best-in-class public Internet service provider and a global private network company. The combination of the two means that customers can count on SAVVIS for both their public and private network needs. Of these two, the private networks appear to be a service that SAVVIS takes very seriously. McCormick says, "When SAVVIS promises customers a private network, it will be private. We built our name in the financial services industry, which is most concerned about security and reliability."

Since SAVVIS's initial public offering in February 2000, the company has been showing its stuff at trade shows in its quest for more identity in the marketplace. This type of branding will be critical to SAVVIS's future success. And trade shows are a great venue to showcase the company's broad range of high-technology products. SAVVIS feels that its combination of smart people, smart networks, and smart customers are just what it needs.

Discussion Questions

1. In the types of industries SAVVIS competes in, would a mechanistic- or an organic-type organization design be more appropriate? Explain your answer.
2. With what types of legal issues might SAVVIS have to deal as it carries out its business?
3. SAVVIS has dual headquarters—in St. Louis, Missouri, and in Herndon, Virginia. What types of organizational design challenges does this type of arrangement present? How could SAVVIS's decision makers ensure that their organizational design continues to work effectively and efficiently?
4. Research the concept of branding. What is it? How can organizations brand? Why does SAVVIS feel that branding is important?

Sources: Company information from company Web site (**www.savvis.com**), July 10, 2002, and Hoover's Online (**www.hoovers.com**), July 10, 2002; and *Business Now* video segment.

ENDNOTES

1. Company Web site, **www.strawberryfrog.com**, June 3, 2002; and S. Ellison, "Ad Firm Strawberry Frog in Amsterdam Thinks Big But Wants to Stay Small," *Wall Street Journal*, April 3, 2000, pp. A43D+
2. L. Saunders, "Freedom Day for Small Businesses," *Forbes*, February 22, 1999, pp. 128–30.
3. "Ask Success," *Success*, August 1998, p. 29.
4. W. D. Keller, *The Essentials of Business Law, I* (Piscataway, NJ: Research and Education Association, 1998), pp. 64–74.
5. See, for example, R. L. Daft, *Organization Theory and Design*, 7th ed. (Cincinnati, OH: South-Western Publishing, 2000).
6. D. A. Morand, "The Role of Behavioral Formality and Informality in the Enactment of Bureaucratic versus Organic Organizations," *Academy of Management Review*, October 1995, pp. 831–72; and T. Burns and G. M. Stalker, *The Management of Innovation* (London: Tavistock, 1961).

7. For additional readings on boundaryless organizations, see "The Boundaryless Organization: Break the Chains of Organizational Structures," *HR Focus,* April 1996, p. 21; R. M. Hodgetts, "A Conversation with Steve Kerr," *Organizational Dynamics*, Spring 1996, pp. 68–79; and J. Gebhardt, "The Boundaryless Organization," *Sloan Management Review*, Winter 1996, pp. 117–19. For another perspective on boundaryless organizations, see B. Victor, "The Dark Side of the New Organizational Forms: An Editorial Essay," *Organization Science*, November 1994, pp. 479–82.
8. R. W. Keidel, "Rethinking Organizational Design," *Academy of Management Executive*, November 1994, pp. 12–27; R. Ashkenas, D. Ulrich, T. Jick, and S. Kerr, *The Boundaryless Organization: Breaking the Chains of Organization Structure* (San Francisco: Jossey-Bass, 1995); P. LaBarre, "The Seamless Enterprise," *Industry Week*, June 19, 1995, pp. 22–34; D. Ulrich and S. Kerr, "Creating the Boundaryless Organization: The Radical Reconstruction of Organizational Capabilities," *Planning Review*, September–October 1995, pp. 41–45; and A. Majchrazk and Q. Wang, "Breaking the Functional Mindset in Process Organizations," *Harvard Business Review*, September–October 1996, pp. 93–99.

6 Launching the Venture

LEARNING OBJECTIVES

After reading and studying this chapter, you should be able to:

1. Explain the purposes of goals.
2. Describe the kinds of goals that entrepreneurial ventures might pursue.
3. Describe the characteristics of well-written goals.
4. Explain how to set goals.
5. Discuss the importance of strategies to entrepreneurial ventures.
6. Describe the coordinative relationship between goals and strategies.
7. Explain specific operations management and technology, marketing, information systems, and financial and accounting strategies.
8. Discuss the role of quality in an entrepreneurial venture.

ENTREPRENEURSHIP IN ACTION

Nicholas Graham is the king of underwear and the self-proclaimed "Chief Underpants Officer."[1] His Joe Boxer brand of underwear has grown into a global brand on the strength of its wacky and fun boxers and briefs. Underwear, sleepwear, and loungewear for men, women, and kids represent the company's core business. However, other products, such as bedding, sportswear, and accessories (watches and mouse pads are two such products that come to mind) are produced under license to other companies.

The San Francisco–based Joe Boxer Company (**www.joeboxer.com**) was founded in 1985 on the premise that the most basic and utilitarian element of men's clothing should be remade to reflect humor, fashion, and the shifting trends in American culture. Over the years, Graham has guided his company with a bold plan and specific goals. He understood that the clothing industry (even the

You might be saying to yourself about now, "What a strange company!" However strange and wacky it may appear, Nicholas Graham's Joe Boxer Corporation has carved a successful niche for itself. From his original idea to change the way the world looked at men's underwear to the unique Joe Boxer Cab program, Graham has fashioned an assortment of strategies to launch and operate his entrepreneurial venture. In this chapter, we're going to look at the process of launching an entrepreneurial venture. Once the venture has been planned and organized, it's time to get it going. Doing that involves establishing goals and strategies for the organization's key work activities. These key work activities include technology and operations methods, marketing, information systems, and financial and accounting systems. As we look at each of these areas, we'll be examining the specific types of strategies that entrepreneurs might use. Before we get into the specifics of these areas, however, we need to explore what's involved with establishing goals and strategies.

ESTABLISHING ORGANIZATIONAL GOALS AND STRATEGIES

Without goals and strategies, there would be no coherent organizational decisions or direction. Once the vision and mission are outlined, the business plan crafted, and the organization's legal and structural decisions made, it's time for the entrepreneur to think about more specific issues of what the entrepreneurial venture hopes to accomplish and how it will do so. Rather than rushing headfirst into the unknown with no thought given to the future (even in the dynamic, often chaotic environments of entrepreneurial ventures), it's important to take the time to establish goals and strategies. In this section, we're going to discuss what goals and strategies are and the process entrepreneurs use in developing them.

Organizational Goals

Remember that we defined **goals** earlier in Chapter 4 as outcomes or end results that are desired by individuals, groups, or entire organizations. Although some individuals make a distinction between goals and objectives—they maintain that goals are more general and objectives are more specific—we're going to use the terms *goals* and *objectives* interchangeably. But no matter what we call them, why is it important to have goals? Goals serve three main purposes. (See Exhibit 6-1.)

"under" clothing industry) was intensely competitive and that being successful in such an environment would require bold strategic choices.

The company firmly believes in innovation and creativity and emphasizes these core values in product design, merchandising, marketing, customer service, and all business functions. However, in this business, marketing and publicity strategies are the bread-and-butter of Joe Boxer's operation. And they've done some pretty wacky things. From the world's largest e-mail message center on a billboard in New York's Times Square to the Joe Boxer Cab that cruises the streets of New York and San Francisco, Graham states, "I guess the more people talk about you, the better. Joe Boxer is very eccentric." To continue its growth, the company's newest strategy was an exclusive distribution arrangement with Kmart that started in July 2002.

EXHIBIT 6-1 Why Have Goals?

Goals

1. Direct All Organizational Work Toward Common and Unified Purpose
2. Act as Targets for Motivating People
3. Serve as Criteria Against Which Work Accomplishments Are Measured

Purposes of Goals. First, goals direct the entrepreneur and other organizational members toward a common and unified organizational purpose (remember that this common and unified purpose is known as the organizational vision). Goals can help organizational members understand where the organization is going and why it's vital to get there. This is particularly important for entrepreneurial ventures in which, in a chaotic and uncertain environment, it may be easy to lose sight of what we're doing. Another reason goals are important is that they provide targets organizational members may be motivated to work toward accomplishing.[2] Motivation, very simply, is the willingness to put forth effort in the accomplishment of some activity. Don't you work a little harder, aren't you a little more motivated, when you have a goal you're trying to reach? Maybe it's getting an A in a course you're taking or maybe it's getting that term paper done one week before it's actually due. Whatever the goal might be, it serves as a target for which you put forth effort and work hard to meet. The same is true for organizational goals, except in this case, the goals may revolve around completing an advertising campaign for a new product or finding ways to lower shipping expenses. Finally, goals serve as criteria against which work accomplishments and performance are measured. How do you know how efficiently or effectively you're doing something if there's nothing against which to measure? Goals provide that measurement standard. They give us some guide as to what we should be working to accomplish. How would an entrepreneur know whether he has been successful in his efforts without some way of measuring and comparing what was done? Goals serve as a way to measure success. Actual work outcomes and results are measured against whatever goals were established. For example, did revenues increase by *x* amount? Was the product development schedule met? Was cash flow positive? Without something against which to measure, we'd never know whether what we're doing is the best thing for us to be doing or whether we're doing it the best possible way. Eddie Cheever, well known in the world of racecars, founded Alleanza Marketing Group in 2001 to handle sponsorship campaigns for his racing team. Although he had no formal business training, Cheever recognized the role of goals in success. He said, "The most important thing for both a race team and a company is to know what the goal is. In racing, everybody understands that the goal is to win races. The primary goal of our marketing company is whatever our sponsors are trying to achieve."[3]

As you can see, goals play an important role in an entrepreneurial venture for several reasons. But it's also important to understand that there are different types of goals an entrepreneur needs to establish.

Types of Goals. At first glance, it might seem that a business organization would have only one objective—to make a profit. However, it's not quite that simple. All organizations have different types of goals. Because there are a variety of work activities to be pursued in an entrepreneurial venture, and because no one single measure can evaluate whether an organization is successful, entrepreneurs need to establish several goals. (See Exhibit 6-2.)

EXHIBIT 6-2 Types of Goals

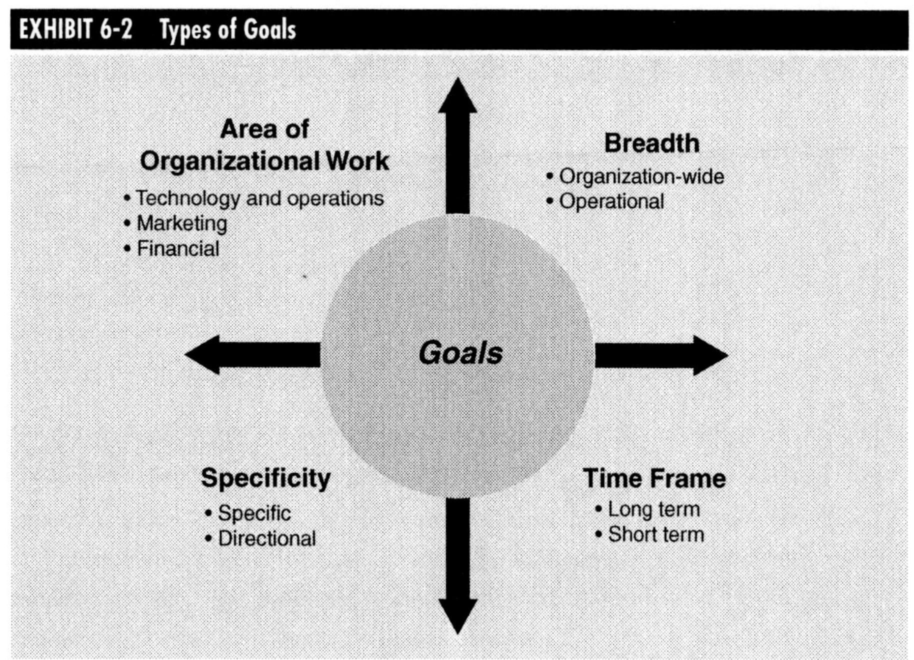

As you can see, there are four ways to describe the goals of an entrepreneurial venture: breadth, time frame, specificity, and area. The breadth category covers how broad-based or narrow the organizational goals are. **Organization-wide goals** are ones that establish broad purposes, apply to the entire entrepreneurial venture, and seek to position the venture successfully in terms of its environment. These goals are broad in nature and tend to encompass the entire spectrum of what the entrepreneurial venture hopes to accomplish. These organization-wide goals stem from the organizational vision and provide broad targets for organizational members to accomplish. On the other hand, **operational goals** are ones that specify details associated with accomplishing the organization-wide goals. The operational goals are much narrower in focus and serve to divide the organization-wide goals into more specific targets.

Time frame is another way to describe an entrepreneurial venture's goals. By definition, a goal is something to be accomplished in the future. What this category of goals describes is how far away that "future" is. The difference in years between short term and long term has shortened considerably. It used to be that long term meant anything over seven or even ten years. Try to imagine what you want to be doing in seven years, and you can begin to appreciate the difficulty of establishing goals that far into the future. Therefore, we're going to define **long-term goals** as ones with a time frame beyond three years.[4] **Short-term goals** are ones that cover one year or less. Although these time classifications (that is, three years and one year) are fairly common, any desired time frame can be used by an entrepreneur. Whatever time frame is used, entrepreneurs do need to have both long- and short-term goals. Long-term goals provide a coherent and unified future target for the entrepreneurial venture whereas the short-term goals provide the stepping stones to the future. It's like building a house, for which you have the long-term goal of having a solid, functional, and enjoyable living space. But to get

Entrepreneurs in Action

Wiley Mullins is a good example of how entrepreneurs must set goals on the road to success. He knew his Healthy Southern Classics (**www.unclewileys.com**) line of food seasonings was a winner if he could just get supermarkets to sample them. But first he had to overcome their reluctance to try fat-free and cholesterol-free versions of seasonings for traditional southern cooking. With no proven track record of demand for his products, Mullins had an uphill battle. However, he first set a short-term goal to get into one major food chain and to work from there. He also had a long-term goal of seeing his face on his packages smiling down at customers from gleaming grocery shelves all across the country. Today, Mullins has around 15 employees and around $1.5 million in annual revenues. You can see Wiley's smiling face on his packages found in a number of top grocery chains, including Safeway, Stop & Shop, and Wal-Mart.

Sources: Company information from company Web site (**www.unclewileys.com**), June 11, 2002; Hoover's Online (**www.hoovers.com**), June 11, 2002; and B. Deterline, "A Man for All Seasonings," *Smart Money*, April 1999, pp. 155–58.

to that point, you have to accomplish certain short-term goals along the way, such as getting the foundation poured, the plumbing installed, and the floors carpeted. The accomplishment of these short-term goals contributes to the accomplishment of the long-term goal. It's the same thing for an entrepreneurial venture, in which it's important to accomplish the short-term goals in order to reach the long-term goals.

The next category describes how specific organizational goals are. **Specific goals** are ones that are clearly defined and leave no room for interpretation. There's no ambiguity and no problem with misunderstanding what is intended to be accomplished. Although it may seem preferable to have goals be as specific as possible, there are drawbacks to having specific goals. They require clarity and a sense of predictability that typically do not exist in an entrepreneurial environment. When uncertainty is high and decision makers must be flexible in order to respond to unexpected changes, it is preferable to use **directional goals**, which are flexible enough to provide focus and general guidelines but do not lock entrepreneurs into specific courses of action. The flexibility of directional goals must be weighed against the loss of clarity provided by specific ones.

One thing that you may have noticed after reading the descriptions of these first three categories of goals (organization-wide vs. operational, long-term vs. short-term, and directional vs. specific) is the similarity among them. Well, you're very perceptive! In fact, organization-wide goals tend to be long-term and directional and operational goals tend to be short-term and specific. The important thing to recognize is that entrepreneurs need to establish both broad, directional, long-term goals *and* narrow, specific, short-term goals. All these different types of goals are needed in the last category of goals we need to examine—areas of organizational work.

The final types of goals are those established for the various organizational work areas. The most common organizational work areas include technology and operations methods, marketing, and financial. (Please note that the human resource area is an important work area, also. However, because it encompasses such a wide array of issues, we'll cover it in Chapter 8.) Therefore, an entrepreneur would want to set technology and operations goals, marketing goals, and financial goals. But, be aware that not all organizations do the same type of work. Entrepreneurs should establish goals for the particular types of work activity that characterize their entrepreneurial ventures. So whether the venture is a restaurant, a software design firm, or a medical equipment laboratory, these goals should reflect the specialized work that is done.

Now that we've discussed all the types of goals that are important for an entrepreneur to establish, we need to look at how these goals are developed. What's involved in setting goals? However, before we explain the steps in the goal-setting process, we need to look at the characteristics of "well-written" goals.

Characteristics of Well-Written Goals. Goals are not all created equal! Some goals are better than others. How do you tell the difference? What makes a goal a "well-written" goal? Exhibit 6-3 outlines the characteristics of well-written goals.

A well-written goal should be written in terms of outcomes rather than actions. The desired end result is the most important element of any goal; therefore, the goal should be written to reflect this. Next, a goal should be measurable and quantifiable. It's much easier to determine if a goal has been met if it's measurable. For instance, suppose one of your goals is to "produce a high-quality product." What exactly do you mean by "high quality"? Because there are numerous ways to define quality, you should be stating specifically how you will measure whether the product is high quality. This means that even in areas in which it may be difficult to quantify your intent, you should try to find some specific way or ways to measure whether that goal is accomplished. Why have the goal if you can't measure whether it's been met?

In line with specifying a quantifiable measure of accomplishment, a well-written goal should also have a clear time frame. Although open-ended goals may seem preferable because of the supposed flexibility they give, in fact, goals without a time frame make an organization less flexible because you're never sure when the goal has been met or when you should call it quits because the goal will never be met regardless of how long you work at it. A well-written goal will specify a time frame for accomplishment.

Next, a well-written goal should be challenging yet attainable. Goals that are too easy to accomplish are not motivating; neither are goals that are not attainable even with exceptional effort. To provide high levels of individual motivation, goals should be challenging yet attainable.

EXHIBIT 6-3 Characteristics of Well-Written Goals

- Written in terms of outcomes rather than actions
- Measurable and quantifiable
- Clear as to a time frame
- Challenging yet attainable
- Written down
- Communicated to all organizational members

The Grey Zone One potential ethical dilemma of which entrepreneurs need to be aware as they work on establishing goals is the focus on outcomes rather than on actions. Although it's important in writing goals to identify the desired end result, you don't want to give the impression that achieving this goal is important even if you have to act unethically or irresponsibly to do so. When organizational (or individual) performance results are evaluated only on outcomes, there are increased pressures to do "whatever is necessary" to look good by achieving the desired outcomes. How can entrepreneurs get the best of both worlds—the desired focus on end results and being ethical and responsible while achieving these ends? What would you recommend that entrepreneurs do to deal with this ethical dilemma?

Well-written goals are written down. Although actually writing down goals may seem a ridiculous waste of time, the process of writing the goals forces the entrepreneur to think them through. In addition, the written goals become visible and tangible evidence of the importance of working toward something—something specific that is important to the entrepreneur to accomplish. After all, if it isn't important enough to identify and accomplish, why have the goal in the first place?

Finally, well-written goals are communicated to all organizational members. This may not be necessary in an entrepreneurial venture with one person (the entrepreneur), but it becomes extremely important as people join the organization. It's important that these individuals know what end results are being pursued. Particularly in a growing entrepreneurial venture, goals need to be communicated so that everyone is aware of them. This, in turn, helps ensure that all organizational members are "on the same page" and that they are working in ways to ensure the accomplishment of the organizational goals.

The question now becomes How do I establish goals? What process should I follow? Exhibit 6-4 illustrates the seven steps in the goal setting process.

The Goal Setting Process. Sitting down and writing out goals is not something most entrepreneurs look forward to doing. However, as we've discussed, it *is* important to have written goals. The process of writing goals can be made easier by following these seven steps.

EXHIBIT 6-4 The Goal-Setting Process

Steps

1. Review the organizational vision and mission(s)
2. Evaluate available resources
3. Determine broad, long-term organization-wide goals
4. Write down the organization-wide goals
5. Determine specific, short-term operational goals
6. Write down the operational goals
7. Review results

Goals

Step 1. Review the organizational vision and mission(s). These broad statements of the entrepreneurial venture's purpose and what it hopes to accomplish provide an overall guide to what the entrepreneur and other organizational members think is important. As we stated in Chapter 4, the vision and mission are future-oriented (just as goals are). Therefore, it's important to review these statements before writing goals because organizational goals should be established in light of the vision and mission statements.

Step 2. Evaluate available resources. You wouldn't want to set goals that are impossible to achieve given your available resources.

Even though goals should be challenging, they should also be realistic. If your resources won't allow you to achieve a goal no matter how hard you try or how much effort is put forth, that goal shouldn't be set. That would be like the person with a $50,000 annual income and no other financial resources setting a goal of building a $1 million house in two years. No matter how hard he or she works at it, it's not going to happen!

Step 3. Determine individually or with input from other organizational members broad, long-term, and organization-wide goals. In order for these organization-wide goals to provide an entrepreneur with a sense of what the overall entrepreneurial venture hopes to achieve, they should be measurable and indicate a time frame. For instance, achieving a 2 percent market share penetration within three years or bringing out a new product every year for the next four years.

Step 4. Write down these organization-wide goals. You already know why written goals are important!

Step 5. Determine specific, short-term, operational goals individually or with input from other organizational members. These goals reflect the desired outcomes in the various areas of operational work activities and are congruent with the organization-wide goals. They should be measurable, specific, and include a time frame.

Step 6. Write down these operational goals.

Step 7. Review results and whether goals are being met. Make changes as needed. Given the fast-paced dynamic nature of entrepreneurial organizations, this can be a real challenge. However, to keep from focusing resources and efforts on unimportant activities and to keep from wasting resources, it's important to know

Entrepreneurs in Action

John Kowalski had a dream about a mean-looking, bristle-backed and crimson-eyed pig lurching from beneath the bed of a pickup truck. Although a dream like this would frighten most people, Kowalski woke up and drew the image on paper. The next day he took his rough sketch to an artist, who transformed it into the logo for Kowalski's company, Load Hog Industries (**www.loadhog.com**). The logo was actually the easy part of launching the business. Most entrepreneurs assume that they'll get their ventures up and running in a fairly short time, even with setbacks. However, it's taken Kowalski nine long years to do so. Yet, the experiences have made the company stronger. In fact, Kowalski's strategy is to extend his product's application well beyond its original market, which should help ensure the company's future success.

Sources: Company Web site (**www.loadhog.com**), June 13, 2002; and L. Buchanan, "Pickup Artist," *Inc.*, June 2001, pp. 68–73.

whether the established goals are being achieved. Because the established goals serve to direct efforts, energies, and resources in appropriate ways, if we know that the goals aren't being met, we can redirect our activities and resources.

Now that we have a well-defined set of goals, what next? At this point, the entrepreneur should develop specific strategies to accomplish the goals.

Organizational Strategies

What exactly is a **strategy**? It's a plan of action for accomplishing goals. Specific strategies need to be developed so the venture's long-term organization-wide goals and the short-term operational goals can be achieved. They do, indeed, play an important role in how well the entrepreneurial venture ultimately performs.[5]

Why *are* strategies important to entrepreneurial ventures? They are important to develop because they provide the "hows" of goal achievement. Whereas the goals themselves indicate "what" the entrepreneur hopes to accomplish, the strategies outline "how" the goals are going to be met. The goals and strategies must be coordinated with each other for the venture to be successful. How should this relationship work?

As we've stated many times, the organizational vision and mission statements provide a broad overview of what the entrepreneurial venture is going to do and how it's going to do it. Using the vision and mission statements as guides, organization-wide goals are developed. From these broad goals, operational goals are developed. The operational goals are pursued through the implementation of various strategies. If the strategies are effective, the operational goals are achieved. As these operational goals are achieved, the organization-wide goals also are achieved. The whole process links the venture's vision/mission, goals, and strategies. Using our previous example of an organization-wide goal of achieving a 2 percent market share penetration within three years, we would need to specify operational goals and strategies probably in the areas of marketing, product development, and technology and operations methods (or in whatever other operational areas we feel are critical) in order to be able to achieve that organization-wide goal. If the short-term operational goals aren't achieved through the implementation of various operational strategies, there's no way that the long-term organization-wide goals are going to be met. The strategies are the ways organizational goals are pursued and ultimately achieved. For example, Debra Stark's goals and strategies for her natural-foods store Debra's Natural Gourmet in Concord, Massachusetts, are clear-cut. Her goal: successfully compete with the large competitors by slathering attention on every single customer. Her strategies to do this: employing a registered nurse to make sure natural remedies won't interfere with customers' use of other medicinal products, looking out for bogus product claims and explaining those to customers, giving every employee a management role and making them responsible for some aspect of the store's operation, prominently posting daily and monthly

Rapid Review ◀◀|

- ✔ What are goals?
- ✔ What purposes do goals serve?
- ✔ Describe the four categories of organizational goals and the types of goals within each category.
- ✔ What are the characteristics of well-written goals?
- ✔ Outline the steps in the goal-setting process.
- ✔ What is a strategy?
- ✔ Why are strategies important to entrepreneurial ventures?
- ✔ Describe the connection between goals and strategies.

sales reports, and distributing 20 percent of after-tax profits every quarter to employees. By pursuing her goal using these strategies, Stark has a loyal customer following and has achieved 11 consecutive years of double-digit revenue growth.[6]

What we need to look at next are the various work areas that entrepreneurs must address in launching the venture. As we study these, we'll be discussing the various strategic choices that entrepreneurs might consider.

DESIGNING THE VENTURE'S PRODUCTION AND OPERATIONS MANAGEMENT FUNCTION

By this point in your life, you've obviously purchased and used an incredible number and variety of products and services. Where do these products come from? How do they get made? You may have produced some yourself—for example, if you've ever grown produce in a garden, built a bookshelf out of wood and bricks, fashioned a wreath out of twigs and grapevines, or baked a loaf of bread—but most of the products we consume and use are produced (made) by someone else. The process of creating products (goods and services) in which organizational inputs (resources) are transformed into outputs is called **production**. The production process used to create physical (tangible) products is fairly obvious. You can see raw materials being transformed into an actual product. However, even the creation of services requires some types of transformation activities. What are these *transformation activities* used to create products and services? Very simply, they are the various technology and operations strategies.

Operations Management and Technology Strategies

Whether the entrepreneurial venture is producing goods or services, we need to decide what technology and operations strategies we'll use to produce our product or service. What we'll look at in this section are some of the common strategic choices in this area. Exhibit 6-5 illustrates the various operations management and technology strategies.

Production Process Strategies. How are you going to transform your available resources into the products or services that your entrepreneurial venture will market? In other words, what's the "best way" to produce the desired products?

EXHIBIT 6-5 Technology and Operations Strategies for Entrepreneurial Ventures

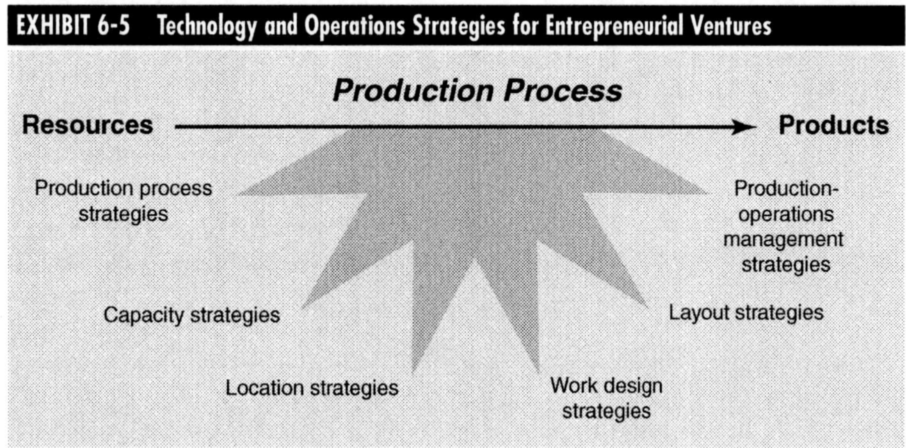

Different organizations use different approaches, but all involve a certain production process strategy. The decision about production process strategy focuses on the approach that the entrepreneurial venture will use to transform resources into goods and services. The goal of your production process strategy is to find a way to produce your products or services so that they meet (or exceed) customer expectations in light of cost and other organizational constraints. Your decision(s) in this area involve choosing the most appropriate production process strategy given the nature of your product. The type of process strategy you choose will have a long-term effect on how efficient your production activities are as well as the flexibility, cost, and quality of the products you're producing. There are three possible choices:

1. The *process-focused* strategy is one in which the organization's technology and operations methods are organized around the processes necessary to produce a customized product or service. This strategy would be appropriate for situations in which the entrepreneur is producing high-variety, low-volume products such as gourmet meals, specialized print jobs, or custom-designed Web pages. In this strategy, the most important production decisions are focused on the actual processes used in producing the custom-made, specialized products. That is, the entrepreneur must carefully consider the way the product or service is produced and make sure that production process design decisions are focused on the actual process.
2. A *product-focused* strategy is one in which the organization's technology and operations methods are organized around the products or service. This strategy would be appropriate for producing high-volume, low-variety products—for example, computer chips, potato chips, or wood chips. With this strategy, the most important production decisions are focused on the actual products, not on the process used to make them. The production process would not be complex because the products being produced are not complex. Instead, this approach is focused on making sure that the production process supports the efficient production of these products.

Entrepreneurs in Action

Payam Zamani, CEO of PurpleTie Inc. uses a process-focused strategy in his dry cleaning business. Customers use the phone or their computer to order pickup of their dirty clothes by PurpleTie's fleet of vans. After picking up the order, the company takes the soiled clothes to a centralized facility where they are cleaned and then returns them to the customer. Although this central-hub approach poses some logistics challenges, Zamani argues that it creates immense savings by cutting real estate costs. By using a centralized facility, the company doesn't need to invest in various cleaning facilities throughout the market.

Source: M. Hofman, "An Opportunity to Clean Up," *Inc.*, January 2001, pp. 21–23.

3. The *repetitive-focused* strategy is one that falls somewhere between process-focused and product-focused. In this production approach, standardized component parts, typically called modules, are used to assemble standardized products. There's more customizing of the product than in the product-focused strategy, but not as much as in the process-focused approach. An example would be an assembly line on which motorcycles are produced to customer specifications using standardized component parts. Another example might be a fast-food restaurant where the product is assembled to a customer's order using standardized components (same-size buns, same-size hamburger patty, and measured amounts of condiments).

The production process strategy most appropriate for the entrepreneurial venture depends on the volume and variety of products being produced. The entrepreneur also must consider factors such as how important it is to keep costs low, to provide high levels of quality, or to meet specialized customer needs better. Looking at all these factors is important in choosing the most appropriate production process strategy.

Capacity Strategies. Another important technology and operations strategy involves production capacity. Capacity is the maximum possible output of an organization in a given time period. It's a constraint on how much product can be produced by the entrepreneur or the entrepreneurial venture. Capacity influences how much physical space and how much equipment will be needed to produce the desired number of products. After all, you don't want to have too much or too little capacity. That could prove to be a significant financial drain on your entrepreneurial venture—either you're losing money because you don't have enough product because of the lack of space to produce more or you're paying for space that you don't need. Some strategic decisions associated with determining appropriate production capacity include demand management and capacity management. Let's look first at demand management.

How do entrepreneurial organizations "manage" demand? They'll use strategies such as staffing changes (adding or laying off employees), adjusting equipment (purchase, lease, or sell), improving work methods to be more efficient, or redesigning the product so more (or fewer) can be produced. Another factor that may need to be considered in managing demand is whether there's a seasonal demand for your venture's products. If there is, capacity will likely need to expand during the time of high demand (unless you happen to have excess capacity) and shrink during nonseasonal times. It's important for the entrepreneur who is considering demand-management strategies to also consider strategies for managing capacity. These strategic choices work hand in hand and should complement each other.

Capacity management involves decisions about how to effectively and efficiently use the current facilities and equipment. Part of this strategy involves knowing break-even point, which we discussed in Chapter 3. You want to make sure you have enough capacity to support the production level necessary to reach break-even point. On the other hand, though, you don't want to have too *much* capacity, either. Paying for excess capacity and equipment would not be a wise use of an entrepreneurial venture's often limited resources. Finally, part of the capacity-management strategy may involve forecasting future capacity requirements in order to ensure that facilities and equipment are available when needed. It's important to do some planning in order to have the necessary space and equipment.

Location Strategies. One of the most important technology and operations decisions for entrepreneurs is where to locate. This decision basically boils down to: Will you operate your entrepreneurial venture out of your home or from another location? Because the choice of location significantly influences costs and revenues, the objective of your location strategy should be to maximize the benefits and minimize the costs of locating in a particular area. What factors may affect the location strategy of an entrepreneurial venture? It's important to consider labor costs and availability (if your organization needs or may someday need additional employees), proximity to needed raw materials and suppliers, proximity to markets (customers), state and local government policies and regulations, environmental regulations, availability and cost of utilities, site costs (lease or

FYI

Designing Effective Work Spaces

Do you study better in some places than in others? What would your ideal study place look like? It used to be that organizational architects were directed to squeeze as many workers as possible into the smallest space possible to balance the cost of expensive real estate. However, today many organizations are discovering that the design of their work spaces can have a significant impact on what employees do and how they accomplish their work. For example, Austin-based Future Protocol, Inc., a computer network design company, moved into an abandoned adult-movie theater. To convert the former "porno-palace" into a high-tech workplace, Future Protocol installed windows into the walls, added skylights, and tore out the theater's seats so workstations could be installed. The theater's balcony was extended to add a second level of offices and conference rooms. The theater's marquee is now used for free advertising. CEO Jennifer Hussey says that the company's employees love it. "I've seen the motivation level climb to a new height. People seem to get here a little earlier, stay a little longer."

Why would an organization go to this type of effort to create such a work environment? There are several reasons why. First of all, office and work space design has become an important recruiting tool. Potential employees judge the look and feel of their work spaces and consider it third most important in job choice after salary and benefits. Another reason for designing desirable work spaces is the belief that it will lead to more communal bonds among employees. Fostering this community feeling is conducive to employee interaction, trust, and openness. Finally, work space design can be used to foster creativity and innovation, something that's important to entrepreneurial ventures. When work spaces are open, flexible, and designed for social interaction, employees mingle and move about. The impromptu conversations and "chance encounters" can lead to the sharing of information and new insights—all hallmarks of an innovative organization. Can work space design give an organization a competitive advantage? The answer would have to be "not by itself," but having well-designed work spaces can be an important component of a venture's strategies.

Sources: L. Kanter, "Dream Offices," *Business Week Frontier,* November 6, 2000, pp. F18–F28; and M. McDonald, "The Latte Connections," *U.S. News and World Report,* March 29, 1999, pp. 63–66.

buy), transportation availability, and quality-of-life issues. Each of these factors can influence the most appropriate choice for locating the entrepreneurial venture. Keep in mind that one or some of these factors may be more critical to your organization than others and thus may be more important to your decision about where you choose to locate your business.

Work-Design Strategies. What are work-design strategies, and why are they important to the technology and operations decisions of the entrepreneurial venture? First of all, these strategies are important to the technology and operations methods of the entrepreneurial venture because they determine who can do what work, when they can do it, and under what conditions. Very simply, they address the way your entrepreneurial venture's work is going to be done. Some of the more common work design strategies that entrepreneurs may choose involve job specialization (tasks are divided up into specialized components, with organizational employees performing one or a couple of these specialized components), job enlargement (organizational employees are given a number of tasks to do rather than specializing in just one), job enrichment (organizational employees are given the responsibility for doing the task *and* responsibilities for planning the work and measuring work performance), ergonomics (designing physically efficient and safe work approaches), work methods (determining the processes and procedures for performing tasks), and motivation and incentive systems (deciding how individuals will be rewarded for their efforts in completing assigned tasks). Work design often also involves establishing performance standards for different jobs. Organizational employees need to know what work output (quantity and quality) is desired and expected.

Layout Strategies. How a facility is arranged has a significant impact on how efficiently work gets done. The objective of an entrepreneurial venture's layout strategy is to design a layout that's economical and meets the requirements of product design and volume, process equipment and capacity, quality of work life for employees, and building and site constraints. There are six potential layout strategies:

1. The *fixed-position layout* is one in which the product remains stationary and requires workers and equipment to come to the work area. Some examples include building a bridge, erecting an apartment building, building sailboats, or dousing a burning oil well fire.
2. The *process-oriented layout* is appropriate for low-volume, high-variety products for which the focus is on the processes being used to create the product or service. Some examples might include a medical clinic, a cafeteria kitchen, or a job shop that produces thermostats. For example, O. C. Tanner Company of Salt Lake City, Utah, produces 10,000 pieces of jewelry a day, primarily for employee-recognition programs. The average order size ranges from 2 to 30 pieces. However, for the 2002 Winter Olympics, Tanner had a special job—manufacturing the more than 800 gold, silver, and bronze medals for the winning athletes. Because the medals had to be absolutely perfect, the company knew how important it was to have a layout design that met those requirements. It invested 2,175 hours to develop the techniques and processes needed to produce the medals that would be a source of pride for the host country, the United States.[7]

3. The *office layout* positions workers, equipment, and office spaces to provide for movement of information. Some examples include an insurance company, an advertising agency, or a computer software design firm.
4. The *retail/service layout* arranges people and equipment according to customers' needs and behaviors. Obviously, the objective behind any retail layout is to maximize profitability per square foot of shelf space or floor space—that is, putting the products where customers are going to buy them. Examples might include a grocery store, a clothing store, or an office products store.
5. The *warehouse layout* is designed to find the optimal tradeoff between product-handling cost and warehouse space. Examples include any type of warehouse, storage, or distribution facility.
6. The *product-oriented layout* is organized around a product or group of similar high-volume, low-variety products. In this type of repetitive, continuous production, it's important to have layout arrangements that maximize person and machine use. Examples include a meat packing facility or a furniture manufacturer.

By looking at the various options, an entrepreneur can determine which layout strategy will best fit the demands and requirements for producing the products or services of the entrepreneurial venture. An appropriately designed layout strategy can make the production process as efficient as possible.

Operations-Management Strategies. An entrepreneur might want to use other types of operations-management strategies that are associated with the production process. For instance, the entrepreneur may need to make some strategic decisions about using a just-in-time production system, purchasing-management procedures, inventory-management systems, project-management procedures, or maintenance management. Each of these strategies is aimed at making the venture's production process as efficient and effective as possible. For instance, Jeffrey

Entrepreneurs in Action

O'Reilly Auto Parts, an auto parts retailer based in Springfield, Missouri, knew that its inventory-management system wasn't adequate to support the organization's expansion from 260 to over 700 retail stores. Changes to items had to be made manually, and as the number of stocked products increased, employees were completely overwhelmed. Their solution—a major investment in sophisticated inventory-management software that could forecast demand levels based on historical sales patterns, track the performance of suppliers, and determine how much stock to order based on special discounts, current inventory levels, and planned price increases. In place since 2000, the inventory-management system has meant some $50 million a year in savings for the company. Bottom-line proof that inventory management strategies count!

Source: S. Clifford, "O'Reilly Auto Parts," *Business 2.0*, August/September 2001, p. 143.

Hochman of GW Trading Company, a St. Louis–based clothing recycling business, is using a strategy of teaming up with his competitors to buy materials, such as the steel strapping that's used to wrap bales of clothing. Why? To cut costs in an uncertain economy.[8] One operations management and technology strategy that's becoming increasingly important for entrepreneurs has to do with managing quality.

The Important Role of Quality

$2.1 billion. That's the amount that Toshiba Corporation paid to settle a lawsuit over defects in its laptops. Palm, Inc., the leading manufacturer of personal digital assistants (PDAs), revealed that its first model with a color screen—first offered for sale in February 2000—had a tendency to crack. It offered customers free replacements for cracked units. These are just a few of the quality problems being experienced by businesses. There is no doubt that quality is important to organizations, especially entrepreneurial ones. Many experts believe that organizations that do not produce high-quality products will be unable to compete successfully in the global marketplace. In fact, in an annual census of U.S. manufacturers conducted by *Industry Week* (**www.industryweek.com**), a majority of corporate and plant-level executives said that strategic initiatives that promoted quality and continuous improvement were critical to manufacturing excellence and their ultimate success.[9] One respondent, the vice president and general manager of Bettis Corporation (**www.bettis.com**) in Waller, Texas, said, "I am a believer that you cannot afford not to focus on quality. You're just going to pay the price when something bad happens. A failure in the quality of our product could shut down a customer's plant. Continuous improvement is something we have to do to survive in the marketplace."[10]

EXHIBIT 6-6 Quality Dimensions of Goods and Services

Product Quality Dimensions

1. Performance—Operating characteristics
2. Features—Important special characteristics
3. Flexibility—Meeting operating specifications over some period of time
4. Durability—Amount of use before performance deteriorates
5. Conformance—Match with preestablished standards
6. Serviceability—Ease and speed of repair or normal service
7. Aesthetics—How a product looks and feels
8. Perceived quality—Subjective assessment of characteristics (product image)

Service Quality Dimensions

1. Timeliness—Performed in promised period of time
2. Courtesy—Performed cheerfully
3. Consistency—Giving all customers similar experiences each time
4. Convenience—Accessibility to customers
5. Completeness—Fully serviced, as required
6. Accuracy—Performed correctly each time

Sources: Adapted from J. W. Dean, Jr., and J. R. Evans, *Total Quality: Management, Organization and Society* (St. Paul, MN: West Publishing Company, 1994); H. V. Roberts and B. F. Sergesketter, *Quality Is Personal* (New York: The Free Press, 1993); D. Garvin, *Managed Quality: The Strategic and Competitive Edge* (New York: The Free Press, 1988); and M. A. Hitt, R. D. Ireland, and R. E. Hoskisson, *Strategic Management*, 4th ed. (Cincinnati, OH: South-Western, 2001), p. 211.

What is quality? When you consider a product or service to have quality, what does that mean to you? Does it mean that the product doesn't break or quit working—that it's reliable? Does it mean that the service is delivered in a way that you intended? Does it mean that the product does what it's supposed to do? Or does quality mean something else? Exhibit 6-6 provides a description of several quality dimensions. We're going to define **quality** as the ability of a product or service to reliably do what it's supposed to do and to satisfy customers' expectations.

How can entrepreneurs ensure that quality is a priority in their ventures? One thing they can do is to adopt a total quality management culture. **Total quality**

EXHIBIT 6-7 What Is TQM?

1. Intense focus on the *customer*. The customer includes not only outsiders who buy the organization's products or services but also internal customers (such as shipping or accounts payable personnel) who interact with and serve others in the organization.
2. Concern for *continual improvement*. TQM is a commitment to never being satisfied. "Very good" is not good enough. Quality can always be improved.
3. *Process-focused*. TQM focuses on work processes as the quality of goods and services is continually improved.
4. Improvement in the *quality of everything* the organization does. TQM uses a very broad definition of quality. It relates not only to the final product but also to how the organization handles deliveries, how rapidly it responds to complaints, how politely the phones are answered, and the like.
5. *Accurate measurement*. TQM uses statistical techniques to measure every critical variable in the organization's operations. These are compared against standards or benchmarks to identify problems, trace them to their roots, and eliminate their causes.
6. *Empowerment of employees*. TQM involves the people on the line in the improvement process. Teams are widely used in TQM programs as empowerment vehicles for finding and solving problems.

management (TQM) is a philosophy of management that is driven by customer needs and expectations and focuses on continual improvement in the way employees do their work. Exhibit 6-7 describes six characteristics of TQM. From focusing intensely on the customer to measuring accurately to empowering employees, TQM promotes the pursuit of quality throughout the organization. For example, employees at the Aeroquip-Inoac Company facility in Livingston, Tennessee, are dedicated to continuous improvement in how they do their jobs. They use employee suggestions and **benchmarking** (the search for the best practices among competitors or noncompetitors that contribute to their superior performance) and have built a reputation for delivering high-quality products. The company's current quality assurance environment supports defect *prevention* rather than defect *detection*. Quality is the responsibility of *all* employees. Employees and supervisors work together to solve quality problems and to provide customers with the quality products they value.[11]

Yes, quality is an important issue for entrepreneurs to address as they design appropriate strategies for the production and operations management area of their venture. Once these strategies have been determined, the entrepreneur is ready to look at developing some appropriate marketing strategies. We know how the product is going to be produced, now how do we market it? That's the area we will look at next.

Rapid Review 

- ✔ Describe transformation activities and how they relate to production.
- ✔ What are the three possible production process strategies and how are they different?
- ✔ What are the strategic decisions associated with capacity?
- ✔ What factors affect the location strategy of an entrepreneurial venture?
- ✔ What are the different work design strategies, and why are they important to entrepreneurial ventures?
- ✔ Describe the six potential layout strategies.
- ✔ What types of strategies might be needed in the area of managing operations?
- ✔ What is quality? How can entrepreneurs ensure that quality is a high priority in their ventures?

FYI

Quality Certification Goals

To publicly demonstrate their commitment to quality, many organizations worldwide pursue quality certification. The two best-known of these quality certifications are ISO 9000 and Six Sigma.

ISO 9000. **ISO 9000** is a series of international quality management standards established by the International Organization for Standardization (**www.iso.ch**) that set uniform guidelines for processes to ensure that products conform to customer requirements. These standards cover everything from contract review to product design to product delivery. The ISO 9000 standards have become the internationally recognized standard for evaluating and comparing companies in the global marketplace. In fact, this type of certification is becoming a prerequisite for doing business globally. Gaining ISO 9000 certification provides proof that a quality operations system is in place in an organization. Why would companies want to pursue ISO 9000 certification? Some reasons include: customers are demanding and expecting quality products, being able to gain market advantage, fending off competitive pressures, controlling production costs, improving quality of processes and products throughout the organization, and pursuing an important piece of the organization's overall strategy.

Six Sigma. Motorola Corporation popularized the use of stringent quality standards more than 30 years ago through a trademarked quality program called Six Sigma. Very simply, **Six Sigma** is a quality standard that establishes a goal of no more than 3.4 defects per million units or procedures. What does the name mean? *Sigma* is the Greek letter that statisticians use to define a standard deviation from a bell curve. The higher the sigma, the fewer the deviations from the norm—that is, the fewer the defects. At One Sigma, two-thirds of whatever is being measured falls within the curve. Two Sigma covers about 95 percent. At Six Sigma, you're about as close to being defect-free as you can get. It's an ambitious quality goal! Although it may be an extremely high standard to achieve, many quality-driven businesses are pursuing it and are using it to judge their suppliers.

Although it's important for entrepreneurs to recognize that many positive benefits can accrue from attaining quality certification goals, the key benefit comes from the quality-improvement journey itself. In other words, the goal of quality certification should be having work processes and a technology and operations system in place that enables an organization to meet customers' needs and for employees to perform their jobs in a consistently high-quality way.

Sources: International Organization for Standardization Web site (**www.iso.ch**), June 13, 2002; G. Hasek, "Merger Marries Quality Efforts," *Industry Week*, August 21, 2000, pp. 89–92; and C. H. Deutsch, "Six Sigma Enlightenment," *New York Times*, December 7, 1998, pp. C1+.

ESTABLISHING THE VENTURE'S MARKETING FUNCTION

Henry and Lisa Lovejoy knew they would have to build a brand for their wholesale fish business if they wanted to survive in an industry in which the products are viewed as commodity slabs of flesh displayed in a glass-enclosed counter.[12] What to do? They decided to take advantage of people's rising concern over endangered fish populations by wholesaling only ecologically acceptable products.

EXHIBIT 6-8 Marketing Strategies for Entrepreneurial Ventures

Segmentation Strategies

- Geographic
- Demographic
- Psychographic
- Behavioral

Target Market Selection Strategies

- Single segment concentration
- Selective specialization
- Product specialization
- Market specialization
- Full market coverage

Differentiation Strategies

- Product itself
- Services
- Personnel
- Image

Marketing Mix Strategies

- Product
  - New product development
  - Product line
  - Brand
  - Packaging and labeling
  - Product life cycle decisions
- Pricing
  - Markup pricing
  - Target return pricing
  - Perceived-value pricing
  - Value pricing
  - Going-rate pricing
  - Sealed-bid pricing
  - Geographical pricing
  - Price discounts and allowances
  - Promotional pricing
  - Product mix pricing
- Promotion
  - Advertising
  - Billboards
  - Point-of-purchase displays
  - Symbols and logos
  - Packaging inserts
  - Sales promotion
  - Public relations
  - Personal selling
  - Direct marketing
- Place
  - Channel choice
  - Market logistics
  - Inventory
  - Transportation modes/carriers

They decided to call their business EcoFish Inc. (**www.ecofish.com**); they developed a splashy five-color logo to establish their business as a trusted and socially responsible supplier of fish products. As this example shows, an entrepreneurial venture's marketing strategies are critical. **Marketing** is defined as a process of assessing and meeting individual's or group's wants and needs by creating, offering, and exchanging products of value. The two biggest factors in marketing are the two Cs—customers and competitors. All of an entrepreneurial organization's marketing strategies are directed at effectively and efficiently managing these two groups. The main marketing strategies we're going to discuss involve segmentation or target market selection, differentiation, and marketing mix (the 4 Ps: product, pricing, promotion, and place). Exhibit 6-8 shows the most common strategic options in each of these areas.

Segmentation or Target Market Selection Strategies

As an entrepreneur researches the feasibility of the venture and prepares the business plan, he or she must think about who will buy the organization's products. Who are these people? Every market consists of potential or actual customers who may differ in one or more ways. These differences can be used to segment a market. Market segments are large, identifiable groups within a market. At the most basic level, an entrepreneurial venture may choose a marketing strategy to either segment (divide) the market into different groups or treat it as one homogeneous market. If entrepreneurs choose to segment their markets, they can select from several different segmentation variables including *geographic* (region, city or metropolitan area, population density, and climate); *demographic* (age, gender, family size, family life cycle, income, occupation, education, religion, race, and nationality); *psychographic* (social class, lifestyle, attitudes toward various societal situations, and personality); and *behavioral* (occasion of product use, benefits, user status, usage rate, loyalty status, readiness to purchase, and attitude toward product). If the venture sells products or services to the business market rather than the consumer market, the major approaches to segmenting these markets include demographic (industry type, company size, and location); operating variables (technology, user–nonuser status, and customer capabilities); purchasing approaches (purchasing department, power structure, nature of existing relationships, general purchasing policies, and purchasing criteria); situational factors (urgency, specific applications, and size of order); and personal characteristics (buyer–seller similarity, attitudes toward risk, and loyalty). Once possible customer segments have been identified, the next step is to determine which ones are the most attractive targets for selling your product.

Target market selection can use one of five possible approaches: (1) *Single segment concentration* is when the entrepreneur selects a single segment (out of all possible segments) to target. (2) *Selective specialization* is when the entrepreneur chooses to serve a number of equally attractive and appropriate segments that have little or no common characteristics. (3) The *product specialization* strategy is one in which the entrepreneurial venture concentrates on making a certain product that's sold to several segments. (4) In the *market specialization* strategy, the organization serves many needs of a particular segment or customer group. (5) The *full market coverage* strategy means that the entrepreneurial venture is attempting to serve all customer groups (segments) with all the products they might need or desire.

After deciding the segmentation and target market selection strategies for the venture, an entrepreneur has a good idea of the customer group (or groups) that he or she hopes to target. However, the design of appropriate marketing strategies doesn't stop here. Now, the entrepreneur must decide how to get that customer group to notice his or her product over others' products. That's where the differentiation strategies come in. Think back to our chapter-opening case. In the intensely competitive fashion industry, Nicholas Graham had to design some way to make his products stand out.

Differentiation Strategies

How important are differentiation strategies? Quite important! Studies of new ventures suggest that differentiation is the most direct means to success.[13] Because the vast majority of marketing takes place in competitive markets, entrepreneurs must look for ways to differentiate their products from competitors. How? Four basic differentiation strategies have been identified: (1) *Differentiating the product itself* by emphasizing features, performance, conformance, durability, reliability, repairability, style, and design. (2) *Differentiating on the basis of services offered* such as delivery, installation, customer training, consulting service, repair, and other miscellaneous factors. For example, Harlan J. Hall, CEO of the SALT Group, a tax consulting business in Kerrville, Texas, holds free tax seminars for

Entrepreneurs in Action

We don't often think about differentiation when it comes to industrial products. However, when Brooks Instrument, a Pennsylvania-based manufacturer developed its new Quantim precision mass flow controller, Tim Scott, the company's vice-president for business development, took an unusual step. A team composed of two Brooks's employees, the president of Brooks's marketing firm, and a freelance copywriter came up with a cartoon superhero, Dr. Direct, to promote the new product. Dr. Direct debuted as an on-line comic strip (**www.quantim.com**) in May 2001 and was an immediate hit among the engineers and scientists who made up the potential market. In addition to the online comic, the team designed a 14-page color comic book that it used to promote the product at industrial trade shows and conferences. Although there was always the risk that potential customers would think Brooks's approach silly, the marketing campaign used to differentiate its new product appears to have been a hit!

Sources: Company Web site (**www.quantim.com**), June 12, 2002; and T. Raz, "I Read It In The Funny Papers," *Inc.* May 2002, pp. 114–115.

potential customers at different locations of the Wells Fargo Bank Texas N.A. SALT benefits from Wells Fargo's name recognition and gets a free space to hold seminars. The bank gets increased business traffic.[14] (3) *Differentiating by personnel* because of their competency, courtesy, credibility, reliability, responsiveness, and communication ability. (4) *Differentiating by image* through focusing on symbols such as a logo, color identifier, or famous person; through written and audiovisual media; through atmosphere features such as building design, interior design, layout, colors, or furnishings; or through sponsored events or causes. In Columbus, Ohio, for example, employment agency Team 2000 Staffing Services was faced with formidable competition. To differentiate itself, CEO Keith Stevens decided to purchase a used Winnebago recreational vehicle (RV) and go to where the workers were. Team 2000's employees drive the Winnebago to parking lots, give away free food or sports bottles and take applications right there in the RV. In fact, Team 2000 has another interpretation for RV—recruitment vehicle. The company still makes monthly recruiting trips around the city and an employee drives the RV around town once a week to "raise visibility."[15]

Although the choice of differentiation strategy is obviously an important one, there's more for the entrepreneur to decide. That "more" is the marketing mix strategies.

Marketing Mix Strategies

When Mi8 Corporation (**www.mi8.com**), a Manhattan-based application service provider, decided to raise prices for its services, it was dealing with part of its marketing mix strategies. The marketing mix strategies get into the specific details of what product is going to be offered to customers, how it will be priced, how it will be promoted, and where it will be placed so customers can get it. These are the 4 Ps often referred to in marketing—that is, product, price, promotion, and place. We'll look at each separately.

Product Strategy. An entrepreneurial venture's *product* strategy involves several aspects. An important one is how the venture will approach new-product development. New products can include original products, improved products, modified products, or new brands. Strategic product decisions involve product line width (how many different product lines to offer), product line depth (how many variations of a product to offer), product line length (how many different products to offer within the product line), and product line consistency (how closely related the product lines and products are). There also may be product strategy choices that involve brand decisions such as whether to use a brand name, a brand sponsor, and what type of brand strategy to pursue. Other product strategies involve packaging and labeling decisions. Once the product is on the market, product strategies concern managing the various stages in the product life cycle (PLC). The PLC concept is a recognition that a product's sales rise and decline, bringing about the need for different strategies for coping with these ups and downs. (See Exhibit 6-9 for an example of what a typical PLC curve looks like.) The various stages of the PLC might require changes in the product strategy, as well as in the other P strategies.

Pricing Strategy. Most entrepreneurs tend to set prices too low when they first launch their ventures.[16] They're not quite sure what customers are willing to pay or how much they value what they're getting. Along with the uncertainty, there's the element of fear. Entrepreneurs fear that if they charge too much, they might lose a customer or they worry about pricing their product out of the market. So, the choice of a *pricing* strategy is an important one! It depends on the entrepreneur's pricing objectives (survival, maximum current profit, maximum current revenue, maximum sales growth, maximum market skimming, product-quality leadership, or other). It also is influenced by the customers' demand for

EXHIBIT 6-9 Product Life Cycle

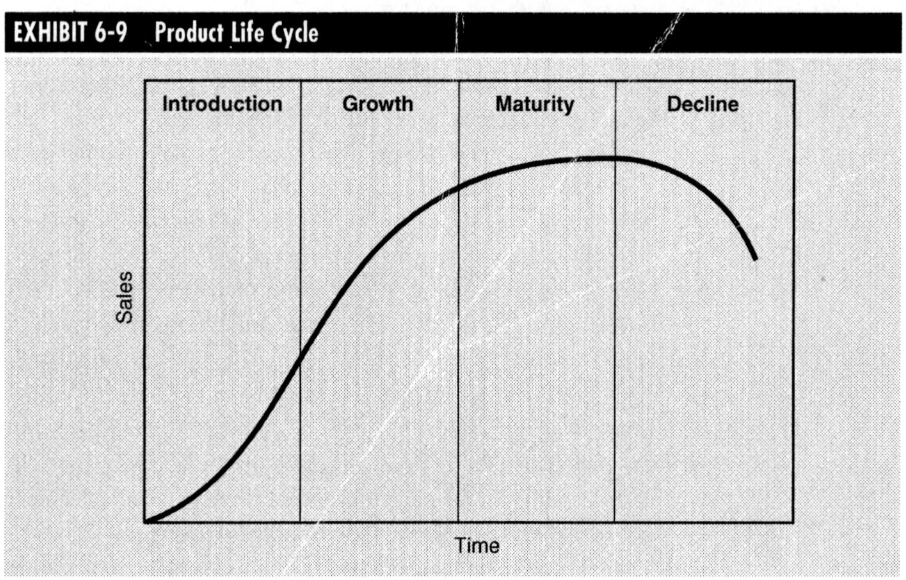

Entrepreneurs in Action

In an expanding market saturated with products, how does a new company with no profits and little to spend on marketing get customers' attention? Product packaging was the answer for Fountainhead Water Company (**www.fountainheadwater.com**). Company President Kevin McClanahan wanted a product packaging breakthrough—a design with dual appeal—one that was an unusual two-liter size (the recommended daily amount to drink) and elegant enough for the dinner table. The first package prototype turned off customers, who said it looked too much like a bottle of bleach. The company's second choice was a tall, elegant-looking fluted bottle. This design has won awards from industry groups and kudos from consumers. As one of Fountainhead's distributors said, "You can have the best water, from a 3,000-year-old well, but that doesn't sell it. The bottle does." Although its product package strategy has been important to Fountainhead's success, the other marketing mix strategies have played an important role, also.

Sources: Company Web site (**www.fountainheadwater.com**), June 12, 2002; and E. Updike, "Selling the Sizzle of Water," *Business Week Enterprise,* April 27, 1998, p. ENT12.

the product, costs of producing and marketing the product, and competitors' prices. Based on these factors, the entrepreneur may choose one of the following pricing strategies: *markup pricing* (pricing by adding a standard markup), *target return pricing* (pricing to achieve a targeted or desired return), *perceived-value pricing* (based on the customers' perception of value), *value pricing* (based on charging low prices for high-quality products), *going-rate pricing* (based largely on what competitors are charging), or *sealed-bid pricing* (used in bid situations and based on expectations of how competitors will bid). Other pricing strategy decisions an entrepreneur will face include whether to use geographical pricing (charging different prices for different locations), price discounts and allowances (giving discounts or allowances to certain customers), promotional pricing (running special promotion pricing events), or product mix pricing (pricing according to whether a customer buys one or several products in the product line). Also, even though an entrepreneur may establish what he or she believes is an effective pricing strategy, competitive and marketplace dynamics may require increasing or lowering prices, thus creating a need to change the current pricing strategy from time to time.

Promotion Strategy. A good overall marketing strategy requires strategies for *promoting* the product. Common strategies for promotion involve the use of the various marketing communication tools. These include advertising (print and broadcast media ads, brochures and booklets, posters and leaflets, billboards, point-of-purchase displays, symbols and logos, packaging inserts, and many others); sales promotion (contests, games, sweepstakes and lotteries, premiums

Entrepreneurs in Action

Diamond wholesaler Glenn Rothman faced a signi
challenge. As one of several thousand diamond w
to find a way to create a consumer brand. That w
Japanese method of cutting diamonds. With this p
stones viewed under low magnification refracted li
appeared to give off a pattern of eight heart-shap
bottom of the diamond and eight arrow-shaped fir
the top. Diamonds cut this way are called "hearts-and-arrows" dia-
monds. Rothman knew he had found his marketing strategy. He changed the name of his company from Di-Star to Hearts on Fire (**www.heartsonfire.com**). Then, to get customers to pay more for his branded Hearts on Fire diamonds, Rothman started distributing a handheld cylindrically shaped magnifying glass so they could see the pattern of hearts and arrows. He also started giving training sessions for the stores that carried his line of diamonds. These marketing strategies helped Rothman increase his overall sales and his gross profit margins. Today, his Hearts on Fire company sells diamonds to the tune of annual sales of over $5 million.

Sources: Information on company from company Web site (**www.heartsonfire.com**), June 12, 2002 and Hoover's Online (**www.hoovers.com**), June 12, 2002; and B. Nelson, "Stones on Fire," *Forbes*, August 9, 1999, pp. 74–78.

and gifts, sampling, fairs and trade shows, exhibits, demonstrations, coupons, rebates, trading stamps, product tie-ins, and others); public relations (press kits, speeches, annual reports, charitable contributions, sponsorships, community relations, lobbying, community events, company magazine, and others); personal selling (sales presentations, sales meetings, incentive programs, samples, and others); and direct marketing (catalogs, mailings, telemarketing, electronic shopping, or TV shopping). What are the most appropriate promotional strategies? It depends on the target audience and the marketing communication objectives. What do I want to communicate to whom? Once this is determined, the appropriate message, communication channels, promotion budget, and promotion mix strategies can be designed.

Place Strategy. The final aspect of the marketing mix strategies involves specific *place* or distribution strategies. What's involved with the place strategy? One important aspect for the entrepreneur to determine is the choice of channels for distributing the venture's product or service. Strategic alternatives include the *type* of intermediary to use (such as, wholesaler, dealer, direct sales, value-added reseller, mail-order marketer, etc.) and the *number* of intermediaries to use (exclusive distribution, selective distribution, or intensive distribution). Another important aspect of the place strategy involves the actual physical distribution of the product—also referred to as market logistics. Normally, there are four logistics strategies to decide. The first is determining how customer orders will be

Rapid Review ◀◀|

- Define marketing.
- ✔ What are the two Cs of marketing?
- ✔ Describe the segmentation strategies for consumer markets and for business markets.
- ✔ What are the five possible strategic approaches to target market selection?
- ✔ How could entrepreneurs differentiate their products from competitors?
- ✔ Describe the specific strategies associated with each of the 4 Ps of the marketing mix.

processed. Next, is determining what warehousing arrangements (if any) are most appropriate. Then, decisions about inventory (when to order and how much to order) must be addressed. Obviously, decisions about the inventory strategy must be coordinated with the venture's technology and operations strategy so that finished products are available when needed, in the style and design needed, and at an appropriate cost. Finally, the place strategy involves decisions about transportation modes and carriers that will get the product to where it's needed. For instance, Leslie Blodgett chose to use the QVC cable television shopping channel to sell her cosmetics products Bare Escentuals (**www.bareescentuals.com**). It was obviously a good strategic choice as more than 3 million women tune into her program every other month.[17]

Choosing appropriate marketing strategies in all these areas is obviously important for the entrepreneur. Effectively managing customers and competitors through well-designed marketing strategies should help an entrepreneurial venture achieve its goals. The next major types of strategies we want to look at are the information system strategies.

DESIGNING THE VENTURE'S INFORMATION SYSTEMS

You'd probably agree that information affects how effectively and efficiently you get your schoolwork done. Well, it also affects how organizational members do their work and how effectively and efficiently they get it done. Without information, a payroll clerk wouldn't know what deductions to make from paychecks; a sales representative wouldn't know what prices to quote a potential customer; or a production manager wouldn't know how this month's quality levels compared to last month's. It's essential to have information to make decisions and to carry out work duties. How does an entrepreneur get information? If there are other organizational members, how will they get information? That's what an information system does. An **information system** is defined as a set of interrelated components used to collect, process, store, and disseminate information to support decision making, analysis, and control in organizations. Two strategic decisions associated with the entrepreneur's choices of an information system are the choice of system technology and the choice of what type (or types) of information system to have. Exhibit 6-10 summarizes possible information system strategies.

System Technology

The choice of system technology is actually pretty simple—the information system can be either manual or computer-based. A manual system uses simple pencil-and-paper technology to collect, store, process, and disseminate information. A computer-based system relies on computer hardware and software to do the same. Which approach an entrepreneur chooses to use depends on how important the collection and manipulation of information is to effectively and

EXHIBIT 6-10 Information Systems Strategies for Entrepreneurial Ventures

System Technology	Type of Information System
• Manual	• Transaction processing system
• Computer based	• Office automation system
	• Knowledge work system
	• Management information system
	• Decision support system
	• Executive support system

efficiently running the business. For instance, is it critical that the entrepreneur have rapid access to information from all operational areas? Is it critical that other organizational members have rapid access to information to help them do their jobs effectively and efficiently? Is it critical that organizational units share information? All these factors will influence the extent to which an entrepreneurial venture uses a computer-based or a manual system. As prices of computer-based systems continue to fall and computing power continues to rise, many entrepreneurial ventures have chosen a computer-based information system because of the easy access to information and the more sophisticated analyses that can be done with the information. For example, Bob Shallenberger, an oriental rug retailer from St. Louis, invested in a computer system that gives him customized information on inventory, customers, finances, and suppliers. He says, "It's wholly empowering. We're in the game now."[18]

Types of Information Systems

An entrepreneurial venture's information system isn't just one single system because no one system can provide all the information needed. Instead, an organization will have many different types of information systems that satisfy different information needs. Six different types of information systems are possible strategic choices. The first type is called a *transaction processing system (TPS)*. This type of information system tracks day-to-day work (transactions) being completed in various work areas such as payroll, sales tracking, or production scheduling. The next type of information system is an *office automation system (OAS)*. This system includes any of the organization's paperwork such as letters, invoices, press releases, newsletters, schedules, and so forth. More and more, this type of information gathering and exchange is done through word processing, electronic mail, and desktop publishing software. The remaining types of information systems are more sophisticated in what they do. Although they may not be entirely appropriate for an entrepreneurial venture, we need to introduce them. A *knowledge work system (KWS)* is used primarily by an organization's knowledge workers (engineers, analysts, designers, research scientists, and so forth). A KWS provides ways to promote and use new knowledge and innovations in the organization through elements such as product design graphics, legal database searches, or financial data analysis. A *management information system (MIS)* is used by an organization's managers for planning, controlling, and decision making. An MIS typically summarizes and reports the organization's work activities but differs from the TPS because it summarizes a series of time periods, not simply the day-to-day transactions. A *decision support system (DSS)* allows for powerful data analysis and allows decision makers to change assumptions and information to see what impact these changes have on the outcomes. The last type of information system is an *executive support system (ESS),* which would be used by an organization's upper-level managers to aid in making unstructured, comprehensive, broad, and complex decisions. Although a start-up venture may not need the sophisticated types of analyses offered by a KWS, MIS, DSS, or ESS, an entrepreneur *is* likely to use some type of transaction processing system and office automation system.

It's important for an entrepreneur to choose appropriate strategies for the efficient and effective collection and use of information. Without information, it's going to be hard to run the business successfully. One area that provides important information for the entrepreneurial venture is the financial and accounting area, which we discuss next.

ESTABLISHING THE VENTURE'S FINANCIAL AND ACCOUNTING SYSTEMS

This last group of strategies concerns choices about how financial and accounting data are collected and used. The four broad areas we'll be looking at are evaluating financial performance; financial forecasting, planning, and budgeting; financing mix; and other financial management decisions. Possible financial/accounting strategies are summarized in Exhibit 6-11.

Evaluating Financial Performance

After the events of September 11, 2001, many tourism-based organizations saw their business revenues decline. Entrepreneurs across the United States began

EXHIBIT 6-11 Financial and Accounting Strategies for Entrepreneurial Ventures

Evaluating Financial Performance

- What type of analysis?
- How much analysis?
- How often to analyze?

Financial Forecasting, Planning, and Budgeting

- What type of forecast?
- How often to forecast?

Financing Mix

- Short-term versus long-term funding sources
- Permanent or temporary sources

Other Financial Management Decisions

- Capital budgeting
- Stock dividend policy
- Cash flow management
- Cash and marketable securities management
- Accounts receivable and inventory management
- Term loans or leases

evaluating the impact—good and bad—on their business's finances. How is an organization's financial performance usually evaluated? By looking at the financial statements and evaluating the information that's on them. These financial statements include specific pieces of information about the organization's operations. The typical financial statements include the income statement, the balance sheet, and a cash flow statement. By themselves, the financial statements show only results. To evaluate financial performance, we have to look more closely at what the statements are telling us. Financial ratios are the principal tool for financial analysis. The financial ratios standardize financial information so that comparisons can be made from time period to time period or of the organization to its industry. The strategic choices in terms of evaluating financial performance revolve around what types of analysis to do, how often to analyze, and how much analysis to do. Quite often, this is dictated by securities laws and regulations and is not entirely open to individual choice, particularly for entrepreneurial ventures whose stock may be held publicly. Even if financial analysis isn't mandated, though, the fact remains that an organization needs to have in place some mechanism and procedure for evaluating financial performance. Without this information, an entrepreneur would have little knowledge of how the organization is performing, at least from a quantitative and financial standpoint. We'll cover the basic financial analysis techniques in the next chapter as we discuss ways to measure performance.

Financial Forecasting, Planning, and Budgeting

Financial forecasting is used to estimate an entrepreneurial venture's future financial needs. Once forecasts are developed, an entrepreneur can plan and budget according to the forecasts. The most popular type of financial forecast—because it's fairly easy to do—is the percent of sales method. With this approach, you would first convert each expense, asset, or liability to a percentage of current sales. Then, you would forecast the future level of sales. Using this forecasted level of sales, you would estimate the levels of an expense, asset, or liability using that same calculated percentage of sales. The resulting numbers provide the basis for operational planning and budgeting. This approach can help an entrepreneur identify the changes that result from an increasing (or perhaps even, a decreasing) level of sales. With this information, plans and budgets can be developed to support the expected level of sales.

Other types of financial forecasting models tend to be more sophisticated and may not be entirely appropriate for the unique situations facing entrepreneurial ventures. The strategic choices in terms of financial forecasting, planning, and budgeting—just as with the strategic choices in evaluating financial performance—revolve around the choice of financial models and how often they're used.

Financing Mix

The financial mix strategies concern decisions about the entrepreneurial venture's financial and capital structure. In making decisions about the optimal financial structure, entrepreneurs must look at (1) how they want to divide total funding sources between short- and long-term components and (2) what proportion of total financing they want to be from permanent sources. Answers to these two

FYI

Budgeting Basics

Most of us have had some experience, as limited as it might be, with budgets. We probably learned about them at a very early age when we discovered that unless we allocated our "revenues" carefully, our weekly allowance was spent on "expenses" before the week was half over.

A **budget** is a numerical plan for allocating resources to specific activities. An entrepreneur likely will need to use budgets in his or her entrepreneurial venture. What's involved with budgeting? The following suggestions will help you be better at budgeting.

1. *Determine which work activities are going to be pursued during the coming time period.* An organization's work activities are the result of the goals that have been established.
2. *Decide what resources will be necessary to accomplish the desired work activities and thus meet the goals.* Although there are different types of budgets, the most common ones involve monetary resources. However, you also may have to budget time, space, material resources, human resources, capacity utilization, or units of production.
3. *Gather cost information.* You'll need accurate cost estimates of needed resources. Previous budgets may be of some help, but if you don't have previous budgets, you'll have to research the costs of various resources.
4. *Once you know what resources will be available, assign the resources as needed.* The budget should detail what resources are available and which will be used where.
5. *Review the budget periodically.* It's always a good idea to review the budget periodically to see if things are going along as planned. Don't wait until the end of the time period to determine whether you're over or under budget.
6. *Take action if you find you're not within budget.* Remember that a budget is a good control tool. If resources are being consumed more quickly than budgeted, you may need to find out why and fix it.
7. *Use past experience as a guide when developing your budget for the next time period.* Although circumstances may change, you can still use past experience as a good guide in establishing future budgets.

Source: S. P. Robbins and M. Coulter, *Management,* 7th ed. (Upper Saddle River, NJ: Prentice Hall, 2002), pp. 585–586.

questions will determine what financing mix strategies the entrepreneur uses. Other factors that may influence this strategic choice include how much debt capacity the venture has, whether or not it has reached its optimal amount of debt, the stage in the business cycle, and the amount of risk the venture faces. All factors will affect the types and maturities of the various financing options an entrepreneur selects.

Other Financial Management Decisions

Other possible financial management strategic decisions involve choices about investing in long-term assets (capital budgeting decisions—when and how), stock dividend policy (how much, how often), cash-flow management (how much, how often), cash and marketable securities management (What do we do with our

Rapid Review

- ✔ What is an information system?
- ✔ What are the two possible strategic choices in information system technology?
- ✔ Describe the six different types of information systems.
- ✔ What strategic choices are there in terms of evaluating financial performance?
- ✔ What strategic choices are there in terms of financial forecasting, planning, and budgeting?
- ✔ Describe what financial mix strategies cover.
- ✔ What other financial management strategies might entrepreneurs need?

excess cash—put it in the bank or invest it in marketable securities?), accounts receivable and inventory management (How do we efficiently and effectively collect accounts receivable, and how do we efficiently and effectively manage our inventory?), and lease/purchase decisions (Do we buy or do we lease needed equipment and facilities?). In each of these financial areas, there are strategic choices to make. The entrepreneur must decide what to use and how to implement it.

Appropriate strategies are important for each of the operational areas we've looked at. Without appropriate strategies in these areas, the short-term operational goals will not be met, nor will the organizational goals be achieved. It's doubtful that the Joe Boxer Company would have achieved the levels of success that it has without goals and strategies. Although we've discussed goals and strategies from the perspective of launching the entrepreneurial venture, keep in mind that setting goals and pursuing them through appropriately chosen strategies is an ongoing task for entrepreneurs.

CHAPTER SUMMARY

This summary is organized around the chapter-opening objectives.

1. Goals are outcomes or end results that are desired by individuals, groups, or entire organizations. They serve three main purposes. First, goals direct the entrepreneur and other organizational members toward a common and unified organizational purpose. Next, goals provide targets organizational members may be motivated to work toward accomplishing. Finally, goals serve as criteria against which work accomplishments and performance are measured.
2. An entrepreneurial venture will have the following types of goals: organization-wide goals (those that establish broad purposes, apply to the entire entrepreneurial venture, and seek to successfully position the venture in terms of its environment); operational goals (ones that specify details associated with accomplishing the organization-wide goals); long-term goals (ones with a time frame beyond three years); short-term goals (those that cover one year or less); specific goals (ones that are clearly defined and leave no room for interpretation); directional goals (those that are flexible enough to provide focus and general guidelines but do not lock entrepreneurs into specific courses of action); and, finally, goals established for the various organizational work areas.
3. Well-written goals are written in terms of outcomes rather than actions, are measurable and quantifiable, are clear as to a time frame, are challenging yet attainable, are written down, and are communicated to all organizational members.
4. The goal-setting process consists of seven steps: review the organizational vision and mission(s); evaluate available resources; determine broad, long-term organization-wide goals; write down the organization-wide goals;

determine specific, short-term operational goals; write down the operational goals; and review results.

5. A strategy is a plan of action for accomplishing goals. Strategies are important to entrepreneurial ventures because they are how the goals are going to be achieved.
6. Goals and strategies must be coordinated with each other for the entrepreneurial venture to be successful. Using the vision and mission statements as guides, organization-wide goals are developed. From these broad goals, operational goals are developed. The operational goals are pursued by implementing various strategies. As these operational goals are achieved, the organization-wide goals are achieved. The whole process links the venture's vision/mission, goals, and strategies.
7. Operations management and technology strategies include production process strategies (process-focused, product-focused, and repetitive-focused) capacity strategies, location strategies, work design strategies, layout strategies (fixed-position, process-oriented, office, retail-service, warehouse, and product-oriented), and operations management strategies. Marketing strategies include segmentation strategies (geographic, demographic, psychographic, and behavioral), target market selection strategies (single segment concentration, selective specialization, product specialization, market specialization, and full market coverage), differentiation strategies (product itself, services, personnel, and image), and marketing mix strategies (product, price, promotion, and place). Information system strategies include the choice of system technology (manual or computer-based) and type of information system (transaction processing system, office automation system, knowledge work system, management information system, decision support system, and executive support system). Financial and accounting strategies include decisions about evaluating financial performance (what type of analysis, how often to analyze, and how much analysis); financial forecasting, planning, and budgeting (what type to use and how often to use); financing mix (short-term vs. long-term funding sources and permanent or temporary sources); and other financial management decisions (capital budgeting, stock dividend policy, cash flow management, cash and marketable securities management, accounts receivable and inventory management, and term loans or leases).
8. Quality is the ability of a product or service to reliably do what it's supposed to do and to satisfy customer expectations. Quality is important to entrepreneurial ventures and can be pursued by adopting a total quality management (TQM) culture. TQM is a philosophy of management that's driven by customer needs and expectations and focuses on continual improvement in the way employees do their work.

KEY TERMS

- *Goals:* Outcomes or end results that are desired by individuals, groups, or entire organizations.
- *Organization-wide goals:* Goals that establish broad purposes, apply to the entire entrepreneurial venture, and seek to successfully position the venture in terms of its environment.

- *Operational goals:* Goals that specify details associated with accomplishing the organization-wide goals.
- *Long-term goals:* Goals with a time frame beyond three years.
- *Short-term goals:* Goals that cover one year or less.
- *Specific goals:* Goals that are clearly defined and leave no room for interpretation.
- *Directional goals:* Goals that are flexible enough to provide focus and general guidelines, but do not lock entrepreneurs into specific courses of action.
- *Strategy:* A plan of action for accomplishing goals.
- *Production:* The process of creating products (goods and services) in which organizational inputs (resources) are transformed into outputs.
- *Quality:* The ability of a product or service to reliably do what it's supposed to do and to satisfy customers' expectations.
- *Total quality management (TQM):* A philosophy of management that's driven by customer needs and expectations and focuses on continual improvement in the way employees do their work.
- *ISO 9000:* A series of international quality management standards established by the International Organization for Standardization that set uniform guidelines for processes to ensure that products conform to customer requirements.
- *Six Sigma:* A quality standard that establishes a goal of no more than 3.4 defects per million units or procedures.
- *Benchmarking:* The search for the best practices among competitors or noncompetitors that contribute to their superior performance.
- *Marketing:* A process of assessing and meeting individual's or group's wants and needs by creating, offering, and exchanging products of value.
- *Information system:* A set of interrelated components used to collect, process, store, and disseminate information to support decision making, analysis, and control in organizations.
- *Budget:* A numerical plan for allocating resources to specific activities.

SWEAT EQUITY

1. Investments in information technology can be a big boon to entrepreneurial ventures. How can entrepreneurs get the most out of their dollars spent on information technology? Research the topic of how businesses can benefit from information technology. Write a report summarizing your findings. Be sure to cite your sources.
2. During the first part of this century, e-commerce (electronic commerce) was viewed as a sure thing. Research the topic of e-commerce and how it relates to entrepreneurial ventures. Is e-commerce still a viable strategy for organizations? What does it take to have a successful e-commerce strategy? Write a two- to three-page bulleted list that identifies key points about e-commerce, its potential, its drawbacks, and any other relevant information. Be sure to cite your sources.

3. Pricing is something that many entrepreneurs don't put a lot of thought into. However, determining how much to charge for a product or service can spell the difference between financial success or failure. Interview three to five entrepreneurs (preferably from different types of businesses and industries) and ask how they established their pricing strategy. Your survey results will be combined with others in your class. Then, graph the totals and write a short report on pricing strategy for entrepreneurial ventures.
4. Here are some ideas suggested as ways to fire up an organization's marketing strategies:
   - Start a product-of-the-month program.
   - Offer short educational classes to actual and potential customers on how to use your product or service.
   - Insert lottery tickets into mailings to customers and make follow-up calls with the winning number.
   - Keep the reception desk area stocked with candy and toys so customers and employees perceive that everyone is relaxed and having fun.
   - Conduct online focus groups to find out what customers think.

   What do you think of these suggestions? Now, break into small groups, identify a type of entrepreneurial venture, and come up with your own list of creative marketing strategies. (Be sure to think in terms of the 4 Ps and the other marketing strategies.) Be prepared to share your ideas with the class.
5. How important is reputation to a business? Research the topic of business reputation and how it might be used in a venture's marketing strategies. Write a short report summarizing your findings.
6. Many large organizations use customer loyalty programs to reward their best customers for their continued patronage. Could customer loyalty programs be used by entrepreneurs? Research customer loyalty programs. Find three examples of customer loyalty programs used by organizations (large or small). Write a bulleted list of your findings.
7. What help does corporate America offer entrepreneurs? Large businesses may view the entrepreneurial market as an attractive one. Find three examples of corporations that have targeted entrepreneurial/small businesses. Describe *and* evaluate what products or services they're offering.
8. One important aspect of a venture's operations management and technology strategies is ensuring that your workplace is safe. Research the topic of workplace safety. Write a two- to three-page report explaining what workplace safety involves and what entrepreneurs need to do to have safe workplaces.
9. A popular marketing strategy used by large and small organizations alike is cause-related marketing (the practice of designating a portion of sales or profits to a not-for-profit cause and aggressively publicizing it). Research the topic of cause-related marketing. Find examples of companies that are using cause-related marketing strategies. Compile a bulleted list outlining your findings about the topic.
10. Staying in touch with customers. This would seem to be a pretty important strategy for entrepreneurs. dELiA*s (**www.delias.com**), a teenage girls' fashion and accessories company with a popular online teen site, recognizes how important it is to stay in touch with its customers.

a. Find some data on the number of teenage girls and their levels of disposable income. Is it increasing or decreasing? What are the implications for dELiA*s and its strategies?

b. Go to the company's Web site. What's your assessment of the site? Is it a good marketing tool? Why or why not?

ENTREPRENEURSHIP IN ACTION CASES

Joe Boxer Company (www.joeboxer.com)

This case can be found at the beginning of Chapter 6.

Discussion Questions

1. Put yourself in Nicholas Graham's place. What types of long-term goals might you have for the company?
2. Which of Joe Boxer's strategies appear to the strongest and most effective? Support your answer.
3. What other strategies would be important to a company such as Joe Boxer?

Western Digital Corporation (www.westerndigital.com)

Digital dilly-dallying. Cyberloafing. As more and more organizations look to provide employees with the latest in technology and online access, the potential for workplace abuse of these tools and the time that it takes away from doing a job, grows. More than any other recent technological development, the Internet has created opportunities for on-the-job loafing. Over 90 percent of employees surveyed by an online career information specialist said they have surfed non-work-related Web sites at some point during the workday. But that's not the only shocking statistic—37.1 percent of these individuals say they continuously surf the Web at work; 58.8 percent say they have received sexually explicit or otherwise improper e-mail at work; 24 percent say they take preventive measures to keep their bosses from catching them surfing; and 54 percent of employers say they have caught employees surfing non-business-related Web sites at work.

From the cyberloafer's point of view, the Internet is a perfect substitute for work because an employee can look busy while goofing off! After all, Web searches and e-mail can look like serious business. Although not every log-on to e-mail or visit to a Web site involves an employee's goofing off, many organizations are beginning to recognize that they need to establish some controls for these technologies.

At Western Digital Corporation, a global provider of information storage products and services based in Irvine, California, managers weighed the pros and cons of providing Internet access to its 8,000+ employees worldwide. Its mission states, "Western Digital's mission is to satisfy our customers' requirements by providing world-class computing products and services. We will accomplish this mission through investments in people and technologies that generate sustained profitability." Employees carry out this vision doing their work using stated corporate values: integrity, leadership, customer satisfaction, individual responsibility, quality and continuous process improvement, and teamwork.

Discussion Questions

1. Would an Internet usage policy be an important part of a venture's information system strategies? Why or why not?
2. What types of work benefits aside from internal communication and customer service might be possible from Western Digital employees having access to the Internet? Would these same types of benefits be applicable to other types of organizations?
3. Write a set of guidelines for Western Digital that address employees' use of the Internet at work.
4. What recommendations would you give to entrepreneurs who want to develop an Internet usage policy?

Sources: Company information from Company Web site (**www.westerndigital.com**), June 13, 2002, and Hoover's Online (**www.hoovers.com**), June 13, 2002; M. A. Verespej, "Everybody's Gone Surfing," *Industry Week*, January 10, 2000, p. 11; and "Western Digital Corporation's Internet Access Policy," *Workforce Tools: Supplement to the January 1997 Issue of Workforce*, January 1997, pp. 1–3.

Bass Pro Shops, Inc. (www.basspro.com)

The most popular tourist site in Missouri isn't what you might expect. It's not the Gateway Arch in St. Louis, nor is it Harry Truman's home in Independence. Instead, you'd have to travel to the southwest corner of Missouri to Springfield to Bass Pro Shops Outdoor World. More than 4 million people visit this store annually. Although most of the visitors are hunting and fishing enthusiasts, many come just to see the incredible sights in the store. There's a four-story waterfall, rifle and archery ranges, four aquariums, an indoor driving range, a putting green, and a 17,000-square-foot wildlife museum with a world-class collection of stuffed animals. Visitors can get their hair cut at the barbershop and then arrange to have a fishing lure made out of the hair clippings. They can eat at McDonald's or at the Hemingway's Blue Water Café, whose showpiece is a 30,000 gallon saltwater aquarium. However, despite all these fascinating attractions, the heart (and soul) of the store is row after row of guns, decoys, tents, rods, reels, lures, campers, clothing, and other sports and outdoors equipment and apparel. One floor of the massive store also showcases boats—speedboats, houseboats, pontoon boats, fiberglass boats, and aluminum boats. There's something for everyone to gaze at and enjoy.

Johnny Morris, the founder of Bass Pro Shops, was born and raised in Springfield. He opened the original store in a small corner of his father's liquor store. From that humble beginning, the company has grown to be a dominant player in the sports and outdoors market. Morris did it through a strategy of never allowing the customer to have a dull moment. His retailing approach has been one of excitement and entertainment. The flagship store's design (and ultimately the design of all the other stores) was developed from trips to different stores to pinpoint their appeal. One visit to L. L. Bean in Freeport, Maine, was particularly memorable. Morris felt that if that store could draw well over 3.5 million visitors a year to the middle of nowhere, then he could do that, and better, in Springfield.

The privately owned Bass Pro Shops, Inc., is now pursuing a strategy of trying to duplicate the flagship store's success. There are now 15 stores—three in Florida, two in Missouri, two in Tennessee, two in Texas, and one each in Georgia, Illinois, Maryland, Michigan, North Carolina, and Ohio. Three new locations are planned: Bossier City, Louisiana, Oklahoma City, and Kansas City, Missouri. Each of these new sites was chosen with a discerning eye for location. And, each of the stores is enormous, complete with waterfalls and aquariums—all the ways to keep customers entertained. There's also a new aspect to the original store in Springfield. Right next to it, the American National Fish and Wildlife Living Museum and Aquarium opened in 2001. This museum has been attracting a large number of visitors. Morris also continues to look for new opportunities. He says, "I'd be happy to add two or three stores a year, if we can resist the temptation to grow faster than our ability to maintain our quality."

Discussion Questions

1. What role do you think goals and strategies have played in the success of Bass Pro Shops, Inc.? Give some examples.
2. To be a successful entrepreneurial venture in this industry, which strategies would have to be particularly effective? Now, using information in the case and from the company's Web site, how do Bass Pro Shops' strategies seem to measure up? Explain your answer.
3. Evaluate Johnny Morris's statement at the end of the case. What do you think it means? What are the implications for setting goals and strategies?

Sources: **Company information from Company Web site (www.basspro.com), June 13, 2002, and Hoover's Online (www.hoovers.com), June 13, 2002; E. McDowell, "Adventures in Retailing," *New York Times*, March 20, 1999, p. B1; and author's personal experiences at Bass Pro Shops.**

Ace Wire and Super Clip (www.acewire.com)

Linda Froelich's dream has turned out to have nightmarish overtones. She had created a product and, convinced that it was a winner, set about getting her patented invention onto store shelves only to find the shelves soon crowded with knockoffs of her invention. Her product is a simple paper clip design that she called the SuperClip. The SuperClip is little more than a very large paper clip. However, it neatly holds up to 100 sheets of paper, is easier to use, and is less bulky than the standard bulldog or butterfly clips.

Even with a simple product, Froelich believed that she had done everything right. She was awarded a patent in 1994 (No. 5329672) for her unique design, which was a quantum leap over the prior design. With an early sale to Office Depot (a national office-supply chain with over 1,000 stores), she was convinced that she was about to crack the mainstream office-supply market. However, she soon discovered that the office-supply industry is dominated by a handful of very large companies. These companies have found it easy to design around her patent and have not hesitated to do so. Froelich was stunned. She says, "I felt everyone would love this product as I have. I was naive. I believed this product was so good I wouldn't have a problem."

The SuperClip is produced by Froelich and her husband through their family business, Ace Wire Spring & Form Company (**www.acewire.com**), based in McKees

Rock, Pennsylvania. For over 60 years, Ace has custom-manufactured wire forms such as bucket handles, paper racks, and springs that go into varied products from screen doors to M-1 military tanks. The company has annual sales of more than $5 million. Although these markets were not at all similar to the office-supply business, Linda felt that her paper clip design was unique and so superior that it was worth pursuing. The realities have been a harsh lesson.

With imitation supersize clips found everywhere, pallet on pallet of the SuperClips languished in the back storeroom of Ace. The large office-supply competitors priced their imitations so much lower that Linda's product was having a hard time competing. However, she didn't give up. Although Linda and her husband prided themselves on being American manufacturers, they made the decision to produce the SuperClip offshore. That way they'd be able to meet competitors' prices and hopefully be able to provide better quality. In addition, they decided to expand the product line by introducing the SuperClip in various colors to appeal to school and office markets. Ace landed contracts with the federal government for the SuperClip and the Arthritis Foundation endorsed it because of its ease of use for people with arthritis.

Discussion Questions

1. What do you think went wrong with Linda's entrepreneurial venture?
2. Could goals and strategies have prevented the problems? Explain.
3. Ace Wire's Web site proudly boasts its ISO 9002 certification. Find out what you can about ISO 9002 certification and summarize your findings in a bulleted list. Why might this type of certification be important for a manufacturer?
4. What advice might you give the Froelichs? What could you learn from the Froelich's experiences?

Sources: Company information from Company Web site (**www.acewire.com**), June 13, 2002, and Hoover's Online (**www.hoovers.com**), June 13, 2002; and E. O. Welles, "Clipped," *Inc.*, December 1997, pp. 96–109.

Panera Bread Company (www.panerabread.com)

Out of the Heartland of America comes bread baked with heart. Panera Bread, based in Richmond Heights, Missouri (a suburb of St. Louis), bakes handcrafted breads fresh each and every day. At its more than 370 bakery cafés, people enjoy 15 flavorful, hearty varieties of bread. Panera Bread bakes more bread every day than any other bakery–café operation in the United States. CEO Ron Shaich's goal is to put "a loaf of bread in every arm."

At the company's mostly suburban locations, patrons can purchase freshly baked sourdough bread and other bakery goods, including bagels, cinnamon rolls, muffins, and filled pastries. In addition, Panera Bread and its St. Louis Bread units serve up a menu featuring sandwiches, soups, and specialty coffees. The interiors are stylish, with fashionable décor, hardwood floors, and food served on china dinnerware. Customers often linger over their meals enjoying the food, the conversation, and the ambience.

The company has been on a roll recently. Shaich has overseen Panera's growth and intends to emulate Starbucks' expansion strategy. In fact, he plans to open more than 500 new franchises over the next several years. Revenues in 2001 were over $201 million (one-year sales growth was 32.8 percent) and net income was over $13 million (one-year net income growth was 91.3 percent). During the first quarter of 2002, the torrid pace continued as sales increased 48 percent. At Panera Bread, it isn't just the bread that's rising!

Discussion Questions

1. What type of production process strategy would be appropriate for one of Panera Bread's café–bakeries? What type of layout strategy would be most appropriate? Explain your choices.
2. What type(s) of information system(s) would Panera Bread's home office probably want to have in place? How about one of Panera's café–bakeries? Explain your choices.
3. Check out Panera Bread's Web site. Is it a good marketing tool? Why or why not?
4. Using information from the company's Web site, how many franchised café–bakeries are there? Do some research on franchise ownership (in general, not just for Panera Bread). Would the need for technology and operations strategies, marketing strategies, information systems strategies, and financial and accounting strategies change just because of the franchise relationship? Explain.

Sources: Company information from Company Web site (**www.panerabread.com**), May 23, 2002, and Hoover's Online (**www.hoovers.com**), June 13, 2002; and M. Krantz, "Small-Cap Stars," *Business Week*, The Business Week 50, Spring 2002, pp. 147–150.

BUSINESS PLAN PRO

EXERCISE 6-1: Your Target Market

Business Plan Pro includes a market analysis table you can use to add detail to your market analysis by adding up the potential customers in various market segments.

- Note how this computer reseller divides its market into several different segments. Read the related texts in this sample plan to see how those segments are defined. Note that the numbers in this plan refer to total potential customers, not actual customers reached.
- Compare the AMT market segmentation to the Market Analysis table included in the Metolius Graphics sample plan. It's listed in the Sample Plan Browser as "Graphic Services," SIC code 7336.
- Using any one of the business plans you've worked on for previous exercises, or a new plan of your choosing, use the Easy Plan Wizard, the Plan Outline, or the **View>Tables>Market Analysis** command to view to find the Market Analysis table and fill it in.
- As you do, be creative about market segmentation. The better you define different groups of customers, the better the lead-in to marketing strategy.

EXERCISE 6-2: Your Marketing Plan

Business Plan Pro's list of business plan tasks in the Easy Task Wizard includes a section called "Your Marketing Plan," which includes several topics related to the content of this chapter.

- Consider the marketing plan described in the AMT plan in Exercise 6-1, above. Use the Easy Plan Wizard to find both the "Your Market" and the "Your Market Strategy" sections of this plan. In what ways might this plan, which was written in 1995, be obsolete in today's economy? What tools would a present-day AMT have that the 1995 AMT didn't have?
- Access the Metolius Graphics business plan using the Sample Plan Browser. It's listed in the Sample Plan Browser as "Graphic Services," SIC code 7336. Compare its market analysis to the AMT market analysis. Are these two businesses selling to the same kinds of market segments? How are their marketing plans different? Which one seems most likely to succeed?
- Using any one of the business plans you've worked on for previous exercises, or a new plan of your choosing, use the Easy Plan Wizard view to find the "Your Marketing Plan" section and fill in the marketing plan topics.

Spherix

Spherix (**www.spherix.com**) knows very well the importance of innovation. A diverse Maryland company with three divisions—Biotechnology, Information Services, and Information Technology—Spherix has been in business for over 35 years. Gilbert Levin, Ph.D., founder and CEO, has interests that know no bounds, as evidenced by its wide-ranging product lines. The company's Biotechnology division makes FlyCracker, a pesticide that's safe for humans. Its newest product is a low-calorie sugar substitute called Tagatose. Tagatose is creating all kinds of buzz in the medical community and in the investor community because of its application for conditions such as anemia, hemophilia, and diabetes. The company's Information Services division consists of call centers that handle questions on public and environmental health issues and other topics for U.S. drug companies and government agencies. The company's third division, the Information Technology division, has been the income provider that supports the biotechnology efforts. The centerpiece of the IT business is reserveworld.com, an online reservations site that handles tickets and reservations for a large number of tourist destinations (over 64,000), including the Statue of Liberty. However, with the buzz about Tagatose, the pharmaceutical side of Spherix may become just as big as the IT side.

Everyone at Spherix knows how important innovation and creativity are. The company is dedicated to the pursuit of innovative ideas in any line of business. After all, look at the company's track record—pesticides, tourist reservations, and sugar substitutes. Spherix's president says, "Creative innovation and a diligent commitment to quality—that's what sets Spherix apart. We have a rich pipeline of new ideas for technology products and services, and a staff that's dedicated to working with industry to bring those ideas to fruition. At Spherix, we're not riding the wave of technology, we're helping to create it."

Discussion Questions

1. Given the diversity of its divisions, what could Spherix do to ensure that its goals are compatible? Or in setting goals, would it even matter that its business divisions are so diverse?
2. How important do you think quality is to this company's strategies? How can it ensure that quality is part of all that it does?
3. Log on to Spherix's Web site (**www.spherix.com**). Find its statement of mission. Describe how the company's stated mission will affect the company's production and operations management function, the marketing function, its information systems, and its financial and accounting systems.

Sources: **Company information from company Web site (www.spherix.com), July 10, 2002, and Hoover's Online (www.hoovers.com), July 10, 2002; and *Business Now* video segment.**

ENDNOTES

1. Information on company from company's Web site (**www.joeboxer.com**), June 10, 2002, and Hoover's Online (**www.hoovers.com**), June 10, 2002; and "Photo Opportunities," *Inc.,* May 1999, pp. 104–105.
2. M. E. Tubbs, D. M. Boehne, and J. S. Dahl, "Expectancy, Valence, and Motivational Force Functions in Goal-Setting Research: An Empirical Test," *Journal of Applied Psychology,* June 1993, pp. 361–73; E. A. Locke, "Facts and Fallacies About Goal Theory: Reply to Deci," *Psychological Science,* January 1993, pp. 63–64; and J. C. Naylor and D. R. Ilgen, "Goal Setting: A Theoretical Analysis of a Motivational Technique," in *Research in Organizational Behavior,* vol. 6, ed. B. M. Staw and L. L. Cummings (Greenwich, CT: JAI Press, 1984), pp. 95–140.
3. A. Raskin, "Secrets from the Fast Lane," *Inc.,* June 2002, pp. 36–37.
4. J. D. Hunger and T. L. Wheelen, *Strategic Management,* 5th ed. (Reading, MA: Addison-Wesley, 1996), p. 143.
5. D. J. Ketchen Jr., J. B. Thomas, and R. R. McDaniel, "Strategic Planning and Firm Performance: A Synthesis of More Than Two Decades of Research," *Academy of Management Journal,* December 1994, pp. 1649–65; S. Hart and C. Banbury, "How Strategy-Making Processes Can Make a Difference," *Strategic Management Journal,* May 1994, pp. 251–69; and N. Capon, J. U. Farley, and J. M. Hulbert, "Strategic Planning and Financial Performance: More Evidence," *Journal of Management Studies,* January 1994, pp. 105–10.
6. D. M. Osborne, "The Store That Stark Built," *Inc.,* August 2001, pp. 46–47.
7. D. Drickhamer, "Manufacturer Goes for the Gold," *Industry Week,* February 2002, p. 27.
8. E. Barker, "Hot Tips," *Inc.,* August 2001, p. 74.
9. J. Jusko, "Tried and True," *Industry Week,* December 6, 1999, pp. 78–85.
10. Ibid., p. 78.
11. G. Hasek, "Extraordinary Extrusions," *Industry Week,* October 16, 2000, pp. 79–80.
12. Company Web site (**www.ecofish.com**), June 12, 2002; and J. Grossmann, "Sea Change," *Inc.,* January 2002, p. 22.
13. A. Amason, H. Sapienza, and J. Almeida, "Strategy and New Venture Performance: Low Cost and Differentiation Advantage in High Potential New Ventures," *Academy of Management Proceedings,* 2001, Entrepreneurship Division Abstracts, p. 14.
14. S. Greco, "Hot Tips," *Inc.,* August 2001, p. 74.
15. L. Buchanan, "Winnebago Take All," *Inc.,* May 2001, pp. 66–67.
16. N. Brodsky, "The Right Price," *Inc.,* April 2001, p. 25.
17. E. Brown, "What Women Want," *Forbes,* November 12, 2001, p. 124.
18. J. H. Maxwell, "With a Little Help from My Friends," *Inc.,* November 2001, pp. 116–117.

7

SECTION 3 MANAGING THE ENTREPRENEURIAL VENTURE

Managing Processes

LEARNING OBJECTIVES

After reading and studying this chapter, you should be able to:

1. Describe the steps in the decision-making process.
2. Explain the different styles of decision making.
3. Describe different ways to measure and evaluate performance.
4. Describe the commonly used financial statements and financial ratios.
5. Explain cash flow analysis.
6. Detail what is involved in a SWOT analysis.
7. Tell why stimulating change is important to entrepreneurial ventures.
8. Describe the different roles entrepreneurs play as change agents.
9. Explain how innovation and creativity can be managed.
10. Explain why it's important to manage customer service and how customer service can be managed.
11. Differentiate the various types of e-businesses.
12. Explain the characteristics of a world-class organization.

ENTREPRENEURSHIP IN ACTION

Its bicycles are loved by customers and respected by competitors. Cannondale Corporation (**www.cannondale.com**) based in Bethel, Connecticut, is the world's leading manufacturer of high-performance bicycles.[1] However, not content to stay on a gentle, smooth, and predictable path, CEO Joe Montgomery decided to go in a new direction by introducing a new line of off-road motorcycles in the spring of 2000. He hoped that the company's new push into motorized products would help double sales and give a boost to the stock price that had been languishing around $3 a share after hitting a high of $27 in October 1997. However, to accomplish these goals, the company was going to have to steal market share from some serious competition: Yamaha, Suzuki, Kawasaki, and Honda. Yet, there was some

Should Joe Montgomery be concerned about his company's performance? At what point might he have to make a decision about changing the company's direction? At some point, all entrepreneurial ventures face decisions such as this. Once an entrepreneurial venture is launched, there will continually be situations that need the attention of the entrepreneur. The successful entrepreneur needs to be able to manage the various processes of an ongoing venture. Managing processes is what we're going to look at in this chapter. We'll first examine the all-important decision-making process and look at some characteristics of different decision-making styles. Next, we'll look at different ways of measuring and evaluating performance. Based on performance results, the entrepreneur may need to stimulate and manage change, which is also a topic we'll look at. Finally, we're going to discuss some contemporary issues facing entrepreneurs as they manage the processes of an ongoing business. These include managing innovation and creativity, managing customer service, initiating e-business strategies, and becoming a world-class organization. Because everything that an entrepreneur does in managing processes involves making decisions, we need to understand how that important process takes place.

MAKING DECISIONS

One thing that all entrepreneurs do, regardless of size, type, location, or age of their entrepreneurial ventures, is make decisions. A **decision** is a choice made between two or more alternatives. When you choose where to eat for lunch, you're making a decision. When you choose which classes to take with which professors, you're making decisions. Entrepreneurs are faced with making decisions day in and day out, although their decisions aren't usually as simple as deciding between tacos or cheeseburgers. How are decisions made? What's involved with making decisions? Let's look at the decision-making process to better understand these issues.

good news. Recreational off-road biking was extremely popular, with the consumer boom being fed by televised motocross competitions.

The path to the introduction of the new motorcycle was about as unpredictable and bumpy as some of the trails that the company's customers love to traverse. Bringing a new product out is a difficult proposition for any company, and Cannondale's product development expertise, although extremely proficient in high-performance bicycles, was put to the test. Cannondale so far has invested nearly $65 million in the motorsports division. Company sales declined in 2000 and 2001 and the company had net losses both of these years, as well. However, Montgomery still feels that it's one of the best investments he's made.

The Decision-Making Process

From the initial context analysis to determine and evaluate entrepreneurial opportunities to the point of designing and implementing strategies, the entrepreneur has been making decisions. The decision making doesn't stop there. Decisions are continually being made in the day-to-day ongoing operation of the entrepreneurial venture. Although many of these decisions may be relatively simple and straightforward, they still involve making

EXHIBIT 7-1 The Decision-Making Process

Steps

1. Recognizing the need to make a decision
2. Identifying decision criteria
3. Weighting the criteria
4. Developing alternatives
5. Analyzing and evaluating each alternative
6. Selecting an alternative–making a decision!

a choice. How are decisions made? The process of making decisions involves a series of six steps. (See Exhibit 7-1.)

Step 1 is *recognizing the need to make a decision.* The need to make a decision comes about because of a problem or an opportunity. A **problem** is a situation in which there's an inconsistency between actual and desired results. An **opportunity** is an optimistic possibility or positive trend. In either situation, the entrepreneur must recognize that a decision needs to be made—that is, he or she must recognize that performance is not up to par or that performance can be improved if opportunities are exploited. (In later sections of this chapter, we're going to discuss ways to analyze and evaluate performance results and trends.) Once the entrepreneur has identified a problem or opportunity that needs attention, step 2 is *identifying decision criteria* that will be important in addressing the situation. That is, the entrepreneur must determine what's relevant or important in making a decision. Whether they are explicitly stated or not, every decision maker has criteria that guide his or her decisions. These criteria reflect the entrepreneur's interests, values, and personal preferences. Keep in mind that not all the criteria identified will be equal in importance. So step 3 in the decision-making process is *weighting the criteria* so they have the appropriate priority in making choices. Step 4 is *developing alternatives,* which often demands creative and innovative thinking. In step 5, the entrepreneur needs to critically *analyze and evaluate each alternative.* He or she would do this by appraising the alternative against the criteria identified earlier. The strengths and weaknesses of each alternative become apparent as they're compared to the weighted criteria. Step 6 in the decision-making process is *selecting an alternative.* Once an alternative has been selected, it would be implemented and, after an appropriate period of time, evaluated to see whether the problem or opportunity had been addressed.

Now, how realistic is this decision-making process? Is that actually what an entrepreneur should—or would—do every time there's a decision to be made? The answer probably would be "yes" if every decision-making situation was one in which the decision maker could be this rational because this approach would lead to a wide variety of choices from which the best alternative is chosen. However, in reality, several factors limit just how rational a decision maker can be. We certainly don't want to imply that the decision-making process just presented is useless. It isn't, and most entrepreneurs probably *do* try to be as rational as possible as they make decisions. In addition, many types of entrepreneurial decisions do lend themselves to the preciseness and thoroughness of the rational decision-making process. But, we also need to recognize that there are certain factors that influence just how rational decision makers are (and can be) as they make decisions.

Entrepreneurs in Action

Anne DeGrott, CEO of Epivax, Inc. (**www.epivax.com**) is certainly accustomed to dealing with vast amounts of information. In 1983 in her last year of medical school, she first read about the new "mystery killer" disease AIDS and was immediately hooked. Developing vaccines for AIDS and tuberculosis became her passion. When the university research settings she was working in became too confining and structured, she started her own biotech company. Today, her company, Epivax, uses computers to decipher those pieces of a virus, called epitopes, that stimulate the immune system. It makes those epitopes and tests them in the lab. Epivax makes money by doing epitope analysis for vaccine companies on a fee-for-service basis. She believes that, "It's a great revenue model. If we succeed, we're going to get a lot of other business. Infectious diseases are a growth area."

Sources: Company Web site (**www.epivax.com**), June 18, 2002; and T. Singer, "Mission Critical," *Inc.*, January 2001, pp. 68–69.

Factors That Influence the Rationality of Decision Making

We're going to look at four factors that influence how rational an entrepreneur can be in making decisions. These include individual differences in information-processing ability and capacity, individual decision-making style, the role of intuition, and the type of decision-making condition.

Individual Differences in Information-Processing Ability. The first factor we want to discuss that determines rationality in making decisions is individual differences in the ability to process information. Think about how you respond when you're presented with large amounts of information. Then, think of someone close to you. Does this person respond in the same way? Some people would stress out under these circumstances; others would break the information into smaller parts and deal with it that way; still others might be able to process the information without any problem whatsoever. People differ in their ability to absorb, analyze, and process information. Some people reach what is known as "information overload" more quickly than do others. In an entrepreneurial venture, the entrepreneur is juggling a number of problems and taking in so much information that it's impossible to always follow a rational systematic decision-making process. Instead, more realistically, entrepreneurs cope with the complex information demands of decision making by behaving in a way that allows them to be rational within certain limits. This approach to decision making was described by Herbert Simon (an expert on decision-making processes who won a Nobel prize in economics in 1978 for his groundbreaking work), who proposed that our rationality is "bounded." **Bounded rationality** refers to the concept that individuals have the time and cognitive ability to process only limited amounts of information as they make decisions.[2] According to this concept, rather than conduct an all-out search for the absolute best alternative, the decision maker will review feasible alternatives until he or she finds one that is good enough. In decision making, this is known as **satisficing**—seeking out alternatives that are satisfactory and sufficient. This concept can be explained by asking how you found the "significant other person" in your life. Did you review all possible alternatives or did you "accept" one that met your needs? Although you may laugh about this, the point is that we don't have the capacity, ability, or time to analyze all possible alternatives. We can be rational up to a certain point—the point at which we begin to look at alternatives. Then, because of information-processing limitations, we limit our search. This does not, by any means, suggest that entrepreneurs don't approach decision making seriously. They must and for the most part do. But, it does mean that individual differences in processing information and the resulting constraint of bounded rationality do play roles in determining how rational an entrepreneur can be in making decisions.

Individual Decision-Making Style. Another factor that influences the rationality of decision making is a person's style of making decisions. Entrepreneurs have different styles when it comes to making decisions and solving problems. One view of decision-making styles proposes that individuals approach problems in three ways—as problem avoiders, problem solvers, or problem seekers.[3] A **problem avoider** approaches problems by avoiding or ignoring information that points to a problem. Problem avoiders are inactive and do not want to confront problems. A **problem solver** is a person who addresses problems by trying to solve them as they come up. Solvers are reactive; they deal with problems after they occur. The **problem seeker** is proactive; he or she approaches problems by actively seeking out problems or new opportunities. Which of these styles is the best? Actually, entrepreneurs should probably use all three approaches. There are times when ignoring a problem is the best response. At other times, being reactive may be the only option because the problem happens so quickly. Then, there are times, particularly when searching out opportunities and finding ways to do things better, that entrepreneurs need to be proactive; that is, they need to actively seek these situations out. Think back to our chapter-opening case. As Joe Montgomery evaluated future directions for Cannondale, was he acting as a problem avoider, problem solver, or problem seeker?

Another perspective on decision-making styles proposes that people differ along two dimensions in the way they approach decision making.[4] One is their *way of thinking*. Some people tend to be rational and logical in the way they think or process information. A rational "type" tends to look at information in an orderly way and makes sure that it's logical and consistent before making a decision. Other people tend to be creative and intuitive. These intuitive types don't have to process information in a certain order but are comfortable looking at it as a whole. The other dimension describes a person's *tolerance for ambiguity*. Again, some people have a low tolerance for ambiguity and must have consistency and order in the way information is structured so that ambiguity is minimized. Others can tolerate high levels of ambiguity and are able to process many thoughts at the same time. When these two dimensions are diagrammed, four different decision-making styles are formed. (See Exhibit 7-2.) Let's look briefly at each style.

EXHIBIT 7-2 Decision-Making Styles

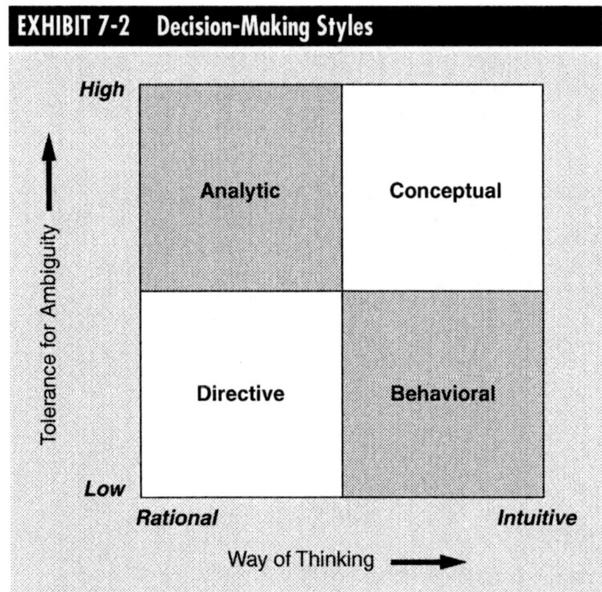

Source: *Supervision Today*, 1998, 2nd ed., by Robbins/DeCenzo. Reprinted by permission of Prentice Hall Inc., Upper Saddle River, NJ.

The **directive style** of decision making is characterized by a low tolerance for ambiguity and a rational way of thinking. These types are efficient and logical. They make fast decisions and focus on the short run. Their efficiency and speed in making decisions often results in making decisions with minimal information and assessing few alternatives. The **analytic style** is characterized by a high tolerance for ambiguity and a rational way of thinking. These types have much greater tolerance for ambiguity than do directive types. They want more information before making a decision and they consider more alternatives. Analytic decision makers are best characterized as careful decision makers with the ability to adapt to or cope with unique situations. The **conceptual style** is one characterized by a high tolerance for ambiguity and an intuitive way of thinking. Individuals with this style tend to be very broad in their outlook and will look at many alternatives. They focus on the long run and are very good at finding creative solutions to problems. Finally, the **behavioral style** is a decision-making style characterized by a low tolerance for ambiguity and an intuitive way of thinking. These decision makers work well with others. They're concerned about the achievements of those around them and are receptive to suggestions from others. They often use meetings to communicate, although they try to avoid conflict. Acceptance by others is important to the behavioral style decision maker.

Which is the best style? There *is* no "best" style. What's important is that entrepreneurs recognize their style of making decisions, are aware of the characteristics of that style and how it influences their decision making, and acknowledge that others in the organization may approach decision making in their own unique way.

The Role of Intuition. How does intuition affect the rationality of decision making? Studies have shown that intuition is used regularly in decision making and may actually help improve decision making.[5] **Intuitive decision making** is a subconscious process of making decisions on the basis of experience and accumulated judgment. Researchers studying intuitive decision making have identified five aspects of intuition, which are described in Exhibit 7-3. Making decisions on the basis of "gut feeling" doesn't necessarily happen independently of rational analysis; rather, the two complement each other. An entrepreneur who has had experience with a particular, or even a similar, type of problem or opportunity often can act quickly with what appears to be limited information. Under these circumstances, the entrepreneur doesn't rely on a systematic and thorough analysis of the problem or opportunity and evaluation of alternatives, but instead uses his or her experience, knowledge, and judgment to make a decision.

Decision-Making Conditions. The last factor that can affect how rational the entrepreneur is in making decisions is the circumstances surrounding the

EXHIBIT 7-3 What Is Intuition?

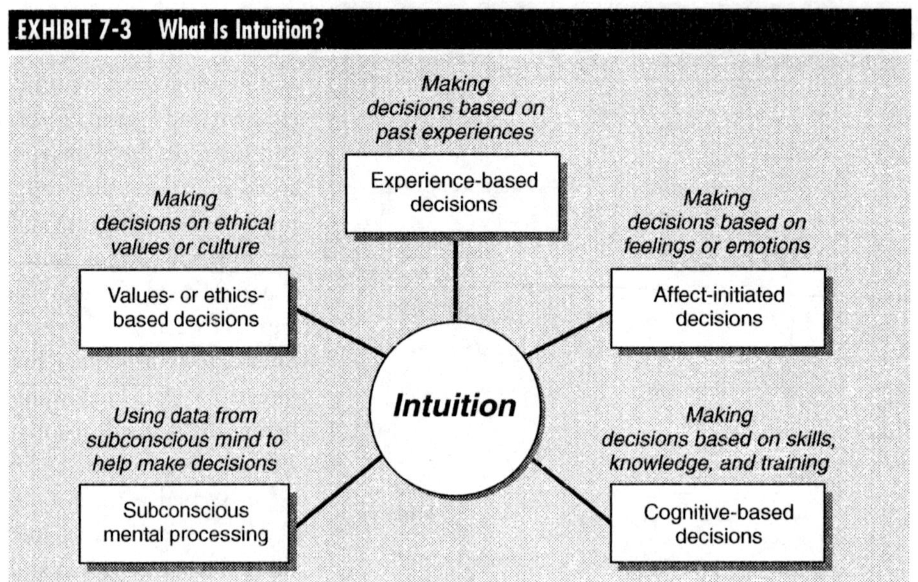

Source: Based on L.A. Burke and M.K. Miller. "Taking the Mystery Out of Intuitive Decision Making." *Academy of Management Executive.* October 1999. pp. 91–99.

decision to be made. Entrepreneurs face three potential conditions as they make decisions: certainty, risk, and uncertainty. **Certainty** is a situation in which an entrepreneur can make accurate assessments of which alternative is best because every possible outcome is known. For instance, if the entrepreneur is trying to get the best rate of return from local financial institutions on excess funds, he or she can investigate how much interest each financial institution is offering. The outcome of each and every alternative is known, so the entrepreneur can approach the decision rationally and systematically. As you might expect, this decision-making condition isn't characteristic of most situations faced by most entrepreneurs! A far more common situation is one of **risk**, which describes conditions in which the decision maker can estimate the likelihood of certain outcomes. The ability to assign probabilities to outcomes may be the result of personal experience or secondary information. Under the conditions of risk, the entrepreneur has historical data or personal experience allowing him or her to assign statistical probabilities to different alternatives. Under this decision-making condition, the entrepreneur can be partly rational because at least he or she can attempt to define reasonable probabilities of the likelihood of certain outcomes. However, keep in mind that these *are* just probabilities—they're not certain outcomes. But at least *some* guidelines can be developed to help make a rational decision, unlike our last type of decision-making situation. The final type of decision situation is one of **uncertainty**, which describes a situation in which the decision maker is neither certain about outcomes nor able to make reasonable probability estimates. Many decision-making situations that entrepreneurs face are ones of uncertainty. Under these conditions, the choice of alternatives is influenced by the limited amount of information available to the decision maker and by the entrepreneur's desire to maximize potential gains, satisfice with an acceptable gain, or minimize potential losses. Uncertainty often forces entrepreneurs to rely more on hunches, intuition, creativity, and "gut feelings."

Rapid Review

- ✔ What is a decision? Describe the six steps in the decision-making process.
- ✔ Differentiate between a problem and an opportunity.
- ✔ How do individual differences in information-processing ability influence the rationality of decision making?
- ✔ What is bounded rationality? What is satisficing?
- ✔ Describe the three different styles of approaching problems in the workplace.
- ✔ What two dimensions affect the way individuals approach decision making? Describe the four different decision-making styles that result because of the interaction of these two dimensions.
- ✔ What role does intuition play in decision making?
- ✔ Differentiate the three conditions entrepreneurs face as they make decisions.

One area in which entrepreneurs put their decision making to work in managing the processes of the up-and-running entrepreneurial venture is in measuring and evaluating organizational performance. That's the next topic we want to look at.

MEASURING AND EVALUATING ORGANIZATIONAL PERFORMANCE

The entrepreneurial venture is launched! The entrepreneur and other organizational members are performing their work. The floral arrangements are being designed and delivered, the Web pages are being created and posted, the bicycles and motorcycles are being built and shipped, or the work is being done for whatever the venture's output may be. What now? Do we just assume that things are running smoothly and are going as planned? Well, that may happen in some other alternate realm! But, the reality of managing the entrepreneurial venture isn't that simple. Things don't always go as planned and results don't always measure up, but the only way we're going to know this is to measure and evaluate performance. In this section, we want to discuss what performance results might be important to entrepreneurs and then look at some tools and techniques that entrepreneurs might use to measure and evaluate performance.

What Performance Results Are Important?

Working at something, anything, results in some level of performance—good, poor, fair, or whatever. This is just as true on the individual level (and we'll discuss the basics of individual performance appraisal in the next chapter as we look at managing people) as it is on the organizational level. What we're concerned with here is measuring and evaluating performance on the organizational level. **Organizational performance** is defined as the organization's success at achieving its goals effectively and efficiently. On the organizational level, what performance results might be important for the entrepreneur to know? Before we look at specific organizational performance measures, we need to recognize that these measures can be either quantitative or qualitative. **Quantitative measures** are stated as numbers. They're quantifiable and can be easily assembled, calculated, and compared. **Qualitative measures**, on the other hand, define organizational activities that are hard to quantify. Some activities that the entrepreneurial venture might be doing may not easily be reduced to quantitative terms, so qualitative assessments would be appropriate; for instance, in evaluating whether the organization is being socially responsible and ethical, if that's an important goal. Although quantitative data are easier to collect and compare, keep in mind that qualitative measures might be appropriate indicators of performance, as well.

Now, with that said, there are a couple of different types of organizational performance results we want to describe that entrepreneurs might be interested in measuring and evaluating.

Organizational Efficiency and Effectiveness. First, entrepreneurs may want to assess organizational efficiency and effectiveness. **Efficiency** concerns the amount of resources that are being used to meet the stated goals. It refers to the relationship between inputs (resources) and outputs. If you can get more output from the given inputs, you have increased efficiency. Likewise, if you can get the same level of output from fewer inputs, you're also increasing efficiency. Because most entrepreneurial ventures have limited resources, using them efficiently is an important organizational performance concern. Efficiency is often referred to as "doing things right"—that is, not wasting resources. On the other hand, **effectiveness** concerns whether an organization is meeting its stated goals. Effectiveness is often described as "doing the right things" because the entrepreneur wants to concentrate on doing the things that will help the entrepreneurial venture reach its goals. Whereas efficiency is concerned with the "means" of getting things done, effectiveness is concerned with the "ends," or the attainment of organizational goals.

Efficiency and effectiveness should go hand in hand. Yes, it's easier to be effective if you ignore efficiency. You could expend whatever resources are needed to achieve the goals. Although you'd be getting the job done, it would be at a high cost. Likewise, an organization can be efficient, but not effective. It can do the wrong things, but do them well. Some goals might be achieved, but be the wrong goals. Entrepreneurs should strive for both high effectiveness (high goal attainment) *and* high efficiency (low waste of resources). Successful entrepreneurial ventures typically have achieved high levels of both efficiency and effectiveness.

Financial Performance. One of the primary purposes of business organizations is to earn a profit. Profit data and other types of financial data serve to describe and summarize in monetary terms what the entrepreneurial venture is doing and how well it is doing. Because of the importance of doing well financially, financial results serve as a significant measure of organizational performance. In addition, much of the financial data is used to calculate efficiency measures. For instance, total sales divided by number of employees (a measure of sales per employee) is one measure of efficiency, as is gross profit margin (cost of goods sold and direct labor expenses calculated as a percentage of sales). Other financial measures will be discussed in the next section as we look at the performance measurement tools and techniques that entrepreneurs might use.

Tools and Techniques for Measuring and Evaluating Organizational Performance

Now that we know what performance results might be important for entrepreneurs to look at, how can these performance areas be measured and evaluated? We want to describe four important measurement tools: financial statement analysis, financial ratio analysis, cash flow analysis, and SWOT analysis.

Financial Statement Analysis. Keeping up-to-date and thorough financial records is important for entrepreneurs. Why? These records provide accurate information regarding the financial health of the business. An organization's financial results are reflections of how efficiently and effectively it's been doing its

Cut the Chaos

An entrepreneur's workspace and workday can easily erode into chaos. How can you be more efficient and effective? Here are some ways to cut the chaos:

Handling E-Mail

- Be brief. If you need to send something longer, send it only to those who absolutely need it.
- Respond quickly. The value of e-mail is that it allows quick responses. Don't sit on a message for more than a few days.
- Use the subject line. Don't use generic headings such as "follow-up." Describe your message precisely so it will be clear to the receiver also.
- Filter the spam. There are software filters or you can do it yourself. Delete the spam mail without opening it.
- Be judicious about what e-mail groups you join. Some groups send so much e-mail to their members that it can be overwhelming. Ask yourself if you're really getting anything out of all that information.
- Handle e-mail as few times as possible. Your options: respond to it or file it.

Handling Paper

- Stop it before it arrives. Cancel magazines and newspapers you don't read; toss junk mail without opening it, and ask to be removed from routing lists.
- Attempt to handle paperwork only once. Take care of correspondence at the time you receive it. Don't pick up a piece of paper until you're ready to do something with it. Your options: recycle, refer, record, act, or file.

Handling Workday Interruptions

- Keep in mind that not every interruption is an interruption—some may be absolutely necessary.
- Give people the information they need before they interrupt you.
- Close your door to interruptions for part of the day.
- Evaluate your interruptions. Keep a log for two weeks and see if certain people are the source of interruptions. Ask for their help in keeping you focused.

Handling Filing

- Think carefully about what you file. Many times you never look at what you file away. Ask yourself, If I need this piece of paper and don't have it, how much trouble will it cause? If the answer is a lot, then file it.
- File, don't pile. Get paperwork off your desk so it won't distract you.
- For those papers you do choose to file, file in one of two places: action or standing. Action files are ones you use often and may want to keep on your desk. Standing files are those that go in a file drawer or cabinet.

work. In addition, information from financial records is needed to prepare federal and state tax returns and also may be needed by banks and other financial institutions if the entrepreneurial venture requires additional capital. Unless the entrepreneur is able—and willing—to put these important financial records together, professional accounting or bookkeeping help and advice may be necessary. No matter *who* puts them together, one thing that's important in the creation of the venture's financial records is following **generally accepted accounting principles (GAAP)**, standards developed by the Financial Accounting Standards Board

(FASB) to ensure that all businesses create uniform financial statement formats. Even though these standards provide a measure of uniformity, some flexibility is allowable as long as consistency is maintained within the business's financial records.

Keeping financial records begins with the creation of journals and ledgers. (As we discuss the creation and use of the various financial records, keep in mind that any of these tools can be manual or computer-based.) Raw data from sources such as sales slips, check stubs, or purchase invoices are recorded in an **accounting journal**, which is simply a chronological record of a business's financial transactions. The entrepreneur may have several accounting journals, such as a sales journal, a purchases journal, a cash receipts journal, and a cash disbursements journal. These journals are the backbone of the venture's financial records, and the entrepreneur needs to keep these journals accurate, timely, and safe. Depending on the frequency and complexity of financial transactions, the entrepreneur may need to do these daily, every other day, or maybe even weekly. Then, at some regular time interval—usually at the end of a month—the financial transactions are divided into separate accounts and posted into a **general ledger**, which provides a summary record of financial transactions. At the end of an accounting period (month, quarter, year), each individual account in the ledger is closed and totaled. This information is compiled into commonly used financial statements that show an entrepreneur how his or her venture is doing financially. What are these financial statements?

The **income statement** (also called the **profit and loss** or **P&L**) is a financial statement that shows the revenues and expenses of a business and the resulting profit or loss over a specific period of time. The income statement shows the financial condition of a business over time—that is, it provides a "moving picture" of the venture's financial performance. The main sections of the income statement that can be analyzed by the entrepreneur include sales (or revenues or income); cost of goods sold (the total costs of products or services sold during the time period); gross profit; operating, general, and other expenses of the entrepreneurial venture not associated with the cost of goods sold; and net income (or loss). How can the entrepreneur use this information to help measure performance? One thing he or she can do is calculate the percentage relationship of each item of expense to sales. This results in what is known as a **common-size income statement**, a valuable tool for checking the efficiency of the entrepreneurial venture. A common-size income statement measures the changes in the use of resources because resource use is indicated by its cost or expense. Another way the entrepreneur can measure performance is by looking at the trends in sales, expenses, and income using both the regular income statement and the common-size income statement. If sales show a downward trend or if expenses (actual or percentage) show an upward trend without an accompanying upward trend in sales, the entrepreneur needs to evaluate what's happening. Is there a problem that needs to be addressed? By continually measuring and analyzing the financial information on the income statement, an entrepreneur is alerted to actual and potential problems in the actual working operations of the business.

The second primary financial statement is the **balance sheet**, a financial statement that shows the value of an organization's assets, liabilities, and owner's equity. This financial statement provides a snapshot of the entrepreneurial venture

Entrepreneurs in Action

On a wall in his office is a sign that says "Profit equals revenues minus expenses" and an upward-pointing arrow next to the word *revenues* and a downward-pointing arrow next to the word *expenses*. Rick Sapio, CEO of Dallas-based Mutuals.com never really thought about keeping an eye on expenses when he first started his business, which provides mutual-fund advisory services and account management to customers for a flat fee. But then, he had been able to raise an astonishing $14 million from angel and institutional investors. Having all that cash may not have been a good thing. The company was focused on growing revenues, not on controlling expenses. However, when the stock market began its downward slide, Sapio found it more difficult to raise funds. All of a sudden, the expense side of the income statement became extremely important, and Sapio's focus on the bottom line has helped Mutuals.com become a more efficient, and effective, organization.

Sources: Company Web site (**www.mutuals.com**), June 19, 2002; and E. Barker, "Cheap Executive Officer," *Inc.*, April 2002, pp. 114–116.

at any given point in time (usually at the end of a financial period—month, quarter, or year). The two main sections of the balance sheet show the value of the assets the venture owns and the claims against those assets in the form of liabilities (the value of what is owed to others) and owner's equity (the value of the owner's stake in the business). This information also can be shown in a **common-size balance sheet**, which takes each section separately (assets, liabilities, and equity), sets the total equal to 100 percent, and then shows each item in that section as a percentage of the total. As with the common-size income statement, these percentages can indicate areas of concern. Both actual numbers and trends can be measured and evaluated to see if there are any current or potential problems.

The third primary financial statement needed by entrepreneurs for measuring and evaluating performance is the **cash-flow statement**, which is a financial statement that shows cash inflows and outflows of a business. You probably personally know the importance of keeping track of cash inflows and outflows if you've ever run out of money (cash) to pay your bills or to buy necessities. Keeping track of cash flow is critical to the survival of entrepreneurial ventures, maybe even more critical than profits. Many businesses show a profit, but have problems paying their bills on time because they have a cash-flow problem. Negative cash flow (more cash going out than coming in) is common for new businesses. This situation isn't alarming as

The Grey Zone

What happens if one of your key employees leaves your company and goes to work for a competitor? What if that employee knows your customers, contacts, trade secrets, and important financial information? How can you protect yourself against such a circumstance? What ethical considerations, if any, would there be in safeguarding your intangible assets?

Rapid Review

- ✔ How is organizational performance defined?
- ✔ Which are more important, quantitative performance measures or qualitative performance measures?
- ✔ What types of organizational performance results might entrepreneurs be interested in measuring and evaluating?
- ✔ What does it mean for an organization to be efficient? Effective?
- ✔ Why is it important to measure and evaluate financial performance?
- ✔ What are generally accepted accounting principles? Why are they important?
- ✔ What types of financial records should an entrepreneurial venture keep? How are an accounting journal and a general ledger related?
- ✔ Describe the common types of financial statements.

long as it happens infrequently or the business is very young. But, if these situations aren't the case, then there's a problem of inadequate cash flow. Managing cash flow is such an important performance analysis and measurement tool for entrepreneurs that we've got a whole chapter section devoted to it. We'll get to it after we discuss financial ratio analysis.

Financial Ratio Analysis. With the information from the two primary financial statements—that is, the income statement and the balance sheet—the entrepreneur can measure and evaluate changes in financial performance through **financial ratio analysis**—a way to express relationships between key accounting elements from the financial statements and a convenient and relatively easy technique for doing a financial analysis. By watching the trends in the financial ratios, an entrepreneur can spot "red flags" in performance and take appropriate action(s), if necessary, before they become critical.

There are four major categories of financial ratios. (See Exhibit 7-4 for a description of these ratios and how they're calculated. We're not going to go into a detailed explanation of these ratios under the assumption that you've covered or will cover this information in an accounting or finance course.) The **liquidity ratios** measure the organization's ability to meet its current debt obligations with its current assets. The two main types of liquidity ratios are the current and the quick (or acid test). **Leverage ratios** examine the organization's use of debt and the use of equity to finance its assets—in other words, they're measures of the firm's use of leverage. In addition, one other key leverage ratio examines whether the organization is able to meet interest payments on any debt. As you know from the balance-sheet format, an organization's assets can be financed in only two ways—through debt or through equity. Remember the accounting equation: assets = liabilities + owner's equity. These ratios measure the organization's asset financing provided by the owners and that provided by creditors. The main leverage ratios include the debt-to-assets, debt-to-equity, and times interest earned. These ratios reflect important decisions about the type of financing used by the entrepreneur. The next major category of financial ratios is the **operating ratios**, which measure how efficiently the organization is using its assets—in other words, how efficiently is the venture operating? The key operating ratios are inventory turnover, total asset turnover, fixed asset turnover, average collection period, average payable period, and working capital turnover. For each of these operating ratios, you're calculating a measure of the efficiency of asset use. After all, the only reason an entrepreneurial venture has assets is to help it earn revenues (and hopefully, profits). These operating ratios indicate how efficiently the organization is using its assets to do this. The final category of financial ratios is the **profitability ratios**, which measure how profitable the organization is. Very simply, the profitability ratios are a proxy of the venture's efficiency *and* effective-

EXHIBIT 7-4 Selected Major Financial Ratios

Category	Ratio	Calculation	Objective
Liquidity	Current ratio	Current assets / Current liabilities	Tests the organization's ability to meet short-term obligations
	Quick or acid test	Current assets minus inventories / Current liabilities	Tests liquidity more accurately when inventories turn over slowly or are difficult to sell
Leverage	Debt-to-assets	Total debt / Total assets	Indicates the amount of the organization's assets being financed by debt; the higher the ratio, the more leveraged the organization
	Debt-to-equity	Total debt / Total equity	Shows the relationship of the organization's use of debt versus its use of equity
	Times interest earned	Profits before interest and taxes / Total interest expenses	Measures how many times the organization can cover its interest expenses
Operating	Inventory turnover	Sales / Inventory	Measures how many times the organization turns over (sells) its inventory
	Total asset turnover	Sales / Total assets	Shows how efficiently the organization is using its assets to generate sales
Profitability	Profit margin	Net income / Sales	Identifies how much is being made in profit for every dollar of sales
	Return on investment (ROI) or Return on assets (ROA)	Net income / Total assets	Identifies the profits per dollar of assets
	Return on stockholders' equity (ROE)	Net income / Total stockholders' equity	Identifies the profits per dollar of stockholders' equity
	Earnings per share (EPS)	Net income / Number of shares of common stock outstanding	Provides a measure of earnings available to the owners of common stock
	Price earnings ratio	Market price per share / Earnings per share	Provides an indicator of the attractiveness of the organization to equity markets

ness, and are critical indicators of performance. The main profitability ratios are the profit margin (both net and gross), return on investment (or return on assets), return on equity, and price earnings ratio.

Although it's important to calculate the financial ratios on a regular basis (usually quarterly and annually), the fact that the entrepreneur calculates financial ratios isn't enough! By themselves, the ratios are nothing more than a series of numbers and percentages reflecting an organization's financial performance for a certain period of time. The entrepreneur must understand how to interpret what the ratios are showing and apply this performance information to managing the venture's work processes more effectively and efficiently. Interpreting the ratios involves comparing them to industry ratios and to trends both for the organization and for the industry. However, a cautionary note needs to be made regarding any comparison of organization ratios to industry ratios. The industry ratios are simply averages of financial information reported to the various data-gathering companies. Although knowing the industry average gives an entrepreneur *some* standard of comparison, the goal should be to manage the entrepreneurial venture so that work performance (and the resulting financial results) is *better than* the average. In addition, when a financial ratio is substantially out of line with the industry ratio, it's important for an entrepreneur to carefully assess *why* there's a discrepancy before making any drastic changes in what is being done and how. You *must* know what the ratios are showing and what they reflect.

Cash-Flow Analysis. Cash. It's an absolutely vital economic unit of exchange. Unless you barter for your essentials of daily living, you know that cash is critical! Although bartering for goods and services may be something that entrepreneurs engage in occasionally, they also need cash to run their businesses. Without cash to purchase needed resources, to resolve unanticipated problems, or to invest in opportunities, the entrepreneur would be extremely limited in what could be done and how.

We're going to define **cash flow** as the actual amount of cash an organization brings in and the actual amount of cash it pays out during a given time period. Positive cash flow is when the amount of cash coming in is greater than the amount of cash going out; negative cash flow is when the amount of cash going out is greater than the amount of cash coming in.

The major challenge in managing cash flow is timing. The goal of good cash-flow management is making sure there's enough cash on hand when you need it. Having a positive cash balance three months from now doesn't matter if you have payroll, utility bills, and suppliers that need to be paid today. Although some cash inflows and outflows occur on a regular schedule, other cash flows do not. Fortunately, entrepreneurs can use certain cash-flow management tools and techniques. In the process of managing cash flow, entrepreneurs do play different and important roles. (See Exhibit 7-5.) In these roles, an entrepreneur can use different cash flow management tools such as the cash budget and ways to manage accounts receivable, accounts payable, and inventory.

The cash budget (or cash forecast) is a way for the entrepreneur to plan the venture's short-term cash needs. It shows the amount and timing of cash receipts and cash disbursements on a daily, weekly, or monthly basis. Keep in mind that a cash budget is just a forecast of cash inflows and outflows. It will never be completely accurate. However, it does

EXHIBIT 7-5 Key Cash Management Roles Played by Entrepreneurs

Role 1: Cash Finder
- Most important role played by entrepreneur
- Making sure there's enough cash to pay present and future bills
- An ongoing job

Role 2: Cash Planner
- Making sure cash is used properly and efficiently
- Requires keeping track of cash and planning for its use
- Forecasting cash inflows and outflows

Role 3: Cash Distributor
- Controlling the cash used to pay bills and other obligations
- Keeping on top of priority and timing of these cash payments
- Making sure cash is available when needed

Role 4: Cash Collector
- Collecting the cash that's due
- Making sure it's collected on time

Role 5: Cash Conserver
- Getting maximum value for cash being spent
- Getting the most for your money
- Avoiding unnecessary expenditures

Source: Based on B. J. Blechman, "Quick Change Artist," *Entrepreneur*, January 1994, pp. 18–21.

give the entrepreneur a pretty good idea of cash balances for th
How often an entrepreneur does a cash budget would depend c
the business. If the venture's cash flows are uncertain, it would b
more cash budgets in order to maintain some sense of control. U
cash budgets is quite common, but some organizations may requ
budgets.

There are five steps to preparing a cash budget. (See Exhibit
determine the desired cash balance to keep on hand. The entrepreneu
decide what amount of cash he or she wishes to keep as a reserve. ... should not be excessive because the cash may be put to better, more productive uses, but it also should not be so small that the entrepreneur worries every time period whether there's going to be enough cash to pay the bills. Probably the best way to determine this amount is based on experience. Step 2 is to *identify the beginning cash.* The entrepreneur must know what cash is on hand at the start of the time period. In step 3, you should *forecast cash receipts.* This forecast is an important element in the cash budget. Cash receipts includes cash sales, payment of any accounts receivables (amounts people owe you), interest payments, cash contributions by owner(s), and any other cash inflows. You want to have a good idea of what cash is coming in, but it's not always easy to do this. Entrepreneurs in new entrepreneurial ventures and ones in highly uncertain industries may find it particularly challenging to forecast cash receipts. In step 4, you should *forecast cash disbursements.* This is relatively easy for an established business because the patterns of cash disbursements, for the most part, should be pretty similar. However, it's probably better to *over*estimate cash disbursements (within reasonable amounts) to ensure that enough cash is on hand in case expenditures are

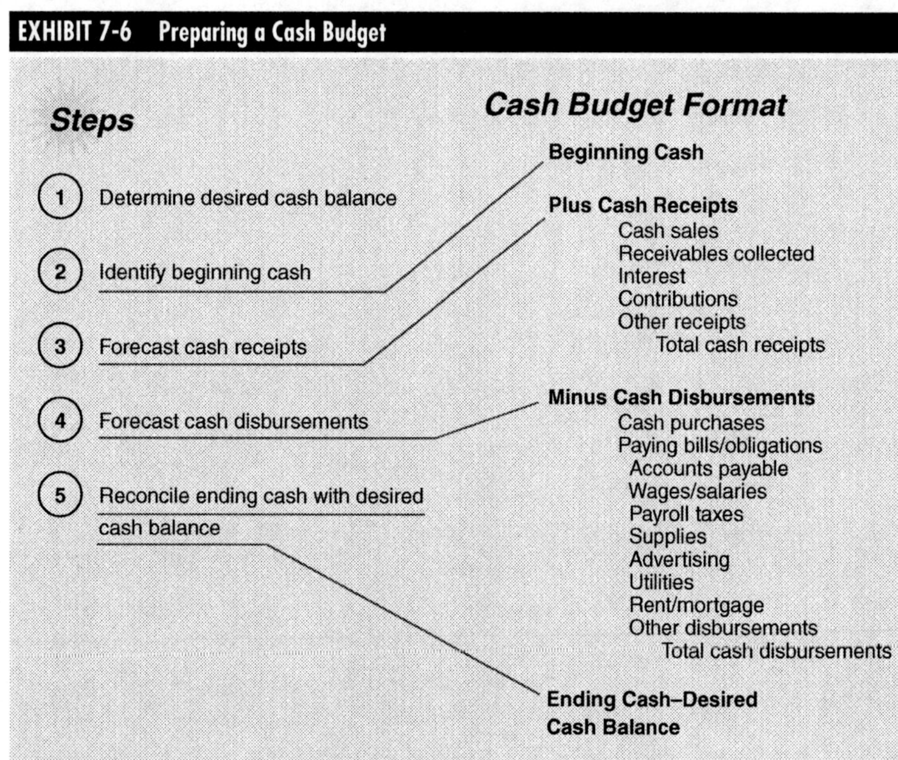

higher than expected. Finally, in step 5, you should *reconcile ending cash with the desired cash balance.* If the ending cash figure is more than the desired cash balance, the entrepreneur has excess cash to invest or pay down loans. If there's a negative difference, the entrepreneur will have to arrange for financing or look for other sources of cash.

Other cash-flow-management techniques revolve around managing the "big three" of an organization's cash flow: accounts receivable, accounts payable, and inventory.[6] Accounts receivable are amounts owed to your business because customers have purchased on credit; that is, they get the product or service, but don't pay for it until a later time. Selling on credit is a common practice in business,

FYI

Tips for Managing the Big Three

The "big three" of cash-flow management are accounts receivable, accounts payable, and inventory. There's bound to be significant cash flow in and through all of these areas. An entrepreneurial venture should always try to get cash in as fast as possible from accounts receivable and to stretch out the payables. So, how can each of these areas be "managed" for the most efficient and effective use of your entrepreneurial venture's often scarce cash?

Accounts Receivable Tips. Here are some tips to help get your cash in quicker: (1) Have a clear and well-thought-out credit and collection policy. (2) Speed up getting customer orders by offering fax services or online ordering. (3) Process customers' orders as quickly as possible, but do so accurately. (4) Prepare the customer invoice the same day the order is received. Make sure it is clear and accurate. State payment terms exactly and clearly. (5) Mail the invoice the same day it is prepared. The sooner the bill is in the mail, the sooner you're going to see your cash. (6) Use aging schedules (a list of accounts receivables sorted by when they're due—also known as the "age" of the account.) (7) Don't wait too long to start collection of a customer's unpaid bill.

Accounts Payable Tips. Here are some tips for managing what you owe: (1) Set up a monthly payment calendar so you know what is due when and so you can take advantage of early payment discounts. It's usually to your benefit to take advantage of these cash discounts. (2) Keep all bill-paying paperwork organized. (3) Verify all invoices before paying. (4) If possible, stagger payments so you aren't paying several bills all at once. That can be a significant drain on cash flow. (5) Keep on the lookout for early warning signs that your cash flow is in trouble.

Inventory Tips. Purchasing and holding inventory can be a significant drain on cash flow. You want to have enough inventory on hand to meet your operational and customer needs, but not too much that it's lying around not generating any return. In addition, unused inventory has to be stored, which can be another cash expense. Here are some tips for managing your inventory: (1) Make sure you have the right kind of inventory. (2) Keep inventory lean and turn it over frequently. (3) Use markdowns to get rid of inventory, if necessary. (4) Schedule inventory deliveries at the latest possible date to stretch out the time when the payment is due. (5) Other things being equal (that is, quality and price), order from the fastest supplier so you can keep inventory levels fairly low.

Sources: T. S. Hatten, *Small Business* (Upper Saddle River, NJ: Prentice Hall, 1997), pp. 468–469; T. W. Zimmerer and N. J. Scarborough, *Essentials of Entrepreneurship and Small Business Management* (Upper Saddle River, NJ: Prentice Hall, 1998), pp. 232–239; and "Steps for Improving Your Firm's Cash Flow," *Nation's Business* November 1998, p. 12.

but it's an expensive one. It's important for an entrepreneur to establish an effective and efficient collection approach. Remember that this is *your* cash. You want to get what's owed you. (The FYI Box in this section provides some practical advice for entrepreneurs in managing accounts receivable, accounts payable, and inventory.) Accounts payable are amounts that you owe to others. These amounts reflect what you have purchased on credit. The objective behind effectively and efficiently managing accounts payable is the opposite from that of the accounts receivable. When you *owe* money, you want to take as long as possible to pay without damaging your venture's credit rating. Finally, how the entrepreneurial venture's inventory (both raw materials and finished goods) is managed can affect cash flow. You want to make sure you have the right type and amount of inventory to meet customers' needs. Carrying items in inventory can be expensive, especially if it sits there for a long time. The inventory needs to be turned into cash.

SWOT Analysis. SWOT. What an odd "word!" The letters actually are an acronym for **s**trengths, **w**eaknesses, **o**pportunities, and **t**hreats. More importantly, though, SWOT analysis is a tool that entrepreneurs can use in assessing the work being done in their entrepreneurial venture and how organizational performance is measuring up.

An analysis of the venture's work activities and processes identifies strengths and weaknesses. **Strengths** are activities that the organization is doing well. Organizational strengths should be reinforced and nurtured because they influence how well the organization ultimately performs its work. In addition, strengths can be important potential competitive weapons. **Weaknesses** are things that the organization does not do well. Organizational weaknesses need to be corrected if they're in critical areas that are affecting the venture's performance and its ability to be competitive. This internal analysis is typically done using an **internal audit**, which very simply is a thorough assessment of the venture's internal work areas. It usually includes an evaluation of the activities, processes, and strategies in production and operations, marketing, human resource management, research and development, information systems and technology, and financial. Obviously, however, the internal audit should cover a venture's own specific and unique work areas. An internal audit looks at what is being done in each area and assesses how efficiently (low waste of resources) and effectively (meeting goals) that particular area's work is being done. Depending on what the internal analysis shows, the entrepreneur may need to make some decisions about correcting problems (weaknesses) or exploiting strengths. Although the internal analysis is a significant part of measuring and evaluating organizational performance, it's also important to look externally because there are things happening there that can have an impact on a venture's current and future performance.

An analysis of the trends and changes happening outside the organization provides an indication of potential opportunities and threats. Opportunities (as we defined them earlier in this chapter and in previous chapters) are positive and favorable external trends or changes of which the entrepreneur might want to take advantage. **Threats**, then, are negative and unfavorable external trends and changes that the entrepreneur will probably want to avoid or at least buffer against. The external analysis assesses what's happening outside the organization by examining trends and changes in the economic, technological, demographics,

FYI

Keeping Score

Do you keep track of your points earned in the various classes you're taking? Would basketball (or football, baseball, hockey, soccer) be as fun to follow if no scores were recorded? Keeping score provides a way to judge how you (or your favorite team) are doing. Entrepreneurs are discovering that keeping track of their company's performance can be as easy as keeping a scorecard.

Scorecards serve many purposes. They help entrepreneurs clarify strategic goals. You have to decide what's important and then identify the things you're going to track to ensure that performance in those areas is making a difference. In addition, scorecards help communicate those objectives to other people in the organization. Through the scorecards, there are no misunderstandings about the standards used in measuring nebulous organizational performance concepts such as customer satisfaction. Finally, because of their design, scorecards can provide rapid, easily understood feedback about how the entrepreneurial venture or any of its work areas are doing.

What should a scorecard include? The process starts with deciding organizational goals and then translating those goals into specific, concrete measures. Some experts recommend a scorecard that scores four areas: (1) financial scores, which cover things such as sales growth and profitability; (2) customer scores, which include rankings for market share, customer satisfaction, and so forth; (3) learning and growth scores, which measure things such as employee turnover, productivity, and other types of employee and organizational learning; and (4) an internal business process score, which measures product development, innovation, efficiency, and so forth. The choice of what to score should be determined by an organization's specific markets, strengths, and strategies. Once you've decided what the scorecard should keep track of, then it's just a matter of getting good information. You have to measure performance in the areas you've decided are important. Then, after a certain period of time (monthly, quarterly, semiannually, annually, or whatever), you'll need to show the performance results on a scorecard. The scorecard itself should be designed to present the "scores" as clearly and briefly as possible. The intent of the scorecard is not to be a long, involved performance measurement report, but a clear, succinct summary of the most critical performance measures.

Scorecards are tools that help entrepreneurs communicate the vision to all levels of an organization. As one proponent said, "It keeps you in tune with what's going on."

Sources: T. Leahy, "Tailoring the Balanced Scorecard," *Business Finance*, August 2000, pp. 53–56; J. Case, "Keeping Score," *Inc.*, June 1998, pp. 80–86; and M. Henricks, "Who's Counting?" *Entrepreneur*, July 1998, pp. 70–73.

social–cultural, global, and political–legal arenas. By assessing these external factors, the entrepreneur attempts to pinpoint what changes may be necessary in the organization to exploit the opportunities and to keep away from the threats. These changes will affect what work is being done and how it's being performed.

All of the performance-measurement tools and techniques that we've discussed in this section—financial statement analysis, financial ratio analysis, cash-flow analysis, and SWOT analysis—provide a picture of how efficiently and effectively the entrepreneurial venture is performing. What happens next? Depending on performance results, it may be necessary for the entrepreneur to

Rapid Review

- ✔ Describe the four categories of financial ratios and the major ratios in each of the four categories.
- ✔ Why isn't calculating financial ratios sufficient for measuring performance?
- ✔ What is cash flow? What cash-management roles do entrepreneurs play?
- ✔ What is a cash budget? Outline the five steps to preparing one.
- ✔ How can entrepreneurs manage the big three for the most efficient cash flow?
- ✔ What does SWOT stand for? How is it a performance measurement tool?
- ✔ How can a performance scorecard be useful? What does a scorecard measure?

make changes to what the venture is doing and how work is being done. That's the topic we want to look at next—stimulating and making changes.

STIMULATING AND MAKING CHANGES—BEING A CHANGE AGENT

Change—the only thing constant about it is the fact that it *is* constant. We know from earlier discussions that the context facing entrepreneurs is one of dynamic change. Both external and internal forces may bring about the need to make changes in the entrepreneurial venture. External forces for change include changes in technology, global competition, economic trends, or any other number of external factors. Internal forces for change may include any decisions and actions taken by organizational members in response to not meeting performance goals, developing and implementing a new strategy, or adapting to other changing organizational circumstances. Any of these changing external or internal forces may bring about the need to stimulate organizational change. What exactly is **organizational change**? We're going to define it as any alterations in what an organization does or how it does it. Entrepreneurs need to be alert to problems and opportunities that may create the need to change. In so doing, the entrepreneur may have to act as a **change agent**, a person who's a catalyst for change and who also manages the change process.

Entrepreneurs in Action

Ray Ferguson, CEO, and Ed Moody, vice president, of high-end sunglass manufacturer Costa Del Mar (**www.costadelmar.com**) are well aware of the important roles they play in stimulating and implementing changes. Competing in the tough sunglasses business, they've had to make a number of changes over the years. One of their most recent changes was when they pulled their sunglasses out of the Totes retail chain. Although having their product in so many retail outlets across the United States seemed like a good idea at the time they made the decision, it actually wasn't a good one at all. So, they changed. Their new push is toward outdoors retailers such as Sports Authority and Galyans. But if that doesn't work out, Ferguson and Moody know that they can change direction at any time.

Sources: Company Web site (**www.costadelmar.com**), June 18, 2002; and R. Wherry, "Full Speed Ahead," *Forbes*, January 7, 2002, p. 142.

Of the many hats an entrepreneur wears, that of change agent may be one of the most important.[7] If changes are needed in the entrepreneurial venture, often it is the entrepreneur who first recognizes the need for change and acts as the catalyst, coach and cheerleader, and chief change consultant. Change isn't easy in any organization, but it can be particularly challenging for entrepreneurial organizations. Even if a person is comfortable with taking risks, as entrepreneurs usually are, change can be hard. That's why it's important for the entrepreneur to recognize the critical roles he or she plays in stimulating and implementing change.

As a change agent, the entrepreneur plays different roles. First and foremost, the entrepreneur is a catalyst for change. He or she should be alert to signals that change is needed—signs from external or internal circumstances and situations or signs from organizational performance results. Often, the entrepreneur is the first person who, while managing the organizational processes, recognizes the need for change and moves to take action. What kinds of organizational change efforts might the entrepreneur have to initiate? Organizational change may be necessary in any or all of the following organizational areas: strategy, technology, products, structure, or people and culture. Changes in strategy may range from minor adjustments to major alterations in the way that organizational goals are pursued using various strategies. Changes in technology usually involve the introduction of new equipment, tools, or methods; automation; or computerization. Product changes involve any innovations or creative developments in current or new products. (The process of managing innovation and creativity is a significant part of managing the venture's overall processes, and we'll look at it more in depth in the next section.) Changes in structure involve any alteration in the way the venture is designed and structured. Remember from Chapter 5 that organizational design includes decisions about work specialization, chain of command, departmentalization, span of control, centralization and decentralization, and formalization. Alterations in any of these aspects would involve structural change. Finally, changes in people or culture include any changes in organizational members' values, attitudes, beliefs, norms, or behaviors—that is, a change in the culture. These types of "people" changes may be among the most difficult that entrepreneurs make because people are often reluctant and unwilling to change. However, resistance to organizational change efforts is to be expected. Managing resistance brings up the second role that entrepreneurs may have to play as change agents—that of being a cheerleader and coach.

During any organizational change, the entrepreneur may have to act as chief cheerleader and coach. Think about what coaches and cheerleaders do. They encourage, they support, they explain, they get you excited, they build you up, and they motivate you to put forth your best efforts. Organizational change of any type can be disruptive and scary. If there are other employees in the entrepreneurial venture, they may resist making changes. Thus, the entrepreneur must assume the role of explaining the change and encouraging change efforts by being a coach and cheerleader. Overcoming any resistance to change requires intense interpersonal efforts and support. If the entrepreneurial venture has a fairly open and flexible structure, the entrepreneur may find that being candid about the change, allowing organizational members to participate in the change, providing facilitation and support, and educating organizational members about the change may work best. If the entrepreneurial venture's structure isn't quite as open or

Rapid Review

- ✔ What is organizational change?
- ✔ What brings about the need for organizational change?
- ✔ Why might the role of change agent be one of the most important an entrepreneur plays?
- ✔ Describe the different roles an entrepreneur might play in stimulating and implementing change.
- ✔ What types of organizational change might an entrepreneur have to initiate?

flexible, the entrepreneur may need to rely more on telling people what to do. In either case, this role of being chief coach and cheerleader is an important one because it gets at the heart of making changes—getting people to accept and embrace the change.

Finally, the entrepreneur may have to act as the primary organizational change consultant if fees for hiring outside change consultants are beyond the venture's available financial resources. A change consultant guides the actual change process as changes in strategy, technology, products, structure, or people are being implemented. In this role, the entrepreneur answers questions, makes suggestions, gets needed resources, facilitates conflict, and does whatever else is necessary to get the change(s) implemented. In addition, in this role, the entrepreneur would evaluate the success of the change implementation—that is, would evaluate whether the change has been implemented efficiently and effectively—and then take any necessary action.

A predictable part of managing the ongoing processes of the entrepreneurial venture is stimulating and making changes. Whether the changes are in response to performance results that don't quite measure up or are made to exploit opportunities, the entrepreneur plays important roles as a change agent. In addition to the topics we've just covered that are part of managing the venture's processes, there are some contemporary issues that entrepreneurs face because they do manage processes.

CONTEMPORARY ISSUES IN MANAGING THE VENTURE

Throughout the ongoing organizational processes of making decisions, measuring and evaluating organizational performance, and stimulating and making changes, the entrepreneur is focused on making sure the venture is operating as efficiently and effectively as possible. However, in today's intensely competitive climate, the entrepreneur also must be aware of the importance of managing innovation and creativity, managing customer service, initiating e-business strategies, and becoming a world class organization. We're going to discuss these important contemporary issues in this section.

Managing Creativity and Innovation

In today's dynamic, chaotic world of global competition, organizations must continually innovate new products and services if they want to compete successfully. We know from earlier chapters that innovation is a characteristic of entrepreneurial organizations—entrepreneurial organizations are continually innovating. In fact, you can say that innovation is what makes the entrepreneurial organization "entrepreneurial." In a sense, creativity and innovation involve change—change in *what* the organization makes or change in *how* it makes its products. We defined **creativity** in Chapter 2 as the ability to combine ideas in a unique way or to

EXHIBIT 7-7 The Right Environment for Innovation

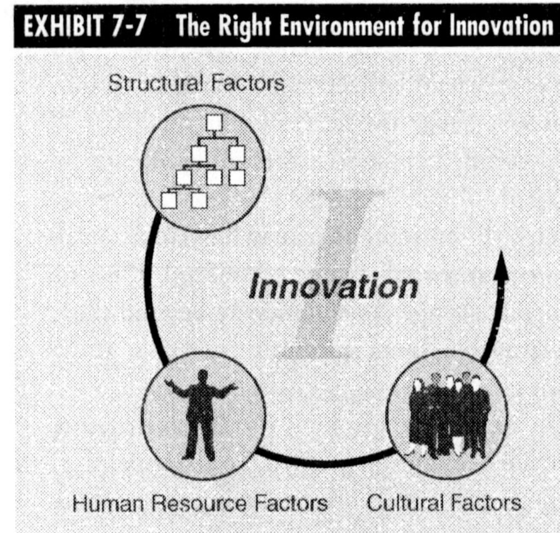

make unusual associations between ideas.[8] On the other hand, **innovation** was defined as the process of taking a creative idea and turning it into a useful (marketable) product, service, or method of operation. We're making a distinction between the two seemingly similar terms because creativity, by itself, isn't enough to make an entrepreneurial venture successful. That creativity has to be channeled into some product or process from which the organization can benefit. An innovative organization is characterized by its ability to turn creativity into valuable outcomes. How can innovation be cultivated in the entrepreneurial venture?

Cultivating Innovation. If an entrepreneur wants to encourage innovation in the organization, it's important to have creative individuals or groups planted in the right environment. Just as it takes the right environment for a flower to grow beautiful blooms, it takes the right environment for innovation to take hold and prosper. What does this kind of environment look like? Three factors have been found to stimulate innovation in organizations.[9] These include structural factors, cultural factors, and human resource factors. (See Exhibit 7-7.)

An organization's structure can have a significant impact on whether innovation blooms. Extensive research into the effect of structural variables on innovation has shown three things.[10] First, organic-type structures have a positive effect on innovation. Remember from Chapter 5 that this type of organization is low in formalization, centralization, and work specialization. It's a highly open, free-flowing, and flexible type of structure. The organic design facilitates the flexibility, adaptability, and cross-fertilization among people and work units that are necessary for creativity and innovation to occur and thrive.

The second structural factor that's been shown to have a positive impact on innovation efforts is having sufficient resources to support the innovation process. Why are resources important? Resources—financial resources, in particular—

Entrepreneurs in Action

CHIFF is the spirit that permeates Cranium Inc. (**www.playcranium.com**). CHIFF is an acronym for "clever, high-quality, innovative, friendly, and fun." The company created the game Cranium, and it became the fastest-selling independent board game in U.S. history. Despite their success with this game, founders Whit Alexander and Richard Tait are approaching their venture as a game of skill, not luck. And creating an organizational culture that's conducive to fostering human ingenuity is important to them. Says Tait, "Our survival and success will come from optimizing fun, focus, passion, and profits. That takes smarts and we thrive on that."

Sources: Company Web site (**www.playcranium.com**), June 18, 2002; and J. Bick, "Inside the Smartest Little Company in America," *Inc.*, January 2002, pp. 56–61.

allow entrepreneurs to purchase innovations, pay the expenses associated with implementing innovations, or absorb the costs of unsuccessful innovations. However, this may be the most difficult structural factor for the entrepreneur to control. Financial resources may be limited. But even with the constraint of limited resources, innovation processes are too important to ignore. An investment in innovation is vital for the long-term survival and ultimate success of the entrepreneurial organization.

The third structural factor that's important to the innovation process is encouraging frequent communication among the organization's various work units (departments, divisions, or whatever). Free-flowing and continual cross-communication has been shown to help break down barriers to innovation.[11] Sharing information and openly collaborating on ideas can create an environment that's conducive to high levels of creativity and innovation. Although the structural factors are important, they're just one aspect of nurturing innovation. Now let's look at the cultural factors.

Innovative organizations tend to have similar cultures.[12] They encourage experimentation, reward both successes and failures, and celebrate mistakes. An innovative culture is likely to have the following characteristics:

- *Acceptance of ambiguity.* Too much emphasis on objectivity and specificity constrains creativity.
- *Tolerance of the impractical.* Individuals who come up with impractical, even foolish, answers to what-if questions are not stifled. What at first seems impractical might lead to innovative solutions.
- *Low external controls.* Rules, regulations, policies, and similar organizational controls are kept to a minimum.
- *Tolerance of risk.* Employees are encouraged to experiment without fear of consequences if they fail. Mistakes are treated as learning opportunities.
- *Tolerance of conflict.* Diversity of opinions is encouraged. Harmony and agreement between individuals or groups are not assumed to be evidence of high performance.
- *Focus on ends rather than means.* Goals are made clear, and individuals are encouraged to consider alternative routes toward meeting the goals. Focusing on ends suggests that there might be several right answers to any given problem or opportunity.
- *Open-system focus.* The entrepreneur closely monitors the environment and responds rapidly to changes as they occur.

Each of these cultural characteristics contributes to an atmosphere in which creativity and innovation can flourish. But culture is just a reflection of the people who comprise the entrepreneurial venture. What about the people factor? What role does it play in the innovative organization?

Innovative organizations understand the importance of the people who work there. Innovative organizations do many things to support the innovation efforts of their members, such as actively training and developing people so that their knowledge remains current, offering their employees high levels of job security to reduce the fear of getting fired for making mistakes, and encouraging individuals to become champions of new ideas. These **idea champions** are individuals who actively and enthusiastically pursue new ideas, build support, overcome resistance, and ensure that an innovation is implemented. Having idea champions throughout the entrepreneurial organization goes a long way toward ensuring that creative and innovative thinking (and doing) will thrive. It's not only the entrepreneur who should play the role of idea champion. In a truly innovative organization, idea champions will be found in different areas. They'll be those individuals who are willing to take a stand, to try something different, and to passionately pursue different and unique ideas. Nurture them, support them, and reward them—these individuals can be valuable to your entrepreneurial organization.

Managing creativity and innovation are important issues for entrepreneurs to recognize. Another contemporary issue entrepreneurs must understand is managing customer service.

Managing Customer Service

Joe Fulmer's Stitching Post in Dayton, Ohio, is a seamstress's paradise.[13] It's a place where customers come to socialize, to learn, to advise, and, of course, to buy. And boy, do they buy—the Stitching Post is a thriving $11 million company with 115 employees. Fulmer keeps his customers happy by providing outstanding customer service. Take, for example, his education program. Any customer can learn basic sewing, advanced tailoring, and anything in between. However, buy a sewing machine and you'll get free lifetime instruction about how to use it. Fulmer believes that by offering to teach customers sewing techniques, he can entice them to upgrade to more expensive models. When a customer does decide to upgrade, Fulmer applies the full cost of a sewing machine purchased within a year toward a better model. By creating a place where customers want to drop in again and again, Fulmer has built a successful business.

As this example shows, taking care of your customers can be valuable. What do entrepreneurs need to know about managing customer service? Let's look first at why customer service is important.

Why Managing Customer Service Is Important. Managing customer service *is* important. Why? One reason is that customers are the source of a venture's revenues.

All businesses need customers. Without customers, your entrepreneurial venture won't survive for long. And, it's not just getting customers, it's keeping those customers by taking care of them. Customers shouldn't be viewed as a one-time-only proposition. When customers stop frequenting a business, not only is a current source of revenue lost, but so is a future stream of revenue. Research has shown that companies can improve profits anywhere from 25 percent to 85 percent when they reduce customer defections.[14] Retaining customers by effectively managing customer service is simply good business.

Another reason that managing customer service is important is that when customers aren't treated well, it can have a ripple effect. A series of studies completed by the Technical Assistance Research Program (TARP) in Washington, D.C., found that the average business never hears from 96 percent of its dissatisfied customers.[15] Basically what this means is that if your business has 100 unhappy customers, you'll hear from only about four of them. But that doesn't mean that the other 96 simply have disappeared. Quite the contrary! TARP also found that although the company may not hear from those other 96 dissatisfied customers directly, they're out there telling others about their experiences. Each of

Entrepreneurs in Action

As Chief Executive Bear, Maxine Clark has built a business that knows how to take care of its customers. Her Build-A-Bear Workshops (**www.buildabear.com**) are interactive retail experience stores where kids and adults go to create their own bears from scratch. The philosophy guiding the bear workshops found across the United States is that "there is nothing a store manager cannot do for a customer." They want customers to leave happy and feeling that they have had an "un-bear-lievable" experience. How has Clark implemented this type of differentiation strategy? She is a fanatic about training. All Build-A-Bear Workshop employees go through a three-week training program at Bear University. Also, to help keep employees focused on customers, Build-A-Bear sends out surveys of employee performance to at least 40 customers in each store every week. Employees have to score a rating of at least 80 percent to earn a bonus. And Clark must be doing something right. In 2000 her business won an Arthur Andersen Best Practices Award for exceeding customer expectations.

Sources: Company Web site (**www.buildabear.com**), June 18, 2002; S. Nelton, "Building an Empire One Smile at a Time," *Success*, September 2000, pp. 34–37; and "Saluting the Global Awards Recipients of Arthur Andersen's Best Practices Awards 2000," accessed at *Fortune Online* (**www.fortune.com**), February 2, 2001.

them will tell an average of 9 or 10 people about their problems with the company. For example, think about what you did when you had a bad experience at a restaurant or retail establishment. If you didn't complain directly to the business, did you tell your friends or family members about your experiences and advise them never to go there? Most of us probably have done this. Bad service affects not only current customers but also potential customers.

The final reason that managing customer service is important is that exemplary customer service can be a competitive advantage. An entrepreneurial venture can differentiate itself from competitors through the way it takes care of its customers. This type of customer service differentiation strategy has been shown to have a positive impact on an organization's performance.[16]

How to Manage Customer Service. The first and most important thing entrepreneurs must understand in managing customer service is that customer service is everyone's job. Everyone in the venture must accept the philosophy that taking care of customers is something that each and every person does, no matter what their job responsibilities are. But it's not enough to espouse customer service, you have to do it. What's involved? Entrepreneurs should focus on three aspects: a service strategy, customer-friendly systems, and customer-oriented frontline people.[17]

A service strategy focuses the attention of all organizational members toward discovering, understanding, meeting, and exceeding the real priorities of customers. How do you discover what customers want? One thing an entrepreneur might use is a **customer report card**, a type of customer service audit that lists what customers are looking for (such as convenient parking, 30-day return policy, short waiting times, or whatever service attributes might be appropriate for a particular type of business), their priority for each of these attributes (high, medium, or low), and how customers score your business on these attributes. It's a grade card for a business. It can provide an entrepreneur with valuable information that can be used to design an appropriate customer service strategy. Another thing an entrepreneur might do is simply ask customers what they want. It's what you learn in every basic marketing class—find out what customers want (or need) and provide it. There's nothing complicated about such a strategy, but many entrepreneurs forget the basics. David Horowitz, CEO of a small Canadian manufacturer called Priva, Inc., didn't forget. His company had racked up considerable losses in its first three years of operation. Then, he decided to simply ask customers what they wanted. They started putting postage-paid envelopes into every product package. Customers responded back, and Priva was better able to meet their needs. The outcome? Since 1996 Priva has been ranked five times on *Profit* magazine's annual list of the top 300 growth companies in Canada.[18]

The next thing entrepreneurs need to do in managing customer service is to implement customer-friendly systems. These systems should be designed so that a customer can complete any transaction any time (in person, by phone, on the Internet, or whatever) reliably, hassle-free, and quickly. The venture's delivery system—that is, the way your goods or services are delivered to the customer—should be designed for the convenience of the customer, not the convenience of your organization. All physical facilities, procedures, methods, communication processes, and policies should be designed to meet customers' needs.

Finally, managing customer service means having customer-oriented employees. As we said earlier, customer service is the responsibility of everyone in the organization. However, don't just assume that employees know about customer service. You have to educate employees on how to service customers. Clarify your expectations regarding how customers are to be treated. Provide employees with training on how to treat customers and how to deal with various customer situations. An important part of having customer-oriented employees is empowering employees to be able to deal with customer problems. Then, evaluate employees on how well they treat customers. Reward employees who treat customers the way you want them treated.

With a well-designed customer service strategy, customer-friendly systems, and customer-oriented employees, an entrepreneur will be well on his or her way to effectively managing customer service.

Initiating E-Business Strategies

Not all that many years ago, you probably kept in touch with friends using the telephone. Now, chances are you use e-mail as one of your main ways to communicate. Web addresses are a common feature on product packages and in advertising. As a student, your learning increasingly may be taking place in an electronic environment. Everywhere you look, organizations are becoming e-businesses. Today's entrepreneurs do business in an e-world.

E-business (electronic business) is a term describing the way an organization does its work by using electronic (Internet) links with its key constituencies

Building Customer Loyalty

One philosophy that successful organizations are following is customer relationship marketing, which is a process of building long-term, trusting, "win–win" relationships with valued customers. This strategy emphasizes the importance of building solid and valuable relationships with customers. How can organizations do this? Three approaches have been identified.

1. Adding financial benefits to the customer relationship through programs such as frequent buyers, collectors' societies, kids clubs, and so forth. For instance, Harley-Davidson sponsors the Harley Owners Group (HOG), whose members pay an annual fee to receive a magazine (*Hog Tales)*, an emergency pickup service, touring guides, theft reward service, discount hotel rates, and so forth.
2. Adding social benefits to the financial benefits by bonding with customers and building personalized relationships with them through events such as customer appreciation days or hosting a party just for customers. In addition, in today's wired world, customer connections don't even have to be real, they can be virtual. Many organizations have created online communities—constantly changing groups of people who collaborate, share ideas, and build relationships online.
3. Adding structural ties as well as financial and social benefits through such activities as supplying customers with special equipment or computer links.

Sources: N. Paley, "Romancing Your Customers," *Sales and Marketing Management*, March 1996, pp. 30–32; and L. L. Berry and A. Parasuraman, *Marketing Services: Competing through Quality* (New York: Free Press, 1991), pp. 136–42.

in order to efficiently and effectively achieve its goals. It's more than e-commerce, although e-business can include e-commerce. **E-commerce (electronic commerce)** is any form of business exchange or transaction in which the parties interact electronically.[19] Companies such as Dell (computers), Varsitybooks (textbooks) , and JustFlowers.com (flowers and other gifts) are engaged in e-commerce because they sell products over the Internet. Exhibit 7-8 explains the main forms of e-commerce transactions. Although e-commerce applications will continue to grow in volume, they're only one part of an e-business.

Not every organization is or needs to be a total e-business. Exhibit 7-9 illustrates three types of e-business involvement. The first type is known as an e-business-*enhanced* organization, a traditional type of organization that establishes e-business capabilities, usually e-commerce, while maintaining its traditional business structure. Many large *Fortune 500* companies are evolving into e-businesses using this approach. They use the Internet to *enhance* (not to replace) their traditional ways of doing business. Organizations such as Sears, Merrill Lynch, Office Depot, Starbucks, Tupperware, and Whirlpool are e-business enhanced organizations.

Another type of e-business involvement is an e-business-*enabled* organization. In this type of e-business, an organization uses the Internet to do its work better but not to sell anything. In other words, the Internet *enables* organizational members to do their work more efficiently and effectively. For instance, Levi Strauss & Company (the jeans company) uses its Web site to interact with

EXHIBIT 7-8 Types of E-Commerce Transactions

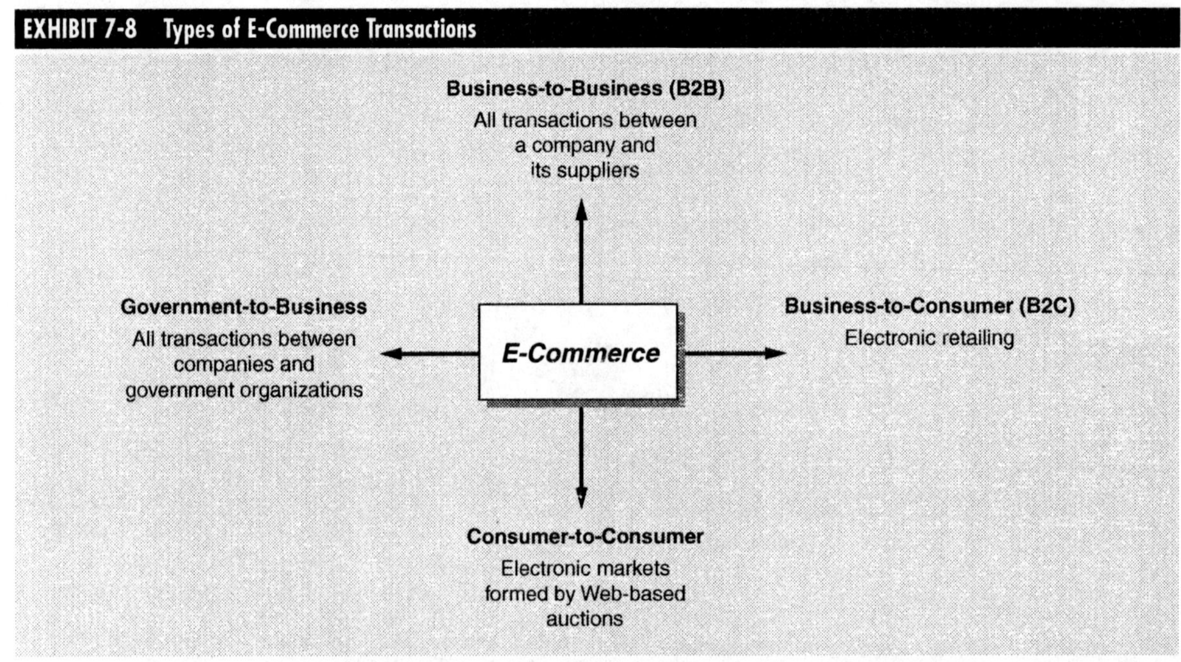

EXHIBIT 7-9 Categories of E-Business Involvement

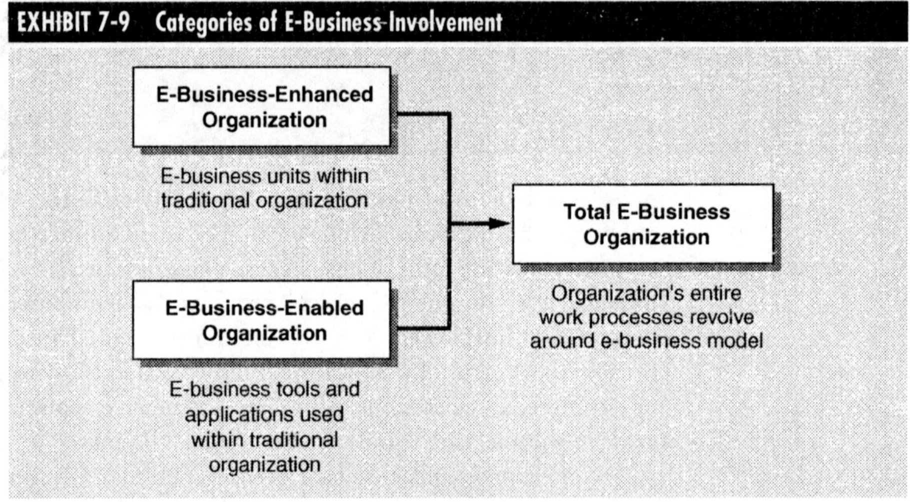

customers, providing them with information about the company and its products, but not to sell jeans. It also uses an **intranet**, an internal organizational communication system that uses Internet technology and is accessible only to organizational employees, to communicate with its workforce. Other organizations use enterprise-wide software solutions such as database management software or customer relationship management software to link together all organizational areas. These organizations have found that being an e-business-enabled organization makes them more competitive. But, it's not only the big companies harnessing the power of the Internet to be more efficient and effective. For instance, 1-800-GOT-JUNK, a trash-removal business based in Vancouver, British Columbia, designed and implemented an intranet called JunkNet for its franchisees and saw its revenues jump from $2 million in 1999 to $10 million in 2001.[20]

EXHIBIT 7-10 Guidelines for Initiating E-Business Strategies

- The old rules for being a successful organization (economies of scale, offering a wide array of products, efficiency of operations, market share, and vertical integration) are no longer sufficient.
- The challenge for entrepreneurs is bridging the gap between the "physical" and the "digital" worlds.
- E-business requires new business designs and new organizational capabilities.
- These new business designs must efficiently and effectively integrate the business's functions, technologies, and work processes.
- The choice of e-business design is dictated by the customers: what they value and what they care about.
- Customer needs and the ability to satisfy those needs are at the core of a successful e-business model.
- Building customer relationships and connections is an important capability.
- Becoming customer-focused doesn't simply mean improving customer service. It means having consistent, dependable, and convenient interactions with customers in every single encounter—physical and virtual.
- Technology must be imbedded in an effective e-business design. Technology is not the end, but the means to an end.
- Software applications must be cross-functional and integrated.
- Formulating an e-business strategy involves the following: *knowledge-building,* which helps an organization understand what the customer is looking for and where the industry is going; *capability evaluation,* which defines the existing business and identifies what capabilities it has today and what capabilities it needs for tomorrow; and *e-business design,* which asks what products, services, or experiences a business needs to provide to take advantage of digital capabilities.

The last type of e-business involvement is when an organization becomes a total e-business. Many entrepreneurial organizations—such as Amazon.com, Yahoo, E*Trade, and eBay—started as total e-business organizations. Total e-business organizations combine the elements of e-enhanced and e-enabled organizations. Their whole existence is made possible by and revolves around the Internet. Other organizations, such as Charles Schwab & Company have evolved into e-business organizations that seamlessly integrate traditional and e-business functions.

Successful entrepreneurial organizations of the twenty-first century are going to have to understand e-business strategies. The environment in which entrepreneurs do business will not be the same tomorrow as it is today. To succeed in this type of environment means finding out all you can about how e-business is changing. Exhibit 7-10 lists some guidelines for initiating e-business strategies.

It's apparent that managing customer service and initiating e-business strategies are important considerations for today's entrepreneurs. But there's one more topic we want to look at in this chapter that's important for entrepreneurs to understand—the concept of world-class organizations.

Becoming a World-Class Organization

What is a **world-class organization**? It's an organization that is continually looking for ways through its decisions and actions to be the best in the world at what it does. Even if an organization operates in a single geographic location, it should still strive to be the best at what it does in its own little "world." As you can well imagine, becoming a world-class organization means excelling in many areas. What characteristics does a world-class organization have? The major ones are shown in Exhibit 7-11.

EXHIBIT 7-11 Major Characteristics of World-Class Organizations

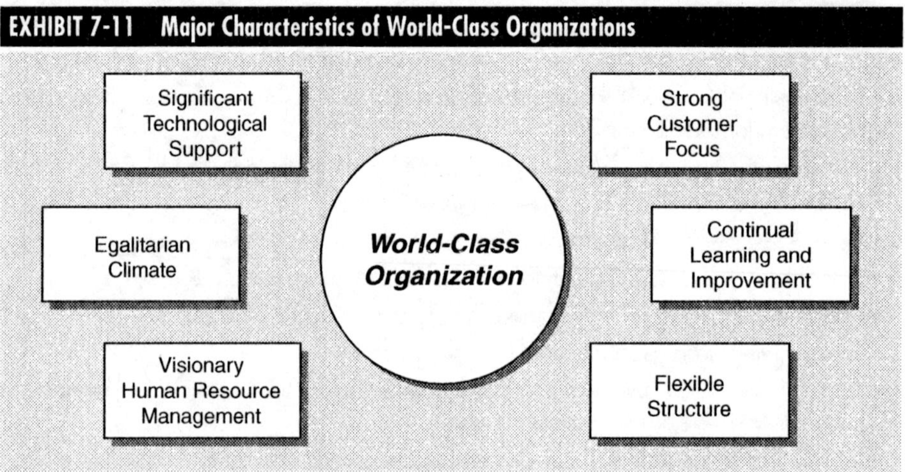

Source: Based on R. M. Hodgetts, F. Luthans, and S. M. Lee, "New Paradigm Organizations: From Total Quality to Learning to World Class," *Organizational Dynamics,* Winter 1994, p. 15.

As our earlier discussion on managing customer service made clear, customers are important. A strong customer focus is by far the most important characteristic of a world-class organization. At the heart of *what* a world-class organization does and *how* it does it is what customers (external or internal) need now or in the future. After all, an entrepreneurial venture is not in business to please itself, but to delight its customers. If you don't do this, you won't be in business for long. A strong customer focus guides everything the venture does and is critically important for being a world-class organization.

Another distinctive characteristic of world-class organizations is their emphasis on continual learning and improvement. Whether it's finding ways to be faster or more efficient and effective than competitors, world-class organizations look for ways to continuously improve. As we know from previous discussions of organizational change and total quality management, you can't stand still! You have to continually look for ways to improve what you do and how you do it.

Another characteristic of a world-class organization is that it has a fluid and flexible organizational structure that allows it to respond quickly, decisively, and intelligently to internal and external changes and trends. World-class organizations don't get hung up on rigid job classifications, duties, or relationships. Instead, their organizational structure facilitates open, responsive, and flexible approaches to resolving problems or pursuing opportunities.

A world-class organization also has visionary and creative human resource management policies, programs, and practices. Organizational members are valued and are treated in ways that they know their contributions are valued and appreciated. Most importantly, world-class organizations effectively energize their employees' creativity in decision making and in the ways they do their jobs. They're encouraged to be innovative and to continually look for ways to learn and improve.

Another attribute of a world-class organization is its egalitarian climate or culture. What does it mean to have this type of culture? It means that the organization and its members value and respect everyone both inside and outside the organization. Everyone and everything from customers, suppliers, fellow

Speed Counts

Today's economic realities of being competitive are that it's not enough to be strong or shrewd, you also have to be swift. Speed and time compression have become considerably important currencies in the new economy. One of the most telling differentiators in business today is how close a company can come to operating in "real time"—that is, having the shortest possible lapse between idea and action, between implementation and result. What can world-class entrepreneurial organizations do to embrace speed? Here are some suggestions: (1) Seize the future. Don't wait until you feel the time is right. Someone else may just beat you to it. (2) Make speed the core of your business. Develop the capabilities to respond instantly—or at least rapidly—to customers' needs. (3) Accelerate your timetables. Make sure all work processes are being done in the best time possible without sacrificing quality. (4) Invest money to cut time. If it's important to move faster, spend the resources to do so. (5) Heed the caution signals. Recognize there are limits to how fast your speed can get. When work tasks become counterproductive, recognize it may be time to reconsider what you're doing and how you're doing it.

Source: D. D. Buss, "Embracing Speed," *Nation's Business*, June 1999, pp. 12–17.

employees, and other stakeholders, to the community and the environment are treated with dignity and respect. World-class organizations recognize the interconnectedness of how they do business and their ultimate success.

The final characteristic of a world-class organization is significant technological support. In a world where speed and flexibility are critical to competitive success, technological support is crucial. But, understand that it's not the technology itself that's important. It's how the organization's people use the technology to serve customers more efficiently and effectively. Chuck James, CEO of Dallas-based PrimeSource Food Service Equipment Inc., understands the importance of technology. Using technology to arrange the logistics, the company ships ovens, refrigerators, and other restaurant gear from its Indianapolis warehouse to customers around the United States.[21]

It's only fitting to end our discussion of world-class organizations by looking at a quote by Peter Drucker, one of the best-known management thinkers and writers of today. In discussing the management challenges for the twenty-first century, he says, "No institution, whether a business, a university or a hospital, can hope to survive, let alone to succeed, unless it measures up to the standards set by the leaders in its field, anyplace in the world."[22] The challenge for you as an entrepreneur is to make sure that as you manage your venture's processes you're doing this.

Rapid Review 

- ✔ Distinguish between creativity and innovation. Why are both important?
- ✔ What three types of factors have been found to stimulate innovation in organizations?
- ✔ Define idea champions. How important are they to innovation?
- ✔ What is customer service? Why is it important to manage customer service?
- ✔ On what three aspects should entrepreneurs focus in order to manage customer service?
- ✔ How are e-business and e-commerce different?
- ✔ Differentiate among e-business enhanced, e-business enabled, and total e-business organizations.
- ✔ What is a world-class organization? Describe the characteristics of world-class organizations.

CHAPTER SUMMARY

This summary is organized around the chapter-opening objectives.

1. There are six steps in the decision-making process. Step 1 is recognizing the need to make a decision. Step 2 is identifying decision criteria that are important. Step 3 is weighting the criteria so they have the appropriate priority in making choices. Step 4 is developing alternatives. Step 5 is to critically analyze and evaluate each alternative. Step 6 is selecting an alternative. Once an alternative has been selected, it would be implemented and, after an appropriate period of time, evaluated to see whether the problem or opportunity had been addressed.
2. The directive style is a decision-making style characterized by a low tolerance for ambiguity and a rational way of thinking. The analytic style is characterized by a high tolerance for ambiguity and a rational way of thinking. The conceptual style is characterized by a high tolerance for ambiguity and an intuitive way of thinking. The behavioral style is characterized by a low tolerance for ambiguity and an intuitive way of thinking.
3. Organizational performance can be measured and evaluated in different ways. Four important performance measurement tools include financial statement analysis, financial ratio analysis, cash-flow analysis, and SWOT analysis. The venture's financial statements (income statement, balance sheet, and cash flow statement) provide accurate information about the financial health of the business. With information from the income statement and balance sheet, an entrepreneur can measure and evaluate changes in financial performance through financial ratio analysis. The four major categories of financial ratios are the liquidity ratios, leverage ratios, operating ratios, and profitability ratios. Cash-flow analysis measures cash flow, the actual amount of cash an organization brings in and the actual amount it pays out during a given time period. The goal of good cash-flow management is making sure there's enough cash on hand when you need it. SWOT analysis is a tool that entrepreneurs can use to assess the work being done in the venture and how organizational performance is measuring up. SWOT stands for strengths, weaknesses, opportunities, and threats.
4. The commonly used financial statements are the income statement (also called the profit and loss or P&L), which shows the revenues and expenses of a business and the resulting profit or loss over a specific period of time; the balance sheet, which shows the value of an organization's assets, liabilities, and owner's equity; and the cash-flow statement, which shows the cash inflows and outflows of a business. The four major categories of financial ratios are the liquidity ratios, which measure the organization's ability to meet its current debt obligations with its current assets; the leverage ratios, which examine the organization's use of debt and equity to finance its assets; the operating ratios, which measure how efficiently the organization is using its assets; and the profitability ratios, which measure how profitable the organization is.
5. Cash-flow analysis measures the inflow and outflow of cash in a business. Positive cash flow is when the amount of cash coming in is greater than the

amount of cash going out. Negative cash flow is when the amount of cash going out is greater than the amount of cash coming in.

6. A SWOT analysis looks at the organization's strengths, weaknesses, opportunities, and threats. Using an internal audit, an entrepreneur can determine the organization's strengths and weaknesses. An analysis of the trends and changes taking place outside the organization provides an indication of potential opportunities and threats.
7. Stimulating change is important to entrepreneurial ventures because both external forces and internal forces may bring about the need for the venture to change. External forces for change include changes in technology, global competition, economic trends, or in any other number of external factors. Internal forces for change may include any decisions or actions taken in response to not meeting performance goals, developing and implementing a new strategy, or adapting to other changing organizational circumstances.
8. As a change agent, an entrepreneur plays different roles. One of these roles is a catalyst for change. An entrepreneur should be alert to signals that change is needed. Another role is chief cheerleader and coach. As a cheerleader and coach, an entrepreneur should explain the change and encourage change efforts. Finally, the entrepreneur may have to assume the role of primary change consultant. In this role, an entrepreneur answers questions, makes suggestions, gets needed resources, facilitates conflict, and does whatever else is necessary to get the change(s) implemented.
9. The most important aspect of managing creativity and innovation is cultivating innovation in the entrepreneurial venture. Three factors have been found to stimulate innovation in organizations: structural factors, cultural factors, and human resource factors. As for structure, we know that organic structures facilitate innovation, that having sufficient resources to support the innovation process is important, and that continual and free-flowing communication among the organization's various work units is important. As for cultural factors, innovative cultures tend to have the following characteristics: acceptance of ambiguity, tolerance of the impractical, low external controls, tolerance of risk, tolerance of conflict, focus on ends rather than means, and open-system focus. Finally, as for the people factor, innovative organizations do many things to support the innovation efforts of their members such as actively training and developing people so that their knowledge remains current, offering employees high levels of job security to reduce the fear of getting fired for making mistakes, and encouraging individuals to become champions of new ideas.
10. It's important to manage customer service because customers are the source of a venture's revenues, an unhappy customer can have a ripple effect, and exemplary customer service can be a source of competitive advantage. The most important thing to remember in managing customer service is that customer service is everyone's job. In managing customer service, entrepreneurs should focus on having a service strategy, designing customer-friendly systems, and having customer service–oriented employees.
11. The three types of e-businesses are e-business-enhanced, e-business-enabled, and total e-business. An e-business-enhanced organization establishes

e-business capabilities while maintaining its traditional business structure. An e-business-enabled organization uses the Internet to do its work better but not to sell anything. A total e-business is one whose entire existence is made possible by and revolves around the Internet.

12. A world-class organization is one that is continually looking for ways through its decisions and actions to be the best in the world at what it does. A world-class organization has six characteristics: strong customer focus, continual learning and improvement, flexible structure, visionary human resource management, egalitarian climate, and significant technological support.

KEY TERMS

- *Decision:* A choice made between two or more alternatives.
- *Problem:* A situation in which there's an inconsistency between actual and desired results.
- *Opportunity:* An optimistic possibility or positive trend.
- *Bounded rationality:* The concept that individuals have the time and cognitive ability to process only limited amounts of information as they make decisions.
- *Satisficing:* Seeking out alternatives that are satisfactory and sufficient.
- *Problem avoider:* A person who approaches problems by avoiding or ignoring information that points to a problem.
- *Problem solver:* A person who addresses problems by trying to solve them as they come up.
- *Problem seeker:* A person who actively seeks out problems or new opportunities.
- *Directive style:* A decision-making style characterized by a low tolerance for ambiguity and a rational way of thinking.
- *Analytic style:* A decision-making style characterized by a high tolerance for ambiguity and a rational way of thinking.
- *Conceptual style:* A decision-making style characterized by a high tolerance for ambiguity and an intuitive way of thinking.
- *Behavioral style:* A decision-making style characterized by a low tolerance for ambiguity and an intuitive way of thinking.
- *Intuitive decision making:* A subconscious process of making decisions on the basis of experience and accumulated judgment.
- *Certainty:* A decision-making situation in which an entrepreneur can make accurate assessments of which alternative is best because every possible outcome is known.
- *Risk:* A decision-making situation in which the decision maker can assess the likelihood (probability) of certain outcomes.
- *Uncertainty:* A decision-making situation in which the decision maker is neither certain about outcomes nor able to make reasonable probability estimates.

- *Organizational performance:* The organization's success at achieving its goals efficiently and effectively.
- *Quantitative measures:* Organizational performance measures that are quantifiable.
- *Qualitative measures:* Organizational performance measures that are hard to quantify.
- *Efficiency:* The amount of resources being used to meet stated goals.
- *Effectiveness:* Whether an organization is meeting its stated goals.
- *Generally Accepted Accounting Principles (GAAP):* Standards developed by the Financial Accounting Standards Board to ensure that all businesses create uniform financial statement formats.
- *Accounting journal:* A chronological record of a business's financial transactions.
- *General ledger:* A summary record of financial transactions.
- *Income statement (profit and loss or P&L):* A financial statement that shows the revenues and expenses of a business and the resulting profit or loss over a specific period of time.
- *Common-size income statement:* A financial statement that measures the changes in the use of resources by calculating the percentage relationship of each item of expense to sales.
- *Balance sheet:* A financial statement that shows the value of an organization's assets, liabilities, and owner's equity.
- *Common-size balance sheet:* A financial statement that takes each section of the balance sheet, sets the total equal to 100 percent, and then shows each item in that section as a percentage of the total.
- *Cash-flow statement:* A financial statement that shows the cash inflows and outflows of a business.
- *Financial ratio analysis:* A way to express relationships between key accounting elements from the financial statements and a convenient and relatively easy technique for doing a financial analysis.
- *Liquidity ratios:* Financial ratios that measure the organization's ability to meet its current debt obligations with its current assets.
- *Leverage ratios:* Financial ratios that examine the organization's use of debt and the use of equity to finance its assets.
- *Operating ratios:* Financial ratios that measure how efficiently the organization is using its assets.
- *Profitability ratios:* Financial ratios that measure how profitable the organization is.
- *Cash flow:* The actual amount of cash an organization brings in and the actual amount of cash it pays out during a given time period.
- *Strengths:* Activities the organization is doing well.
- *Weaknesses:* Things the organization does not do well.
- *Internal audit:* A thorough assessment of the venture's internal work areas.

- *Threats:* Negative and unfavorable external trends and changes that the entrepreneur will probably want to avoid or at least buffer against.
- *Organizational change:* Any alterations in what an organization does or how it does it.
- *Change agent:* A person who's a catalyst for change and who also manages the change process.
- *Creativity:* The ability to combine ideas in a unique way or to make unusual associations between ideas.
- *Innovation:* The process of taking a creative idea and turning it into a useful (marketable) product, service, or method of operation.
- *Idea champions:* Individuals who actively and enthusiastically pursue new ideas, build support, overcome resistance, and ensure that an innovation is implemented.
- *Customer report card:* A type of customer service audit that lists what customers are looking for, their priority for each of these attributes, and how customers score a business on these attributes.
- *E-business (electronic business):* The way an organization does its work by using electronic (Internet) links with its key constituencies in order to efficiently and effectively achieve its goals.
- *E-commerce (electronic commerce):* Any form of business exchange or transaction in which the parties interact electronically.
- *Intranet:* An internal organizational communication system that uses Internet technology and is accessible only to organizational employees.
- *World-class organization:* An organization that is continually looking for ways, through its decisions and actions, to be the best in the world at what it does.

SWEAT EQUITY

1. Every year, Ernst & Young (**www.ey.com**) gives out its Entrepreneur of the Year Awards. The winners epitomize the best of the best and are wonderful illustrations of successful entrepreneurs. Choose one of the winners profiled on E&Y's Web site (you'll have to do some searching to find them!). Write a paper describing this person, his or her entrepreneurial venture, and what this entrepreneur does so well that he or she has been named as "world-class." In your conclusion, provide a bulleted list of ideas that you can share with other members of your class.
2. Surveys consistently point out that small companies create products faster (23 vs. 30 months) and have more successful products (62 percent vs. 58 percent) than do large companies. However, formal product development processes in small organizations are often quite haphazard. Yet, there's help for entrepreneurs who want to be more efficient and effective at this process. The Product Development and Management Association has provided some useful information on its Web site at **www.pdma.org**. Go to the Web site and check out all the information there. Make a bulleted list of important tips you find on this site. Be prepared to share your tips with the class.

3. Dan Leever, chief executive of MacDermid, Inc. (**www.macdermid.com**), a specialty chemical manufacturer based in Waterbury, Connecticut, says his business helps its customers become more efficient. The company's specialty chemicals are used mainly by circuit board makers. For example, a chemical process developed by MacDermid allows companies to save 25 percent in the production of double-sided circuit boards. It also developed a chemical product for Boeing that strips the surface of an airplane before it's painted and is 15 percent faster than traditional hand sanding. CEO Leever has an interesting philosophy about customers as well. He says he will turn down any potential customer who demands big discounts. Because the company helps its customers save money, MacDermid doesn't have to slash prices like most of its competitors. Check out the company's Web site and then answer the following questions.

a. What is MacDermid's philosophy? Do you agree or disagree with it? Explain your answer.

b. Do you think innovation would be important to this company? Why? How could it encourage innovation efforts?

c. What do you think of Leever's statement that he'll turn down any customer who demands big discounts? Do you think this would work for other entrepreneurial ventures? Explain. Why does it work for MacDermid Inc.?

Sources: Company Web site (**www.macdermid.com**), June 19, 2002; and S. Sansoni, "Waste Makes My Guts Churn," *Forbes*, November 2, 1998, p. 228.

4. Change is difficult and stressful. These 10 steps have been suggested for positive change:

- Develop a vision, mission, strategy, and operating plan that offers the greatest potential for success. Involve all organizational members in the planning process and communicate the results.
- Set high expectations with specific goals and objectives, but not unrealistic or unachievable ones. Communicate these, along with the rationale. Embrace people who resist, and carefully consider their reasons.
- Build trust by being totally honest, fair, and trustworthy. Regularly assess how things are going with people who are not key decision makers. Without trust, nothing else works.
- Define each person's roles and responsibilities. Clarify expectations.
- Establish agreed-upon measures so people can track how they and the business are doing. Post these openly and refer to them often.
- Provide frequent, balanced feedback and information about external conditions and how things are going. Provide opportunities for people to contribute ideas. Use collaborative problem-solving. Make necessary resources and technology available.
- Continuously update employees on changes in external environment—customers, markets, competition, etc. Involve them in gathering this information. Inform them of any important news before they hear it from the media.
- Recognize and praise success, but also identify and critique failure. Encourage action. Discourage inaction. Criticize methods or actions, not

individuals. If some individuals aren't willing or able to perform, help them to improve or get rid of them.

- Reward success and desired behaviors. Tie rewards to actions that employees can control.
- Celebrate success and grieve over setbacks together. Maintain an environment of enthusiasm, cooperation, collaboration, and sharing. Emphasize getting the job done, together.

Write a paper discussing each of these points. Do you agree or disagree with them? Do you think they could actually be used by organizations? How would you improve on them?

Source: J. Mariotti, "10 Steps to Positive Change," *IW,* July 20, 1998, p. 82.

5. No one likes to think that employees would intentionally steal, commit fraud, or embezzle funds from an organization. However, it can and does happen. Thus, an important part of managing processes might be protecting against these situations. Research the topic of employee theft, fraud, and embezzlement. Write a paper describing what it is, how often it happens, and what can be done to prevent it. Be prepared to share your findings with your class.

6. Research the topic organizational innovation. Find five sources on organizational innovation and prepare a bulleted list with key points that you find. Be sure to cite your sources.

7. Stanford professor Robert Sutton says that if you want to fill your company with great ideas, you need to fill it with great people. Here are his suggestions for doing that: Hire people who are slow at learning the organizational way of doing things; Hire people who make you uncomfortable, even those whom you dislike; Hire people whom you don't need at the moment; Use job interviews to get new ideas, not just to screen candidates; Encourage people to ignore superiors and peers; and Find happy people and let them fight. What do you think his suggestions mean? How do you think his suggestions would help an organization get great ideas? Do you agree with his suggestions? Why or why not?

Source: P. LaBarre, "Weird Ideas That Work," *Fast Company,* January 2002, pp. 68–73.

8. What can you learn from other entrepreneurs? Log on to **www.allbusiness.com/lessons/index.asp** and choose three of the stories profiled there. Write a paragraph describing each one and what you learned from reading it.

9. Stephen Covey's *The Seven Habits of Highly Effective People* has been a best-selling book for a number of years. What about strategies for effective business? Here is a list of seven proposed strategies for effective business:

- Strategy 1: Be proactive.
- Strategy 2: Begin with the end in mind.
- Strategy 3: Put first things first.
- Strategy 4: Think win–win.
- Strategy 5: Seek first to understand, then to be understood.
- Strategy 6: Synergize.
- Strategy 7: Sharpen the saw by continually improving.

Write a paper explaining what you think each of these strategies means and how each relates to managing processes in an entrepreneurial organization.

Source: K. Cheng, "The Seven Strategies of Effective Business," *Industrial Management*, May-June 1999, pp. 6–8.

10. Find five examples of entrepreneurial businesses that have outstanding customer service (library search, Internet search, personal experience). Describe what these businesses do in servicing customers. What could other entrepreneurs learn from these examples?

ENTREPRENEURSHIP IN ACTION CASES

Cannondale Corporation (www.cannondale.com)

This case can be found at the beginning of Chapter 7.

Discussion Questions

1. What approach to problems does Montgomery appear to exhibit? Explain.

2. Would innovation be important in this type of business? Why? In what areas might innovation be developed?

3. How might Montgomery manage customer service in his business?

Timbuk2 (www.timbuk2.com)

It's a job that few have the stamina or agility to do, especially in cities with lot of hills like San Francisco. However, bicycle messengers perform an important service, hauling bulky loads swiftly from city location to city location. And their bags have to be tough, waterproof, lightweight, and functional—and it's nice if they look great, too! Rob Honeycutt knows well what bike knapsacks needed to be—he was a messenger once himself. Today, his company, Timbuk2 Designs (**www.timbuk2.com**) manufactures bags that appeal to the "hip, young, wacky nuts on bikes."

From its early struggles, Timbuk2, has become a successful entrepreneurial venture. Honeycutt describes his company as more than a bike bag maker. He says it's an ambitious experiment in manufacturing. His goals are to make custom products more efficiently than mass manufacturers and to become competitive with offshore manufacturing. And then, as if those ambitious goal aren't enough, he also hopes to achieve efficiency and profitability while paying the company's workers among the highest wages and best benefits in the apparel industry. So far, the company has achieved several of its goals.

Many bike shops claim that Timbuk2 bags are the best and most popular bags. The company offers what none of its competitors do: a three-panel construction design that allows customers to custom choose from 13 colors for an astounding 2,197 possible color combinations. And, Timbuk2's bags cost no more than mass-produced ones. The company pays its employees more than other apparel makers and offers full medical benefits. The company is debt-free and has financed growth through friends, family, and cash flow. How has it accomplished its goals?

Honeycutt wanted to do what Toyota Motor Corporation eventually was able to do with cars: mass customization or making cars to customers' orders. He thought it might work because manufacturing bags is much simpler than making cars. However, things didn't quite work out on the first try until workers began experimenting with something Honeycutt had seen at a trade show demonstration. That something was the Toyota Sewing System, which calls for each sewing operator to move down a row of task-specific sewing machines instead of performing a single task and passing parts to the next sewing operator. This approach cuts labor costs because no floor assistants are needed to carry partially completed inventory from one machine to the next. In addition, Timbuk2 was able to keep its inventory costs low because it buys only a week's worth of materials and ships out completed bags daily. They have also discovered that the mass customization approach has cut waste because mistakes are caught along the way.

Although there are many things that the company is doing right, Timbuk2 continues to refine its system, relying heavily on employee suggestions and ideas. In 1993 it took 144 minutes to make one bag. Using automated sewing machines and employees' suggestions, they have reduced that time to 16 minutes. The goal is getting that time down to 12 minutes. And, labor costs are about 16% of total costs now and the goal is whittling that down to 12%. So, Timbuk2 continues its pursuit of success.

Discussion Questions

1. What types of performance measures might Timbuk2 want to use? Be as specific as possible.
2. Would you call this company efficient? Effective? Explain your answers.
3. Using information from the written case and from the company's Web site, would you describe Timbuk2 as a world-class organization? Support your answer.

Sources: Company Web site (**www.timbuk2.com**), June 19, 2002; and R. Furchgott, "Success Could Be in the Bag," *Business Week Enterprise,* December 16, 1996, pp. ENT8–ENT9.

California Pizza Kitchen (www.cpk.com)

Lawyers running a pizza restaurant. Now that seems to be as unlikely a combination as tandoori chicken or barbecued chicken on pizza. Yet, Rick Rosenfield and Larry Flax have built a successful company called California Pizza Kitchen (**www.cpk.com**). The two former federal prosecutors decided to trade in the courtroom for the dining room and opened a unique restaurant that offers creative hearth-baked pizzas.

The pair opened their first CPK in Beverly Hills in 1985. Since that time, the company has grown to over 130 units in 25 states and 4 other countries. As owners of the leading premium pizza chain, Rosenfield and Flax have built a successful entrepreneurial venture by carefully managing processes. But things weren't always that way.

In 1992 PepsiCo Inc., bought 67 percent of the CPK chain for $94 million. Rosenfield and Flax pocketed $34 million in cash and kept a 24 percent stake in their company. Both stayed on as co-CEOs and had the go-ahead from Pepsi to grow the company using corporate money for expansion. Pepsi's mandate: Open as many restaurants as possible. The only problem was that no one had a real plan about how to do that. The most restaurant locations the pair had ever opened in one year was seven. Pepsi sent in some corporate accountants to keep an eye on CPK's fairly loose organization. During the first 18 months under Pepsi's ownership, the company opened nearly 40 new restaurants. Although sales revenues doubled, occupancy costs were skyrocketing. Pepsi's accountants responded by cutting corners. Instead of grilled fresh vegetables on the pizzas, frozen vegetables were used. Instead of fresh mozzarella cheese, frozen was used. Customers noticed. Sales revenue growth crashed. Pepsi's decision makers were alarmed, needless to say. They tried several things, but to no avail. For the five years Pepsi owned CPK, the company lost money. Fortunately, Flax and Rosenfield had negotiated a buyout strategy. The cofounders got the company back through a unique buyback arrangement and took immediate steps to improve operations.

The first thing they did was to hire an experienced chief executive, Frederick Hipp, who had run Houlihans, a successful chain of contemporary restaurants. Hipp brought logical planning to the operation. He first shut down the worst-performing locations and revised the growth plans. He wasn't in any rush to open new stores and said, "I'll wait up to two years for the right site." He wants to fill in existing markets by opening sites in malls with strong anchors. In addition, Hipp is bringing back CPK's once notable quality. They made the switch back to fresh ingredients. In addition, they decided to increase the size of the pizzas with no price increase. And, once again, customers noticed. Same-store sales were up eight percent.

Great food and service are crucial for any restaurant wanting to succeed. And, CPK has that and more. By continuing to manage the ongoing operations, they hope to maintain their position as the leading premium pizza chain.

Discussion Questions

1. What might have been some signs of problems and/or opportunities in CPK's operations?
2. Go to the company's Web site. Link to the Join Our Team section and check out the link called ROCK. What's your reaction to this? How do these concepts contribute to CPK's success?
3. Obviously customer service is an important goal of CPK. How would CPK define customer service? How could it manage customer service?

Sources: Company information from company Web site (**www.cpk.com**), June 19, 2002, and Hoover's Online (**www.hoovers.com**), June 19, 2002; K. Morris, "How to Have Your Pie and Eat it, Too," *Business Week*, November 16, 1998, pp. 100–102; and A. Linsmayer, "Smothered by Money," *Forbes*, November 30, 1998, pp. 138–140.)

Getty Images (www.gettyimages.com)

Snapshots. You probably have photo albums filled with them. They capture historical moments and provide visual links to the past—to that brief moment in time when the photo was snapped. Photographs play an important role in telling stories, whether that story is personal, a part of a report for a class, or an illustration in a news story you're reading. With a database of over 70 million photographs and an estimated 30,000 hours of film, Seattle-based Getty Images, Inc., a stock photo company, has one foot firmly planted in the past and another firmly planted in the future. Mark Getty, cofounder and executive chairman of Getty Images, is carefully transforming his company by embracing the new rules of Web-based business and culture. It's not been an easy transition.

When you read a book or a magazine, where do the photos come from? Unless they're custom-shot photos, they're probably from stock photo businesses—companies that purchase photos from numerous professional photographers around the world, organize those photos into categories, and sell to customers (creative and design professionals, other businesses, and consumers). In the "old" economy, it often took days, even weeks for customers to get a photo. They'd have to look through pages and pages of expensively produced color catalogs, trying to find that perfect image for the project on which they were working. If they couldn't find it, they might have to pay a research assistant at an image company to search through many thousands of photos to help find just what they were looking for. After numerous phone calls and selecting that perfect image, a package would show up at the customer's door with the chosen image. It would be on a square of film that would have to be digitized and eventually returned to the stock agency. And if you were working late at night or rushing to meet a project deadline, you were out of luck! Mark Getty perceived that there were opportunities in making this whole inefficient and cumbersome process better through the power of the Internet. He's transforming his company into one that's set to profit in an e-business world.

Getty Image's integrated Web site can be accessed anywhere, anytime by customers. Using a key-word search, customers can receive a series of relevant images. Customers can immediately take a rough image for free and see what it looks like in a page layout. Buying a final image is very simple—enter a credit card number and download the image. But getting the process to this point hasn't been as simple!

Getty Images is a blend of acquired businesses, most of which were competitors. It began with two big acquisitions: London-based Tony Stone Images and Seattle-based PhotoDisc. These two companies couldn't have been more different. Tony Stone, a traditional stock photo company, was known for its superior artistic quality. PhotoDisc was a start-up that pioneered the delivery of images on CDs sold at discount stores and other retailers. Old meets new! As difficult and often unpleasant as the merger between the two companies was, eventually company executives realized they had the opportunity to create something new, unique, and potentially valuable by combining the best of both companies. The process of integrating new businesses has become easier as Getty Images has grown through other acquisitions.

One of the company's innovative approaches is an idea bank committee, a group of 10 people that meets once a month. Their job is to direct ideas from the company's more than 2,600 employees to the person best equipped to decide whether the idea is feasible and how to do it. The group has no formal leader, and it processes between 40 and 80 ideas per month. Some ideas are small; others have had an enormous impact on the company. For instance, based on multiple requests, the group lobbied to allow customers to create customized packages of CDs by choosing their own mix of images. This customization option now accounts for over 40 percent of sales revenue. Then there's the backroom operation of Getty Images, in which two shifts of technicians digitally scan an average of 750 photos every 12 hours. These teams work to add value to the basic photos. For instance, they tag the photo with digital information that customers can use to control their computer settings to get more accurate color. Or the team might create special options in some photo files by, for instance, changing the background.

Through extensive training, radical restructuring, and investments in technology, Getty Images is positioned as a leader and innovator in the visual content market. However, success today doesn't guarantee success tomorrow, especially in a Web-based economy. Mark knows he'll have to keep Getty employees focused on providing customers with the ultimate in imagery.

Discussion Questions

1. What type of e-business would you call Getty Images? Explain your choice.
2. What do you think of Getty's idea bank committee? Would this type of approach work in other entrepreneurial organizations? Why or why not?
3. What examples of customer service do you see in this story? How does what the company does relate to what was discussed in the chapter?
4. What characteristics and ways of managing processes does this company exhibit that might be important for successful entrepreneurial organizations in the twenty-first century?

Sources: Company information from company Web site (**www.gettyimages.com**), June 19, 2002, and Hoover's Online (**www.hoovers.com**), June 19, 2002; and C. Dahle, "Image Isn't Everything," *Fast Company,* June 2000, pp. 346–357.

Martha Stewart Living Omnimedia (www.marthastewart.com)

Martha Stewart. Most people have a definite opinion about America's most famous homemaker—they either love her or hate her. But no matter what you think about the public person you see cooking, decorating, or gardening, you have to admire the fact that she's building an impressive entrepreneurial organization, Martha Stewart Living Omnimedia, Inc.(MSO).

From the publication of her first book on entertaining in 1982 to today's multimedia empire, Stewart has capitalized on what she does best—helping people create a type of quality lifestyle in which the ultimate in cooking, decorating, entertaining, and other homemaking arts is emphasized and celebrated. And Martha's fans are many and loyal. Her various media properties are said to reach over 88 million people a month.

What exactly does MSO do? It's a leading creator of "how-to" content and related products for homemakers and other consumers. Company executives search for ways to leverage the "Martha Stewart" brand name across a broad range of media and retail outlets. The company's merchandise includes more than 3,700 variations of products, including bed and bath products, baby items, interior paints, craft kits, outdoor furniture and garden tools, and a housewares line. The company aims to offer its customers quality, convenience, and choice across a wide range of outlets. Customers can purchase Martha Stewart merchandise at mass market retailers (Kmart, which Stewart is sticking with for now, even given the company's considerable problems), national department stores (Sears, Zellers, and P/Kaufmann), specialty paint stores and specialty craft and fabric stores, the Martha by Mail catalog, and the online Martha by Mail store. Then there are MSO's various media properties including three magazines, the weekly television program, a daily cable television program, books, a weekly askMartha newspaper column, the askMartha radio program, and the company's Web site.

Measuring and evaluating organizational performance given such a wide variety of activities is quite a challenge. Yet, everything they do is aimed at achieving the company's two main goals: (1) providing original "how-to" content and information to as many consumers as possible, and (2) turning consumers into "doers" by offering them the information and products they need for doing things the "Martha Stewart way."

Discussion Questions

1. What types of performance measures might Martha Stewart use to monitor how well the company is doing? Be specific and explain your choices.
2. What type of e-business would you call MSO? Explain your choice.
3. Get a copy of the company's latest income statement and balance sheet (from its Web site, another Web site, or at the library). Calculate the major financial ratios that are illustrated in Exhibit 7-4.
4. How does MSO manage innovation and creativity? How does it manage customer service?

Sources: Company information from company Web site (**www.marthastewart.com**), June 19, 2002, and Hoover's Online (**www.hoovers.com**), June 19, 2002; and D. Brady, "Martha, Inc., *Business Week*, January 17, 2000, pp. 62–72.

BUSINESS PLAN PRO

EXERCISE 7-1: The Milestones Table

The Business Plan Pro manual says the Milestones table is "one of the most important tables in the plan." Why? How does a good milestones table affect decision making, evaluation, and measurement?

- Why does comparing actual results to the original plan increase the value of a business plan process?
- What other tables in a standard business plan lend themselves to plan-vs.-actual analysis (*Hint: sales, profit and loss, others*).

EXERCISE 7-2: Milestones for Graphico

Chapter 3 of the Business Plan Pro includes a graphic tour for a one-person graphics design company. You may have added to this plan in Exercises 2-1, 2-2, and others. If you don't yet have a saved version of this guided tour plan on disk, follow the guided tour and create one now.

- Use the Easy Plan Wizard steps or any other business plan navigation method (*hint:* Plan Outline *view, or* **View>Tables>Milestones** *command*) to access the empty milestones table for the Graphico guided tour plan.

- Add imaginary milestones. Follow the instructions for the table. Be prepared to present them and explain them. Why have you suggested these milestones?
- View the Milestones chart, using either Plan Wizard steps, Plan Outline view, or the commands in the View menu. Does it seem visually useful? What benefit does this visual representation offer to help the planning process?

EXERCISE 7-3: Risks, Contingency Planning, and Course Corrections

Select a business plan from any of the plans in previous exercises.

- Use the Plan Outline view to add additional topics. Add topics for contingency planning, risks, and course corrections (three topics, not one). What kinds of information should be included in these topics? Why would these topics be useful for an ongoing business plan?
- How does the plan improve decision making, evaluating, and measuring achievements of objectives? Can you see how the Profit and Loss table might be important for measurement and tracking? Can you see how the milestones table could be useful for following up with a plan?
- Using the Plan Outline view, add a topic for evaluation and follow-up, an addition to the standard plan outline. How can this added topic help keep the plan alive for course corrections?

Quova, Inc.

Marie Alexander, CEO of Quova, doesn't think there's a glass ceiling holding her down. The "old boys club" hasn't gotten in her way. In fact, she says the only groundbreaking she's doing is through her company's product. And that product is quite innovative. Quova's product "maps" the Internet. It collects data on a Web site's visitors by looking at the Internet provider addresses and uses that to approximate the user's location. Why is that important? Mainly for marketing applications, but there are other important uses.

Geography and location are critical for any marketer. Marketers want to know where their customers are so they can target local advertising and regional sales promotions. With the ability to tie in the Internet with its always-on, always-available element, Quova's product that adds in the element of location becomes a very powerful tool indeed. Other customers are using Quova's geographic mapping for Web analytics—where users are located and what trends are occurring in various geographic areas. But the company has found additional promising applications in the areas of fraud detection and online regulation compliance. You might be wondering whether the ability to pinpoint a user's location is an invasion of privacy. However, Quova assures that its technology doesn't invade users' privacy. A user's location is narrowed down only to a metropolitan area, which is what Quova's customers want.

Marie Alexander says that although Quova's product may be great, that's not enough. History has shown that it takes more than just a better product for a company to be great. To be successful, you have to be able to build a better product *and* build a better company.

Discussion Questions

1. What organizational performance measures might be needed by Quova? Why?
2. On Quova's Web site is the following statement: "At Quova, our success lies in the success of our customers." What do you think this means? What are the implications for managing customer service?
3. What do you think Alexander's statement—"To be successful, you have to be able to build a better product *and* build a better company"—means? What would be the implications as this venture manages its processes?

Sources: Company information from company Web site (**www.quova.com**), July 10, 2002, and Hoover's Online (**www.hoovers.com**), July 10, 2002; and ***Business Now*** video segment.

ENDNOTES

1. Company information from company Web site (**www.cannondale.com**), June 14, 2002, and Hoover's Online (**www.hoovers.com**), June 14, 2002; and The Associated Press, "Cannondale Dives into Dirt Bikes," *Springfield News Leader*, June 4, 2000, p. 12B.
2. J. G. March and H. A. Simon, *Organizations* (New York: Wiley, 1958).
3. J. R. Schermerhorn, Jr., *Management for Productivity*, 4th ed. (New York: Wiley, 1993), p. 150.
4. A. J. Rowe, J. D. Boulgarides, and M. R. McGrath, *Managerial Decision Making*, Modules in Management Series (Chicago: SRA, 1984), pp. 18–22.
5. See L. A. Burke and M. K. Miller, "Taking the Mystery Out of Intuitive Decision Making," *Academy of Management Executive*, October 1999, pp. 91–99; O. Behling and N. L. Eckel, "Making Sense Out of Intuition," *The Executive*, February 1991, pp. 46–47; W. H. Agor (ed.), *Intuition in Organizations* (Newbury Park, CA: Sage, 1989); and K. R. Hammond, R. M. Hamm, J. Grassia, and T. Pearson, "Direct Comparison of the Efficacy of Intuitive and Analytical Cognition in Expert Judgment," *IEEE Transactions on Systems, Man, and Cybernetics SMC-17* (1987), pp. 753–70.
6. T. W. Zimmerer and N. M. Scarborough, *Essentials of Entrepreneurship and Small Business Management*, 2nd ed. (Upper Saddle River, NJ: Prentice Hall, 1998), p. 232.
7. Based on K. D. Godsey, "Back on Track," *Success*, May 1997, pp. 52–54; J. Weiss, "Reengineering the Small Business," *Small Business Reports*, May 1994, pp. 37–43; M. Barrier, "Re-engineering Your Company," *Nation's Business*, February 1994, pp. 16–22; and G. Fuchsberg, "Small Firms Struggle with Latest Management Trends," *Wall Street Journal*, August 26, 1993, p. B2.
8. These definitions are based on T. M. Amabile, "A Model of Creativity and Innovation in Organizations," in *Research in Organizational Behavior*, vol. 10, ed. B. M. Staw and L. L. Cummings (Greenwich, CT: JAI Press, 1988), p. 126.
9. R. W. Goodman, J. E. Sawyer, and R. W. Griffin, "Toward a Theory of Organizational Creativity," *Academy of Management Review*, April 1993, pp. 293–321.
10. G. R. Oldham and A. Cummings, "Employee Creativity: Personal and Contextual Factors at Work," *Academy of Management Journal*, June 1996, pp. 607–34; J. F. Coates and J. Jarratt, "Workplace Creativity," *Employment Relations Today*, Spring 1994, pp. 11–22; S. D. Saleh and C. K. Wang, "The Management of Innovation: Strategy, Structure, and Organizational Climate," *IEEE Transactions on Engineering Management*, February 1993, pp. 14–22; and F. Damanpour, "Organizational Innovation: A Meta-Analysis of Effects of Determinants and Moderators," *Academy of Management Journal*, September 1991, pp. 555–90.
11. W. Burpitt, "Beyond the Shadow of the Entrepreneur: The Influence of Staff Level Contextual Variables on Organizational Level Absorptive Capacity and Performance," *Academy of Management Proceedings*, 2001, Entrepreneurship Division Abstracts, p. 16; and P. R. Monge, J. D. Cozzens, and N. S. Contractor, "Communication and Motivational Predictors of the Dynamics of Organizational Innovations," *Organization Science*, May 1992, pp. 250–74.
12. See, for instance, A. DeGues, "The Living Company," *Harvard Business Review*, March–April 1997, pp. 51–59; T. M. Amabile, R. Conti, H. Coon, J. Lazenby, and M. Herron, "Assessing the Work Environment for Creativity," *Academy of Management Journal*, October 1996, pp. 1154–84; S. G. Scott and

R. A. Bruce, "Determinants of Innovative People: A Path Model of Individual Innovation in the Workplace," *Academy of Management Journal*, June 1994, pp. 580–607; G. Morgan, "Endangered Species: New Ideas," *Business Month*, April 1989, pp. 75–77; R. M. Kanter, "When A Thousand Flowers Bloom: Structural, Collective, and Social Conditions for Innovation in Organizations," in *Research in Organizational Behavior*, vol. 10, ed. B. M. Staw and L. L. Cummings (Greenwich, CT: JAI Press, 1988), pp. 169–211; M. Tushman and D. Nadler, "Organizing for Innovation," *California Management Review*, Spring 1986, pp. 74–92; and T. M. Amabile, "A Model of Creativity and Innovation in Organizations," p. 147.

13. "Common Threads," *Inc.,* August 2001, pp. 51–52.
14. F. R. Reichheld and W. E. Sasser, Jr., "Zero Defections: Quality Comes to Services," *Harvard Business Review*, September–October 1990, pp. 301–07.
15. Ibid.
16. L. Edelman, C. Brush, and T. Manolova, "Resources–Conduct–Performance: The Mediating Role of Strategy on Small Firm Performance," *Academy of Management Proceedings*, 2001, Entrepreneurship Division Abstracts, pp. 23–24; and A. M. Pelham, "Market Orientation and Other Potential Influences on Performance in Small and Medium-Sized Manufacturing Firms," *Journal of Small Business Management*, January 2000, pp. 48–67.
17. K. Albrecht and R. Zemke, *Service America: Doing Business in the New Economy* (Homewood, IL: Dow Jones-Irwin, 1985).
18. M. Gottlieb, "Just Tell Me What You Want," *Industry Week*, March 19, 2001, pp. 42–45.
19. D. A. Menasce and V. A. F. Almeida, *Scaling for E-Business* (Upper Saddle River, NJ: Prentice Hall PTR, 2000).
20. A. Stuart and J. H. Maxwell, "Inside Story," *Inc.,* April 2002, pp. 94–100.
21. C. Hocker, "Fourth-Generation Entrepreneur Back at the Market," *Black Enterprise*, June 2001, p. 46.
22. P. Drucker, *Management Challenges for the 21st Century*, (New York: HarperCollins Publishers, 1999), p. 61.

8 MANAGING PEOPLE

LEARNING OBJECTIVES

After reading and studying this chapter, you should be able to:

1. Discuss the importance of people to organizational performance.
2. Describe the human resource management issues with which entrepreneurs may have to deal.
3. Explain why recruiting employees is important, yet one of the most challenging human resource management tasks that entrepreneurs do.
4. Explain what employee stock ownership plans and stock option plans are.
5. Define motivation and explain why it's important.
6. Describe how entrepreneurs might motivate organizational members.
7. Describe the role of teams and the management of teams in entrepreneurial organizations.
8. Discuss the importance of managing conflict.
9. Explain why empowerment and delegation are important activities of entrepreneurs.

ENTREPRENEURSHIP IN ACTION

How would you feel if you were a new employee, your boss asked you to do something, and you had to admit that you didn't know how to do it? Most of us would feel inadequate and incompetent. Now imagine how strange and uncomfortable it would be if, after experiencing such an incident, you went home with the boss because you two were roommates and have been friends since fourth grade.

This situation was faced by John Kim, an employee at Plumtree Software (**www.plumtree.com**) and his boss, Glen Kelman.[1] Kelman is a cofounder and vice-president of product management and marketing at Plumtree. A third roommate, Conan Reidy, also works at Plumtree. The three roommates are finding that mixing work and friendship can be tricky!

At home, the roommates are equal. They share a single bath-

As your entrepreneurial venture prospers and grows, eventually you're going to have to bring other people on board, maybe even friends. Managing the people in an entrepreneurial organization can be challenging, yet rewarding. The quality of an organization is, to a large degree, merely the summation of the quality of people it hires and keeps. Glen Kelman and Plumtree's other executives know that getting and keeping competent, talented, and motivated employees are critical to the success of their organization. In this chapter we want to look at the various aspects of managing people in the entrepreneurial venture. We'll examine some human resource management issues, look at motivation theories and how to motivate employees, discuss teams and leadership issues, and describe some other interpersonal issues that entrepreneurs may have to deal with.

HUMAN RESOURCE MANAGEMENT ISSUES

Until they get to a certain size, entrepreneurial organizations are unlikely to have a separate human resource management (HRM) specialist or department. That means that as the organization grows the entrepreneur personally may have to handle human resource activities until the point at which it's necessary to hire a specialist in this area. An entrepreneur should be aware of a number of HRM issues.

Strategic Human Resource Management

How often have you heard or read about companies making the statement that "Our people are our *most* important asset"? Is it just a nice thing to say or is there some truth to the statement? How important *are* people to an organization's success? According to Jeffrey Pfeffer, a management professor who has spent his career studying people and organizations, they're *very* important![2] He asserts that what differentiates high-performing organizations from others is the way they treat their people. These high-performance organizations have people strategies that reward teamwork, commitment, excellence, integrity, and other essential behaviors. The people philosophy of these high-performance organizations revolves around treating people appropriately by giving them the tools, training, and incentives they need to do their jobs. And guess what? They (both the individuals and the organization) excel! The common thread in these **high-performance work practices**—that is, human resource policies and practices that lead to high levels of both individual and organizational performance—seems to be a

room and housework. However, at work, equality is out the door! For instance, a problem with office assignments erupted when Plumtree moved into new headquarters. As part of the four-person management team, Kelman got a corner office with a window. Reidy, who works in an office cubicle, was annoyed at Kelman for not standing up for him when offices were assigned. Another problem is that the roommates compete to outlast one another working late. Reidy's boss worries that he's going to burn out. Then, there's the issue of Kelman's financial wealth as Plumtree went public in June 2002. What happens now? Although it might seem easy to say "move," it's too expensive in San Francisco, and these guys are good friends.

EXHIBIT 8-1 Seven Important People Practices of Successful Organizations

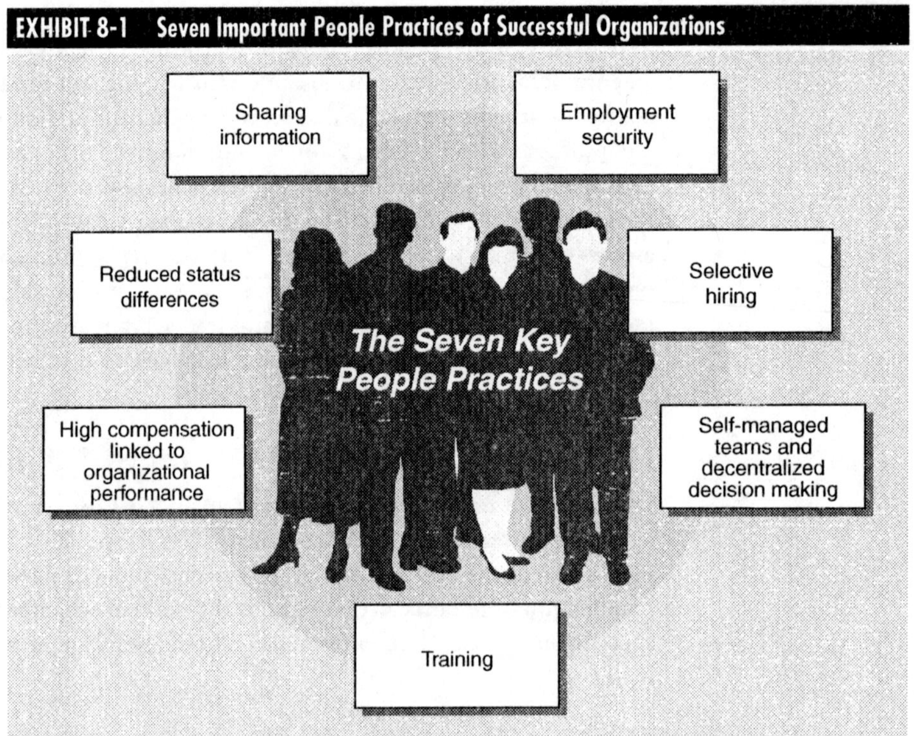

Source: Based on J. Pfeffer, *Competitive Advantage through People* (Boston: Harvard Business School Press, 1994).

commitment to improving the knowledge, skills, and abilities of the organization's current and potential employees; increasing their motivation; reducing loafing on the job; and enhancing the retention of quality employees while encouraging nonperformers to leave the organization. Pfeffer identifies seven people practices that he believes are key to a successful organization. (See Exhibit 8-1.) These seven practices include: employment security, selective hiring, self-managed teams/decentralized decision making, training, high compensation linked to organizational performance, reduction of status differences, and sharing information.

When all is said and done, however, what impact *do* such high-performance work practices have? Studies that have looked at the link between HRM policies and practices and organizational performance have found that these types of people-friendly HRM policies and practices tend to have a positive impact on performance.[3] What type of positive impact? One study reported that if an average company implemented these high-performance work practices, it could potentially add annually (per employee) $27,044 more in sales, $3,814 in profits, and $18,641 in market value.[4] Now multiply these figures by 5 or 10 or 100 employees and ask yourself if it might be worthwhile to take managing employees seriously? Another study reported that significantly improving an organization's HRM practices could increase its market value by as much as 30 percent.[5] It would appear that a philosophy of managing employees in a way that encourages, supports, and recognizes their contributions might be a pretty good one! But, now that we know something about the important strategic role that an organization's human resources play, what types of human resource management issues do entrepreneurs have to deal with? These issues include bringing people on board and managing them once they are on board.

Bringing People on Board

Jeff Soderberg, founder and president of Software Technology Group (**www.stg.com**) knows how important it is to have the right people in his organization. He has a core group of staffers who not only work hard, but play hard. His employees are intensely devoted to practicing their chosen sports—fly fishing, golfing, or bike racing, among others, and he supports their off-hours pursuits because he feels it makes them better employees.[6] Having a "dream team" of dedicated, hard-working employees doesn't happen just by luck or chance. Not at all! There are things that any entrepreneur must do to ensure that the venture has the people it needs to do the work that's required. These include human resource planning, recruiting and hiring, and having in place a process for dealing with situations when the same number of employees may no longer be needed or with employees who aren't working out. We're going to look at human resource planning first.

Human Resource Planning. The first step in bringing people on board is knowing something about the types of people needed (that is, what skills, abilities, experiences, education, and knowledge are needed) and how many people are needed. As an entrepreneur you should do some **human resource planning**—assessing current and future human resource needs—before even thinking about hiring. In this way, you can work toward ensuring that you have the right number and right kinds of people in the right places and at the right times. What's involved with human resource planning? Although some of the activities we're going to look at might seem overly cumbersome at times, keep in mind that managing the entrepreneurial venture's human resources effectively and efficiently takes more than a haphazard halfhearted effort. Continually remind yourself of the importance of having employees who are exceptionally capable and motivated.

One of the first things an entrepreneur should do is inventory current employees by getting information on their education, training, prior employment, languages spoken, special abilities, and specialized skills. This inventory provides an important summary of talents and skills currently available in the organization. It supplies information on what current employees can do. If your entrepreneurial venture is just at the point at which it's necessary to hire individuals, it would make sense to start and keep this inventory from the very beginning.

Another important part of human resource planning is a **job analysis**, which is an assessment that defines jobs and the behaviors necessary to perform them. Just as the human resource inventory provides fundamental information about the organization's people, the job analysis provides fundamental information about the organization's jobs—that is, the work that needs to be done. It defines the minimal knowledge, skills, and abilities necessary to perform each and every job adequately. Two important human resource documents created with the information from the job analysis are the job description and the job specification. A **job description** is a written statement of the work a jobholder does, how it is done, and why it is done. It typically describes job content and focuses on the *job*. The **job specification** states the minimum acceptable qualifications that a jobholder or job seeker must possess to perform a given job successfully. It focuses on the *person*. These two documents are important to the efficient and effective functioning of the entire HRM process because they're focused on the key reason for

Rapid Review

- ✔ What are high-performance work practices?
- ✔ Explain the people practices that successful organizations tend to have.
- ✔ What type of impact have these high-performance work practices been shown to have?
- ✔ Why should an entrepreneur do some human resource planning, and what should be done during it?
- ✔ Differentiate among job analysis, job description, and job specification.
- ✔ Why are job descriptions and job specifications important documents?

having employees in the first place—having competent and motivated people performing job duties that are critical to the work of the organization.

The foundation for a successful HRM program (one that brings in and keeps on board capable and motivated employees) occurs during the human resource planning process. Without the information provided by the human resource inventory and the job analysis, bringing people on board would be more difficult and certainly less effective. Although these initial HR activities take time, the effort and resources expended will be worth it. The payoff will be a core of competent, dedicated, and skilled individuals who will be able to initiate and drive the entrepreneurial venture's successful growth. However, the human resource inventory and the job analysis are just the first steps in making this happen. The next thing the entrepreneur must do is the actual recruiting and hiring.

Recruiting, Selecting, and Hiring. To bring people into the organization, you have to first find acceptable candidates. **Recruiting** is the process of locating, identifying, and attracting capable job applicants. It can be a frustrating process for entrepreneurs, particularly if the labor market is tight (that is, there are more jobs than qualified job seekers) and if the entrepreneurial venture can't offer the same types and amount of compensation and benefits that larger organizations can. However, the entrepreneur should approach recruiting with the perspective that what (in this case, *who*) comes into the organization affects what goes out of the organization (that is, its products and services). If your recruiting activities are done halfheartedly and with little thought or preparation, you're going to get below-average job applicants, and the resulting work performance is going to be below average. (Computer types like to classify this phenomenon as GIGO—garbage in, garbage out.) The point is that an entrepreneur should take the recruiting process seriously because the organization's ultimate performance levels are a reflection of the quality of people brought in. We can't hire quality people if we don't locate, identify, and attract them. What types of recruiting sources might entrepreneurs use? Exhibit 8-2 portrays eight sources.

The first type of recruiting source is employee referrals—that is, asking your current employees for the names of potential job candidates. One benefit of this approach is the fact that the current employee knows the type of person who would be a good fit for the organizational culture and performance expectations. In addition, the current employee will want to refer someone who's going to reflect well on them. After all, a person isn't going to recommend someone who's likely to fail. That would make the current employee look bad, also. However, if you're just beginning to add employees to your entrepreneurial venture, this approach obviously won't work until you have current employees to ask for referrals. Another recruiting source is to use job advertisements in newspapers or other paper sources. Although this approach targets a wide audience, it's likely to generate many unqualified job applicants. A variation to advertisements in paper sources is advertising jobs on Web job posting boards. Again, these job postings

EXHIBIT 8-2 Sources for Recruiting Job Applicants

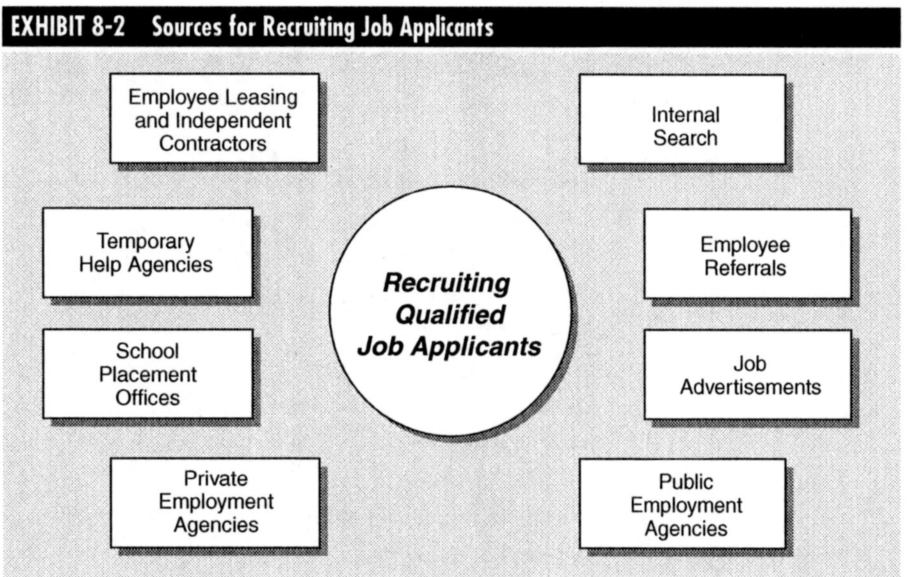

will reach a vast global audience, but not everyone in that audience is going to be a qualified applicant. Another source for recruiting is to use public or private employment agencies. Although public agencies (usually run by a state labor office) are free or may charge only a nominal fee, they tend to attract unskilled or minimally trained candidates. On the other hand, private employment agencies often attract higher-skilled individuals and will carefully screen job applicants for applicable skills, but there's typically a high cost for this type of service. School placement offices can be another source for job applicants. Although these sources can provide the entrepreneur with a large pool of potential candidates, the job applicants typically are new participants in the labor force who don't have a lot of relevant work experience. Another source for recruiting would be temporary help agencies. If the entrepreneurial venture needs employees for short periods when, say, for instance, there's seasonal demand for the venture's products or services, these agencies can be a good choice. However, their services tend to be expensive. In addition, keep in mind that temporary employees generally will have a limited understanding of the organization's goals, activities, and culture. A type of temporary help service is employee leasing firms and independent contractors that typically deal with higher-skilled workers. These sources of job applicants often are used by organizations that have specific work projects that need to be completed. Rather than hiring permanent employees, the organization may look to lease employees or hire an independent contractor. Although this approach can help fill temporary needs, these employees typically will not have any commitment to the organization other than completing the current project. Finally, if the entrepreneurial venture is currently large enough, looking inside the organization for job applicants—an internal search—may be appropriate for filling positions as they open up. Obviously, the advantages of this type of recruitment are that it has relatively low cost, helps build employee morale because employees see that there are career opportunities within the organization, and results in candidates who are quite familiar with the organization. However, the main drawback of an internal search is the limited supply of applicants, particularly if the venture doesn't

Entrepreneurs in Action

Unicru (**www.unicru.com**) has developed a smart-assessment program—a fast-paced, real-time screening system that customers such as Blockbuster, Target, ServiceMaster, and Shoe Carnival use to make their hiring process more efficient and effective. The automated process has helped its customers reduce their hiring cycle (the time from the initial interview to a new employee's start date) by an average of 7 days. Unicru's CEO, Bob Gregg, says there are five ingredients for employee recruitment and retention success: (1) Walk in your employees' shoes on a regular basis so you understand the needs of the people you're hiring. (2) Job performance and tenure do not correlate—there are good and poor performers at both ends of the tenure continuum. (3) There is no such thing as a good or bad employee, just a good or bad fit. (4) Always save your data. (5) Use interviews to probe, not to screen.

Sources: Company information from company Web site (**www.unicru.com**), June 21, 2002; and A. Overholt, "True or False: You're Hiring the Right People," *Fast Company,* February 2002, pp. 110–114.

currently have a large number of employees. And, filling a job internally leaves another open position to be filled. Yet, as the venture grows and as more jobs open up, this approach can be a good one.

Using the various recruitment sources, we've now assembled a pool of job applicants. What comes next is selecting the best candidates. **Employee selection** is a process of screening job applicants to ensure that the best individuals are hired. Employee selection is an exercise in prediction. What you want to predict is which job applicants will be successful performers if hired. How can you do this? By using any number of selection devices that can help pinpoint important, relevant information about the job applicants. The most commonly used ones include job applications, written tests, performance-simulation tests, interviews, reference and background checks, and physical examinations. Let's look at what each of these selection devices does.

The job application is used by almost all organizations. It may be a simple sheet of paper on which the job applicant gives his or her name, address, and telephone number. Or it might be a more comprehensive printed form on which the person provides relevant biographical information and details of their activities, skills, and accomplishments. Although the job application is a popular employee selection instrument, typically only a couple of items on the application form prove to be good predictors of job performance. Its use is probably best limited to information gathering because the process of determining which items on the application form are good predictors of job performance is difficult and expensive.

Written tests include tests of intelligence, aptitude, ability, and interest. These types of tests have been used for years, although their popularity tends to run in cycles. Decision makers have become increasingly aware that poor hiring

Many prospective employees commonly provide a résumé summarizing their background, education, work experiences, and other accomplishments. A number of these résumés are "creatively enhanced." A survey of 2.6 million job applicants discovered that 44 percent of all résumés contained at least some lies. For instance, a person might indicate that they were making more money at their previous job than they really were. Or they might describe job responsibilities as more impressive than they really were. Are these types of "creative enhancements" wrong? What are the ethical implications for job applicants? For entrepreneurs wanting to hire the best employees?

Source: J. Kluger and S. Song, "Pumping Up Your Past," *Time,* June 10, 2002, p. 46.

decisions are costly and that properly designed tests could reduce the likelihood of poor decisions occurring. In addition, the costs associated with developing and validating a set of written tests for a specific job also has decreased significantly. Yet, there are still some concerns about whether a test score can be a good indicator of how well an applicant will perform on a job. This criticism has led to an increased use of performance-simulation tests.

What better way is there to find out whether a person applying for a technical writing position can write technical manuals than by having him or her do it? Performance-simulation tests use actual job behaviors to assess a candidate's skills and abilities. The two most popular performance simulation tests are work sampling and assessment centers. **Work sampling** involves having job applicants perform tasks in a simulated model of a job. Applicants demonstrate they have the necessary skills and abilities by actually doing the simulated tasks. Work sampling is more appropriate for routine type jobs. **Assessment centers** are places where job applicants undergo more elaborate performance simulation tests by performing exercises that simulate real problems they might encounter on the job. These tests are more appropriate for selecting people for professional or managerial positions. Research on both work sampling and assessment centers has shown that both tend to be good predictors of future job performance.[7]

Have you ever gotten a job without one or more interviews? Probably not! The job interview, like the job application form, is an almost universal selection device, yet unless it's done effectively, the interview is questionable as a good predictor of job performance. How can interviews be done effectively? When interviews are structured and well organized, and when interviewers ask common questions, interviews have been shown to be effective predictors of future job performance.[8] Unfortunately, the typical interview—in which job applicants are asked a varying set of essentially random questions in an informal setting—usually provides little in the way of valuable information. A review of the research on interviews leads us to the following conclusions:

1. Prior knowledge about the applicant will bias the interviewer's evaluation.
2. The interviewer tends to have a stereotype of what represents a "good" applicant.
3. The interviewer tends to favor applicants who share his or her own attitudes.
4. The order in which applicants are interviewed will influence evaluations.
5. The order in which information is elicited during the interview will influence evaluations.
6. Negative information is given unduly high weight.

7. The interviewer often makes a decision concerning the applicant's suitability within the first 4 or 5 minutes of the interview.
8. The interviewer forgets much of the interview's content within minutes after its conclusion.
9. The interview is most valid in determining an applicant's intelligence, level of motivation, and interpersonal skills.
10. A "cold" interviewer (one who's extremely formal and serious) can have a devastating effect on the verbal and nonverbal behaviors of applicants with low self-esteem.[9]

What do these research findings tell us? We can use what these studies have shown us to identify some ways to make employment interviews more effective. Exhibit 8-3 lists some specific suggestions. However, even if you follow these suggestions, keep in mind that another important factor in interviewing job applicants is the legality of certain interview questions. Certain interview questions should *not* be asked because they potentially could expose the organization to lawsuits by job applicants. Exhibit 8-4 lists some examples of "no-no" interview questions.

EXHIBIT 8-3 Suggestions for Effective Interviewing

1. Structure a *fixed set of questions* for all applicants.
2. Have *detailed information about the job* for which applicants are interviewing.
3. *Minimize any prior knowledge* of applicants' background, experience, interests, test scores, or other characteristics.
4. *Ask behavioral questions* that require applicants to give detailed accounts of actual job behaviors.
5. Use a *standardized evaluation form.*
6. *Take notes* during the interview.
7. *Avoid short interviews* that encourage premature decision making.

Source: Based on D. A. DeCenzo and S. P. Robbins, *Human Resource Management*, 4th ed. (New York: John Wiley, 1994), pp. 208–9.

EXHIBIT 8-4 "No-No" Interview Questions

- What is your date of birth?
- Have you ever filed a workers' compensation claim?
- What is your place of birth?
- Do you own a home?
- What is your native language?
- Do you have children? Plan to have children? Have child care?
- Do you have a physical or mental disability that would prevent you from doing this job?
- What religion do you practice?

Sources: Based on J. S. Pauliot, "Topics to Avoid with Applicants," *Nation's Business*, July 1992, pp. 57–58; and L. M. Litvan, "Thorny Issues in Hiring," *Nation's Business*, April 1996, pp. 34–36.

Background and reference checks usually include verifying data on the application form and contacting the applicant's references. Several studies indicate that going to the trouble of verifying facts provided on the job application is worthwhile. A significant percentage of job applicants—upwards of 44 percent—exaggerate or misrepresent dates of employment, job titles, past salaries, or reasons for leaving a prior position.[10] In addition, organizations must consider the liability that potential employees may create and get as much background information as possible.[11] Although background checks can be useful, reference checks are difficult to justify even though most organizations still ask for references. Whether work-related or personal, references provide little valid information. Previous employers often are reluctant to give candid evaluations of a former employee's job performance for fear of legal action by the ex-employee. Personal references are no better because these people are likely to provide biased information. After all, who's going to put down as a reference someone who might give a bad report?

The last type of selection device we want to look at is the physical examination. Although there may be jobs that have certain physical requirements, you have to be careful to ensure that these physical requirements are actually job-related and do not discriminate. Some physical requirements may exclude disabled persons or individuals with physical limitations, when, in fact, such requirements do not affect job performance. Because of the legal questions, the physical examination today is used mostly for insurance purposes. Organizations want to be sure that new employees will not submit insurance claims for injuries or illnesses that they had before being hired.

Based on what we've just discussed, what *should* an entrepreneur do to select the best job applicants? Performance-simulation tests, structured and well-organized interviews, and background verifications of biographical information are likely to provide the entrepreneur with the best information for making effective selection decisions. The job application should be used mainly for obtaining biographical information about the job applicant. Written tests are unlikely to provide effective information, so the entrepreneur probably would not want to use

FYI

Get Real

To increase job satisfaction among employees and reduce turnover, which can be expensive, an entrepreneur should consider providing a realistic job preview (RJP). An RJP includes both positive and negative information about the job and the company. For instance, in addition to the positive comments typically expressed during an interview, the job applicant might be told that there are limited opportunities to talk to co-workers during work hours, that promotional advancement is slim, or that work hours fluctuate so erratically that employees may be required to work during what are usually off-hours (nights and weekends). Research indicates that job applicants who have been given a realistic job preview hold lower and more realistic job expectations for the jobs they will be performing than do applicants who have been given only inflated information. After spending time and money performing a job search, the result can be fewer unexpected resignations by new employees and having to start all over again.

EXHIBIT 8-5 Decruitment Options

Option	Description
Firing	Permanent involuntary termination
Layoffs	Temporary involuntary termination; may last only a few days or extend to years
Attrition	Not filling openings created by voluntary resignations or normal retirements
Transfers	Moving employees either laterally or downward; usually does not reduce costs but can reduce intraorganizational supply–demand imbalances
Reduced workweeks	Having employees work fewer hours per week, share jobs, or perform their jobs on a part-time basis
Early retirements	Providing incentives to older and more senior employees for retiring before their normal retirement date
Job sharing	Having employees share one full-time position

these. In addition, asking for references (employment and personal) is unlikely to prove useful in selecting the best employee. Finally, physical examinations should be used for insurance purposes only. What happens next?

At this point, the entrepreneur is ready to make the hiring decision(s). After looking at and carefully evaluating the information gathered and provided during the selection process, the entrepreneur should make a decision about who would best fit the job criteria. But, even given this careful consideration, sometimes things just don't work out. Or, sometimes the entrepreneur may find that the level of business isn't enough to justify the number of employees already on board. What then? This is where the process of decruitment comes in to play.

Decruitment. **Decruitment** describes techniques for reducing the number of employees within an organization. Although asking employees to leave the organization isn't a pleasant task, doing so sometimes may be absolutely necessary for the best interests or even the survival of the organization. There are a number of decruitment options. Exhibit 8-5 summarizes the major ones.

Now that the entrepreneurial venture has on board the numbers and types of people it needs to do the work, is that all there is to managing the organization's human resources? You probably know the answer to that question already! We next want to look at managing people once they're on board.

Rapid Review 

- ✔ What is recruiting? Why is it an important process, even in entrepreneurial ventures?
- ✔ Describe each of the eight recruiting sources.
- ✔ What is employee selection? Why is employee selection an exercise in prediction?
- ✔ Describe each of the six selection devices.
- ✔ What is decruitment, and what options are there for decruitment?

Managing People on Board

Getting competent, qualified people into the organization is just the first step in effectively managing the human resources. Other HRM activities that an entrepreneur must be familiar with include orienting, performance appraisal, employee training, and compensation and benefits. We're going to discuss each of these important activities.

Orienting. A person starting a new job needs some introduction to that job. This introduction is called **orientation**. The major goals of employee orientation are to reduce the initial anxiety all new

Entrepreneurs in Action

Rene Larrave, cofounder of Dallas-based consulting company Tactica (**www.tactica.com**), believes that hiring any employee without planning for his or her future is a drastic mistake. From the moment a new employee comes in the door, he or she learns how to get promoted. Employees know the expectations if they want to move from consultant to associate to manager and finally to principal. Although the company's system may seem overly structured, he explains that, "The type of people we want to attract are very driven, type A people, and achievement and progression through the ranks is important to them. It drives them. So having the promotion plan well laid out is critical for them."

Sources: Company information from company Web site (**www.tactica.com**), June 21, 2002; and K. O'Sullivan, "Why You're Hiring All Wrong," *Inc.*, February 2002, p. 86.

employees feel as they begin a new job; to familiarize new employees with the job, the work unit, and the organization; and to facilitate the transition from being an outsider to becoming an insider. Orientation expands on the information the employee received during the recruitment and selection processes. The three main areas that the orientation should cover are the job, the work unit, and the organization.

In the job orientation, the new hire's specific duties and responsibilities are clarified, as are the performance expectations and performance evaluation techniques to be used. This is also the time to resolve any unrealistic expectations that new employees might have about the job. In the work unit orientation, the new employee is introduced to the goals of the work unit, to how his or her job contributes to the unit's goals, and to co-workers. The organization orientation should cover information about the organization's goals, history, philosophy, procedures, and rules. In addition, this is the time to cover relevant human resource policies and benefits such as work hours, pay procedures, overtime requirements, and fringe benefits. A tour of the entire organization might also be done. Each of these different orientations provides a unique perspective of the person's new work environment. However, if the entrepreneurial venture is still relatively small, all of these aspects may be covered (*should* be covered) in one generalized orientation. But, even in the smallest entrepreneurial ventures, the entrepreneur has an obligation to make the integration of new employees into the organization as smooth and as free from anxiety as possible. It is in the organization's and the new employee's best interests to get the person up and running in the job as soon as possible. A successful orientation, whether formal or informal, results in an outsider–insider transition that makes the new member feel comfortable and fairly well adjusted, lowers the likelihood of poor work performance, and reduces the probability of a surprise resignation by the new employee a short time after starting the job.

FYI

Combating Sexual Harassment

You might think "It can't happen here," but that type of attitude about sexual harassment can bring on a nasty legal surprise. What is **sexual harassment**? It's defined as any unwelcome sexual advance, behavior marked by sexually aggressive remarks, unwanted touching, requests for sexual favors, or other verbal or physical conduct of a sexual nature. And, sexual harassment in the legal sense may be broader than you think. The Equal Employment Opportunity Commission has made it clear and courts have agreed, that sexual harassment can occur in either of two ways: "quid pro quo" sexuality—a supervisor tells an employee that a condition of continued employment is that he or she perform sexual acts; and hostile work environment—includes sexual comments, jokes, pictures, pornography, or derogatory comments about one gender. These definitions are fairly broad, and the potential for sexual harassment lawsuits should make any entrepreneur sit up and take notice, especially because legal judgments can be in the millions of dollars, and the average judgment in a sexual harassment case is $350,000. But, there are steps you can take to fight sexual harassment in your organization. These steps include education, company policy, and procedure. First off, training programs should educate employees as to what sexual harassment is and should raise employees' awareness of what might be sexually offensive to others. And, these training programs should educate employees about what to do. In addition, your organization needs stated policies and procedures regarding sexual harassment. The policy should clearly state that sexual harassment will not be tolerated in the workplace, identify the responsibilities of employees in preventing harassment, specify the sanctions and penalties for violations, and spell out the procedures for reporting incidents of sexual harassment. Take sexual harassment seriously—it *is* a serious human resource issue.

Sources: C. K. Goodman, "Sexual Harassment Cases Growing More Frequent," *Upstate Business*, November 24, 1996, pp. 4–5; K. Donovan, "Avoiding a Time Bomb: Sexual Harassment," *Business Week Enterprise*, October 13, 1997, pp. ENT20–ENT22; R. K. Robinson, et al., "U.S. Sexual Harassment Law: Implications for Small Businesses," *Journal of Small Business Management*, April 1998, pp. 1–13; R. McGarvey, "Hands Off!," *Entrepreneur*, September, 1998, pp. 85–87; and K. Kelly, "Keeping Peace on the Floor," *Business Week Enterprise*, October 12, 1998, p. ENT20.

Performance Appraisal. After orientation, the new employee starts performing the job duties he or she was hired to do. After a certain period, it's important to appraise the person's performance. Is the new employee's job performance up to expectations? Are there areas in which the individual's performance is lacking and needs improvement? Are there areas in which the individual's job performance exceeds expectations and have they been recognized for their accomplishments? **Performance appraisal** is the process of evaluating an individual's work performance. How is employee performance appraised?

An entrepreneur might use different performance appraisal methods. (See Exhibit 8-6.) The **graphic rating scale** is a popular method of appraisal in which an evaluator uses an incremental numerical scale to rate an employee on a set of performance factors. This appraisal approach is widely used because the numerical scales are relatively easy to create and use, but unfortunately it doesn't provide the depth of information that other methods do. **Written essays** are a performance

EXHIBIT 8-6 Performance Appraisal Methods

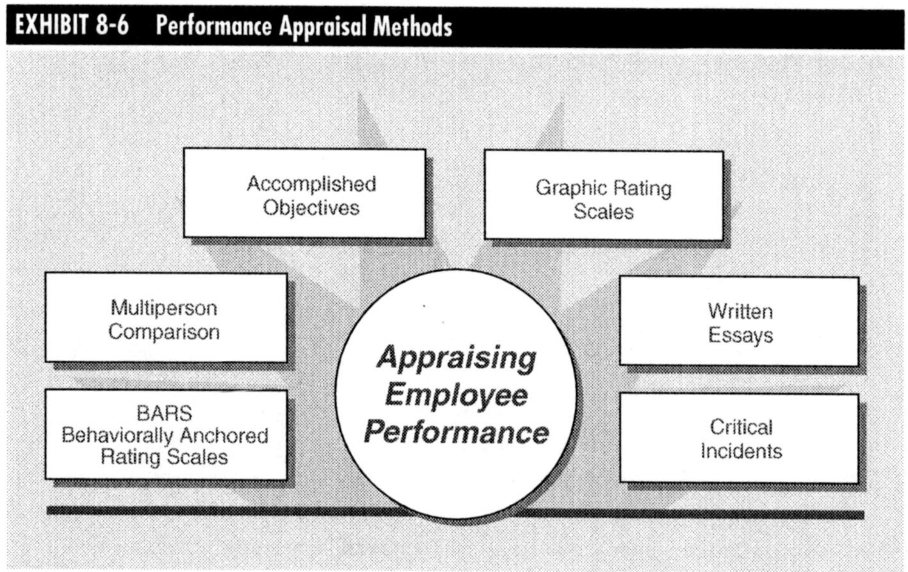

appraisal technique whereby an evaluator writes a description of an employee's strengths, weaknesses, past performance, and potential, and then makes suggestions for improvement. This is probably the simplest method of appraisal since it requires no complex forms to fill out or extensive training to complete. However, a drawback is that a good or bad appraisal may be determined as much by the evaluator's writing skill as by the employee's actual performance. The **critical incidents** approach is one in which an evaluator lists specific key behaviors that separate effective from ineffective job performance. A list of critical incidents for a given employee provides a rich set of examples that can be used to point out desirable and undesirable behaviors. Although listing specific examples of an employee's work performance provides good information, keeping a record of these critical incidents can be quite time-consuming. Another performance appraisal approach that's received a lot of attention is **behaviorally anchored rating scales (BARS)**. This is a technique in which an evaluator rates employees using a numerical scale, just like a graphic rating scale. But the difference is that the BARS focus on specific and measurable job *behaviors*, as opposed to general descriptions or traits. Key elements of jobs are broken down into performance dimensions and then specific illustrations of effective and ineffective behaviors are identified for each performance dimension. The result is behavioral descriptions that capture the essence of what doing that particular job is all about. By appraising an individual using these behaviorally anchored dimensions, you get a good feel for how well the person is performing. This approach is quite effective, but the biggest drawback is the amount of time it takes to create the behaviorally anchored rating scales. The **multiperson comparison** approach is a performance appraisal technique in which individuals are compared to other individuals in the work group. Although this approach would provide a good indicator of an individual's performance in relation to relevant others, it can be quite cumbersome to complete. Finally, there's a performance appraisal technique that evaluates a person's performance on the basis of how well he or she met established goals.

Because this approach puts the emphasis on goal accomplishment by assessing whether goals have been met, other important job performance factors may be overlooked.

The results of an employee's performance appraisal are used for different things. For instance, if the individual's work performance isn't up to expectations, the performance appraisal will pinpoint areas in which improvement is needed. It may simply be a matter of the individual needing additional direction or closer supervision. Or it may be that the individual needs additional training and development. The performance appraisal is also used to highlight performance accomplishments that may be used for recognition purposes, for promotion purposes, or for compensation and reward purposes. Keep in mind that regardless of whether the performance appraisal process is relatively formal or informal and no matter what type of appraisal instrument is used, *some* form of performance appraisal needs to be done, particularly as the entrepreneurial venture grows and adds employees. The performance appraisal acts as a scorecard. If employees aren't performing at or above expected levels, you want to know it and take the necessary actions. Otherwise, the organization will find it difficult to be competitive and to achieve the kinds of performance results that will ensure the venture's continuing success.

Employee Training. An important HR activity that ensures the continued skills and capabilities of an organization's human resources is employee training. It's been estimated that U.S. businesses spend $54 billion on formal courses and training programs to build workers' skills.[12] Obviously, employee training is big business and is big *for* business. Although entrepreneurs may feel that they can't afford the money or time to have an ongoing formal program of employee training, the real question is can they afford *not* to have such a program? Given today's dynamic and intensely competitive environment, it's important to keep employees well trained, like finely tuned machines or racehorses—ready to put their skills and abilities to the test at a moment's notice. What types of employee training might entrepreneurs want to implement? Employee skills training can be grouped into three categories: technical, interpersonal, and problem solving. Most employee training activities seek to modify an employee's skills in one or more of these categories.

Technical training involves upgrading and improving an employee's fundamental technical skills such as math, reading or writing, and job-specific competencies. For instance, many jobs require an individual to be able to use computerized equipment, digitally controlled machines, or other types of sophisticated technology, and they need basic math, reading, and computer skills to be able to do so. Technical training can provide the necessary tools and skills in these areas. Interpersonal training involves helping employees develop their skills and abilities at interacting effectively with co-workers—otherwise known as people skills. Interpersonal training might include things such as learning how to be a better listener, how to communicate ideas more clearly, or how to reduce conflict. Finally, training in problem solving helps employees to be better problem solvers. This might include developing the ability to define problems, assess causes, develop alternatives, be creative, analyze alternatives, and select appropriate solutions.

EXHIBIT 8-7 Typical Employee Compensation Components

Source: Based on L. R. Gómez-Mejía, D. B. Balkin, and R. L. Cardy, *Human Resource Management* (Upper Saddle River, NJ: Prentice Hall, 1995), p. 357.

Each of these training categories addresses an important employee skill, ability, or competency. Organization-provided training opportunities can be a significant benefit for employees, particularly in entrepreneurial organizations in which other types of benefits may not be available. Employee compensation and benefits are the next HRM topics we need to look at.

Compensation and Benefits. The purpose of designing an effective and appropriate compensation system is to attract and retain competent and talented individuals who can help the organization accomplish its mission and goals. In addition, an organization's compensation system has been shown to have an impact on its strategic performance.[13] Entrepreneurs must develop compensation systems that reflect the changing nature of work and the workplace in order to keep employees motivated, committed, and excited. Compensation can include many different types of rewards and benefits. Exhibit 8-7 outlines the typical compensation components an organization may provide.

The base wage or salary is the fixed dollar amount that an individual receives on a regular basis for performing a job. This wage or salary is usually paid weekly, biweekly, or monthly. Benefits consist of a wide variety of compensation programs such as insurance (health, life, dental, or other), vacations, unemployment benefits, stock options, and so forth. Pay incentives are compensation programs designed to encourage and reward good work performance. These incentives may be in the form of merit pay, bonuses, profit sharing, or some other type of reward. Deciding which forms of compensation to use to attract and keep talented employees is an important decision for entrepreneurs because scarce resources may preclude offering high salaries or a wide variety of typical benefits. Many entrepreneurial organizations will offer other incentives, such as stock options, to attract skilled and competent employees. Although granting employees stock options may seem like a wonderful solution to a complicated and complex dilemma, entrepreneurs need to think about some issues before jumping in and doing so. The FYI box in this section provides basic information about stock option plans and ESOPs (employee stock ownership plans).

The decisions on compensation and benefits play an important role in attracting and keeping talented employees. It's also crucial to keep talented employees motivated to perform their jobs. Although motivating employees is not considered a specific HRM activity, it *is* an extremely important consideration in managing people.

Rapid Review

- ✔ What is orientation, and why is it important? What should be covered in each of the three main areas of orientation?
- ✔ Why is performance appraisal important?
- ✔ Describe the different performance appraisal methods an entrepreneur might use.
- ✔ What might the results of a performance appraisal be used for?
- ✔ Why is employee training important even in entrepreneurial organizations?
- ✔ What are the typical compensation components an organization might provide?

FYI

Taking Stock

We've all heard the news stories of employees making millions off their stock options, particularly at dot.com companies. Although not every stock option plan put in place makes millionaires of employees, these plans can be an excellent way to attract and retain talented employees, particularly if other compensation levels tend to be less than competitive. Stock option plans give employees the right to purchase a certain number of their company's shares at a fixed price for a certain period of time. Most options usually begin partially vesting after 1 year and vesting fully after 4 years. Once an option is vested, the employee can "exercise" it, which means purchasing from the company the allotted number of shares at the price that's been set (the strike price) and then either hold the stock or sell it on the open market. The difference between the strike price and the market price of the shares at the time the option is exercised is the employee's gain in the value of the shares. When an employee exercises an option, the company must issue a new share of stock that can be publicly traded. The intent behind stock options is that employees will be motivated to continue performing at high levels, thus increasing the company's performance and the value of its stock. However, even though they're touted as being an effective incentive to keep employees motivated to achieve the long-term goals of an organization, often they bring about the opposite result. Employees may cash in (exercise) their stock options at the earliest possible point rather than waiting for the desired long-term increase in value, and other talented employees may still job-hop looking for the best payoff. Another way to compensate and motivate employees is through an **employee stock ownership plan**, which is a program in which employees become part owners of an organization by receiving stock as a performance incentive. According to the National Center for Employee Ownership, about 11,000 ESOPs are in effect. The research on ESOPs indicates that they can increase employee satisfaction and frequently result in higher performance. However, that potential will be realized only if employees are treated as owners by keeping them regularly informed about the status of the business and giving them opportunities to influence business decisions. Whether you decide that a stock option plan or an ESOP will work best for you, it's extremely important to get good legal and accounting advice. There are a number of tax and legal issues that would need to be addressed before setting up either a stock option plan or an ESOP.

Sources: P. Weaver, "An ESOP Can Improve a Firm's Performance," *Nation's Business*, September 1996, p. 63; S. Kaufman, "ESOPs' Appeal on the Increase," *Nation's Business*, June 1997, pp. 43–44; E. O. Welles, "Motherhood, Apple Pie, and Stock Options," *Inc.*, February 1998, pp. 84–97; and S. Gruner, "Stock Options & Equity," *Inc.*, February 1998, pp. 110–113.

MOTIVATING EMPLOYEES

When you're motivated to do something, don't you find yourself energized and willing to work hard at doing whatever it is you're excited about? Wouldn't it be great if all a venture's employees were energized, excited, and willing to work hard at their jobs? That's what we want to look at in this section—getting employees energized and excited about performing their jobs at or above expected levels. As an entrepreneur, you'll need to understand what motivation is and how to motivate employees.

What Is Motivation?

Motivation is the willingness of an individual to exert high levels of effort in doing a job in order to help the organization reach its goals. Although motivation can also refer to a person's efforts toward reaching personal goals, we're primarily interested in motivation as it relates to the workplace. If an entrepreneurial venture is going to achieve its goals, it's going to need motivated employees—that is, employees who are willing to exert high levels of effort to help the venture achieve its goals.

Motivation is one of the most thoroughly researched and studied topics in management and organizational behavior. Although we're not going to examine all the various motivation theories in depth, we do want to describe briefly some of the more important ones. If you want to know more about any of these motivation theories, you can pick up any introductory management or organizational behavior textbook for additional information.[14]

Early motivation theories focused on trying to describe *what* it was that motivated individuals. The best known of these theories is **Maslow's hierarchy of needs**, which states that there is a hierarchy of five human needs (physical needs on the bottom of the hierarchy and moving up through safety, social, esteem, and at the top of the hierarchy, self-actualization) that serve to motivate a person to exert effort.[15] According to Maslow's theory, as each need is satisfied, the next need becomes dominant. In addition, a need that has been satisfied will no longer motivate an individual. Using Maslow's hierarchy, if you wanted to motivate someone, you'd have to understand what need level that person was on and focus on satisfying needs at or above that level.

Another early motivation theory is **Herzberg's motivation–hygiene theory** or the **two-factor theory of motivation**.[16] This motivation theory proposed that the job factors that contribute to *job satisfaction* (or being motivated to perform) are not the same as the job factors that contribute to *job dissatisfaction*. Herzberg called the job factors that caused people to feel satisfied with their jobs and thus

Entrepreneurs in Action

Auto shops aren't exactly a growth industry. Robert Gross, the CEO of Monro Muffler Brake garages around the northeastern and midwestern United States, has a tough motivational job. If he doesn't push stores to sell extra services, the company's sales will falter. If he pushes too hard and the stores sell products customers don't need, the chain could alienate customers or even worse, be accused of defrauding customers. Gross takes the stick-and-carrot approach to motivating his employees. He gives store managers considerable freedom to run the stores as if they were their own, and managers can earn incentive bonuses as well as stock options if they meet goals. But there are also punishments if the managers don't meet their goals, including losing their jobs.

Source: N. Ridgway, "Tailpipe Dreams," *Forbes*, June 11, 2001, pp. 136–137.

more motivated to perform, the *motivators*. These motivators encompassed job content (the job itself) and included things such as the opportunity to achieve, recognition for work, taking on additional responsibility, opportunity for advancement, and so forth. The job factors that caused people to feel dissatisfied with their jobs were called *hygiene* factors and encompassed job context—things surrounding the job, such as the type and quality of supervision, relationship with supervisor, salary, organizational policies and administration, working conditions, relationships with co-workers, and so forth. According to Herzberg's theory, providing for the hygiene factors would do nothing to motivate employees; it would simply keep them from being dissatisfied with their jobs. In order to motivate employees, you had to look at creating opportunities for them to achieve by focusing on job content.

Although these early theories of motivation got managers and entrepreneurs thinking about motivation, researchers began to recognize that the emphasis on what motivates individuals was misdirected because what motivates each of us is different. What motivates you is different from what motivates the person sitting next to you and is different from what motivates your close friends. Rather than trying to understand and describe motivation from the perspective of *what,* the emphasis switched to understanding *how* motivation takes place. These theories focused on understanding the process of motivation and proposed that by understanding how motivation takes place, motivation efforts could then be individually tailored to each person. We'll look briefly at three of these motivation theories: goal-setting theory, reinforcement theory, and expectancy theory.

We know that an individual's intention to work toward a goal is a major source of job motivation.[17] The **goal-setting theory** of motivation proposes that specific goals increase performance and that difficult goals, when accepted by an individual, result in higher performance than do easy goals. Studies on goal setting have demonstrated the superiority of specific and challenging goals in moti-

FYI

Improving Worker Performance

An entrepreneurial venture that wants to grow (and survive) has to get continually improving performance from its employees. Because the work performance of a venture's human resources is the only resource that competitors cannot duplicate, you've got to understand how to improve your employees' performance. But what can you do to motivate your employees to do their best? Here are some questions that you might ask to see if you're creating an environment in which employee performance is enhanced: (1) Do you try to make sure there's the right fit between employee and job? (2) Do you search for ways to put your employees in direct contact with your customers? (3) Does your company's culture encourage employees to strive for high performance levels? (4) Do you seize opportunities to offer informal rewards and recognition to your employees? (5) Do you try to tailor rewards and recognition to individual employees? (6) Do you recognize that many employees may find their greatest reward in the work itself and allow them to do their jobs the way they think is best?

Source: M. Barrier, "Improving Worker Performance," *Nation's Business,* September 1996, pp. 28–31.

vating individuals. When people are given specific challenging goals, they produce a higher level of output than when they're simply told to "Do your best." Another important element of goal-setting theory is understanding employee participation in setting goals. Will employees try harder if they've had the opportunity to participate? We can't say that having employees participate in the goal-setting process is *always* desirable. In some cases, research showed that participatively set goals elicited superior performance, although in other cases, individuals performed best when goals were assigned by someone else. However, the fact that individuals may better accept goals when they've had a chance to participate in setting them would seem to indicate that allowing employees to participate in goal setting might be a desirable approach. What can we conclude about goal-setting theory and the role it plays in understanding how individuals are motivated? An overall conclusion from goal-setting theory is that a person's intentions to work toward a goal are powerful motivators. Channeled and used properly, using goals as motivators can lead to higher performance.

The next motivation theory we need to look at is **reinforcement theory**, which proposes that an individual's behavior is a function of its consequences. According to reinforcement theory, what controls an individual's behavior are the consequences (or reinforcers) that follow that behavior. Reinforcement theory was first proposed by B. F. Skinner, who said that people will most likely engage in a desired behavior if they are rewarded for doing so. These rewards are most effective if they immediately follow a desired behavior, and behavior that isn't rewarded, or is punished, is less likely to be repeated.[18] As a motivation theory, reinforcement theory proposes that you can influence an employee's behavior by reinforcing work actions that you see as favorable (that is, actions that contribute to the accomplishment of the venture's goals). Although research indicates that

Entrepreneurs in Action

Fran Flood, president of Gentner Communications, a manufacturer of high-end audioconferencing equipment, had a critical motivational problem. Her company was losing money and the sales force was lethargic and unmotivated. Flood's unique solution—hokey movie-themed cheerleading. For instance, she came up with a "Mission: Possible" theme, leaving voice mail messages with each sales rep outlining their targets and rewards for meeting them. She also distributed "wolf bucks"—part of the company's "Hungry Like the Wolf" theme—that were redeemable for cash and prizes at the end of the year if the company met its earnings targets. Every time a large deal was closed, wild wolf howls echoed in the company's hallways. Then, there was the *Matrix* theme that used slogans such as "We won't conduct business as usual! We won't get sucked into the Matrix." Has it worked? Flood has seen the company's sales and earnings growth take off.

Source: L. Goldman, "Over the Top," *Forbes*, October 29, 2001, pp. 146–147.

EXHIBIT 8-8 Expectancy Theory of Motivation

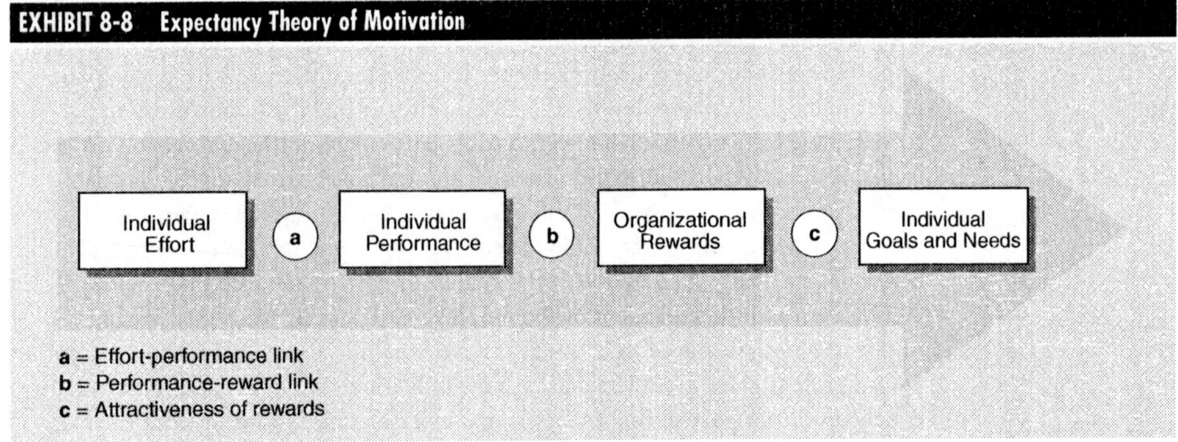

external reinforcement is undoubtedly an important influence on how motivated an employee is, understand that it isn't the only explanation for differences in employee motivation.

The most comprehensive explanation of how motivation takes place is **expectancy theory.**[19] This theory proposes that an individual tends to act in a certain way based on the expectation that the behavior will be followed by a given outcome and on the attractiveness of that outcome to the individual. It includes three variables or relationships (see Exhibit 8-8):

1. *Expectancy* or *effort-performance linkage*, which is the probability perceived by the individual that exerting a given level of effort will lead to a certain level of performance.
2. *Instrumentality* or *performance-reward linkage*, which is the degree to which the individual believes that performing at a certain level is instrumental in leading to the attainment of a desired outcome.
3. *Valence* or *attractiveness of reward*, which is the importance that the individual places on the potential outcome or reward that can be achieved. Valence considers both the goals and the needs of the individual.

Although this theory of motivation might sound complex, it really isn't that difficult to visualize. It can be summed up in the following questions: How hard do I have to work to achieve a certain level of performance, and can I actually achieve that level? What reward will performing at that level get me? How attractive is that reward to me, and does it help me achieve my goals? Whether you are motivated to put forth effort (that is, to work) at any given time depends on your particular goals and your perception of whether a certain level of performance is necessary to attain those goals. Think of how hard you work in a particular class for a grade. Isn't it based on your beliefs about what type of effort (studying, doing homework, coming to class, etc.) it takes to achieve a certain level of performance, the "reward" or grade for achieving that level of performance, and how important that reward or grade is to you? If getting an "A" is important to you, you'll put forth whatever effort it takes to achieve the level of performance (maybe 90% or above) it takes to get that A. The key to expectancy theory as an explanation of motivation is understanding an individual's goals and the links between

Entrepreneurs in Action

Sapient Corporation builds Internet and software systems for e-commerce and for automating back-office tasks such as billing and inventory. It's a people-intensive business, and cofounders Jerry Greenberg and J. Stuart Moore recognized that employee motivation was critically important to their company's ultimate success. They designed their organization so that individual employees are part of an industry-specific team that works on an entire project rather than on one small piece of it. Their rationale was that people often feel frustrated when they're doing a small part of a job and never get to see the whole job from start to finish. They figured people would be more productive if they got the opportunity to participate in all phases of a project.

Sources: Company information from company Web site (**www.sapient.com**), June 20, 2002, and Hoover's Online (**www.hoovers.com**), June 20, 2002; and S. Herrera, "People Power," *Forbes*, November 2, 1998, p. 212.

effort and performance, between performance and rewards, and between rewards and individual goal satisfaction. Individuals will be motivated if they see a link between the amount of effort exerted, the resulting performance level, and the rewards received because of that level of performance.

Each of the motivation theories just described provides clues to understanding employee motivation. But, practically speaking, how can an entrepreneur take what is known about motivation and apply it in real life to actually motivating employees?

How to Motivate Employees

Although there's no simple answer to the question of how best to motivate employees, we do know some things about increasing the likelihood of successfully motivating employees. First of all, *recognize individual differences.* Almost every contemporary motivation theory recognizes that employees aren't the same. They have different needs. They also differ in terms of attitudes, personality, and other important personal variables. Try to understand what's important to individual employees. This also means that you should *individualize rewards.* Because employees have different needs, what acts as a reinforcer for one may not be so for another. Use your knowledge of employees' differences to individualize the rewards they can get. Another suggestion is to *match people to jobs.* A great deal of evidence shows the motivational benefits of carefully matching people to jobs. For instance, high achievers will do best in jobs that provide opportunities to participate in setting challenging goals and that involve autonomy and feedback. However, others will not be motivated by those kinds of jobs or job responsibilities. The fourth suggestion is to *use goals.* The research on goal-setting theory suggests that employees should have challenging, specific goals and feedback on how well they're doing in accomplishing those goals. If you expect resistance to the

Entrepreneurs in Action

Employees at Technology Professionals Group, a technology staffing company based in Grand Rapids, Michigan, find that their rewards for doing good work are tailored to their own unique situations. Linda Connor, vice-president of corporate culture, constantly collects tidbits of information about the company's employees. She takes that information, thinks about it for a while, and then pulls out unusual ideas for customized rewards. For instance, one employee got the opportunity to fly on an F17 bomber. Connor updates her employee profiles over time with information pulled from routine interactions. She says, "Every time I meet an employee or I hear about a meeting someone else had, I take mental notes so we are prepared to do things that are very timely for their current interests or needs."

Source: L. Buchanan, "Managing One-to-One," *inc.*, October 16, 2001, pp. 83–89.

goals, use participation to increase acceptance. Next, *ensure that goals are perceived as attainable.* Regardless of whether goals are actually attainable, employees who see goals as unattainable will reduce their effort. Their attitude is "why bother, it won't do any good to work hard." Be sure, therefore, that employees feel confident that increased efforts *can* lead to achieving work goals. Another suggestion is to *link rewards to performance.* Entrepreneurs should attempt to make rewards contingent on performance. Rewarding factors other than performance will only reinforce those other factors. Entrepreneurs should also look for ways to increase the visibility of rewards. If employees can see what types of behaviors and performance levels are being rewarded, this can serve to motivate others. Next, *check the system for fairness.* Employees should perceive that rewards or outcomes are fair and equitable and relate to the amount of effort expended in doing the work. Finally, *don't ignore money.* It's so easy to get caught up in setting goals, creating interesting jobs, and providing opportunities for participation that you overlook the fact that money is a major reason why most people work. Thus, the allocation of performance-based wage increases, bonuses, and other pay incentives is important in determining employee motivation. We're not saying that your motivation techniques should focus solely on money. Rather, we're simply stating the obvious—that is, if money is removed as an incentive, people aren't going to show up at work. You can't say the same for removing goals, enriched work, or participation.

Having motivated employees is an important goal for any entrepreneurial venture. Another important aspect of managing people, however, is dealing with employee teams and leadership issues. Those are the topics we're going to look at next.

Rapid Review 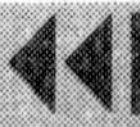

- ✔ What is motivation? Why is it important?
- ✔ Describe Maslow's hierarchy of needs theory and Herzberg's motivation–hygiene theory.
- ✔ How does goal-setting theory approach motivation?
- ✔ What does reinforcement theory say about motivation?
- ✔ Describe expectancy theory and how it relates to motivation.
- ✔ Explain how entrepreneurs can motivate employees.

EMPLOYEE WORK TEAMS AND LEADERSHIP

Many organizations, entrepreneurial and otherwise, are using work teams to perform organizational tasks, create new ideas, and resolve problems. Work teams are popular and likely to continue being used. In this section, we want to discuss what a work team is, the different types of work teams an organization might use, how to develop and manage effective work teams, and how to lead a work team.

What Is a Work Team?

Most of us are probably pretty familiar with teams, especially if we have ever participated in or watched any type of organized sports activity. Although an athletic team has many of the same characteristics as a work team, work teams are different and have their own unique traits. Just what are **work teams**? They're formal work groups made up of interdependent, interacting individuals who are responsible for the attainment of work goals.

Types of Work Teams

Although there are several ways to categorize work teams, we're going to describe them in terms of four characteristics: purpose, duration, membership, and structure.[20] Let's look at each of these characteristics in more detail.

Work teams can vary in their purpose or goal. Examples abound of the variety of work activities teams have tackled in entrepreneurial organizations. For instance, a team might be involved in product development, problem solving, or any other work-related activity. So, one way work teams can be described is in terms of what they're set up to do. In addition, teams can also be classified in terms of duration as either permanent or temporary. Teams that are formal, ongoing components of an organization's structure would be classified as permanent. Many entrepreneurial organizations that have adopted the work-team concept have an organizational structure designed around these permanent teams. On the other hand, temporary teams would include ad hoc task forces, project teams, or any other type of short-term team created for a specific purpose that will disband once that purpose or goal is accomplished. The next characteristic that can be used to classify teams is that the team's membership can either be function-based—that is, composed of people from a particular organizational functional area or department—or it could be a **cross-functional team**, which has team members from various organizational functional areas or departments. Finally, teams can be classified as either supervised or self-managed. A supervised team is one that's under the direction of some person who is responsible for guiding the team in setting goals, in performing the necessary work activities, and in evaluating performance. A self-managed team, as its title suggests, assumes these responsibilities as it manages itself.

Although knowing how to describe work teams in terms of their characteristics is important, what we're really interested in is how to make sure that these work teams perform their work at the highest levels of efficiency and effectiveness. What's involved with that?

Developing and Leading Effective Teams

One thing you need to realize is that using work teams doesn't automatically lead to increases in productivity. If the team isn't effective, their performance accomplishments are likely to be disappointing as well. However, an entrepreneur's goal should be to have the venture's work teams achieving more than individuals working separately (even if their work is coordinated) can achieve. An effective team can do this! Therefore, we need to know what makes a team effective. Research on teams provides insights as to what characteristics an effective team has.[21] (See Exhibit 8-9.)

First, an effective team will have *clear goals.* High-performance teams have both a clear understanding of the goal to be achieved and a belief that the goal embodies a worthwhile or important result. In effective teams, members are committed to the team's goals, know what they're expected to accomplish, and understand how they will work together to achieve those goals. The next characteristic of effective teams is *relevant skills.* Effective teams are composed of competent and talented individuals. They have the necessary technical skills and abilities to achieve the desired goals, and the interpersonal skills required to achieve excellence while working well with others. High-performing teams have members who possess *both* technical and interpersonal skills. Next, effective teams exhibit *mutual trust.* Team members must believe in one another's integrity, character, and ability. However, this trust is fragile. It takes a long time to build and it can be easily destroyed. But ultimately, to be effective, the team members must have this mutual trust.

Another characteristic of effective teams is *unified commitment.* Members of an effective team exhibit intense loyalty and dedication to the team. They're willing to do whatever it takes to help the team succeed. We call this loyalty and dedication "unified commitment." Next, effective teams exhibit *good communication.* It shouldn't surprise you that effective teams are characterized by good communication. Team members are able to convey messages between each other in ways that are readily and clearly understood. This includes nonverbal as well as spoken

EXHIBIT 8-9 Characteristics of an Effective Team

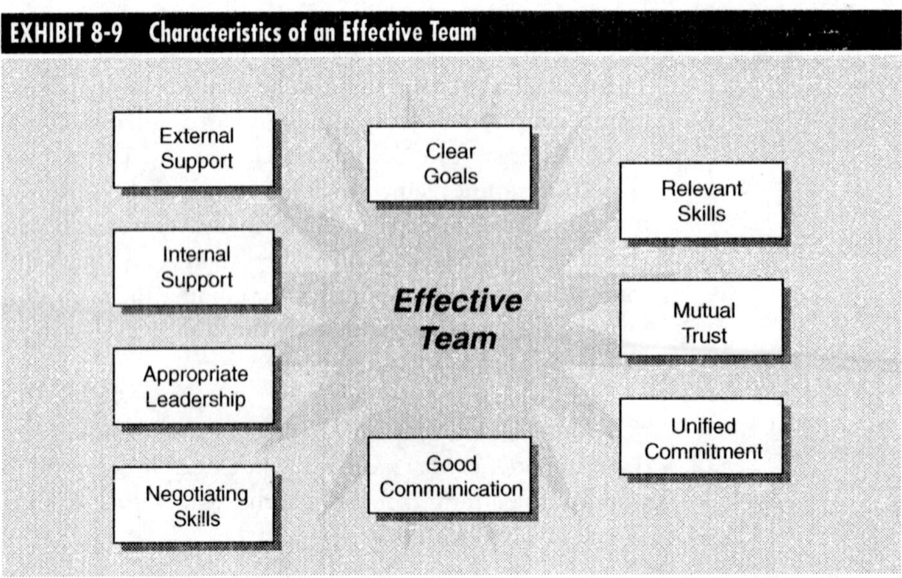

Entrepreneurs in Action

In a suburb outside Cleveland, CEO Joseph P. Keithley, manages a Silicon Valley–like organization in which the organizational culture embodies an entrepreneurial spirit and Midwestern work ethics and values. The company, Keithley Instruments Inc. (**www.keithley.com**), manufactures test and measurement devices for the wireless communications, optoelectronics, and semiconductor markets. Keithley has created a cultural climate in which employees trust one another. He believes so strongly in this type of environment that he shares quarterly results with employees at a mass employee meeting. In addition, every couple of weeks, he invites small groups to join him for lunch, at which they discuss their jobs, company issues, and any other topics that are of interest to the employees.

Sources: Company information from company Web site (**www.keithley.com**), June 21, 2002; and T. Stevens, "Profiting from Precision," *Industry Week*, July 16, 2001, pp. 45–47.

messages. Good communication also means the team engages in relevant and continual feedback among team members and between the team and any other individuals or teams. The next characteristic of an effective team is *negotiating skills*. When a team has negotiating skills, it means that the team is flexible and continually making adjustments. Team members are able to negotiate among themselves and with others outside the team. Because problems and relationships are regularly changing in a team, members must be able to confront and reconcile differences.

Next, effective teams will have *appropriate leadership*. Effective teams need effective leaders. Effective leaders can motivate a team to follow them through the most difficult situations. How? They help clarify goals. They demonstrate that change is possible. They increase the self-confidence of team members, helping members to realize their potential more fully. Increasingly, effective team leaders are taking on the role of coach and facilitator. They help guide and support the team, but don't control it.

Finally, effective teams are going to have *internal and external support*. An effective team needs a supportive climate. Internally, the team should have proper training, an understandable measurement system that team members can use to evaluate their overall performance, an incentive program that recognizes and rewards team activities, and a supportive human resource system. The internal climate should support team members and reinforce behaviors that lead to high levels of performance. Externally, the team needs to be provided with the resources needed to get the job done. External support is an important requirement of effective teams.

Knowing what characteristics make a team effective isn't enough, though. As entrepreneurs, we need to understand how effective teams are developed and managed so that our entrepreneurial venture can capitalize on the positive gains that can come from work teams. What's involved in developing and managing a work team? It's probably most logical to think in terms of the planning, organizing, leading, and controlling activities that must occur.[22]

Planning for and by the team is an important activity. The team must take the time to determine goals and establish plans. As we pointed out previously, effective teams have clear goals. Team members must also understand and accept the team's goals.[23] Whether the goals are provided for the team or whether the team develops its own goals, every team member needs to know and accept the goals.

Once the team's goals have been agreed on, organizing tasks involve clarifying authority and structural issues. One of the key questions for the team is, "How much authority do we have?" If the team is a self-directed or self-managed team, it's already been empowered with the authority to make certain decisions and perform specific work activities. However, even if a team isn't self-managed, questions will come up regarding what it can and cannot do. It's important that these authority issues be addressed early so that a team knows its parameters and constraints. Structural issues also need to be resolved within the team itself. Has a leader been appointed or will the team designate one? What tasks should be done to accomplish the team's goals? What are the most effective and efficient ways to do the work? Who's going to do what tasks? How will work assignments be made? These are the types of organizing questions that must be answered.

Important leading issues that a team must address include, among others, what role the team's leader will play, how conflict will be handled, and what communication processes will be used. Although the team leader often plays an important role in directing the efforts of the team, team leaders are increasingly assuming the roles of facilitator and coach rather than of "person in charge." If the entrepreneur is the person leading the team, he or she wants to make sure not to dictate what the team is doing and how it should do its work. Sometimes it's hard to let go and let others make decisions, yet an effective leader should know when to step in and when to step back. If the team leader is not the entrepreneur, the person who *is* put in charge of the team must have the "right stuff" to help the team achieve its maximum potential. This means having (1) sufficient technical knowledge to understand the team's duties and (2) having strong interpersonal skills to be able to deal with encouraging individual participation, motivating outstanding performance, resolving conflicts, and gaining consensus on key issues. Exhibit 8-10 lists some key people skills that have been found to be important in leading a team.

Finally, two of the most important controlling issues in managing teams are: How will the team's performance be evaluated, and what type of reward system will be used? As entrepreneurial organizations make greater use of work teams, they're going to have to address these issues and make changes in their performance appraisal and reward systems. Performance criteria may need to be modified to incorporate teamwork behaviors in employee evalu-

Rapid Review

- ✔ What is a work team?
- ✔ How can work teams be categorized?
- ✔ What is unique about a cross-functional team?
- ✔ Describe the characteristics of an effective team.
- ✔ What's involved with developing and managing an effective team?
- ✔ How do planning, organizing, leading, and controlling issues play a role in developing and managing an effective team?

EXHIBIT 8-10 Key People Skills in Leading a Team

- Ask appropriate questions to bring out ideas and stimulate discussion.
- Listen closely and intently to members' ideas and concerns.
- Manage group discussions to encourage shy team members to participate.
- Establish an informal and nonthreatening climate so members feel free to speak their thoughts candidly.
- Use the consensus method to reach decisions on key team issues.
- Involve team members in setting goals.
- Implement meeting guidelines to minimize wasted time in group meetings.
- Encourage respect for each other so each member knows that his or her contributions are valued.
- Identify and deal with dysfunctional behaviors immediately.
- Celebrate the achievement of milestones and other team accomplishments.
- Use recognition, task assignments, and other techniques to motivate team members.

Source: Based on G. M. Parker, *Cross-Functional Teams* (San Francisco: Jossey-Bass, 1994), pp. 57–58.

ations. Not only should individual performance be evaluated, but factors that indicate how well the individual works in the team context also should be considered. In addition, entrepreneurs may have to look at how teams are rewarded for their efforts and performance levels. Group incentive plans may be an answer. Under these systems, group rewards are directly related to performance. If the team succeeds, team members will be rewarded. In addition, teams may be rewarded with one-time bonuses, team incentives, or informal team recognition. Whatever approach is used, the entrepreneur needs to look to the work teams for direction in deciding what types of rewards and recognition are important.

Developing and leading effective work teams are important "people" issues that entrepreneurs may have to deal with as the venture grows. There are two final people issues that we need to discuss in this chapter.

OTHER PEOPLE ISSUES

Although managing the entrepreneurial venture's people may be one of the most challenging things an entrepreneur does, it can also be one of the most rewarding. In addition to the people topics we just looked at, you need to understand two other people issues. One is managing conflict and the other is empowering employees and delegating duties.

Managing Conflict

Look back at our chapter-opening case. The work and home situations faced by the three roommates at Plumtree Software had already led to some conflicts. When you have people working together, conflict is inevitable. **Conflict** refers to any perceived disagreements or differences that result in interference or opposition. Whether the disagreements or differences are real or not is irrelevant. If people perceive that disagreements and differences exist, then a conflict exists.

Our perception of conflict has evolved from a view that all conflict is bad and must be avoided to a view that some conflict is necessary for a work team to perform effectively. However, we're not so naive as to think that all conflicts

Entrepreneurs in Action

Conflict is managed well at Higher Octave, a New Age record label based in Malibu, California. Lunchtime involves recreation at the beach, and a massage therapist pays a weekly visit. The relaxed environment makes employees want to stay. And they do stay—employee turnover is almost zero. Cofounders Matthew Marshall and Daniel Selene have created an organization in which popular songs aren't referred to as "hits" and the word *deadline* is banned because both conjure up images of destruction and death. But even with the company's laid-back, mellow approach, employees bring out almost 20 albums a year, and Higher Octave has reached the number-one spot on *Billboard* magazine's New Age chart for 8 of the past 10 years. That's not a bad record for an organization that epitomizes calm and serenity.

Sources: Company information from company Web site (**www.higheroctave.com**), June 21, 2002, and Hoover's Online (**www.hoovers.com**), June 21, 2002; and A. Marsh, "Malibu Mellow," *Forbes*, August 10, 1998, pp. 62–64.

within a group are good. Some conflicts support a group's goals, whereas others prevent a group from achieving its goals. Unfortunately, the difference between whether a conflict is functional (good) or dysfunctional (bad) isn't clear or precise. No one level of conflict can be assumed good or bad under all conditions. The type and level of conflict that will promote a healthy and positive interchange of ideas and involvement toward the team's goals may, in another group or in the same group at another time, be highly dysfunctional. As an entrepreneur, you want to create an environment in which team conflict is healthy but not allowed to run to extremes. If the work team is apathetic, unresponsive to change, lacking new ideas, or stagnant, you may need to stimulate conflict. However, if conflict has caused the team to become disruptive, chaotic, and uncooperative, you need to minimize the amount of conflict because at this point, it's a disruptive force.[24] If conflict levels have become too high (i.e., it is having a negative impact on performance), then you may need to take steps to manage the conflict.

Empowering Employees and Delegating Duties

Entrepreneurs are strongly self-reliant, and letting others take over decisions and tasks doesn't come easily to them. However, if you truly want to grow your entrepreneurial venture, you're going to have to learn to let go. Letting go entails a managerial philosophy of empowering employees—that is, giving them the power and freedom to do things. It means trusting employees to make good decisions and to work competently and in the best interests of the organization. We introduced the concept of **empowerment** in Chapter 5 when we were discussing the organizational chain of command. We defined it as increasing the decision-making discretion of individuals. In an empowered organization, individual employees are free to resolve problems as they arise, are encouraged to approach their work the way they feel is best because they have more detailed knowledge about it, and are encouraged to think for themselves rather than being told what to do. Empowerment is a philosophical concept you have to "buy into" as you accept and embrace giving employees more control over what they do and how they do it. And this doesn't come easy. In fact, it's hard to do. Your life is tied up in this business. You've built it from the ground up. But continuing to grow your entrepreneurial venture is eventually going to require handing over more responsibilities to your employees. It's going to require accepting and embracing a philosophy of employee empowerment. What's involved?

Entrepreneurs can begin empowering employees in a couple of ways. One way to start is through participative decision making, in which you get employee input into decisions. Although getting employees to participate in decisions isn't quite taking the full plunge into employee empowerment, it is, at least, a way to begin tapping into the amazing array of employees' talents, skills, knowledge, and abilities. If your use of participative decision making is successful, what else can you do? Another way to empower employees is through delegation. **Delegation** is defined as the process of assigning certain decisions or specific job duties to individual employees. By delegating these decisions and duties, you're turning over to someone the responsibility for carrying them out. You're entrusting the accomplishment of these work activities to this person. Delegating effectively means following some simple guidelines. See the FYI box for some advice on effective delegation.

When you're finally comfortable with the idea of empowerment, fully empowering employees means redesigning their jobs so they have discretion over the way they do their work. It's allowing employees to do their work effectively and efficiently by using their creativity, imagination, knowledge, and skills. If the entrepreneur implements employee empowerment properly—that is, with

FYI

Delegate Like a Pro

If your entrepreneurial venture succeeds and grows (which is, of course, what you want it to do), eventually you're going to have to delegate some decisions and duties to other employees. How can you do so effectively? The first thing is to *approach delegation carefully and with some thought.* Although you may finally have accepted that you're going to have to delegate, don't cast off your responsibilities in a rush. Think about who, what, and how. Next, be sure to *choose individuals carefully.* You need to trust the skills and abilities of the person(s) to whom you're going to be delegating. Once you've decided on the individuals who will be taking over certain decisions and duties, *be specific about what you're delegating* to them. Be direct about expectations. Clarify what decisions and duties are being assigned. Next, *communicate.* Let those affected by the delegation of certain decisions and duties know that another person is now handling these. Also establish feedback procedures. This way you can find out what's happening and take care of any problems that might arise. Finally, *make good use of your freed-up time.* An entrepreneur has a lot of things to do. When you've delegated some of your decisions and tasks, use the time to attend to other important aspects of growing your business.

Sources: R. McGarvey, "Ready, Set, Delegate!" *Entrepreneur,* July 1998, pp. 77–79; B. Bernard, "Delegating Duties the Right Way," *Nation's Business,* April 1998, p. 10; and "Do You Delegate As Much as You Can?" *Nation's Business,* July 1996, p. 9.

Rapid Review

- ✔ What is conflict? Is all conflict bad? Explain.
- ✔ What is empowerment?
- ✔ How can an entrepreneur design an empowered organization?
- ✔ What is delegation?
- ✔ What are the advantages and drawbacks of empowering employees?

complete and total commitment to the program and with appropriate employee training—the results can be impressive for the entrepreneurial venture and for the empowered employees. The business can enjoy significant productivity gains, quality improvements, more satisfied customers, increased employee motivation, and improved morale. Employees can enjoy the opportunities to do a greater variety of work that is more interesting and challenging. In addition, employees are encouraged to take the initiative in identifying and solving problems and doing their work. Do be aware, however, that not every employee wants to be empowered. Some will not want the responsibility and others may be afraid of it. Yet, the dynamic, often chaotic, nature of a growing and successful entrepreneurial venture is going to require at some point that the venture's employees take an active role in what work gets done and how. If employees resist empowerment attempts, you may need to recognize that these are not the kind of employees who are going to contribute to the long-term and continued success of your entrepreneurial venture.

CHAPTER SUMMARY

This summary is organized around the chapter-opening objectives.

1. Studies have shown that high-performing organizations treat their employees well. The common thread in these high-performance organizations is high-performance work practices that lead to high levels of both individual and organizational performance. Their people strategies reward teamwork, commitment, excellence, integrity, and other essential behaviors.
2. The human resource management issues that entrepreneurs may have to deal with include bringing people into the venture and managing them once they're there. Bringing people into the venture involves human resource planning; recruiting, selecting, and hiring; and decruiting. Managing people once they're in the venture involves orienting, conducting performance appraisal, providing employee training, and determining compensation and benefits.
3. Recruiting is the process of locating, identifying, and attracting capable job applicants. It is an important process because the venture's ultimate performance is a reflection of the quality of the people it brings in. However, it's a challenging HRM task, particularly if the labor market is tight, because an entrepreneurial venture often can't offer the same types and amount of compensation and benefits that larger organizations can.
4. An employee stock ownership plan is a program in which employees become part owners of an organization by receiving stock as a performance incentive. Stock option plans give employees the right to purchase a certain number of their company's shares at a fixed price for a certain period of time.
5. Motivation is the willingness of an individual to exert high levels of effort in doing a job in order to help the organization reach its goals. It's important

because if an entrepreneurial venture is going to achieve its goals, it's going to need motivated employees.

6. Although there's no easy answer about how best to motivate employees, entrepreneurs might use the following suggestions: recognize individual differences, individualize rewards, match people to jobs, use goals, ensure that goals are perceived as attainable, link rewards to performance, check the system for fairness, and don't ignore money.
7. Many entrepreneurial organizations are using work teams to perform the organization's work. These work teams can have different purposes, be established for different periods of time, be composed of members from the same functional or cross-functional areas, and either be self-managed or have an assigned team leader. Managing work teams involves looking at the planning, organizing, leading, and controlling activities that must occur.
8. It's important to manage conflict because some conflicts support a group's goals whereas other conflicts prevent a group from achieving its goals. As an entrepreneur, you want to create an environment in which team conflict is healthy but not allowed to be dysfunctional.
9. Empowerment and delegation are important activities of entrepreneurs because if an entrepreneur truly wants to grow his or her venture, they're going to have to learn how to let go. Empowerment is increasing the decision-making discretion of individuals so that they're free to resolve problems as they arise, are encouraged to approach their work the way they feel is best, and are encouraged to think for themselves rather than being told what to do. Delegation is the process of assigning certain decisions or specific job duties to individual employees.

KEY TERMS

- *High-performance work practices:* Human resource policies and practices that lead to high levels of both individual and organizational performance.
- *Human resource planning:* Assessing current and future human resource needs.
- *Job analysis:* An assessment that defines jobs and the behaviors necessary to perform them.
- *Job description:* A written statement of the work a jobholder does, how it is done, and why it is done.
- *Job specification:* A written statement of the minimum acceptable qualifications that a jobholder or job seeker must possess to perform a given job successfully.
- *Recruiting:* The process of locating, identifying, and attracting capable job applicants.
- *Employee selection:* A process of screening job applicants to ensure that the best individuals are hired.
- *Work sampling:* A performance-simulation test in which job applicants perform tasks in a simulated model of a job.

- *Assessment centers:* Places where job applicants undergo more elaborate performance-simulation tests by performing exercises that simulate real problems they might encounter on the job.
- *Decruitment:* Techniques for reducing the number of employees within an organization.
- *Orientation:* An introduction of a new employee to a job, the work unit, and the organization that facilitates the transition from being an outsider to becoming an insider.
- *Sexual harassment:* Any unwelcome sexual advance, behavior marked by sexually aggressive remarks, unwanted touching, requests for sexual favors, or other verbal or physical conduct of a sexual nature.
- *Performance appraisal:* The process of evaluating an individual's work performance.
- *Graphic rating scale:* A performance appraisal method in which an evaluator uses an incremental numerical scale to rate an employee on a set of performance factors.
- *Written essays:* A performance appraisal technique whereby an evaluator writes a description of an employee's strengths, weaknesses, past performance, and potential, and then makes suggestions for improvement.
- *Critical incidents:* A performance appraisal technique in which an evaluator lists specific key behaviors that separate effective from ineffective job performance.
- *Behaviorally anchored rating scales (BARS):* A performance appraisal technique in which an evaluator rates employees using a numerical scale with the focus on specific and measurable job behaviors.
- *Multiperson comparison:* A performance appraisal technique in which individuals are compared to other individuals in the work group.
- *Employee stock ownership plan (ESOP):* A program in which employees become part owners of an organization by receiving stock as a performance incentive.
- *Motivation:* The willingness of an individual to exert high levels of effort in doing a job in order to help the organization reach its goals.
- *Maslow's hierarchy of needs:* A motivation theory that states there is a hierarchy of five human needs that serve to motivate a person to exert effort.
- *Herzberg's motivation–hygiene theory (two-factor theory of motivation):* A motivation theory that proposed that the job factors that contribute to job satisfaction (being motivated to perform) are not the same as the job factors that contribute to job dissatisfaction.
- *Goal-setting theory:* A motivation theory that proposes that specific goals increase performance and that difficult goals, when accepted by an individual, result in higher performance than do easy goals.
- *Reinforcement theory:* A motivation theory that proposes that an individual's behavior is a function of the consequences that follow that behavior.
- *Expectancy theory:* A motivation theory that proposes that an individual tends to act in a certain way based on the expectation that the behavior will be fol-

lowed by a given outcome and on the attractiveness of that outcome to the individual.

- *Work teams:* Formal work groups made up of interdependent, interacting individuals who are responsible for the attainment of work goals.
- *Cross-functional team:* A work team that is composed of people from various organizational functional areas or departments.
- *Conflict:* Any perceived disagreements or differences that result in interference or opposition.
- *Empowerment:* Increasing the decision-making discretion of individuals.
- *Delegation:* The process of assigning certain decisions or specific job duties to individual employees.

SWEAT EQUITY

1. When the labor market is tight, companies compete as fiercely for employees as they do for customers. Here are some tips for successfully keeping employees on board: Make it a long-term commitment; hire the right people; offer a competitive salary and benefits package; provide an economic stake in the company; be flexible with work schedules; communicate; encourage creativity and innovation; build a sense of camaraderie; reward individual and group performance; invest in training; and remember that your employees have lives outside the company.

   Take each tip and write an explanation of what you think it means and what you think it would require for an entrepreneur to practice it successfully.

2. At Click Commerce Inc. (**www.clickinteractive.com**), a Chicago-based software design firm, founder Michael Ferro Jr. says he has found a way to bring out the best in his workers: punish them. How? Ferro has what he calls the "penalty box," which simply is a temporary stint in the company's sales department offices. Programmers who are burned out or acting overly arrogant get sent to the penalty box. Part of the punishment is that the person is required to wear professional business attire instead of the usual jeans and T-shirt. (That usually results in some good-natured teasing of the person.) Instead of writing software, the person is sent out to call on customers—after a few hours' coaching by the sales staff.

   Explain Ferro's approach to motivation using the following theories: expectancy theory, reinforcement theory, and goal-setting theory. What do you think the positive motivational aspects of such an approach might be? Negative motivational aspects? Do you think Ferro's approach is good or bad? Explain.

   Sources: Company Web site (**www.clickinteractive.com**), June 24, 2002; and L. Brown, "Spare the Rod ..." *Forbes*, May 18, 1998, pp. 76–78.

3. "Good economic conditions are a double-edged sword for restaurant operators." So says the senior director of research for the National Restaurant Association (**www.restaurant.org**). A booming economy means more people

have more spending money to eat out and are doing so more frequently. However, that same economy shrinks the available labor pool.

Form small teams in class. Your team is getting ready to open its first restaurant. Getting and keeping talented people is going to be crucial to your venture's success. Given the realities of the economy as described above, explain how you will successfully manage the HRM issues (getting people on board and keeping them on board) and the motivational issues. Come up with a bulleted list of specific suggestions for each of these important people issues.

4. Workforce diversity is important for organizations. Research the topic of workforce diversity. Compile a bulleted list of important points about diversity. Then, write a paper explaining these implications for entrepreneurs. Be sure to focus on the "people" implications.
5. Interviewing is one of the employee selection techniques that most entrepreneurs think is easy and that they can do without much preparation. However, preparation is the key to successful interviews. In this assignment, you're going to interview entrepreneurs about their interviewing processes. Interview three to five entrepreneurs. Ask them to describe their interviewing processes. What types of questions do they typically ask? Do they have job applicants do any special assignments? Have they found anything to be particularly effective while interviewing? When you have completed your interviews, write a report of your findings. Be prepared to share them with your class.
6. The potential for telecommuting—a job in which an employee works at home and is linked to the workplace by computer and modem—is one way that entrepreneurial ventures are attracting potential employees. Research the topic of telecommuting and write a paper explaining its advantages and disadvantages for entrepreneurial ventures.
7. One way for entrepreneurs to add people to an organization is to use college interns. Research the internship program at your school. What are the requirements both for students and for the sponsoring organization? If you can, interview two sponsoring organizations that would be described as entrepreneurial. What have been their experiences with interns? If your school does not have an internship program, use secondary sources to research the topic of student internships.
8. Some experts have said that entrepreneurs should not only appraise their employees' work performance but let their employees appraise the owner's performance. This type of performance appraisal is called 360-degree feedback. Research 360-degree feedback. How is it done? What are the benefits and drawbacks? How might an entrepreneur implement such a program?
9. One of the hardest things that an entrepreneur has to do is to let employees go either through firing or through layoffs. Research the best way to do these HRM activities and write a paper with a bulleted list of suggestions for letting employees go.
10. A popular topic in management these days is emotional intelligence. Research this topic. Then, write a bulleted list of key points about emotional intelligence and what entrepreneurs need to know about the subject.

ENTREPRENEURSHIP IN ACTION CASES

Plumtree Software (www.plumtree.com)

This case can be found at the beginning of Chapter 8.

Discussion Questions

1. Do you think Kim and Reidy have a right to be concerned about the inequality of their relationship with their roommate while at work? Explain.
2. What could Kelman do to make the work situation easier for him and his roommates?
3. Do you think it's a good idea for friends to work together? Why or why not? What suggestions can you make for situations in which friends work together?

Rhino Foods Inc. (www.rhinofoods.com)

Would you agree that an organization is nothing without its employees? If you do, then it would seem that the only sustainable competitive advantage an entrepreneurial organization would have for the future would be its employees, right? That human resource management philosophy has worked quite well for Rhino Foods Inc., a specialty dessert manufacturer located in Burlington, Vermont.

Rhino Foods isn't a big corporation, but it has developed a strong competitive advantage that has enabled it to succeed despite continuing intense competition and other types of external challenges. Although Rhino has had its share of ups and downs, its financial and organizational performance results have been above average. What is the source of Rhino's success? Rhino's founder, Ted Castle, points to the company's workforce. How does Rhino manage its employees? What types of human resource management policies and practices has it implemented?

The company's purpose statement asserts:

> The employees and families of Rhino Foods are its greatest assets. The company's relationship with its employees is founded on a climate of mutual trust and respect within an environment for listening and personal expression. Rhino Foods declares that it is a vehicle for people to get what they want.

The words that make up the purpose statement were chosen very carefully as a reflection of Castle's philosophy about both the role of the organization and the role of the employee. Another human resource management practice that symbolizes Rhino's belief about its employees being the source of its success is the strong use of employee empowerment—letting employees have significant control and say over what jobs they do and how they do them. Finally, Rhino uses an unusual approach to challenging its employees. The company's philosophy is that "employees who challenge themselves personally see a difference professionally too." Employees are encouraged to set and achieve goals no matter how intimidating those goals might be. The point is to challenge employees and show them that they can make things happen on their own.

Discussion Questions

1. What do you think Rhino's philosophy might be regarding the role of strategic human resource management? Explain.

2. On the basis of the information included in this case and on the company's Web site, create a recruitment advertisement for a production line position that Rhino Foods might use.
3. How do you think Rhino Foods motivates its employees? Give specific examples and explain them in terms of the motivation theories described in the chapter.

Sources: Company information from company Web site (**www.rhinofoods.com**), June 21, 2002; T. Castle, "A Creative Way to Avoid Layoffs," *Nation's Business*, August 1997, p. 6; G. Flynn, "Why Rhino Won't Wait 'Til Tomorrow," *Personnel Journal*, July 1996, pp. 36–43; and T. H. Naylor and R. Osterberg, "The Search for Community in the Workplace," *Business and Society Review*, Spring 1995, pp. 42–47.

Whole Foods Market Inc. (www.wholefoodsmarket.com)

Who would have ever thought that an aging hippie could build a successful food empire? Well, not just any food empire, but one built by selling natural foods. John Mackey founded and runs an efficiently operated and brilliantly marketed health-food empire that has tapped into society's yearning for healthy living and eating. His Austin, Texas–based Whole Foods Market Inc. has more than 130 stores across the United States and one in Toronto, Canada. Whole Foods is the market leader in the natural foods retailing industry. Its sales are almost four times greater than its largest competitor. Industry sources estimate that Whole Foods has more than 12 percent market share of the total natural foods retailing industry. With these types of performance measures, the company must be doing something right.

The company's motto—Whole Foods, Whole People, Whole Planet—emphasizes that its vision reaches beyond being just a food retailer. The company believes that its success in fulfilling that vision is measured by customer satisfaction, team member excellence and happiness, return on capital investment, improvement in the state of the natural environment, and local and larger community support. The key to Whole Foods' ultimate success is the collective energy and intelligence of its team members.

The Whole Foods culture is based on teamwork. Each store is made up of an average of 10 self-directed teams—teams in grocery, produce, and so forth. These teams, and only the teams, have the power to approve new hires for full-time jobs. Store leaders screen applicants and recommend them for a job on a specific team, but there has to be a two-thirds approval vote by the team before the individual is hired. Needless to say, with this much responsibility placed on work teams, building and sustaining employee trust is an important goal of Whole Foods Market. The company does this in many ways, such as recognizing how important leisure time, family, and community involvement outside of work are for a rich, meaningful, and balanced life; by encouraging participation and involvement by employees at all levels of the organization; and by recognizing and honoring diversity and individual differences.

Discussion Questions

1. What would be the advantages and drawbacks of letting employee work teams have sole decision-making power over who gets hired?
2. Log onto Whole Foods Web site (**www.wholefoodsmarket.com**). Click on "The Company" and check out the section on The Whole Philosophy.

How would you describe Whole Foods' philosophy for managing people? Do you agree with its philosophy? Why or why not? What could entrepreneurs learn from Whole Foods' approach?

3. How would you explain Whole Foods' approach to employee motivation? Do you think it would work in other types of entrepreneurial organizations? Explain.

Sources: Company information from company Web site (**www.wholefoodsmarket.com**), June 24, 2002, and Hoover's Online (**www.hoovers.com**), June 24, 2002; and W. Zellner, "Peace, Love, and the Bottom Line," *Business Week*, December 7, 1998, pp. 79–85.

Semifreddi's

Semifreddi's is an artisan-bread baker (bakers of specialty bread and bread shaped in unusual and artistic ways) in Emeryville, California. CEO Tom Frainier has built a company whose annual revenues are over $7 million. He describes himself as an "accessible, available, communicative guy." However, language barriers are proving to be a challenge for Tom and his workers, most of whom come from Mexico, Laos, China, Peru, Cambodia, Yemen, and Vietnam. Even though his workers have limited English language skills, Tom feels that he communicates sufficiently well with his diverse workforce.

However, when customers began making comments about the lack of parking on one side of the bakery, Tom did what he always does when there were issues to be discussed. He called an employee meeting. He asked workers not to park in the spaces reserved for customers. Some employees misunderstood and thought that he was telling them not to drive to work. Tom said later that his mistake was talking slowly and loudly and assuming that his employees would understand him. However, the miscommunication over the parking issue was minor in comparison to another of Tom's communication challenges.

Tom is a staunch supporter of open-book management, a management approach that entails regularly "opening up the books—the financial statements" to employees and sharing this information with them in order to make them feel more a part of the business. He recently gathered together employees from different work shifts for a meeting and rattled off a bunch of numbers. Then Tom asked everybody if they understood the information, and all heads nodded in agreement. Tom said later, "I didn't realize they were just being polite." His desire to involve employees by letting them see the financial results wasn't having the intended effect.

Discussion Questions

1. Effective communication is an important part of managing employees. How could Tom have communicated better with his employees? What would you tell other entrepreneurs about effective communication?
2. How might workforce diversity affect the types of employee motivation that entrepreneurs use? What are the implications of workforce diversity for designing effective motivational programs?
3. Could open-book management be considered motivational? Explain.
4. How could Tom be more effective in using open-book management? Give specific suggestions.

Source: M. Hofman, "Lost in the Translation," *Inc.*, May 2000, pp. 161–62.

Lipschultz, Levin, and Gray (www.thethinkers.com)

It's not quite what you would expect at the offices of a certified public accounting firm. But at Lipschultz, Levin, and Gray, LLC, in Northbrook, Illinois, they aren't your typical "bean counters." Instead, Steve Siegel, LLG's managing member, has implemented a number of changes that are strikingly entrepreneurial and also a little bit bizarre!

Every telltale sign of what most people consider boring, dull CPA work has been eliminated. Although the firm still delivers traditional accounting, tax, and audit services, it also launched new business consulting services that have been quite successful. However, Siegel has paid the most attention to developing the creativity, talent, and diversity of its staff so that new knowledge could be acquired and shared without getting hung up on traditional organizational relationships or having employees shut away in corner offices.

None of the firm's employees (called team members) or partners has an office or a desk to call his or her own. Instead, everyone who works at LLG is part of a nomadic group who hauls their work stuff (files, phones, laptops) to a new spot every day. This isn't as difficult as it sounds because each piece of furniture is mounted on casters and rolls around easily. Everywhere you look in the company's office, you see evidence of versatility, comfort, and eccentricity. A miniature golf course is located right in the middle of everything. Because Siegel had long felt that the managing partners ought to be accessible to every other team member and his goal was to get people out of their imposed solitude, the golf course serves this purpose nicely. In addition, Siegel was convinced that people do their best intellectual work in nontraditional, perhaps even idiosyncratic, settings. That's the motivation behind the "open" office design in which professionals could gather—on purpose or by accident—without walls, cubicles, or offices to get in the way. To support this open concept, every space is wired with data ports and telephone jacks. There's even some fun stuff, too! There's a giant, wall-mounted abacus (remember, the image of bean counters) made from steel tubes and bright plastic balls. In addition, when clients and visitors first come in, they're greeted by a "Welcome Wall" with a big-screen television that flashes a continuous slide show of one-liners about business, life, and innovation.

Although part of the reason behind LLG's radical open office design was to save money, a bigger objective was to leverage and showcase the company's intellectual capital. Siegel wanted a place where people who were always in contact with each other actually got smarter. It's an unusual approach. But, for these bean counters, it seems to have worked well.

Discussion Questions

1. What people philosophy do you think Steve Siegel and LLG have? Explain.
2. Do you think LLG's open office concept would be motivating to professional accountants? Explain.
3. What implications does LLG's approach have for bringing people on board and managing people on board? Be as specific as possible.

Sources: Company information from company Web site (**www.thethinkers.com**), June 24, 2002; and N. K. Austin, "Tear Down the Walls," *Inc.*, April 1999, pp. 66–76.

BUSINESS PLAN PRO

EXERCISE 8-1: Your Management Team

Access the Graphico or any other business plan you've developed for any of the previous business plan exercises. This doesn't include any of the sample plans.

- Use the Easy Plan Wizard view to find the section named "Your Management Team," which includes several text topics and the personnel plan table.
- Fill in the personnel plan table. You will be guessing. Make logical, reasonable guesses for the number of people needed and salary and compensation for these people.
- Fill in the related topics. Explain a hypothetical management structure and management strategy for a hypothetical business.

EXERCISE 8-2: Management Strategies in Sample Plans

Use the Business Plan Pro Sample Plan Browser to find and open the following sample plans:

1. Southeast Health Plans. The plan name is "Plan Administration—Health." Its SIC code is 6411.
2. The Athlete's Foot. Athletic shoe store chain. The plan name is "Shoe Store—Athletic—Franchise" and its SIC code is 5661.
3. The Daily Perc. The plan name is "Café—Coffee Kiosks" and its SIC code is 5812.

All three plans were funded and the companies they envisioned were actually established. Read through these sample plans for their Management Team chapters. Compare the management of these different real companies using what you can tell from their original business plans.

CESSI

Fred Cherry, founder and president of CESSI (**www.cessi.com**), returned home with new priorities after being a prisoner-of-war in North Vietnam for seven and a half years. That experience gave him a totally different outlook on society, people, and how we should conduct our business. Disabled as a result of torture and war injuries, Cherry founded a company that concentrates on federal information technology and disability issues. He wanted to do everything he could to help people with disabilities function as normally as possible.

The company holds federal contracts under Section 508 of the Federal Rehabilitation Act, which mandates that any information technology the federal government develops, procures, uses, or maintains must be accessible by people with disabilities. Government agencies are starting to assess where they are in terms of compliance and are starting to make changes in policies and practices, but many still have a long way to go. And that's where CESSI comes in. CESSI plays an important role at the federal government's Assisted Technology Centers, where it operates equipment, demonstrates assisted technologies, helps people decide what assisted technology will best accommodate their disabilities, keeps equipment and software upgraded, and does outreach to federal employees who have disabilities to make them aware of the services offered.

Cherry has surrounded himself with good people. CESSI vice president Sheila Newman has extensive experience in disability policy and services. She brings to her job integrity, honesty, experience, sincerity, and love. Also, the company has long practiced what it preaches by hiring people with disabilities. Cherry says, however, that these individuals weren't hired because they had disabilities but because they could do a good job. He further says that although it's important to make money, the goal of his company is to help. He loves to see his people happy and they are.

Discussion Questions

1. How do you think Cherry's background and experiences shaped his human resource management philosophy?
2. Research the topic of worker disability accommodation. What suggestions can you give to entrepreneurs who want to develop policies and practices that accommodate workers with disabilities?
3. Cherry says that he loves to see his people happy. What are the motivational implications of such a statement? How might motivational programs have to be designed to accommodate workers with disabilities?

Sources: **Company information from company Web site (www.cessi.com), July 10, 2002; and *Business Now* video segment.**

ENDNOTES

1. Company information from company Web site (**www.plumtree.com**), June 20, 2002, and Hoover's Online (**www.hoovers.com**), June 20, 2002; L. Kroll, "R-E-S-P-E-C-T," *Forbes,* July 22, 2002, pp. 184-185; and L. Kroll, "The Plumtree Software Soap Opera," *Forbes,* May 29, 2000, pp. 96–100.
2. J. Pfeffer, *Competitive Advantage through People* (Boston: Harvard Business School Press, 1994); J. Pfeffer, "Producing Sustainable Competitive Advantage through the Effective Management of People," *Academy of Management Executive,* vol. 9, no. 1 (1995), pp. 55–69; and J. Pfeffer, *The Human Equation: Building Profits by Putting People First* (Boston: Harvard Business School Press, 1998).
3. J. B. Arthur, "Effects of Human Resource Systems on Manufacturing Performance and Turnover," *Academy of Management Journal,* June 1994, pp. 670–687; M. A. Huselid, "The Impact of Human Resource Management Practices on Turnover, Productivity, and Financial Performance," *Academy of Management Journal,* June 1995, pp. 635–672; M. J. Koch and R. G. McGrath, "Improving Labor Productivity: Human Resource Management Policies Do Matter," *Strategic Management Journal,* May 1996, pp. 335–354; B. Becker and B. Gerhart, "The Impact of Human Resource Management on Organizational Performance: Progress and Prospects," *Academy of Management Journal,* August 1996, pp. 779–801; M. A. Youndt, S. A. Snell, J. W. Dean, Jr., and D. P. Lepak, "Human Resource Management, Manufacturing Strategy, and Firm Performance," *Academy of Management Journal,* August 1996, pp. 836–866; J. T. Delaney and M. A. Huselid, "The Impact of Human Resource Management Practices on Perceptions of Organizational Performance," *Academy of Management Journal,* August 1996, pp. 949–969; and M. A. Huselid, S. E. Jackson, and R. S. Schuler, "Technical and Strategic Human Resource Management Effectiveness as Determinants of Firm Performance," *Academy of Management Journal,* January 1997, pp. 171–188.
4. M. A. Huselid, "The Impact of Human Resource Management Practices on Turnover, Productivity, and Corporate Financial Performance," *Academy of Management Journal,* vol. 38, no. 3, 1995, pp. 635–872.
5. "Human Capital a Key to Higher Market Value," *Business Finance,* December 1999, p. 15.
6. E. Watters, "Come Here, Work, and Get out of Here ... You Don't Live Here. You Live Someplace Else," *Inc.,* October 30, 2001, pp. 56–61.

7. I. T. Robertson and R. S. Kandola, "Work Sample Tests: Validity, Adverse Impact, and Application Reaction," *Journal of Occupational Psychology,* vol. 55, no. 3, 1982, pp. 171–183; and G. C. Thornton, *Assessment Centers in Human Resource Management,* (Reading, MA: Addison-Wesley, 1992).
8. R. L. Dipboye, *Selection Interviews: Process Perspectives* (Cincinnati: Southwestern Publishing, 1992), p. 180.
9. See R. D. Arveny and J. E. Campion, "The Employment Interview: A Summary and Review of Recent Research," *Personnel Psychology,* Summer 1982, pp. 281–322; M. D. Hakel, "Employment Interview," in K. M. Rowland and G. R. Ferris (eds.), *Personnel Management: New Perspectives* (Boston: Allyn and Bacon, 1982), pp. 192–255; E. C. Webster, *The Employment Interview: A Social Judgment Process* (Schomberg, ON: S.I.P. Publications, 1982); M. M. Harris, "Reconsidering the Employment Interview: A Review of Recent Literature and Suggestions for Future Research," *Personnel Psychology,* Winter 1989, pp. 691–726; A. P. Phillips and R. L. Dipboye, "Correlational Tests of Predictions from a Process Model of the Interview," *Journal of Applied Psychology,* February 1989, pp. 41–52; H. G. Baker and M. S. Spier, "The Employment Interview: Guaranteed Improvement in Reliability," *Public Personnel Management,* Spring 1990, pp. 85–87; and R. C. Liden, C. L. Martin, and C. K. Parsons, "Interviewer and Applicant Behavior in Employment Interviews," *Academy of Management Journal,* April 1993, pp. 372–386.
10. J. Kluger and S. Song, "Pumping Up Your Past," *Time,* June 10, 2002, p. 46.
11. N. D. Bates, "Understanding the Liability of Negligent Hiring," *Security Management Supplement,* July 1990, p. 7A.
12. Information from Training Supersite Web site, **www.trainingsupersite.com**, December 13, 2000.
13. L. R. Gomez-Mejia, "Structure and Process of Diversification, Compensation Strategy, and Firm Performance," *Strategic Management Journal,* vol. 13, 1992, pp. 381–397; and E. Montemayor, "Congruence between Pay Policy and Competitive Strategy in High-Performing Firms," *Journal of Management,* vol. 22, no. 6, 1996, pp. 889–908.
14. See, for example, S. P. Robbins and M. Coulter, *Management,* 7th ed. (Upper Saddle River, NJ: Prentice Hall, 2002); and S. P. Robbins, *Organizational Behavior,* 10th ed. (Upper Saddle River, NJ: Prentice Hall), 2003.
15. A. Maslow, *Motivation and Personality* (New York: McGraw-Hill, 1954).
16. F. Herzberg, B. Mausner, and B. Snyderman, *The Motivation to Work* (New York: Wiley, 1959); and F. Herzberg, *The Managerial Choice: To Be Effective or to Be Human,* rev. ed. (Salt Lake City: Olympus, 1982).
17. J. C. Naylor and D. R. Ilgen, "Goal Setting: A Theoretical Analysis of Motivational Technique," in B. M. Staw and L. L. Cummings (eds.), *Research on Organizational Behavior,* vol. 6 (Greenwich, CT: JAI Press, 1984), pp. 95–140; M. E. Tubbs, D. M. Boehne, and J. S. Dahl, "Expectancy, Valence, and Motivational Force Functions in Goal-Setting Research: An Empirical Test," *Journal of Applied Psychology,* June 1993, pp. 361–373.
18. B. F. Skinner, *Science and Human Behavior* (New York: Free Press, 1953); and B. F. Skinner, *Beyond Freedom and Dignity* (New York: Knopf, 1972).
19. V. H. Vroom, *Work and Motivation* (New York: Wiley, 1964).
20. Based on C. E. Larson and F. M. J. LaFasto, *TeamWork* (Newbury Park, CA: Sage Publications, 1989); and E. Sundstrom, K. P. DeMeuse, and D. Futrell, "Work Teams," *American Psychologist,* February 1990, p. 120.
21. See E. Sundstrom, K. P. DeMeuse, and D. Futrell, "Work Teams"; C. Larson and F. LaFasto, *TeamWork;* J. R. Hackman (ed.), *Groups That Work (and Those That Don't)* (San Francisco: Jossey-Bass, 1990); and D. W. Tjosvold and M. M. Tjosvold, *Leading the Team Organization* (New York: Lexington Books, 1991).
22. P. E. Brauchle and D. W. Wright, "Fourteen Team Building Tips," *Training & Development,* January 1992, pp. 32–34; R. S. Wellins, "Building a Self-Directed Work Team," *Training & Development,* December 1992, pp. 24–28; S. T. Johnson, "Work Teams: What's Ahead in Work Design and Rewards Management," *Compensation and Benefits Review,* March–April 1993, pp. 35–41; V. A. Hoevemeyer, "How Effective Is Your Team?" *Training & Development,* September 1993, pp. 67–71; S. G. Cohen and G. E. Ledford Jr., "The Effectiveness of Self-Managing Teams: A Quasi-Experiement," *Human Relations,* January 1994, pp. 13–43; and J. Panepinto, "Maximize Teamwork," *Computerworld,* March 21, 1994, p. 119.
23. D. M. Enlen, "Team Goals: Aligning Groups and Management," *Canadian Manager,* Winter 1993, pp. 17–18; and A. M. O'Leary, J. J. Martocchio, and D. D. Frink, "A Review of the Influence of Group Goals on Group Performance," *Academy of Management Journal,* October 1994, pp. 1285–1301.
24. K. M. Eisenhardt, J. L. Kahwajy, and L. J. Bourgeois III, "How Management Teams Can Have a Good Fight," *Harvard Business Review,* July–August 1997, pp. 77–85.

9 MANAGING GROWTH AND OTHER ENTREPRENEURIAL CHALLENGES

LEARNING OBJECTIVES

After reading and studying this chapter, you should be able to:

1. Describe the various ways organizational growth can be measured.
2. Discuss the various strategies for growing an entrepreneurial venture.
3. Explain the key challenges in pursuing growth.
4. Describe what issues an entrepreneurial venture might face in restrained and rapid growth.
5. Tell how entrepreneurs might recognize downturn situations and factors that contribute to declines.
6. Discuss the strategies an entrepreneur might use in dealing with downturns.
7. Describe the reasons an entrepreneur might wish to exit an entrepreneurial venture.
8. Explain what's involved with exiting an entrepreneurial venture.
9. Discuss the various business valuation methods.
10. Describe how minority- and women-owned entrepreneurial ventures can deal with problems.
11. Discuss the special challenges of family businesses.
12. Explain how entrepreneurs can successfully manage their personal lives.

ENTREPRENEURSHIP IN ACTION

As the brightly-colored and animated JesterBot robot moves around, it brings broad smiles to the faces of disabled kids during their weekly physical therapy exercises. The JesterBot is a robot designed by Corinna Lathan, cofounder of AnthroTronix (**www.anthrotronix.com**).[1] With a masters degree in aeronautics and astronautics and a Ph.D. in neuroscience, all from MIT, Lathan is one smart lady. The robot she designed allows children with physical disabilities to experience a sense of play and control as they exercise. How? The child wears a hat, wristbands, or legbands embedded with sensors and transceivers that send motion and voice data to JesterBot. JesterBot is equipped with a CPU that processes the data, sends it to a data port, and relays it on to a computer, where therapists and teachers can assess the child's range of motion. This type of therapeutic device can be a significant asset to the child's development. However, Lathan is finding that

Growth is what distinguishes an entrepreneurial venture. However, as our chapter-opening case illustrates, growth doesn't come easily. Growing ventures have challenges and issues to deal with in order to be effective and efficient. In this final chapter we're going to discuss managing growth and other entrepreneurial challenges. These "other" challenges include the issues faced during organizational performance downturns, harvest and exit decisions, problems encountered by minority and women entrepreneurs, and issues faced by family businesses. In addition, we're going to look at some of the personal life choices and issues with which entrepreneurs must deal.

MANAGING GROWTH

Growth. It's a natural and desirable outcome for entrepreneurial ventures. In fact, it's part of our definition of entrepreneurship. Remember how we defined entrepreneurship—the process whereby an individual or group of individuals uses organized efforts and means to pursue opportunities to create value *and grow* by fulfilling wants and needs through innovation and uniqueness, no matter what resources are currently controlled. Entrepreneurial ventures pursue growth.[2] An organization that isn't growing but instead is staying the same isn't entrepreneurial. Growing successfully doesn't necessarily occur randomly or by luck. Successfully pursuing growth typically requires an entrepreneur to manage all the challenges associated with growing. That's what we're going to look at in this section—managing growth. We first need to look at how growth is defined and measured.

Introduction

What is growth? When an organization is growing, what does it mean? As it relates to entrepreneurial ventures, **organizational growth** is any increase in the level, amount, or type of the organization's work and outputs. It involves expanding, enlarging, or extending what the venture does. For instance, in our chapter-opening case, Corinna Lathan wanted to grow her company by ramping up production, tripling the size of the staff, and increasing sales and marketing efforts. This idea of growth as increases in size or coverage is a common one. But another dimension to growth encompasses a spirit of vitality and energy.[3] An organization that's growing is vibrant and flourishing. It's striving to be excellent. There's a level of excitement about what is being accomplished in the organization and a strong desire on the part of organizational members to be part of

growing her company isn't child's play.

AnthroTronix, founded in July 1999, is currently located in the business incubator at the University of Maryland. It's focusing on the therapeutic toys market, which Lathan estimates at $2 billion. Toy companies like Mattel and Hasbro have avoided this market, though, because it's so R&D-intensive. But that's what Lathan and her associates do best. Making it go, however, means ramping up production, tripling the size of the staff, and increasing sales and marketing efforts. The biggest hurdle to growing—funding. If Lathan doesn't get the $3 to $5 million in financing she needs, it's going to be difficult for AnthroTronix to get JesterBot in the hands of those who can benefit from it most.

it. So although growth does involve increases and expansions in what the organization does, it also involves a feeling of and a commitment to being all that we can be and being the best that we can. Now that we have a better understanding of what growth is, how is it measured?

A number of variables have been used in measuring organizational growth.[4] The most common measures are financial—increases in sales or revenues, increases in venture capital, increases in profitability, or other financial measures. But growth has also been defined by the number of customers, products, locations, employees, or any other characteristic that could be quantified. As you can see, it's easier to measure growth, if you can quantify the factor. It doesn't matter what the factor is. In fact, it should be one that's important to your specific type of entrepreneurial venture. So look closely at your entrepreneurial venture. Decide how you are going to measure whether your business is growing. Will it be by number of clients served, number of outlets opened, types of products offered, or what? Also, define what financial measures you will use to evaluate whether the growth strategies are working. Will it be sales (revenues), profit, or some combination or variation of these? It doesn't matter which measure(s) you use, but it *does* matter that you use some factors to measure growth that are appropriate for your type of business. Now that we know something about what growth is and how to measure it, we need to look at how to pursue organizational growth—that is, the various growth strategies.

Pursuing Growth

The best growth strategy is a well-planned one.[5] Ideally, the decision to grow doesn't come about spontaneously, but instead is part of the venture's overall business plan. Rapid growth without planning can be disastrous. Do make growth part of your business planning, but don't be overly rigid in your planning. Your plans should be flexible enough to exploit unexpected opportunities that arise. You *want* your entrepreneurial venture to grow. But how? What are some ways that you can grow your business?

One approach to pursuing growth identifies four possible strategies based on combinations of current and new products and customers.[6] Exhibit 9-1 illustrates these various combinations. Let's briefly discuss each option.

EXHIBIT 9-1 Organizational Growth Strategies

Customers \ Products	Current	New
Current	Product–customer exploitation	Product development
New	Customer development	Product–customer expansion

The **product–customer exploitation strategy** describes attempts to increase the sales of current products to current customers. Under this strategy, the entrepreneur might use incentives to get current customers to buy more of the venture's product(s) or might advertise other uses for the product(s). There are a variety of ways to try to get current customers to buy and use more of the current product(s). In fact, that's the primary job of the venture's advertising and marketing function.

The **product development strategy** involves creating new products for use by current customers. A new product may include improved or modified versions of existing products. In addition, new features, options, sizes, and ingredients are often used in developing new products for current customers. For example, in our chapter-opening case, AnthroTronix could add other therapeutic toys to its product line. These would be new products created for current customers.

The **customer development strategy** describes attempts to sell current products to new customers. New customers might come from additional geographic areas or market segments not currently served. For instance, Day Runner, the retail leader in the personal organizer market, developed a line of organizers aimed at 6- to 12-year-olds, a market segment to whom it had not sold previously. This is an example of market development—a current product aimed at new customers. The decision to sell globally would be another example of market development because the venture is moving into additional geographic areas with its current products.

The final growth strategy is termed **product–customer expansion**. Under this approach, the venture attempts to expand both into new products and new customers. This approach tends to be one of the riskiest growth strategies because you're dealing with both new products and new customers. However, it can be a way to continue growing.

These strategies are the ones typically used by entrepreneurial ventures pursuing growth. Actually, they describe what an entrepreneurial venture has to do in order to grow. If you want to increase sales revenues, you must develop new products, pursue new customers, or both. If you "do it right"—that is, effectively and efficiently—revenues and profits should grow also! What's involved with "doing it right"? The key challenges for an entrepreneur in organizing for growth include finding capital, finding people, reinforcing organizational controls, and strengthening the organizational culture.

Entrepreneurs in Action

David Hartstein, CEO of KaBloom (**www.kabloom.com**) wants to grow his company—quickly. He initially planned to do this by opening eye-catching European-style flower shops everywhere—sort of a Starbucks-like strategy. The advantage of such a growth approach is that you're everywhere and growing quickly. However, the drawback is that it takes a lot of financing, and you're seen as running local flower shops out of business. To diminish that negative image and to jump-start the company's growth, Hartstein decided that franchising was a better answer. A franchising consultant hired by the company says, "There's no question that you can expand faster through franchising because you're not using your own capital." Because of its service aspect, KaBloom is likely a good candidate for a successful franchising strategy.

Sources: Company information from company Web site (**www.kabloom.com**), June 26, 2002; and J. H. Maxwell, "Daisy Chain," *Inc.*, April 2002, p. 22.

Organizing for Growth

Having enough capital is a major challenge facing growing entrepreneurial ventures. The money issue never seems to go away, does it? It does take capital to expand. If you want to open new locations or markets or if you want to continue innovating new products, it's going to take capital. You have to decide how much capital is necessary and where the capital is going to come from. Is this the time you'll attempt an initial public offering of stock? Do you have the cash reserves on hand to support your growth? Will you have to go through traditional—or even nontraditional—financing channels? The process of finding capital for pursuing growth is much like going through the initial financing of the venture. However, at this time, hopefully you have a successful track record to back up your request. If you don't, it may be extremely difficult to acquire the capital you need to finance growth. That's why we said earlier that the best growth strategy is a planned one. Part of that planning should be how growth will be financed.

Another important issue that a growing entrepreneurial venture needs to address is finding people. If you're opening additional locations, increasing sales of current products, or innovating, producing, and selling new products, you're going to need additional employees to do the work. We know from Chapter 8 that finding talented, competent, and capable people is a challenge in itself. When the venture is growing quickly, the challenge may be intensified because of the time constraints involved. It's important to plan, as much as possible, the numbers and types of employees you're going to need to support the increasing workload as your entrepreneurial venture grows. Also, it may be necessary to provide additional training and support to employees to help them handle the increased pressures associated with a growing organization.

Another challenge that growing entrepreneurial ventures face is reinforcing already established organizational controls. Maintaining good financial records and financial controls over cash flow, inventory, customer data, sales orders, receivables, payables, and costs should be a priority of every entrepreneur—whether pursuing growth or not. However, it's particularly important to reinforce these controls when the entrepreneurial venture is expanding. It's all too easy to let things "get away" from you or to put off doing them when there's an unrelenting urgency to get things done—like, for instance, when sales orders are coming in so quickly that they're not checked for accuracy. Here's a personal example of why controls are so important during periods of organizational growth. During a recent holiday season, I ordered some merchandise from a well-known online e-commerce retailer. When I received my merchandise, someone else's order was with my shipment. Fortunately, that person's packing slip was wrapped around the merchandise so I went ahead and sent it on to that individual. However, what if that packing slip hadn't been there? Or what if I hadn't wanted to take the time and money to ship it on to that person? There would have been additional expense on the part of the organization to resend the merchandise, and there would probably have been one dissatisfied customer because of all the hassle to get the merchandise she had ordered. Rapid growth—or even slow growth—does not excuse the need to have effective controls in place. In fact, it's particularly important to have established procedures, protocols, and processes and to use them. Even though you'll never entirely eliminate mistakes and inefficiencies, at least you can ensure that every effort is being made to do business effectively and

FYI

When Success Is Failure

How can success ever be failure? You're probably thinking to yourself that success was supposed to be something entrepreneurs strived to achieve. Yet, a history of success can actually make you a failure. How? When you're focused on past successes, you can miss new opportunities or changing conditions. Here are some suggestions for not allowing past successes to lead to failure.

Reward contrarian opinions. Encourage honest criticism of ideas, plans, and strategies. This doesn't mean criticizing a person, but does mean honestly evaluating a person's ideas and work product.

Reduce the risk of all-or-nothing outcomes. If the future of your venture rests on more than one product, strategy, or plan, you'll be better able to get rid of those that are not worthwhile.

Keep in mind that change is a continual reality. Even though predicting the future is impossible, prepare for changes by monitoring the external environment and by having plans in place to deal with change.

Don't assume that when some idea fails that you're a failure, too. People often define themselves by their successes. If one of your ideas doesn't work out, that doesn't automatically make you a loser. What it should do is make you better the next time.

Source: S. Berglas, "Know When to Fold," *Inc.*, March 1998, pp. 31–32.

efficiently. Part of this emphasis on controls and accountability arises from the venture's culture, which is the last challenge we need to discuss associated with managing organizational growth.

When a venture is growing, it's important to create a positive, growth-oriented culture that enhances the opportunities to achieve success, both organizationally and individually. This sometimes can be difficult to do, particularly when changes are happening rapidly. However, employees' values, attitudes, and beliefs—that is, the organizational culture—that are established and reinforced during these times are critical to the entrepreneurial venture's continued and future success. Exhibit 9-2 lists some suggestions that entrepreneurs might use to ensure that their venture's culture is one that embraces and supports a climate in

EXHIBIT 9-2 Suggestions for Achieving a Supportive Growth-Oriented Culture

- *Keep the lines of communication open.* Employees need to be informed about major issues.
- *Establish trust* by being honest, open, and forthright about the challenges and rewards of being a growing organization.
- *Be a good listener.* Find out what employees are thinking and facing.
- *Be willing to delegate duties.* You cannot continue to make every decision.
- *Be flexible.* Although planned growth is desirable, be flexible enough to change your plans.
- *Provide consistent and regular feedback.* Let employees know the outcomes—good and bad.
- *Reinforce the contributions of each person* to the venture's ultimate success. People like to be recognized for the efforts they're putting forth.
- *Continually train employees.* It's important to enhance employees' capabilities and skills.
- *Maintain the focus on the venture's vision and mission.* The organizational vision and mission are the reasons the venture is in business.
- *Establish and reinforce a "we" spirit.* A successful growing entrepreneurial venture takes the coordinated efforts of all the employees.

Entrepreneurs in Action

Convergys (**www.convergys.com**) is a company that's growing fast *and* not sacrificing customer service. It's a good thing, because service is Convergys's business. If you've ever dialed a 1-800 number to reach an organization's customer-service department, chances are you've talked to a Convergys employee. Convergys provides customer services for numerous companies. How is it growing? Its core growth is coming from providing specialized customer service offerings—for instance, having the ability to take calls in 30 languages and having agents who specialize in handling calls for a single company. The company is also branching in new directions. One area of growth is taking over the work of calculating and processing cellular and cable-TV bills for phone and cable companies. Convergys is also starting to handle human resource functions such as benefits administration for large global corporations. Even though the company is growing rapidly, CEO Jim Orr knows how important it is to keep his employees focused on servicing customers.

Sources: Company information from company Web site (**www.convergys.com**), June 27, 2002, and Hoover's Online (**www.hoovers.com**), June 27, 2002; and C. Fishman, "Fast Growth, Great Service," *Fast Company*, December 2001, pp. 44–46.

which organizational growth is viewed as desirable and important. Keeping employees focused and committed to what the organization is doing is crucial to the ultimate success of the venture's growth strategies. If employees don't "buy into" the direction the entrepreneurial venture is headed, it's unlikely the venture's growth strategies will be successful. This shared acceptance of what the organization is doing and how it is doing it will be important to the company's performance. Having a culture that upholds and supports the venture's growth activities is an ongoing challenge in effectively managing that growth. However, even if an entrepreneur successfully manages the challenges associated with growing the venture—that is, finding capital, finding people, reinforcing organizational controls, and strengthening the organizational culture—some special issues are associated with strategies of both restrained and rapid growth.

At the two extremes of growth—restrained versus rapid—the entrepreneur must be prepared to deal with some unique challenges. Restrained growth means making difficult choices about what to do, when to do it, and how much to do. Do you pass up some opportunities because you're not prepared to exploit them, or are you potentially forfeiting a financial gold mine? Do you deliberately choose to limit your venture's financial gains now so that you can better position it for the future? These are tough decisions to which there are no easy answers. Although the decision to grow slowly can be a good one, there are some drawbacks to restraining growth.[7] One is that it might be more difficult to hold on to talented people. Employees who are drawn to the excitement of a rapidly growing entrepreneurial venture might get bored or frustrated if there's not that impas-

FYI

Gazelles

David Birch, a researcher at Cognetics (**www.cognetics.com**) bestowed the term *gazelles* on fast-growing companies. His widely adopted definition: "a gazelle has to grow at least 20 percent a year for four years, from a base of at least $100,000 in revenues." That translates to a doubling in size over that four-year period.

Many misconceptions abound about gazelles. What are those misconceptions and the realities? One misconception is that gazelles are all in high-tech fields. The reality is that close to 30 percent of gazelles are in wholesale and retail trade and another approximately 30 percent are in services. Only about 47 percent of gazelles on the *Inc. 500* list were in computers or electronics. Another misconception is that gazelles get venture capital (VC). The reality is that most gazelles don't get any formal VC at all. Only about 5,000 companies got VC funding in 2000 and there were some 350,000 businesses that could be considered gazelles. Another misconception is that gazelles are all young organizations. The reality shows from Birch's research that as a group, gazelles are somewhat older than small companies in general. Nearly 20 percent of gazelles have been in business 30 years or more. Another misconception is that gazelles are all small. The reality: As a group, gazelles encompass companies of all sizes. The final misconception about gazelles is that they operate in national or international markets. The reality is that some gazelles do go national or global, but most don't. Many gazelles serve local markets.

Sources: "The Gazelle Theory," *Inc. State of Small Business 2001*, pp. 28–29; and "Birch's Bestiary," *Inc., State of Small Business 2001*, p. 29.

sioned level of innovative energy and a continual challenge of their skills and abilities. A venture following the path of restrained growth also may find itself quickly getting out of touch with changing technology and customer trends. This could lead to a deterioration of capabilities in product innovation, customer service, marketing, or in any of the other organizational functional areas. If not managed appropriately, this could lead to the venture's eventual demise. The key to successfully pursuing a path of restrained growth is planning for it. Growing slowly doesn't have to mean no passionate energy, no excitement, or no future. Instead, restrained growth can help an entrepreneur establish a solid foundation for the continued and future success of the venture.

The other extreme growth situation that presents challenges for entrepreneurs is rapid growth. When an entrepreneurial organization is growing at exponential rates, the entrepreneur has some unique issues to deal with. Finding capital and people can be particularly difficult and frustrating. Efficiently managing cash flow, inventory, and other organizational areas becomes exceptionally important. Expanding a company rapidly doesn't mean just coping with the same problems on a larger scale.[8] It entails understanding, adjusting to, and managing a whole new set of challenges. Rapid growth can produce an organization that's much more complex than before. More sophisticated management, processes, and procedures may be needed. The venture's infrastructure will have to change to support the demands of a rapidly growing business. It can be chaotic, frustrating, and at times, overwhelming. But the rewards, and not just the financial ones, can be exhilarating. The key to successfully managing explosive growth, just like

Rapid Review

- ✔ Define organizational growth.
- ✔ What does the concept of growth include other than increases in size or coverage?
- ✔ What variables have been used to measure organizational growth?
- ✔ Why is it important to be able to quantify a measure of organizational growth?
- ✔ Describe the best growth strategy.
- ✔ What are the four possible growth strategies?
- ✔ What does an entrepreneur have to do to organize for growth?
- ✔ Describe the challenges in restrained growth and in rapid growth situations.

restrained growth, is also planning for it. Although some unexpected opportunities may arise that could not be foreseen or predicted, the best way to exploit the explosive growth without the organization falling victim to chaotic out-of-control frenzy is to prepare for it. Have plans in place for securing financing, hiring employees, reinforcing organizational controls, and reinforcing a growth-oriented organizational culture. Even though it's not possible to eliminate every problem associated with rapid growth, you can effectively manage the problems so that you're maximizing the gains and minimizing the risks.

Organizational growth. It's a desirable and important goal for entrepreneurial ventures. What happens, though, when things turn sour—when the growth strategies don't result in the intended outcomes and, in fact, result in a decline in performance? What challenges are there in managing business downturns? That's what we're going to look at in the next section.

MANAGING DOWNTURNS

Nobody likes to fail. Although some might choose to do so for whatever reasons, most entrepreneurs would not deliberately choose to fail. But organizational performance declines—downturns—happen. The entrepreneurial venture is in trouble and something needs to be done or it won't be able to achieve high levels of success, or even in the worst-case scenario, may not survive. How can these down-

Entrepreneurs in Action

Katie B. Tyler, owner of Tyler II, a Charlotte, North Carolina-based interior construction company, is no stranger to dealing with downturns. She survived her first one in the mid-1980s, but just barely. When the economy started showing signs of meltdown in 2001, she immediately swung into action. How? Tyler first talked to her bank about doubling her line of credit. She then increased her business development budget by 50 percent, thinking that it was going to be important to continue developing new business leads. In addition, she promoted her office manager to client-relations manager to make sure that current customers remained satisfied. Plans for a new headquarters were put on hold. Smart entrepreneurs know that downturns can be managed successfully, but it takes being prepared.

Source: J. Friend, "Batten Down the Hatches," *Business Week Frontier,* February 5, 2001, pp. F8–F10.

turns be successfully managed? The first step is recognizing that a crisis is brewing, and the next step is dealing with the situation. Let's look first at recognizing crises.

Recognizing Crisis Situations

An entrepreneur should be alert to the warning signs of a business in trouble. Exhibit 9-3 illustrates some signals of potential performance decline.[9] One of these signals is inadequate or negative cash flow. Although an occasional cash-flow crisis can be triggered by a variety of factors such as seasonal business fluctuations, customers that pay late or not at all, or major equipment breakdowns, what we're concerned about here is the continual cash-flow shortage. When an organization's cash-flow position is chronically inadequate or negative, it's an indication that performance is heading downhill.

Another signal of potential performance decline is an excessive number of employees. How do you know if there is an excessive number of employees? Some entrepreneurs track trends in performance measures such as sales revenue per employee or profits per employee. If these trends worsen, it can be a sign that organizational performance is declining.

Unnecessary and cumbersome administrative procedures may be another sign that performance is declining. Processes and procedures are supposed to help the flow of work go more smoothly, not make it more difficult.

Fear of conflict or taking risks could be particularly critical signs of potential performance decline in entrepreneurial ventures. Why? Conflict (that is, *productive* conflict, not destructive conflict) and risk taking are cornerstones of entrepreneurial vitality. Continual experimentation and questioning the status quo are particularly important in an entrepreneurial venture that's going to be successful. When a venture's employees fear conflicts and disagreements or when they become too cautious in trying new and different things, it can be a signal that performance may soon deteriorate.

EXHIBIT 9-3 Signals of Potential Decline in Organizational Performance

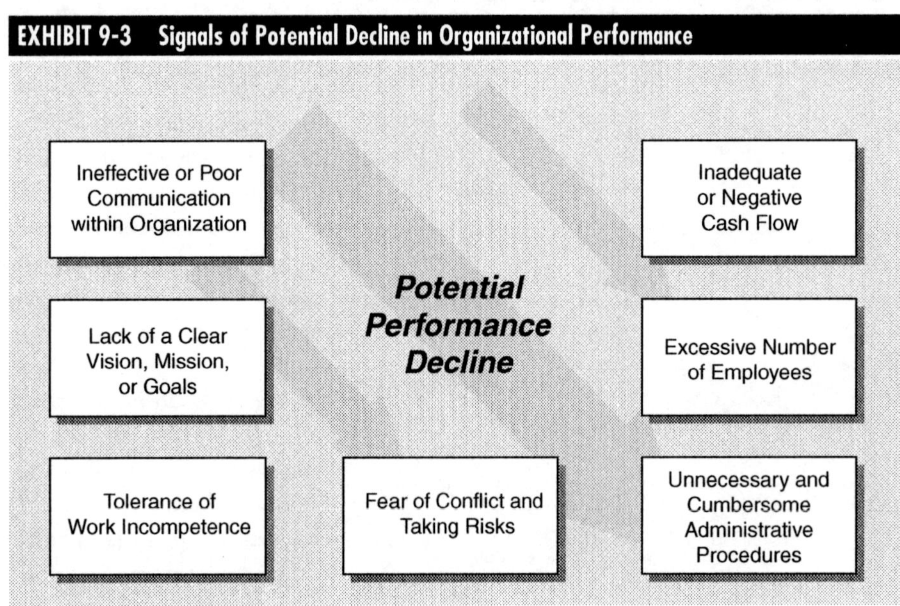

Another signal of potential performance decline is tolerance of work incompetence. It's absolutely foolish to allow incompetent employees to remain in an organization. They're not contributing to and, in fact, in the worst-case scenario, may actually be detracting from, the organization's work. If this type of work incompetence is tolerated, organizational performance will soon suffer.

Lack of a clear vision, mission, or goals may signal a decline in organizational performance. We discussed in earlier chapters the importance of having a clear, specific, and accepted organizational vision, mission, and goals. Without these guiding statements, there will be no coherent direction or coordination to what employees are working on. Then, how can employees know what they're supposed to be doing and whether what they're doing is what's expected? With no clear direction, organizational performance will suffer.

The final signal of potential performance decline as shown in Exhibit 9-3 is ineffective or poor communication within the organization. When employees aren't sharing information, good *and* bad, their attempts to coordinate work efforts will suffer because no one knows what anyone else is doing and no one is trying to learn from coworkers' experiences. This communication breakdown ultimately will lead to individual and organizational performance declines.

Another perspective on recognizing performance declines revolves around what is known as the **"boiled frog" phenomenon**.[10] The "boiled frog" is a classic psychological response experiment. In one case, a live frog that's dropped into a boiling pan of water reacts instantaneously and jumps out of the pan. But, in the second case, a live frog that's dropped into a pan of mild water that is gradually heated to the boiling point fails to react and dies. A small firm may be particularly vulnerable to the "boiled frog" phenomenon because the entrepreneur may not recognize the "water heating up"—that is, the subtly declining situation. When changes in performance are gradual, a serious response may never be triggered or may be done too late to do anything about the situation. So what does the "boiled frog" phenomenon teach us? We need to be alert to the signals that our venture's performance may be worsening. Don't wait to react until the water has reached the boiling point.

Now that we've discussed the signs of organizational performance decline, we need to look at some of the factors that may be contributing to the declining performance. Exhibit 9-4 illustrates some of these possible causes of organizational decline. Each of these possible causes is an indicator that someone—ultimately, the entrepreneur—isn't paying attention. For example, decisions to overexpand or expand too rapidly indicate poor judgment. If the organization has inadequate financial controls or if costs are out of control or too high, the entrepreneur isn't being an effective decision maker. Likewise, there's no excuse for not anticipating new competitors or shifts in customer demand. Although entrepreneurs don't have crystal balls that give them all the answers, they should—as we dis-

EXHIBIT 9-4 Possible Causes of Organizational Decline

- Inadequate Financial Controls
- Uncontrollable or Too High Costs
- New Competitors
- Unpredicted Shifts in Customer Demand
- Slow or No Response to Significant External or Internal Changes
- Overexpansion or Too Rapid Growth
- Culture Clash

cussed in Chapters 2 and 3—systematically scan and evaluate the external environment for significant trends and changes. There's simply no excuse for an entrepreneur not to be aware of what's happening in the external environment. That's being a poor manager. In addition, entrepreneurs who are slow to respond or who never respond to significant changes in their external and internal situations are doing a poor job of managing the venture. Inertia can be a kiss of death in the dynamic and complex competitive environment faced by most entrepreneurial organizations. Finally, when an organization's culture is in turmoil and has turned hostile, employee productivity suffers. Employees stop putting out any effort on behalf of the organization as a whole and do just what's required to get by in their jobs—an attitude that's lethal to the company's performance.

What the entrepreneur does after recognizing the problems is crucial to the venture's future. The decisions made and the actions taken by the entrepreneur at this point can help solidify or doom the business. It's obvious that *something* needs to happen. But what? That's what we're going to look at next.

Dealing with Downturns, Declines, and Crises

Although an entrepreneur hopes never to have to deal with organizational downturns, declines, and crises, there may come a time when he or she must do just that. After all, nobody likes to think about things going bad or taking a turn for the worse. But that's exactly what you should do—think about it before it happens.[11] It's important to have an up-to-date plan for dealing with bad times. It's just like mapping out exit routes from your home in case of a fire. You want to be prepared before an emergency hits. What should this plan focus on? It should provide specific details for controlling the most critical and fundamental aspects

FYI

Preparing for the Worst

As an intelligent entrepreneur, you read news periodicals and you listen to news reports to keep up on what's happening. What if the economists begin predicting an economic downturn? What would you do? What *could* you do? Are there steps you can take to protect your entrepreneurial venture? Financial experts say, "Yes, there are!" The first thing they recommend is *not to over-worry.* Instead, review your venture's financing structure and business plan. Make sure that you've covered important details. If you have a bank line of credit, check for any clauses that might permit cancellation in an economic downturn and consider re-negotiating the loan. The next suggestion is to *think conservatively.* Make cash flow a priority. Build up a cash reserve. Look at your balance sheet and if you are carrying too much debt, use some cash to pay it down. Their next recommendation is *don't wait to lock in financing.* If you had been planning new financing, finish it up now, while the loan terms are still fairly flexible and borrowing rates low. You might also want to think about refinancing old debt to take advantage of the current rates. Finally, *stretch out the time.* Look at your current debt structure. If you have shorter-term debt, replace it with longer maturities. Consider borrowing against any real estate owned to get a 20- to 25-year loan. When economic conditions improve, you can always pay down these long-term loans.

Source: H. Rosenberg, "Shoring Up Your Finances Is a Capital Idea," *Business Week Enterprise,* November 9, 1998, pp. ENT4–ENT6.

of running the venture—cash flow, accounts receivable, costs (expenses), and debt. Beyond having a plan for controlling the venture's critical inflows and outflows, what specific actions might entrepreneurs take in dealing with downturns, declines, and crises? We can look to the strategic management literature for some guidance in dealing with these situations.

Entrepreneurs can use two main types of strategies to halt the organization's declining performance in an attempt to return it to more positive performance levels. The first strategy is called a **retrenchment strategy**, which is a common short-run strategy designed to address organizational weaknesses that are leading to performance declines. In a retrenchment situation, the venture may not necessarily have negative financial returns. Although it may have had some times when revenues didn't cover expenses, this isn't the typical sign that an organization needs to retrench. Instead, the usual situation for retrenchment is that the business hasn't been able to meet its goals in whatever performance areas are being measured. Revenues and profits may be declining but aren't necessarily negative. However, the entrepreneur needs to take some actions to reverse the slide or the venture may soon face significant performance declines. *Retrenchment* is a military term that describes situations in which a military unit "goes back to the trenches" in order to stabilize, revitalize, and prepare for entering battle again. That's pretty descriptive of what entrepreneurial organizations must do, as well, in retrenching. The organization's decision makers must stabilize operations, replenish or revitalize organizational resources and capabilities, and prepare to compete once again in the marketplace battlefield.

The second type of strategy an entrepreneur might use is a **turnaround strategy**, which is a strategy designed for situations in which the organization's performance problems are much more serious, as reflected by its performance measures. Financial results are negative and other measures of performance are usually seriously declining as well. In a turnaround situation, the organization is facing severe external and internal pressures. In this type of situation, something must be done or the organization may well find itself forced out of business.

Implementing both retrenchment and turnaround strategies is dependent primarily on two actions: cutting costs and restructuring. Retrenchment typically will not involve as extensive a use of these actions as a turnaround strategy will. The retrenchment strategy may, in fact, require only selected cost cutting to get organizational performance back on track. Let's look at each of these actions more closely.

Cutting costs is an action to bring the venture's financial performance results back in line with expectations. You want to avoid cutting costs in critical areas that contribute to the venture's competitive advantage, however weak that advantage may be. Instead, the intent in cutting costs is to revitalize the organization's performance (retrenchment) or to save the organization (turnaround).

To cut costs, an entrepreneur can either implement across-the-board cuts (all areas of the venture) or selective cuts (selected areas of the venture). Obviously, in a turnaround situation, the cost cuts need to be more extensive and comprehensive.

What are some ways to cut costs? Entrepreneurs should look closely at work tasks and activities to see if there any wastes, redundancies, or inefficiencies that could be eliminated. They should also determine if there are resources that could be eliminated or used more efficiently. One study of small firms facing downturns proposed that effective cost cutting should focus on carefully managing the costs in the research and development and product development functions.[12] But, the tendency for most entrepreneurs is to start slashing advertising and marketing costs because you can usually see immediate results from these actions. However, this same study of how businesses dealt with downturns also found that it can be counterproductive to overemphasize cost cutting in advertising and sales-related areas.[13] In general, if additional cuts are needed to keep performance from declining further, the entrepreneur may have to look at reducing or eliminating certain work tasks and activities or even entire departments, which is part of what the next option—restructuring—is all about.

Restructuring is the other option an entrepreneur might use in retrenching or turning around the venture. One restructuring action might be **reengineering**, which is a radical redesign of the organization's business processes.[14] Reengineering forces the venture's decision makers to question traditional assumptions and approaches. You throw out everything you know and believe about the way your business operates and start from scratch. Can the work processes be designed better—that is, to be more efficient and effective? Although this type of radical and drastic change may be necessary to get the venture back on track, it's not an easy thing to do and may not have the desired effect.

Downsizing is another restructuring action that involves laying off employees from their jobs. Downsizing can be a quick way to cut costs, but simply cutting the number of employees without some type of analysis of where employee cuts might be most beneficial is dangerous.[15] Downsizing is a serious decision. Numerous issues are associated with a decision to downsize an organization, both for the individuals who will be laid off as well as for those who will remain with the organization. Any downsizing actions should be approached carefully and with some thought.

Another restructuring action is **bankruptcy**, which involves dissolving or reorganizing a business under the protection of bankruptcy legislation. It's typically the result of significant performance declines for which other restructuring or cost-cutting actions have had little effect. What happens when an organization "goes bankrupt"? With the passage of the Bankruptcy Reform Act, business firms were encouraged to reorganize (Chapter 11 bankruptcy) rather than liquidate their assets (Chapter 7 bankruptcy).[16] Therefore, the aftermath of filing for bankruptcy depends on which type is used. An organization in Chapter 11 bankruptcy reorganizes its debts and is protected from creditors collecting on their debts until such time as the business can emerge from bankruptcy. An organization in Chapter 7 bankruptcy will have its assets liquidated by a bankruptcy court, with the proceeds used to pay off all outstanding debts. Although bankruptcy

Rapid Review

- ✔ What are some signals of potential performance decline? What factors might be contributing to a performance decline?
- ✔ Explain the "boiled-frog phenomenon" and how it relates to recognizing performance declines.
- ✔ How is the retrenchment strategy different from the turnaround strategy?
- ✔ What two actions are used to implement retrenchment and turnaround strategies?
- ✔ How can costs be cut?
- ✔ What is reengineering? What is downsizing?
- ✔ Explain the bankruptcy option.

may not be a preferred option, if a venture's turnaround strategy hasn't worked, it may be the *only* option open to the entrepreneur.

The final action an entrepreneur might use in restructuring is exiting the business. However, exiting the business isn't used only in situations when performance is declining. We're going to discuss the exit decision and all its aspects next.

EXITING THE VENTURE

Getting out of an entrepreneurial venture might seem a strange thing to discuss in a book devoted to explaining and championing the development and management of a thriving, growing business. However, there may come a point when the entrepreneur decides it's time to move on. That decision may be based on the fact that the entrepreneur hopes to capitalize financially on the investment in the venture—called **harvesting**—or that the entrepreneur is facing serious organizational performance problems and wants to get out, or even on the desire of the entrepreneur to focus on other pursuits (personal and/or business). The issues involved with making the exit decision effective and successful are choosing a proper business valuation method and knowing what's involved in the process of selling a business.

Business Valuation Methods

"If you value your business . . . value your business."[17] Knowing what your entrepreneurial venture is worth is important. All sorts of events could trigger the need for a valuation. (See Exhibit 9-5.) For instance, it's particularly important when exiting the business to get an accurate and fair valuation of its worth. However, setting a value on a business can be a little tricky. In many cases, the entrepreneur has sacrificed much for the business and sees it as his or her "baby." Calculating

Entrepreneurs in Action

Steve Christini had invented a clever design for a two-wheel-drive bicycle. After obtaining a patent, getting financing, building prototypes, and putting together a distribution deal to sell the bikes, Christini faced a choice: get additional financing to build the bikes himself or sell his business. He chose to sell the business to a large bike company. But he won't be pedaling off into the sunset with his cash. Instead, he'll be running his own small group of engineers and product developers as a tiny unit of the well-financed large company. Although selling out and staying on may seem like the worst of both worlds to many entrepreneurs, it was a perfect solution for Christini. He viewed the sale of his company as a long-term investment to help take his business to the next level rather than as a get-rich-quick exit strategy.

Source: E. Neuborne and M. Perton, "Selling Out," *Business Week Frontier,* November 6, 2000, pp. F38–F46.

EXHIBIT 9-5 Why the Need for a Business Valuation?

Business Valuation

- Selling the Business
- Entering Bankruptcy
- Getting a Divorce
- Breaking Up a Partnership
- Creating a Company Stock Distribution Plan
- Doing Estate or Gift Planning
- Planning for an Initial IPO
- Conducting a Major Strategy-Planning Initiative
- Disputing an IRS Audit
- Seeking Outside Investors
- Applying for Credit or a Loan

Source: Based on J. A. Fraser, "What's Your Company Worth?," *Inc.*, November 1997, p. 111.

the value of the baby based on objective standards like cash flow or some multiple of net profits can sometimes be a shock. For a true and accurate value of your entrepreneurial venture, you'll want to get a comprehensive business valuation prepared by professionals. What are some of the approaches that might be used to place a value on a business?

Because there are many approaches to valuing a business, the approach used usually depends on what's accepted practice in the industry. Valuation techniques generally fall into three categories: (1) asset valuations (2) earnings valuations, and (3) cash flow valuations.[18]

Asset valuations are also known as book value because they're based on the value of the assets as listed in the books or financial statements. The argument for asset valuations is based on the fact that it's the assets of a business that allow it to generate income so the assets reflect the organization's true value. However, many experts contend that asset valuations aren't appropriate because a business with high earnings and low asset value is worth more than a business with low earnings and high asset value. This brings us to an approach that uses earnings as a base for the valuations. These are based on the belief that an organization's value derives from the earnings stream generated. However, the decision here is what earnings measure is the most appropriate—gross sales, projected earnings, some multiple of net profit, or some derivation of these? Although earnings valuations do focus on the ability of the business to generate earnings, the challenge is choosing which earnings measure represents the business's value most appropriately and fairly.

The last method of business valuation is based on the cash flow of the business. In this approach, you're focusing on the amount and timing of cash returns to establish a value of the business. Although this approach provides an indication of the actual cash return provided to the owner—as opposed to valuing the assets of the business or the earnings potential—determining which cash-flow measure is most appropriate (net cash flow, cash-flow multiple, timing of cash flow) can be a problem. The key to business valuation is knowing your options and getting good professional advice.[19]

Although establishing a venture's value can be a challenge, this is just the first consideration in the process of exiting a business. Let's take a closer look at the other factors in the process.

Important Considerations in Exiting the Venture

We've already looked at what is typically the hardest part of preparing to exit a business—valuing it. However, there are some other factors that should be considered.[20] First of all, you want to *be prepared.* Because you never know when you might be approached by someone interested in buying your business or when

Questions to Ask When Selling

When the time comes to sell your business, you should ask yourself certain questions. Asking these questions forces you to think about important issues associated with both the process of selling and the aftermath of the sale. Here are the questions:

- Why am I selling?
- Is this the best time to sell?
- What type of advisor should I hire?
- What valuation method would be best?
- Who's the best buyer?
- What should the terms of sale specify?
- What should I do with the sale proceeds?
- How involved will I be with the business after the sale?

Source: T. Gutner, "Putting Your Company on the Block," *Business Week*, January 26, 1998, pp. 96–97.

circumstances might dictate your exiting the business, you should have on hand a good business plan and at least three to four years of audited financial statements. Next, decide *who will sell the business.* Although you may feel like you know the ins and outs of your business better than anybody else, stop and consider if selling the business is really your area of expertise. It makes more sense to use someone whose expertise is selling businesses. Like a successful real-estate agent, a good business broker knows where the buyers are, what they're looking for, and how to make your venture stand out from others. Another factor to take into account is the *tax considerations.* The choice of legal business organization decided back when you organized the venture (sole proprietorship, partnership, LLC, or whatever) will have an impact on the tax consequences of selling the venture. Look at these consequences carefully before deciding how to sell your business. Another factor to consider is *screening potential buyers.* Even if you use a professional business broker to screen out unqualified buyers, you also should carefully screen the prospective purchasers to make sure you're not disclosing any business secrets to potential competitors. Finally, you must decide whether to *tell employees.* The drawback of telling employees is that they might be uncertain about their future and either look for another job or be distracted from their work, making them less productive, which may affect both individual and organizational performance. On the other hand, the drawback of not telling is that employees may find out anyway and be upset over the lack of communication with them about such an important issue. Only the entrepreneur will have a feel for what is the best thing to do in his or her particular situation.

The process of exiting the entrepreneurial venture should be approached as carefully as the process of launching it. If you're selling the venture on a positive note, you want to realize the value you have built in the business. If you're selling the venture because of declining performance, you want to maximize the potential return. The next topic we want to look at involves some of the challenges facing minority- and women-owned businesses.

Rapid Review 

- ✔ Why might an entrepreneur decide to exit a business?
- ✔ What is harvesting?
- ✔ What events could trigger the need for a business valuation?
- ✔ Describe each of the three categories of business valuation techniques.
- ✔ What factors should be considered when preparing to exit a business?

MINORITY- AND WOMEN-OWNED BUSINESSES

Minority- and women-owned businesses are playing a significant role in the surge of entrepreneurial activity in the United States. Minority-owned businesses are a rapidly growing segment of the U.S. economy. By 1997 (the most current information available) there were an estimated 3.25 million minority-owned businesses in the United States.[21] This number was up 168 percent from 1987. These businesses generated $591 billion in revenues (an increase from 1987 of 343 percent) and employed nearly 4.5 million workers (an increase from 1987 of 362 percent). Women-owned businesses also increased, although not as dramatically. The Center for Women's Business Research says that the number of majority-owned, privately held women-owned businesses increased 14 percent, to 6.2 million in 2002, from 5.4 million in 1997.[22] These businesses employed almost 9.2 million people and generated over $1.15 trillion in sales. The Small Business Administration Office of Women's Business Ownership has different numbers for women-owned businesses: 9.1 million women-owned businesses employing 27.5 million people and contributing $3.6 trillion to the economy.[23] The difference in numbers is likely due to the fact that the Center for Women's Business Research focuses on privately held women-owned firms. However, no matter what numbers are used, it's clear that the contributions of minority and women entrepreneurs to the economic prosperity of the United States cannot be ignored. Yet, these entrepreneurs face significant challenges as they attempt to manage their ventures successfully. Let's look at some of these challenges.

Challenges Faced by Minority and Women Entrepreneurs

Being an entrepreneur—let's add being a *successful* entrepreneur—is hard. Face it. It's not easy to research, plan, organize, launch, and manage an entrepreneurial venture successfully. With all the challenges to being a successful entrepreneur, facing additional obstacles because of your race or your gender seems unbelievable. Yet, minority and women entrepreneurs do face all sorts of challenges.

EXHIBIT 9-6 Limited Access to Capital for Minorities

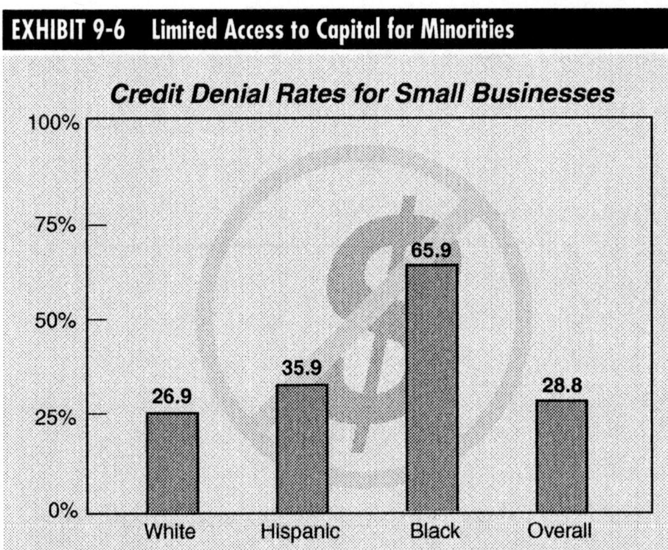

Source: Republished with permission of *The Wall Street Journal*, from "Small-Business Lenders Rebuff Blacks," by J. Tannenbaum, *Wall Street Journal*, July 7, 1999.

Punita Pandey, the founder of netCustomer.com Inc. (**www.netcustomer.com**) seemed to have it all. With an MBA from Berkeley and an engineering diploma from one of India's most prestigious schools, she also had an impressive work background. However, when she went looking for funding for her new business, she ran into a brick wall. The main challenge minority and women entrepreneurs face is getting the funding they need to start and grow their businesses.[24] Access to capital is a serious issue for minority and women entrepreneurs. A study by the Federal Reserve System of small-business financing patterns found that minority small-business owners have an extremely hard time getting credit.[25] Exhibit 9-6 shows the disparity in credit denial rates for small-business owners. The statistics are quite telling! Women also have problems getting credit lines for starting and growing their businesses. Studies have shown that they have lower levels of available credit than do their male counterparts.[26] Minority women business owners face credit obstacles that white female business owners do not. So, the capital problem is definitely real and very serious. Access to capital to start and grow their entrepreneurial ventures is an extremely difficult barrier for minority and women entrepreneurs.

Another challenge that women entrepreneurs, particularly, face is the conflict between work and family. Although this issue can, and does, arise for male entrepreneurs also, it's especially acute for women because many child-rearing and family responsibilities fall on them. Being an entrepreneur can be a 24–7 (24 hours a day, 7 days a week) commitment. Running a successful business often means finding a healthy balance between work and family lives. (We'll discuss this issue again when we get to the section on being an entrepreneur and managing your personal life.)

Finally, minority and women entrepreneurs face the challenges of managing business growth successfully, finding and keeping qualified employees, and keeping up with technology and other marketplace changes. These are challenges that *all* entrepreneurs face. However, because of society's slowly changing attitudes toward minority and women entrepreneurs, they often face additional hurdles in dealing with these issues. Some people may question whether women or minorities have what it takes to succeed and be reluctant to go to work for them, or these entrepreneurs may have to prove themselves before some people will do business with them. Although these attitudes may seem out of place in today's multicultural and increasingly tolerant society, these issues are real for minority and women entrepreneurs. However, even with the additional challenges they face, minority and women entrepreneurs are "making it." Let's take a look at some of the government programs and other help available to minority and women entrepreneurs.

Making It as a Minority or Woman Entrepreneur

Assistance is available for minority and woman entrepreneurs who want to make their ventures successful. One of the best sources for free advice and assistance is

Entrepreneurs in Action

Microlenders may be the answer to entrepreneurs who are shut out of the usual financial channels because of a language barrier, a lack of education, or a poor credit history. Microlenders provide small loans (typically less than $25,000) to existing and prospective small-business owners. Boston-based Accion USA is one of the largest microlenders. Robin Ratcliffe, vice president of communications for Accion says that many of her company's clients are low-income immigrants or minorities who start businesses to supplement or replace minimum-wage jobs.

Source: "Small Change," *Inc.'s State of Small Business*, May 29, 2001, p. 99.

SCORE—the Service Corps of Retired Executives, a nonprofit organization and resource partner with the U.S. Small Business Administration that is dedicated to helping entrepreneurs in the formation, growth, and success of small business nationwide.[27] These retired business executives (some SCORE counselors are still employed) consult with and advise business owners on any and all issues faced in running a business. These people have "been there and done that," and their years of business experience and exposure to all sorts of problems are invaluable to entrepreneurs who need this advice and assistance. It's a wonderful program that can help guide minority and women entrepreneurs as they launch and manage their businesses. SCORE can be contacted through its Web site (**www.score.org**).

Another government program that minority and women entrepreneurs may tap into is the Small Disadvantaged Business (SDB) program, run under the direction of the U.S. Small Business Administration. The SDB program was created in the 1980s to help businesses owned by socially and economically disadvantaged individuals get a bigger share of federal contracts. Because of ongoing issues with fraud in determining who fit the guidelines of being socially and economically disadvantaged, the program has implemented stricter guidelines on race- and gender-conscious federal contracting goals. These new regulations make the application more complex. Yet, the Small Business Administration says these changes will ensure that federal contracts go to the business owners who really need SDB help. This might be a program worth checking into, especially if you're interested in selling to the government.

The U.S. Small Business Administration has also committed itself to promoting business ownership by minority groups by increasing the share of SBA-backed business lending to them. This includes the SBA's 504 program, which provides long-term fixed-rate financing for major fixed assets. This type of assistance is welcomed by minority entrepreneurs, who may have trouble getting capital from traditional sources to start or grow their businesses.

Another government agency that provides assistance to minority businesses is the Minority Business Development Agency (MBDA), which is part of the U.S. Department of Commerce. (Check out its Web site at **www.mbda.gov**.) This agency was created specifically to foster the creation, growth, and expansion of minority-owned businesses in the United States. Assistance in business plans, marketing, management, technical areas, and financial planning are provided in centers located in areas with large concentrations of minority populations and large numbers of minority businesses.

Women entrepreneurs can tap into the Women's Business Center program, an offshoot of the U.S. Small Business Administration program. The WBC program helps female entrepreneurs focus their business plans through courses, workshops,

The Grey Zone

Judy Y. Wiles, founder and owner of First Impressions, Inc., a restaurant and food-service employment agency based in Detroit, has dealt with the prejudices of being a minority in her own way. When she sends someone to close a deal with a suburban client, she sends one of her employees who is white, even though one of her minority workers did the client research, helped develop the sales strategy, and made the initial contact. Judy herself is a minority female. What do you think about this? Do you agree with her approach? What are the advantages and drawbacks to her approach?

Source: A. B. Henderson, "Black Entrepreneurs Face a Perplexing Issue: How to Pitch to Whites," *Wall Street Journal*, January 26, 1999, pp. A1+.

and mentoring services, and provides access to capital and financing sources. (Check out its Web site at **www.onlinewbc.gov**, which provides free information, interactive tools, personalized counseling, topic forums and newsgroups, an extensive data resource guide, market research, and much more.)

Another thing that successful minority and women entrepreneurs are doing that's not part of any government-sponsored program is creating their own reliable network of business advisors.[28] Although entrepreneurship may seem to be a solitary pursuit, it's not. Having a network of people whose advice you trust can be a definite asset. It's valuable to be able to tap into the collective knowledge and wisdom of individuals who can get you to question, to shake things up, or to think differently.

As you can see, there are many sources of help and assistance for minority and women entrepreneurs who want to make it. Although we've described just a few here, there are numerous others. Another group of entrepreneurs that faces unique challenges are family businesses. That's what we want to look at next.

FAMILY BUSINESSES

In some respects, every entrepreneurial venture is a family business, started and managed by an entrepreneur who's a member of some "family." But that's not really what is meant by a family business. What *is* a family business? Entrepreneurship researchers have noted some problems with defining a family business—such as how many members of the family have to be involved, what roles do family members have to play, how many generations does it have to cover, and so on.[29] We're going to define a **family business** as one that includes two or more members of the same family who control, are directly involved in, and own a majority of the business.

As one person said, "When it works right, nothing succeeds like a family firm. The roots are deep, embedded in family values. The flash of the fast buck is replaced with long-term plans. Tradition counts."[30] A family business can be an exceptionally successful and satisfying experience for all involved. However, family businesses face serious challenges in the pursuit of being successful entrepreneurial ventures.

Challenges Faced by Family Businesses

Although family businesses are an integral part of our economy, they face two major challenges. The first challenge is the complex interrelationships that arise, and the second challenge is management succession.

In a family business, the boundaries between work and family are quite complex and multifaceted. Entrepreneurship researchers have proposed that three overlapping perspectives influence the decisions and actions of family business owners.[31] One perspective is from that of the family wanting to take care of family members. Another perspective is from that of ownership, where the concern is doing what's in the best interests of the business. And, then there's the perspective of management, where the concern is doing what's in the best interests of other organizational employees. How can these three overlapping perspectives create challenges? For example, let's take a fairly common business situation—a family member needs a job. From the family perspective, you probably would see this as

FYI

All in the Family

Quentin J. Fleming, author of *Keep the Family Baggage Out of the Family Business* (Simon & Schuster, 2000) says there are seven deadly sins that can run family businesses into the ground or make them less valuable in the marketplace. What are these seven deadly sins and the consequences for the family business?

1. "It's the same old song." The consequence for a family business is that family members' childhood behaviors and beliefs follow them into the business.
2. "We're one big, happy family." The consequence for a family business is the failure to recognize that running a business requires different practices than running a family.
3. "They may have become adults, but they'll always be my children." The consequence for a family business is that parents are unable to accept and treat their grown children as adults.
4. "You're not loyal to this family if you insist on being selfish." The consequence for a family business is this failure to acknowledge and treat family members as individuals.
5. "Father knows best." The consequence for a family business is that founders usually possess dominating personalities and may be totally consumed by the business.
6. "Maybe it will go away if we ignore it." The consequence for a family business is that ignoring problems only adds to their destructive potential.
7. "Tell me about your childhood." The consequence for a family business is that children often enter the business before resolving childhood issues, which can affect the way that they work.

Source: P. Hernan, "Finding the Exit," *Industry Week*, July 17, 2000, pp. 55–61.

a chance to help out someone in the family. From the ownership perspective, you might be concerned about the impact of an additional employee on organizational expenses and profits. From the management perspective, you might be concerned about the effect of the hiring on other nonfamily employees. Each of these perspectives is valid, but which takes precedence? Keep in mind that we're not trying to imply that these three perspectives have to be mutually exclusive all the time. But, there will be situations in which the decision or action is going to be influenced more strongly by one of the perspectives. The entrepreneur behind a successful family business needs to be able to balance all three perspectives simultaneously in managing the complex interrelationships.

The second major challenge facing family businesses is management succession. Studies of family firms have shown that, on average, only 30 percent of family businesses survive to the second generation, and only 10 percent make it to the third generation.[32] Those are pretty alarming statistics, aren't they? Many entrepreneurs dream of passing on the family business to their children or other family members. Unfortunately, human traits such as jealousy, lack of interest, or incompetence may get in the way.

Even though complex interrelationships and management succession pose challenges to the family business entrepreneur, there are ways to make it work. Let's look at some of the things that family businesses can do to be successful.

Making It as a Family Business

One study of successful family firms discovered some "best practices" characteristics that these businesses shared.[33] One of these characteristics was *a focus on business, not family, needs.* Although a family business entrepreneur may feel an obligation to take care of all family problems, the business shouldn't be used as a family employment agency or loan center. Another best practices characteristic was *reinvestment in the business.* Profits should be plowed back into building and sustaining the business. The company's revenues shouldn't be "sucked dry" just to support family wants and desires. Next, *use caution with family.* Think about and discuss relevant issues of employment and money before hiring family members or giving out generous severance packages to family members. Try to forestall potential conflicts by being cautious. Another characteristic of these successful family businesses was *delegation of decisions.* A family business entrepreneur who makes all decisions and never delegates will be viewed as a control freak. Decisions should be delegated to those who are capable of making them. The final best practices characteristic identified was *a big-picture view.* In making decisions, successful family business entrepreneurs considered all stakeholders—from nonfamily employees to local community to family. This supports what we were discussing earlier about balancing the three perspectives—family, ownership, and management—when making decisions and taking action.

The other important thing for family businesses is having a good management succession plan. An effective succession plan will consider six important factors.[34] (See Exhibit 9-7.) These six factors include the role of the owner during the transition; family dynamics, relationships and new roles; income for family members employed in the business and other shareholders; business conditions during transition; treatment of long-term, loyal employees; and tax consequences. Each of these factors affects the choices made during the transition and can influence whether the outcome is smooth, functional, and effective. If no family member wishes to be involved with the business and the decision is made to transfer the business to a nonfamily member, the key question to be answered is ownership—what type and how much (if any) will be retained by the family? These issues do need to be addressed. The main thing in either circumstance—transferring the business to family members or transferring it to nonfamily—is planning ahead. You don't want to wait until something happens and then be forced to make rash and ill-advised decisions.

EXHIBIT 9-7 What Effective Management Succession Plans Should Consider

- The role of the owner during the transition stage
- Family dynamics
- Income for family members employed in the business and shareholders
- Business conditions during the transition
- Treatment of loyal long-term employees
- Tax consequences

A successful and satisfying family business can be a thing of joy for a family. One thing that all entrepreneurs and their families have to deal with, however, is managing the personal demands of being an entrepreneur. We're going to look at this important topic next.

MANAGING YOUR PERSONAL LIFE

Being an entrepreneur is extremely exciting and demanding. There are long hours, difficult demands, and high stress. But, as we've discussed in earlier chapters, being an entrepreneur has many rewards as well. In this last section of the textbook we want to take a look at how to manage your personal life. How can you make it work—that is, how can you be a successful entrepreneur and effectively balance the demands of your work and your personal life?

Making It Work

Entrepreneurs are a special group. They are focused and persistent, hardworking, and intelligent. Because they put so much of themselves into launching and growing their entrepreneurial ventures, many may neglect their personal lives. You will have to make certain sacrifices to pursue your entrepreneurial dreams. However, you can make it work. You can balance your work and personal life. Some suggestions for doing just that follow.

One of the most important things you can do as an entrepreneur to balance your work and personal life is to *become a good time manager*. Prioritize what needs to be done. Use a planner (daily, weekly, monthly) to help you schedule your priorities. Some entrepreneurs don't like taking the time to plan or prioritize, or they think it's a ridiculous waste of time. Yet, identifying the important duties and distinguishing them from those that aren't so important actually makes you a more efficient and effective manager. In addition, part of being a good time manager is delegating to trusted employees the decisions and duties that you don't

Entrepreneurs in Action

Karen Borgnes, president of Seattle-based Pacific Aerotech (**www.pacificaerotech.com**) is a good role model for creating a more sane work environment. She has created a wonderful work life–personal life balance for herself. Having the time to take her daughters to dance class or to serve on two other corporate boards is important to her. However, Borgnes isn't concerned just about balance in her own life; she is sensitive to her employees' personal needs as well. If they want to, they can work four 10-hour days, part-time, or earlier shifts. In addition, all employees get Christmas week off. And, on the first sunny June day (which is a big deal in Seattle), Borgnes has been known to send her employees home early to enjoy the day. Needless to say, employee turnover is low.

Sources: Company information from company Web site (**www.pacificaerotech.com**), June 27, 2002; and R. D. Schatz, "Balance for the Boss," *Business Week Frontier*, October 9, 2000, p. 48.

Rapid Review

- ✔ What type of economic impact are minority and women entrepreneurs having?
- ✔ Describe the main challenges that minority and women entrepreneurs face.
- ✔ What types of programs are available to help minority and women entrepreneurs "make it"?
- ✔ What is a family business?
- ✔ Describe the two main challenges faced by family businesses.
- ✔ What are the best practices characteristics that successful family businesses share?
- ✔ How should an effective management succession plan be developed?
- ✔ What are some suggestions for balancing your work as an entrepreneur and your personal life?

need to be personally involved in. It may be hard to let go of some of the things you've always done, but if you delegate effectively (look back at our discussion in Chapter 8), your personal productivity level will probably rise. Another suggestion for finding that balance is to *seek professional advice* in the areas of business in which you may need it. Although you may be reluctant to spend scarce cash, the time, energy, and potential problems you save in the long run are well worth the investment. Competent professional advisors can provide you information to make more intelligent decisions. Use these professionals' expertise. To achieve that work life–personal life balance, it's also important to *deal with conflicts* as they arise. This includes both workplace and family conflicts. If you don't deal with conflicts, negative feelings are likely to crop up and lead to communication breakdowns. When communication breaks down, vital information may get lost and people (employees *and* family members) may start assuming the worst. It can turn into a nightmare situation that feeds upon itself. So, the best strategy is to deal with conflicts as they come up. Talk, discuss, argue (if you must), but don't avoid the conflict or pretend it doesn't exist. Another suggestion for achieving that balance is to *develop a network of trusted friends and peers*. Having a network of people you can talk to is a good way to think through problems and issues. You might want to develop both a professional network of entrepreneurs and businesspeople and a personal network of friends. The support and encouragement from these groups of people can be an invaluable source of strength for an entrepreneur. The final suggestion for achieving work life–personal life balance is to *recognize when your stress levels are too high*. Entrepreneurs *are* achievers. They like to make things happen. They thrive on working hard. Yet, too much stress can lead to significant physical and emotional problems. You have to learn to recognize when the stress is overwhelming you and do something about it. After all, what's the point of growing and building a thriving entrepreneurial venture if you're not around to enjoy it?

Hopefully, you're just as excited now about entrepreneurship as when you first started reading this book. Keep in mind that being an entrepreneur isn't easy, yet it's one of the most exciting and rewarding paths you can take. Good luck in your pursuit! May your entrepreneurial experiences be all that you dream!

CHAPTER SUMMARY

This summary is organized around the chapter-opening objectives.

1. A number of variables can be used to measure organizational growth. The most common measures are financial, such as increases in sales or revenues, increases in venture capital, increases in profitability, and so forth. Growth can also be defined by measures such as number of customers, products, locations, employees, or other characteristics that could be quantified.

2. Growing an entrepreneurial venture can be accomplished by following one of four strategies that are based on combinations of current and new products and customers. The product–customer exploitation strategy describes attempts to increase sales of current products to current customers. The product development strategy involves creating new products for use by current customers. The customer development strategy describes attempts to sell current products to new customers. The product–customer expansion strategy is an attempt to expand both into new products and new customers.
3. The key challenges for entrepreneurs in pursuing growth are finding capital, finding people, reinforcing organizational controls, and strengthening the organizational culture.
4. The issues an entrepreneur might face in restrained growth are how to keep talented people and how to stay on top of changing technology and customer trends. The issues an entrepreneur might face in rapid growth include finding capital and people and efficiently managing cash flow, inventory, and other organizational areas.
5. The signals of potential performance decline include inadequate or negative cash flow; an excess number of employees; unnecessary and cumbersome administrative procedures; fear of conflict and taking risks; tolerance of work incompetence; lack of a clear vision, mission, or goals; and ineffective or poor communication within the organization. Factors that contribute to organizational decline include inadequate financial controls, uncontrollable or too high costs, new competitors, unpredicted shifts in customer demand, slow or no response to significant external or internal changes, overexpansion or too rapid growth, and organizational culture turmoil or hostility.
6. Entrepreneurs can use two types of strategies to deal with downturns. A retrenchment strategy is a short-run strategy designed to address organizational weaknesses. In retrenching, the organization's decision makers stabilize operations, replenish or revitalize organizational resources and capabilities, and prepare to compete once again in the marketplace. The second strategy is a turnaround strategy, which is a strategy designed for situations in which the organization's problems are much more serious. In this situation, something must be done or the organization may well find itself out of business. Implementing both strategies is dependent on two actions: cutting costs and restructuring. Cutting costs can either be across-the-board or selective. Restructuring options include reengineering, downsizing, bankruptcy, or exiting the business.
7. An entrepreneur might wish to exit an entrepreneurial venture for the following reasons: harvesting (capitalizing financially on the investment in the venture), serious organizational performance problems, or the desire of the entrepreneur to focus on other pursuits.
8. There are two main aspects to exiting an entrepreneurial venture. The first is choosing a proper business valuation method and the second is being prepared for the exit.
9. Business valuation techniques can fall into three categories. Asset valuations (book value) are based on the value of the assets as listed in the books or financial statements. Earnings valuations are based on the value derived from

the earnings stream generated by the venture. Cash-flow valuations are based on the cash flow of the business.

10. Minority and women entrepreneurs face problems that include getting financing (access to capital); resolving conflicts between work and family; managing business growth successfully; finding and keeping qualified employees; and keeping up with technology and other marketplace changes. These entrepreneurs can deal with these problems by getting advice and assistance from sources such as SCORE, the Small Business Disadvantaged program, the U.S. Small Business Administration's 504 program, the Minority Business Development Agency, or the Women's Business Center Program. They can also develop their own reliable network of trusted business advisors.
11. Family businesses face two major challenges: the complex interrelationships that arise and management succession. The complex interrelationships involve three perspectives—the perspective of the family, the perspective of ownership, and the perspective of management.
12. Entrepreneurs can successfully manage their personal lives by becoming good time managers, seeking professional advice in the business areas in which they may need it, dealing with conflicts as they arise, developing a network of trusted friends and peers, and recognizing when stress levels are too high.

KEY TERMS

- *Organizational growth:* Any increase in the level, amount, or type of the organization's work and outputs.
- *Product-customer exploitation strategy:* An organizational growth strategy that describes attempts to increase sales of current products to current customers.
- *Product development strategy:* An organizational growth strategy that involves creating new products for use by current customers.
- *Customer development strategy:* An organizational growth strategy that describes attempts to sell current products to new customers.
- *Product–customer expansion strategy:* An organizational growth strategy that involves expanding both into new products and new customers.
- *"Boiled frog" phenomenon:* A description of a situation in which negative changes in organizational performance are so gradual that the entrepreneur may miss the signs.
- *Retrenchment strategy:* A short-run strategy designed to address organizational weaknesses that are leading to performance declines.
- *Turnaround strategy:* A strategy designed for situations in which the organization's performance problems are more serious, as reflected by its performance measures.
- *Reengineering:* A restructuring action in which an organization's business processes are radically redesigned.
- *Downsizing:* A restructuring action that involves laying off employees from their jobs.

- *Bankruptcy:* A restructuring action that involves dissolving or reorganizing a business under the protection of bankruptcy legislation.
- *Harvesting:* A decision to exit a business based on the fact that an entrepreneur hopes to capitalize financially on the investment in the venture.
- *SCORE (Service Corps of Retired Executives):* A nonprofit organization and partner with the U.S. Small Business Administration composed of retired business executives who consult with entrepreneurs in the formation, growth, and success of their businesses nationwide.
- *Family business:* A business that includes two or more members of the same family who control, are directly involved in, and own a majority of the business.

SWEAT EQUITY

1. *Nanomanagement* is a term used to describe an entrepreneur trying to manage all the details in a small organization. It's a problem that should be addressed before it stifles organizational growth. Why do you think entrepreneurs nanomanage? What suggestions would you make to entrepreneurs for controlling the tendency to nanomanage?

   Source: L. Formichelli, "Letting Go of the Details," *Nation's Business*, November 1997, pp. 50–52.

2. A study of family businesses showed that parents' actions have a direct influence on their kids' becoming entrepreneurs. The findings showed that 32 percent of the sons with entrepreneurial fathers started a business, compared with 12 percent of sons without self-employed fathers. The study also showed that 24 percent of daughters with entrepreneurial mothers also became entrepreneurs, whereas 13 percent of daughters whose mothers weren't self-employed did so. The study also showed that children of entrepreneurs don't start more businesses because they get money from their parents. A more likely explanation is the attitudes that entrepreneurial parents instill in their children, such as the value of being your own boss, and specific talents they pass on.

   Your assignment is to find a father–son or mother–daughter duo both of whom are entrepreneurs. Talk to them about their experiences. Are they in the same line of business? Did the son or daughter always want to be an entrepreneur? What made each (father and son or mother and daughter) want to be an entrepreneur? Do they learn from each others' experiences? Write a paper describing your findings and be prepared to present it to your class.

   Alternative Assignment. Because your access to father–son or mother–daughter entrepreneurs may be limited, here's an alternative assignment that your professor may have you complete. Co-preneurs (husband and wife entrepreneurs) are a special subset of family businesses. Do some research on co-preneurs and the challenges they face. Write a paper that describes those challenges and how co-preneurs are dealing with them.

3. The Gooseberry Patch Company catalog is one of thousands of catalogs mailed annually in the United States. The catalog industry is extremely competitive, and the cofounders behind Gooseberry Patch, Jo Ann Martin and Vickie L. Hutchins, are trying to make good decisions to keep their company growing. Check out their Web site at (**www.gooseberrypatch.com**). Do some research on the direct-marketing industry by going to the Direct Marketing Association Web site (**www.the-dma.org**). Come up with a bulleted list of recommendations you would make to Martin and Hutchins to continue growing their company. Try to be as specific as possible.
4. "Turning down business can help your company grow." What? How can turning away customers help your business grow? A business performance measure called *return on management,* or ROM, explains it all. Read the article "How High Is Your Return on Management?" by Robert Simons and Antonio Davila in the January–February 1998 issue of *Harvard Business Review*. Then write a paper (your professor will tell you the expected length) explaining the concept of ROM and how it relates to entrepreneurship. Be sure to indicate what you see as the advantages and drawbacks of this concept and whether it is still relevant in today's economy.
5. Stress and burnout are serious problems for entrepreneurs. Research the topics of stress and burnout. Focus on finding out what causes stress and burnout for entrepreneurs and how to deal with them. Create a presentation that illustrates the main points you uncover. (Make the presentation with PowerPoint, other software-based transparencies, or posters.) Be prepared to give your presentation in class.
6. A study of family businesses said that family business CEOs have five main concerns about their businesses (the most important concern is listed first): loyalty and commitment of nonfamily managers, succession planning, preserving the family's financial resources, exit from management or ownership, and day-to-day management of family involvement. How does this list relate to what was discussed in the chapter? How could family business entrepreneurs deal with each of these concerns?
7. Many entrepreneurs work out of their homes. But working at home has both advantages and drawbacks. Research this topic and create a bulleted list outlining suggestions for making work at home effective and efficient.
8. "You can't turn around the *Queen Mary* quickly, but you can turn around a kayak very fast." What do you think this quote means as far as an organization's ability to respond to a declining situation? What are the implications for entrepreneurs?
9. Succession planning is especially important in family businesses. Research the topic of succession planning. Create a presentation outlining the key points you find. Be prepared to give your presentation in class.
10. A survey of small business owners found that 38 percent of them had never considered how they will leave their businesses. What are the implications? What would you say to these 38 percent?

ENTREPRENEURSHIP IN ACTION CASES

AnthroTronix (www.anthrotronix.com)

This case can be found at the beginning of Chapter 9.

Discussion Questions

1. If you were Corinna Lathan, how would you measure growth in your business? Why would these measures be important?
2. Do you think slow, cautious growth would be a good strategy in the industry AnthroTronix is in? Explain.
3. AnthroTronix is housed in a business incubator. If your school has a business incubator, find out what services it offers. Write a report summarizing your findings. If your school does not have a business incubator, research the topic of business incubators and write a report summarizing your findings.
4. As a women-owned business, AnthroTronix faces obstacles that other businesses do not. If Lathan came to you for advice, what suggestions might you give her?

Claudia Schiffer

Claudia Schiffer has one of the world's most beautiful and most recognized faces and bodies. Yet, she's not just a pretty face. She's also a very smart entrepreneur. She has built a business venture with revenues believed to be between $8 million and $14 million a year. Her business is herself. She is continually looking at ways to grow her business investment.

Schiffer isn't the first supermodel to recognize the importance of maintaining her "brand." Cindy Crawford, another supermodel, combined good looks with marketing savvy to become a successful entrepreneur. Crawford founded her own company, called Crawdaddy, to oversee her interests, which included a series of successful exercise videos, calendars and other items that carried her photo, and the launch of her own line of makeup. Crawford also teamed up with companies like Blockbuster Video, Kay Jewelers, and Pepsi to become their spokeswoman. In fact, an advertisement for Pepsi running in the summer of 2002 features an older, but still beautiful Crawford. These choices have kept her face and name in the public eye.

Schiffer also recognized the importance of marketing herself in various ways commercially. She, too, has diversified the selling of her image. Like Crawford, she has used calendars, movies, books, television shows, exercise videos, spokesperson contracts, and other means to keep her image out there in the public eye.

However, don't think that building a mini–beauty conglomerate is easy. There are no guarantees that just because you have a famous face and name that your products will sell. For instance, one of Schiffer's partners in the Fashion Café (**www.fashion-café.com**) international chain of theme restaurants, Naomi Campbell, tried to market a music CD and a novel she had written. Both flopped. Industry experts attribute this to the fact that the CD and novel weren't really Campbell's strong areas of expertise. So, even supermodels have to make good decisions about how to grow their businesses.

So to what can Schiffer's success be attributed? Schiffer herself says it's because she's "interested." She's very hands-on and likes to know what's happening both within and outside the business. She's very focused and has a strong competitive desire to remain at the top. In addition, Schiffer is a hardworking individual and a dedicated CEO. She puts in seven day weeks if needed and expects those who work for her to do the same if there are pressing issues and tasks. She also believes that fun is the key to getting herself and her staff to produce the most. But one other thing that characterizes Schiffer's business approach is her caution in her business dealings. She does a lot of research, preparation, and reading the fine print. She also is highly involved in decisions and is almost obsessed with controlling all aspects of her business. Schiffer says, "If I put my own money in, I make sure that I will never lose it."

Discussion Questions

1. What type of growth strategy would you say Schiffer is pursuing? Explain your choice.
2. How would you value a business such as Schiffer's that's based primarily on name and image?
3. What are the advantages and drawbacks of being "obsessed" with controlling all aspects of your business?

Source: D. Carnoy, "Claudia Schiffer," *Success*, August 1998, pp. 52–55.

Colony Beach and Tennis Resort (www.colonybeach.com)

One of the biggest problems for a family business is when the older family member turns over the reins of the business to one of the children but finds it hard to let go of the business that he or she has built. This problem is being played out at the Colony Beach and Tennis Resort in Longboat Key, Florida. Murray Klauber, the Colony's founder and patriarch, may have retired from the presidency and day-to-day operating responsibilities, but he has found it difficult to really let go. Klauber turned over the management of the business to his daughter, Katie Moulton, over 12 years ago. But, his strong and close presence sometimes gets a little *too* close for her comfort. For instance, one morning Mr. Klauber sought out his daughter at breakfast in one of the resort's restaurants to tell her that he thought the maintenance director was doing just a fantastic job. Mrs. Moulton, who had been addressing some unresolved issues with the maintenance director, told her father that she hoped he hadn't told the maintenance director his thoughts. That could have made it extremely difficult for her to address the problems she was having with the person.

Another issue is that Mr. Klauber lives in a suite near the resort's lobby and finds it convenient for "patrolling" the property. But, it's not only Mrs. Moulton who endures the continued attentions of her father. He constantly makes suggestions to Colony employees with his ideas for improving the place. Often, he'll put his thoughts into memos with a red-ink stamp that says, "Do It Now." Klauber doesn't apologize for his actions, but says that, "It's my life's work."

The generational succession issue is getting more difficult for family businesses, particularly because so many founders are living longer and leading more vigorous lives. Says one expert on family businesses, "When they're that energetic, it's hard for them to completely let go of the reins even after they hand them over." The Klauber family is making it work by informally negotiating an understanding that transcends titles, organizational charts, and egos. Mrs. Moulton listens to her father's ideas, but isn't afraid to tell him that they're too off-the-wall. She never intends to have a "showdown" with her father because she understands that he only wants what's best for the business.

Discussion Questions

1. What are the advantages and drawbacks of having the retired founder of a family business stay involved with the business?
2. Based on what this case illustrates, what suggestions might you make to other owners of family businesses?

Source: R. Johnson, "Turning It Over," *Wall Street Journal,* May 24, 1999, pp. A1+.

Blue Nile, Inc. (www.bluenile.com)

Purchasing a diamond engagement ring may be one of the more expensive purchases young adults make. Would you do it online? Well, many people are, and they're purchasing from Blue Nile, the leading online retailer of diamonds and fine jewelry. The company offers luxury-grade jewelry, including loose diamonds, settings, rings (gold and platinum), earrings, necklaces and pendants, bracelets, gemstones (sapphires, rubies, and emeralds), sterling silver jewelry, men's and women's watches, and accessories.

CEO Mark Vadon cofounded the company in 1999 after an unsatisfactory experience purchasing an engagement ring. From the beginning, Blue Nile focused on the "who, what, when, where, and how" of the diamond engagement ring market. What they discovered was that men buy expensive jewelry—not women—and men purchase after getting answers to technical questions. In addition, they found that men want to feel confident about buying, giving, and getting a terrific, quality value. Vadon says that he has built his core business around that group of customers.

As Vadon looks to grow his business, some realities about the jewelry business make it a challenge, especially for an online retailer. One is that jewelry sales tend to be seasonal purchases. Another challenge is the fact that many consumers are reluctant to purchase an expensive product such as jewelry when they can't see or feel it. Then, of course, there's the competition from other online jewelers as well as the brick-and-mortar jewelers. In fact, one of the biggest forces in today's jewelry business is discount retailer Wal-Mart, who's going after the diamond and jewelry market in a big way.

Discussion Questions

1. What types of growth measures might Vadon use in his business? Explain your choices. Why would these measures be important?
2. What types of performance decline signs might an online retailer such as Blue Nile

look for? Are these the same as for brick-and-mortar businesses? Explain.

3. How might Vadon grow his business in light of the challenges facing the jewelry industry in general and an online jewelry business in particular?

Sources: Company information from company Web site (**www.bluenile.com**), February 19, 2002, and Hoover's Online (**www.hoovers.com**), February 19, 2002; and M. S. Foley and T. Melville, "What Men Want," *Success*, April 2001, p. 20.

Thermagon (www.thermagon.com)

Thermal interface products—probably not something with which you're familiar. However, these products help keep important equipment such as computer systems, power-conversion equipment, telecommunications hardware, entertainment products, and automotive electronics cool so they can operate without melting down from the heat generated by the equipment components. Back in 1988, Carol Latham, a staff chemist at British Petroleum, was convinced that polymers (plastic) could help solve the heat problem. However, Latham's bosses didn't share her enthusiasm or excitement. Her appeal for funding to pursue a commercial venture creating polymer-based compounds went nowhere. Rebuffed by her employer, Latham decided to launch a business on her own. With no funding and nothing to sell, but convinced that her basic concept was solid, Latham jumped on the entrepreneurial bandwagon in 1992. She was certain she could develop her idea into an actual product.

As any good entrepreneur should, she drafted (and redrafted) a business plan. With that plan, she was able to raise an initial $70,000 from family, angel investors, and friends. Laboring long hours in her basement using a kitchen blender, cookie sheets, and mixing bowls, she worked on turning polymer-based compounds into commercial products. Soon she had samples of an actual product—superthin polymer sheets designed to fit between computer components. Initial customers, including IBM and Silicon Graphics, loved the product. Now, with those early sales, getting funding wasn't at all difficult. In fact, new investors were fighting to get in.

Now, more than 10 years later, Latham's vision is a company with 12 products sold around the world, approximately 120 employees, and $15 to $20 million in annual revenues. Thermagon supplies thermal solutions that are innovative. Its Web site declares, "If you can imagine it, we can keep it cool." Thermagon has experienced an exciting period of explosive growth and believes that its long-term outlook is rosy.

Discussion Questions

1. Carol Latham is an anomaly. A successful female who has built a thriving entrepreneurial venture in a scientific, high-tech field. To what do you attribute her success?
2. What types of growth challenges might Thermagon experience if it continues its "explosive" growth? How could Latham prepare the company for those challenges?
3. Pretend that you're Carol Latham. What advice would you give other aspiring women entrepreneurs?

Sources: Company information from company Web site (**www.thermagon.com**), June 18, 2002, and Hoover's Online (**www.hoovers.com**), June 28, 2002; and S. Hansen, "You Had Your Chance," *Inc.*, October 30, 2001, pp. 50–55.

BUSINESS PLAN PRO

EXERCISE 9-1: Finish the Graphico Plan

Open Business Plan Pro, retrieve the Graphico business plan file you worked with for several previous exercises. Finish projections for Graphico for the following two years and text necessary to print and publish a complete hypothetical Graphico business plan.

EXERCISE 9-2: Revise the AMT Plan

Open Business Plan Pro, retrieve the AMT business plan file you worked with for several previous exercises (or you can open it from the Sample Plan Browser, as "Computer Hardware – Reseller," SIC code 5040). This plan was originally written in 1995. Revise it to show a hypothetical AMT plan for the present economy and the market conditions in your own town, city, or nearby area. Print and publish the finished plan.

EXERCISE 9-3: Finish Your Own Plan

Use Business Plan Pro to complete your own business plan, for either a hypothetical business you'd like to start, a business you know of because of friends or relatives, or a business that interests you. You may use a business you've used for some of the previous exercises in this book. Print and publish the finished plan.

Sytel

For the past 10 years, 50 to 100 percent every year. That's the growth rate that Sytel (**www.sytel.com**), an aggressive information technology company based in Bethesda, Maryland, has achieved. Sytel's success starts with founder, president, and CEO Jeannette Lee, who came to the United States from Korea at the age of 12. Lee quickly demonstrated a capacity for hard work. As a teen, she worked at a convenience store with 1 day off in nearly 6 years of employment. She says that experience taught her discipline, how to handle stress, and how to manage people. All good lessons that have served her well as she manages her rapidly growing business. As a result of Lee's drive, Sytel has achieved that phenomenal growth rate and a ranking as one of the fastest-growing technology companies in the United States.

Lee has a philosophy that allows her to manage this meteoric growth without sacrificing quality. She says, "I told everyone here what's normal is 40 percent chaos and 60 percent order. In order for us to grow as rapidly as we want, we have to maintain a good balance of both order and chaos." With five divisions serving both government and commercial clients, Sytel now has achieved that critical mass of technology and people to really service customers.

Accomplishing that growth wouldn't be possible without good employees. Lee recognizes that Sytel's employees are the key to its success. She says, "We are fortunate to have smart, dedicated, hard-working people working at Sytel who have been with us for a long time. We take pride in our staff retention rate, which also translates into a very high client retention rate." Sytel still has its very first customer and many of its early employees. Walter Davis, who joined Sytel after a career with some of the nation's largest corporations, says he found a "can-do" attitude at Sytel. He thinks of bigger companies as elephants, but characterizes Sytel as a gazelle—quick, responsive, able to get to target quickly, and able to adjust and adapt to whatever the requirements are.

Discussion Questions

1. How did Lee's background prepare her for growing an entrepreneurial venture?
2. What do you think has contributed to Sytel's ability to grow successfully?
3. How can Lee continue to keep that gazelle-like quality at Sytel as it continues to grow?
4. An interesting thing found on Sytel's Web site (**www.sytel.com**) is a view of its circular organization chart. Take a look at it and describe how you think it has contributed to Sytel's ability to grow.
5. What do you think of Lee's statement about maintaining a good balance of chaos and balance? What are the implications for managing growth?
6. What suggestions would you give to Lee to make sure that she is managing her personal life successfully also?

Sources: Information on company from company Web site (**www.sytel.com**), July 10, 2002; and *Business Now* video segment.

ENDNOTES

1. Company information from company Web site (**www.anthrotronix.com**), June 15, 2002; and N. Ridgway, "Robo-Therapy," *Forbes*, May 14, 2001, pp. 216–218.
2. G. R. Merz, P. B. Weber, and V. B. Laetz, "Linking Small Business Management with Entrepreneurial Growth," *Journal of Small Business Management*, October 1994, pp. 48–60.
3. T. Stevens, "And One to Grow On," *IW*, July 3, 1995, pp. 27–34.
4. Merz, Weber, and Laetz, "Linking Small Business Management with Entrepreneurial Growth."
5. L. Beresford, "Growing Up," *Entrepreneur*, July 1996, pp. 124–128.
6. The discussion of these strategy options has been slightly modified from information found in P. Kotler, *Marketing Management*, 8th ed.(Upper Saddle River, NJ: Prentice Hall, 1994).
7. M. Barrier, "Can You Stay Small Forever?," *Nation's Business*, October 1996, pp. 34R–35R.
8. S. Nelton, "Coming to Grips with Growth," *Nation's Business*, February 1998, pp. 26–32.
9. P. Lorange and R. T. Nelson, "How to Recognize—and Avoid—Organizational Decline," *Sloan Management Review*, Spring 1987, pp. 41–48.
10. S. D. Chowdhury and J. R. Lang, "Crisis, Decline, and Turnaround: A Test of Competing Hypotheses for Short-Term Performance Improvement in Small Firms," *Journal of Small Business Management*, October 1993, pp. 8–17.
11. C. Farrell, "How to Survive a Downturn," *Business Week*, April 28, 1997, pp. ENT4–ENT6.
12. J. K. DeDee and D. W. Vorhies, "Retrenchment Activities of Small Firms during Economic Downturn: An Empirical Investigation," *Journal of Small Business Management*, July 1998, pp. 46–61.
13. Ibid.

14. M. Hammer and J. Champy, *Reengineering the Corporation* (New York: Harper-Collins, 1995).
15. W. McKinley, C. M. Sanchez, and A. G. Schick, "Organizational Downsizing: Constraining, Cloning, and Learning," *Academy of Management Executive*, August 1995, pp. 32–44; and G. D. Bruton, J. K. Keels, and C. L. Shook, "Downsizing the Firm: Answering the Strategic Questions," *Academy of Management Executive*, May 1996, pp. 38–45.
16. C. M. Daily, "Bankruptcy in Strategic Studies: Past and Promise," *Journal of Management*, vol. 20., no. 2, 1994, pp. 263–295; J. P. Sheppard, "Strategy and Bankruptcy: An Exploration into Organizational Death," *Journal of Management*, vol. 20, no. 4, 1994, pp. 795–833; and Y. Chen, J. F. Weston, and E. I. Altman, "Financial Distress and Restructuring Models," *Financial Management*, Summer 1995, pp. 57–75.
17. J. Burton, "Making Sure the Price Is Right," *Business Week Enterprise*, March 29, 1999, pp. ENT10–ENT14.
18. R. W. Price and A. C. Johnson, "The Accuracy of Valuation Methods in Predicting the Selling Price of Small Firms," *Journal of Small Business Management*, October 1997, pp. 24–35.
19. For a concise summary of twelve different business valuation methods, see Price and Johnson (1997), p. 28.
20. D. Rodkin, "For Sale by Owner," *Entrepreneur*, January 1998, pp. 148–153; A. Livingston, "Avoiding Pitfalls When Selling a Business," *Nation's Business*, July 1998, pp. 25–26; and G. Gibbs Marullo, "Selling Your Business: A Preview of the Process," *Nation's Business*, August 1998, pp. 25–26.
21. "Minorities in Business," *Office of Advocacy, Small Business Administration,* (Washington, DC: 2001).
22. "Women-Owned Businesses in the United States, 2002: A Fact Sheet," *National Foundation for Women Business Owners Web Page* (**www.nfwbo.org/key.html**), June 26, 2002.
23. "Online Women's Business Center: About Us," *Office of Women's Business Ownership* (**www.onlinewbc.gov**), June 26, 2002.
24. S. Leibs, "Against the Odds," *IW,* May 1998, pp. 36–40; "Capital Harder to Obtain for Women," *Springfield News Leader,* May 4, 1998, p. 7A; G. Koretz, "Wanted: Black Entrepreneurs," *Business Week*, December 14, 1998, p. 26; J. A. Tannenbaum, "Small-Business Lenders Rebuff Blacks," *Wall Street Journal*, July 7, 1999, pp. A2+; K. Ferguson, "Nothing Ventured," *Business Week Frontier,* July 10, 2000, pp. F28–F34; and S. Coleman, "Access to Capital and Terms of Credit: A Comparison of Men- and Women-Owned Small Businesses," *Journal of Small Business Management,* July 2000, pp. 37–52.
25. Tannenbaum, *Wall Street Journal*, July 7, 1999.
26. "Key Facts," *National Foundation for Women Business Owners Web Page*, (**www.nfwbo.org/key.html**), December 6, 1999.
27. Check out SCORE's Web site at: **www.score.org**.
28. D. Fenn, "A League of Your Own," *Inc. State of Small Business*, 1998, pp. 102–209.
29. R. H. Brockhaus Sr., "Entrepreneurship and Family Business Research: Comparisons, Critique, and Lessons," *Entrepreneurship Theory and Practice*, Fall 1994, pp. 25–38.
30. E. Calonius, "Blood and Money," *Newsweek*, Special Issue 1995, pp. 82–84.
31. F. Hoy and T. G. Verser, "Emerging Business, Emerging Field: Entrepreneurship and the Family Firm," *Entrepreneurship Theory and Practice*, Fall 1994, pp. 9–23.
32. T. W. Zimmerer and N. M. Scarborough, *Essentials of Entrepreneurship and Small Business Management*, 2nd ed. (Upper Saddle River, NJ: Prentice Hall, 1998), p. 17.
33. "How to Avoid a Dysfunctional Family Business," *Business Week Enterprise*, March 2, 1998, p. ENT3.
34. P. Brothers, "Succession Plan Vital for Family Businesses," *The Cincinnati Enquirer*, December 19, 1996, p. S11.

Appendix

SECTION 4

WEB SITES FOR ENTREPRENEURS

The Internet is a treasure trove of information for the new and the experienced entrepreneur. This annotated listing of Web sites is, by no means, complete. The sites included here, though, are a few of the many resources entrepreneurs might use as they research, plan, organize, launch, and manage their ventures. As with any listing of Web sites, the Web site address and information included there can change at any time.

AllBusiness.com: Champions of Small Business

www.allbusiness.com

AllBusiness.com leverages the power of the Internet to be a source for critical business solutions and expertise. AllBusiness.com features sections on forms and agreements, resources and research, business advice, business solutions, e-marketplace, e-seminars, and best of the Web.

American Express Small Business Network

www.americanexpress.com/smallbusiness

The Small Business Network is a community for entrepreneurs. It offers information and resources on financing and growing your business, managing your accounts, connecting with the community, accessing information, and saving on and benefiting from things you use daily.

Benchnet—The Benchmarking Exchange

www.benchnet.com

The Benchmarking Exchange (TBE) is a comprehensive and user-friendly electronic communication and information system designed specifically for use by member individuals and organizations involved in benchmarking and process improvement. TBE provides members with a comprehensive, centralized, and specialized forum for all phases of benchmarking. The site also provides best practice surveys in progress relating to topics such as contract labor, supplier and material management, team-based improvement, organizational chance, facility management, and order fulfillment.

Bloomberg Financial Markets

www.bloomberg.com

Bloomberg.com is a comprehensive financial services and financial management site. The site provides current interest rates, mortgage rates, and currency rates. Finally, Bloomberg provides stock quotes and an audio commentary that allows users to hear from experts.

Bplans.com—The Planning People

www.bplans.com

Bplans.com offers resources on creating business plans, such as the Plan Wizard, which helps users find business-relevant sample plans. The site also provides features such as the business planning resource center and advice for starting a business, marketing your business, and taking your business online.

The Business Forum Online

www.businessforum.com

The Business Forum Online equips emerging businesses and entrepreneurs with two unique resources. An Internal Index offers a compendium of two year's of weekly columns addressing a broad range of issues and opportunities of immediate and practical interest to the owner-manager of the emerging business. An External Index offers wide-ranging links to approximately 100 important informational and professional resources throughout the world to meet the needs of emerging businesses and entrepreneurs.

MoreBusiness—By Entrepreneurs, For Entrepreneurs

www.morebusiness.com

MoreBusiness provides information regarding start-up, running your business, news, and business plans. It provides feature articles, templates, and tools, as well as a marketplace. Users can register to receive a free e-mail newsletter that provides business and product news, tips, articles, and other information to help manage a business.

Business Week Online: Small Business

www.businessweek.com/smallbiz

Business Week Online keeps entrepreneurs up-to-date with recent stories and a news center. The site provides financial, technological, market research, and personal business resources. Business Week also provides services for travel, free e-mail, and a job bank. Finally, the site has a Toolbox of free expert help, a contact search, and free archives.

CEO Express: The Executives' Internet

www.ceoexpress.com

CEO Express provides links to sites regarding daily news and information, business research, industries, office tools, travel, and leisure activities. The site also provides a bookshop, a career center, and feedback. Members can customize CEO Express and suggest additional links. Finally, CEO Express provides information on financial topics, companies, government, international business, statistics, small business, law, cutting edge technology, marketing, and many other business topics.

CIA—The World Factbook
www.odci.gov/cia/publications/factbook
The CIA World Factbook provides country-specific information that is useful for international business owners. Information about geography, people, government, economy, communications, transportation, and military and transnational issues is provided for each country. The Factbook also provides a reference map as well as notes and definitions.

Cross Cultural Communication for Business and Industry
www.bena.com/ewinters/xculture.html
This Web site provides practical tips for those who develop material, services, or products for translation or export. It is produced as a service for the international Internet community and covers topics such as culture and information, document design, technology and infrastructure in target cultures, writing for translation, and internationalization of documentation and Internet communication.

Dow Jones
www.dowjones.com
Dow Jones provides comprehensive coverage of financial topics. The Search function allows users to select topics of interest.

Employee Stock Ownership Plan (ESOP), Stock Options, The NCEO
www.nceo.org
The National Center for Employee Ownership (NCEO) is a private, nonprofit membership and research organization that serves as the leading source of accurate, unbiased information on employee stock ownership plans (ESOPs), broadly granted employee stock options, and employee participation programs. Users can read articles in the library and the columns by leading experts, sample NCEO publications and become involved in workshops, conferences, and other events.

Entrepreneur Magazine
www.entrepreneurmag.com
Entrepreneur Magazine provides feature articles about small business topics. The site also provides small business tools such as an Internet print shop, trade show information, a software library, and free business forms. Other features include information on franchising, business opportunities, money, marketing, management, e-biz, and technology.

Entrepreneurial Edge
www.lowe.org
Entrepreneurial Edge resources include tutorials, a bookstore, electronic documents, researched Internet sites, and an e-mail subscription newsletter. This site also provides an interactive forum for users to compare processes and interact with financial management models. Entrepreneurial Edge is associated with the Edward Lowe Foundation, which creates peer-learning environments for entrepreneurs and provides access to information, solutions, and resources to grow a company.

The Entrepreneur's Mind

www.benlore.com

The Entrepreneur's Mind is a Web resource that presents an array of real-life stories and advice from successful entrepreneurs and industry experts on the many different facets of entrepreneurship and emerging business. Each story in the EM presents in-depth profiles of entrepreneurs and how they grew their successful companies, as well as interviews with industry professionals discussing an aspect of starting and growing a new business venture.

EntreWorld: A World of Resources for Entrepreneurs

www.entreworld.org

EntreWorld is an online information resource for entrepreneurs and supporters of entrepreneurship. EntreWorld provides a solution to information overload on the Web by providing highly filtered information coded by stage of business development. This site provides resources for each stage of a small business: start-up, growth, and entrepreneurship support.

EPI DataZone

www.epinet.org

The Economic Policy Institute (EPI) provides national, state and regional data on historical employment and earnings. Spreadsheet tables can be downloaded.

eWeb

eweb.slu.edu/default.htm

EWeb's mission is to provide support to students and faculty interested in starting, running, and growing businesses—whether you call them entrepreneurial firms, SMEs, small businesses, family businesses, home-based businesses, or new businesses. Entrepreneurs, potential entrepreneurs (including students), and those who consult for or train or educate entrepreneurs will find many resources on this site. EWeb offers book recommendations, business plan help, "how-to" guides, a list of entrepreneurial centers, a list of "core" journals of entrepreneurship, and Ph.D. education resources.

fambiz.com

www.fambiz.com

fambiz.com is the Internet's leading Web site for family business executives and owners. Individuals associated with family businesses will find several resources on this Web site.

Federation of International Trade Associations

www.fita.org

The Federation of International Trade Associations (FITA), founded in 1984, fosters international trade by strengthening the role of local, regional, and national associations throughout North America that have an international mission. This site has an index of Web resources, a global bookstore and publications center, a trade leads hub, a job bank, an international marketing research library, and a directory of export management companies.

FedWorld Information Network Home Page
www.fedworld.gov
In 1992 FedWorld was established by the National Technical Information Service (NTIS), an agency of the U.S. Department of Commerce, to serve as the online locator service for a comprehensive inventory of information disseminated by the Federal Government. What FedWorld can offer is a comprehensive central access point for searching, locating, ordering, and acquiring government and business information.

Forbes Small Business Center
www.forbes.com/smallbusiness
The Forbes site provides information on entrepreneurship topics found in *Forbes* magazine. You can also sign up for news briefs by e-mail.

Forum for Women Entrepreneurs
www.fwe.org
The Forum for Women Entrepreneurs (FWE) is the leading entrepreneurial forum for women in technology and life science start-ups. FWE offers programs and services that accelerate women entrepreneurs' ability to launch and build world-class companies. Founded in 1993, FWE has offices in the Bay Area and provides women-founded businesses with timely information through a strong online community; access to top-tier funding sources; and connections to a high-caliber community of entrepreneurs, investors, and service providers—resources they need to bridge the venture capital funding gap.

The Foundation for Enterprise Development
www.fed.org
The Foundation for Enterprise Development (FED) is a nonprofit organization that provides leading-edge equity compensation and employee ownership strategies to thousands of entrepreneurs and key executives worldwide who are making critical decisions to improve their companies' bottom lines. The FED site also has a selection of publications and other resources.

FRED—Economic Research
research.stlouisfed.org/fred
FRED provides historical U.S. economic and financial data, including daily U.S. interest rates, monetary and business indicators, exchange rates, balance of payments and regional economic data for Arkansas, Illinois, Indiana, Kentucky, Mississippi, Missouri, and Tennessee. Database categories include business and fiscal data, monthly commercial banking data, monthly monetary data, gross domestic product and components, monthly interest rates, and monthly reserves data.

GovCon
www.govcon.com
GovCon is an online community for government contractors. The site provides current business opportunities and profiled contractors of the week. GovCon has a small business resource center and a consultant procurement service. Finally, the site provides free services such as teaming opportunities, SIC codes, and per diem rates as well as a subscription service.

Idea Café
www.ideacafe.com
The Idea Café provides a fun approach to serious business. The site provides technical review for small business, a financial focus of the day, a bookstore, a venture capital forum, and a Biz Idea of the Day. The Idea Café serves critical information fast, fresh, friendly, and for real.

Inc.com
www.inc.com
Inc.com is the Web site for growing companies. As a full-service electronic consultant to people starting and running businesses, Inc.com goes beyond *Inc.* magazine to present resources and interactive networking opportunities available only on the Web. The full contents of the 14 annual issues of *Inc.* and 4 annual issues of *Inc. Technology* are posted at Inc. Online when the magazines go on newsstands. *Inc.* also provides a broad array of books, videos, software, conferences, seminars, consulting services, and awards programs.

International Business Guide Worldclass Supersite
web.idirect.com/~tiger/supersit.htm
The Worldclass Supersite provides instant access and step-by-step commentary for over a thousand top business sites from around the world, chosen based on their usefulness to world commerce, timeliness, ease of use, and presentation. The Supersite has seven sections: reference, news, learning, money, trade, networking, and world beaters.

International Entrepreneur Association Business Resource Center
www.theiea.com
The International Entrepreneur Association (IEA) is an organization that provides useful tools and promotes the creativity necessary to start and operate any successful organization or venture. Membership benefits include business plans, free business software, business resources, assistance programs, e-mail publications, and a business chat room.

A Global World
www.aglobalworld.com
A Global World provides international information concerning global weather, time zones, global distances, dialing codes, power voltage, global holidays, and a global traveler report. The Global Reporter covers topics such as how to dial between foreign countries, driving abroad and what to expect, clearing customs, and how to send a letter overseas.

Krislyn's Strictly Business Sites
www.strictlybusinesssites.com
Krislyn's Strictly Business Sites provides a broad list of business sources in a wide variety of areas. Many sites link to Krislyn's Strictly Business Sites, including a number of educational institutions. Numerous subjects are found on this Web site, including accounting, banking, business schools, multilevel marketing, philanthropy, public relations, retail, small business–entrepreneurial, and much more.

Microsoft Smallbiz

www.microsoft.com/smallbusiness

Microsoft Smallbiz offers technology guides to getting work done, taking business online, and networking PCs. It offers a buyer's guide to Microsoft software, hardware smart buys, finding a tech consultant, and finding a custom-built PC. This site also provides small business talk with links to success stories, small business resources, and expert advice.

Mind Tools

www.mindtools.com

Mind Tools offers information about time-management skills, techniques for controlling stress, information and study skills, tools to improve your memory, creativity tools, tools for mastering complexity, techniques for effective decision making, and project planning and management skills.

The National Association for Female Executives (NAFE)

www.nafe.com

The National Association for Female Executives (NAFE), the largest women's professional association and the largest women business owners organization in the country, provides resources and services—through education, networking, and public advocacy—to empower its members to achieve career success and financial security. Member benefits include information about insurance, lifestyle, money, online services, travel, and books.

National Women's Business Council

www.nwbc.gov

The members of the National Women's Business Council are prominent women business owners and leaders of women's business organizations. The mission of the council is to promote bold initiatives, policies, and programs designed to support women's business enterprises at all stages of development in the public and private sector marketplaces.

New Venture Café

www.mgt.smsu.edu/nvcafe

New Venture Café—where entrepreneurs spend their nights discussing their dreams. A dazzling and useful site designed by Professor Charles Boyd of Southwest Missouri State University for his entrepreneurship class. It includes a wide variety of information regarding entrepreneurship all arranged around the concept of a café menu.

Online Women's Business Center

www.onlinewbc.gov

By combining the expertise and resources of the U.S. Small Business Administration with several major corporate sponsors, this Web site provides the very best information for running a business. As a "one-stop shopping" site, you can find information about everything from how to start a business to how to operate in the global marketplace. Also, you can find information on business principles and practices, management techniques, mentoring, networking, and business resources.

Patent and Trademark Office Home Page
www.uspto.gov
The Patent and Trademark Office provides information on patents and trademarks as well as databases, inventor resources, kid's pages, download forms, PTO fees, FTP data, public affairs, statistics, acquisitions, jobs at PTO, and document formats. The site is constantly updated to provide "New on the PTO Site" items and related current events.

SBA Office of Advocacy—Research and Statistics on Small Business
www.sba.gov/ADVO/stats
The Office of Advocacy works to reduce the burdens that federal policies impose on small firms and maximize the benefits small businesses receive from the government. This site provides links to the office of economic research, the office of interagency affairs, the office of public liaison, and regional advocates. General small business reports and data include the small business answer card, state small business economic profiles, small business economic indicators, and Small Business Administration–sponsored research.

SBA Small Business Administration Home Page
www.sba.gov
The U.S. Small Business Administration Web site details all the programs and aid offered by the Small Business Administration. This is an excellent site, with a lot of useful information for both new and experienced entrepreneurs and small-business owners.

Small and Home Based Business Links
www.bizoffice.com
This site offers links to topics such as reference, financing, services, news, opportunities, marketing, and franchises. Additional links include a library, a search engine, a business forum, a marketplace, a bookstore, and business forms.

Small Business Advancement National Center
www.sbaer.uca.edu
Small business information is provided to small business clients through the Small Business Advancement Electronic Resource. This connection serves as an extensive electronic link among small business owners, entrepreneurs, foundations, educational institutions, associations, international partners, and local, state, and federal government. The Web site offers information geared toward helping already established businesses as well as those just beginning.

Small Business Innovation Research Awards—Community of Science
fundedresearch.cos.com/SBIR
Many U.S. government agencies award Small Business Innovation Research (SBIR) Awards to small U.S. companies in an effort to promote their growth and development. In effect, the SBIR program is the federal government's venture capital investment program. The SBIR program is administered by the U.S. Small Business Administration (SBA); this site explains the program.

Strategic Business Planning Co.
www.bizplan.com
The mission of the Strategic Business Planning Company is to help organizations define their mission and achieve their objectives by developing business and strategic plans and by periodically conducting a comprehensive review of the environment in which they operate. This site provides information about strategic business planning.

TSCentral
www.tscentral.com
The TSCentral Web site offers information on trade and professional event resources. In addition to comprehensive event data, the site also provides detailed venue information and an event industry suppliers database. TSCentral also specializes in delivering a wide range of management products and services for event organizers, sponsors, and exhibitors, including Web advertising and promotion, online event registration, floor-plan management, event representation, direct marketing, webcast production, premium incentives, and Web site development.

U.S. Business Advisor
www.business.gov
The U.S. Business Advisor exists to provide businesses with one-stop access to federal government information, services, and transactions. Its goal is to make the relationship between business and government more productive. Links on this site include business development, financial assistance, taxes, laws and regulations, international trade, workplace issues, buying and selling, and agencies and gateways.

U.S Census Bureau
www.census.gov
The U.S. Census Bureau is part of the U.S. Department of Commerce and provides timely information about people, business, geography, news, and other special topics. This Web site is a treasure trove of information. Selected reports include County Business Patterns, Current Industrial Reports, Current Population Survey, State and Metropolitan Area Data Book, Surveys of Minority-Owned and Women-Owned Business Enterprises, and economic indicators.

U.S. Treasury Department
www.treas.gov
The U.S. Treasury site provides general information and the latest news regarding the Treasury Department. The main menu links to a business services page that offers information about the office of business and public liaison, the office of procurement, registering a business, a simplified tax and wage reporting system, and small business assistance.

YEO Young Entrepreneurs' Organization
www.yeo.org
As a global, nonprofit educational organization for young entrepreneurs, the Young Entrepreneurs' Organization (YEO) strives to help its members build on their successes through an array of educational and networking opportunities. With more than 4,200 members in 100 chapters and 34 countries around the world, YEO provides its members access to a dynamic network of peers on an international level. Links include the YEO strategic alliances, YEO graduate organizations, and entrepreneur resources.

ADDITIONAL ENTREPRENEURSHIP IN ACTION CASES

Varsity Spirit Corporation (www.varsity.com) and National Spirit Group (www.nationalspirit.com)

The cheerleading industry is big business, and getting bigger every year. With more than a million active participants, millions of dollars in revenues, and nationwide television coverage, the spirit industry has evolved into a growth industry. Cheerleading is becoming more athletic, more competitive, and more expensive. The industry doesn't include just cheerleading squads. It now encompasses school dance teams, pompom squads, dance studio participants, and all-star cheerleading squads (called all-stars) who do not actually cheer for a team but exist only to compete. It's an extremely interesting market segment.

Cheerleading is no longer just a sideline activity during fall and spring. Many cheerleaders practice and attend camps and competitions year-round. The camps, the apparel, the competitions—it all adds up to serious money for participants *and* for the companies who supply them.

The two biggest players in the cheer industry are National Spirit Group (**www.nationalspirit.com**) and Varsity Spirit Corporation (**www.varsity.com**). Both companies have capitalized on the cross-marketing opportunities. First, the cheerleaders come to summer camps. While at camp, the company's special events—that is, the regional and national competitions—are promoted. Then there's the clothing—camp shirts, shorts, hair ribbons, etc.—and the other merchandise. We can't leave out the all-important uniform business. Although uniforms aren't actually sold at the camps, the company's sales representatives are there meeting with customers, making presentations, and taking orders.

Just like any good cheerleaders cheering for their teams, the two industry leaders claim to be the best. And, there's no love lost between the two. Jeffrey G. Webb, the CEO of Varsity Spirit Corporation, based in Memphis, used to work for the National Spirit Group. After working two years at National Spirit he left and formed Varsity Spirit in 1974, setting up summer camps in direct competition with his old employer. Then, in 1979 Webb started manufacturing uniforms, the most lucrative segment of the cheer business because it accounts for about 60 percent of revenues. In 1981 Varsity began national competitions that continue to be televised on ESPN. National Spirit soon followed suit and developed national competitions that are shown on CBS, the USA Network, and Fox. Both Varsity and National Spirit are looking at moving into uniforms for other women's and some men's sports. Varsity took the first step when it signed a U.S. licensing agreement with Umbro Corporation, the British manufacturer of soccer uniforms. Under this agreement, Varsity will manufacture and sell for the next five years male and female soccer uniforms under the Umbro name to American school and league markets. Mr. Webb said he hoped to eventually use the same cross-marketing model of camps, competitions, and uniform sales in the soccer market as they had in the cheerleading market.

Discussion Questions

1. Of the two companies described, which do you think is the industry innovator? Explain your choice.
2. Now, check out the Web sites of both Varsity Spirit Corporation and National Spirit Group. Would your answer to question 1 be the same? Explain.
3. A big fear of entrepreneurs is bringing someone into the business who learns the ins and outs, leaves, and starts his or her venture in the same line of business. What might entrepreneurs do to lessen the likelihood of this occurring?

Sources: Company information from company Web sites (**www.varsity.com**) July 1, 2002, and (**www.nationalspirit.com**) July 1, 2002, and from Hoover's Online (**www.hoovers.com**) July 1, 2002; and E. Yellin, "School Spirit Inc.," *New York Times*, July 17, 1999, pp. B1+.

Cybrel Argentina (www.cybrel.com)

Charly Alberti may seem an unlikely Internet entrepreneur. He's best known as the drummer of the Argentine rock band Soda Stereo. However, with the band's breakup in 1997, Alberti's new gig was the Internet. His entertainment-oriented Web site Cybrel Argentina (**www.cybrel.com**) plays to a much larger potential audience than his former band could ever have packed into a stadium. At Cybrel, you can explore a variety of information from a well-designed, impressive, and energetic Web site.

As have others around the world, Latin Americans have taken to the Internet in droves. The lure of readily available information and communication has attracted millions online. However, getting to that information and communication isn't always easy. Poor dial-up connections and limited access are some of the challenges with which Latin American Internet entrepreneurs are dealing. Shopping online is another area in which Latin American consumers have been cautious. Analysts explain that credit cards (the most frequently used form of payment) are not as widely accepted in this region. However, that isn't stopping people like Alberti. He feels it's just a matter of time before the electronic revolution firmly takes hold, and he wants to be positioned to take advantage of it.

Discussion Questions

1. What things would Charly Alberti have needed to do to get his new venture launched? Be as specific as possible.
2. What does Alberti need to do to take advantage of the growth in the use of the Internet in Latin America? Be as specific as possible.
3. Log on to Cybrel's Web site. Describe and evaluate what's there.

Sources: Company information from company Web site (**www.cybrel.com**) July 1, 2002; and D. Stinson, "Internet Fever," *Latin Trade*, August 1998, pp. 61–64.

Altitunes (www.altitunes.com)

Amy Nye Wolf's first "takeoff" could best be described as a crash landing. When she quit her job as a financial analyst for Goldman Sachs, she started planning a new business—using free-standing kiosks to sell music CDs in airport terminals. Her intention for the business was to be a music and portable entertainment retail outlet for customers on the fly. There were no competitors, relatively low overhead, and a captive audience. What more could an entrepreneur ask for? She convinced officials at New York's LaGuardia Airport to let her open a 150-square-foot kiosk. However, Wolf did not do her homework. Airport officials rejected her initial construction plan. It took her a month to answer all their questions. Another mistake was not inquiring about regulations governing construction. Airport security had to inspect and approve all building materials, and as a result, her construction costs doubled and the project completion time was three months behind schedule. Even after this first turbulent takeoff, the company's problems continued. A construction problem at New York's Kennedy Airport delayed that location's opening by a month, resulting in more than $45,000 in lost revenues and adding $20,000 in costs to satisfy a design concern. Then, at Ronald Reagan National Airport in Washington, D.C., officials objected to her construction design. Although she protested the objections, she lost the protest and ended up having to spend an additional $60,000. But, Wolf carries on as she tries to make AltiTunes a successful business. AltiTunes (**www.altitunes.com**) currently operates in 26 airport locations and has opened an outlet at its first train station located in New York City's Grand Central Terminal.

Each AltiTunes location stocks over 1,000 music titles. The typical inventory includes a variety of music ranging from pop to jazz, rap to gospel, country to classical. All major music categories are stocked with enough products to meet customer demand. In addition to music titles, AltiTunes also sells portable electronics (Walkman, Discman, Palm Pilot), music product accessories, books on tape, and Gameboy bases and cartridges. The electronic products are offered in a variety of price ranges to meet customers' needs. At each location, customers can select their music by using one of the EARports, an interactive listening station. These individual stations are sponsored by a record label or distributor, and equipped with headphones for listening. In addition, each location has a MUZE Station, an interactive computer database that contains detailed information on over 350,000 pieces of published music that's updated monthly. It helps both customers and AltiTunes staff to identify a specific title or artist.

AltiTunes' five-year mission is to become the leading brand for small format, extraordinary-location, music and electronics retailing with an expanding network of domestic and international locations. Wolf plans on taking her company outside of airports and train stations to hospitals, hotels, and travel plazas. She definitely wants her business to fly high.

Discussion Questions

1. Evaluate Wolf's launching of her business, AltiTunes. What would you suggest that she might have done differently?
2. What growth challenges is AltiTunes going to face? How might they deal with these challenges?
3. Go to the AltiTunes Web site and click on the Press Releases. Read the press releases there. What impression do you get from reading these?

Sources: Company information from company Web site (**www.altitunes.com**) July 1, 2002; and C. Mastony, "Turbulent Takeoff," *Forbes*, May 3, 1999, p. 94.

Langlitz Leathers (www.langlitz.colm)

Langlitz Leathers is well known by motorcycling enthusiasts. However, the company's famed leather garments are also worn by rock stars and investment bankers. For more than 50 years, Langlitz jackets have given motorcycle riders a nice fit and a sensation of invulnerability mixed with danger. The jackets aren't cheap. Prices begin at $650. Yet, even at those prices, the company's products are considered good buys. And, the jackets are so popular among thieves that they now bear a serial number for easier tracing.

Langlitz Leathers was started by Ross Langlitz in 1947. Unhappy with the motorcycle jacket he had purchased, Langlitz decided to make his own. His first jacket was so well made that many of his friends wanted ones like it. After a couple years of sewing jackets in his basement after work, Langlitz decided to go into business. His reputation spread quickly. Langlitz's reputation for high-quality custom leathers was born. The basic styles Ross designed in the 1940s are still the mainstay products today. The Columbia style is the flagship jacket and still the company's most popular one. It reflects the traditional look of motorcycling with its classically handsome and extremely practical design. Other products include the Cascade style, which is a sport-touring jacket, leather pants called Westerns, competition breeches, rangers, and other leather-related motorcycle products.

The company not only sticks to tradition in its marketing, it also sticks to tradition in its production area. The shop is small (less than 3,000 square feet) and crowded. There are a total of 15 people who work there, with hundreds of leather garments hanging around. They cut and sew only about six garments a day. Half are custom-created to a customer's measurements. The other half are built to stock pattern sizes for walk-in customers. High demand has caused the production time for custom work to fluctuate from less than half a year to more than a year and a half.

The current president of Langlitz Leathers, Jackie L. Hansen (a family member) says that although the company specializes in custom work, "it is not our desire to build fashion wear. We are a small family business and intend to remain that way for a long time. We currently have a long backlog of work orders. So, please don't ask us to build something we don't normally do. What we do, we do very well . . . and we want to keep it that way."

Discussion Questions

1. Does Langlitz Leathers fit the definition of an entrepreneurial organization? Explain.
2. How can a business with a backlog of orders of up to a year and a half stay in business?
3. What do you think are the keys to Langlitz Leathers' success?

Sources: Company information from company Web site (**www.langlitz.com**) July 1, 2002, and Hoover's Online (**www.hoovers.com**) July 1, 200; and P. Fish, "Western Wanderings," *Sunset*, November 1999, p. 20.

Sterling Autobody Centers (www.sterlingautobody.com)

Jon McNeill started his latest entrepreneurial venture, as many entrepreneurs do, through an unpleasant experience. In his case, he wanted to find an honest, reliable, and efficient car repair shop to fix his wife's car after an accident. The minor repair job ended up taking two months. As a former management consultant who had started an insurance call-center company, McNeill smelled opportunity. Even with no background or experience, he sensed that there had to be a better solution to this common necessity—collision repair.

McNeill and cofounder Bill Haylon, a colleague from the consulting firm, put together a business plan for a national chain of auto body shops that would focus on faster, more reliable service. Aiming to put together the best plan they could, McNeill and Haylon brought Bob Thompson, a longtime body-shop owner, on board as well. Collision repair is a $26 billion industry, and there are about 60,000 body shops around the United States, most of them independently owned. With this type of fragmented industry, McNeill had personally experienced the lack of consistency in quality, technology, and processes. In addition, the repair industry has an often-adversarial opponent—the insurance companies. Given these challenges, McNeill thought that the whole repair process could be better. His idea for a nationwide chain of auto body centers was the solution.

Sterling AutoBody Center shops apply assembly-line discipline to the repair process. Company technicians are encouraged to find ways to improve the work flow and to share their ideas with other shops in the chain. Three of the company's guiding principles are: (1) Do the little things right. You don't want a $4,000 repair stalled over a missing $4 part. (2) Don't start what you can't finish. Rather than start a repair without all the needed parts, Sterling uses a parts broker to ensure that all the needed parts arrive at the same time. Then, and only then, does the actual work begin. (3) Clean is good. Sterling believes that a clean, orderly shop sets the right tone—for customers *and* for the repair technicians. McNeill says, "We're not doing anything fancy. We're doing what Henry Ford did 100 years ago. I've told our guys that in five years, I want to be able to have the bulk of our repairs done in one day. You can't do that by just showing up and doing things the same old way."

Although there are a number of regional auto-body shop consolidators being built around similar principles of efficiency, teamwork, and reliability, Sterling is positioned to be the biggest of the bunch. The company wants to continue its nationwide expansion—its strategy: to do for auto repair what Home Depot did for hardware. Allstate Insurance, the nation's second-largest insurer, liked Sterling's model so much, it purchased the company in 2001.

Discussion Questions

1. Would you characterize this company as entrepreneurial? Explain.
2. What types of challenges will Sterling AutoBody Centers face as it expands nationally? Be specific. How can it address these challenges?
3. Evaluate Sterling's three guiding principles. Could these apply to other types of entrepreneurial organizations? Explain.
4. What do you think has contributed to the success of this company?

Sources: Company information from company Web site (**www.sterlingautobody.com**) July 2, 2002, and Hoover's Online (**www.hoovers.com**) July 2, 2002; and C. Salter, "Crash Course," *Fast Company*, July 2002, pp. 42–46.

Index

D

E

F

L

M

N

O

T

U

V

W

Y

Z